THE NEW TESTAMENT
WITH PSALMS & PROVERBS
in the Language of Today

THIS BIBLE IS PRESENTED TO

_____

_____

BY

_____

ON

_____

"Make them holy by the truth; Your Word is truth."
John 17:17

THE NEW TESTAMENT WITH PSALMS & PROVERBS
in the Language of Today

Copyright 2013 © William F. Beck Estates

Lutheran News Inc.
684 Luther Lane
New Haven, MO 63068
www.christiannewsmo.com
published 2013
Manufactured in the United States of America
Printed in Washington Missouri, Missourian Publishing Co.
ISBN 978-0-9644799-5-1

CPON

THIS IS THE WORD FOR "CROSS" IN PAPYRUS 75, OUR OLDEST MANUSCRIPT OF LUKE. IT IS FOUND IN THIS SPECIAL FORM AT LUKE 9:23; 14:27; 24:7.

IF YOU SPELL OUT THIS GREEK WORD, IT IS STAURON. BUT THE LETTERS AU ARE OMITTED AND THEIR OMISSION IS INDICATED BY THE LINE ABOVE THE WORD. THEN R, WHICH IN GREEK HAS THE FORM OF A P, IS SUPERIMPOSED ON THE T SO THAT WE HAVE A HEAD SUGGESTING A BODY ON A CROSS.

"CROSS" IS THE ONLY WORD IN THE MANUSCRIPT SELECTED FOR SUCH A SPECIAL DESIGN. THE SAVIOR, CRUCIFIED FOR US, IS THE REASON WHY THE BIBLE WAS WRITTEN – AND WHY IT IS HERE TRANSLATED.

THE NEW TESTAMENT
PSALMS & PROVERBS

What Does the Bible Teach About:

1. **Truth** – The Bible contains dogma, doctrine, divinely revealed truth which can be known. John 8:31-32; John 4:18; Mark 5:33; Romans 3:2; 2 Tim. 3:16; John 10:35.
2. **History** – Christianity is founded upon historic facts not myths, fables, and fiction. 1 Tim. 1:4; 1 Tim. 4:7; Matthew 19:4; Matthew 12:30-42; Luke 1:1-4; Luke 2:1,2
3. **The Holy Trinity** – Is the only true God. Matthew 28:19-20; Psalm 115:4-7; Psalm 96:5; Deuteronomy 6:4; 1 Corinthians 8:4; John 1:1-3; Gen. 1:26; Exodus 3:2-4; Isaiah 48:16; Matthew 22:41-45; 2 Corinthians 13:14.
4. **Jesus Christ is true God and true Man**. 1 John 5:20; Psalms 2:12; Isaiah 9:16; Micah 5:2; Matthew 10:13-17; John 10:27-30; John 10:37-38; Luke 22:90; John 5:18; Romans 9:5; John 20:28; Matthew 17:5; John 1:1; John 1:14; John 21:27; Matthew 28:18; John 1:3; Colossians 2:9; Philippians 2:5-11.
5. **Jesus Christ paid the ransom price** for the salvation of all people. The vicarious satisfaction of Christ. 2 Corinthians 5:19; 1 Timothy 2:6; John 2:2; Isaiah 53:4-6; 1 Peter 1:18,19; Romans 3:34-34
6. **People are justified by faith** alone in the saving merits of Jesus Christ and not good works: Romans 3:28; Genesis 15:6; Psalms 32:2; Habakkuk 2:4; Isaiah 24:24; Isaiah 53:11; Galatians 3:24; Ephesians 2:8,9; Philippians 3:9; John 6:47; John 3:16; Romans 4:25.
7. **Jesus Christ was born of a virgin**: Matthew 1:22-23; Isaiah 7:14; Luke 1:26-28.
8. **Jesus Christ rose physically from the dead**. Matthew 28:5-7a; Mark 16; Luke 24; John 20 and 21; Matthew 12:40; Matthew 16:21; Corinthians 15; John 25,26.
9. **The Immortality of the Soul and the Resurrection of the Flesh**: Ecclesiastes 12:7; John 11:25-26; I John 3:2; Matthew 10:28; John 5:28,29; Luke 12:20; Matthew 2:50; 1 Kings 1:22; Acts 2:31-36; Luke 24:37-43; Matthew 28:6; 1 John 3:2; 1 Corinthians 15:48; Philippians 3:21; Job 19:25-27.
10. **The Bible** is God's verbally inspired and inerrant revelation to man. Exodus 32:16; Psalm 40:7; 1 Corinthians 2:13; Romans 16:25-27; John 10:35; 1 Thessalonians 2:13; 1 Corinthians 2:13; 1 Corinthians 14:37; 2 Timothy 3:16; 2 Peter 1:21.
11. **The Old Testament**: Moses wrote the first five books of the Bible. Exodus 24:4; Numbers 32:2; Deuteronomy, 31:24; Joshua 1:7,8; John 5:46,47; Luke 44; The 8th century BC Prophet Isaiah wrote the book of Isaiah. John 12:38; John 12:30-40; Matthew 3:3; the Sixth Century B.C. prophet Daniel wrote the Book of Daniel: Mathew 24:14; The book of Jonah presents historic fact and not fiction. Matthew 12:40-43; Luke 11:29-32; The Old Testament directly predicts a Messiah: Acts 2:29-31; Genesis 3:15; Genesis 4:1; Isaiah 7:14; Psalm 22; Micah 5:2; Isaiah 9:6
12. **God created the heaven and the earth in six days**. Evolution is contrary to the Bible. The book of Genesis presents historic fact not fiction: Genesis 1:1; Exodus 20:11; Psalm 32:6,9; Matthew 1:4; Genesis 1:24-27; 1 Corinthians 15:30; Romans 5:12-13
13. **The Christian Church** in the proper sense of the term is the communion of saints, the sum total of all those who have been called by the Holy Spirit through the Gospel from out of the lost and condemned human race, who truly believe in Christ. Ephesians 1:22,23; John 11:41; Godless persons who have

not accepted Christ as their savior from sin are not members of the church even though they may be affiliated with some denomination: Romans 8:9; John 5:6; The Christian Church practices doctrinal discipline. 2 John 9:10; Titus 3:10-11

14. **Christians are active in mission work**. They recognize that Jesus is the only way to heaven. Christianity is the only saving faith and these who die without saving faith in Christ are lost. Matthew 28:18-20; John 14:6; Acts 4:12; John 3:36; Psalm 96:5; Psalm 115:2-7.

15. **God's law** recorded in the Bible is an absolute unchanging standard. John 14:15; John 14:21: John 14:24; Psalms 1:12; Exodus 20:-3-17. All sex outside a heterosexual marriage is sinful. Matthew 5:27-28; Matthew 5:17-19; Matthew 5:32; Proverbs 6:37; Galatians 5:19-21; 1 Corinthians 3:5-8; 1 Thessalonians 4:3-7; 1 Corinthians 5:13.

16. **Homosexuality is a sin**: Romans 1:22-32; 1 Corinthians 6:9; Jude 7. **Abortion**: unborn children are real persons and entitled to the care and preservation which God's command provides for all mankind. Luke 1:41; Psalm 51:5; Psalm 139:13; Jeremiah 1:5; The Bible forbids a willful setting aside of God's will and command to have children, Gen. 1:28; 1 Tim. 5:15; 2:5; Genesis 8,9,10.

17. **Women pastors**: 1 Corinthians 14:34,,34; 1 Timothy 2:11-17; Titus 1:6.

18. **Holy Communion**: Matthew 26:26-,28; Mark 14:22; Luke 22:19-20; 1 Cor. 11:24-25; 1 C or. 10:15; Matthew 18:6.

19. **Judgment Day and Millennialism**: Acts 1:11; Acts 17:31; Mark 13:21; 2 Peter 3:10; Luke 17:20; Mark 13-21; Revelation 1:1; Revelations 20.

20. **Some Words of Comfort** in sorrow: Psalm 23; Isaiah 41:10; Matthew 11:28; 2 Corinthians 12:9; Romans 8:28-39; Hebrews 12:5,6; Philippians 4:4-7.

THE
NEW TESTAMENT

THE GOOD NEWS AS IT WAS TOLD BY
MATTHEW

1 THIS IS A RECORD showing how Jesus Christ was the Descendant of David and of Abraham:

2   **Abraham** was the father of Isaac,
     Isaac was the father of Jacob,
     and **Jacob** was the father of Judah and his brothers.

3   **Judah** was the father of Perez and **Zerah**, and Tamar was their mother.
     Perez was the father of Hezron,
     Hezron was the father of Ram,

4   **Ram** was the father of Amminadab,
     Amminadab was the father of Nahshon,
     Nahshon was the father of Salmon,

5   and **Salmon** was the father of Boaz, and Rahab was his mother.
     Boaz was the father of Obed, and Ruth was his mother.
     Obed was the father of Jesse,

6   and **Jesse** was the father of King David.
     David was the father of Solomon, and Uriah's wife was his mother.

7   **Solomon** was the father of Rehoboam,
     Rehoboam was the father of Abijah,
     Abijah was the father of Asa,

8   **Asa** was the father of Jehoshaphat,
     Jehoshaphat was the father of Joram,
     Joram was the father of Uzziah,

9   **Uzziah** was the father of Jotham,
     Jotham was the father of Ahaz,
     Ahaz was the father of Hezekiah,

10   **Hezekiah** was the father of Manasseh,
     Manasseh was the father of Amon,
     Amon was the father of Josiah,

11   and **Josiah** was the father of Jechoniah and his brothers when the people were taken away to Babylon. 12After they had been taken away to Babylon,
     Jechoniah was the father of Shealtiel,
     Shealtiel was the father of Zerubbabel,

13   **Zerubbabel** was the father of Abiud,
     Abiud was the father of Eliakim,
     Eliakim was the father of Azor,

[14] **Azor** was the father of Zadok,
  Zadok was the father of Achim,
  Achim was the father of Eliud,
[15] **Eliud** was the father of Eleazar, **Eleazar** was the father of Matthan.
Matthan was the father of Jacob, [16]and **Jacob** was the father of **Joseph,**
the husband of **Mary**; she was the mother of Jesus, Who is called Christ.

[17]So there are, in all, 14 generations from Abraham to David, 14 from
David to the Babylonian Captivity, and 14 from the Babylonian Captivity
to Christ.

An Angel Comes to Joseph

[18]This is how the birth of Jesus Christ took place.

His mother Mary had promised Joseph to be his wife. But before they
were married, Mary realized that she was pregnant — by the Holy Spirit.

[19]Joseph, her husband, was a righteous man and didn't want to disgrace her. So he decided break the marriage agreement secretly.

[20]After he thought about it, he saw an angel of the Lord in a dream,
who said, "Joseph, son of David, don't be afraid to take your wife Mary
home with you; her Child is from the Holy Spirit. [21]She will have a Son,
and you will call Him Jesus, because He will save His people from their
sins." [22]All this happened so that what the Lord said through the prophet
would come true: [23]*"The virgin will conceive and have a Son, and He will be
called Immanuel,"*[a] which means "God-with-us."

[24]When Joseph woke up, he did what the angel of the Lord had ordered
him to do. He took his wife home with him [25]but didn't have sexual relations
with her until she gave birth to a son. And he called Him Jesus.

The Wise Men

2 Jesus was born in Bethlehem in Judea when Herod was king. Then
wise men came from the east to Jerusalem. [2]"Where is the Child Who was
born King of the Jews?" they asked. "We saw His star in the east and have
come to worship Him."

[3]When King Herod heard about this, he became alarmed and all
Jerusalem with him. [4]He called together all of the people's ruling priests
and Bible scholars and tried to find out from them where the Christ was to
be born.

[5]"In Bethlehem, in Judea," they told him, "because the prophet has
written: [6]*And you, Bethlehem,* in the land of Judah, *are* not at all *the least
among the leading towns of Judah, since from you will come a leader Who
will be the Shepherd of My people Israel."*

---

23 Is 7:14; 8:8,10   *6 Mic 5:2,4; II Sam 5:2*

---

a - 23 The New Testament often quotes or alludes to verses or phrases from the Old Testament. Words in italics are quoted in the Old Testament. The references, listed by verse on
each page where these occur, show where such a quotation is to be found in the Old Testament.

[7]Then Herod secretly called the wise men and found out from them the exact time the star appeared. [8]Then he sent them to Bethlehem. "Go and search carefully for the little child," he said. "And when you find him, report to me, so that I too may go and bow down before him."

[9]After hearing the king, they started out. And there was the star they had seen in the east! It led them on until it came to a stop over the place where the Child was. [10]They were overjoyed to see the star. [11]They went into the house and saw the little Child with His mother Mary. Kneeling, they *worshiped Him.* Then they opened their treasure chests and *offered Him gifts: gold, incense,* and myrrh.

[12]But God warned them in a dream not to go back to Herod. So they went home to their country by another road.

To Egypt!

[13]After the wise men left, Joseph saw an angel of the Lord in a dream, who said, "Get up, take the little Child and His mother, and flee to Egypt. Stay there until I tell you. Herod is going to search for the Child to kill Him."

[14]Joseph got up at night, took the little Child and His mother, and went to Egypt. [15]He stayed there until Herod died. In this way what the Lord said through the prophet was to come true: *"I called My Son out of Egypt."*

[16]When Herod saw that the wise men had tricked him, he became very angry and sent men to kill all the boys in Bethlehem and in all the country around it, up to two years old, according to the exact time he had found out from the wise men. [17]Then what was said through the prophet Jeremiah came true:

[18] *A cry is heard in Rama! Weeping and bitter wailing:*
   Rachel crying over her children
      and refusing to be comforted, because they are gone.

[19] But when Herod died, an angel of the Lord appeared to Joseph in Egypt in a dream [20]and told him, "Get up, take the little Child and His mother, and go to the land of Israel. Those who tried to kill the little Child are dead."

[21] Joseph got up, took the little Child and His mother, and came to the land of Israel. [22]But when he heard, "Archelaus has succeeded his father Herod as king of Judea," he was afraid to go back there. And being warned in a dream, he went to Galilee. [23]He came and made his home in a town by the name of Nazareth. And so what was said through the prophets came true: "He will be called a Nazarene."[b]

---

11 Is 60:6; Ps 72:9-11,15 15 Num 24:8; Hos 11:1   18 Jer 31:15

---

b - 23   According to Is 11:1 the Savior would be a *Netzer*, a sprout, growing from the roots of the tree of David.

John Prepares the Way — *Mark 1:1-8; Luke 3:1-18; John 1:19-28*

3 The time came when John the Baptizer appeared in the wilderness of Judea and preached: [2]"Repent — the kingdom of heaven is near." [3]He was the one of whom it was said through the prophet Isaiah:

A voice will be calling in the wilderness,
"Prepare the way for the Lord;
make the paths straight for Him."

[4]John wore clothes of camel's hair and a leather belt around his waist. And he lived on locusts and wild honey.

[5]Then Jerusalem, all Judea, and the whole Jordan valley came out to him. [6]As they confessed their sins, he baptized them in the Jordan River.

[7]He also saw many Pharisees and Sadducees coming for baptism. "Brood of poisonous snakes, who warned you to run away from the punishment waiting for you?" he asked them. [8]"Do the works that show you have repented. [9]Don't think you can tell yourselves, 'Abraham is our father.' I tell you, God can raise up children for Abraham from these stones. [10]The ax is now ready to strike at the roots of the trees, and any tree that doesn't produce good fruit will be cut down and thrown into the fire. [11]I baptize you with water to bring about a change of heart. But the One Who is coming after me is mightier than I. I'm not worthy to carry His sandles. He will baptize you with the Holy Spirit and fire. [12]He has the winnowing shovel in His hand and will clean up His threshing floor. His wheat He'll gather into His barn, but the chaff He'll burn in a fire that can't be put out."

John Baptizes Jesus — *Mark 1:9-11; Luke 3:21-22;*
Compare John 1:29-34

[13]Then Jesus came from Galilee to John at the Jordan to be baptized by him. [14]John tried to stop Him. "I need to be baptized by You," he said, "and You come to me?"

[15]"Permit it now," Jesus answered him. "That is how we should *fulfill all righteousness.*"

Then John gave in to Him. [16]As soon as Jesus was baptized, He stepped out of the water, and now heaven was opened, and He saw *the Spirit of God* coming down *on Him* as a dove. [17]And a voice from heaven said, "This is *My Son*, Whom I *love and delight in.*"

The Devil Tempts Jesus — *Mark 1:12-13; Luke 4:1-13*

4 Then the Spirit led Jesus into the wilderness to be tempted by the devil. [2]He didn't eat anything for 40 days and 40 nights. At the end of that time He was hungry.

[3]The tempter came to Him. "If You're God's Son," he said to Him, "tell

---

3 Is 40:3   15 Is 42:6   16 Is 42:1   17 Gen 22:2; Ps 2:7; Is 42:1

these stones to become loaves of bread."

[4]"It is written," Jesus answered, " *'A man doesn't live on bread alone but on every Word that God speaks.'* "

[5]Then the devil took Him into the Holy City and had Him stand on the edge of the temple. [6]"If You're God's Son," he told Him, "jump down. It is written: *'He will order His angels to help you. They will carry you in their hands and never let you stub your foot against a stone.'* "

[7]"It is also written," Jesus answered him, " *'Don't test the Lord your God.'* "

[8]Then the devil took Him to a very high mountain and showed Him all the kingdoms in the world and their glory. [9]"All this I'll give You," the devil told Him, "if You'll bow down and worship me."

[10]Then Jesus answered him, "Go away, Satan! It is written: *'Worship the Lord your God, and serve Him* only.' "

[11]Then the devil left Him, and angels came and took care of Him.

At Home in Capernaum

[12]When Jesus heard John had been put in prison, He went back to Galilee. [13]Leaving Nazareth, He went and made His home in Capernaum, on the shores of the Sea of Galilee, in the area of Zebulun and Naphtali. [14]And so what was said through the prophet Isaiah was to come true:

[15] *Land of Zebulon and land of Naphtali, the way to the sea, across the Jordan Galilee of the Gentiles!*

[16] *The people sitting in the dark will see a great Light. For those sitting in the land of the shadow of death a Light will rise.*

[17] Then Jesus began to preach. "Repent — the kingdom of heaven is here!"

"Come with Me" — *Mark 1:14-20; Luke 5:1-11; John 1:35-51*

[18]As He was walking along the shore of the Sea of Galilee, He saw two brothers, Simon, also called Peter, and his brother Andrew (who were fishermen), casting a net into the sea. [19]"Come, follow Me," Jesus told them, "and I will make you fishers of men." [20]Immediately they left their nets and followed Him.

[21]He went on and saw two other brothers, James, Zebedee's son, and his brother John. They were in their boat with their father Zebedee, mending their nets. He called them, [22]and immediately they left the boat and their father and followed Him.

Preaching in Galilee — *Mark 1:35-39; Luke 4:42-44*

[23]Then He went around everywhere in Galilee, teaching in their synagogues, preaching the good news of the kingdom, and healing every kind

---

4 *Deut 8:3*   6 *Ps 91:11-12*

7 *Deut 6:16*   10 *Deut 6:13*   *15-16* Is 9:1-2

of disease and sickness among the people.

²⁴The news about Him spread all over Syria. And the people brought to Him all who were suffering from various diseases and were in great pain, the demon-possessed, the epileptics, and the paralyzed, and He made them well. ²⁵Large crowds followed Him from Galilee, the Decapolis [Ten-Towns], Jerusalem, Judea, and the other side of the Jordan.

5 When Jesus saw the crowds, He went up the hill. And when He sat down, His disciples came to Him. ²Then He began to teach them:

3   "Blessed are those who are *poor in spirit* — the kingdom of heaven belongs to them.
4   Blessed are *those who mourn* — they will *be comforted.*
5   Blessed are *those who are gentle* — they *will own the land.*
6   Blessed are those who hunger and thirst to be righteous — they will be satisfied.
7   Blessed are *those who are merciful* —
     they will find mercy.
8   Blessed are *those whose hearts are pure* — they will see God.
9   Blessed are those who make peace — they will be called God's sons.
10   Blessed are those who are persecuted for doing right — the kingdom of heaven belongs to them.
11   Blessed are you when people insult you, persecute you, lie and tell only evil about you on account of Me. ¹²Rejoice and be glad because you have a great reward in heaven. That's how they persecuted the prophets who were before you."

A Salt and a Light — *Mark 4:21-23; Luke 11:33*

¹³"You are the salt of the world. If salt loses its taste, how will it be made salty again? It's no longer good for anything but to be thrown out and trampled on by people.

¹⁴"You are the light of the world. A town can't be hidden when it's built on a hill. ¹⁵And you don't light a lamp and put it under a bucket but on the lampstand, where it gives light to everyone in the house. ¹⁶So let your light shine before people that they may see the good you do and praise your Father in heaven."

Jesus Keeps the Law

¹⁷"Don't think that I came to set aside the Law or the prophets. I didn't come to set them aside but to fulfill them. ¹⁸I tell you the truth, until heaven and earth pass away, not an *i* or the dot of an *i* of the Law will pass away until everything is done. ¹⁹Anyone, then, who sets aside one of the least of these commandments and teaches others to do the same will be called the least in the kingdom of heaven. But anyone who does and teaches what

---

3 Is 57:15   *4 Is 61:25 Ps 37:11; Prov 2:21*
7 II Sam 22:26; Ps 18:25; Prov 11:17; 14:21   *8 Ps 24:4; 51:10; 73:1*

they say will be called great in the kingdom of heaven. [20]I tell you, unless your righteousness is much better than that of the Bible scholars and Pharisees, you will never get into the kingdom of heaven."

Do Not Murder

[21]"You have heard that long ago the people were told: *'Do not murder. Whoever murders must answer for it in court.'*

[22]"But I tell you, anyone who is angry with his brother will have to answer for it in court. Anyone who calls his brother an 'empty-head' will have to answer for it before the highest court. Anyone who calls him a 'fool' will have to answer for it in hellfire.

[23]"So if you're bringing your gift to the altar and remember there that your brother has something against you, [24]leave your gift there before the altar and go. First make up with your brother, and then come and offer your gift.

[25]"If someone wants to sue you be quick to make up with him while you are still on the way with him, or your accuser will hand you over to the judge, and the judge to the officer, and you will be put into prison. [26]I tell you the truth, you will never get out until you pay the last cent."

Do Not Lust

[27]"You have heard it was said: *'Do not commit adultery.'*

[28]"But I tell you, anyone who *looks at a woman to lust after her* has already committed adultery with her in his heart.

[29]"If your right eye causes you to sin, tear it out and throw it away. It is better for you to lose a part of your body than to have all of it thrown into hell. [30]And if your right hand causes you to sin, cut it off and throw it away. It is better for you to lose a part of your body than to have all of it go to hell.

[31]"It was said: 'Anyone who divorces his wife *must give her a divorce paper.'* [32]But I tell you, anyone who divorces his wife, except for her being sexually unfaithful, makes her a partner in adultery. And also the man who marries the divorced woman is living in adultery."

Do Not Swear

[33]"Again, you have heard that long ago the people were told: *'Do not swear falsely, but give the Lord what you swear to give Him.'*

[34]"But I tell you, don't swear at all, not by *heaven — it is God's throne;* [35]nor by *the earth — it is His footstool;* nor by Jerusalem — *it is the city of the great King.* [36]And don't swear by your head, because you can't make one hair white or black. [37]Just say, 'Yes, yes; no, no.' Anything more comes from the evil one."

21 Ex 20:13; Deut 5:17   **27** Ex 20:14; Deut 5:18   **28** Prov 6:25   **31** Deut 24:1,3
33 Lev 19:12; Num 30:2; Deut 23:21; Ps 50:14   **34-35** Is 66:1; Ps 99:5
35 Ps 48:2; Lam 2:1

Love Your Enemies — *Luke 6:27-36*

³⁸"You have heard it was said: *'An eye for an eye,* and *a tooth for a tooth.'*

³⁹"But I tell you, don't oppose an evil man. If anyone slaps you on your right cheek, turn the other cheek to him also. ⁴⁰If anyone wants to sue you for your shirt, let him have your coat, too. ⁴¹If anyone makes you go one mile, go two miles with him. ⁴²If anyone asks you for anything, give it to him, and when anyone wants to borrow from you, don't turn away.

⁴³"You have heard it was said: *'Love your neighbor,* and hate your enemy.'

⁴⁴"But I tell you, love your enemies, and pray for those who persecute you. ⁴⁵In this way you will show you are sons of your Father in heaven. He makes His sun rise on the evil and the good and lets rain fall on the just and the unjust.

⁴⁶"If you love those who love you, do you deserve a reward? Don't tax collectors do that, too? ⁴⁷If you treat only your brothers kindly, are you doing anything extraordinary? Don't the people of the world do that, too? ⁴⁸So *be perfect* as your Father in heaven is perfect."

Don't Blow Your Horn

6 "Be careful not to do your good works before people to be seen by them. If you do, your Father in heaven will not reward you. ²So when you give to the poor, don't blow your horn, as hypocrites do in the synagogues and on the streets to be praised by people. I tell you, that's really all the reward they'll get. ³When you give to the poor, don't let your left hand know what your right hand is doing, ⁴that your giving may be secret. Then your Father, Who sees what is secret, will reward you."

How to Pray

⁵"When you pray, don't be like hypocrites, who like to stand praying in synagogues and on street corners in order to be seen by people. I tell you, that's really all the reward they'll get. ⁶But when you pray, *go into your own room, shut your door, and pray* to your Father, Who is with you when you're alone, and your Father, Who sees what is secret, will reward you.

⁷"When you pray, don't babble like pagans, who think they'll be heard if they talk a lot. ⁸Don't be like them. Your Father knows what you need before you ask Him.

The Lord's Prayer — *Luke 11:2-4*

⁹ "This is how you should pray:
Our Father in heaven —
May Your name be kept holy,
¹⁰ Your kingdom come,

---

38 *Ex 21:24; Lev 24:20; Deut 19:21*   43 *Lev 19:18* 48 *Deut 18:13*
6 *II Kings 4:33; Is 26:20*

And Your will be done on earth as it is in heaven.

[11] *Give us today our daily bread.*

[12] And forgive us our sins as we forgive those who sin against us.

[13] And don't bring us into temptation, But deliver us from evil.[c]

[14] "If you forgive the sins of others, your Father in heaven will also forgive you. [15] But if you don't forgive the sins of others, your Father will not forgive your sins."

Fasting

[16] "When you fast, don't look sad like hypocrites. They disfigure their faces to show people they are fasting. I tell you, that's really all the reward they'll get. [17] But when you fast, anoint your head, and wash your face [18] so that no one will see you fasting except your Father, Who is with you when you're alone. And your Father, Who sees what is secret, will reward you."

Treasures

[19] "Don't store up for yourselves treasures on earth, where moths and rust destroy them and thieves break in and steal. [20] But store up for yourselves treasures in heaven, where no moth or rust destroys them and no thieves break in and steal. [21] Where your treasure is, there your heart will be.

[22] "The eye is the lamp of the body. If your eye is healthy, you have light for your whole body. [23] But if your eye is evil, your whole body will be dark. How dark it is when the light in you is dark!

[24] "No one can serve two masters. Either he will hate the one and love the other or be loyal to the one and despise the other. You can't serve God and money."

Don't Worry! — *Luke 12:22-34*

[25] "So I tell you, don't worry about what you'll eat or drink to keep alive or what you'll wear on your bodies. Isn't life more than food, and the body more than clothes?

[26] "Look at the birds in the air. They don't sow or cut grain or gather anything into barns; but your Father in heaven feeds them. Aren't you worth more than they?

[27] "Can any of you by worrying add a single hour to your life?

[28] "And why worry about clothes? See how the flowers grow in the field, and learn from them. They don't work and they don't spin. [29] Yet, I tell you, even Solomon in all his glory didn't dress like one of these. [30] If that's how God clothes the grass in the field, which lives today and tomorrow is thrown into a stove, how much more certainly will He put clothes on you — you

---

11 *Prov 30:8*

---

c - 13   The doxology is found in later manuscripts: "You are the King who rules with power and glory forever. Amen."

who trust Him so little?

³¹"Don't worry, then, and say, 'What are we going to eat?' or, 'What are we going to drink?' or, 'What are we going to wear?' ³²The people of the world run after all these things. Your Father in heaven knows you need them all. ³³Seek first God's kingdom and righteousness, and all these things will be given to you, as well.

³⁴"So, don't worry about tomorrow. Tomorrow will take care of itself. Each day has enough trouble of its own."

Criticize Yourself — *Luke 6:37-42*

7 "Don't judge, so that you will not be judged. ²The way you judge others, you'll be judged, and the measure you measure with will be used for you.

³"Why do you look at the speck in your brother's eye and don't notice the log in your own eye? ⁴Or how can you say to your brother, 'Let me take the speck out of your eye,' when you have that log in your own eye? ⁵You hypocrite, first remove the log out of your own eye. Then you'll see clearly enough to take the speck out of your brother's eye."

Pearls to Pigs

⁶"*Don't* give anything holy to the dogs or *throw your pearls to the pigs, or they'll* trample them under their feet and then turn and *tear you to pieces.*"

Pray — *Luke 11:5-13*

⁷"Ask, and it will be given to you. Search, and you will find. Knock, and the door will be opened for you. ⁸Anyone who continues to ask receives; anyone who keeps searching finds; and anyone who continues to knock, the door will be opened for him.

⁹"If your son asks you for bread, will any of you give him a stone? ¹⁰Or if he asks for a fish; will you give him a snake? ¹¹Now if you, as wicked as you are, know how to give your children good gifts, how much more will your Father in heaven give good things to those who ask Him?"

The Golden Rule — *Luke 6:31*

¹²"Do for others everything you want them to do for you. That is the Law and the Prophets."

The Narrow Gate

¹³"Go through the narrow gate. The gate is wide, and the way is broad that leads to destruction, and many are going that way. ¹⁴But the gate is narrow, and the way is difficult, that leads to life, and only a few are finding it."

6 Prov 9:7

False Prophets — *Luke 6:43-46*

[15]"Beware of false prophets. They come to you dressed like sheep, but in their hearts they're savage wolves.

[16]"You will know them by what they produce. Can they pick grapes from thornbushes or figs from thistles? [17]No, every good tree bears good fruit, and a bad tree bad fruit. [18]A good tree cannot bear bad fruit, nor a bad tree good fruit. [19]Any tree that doesn't bear good fruit is cut down and thrown into the fire. [20]So you will know them by what they produce.

[21]"Not everyone who calls Me 'Lord, Lord,' will enter into the kingdom of heaven, but only the one who continues to do what My Father in heaven wants. [22]Many will say to Me on that Day, 'Lord, Lord, didn't we *prophesy in Your name,* drive out demons in Your name, and do many miracles in Your name?' [23]Then I will tell them frankly, 'I never knew you. *Get away from Me, you who are so busy doing wrong.'* "

Build on a Rock — *Luke 6:47-49*

[24]"Anyone who hears and does what I say is like a man who had the sense to build his house on a rock. [25]The rain poured down, the torrents came, the winds blew, and they beat against that house. But it didn't collapse, because its foundation was on the rock.

[26]"Everyone who hears the words I speak but doesn't continue to follow them is like a man who was so foolish he built his house on sand. [27]The rains poured down, the torrents came, the winds blew, and they beat against that house. And it went down with a big crash."

[28]When Jesus finished speaking, the crowds were amazed at His teaching. [29]He taught them with authority and not like their Bible scholars.

8 He went down the hill, and large crowds followed Him.

Jesus Heals a Leper — *Mark 1:40-44; Luke 5:12-14*

[2]There was a leper, who went to Him and bowed down to the ground before Him. "Lord, if You want to," he said, "You can make me clean." [3]Jesus stretched out His hand and touched him. "I want to," He said. "Be clean!" Immediately the leprosy left him, and he was clean. [4]"Be careful not to tell anyone," Jesus said to him, "but go, *let the priest examine* you, and offer the sacrifice Moses ordered, to show them you're well."

A Believing Captain — *Luke 7:1-10*

[5]He went to Capernaum. There a captain came to Him and begged Him: [6]"Lord, my servant is lying paralyzed at home. He's suffering terribly."

[7]"I will come and make him well," Jesus said.

[8]"Lord," the captain answered, "I'm not worthy for you to come under my roof. But just say a word, and my servant will be made well. [9]I'm only a man who has to obey others, but I have soldiers under me. I tell one of

them, 'Go', and he goes. And another, 'Come', and he comes. And my servant, 'Do this', and he does it."

[10]Amazed to hear this, Jesus said to the people who were following Him, "I tell you the truth, not even in Israel have I found such faith. [11]I also tell you, many will come *from the east and the west* and will eat with Abraham, Isaac, and Jacob in the kingdom of heaven, [12]but those who were born to be the heirs of the kingdom will be thrown out into the dark. There they will cry and grind their teeth."

[13]"Go," Jesus told the captain. "Let it be as you believed." And the servant was made well in that hour.

Peter's Mother-in-Law — *Mark 1:29-34; Luke 4:38-41*

[14]Jesus went into Peter's home, and there He saw Peter's mother-in-law lying in bed with a fever. [15]He touched her hand, and the fever left her. She got up and waited on Him.

[16]In the evening the people brought Him many who were demon-possessed. He drove out the spirits by speaking to them, and all who were sick He made well. [17]In this way what was said through the prophet Isaiah was to come true: *"He took away our sicknesses and carried our diseases."*

[18]When Jesus saw a crowd around Him, He gave orders to cross to the other side.

"I Will Follow You, but..." — *Luke 9:57-62*

[19]A Bible scholar came to Him and said, "Teacher, I will follow You anywhere You go."

[20]"Foxes have holes," Jesus told him, "and birds of the air have nests, but the Son of Man doesn't have a place to lay His head."

[21]"Lord," another disciple said to Him, "first let me go and bury my father."

[22]But Jesus told him, "Follow Me and let the dead bury their own dead."

Wind and Water Obey Him — *Mark 4:35-41; Luke 8:22-25*

[23]Jesus stepped into a boat, and His disciples went with Him. [24]Suddenly a big storm stirred the sea so that the waves were covering the boat. But He was sleeping.

[25]So they went and woke Him up. "Lord, save us!" they said "We're going to drown!"

[26]"Why are you afraid?" He asked them. "You trust Me so little!" Then He got up and ordered the winds and the sea to be quiet, and they became very calm.

[27]The men were amazed and said, "What kind of man is He? Even the winds and the sea obey Him!"

---

11 Is 49:12; 59:19; Mal 1:11   17 Is 53:4

The Gadarenes — *Mark 5:1-20; Luke 8:26-39*

²⁸He went to the country of the Gadarenes on the other side of the sea. There two demon-possessed men came out of the burial places and met Him. They were so savage no one could go along that road.

²⁹*"Let us alone*, Son of God!" they shouted. *"Did You come* here *to* torture us before it is time?"

³⁰Far away a herd of many hogs was feeding. ³¹"If You mean to drive us out," the demons were begging Jesus, "send us into that herd of hogs."

³²"Go," He told them. They came out and went into the hogs. Then the whole herd stampeded down the cliff into the sea and died in the water.

³³Those who had taken care of the hogs ran away and went into the town, where they told everything, especially about the demon-possessed men. ³⁴Then the whole town came out to meet Jesus. When they saw Him, they begged Him to leave their country.

Jesus Forgives Sins — *Mark 2:1-12; Luke 5:17-26*

9 Jesus got into a boat, crossed over, and came to His own town. ²There people brought Him a paralyzed man, lying on a bed.

When Jesus saw their faith, He said to the paralytic, "Cheer up, son! Your sins are forgiven."

³Then some of the Bible scholars said to themselves, "He's blaspheming."

⁴Jesus knew what they were thinking. "Why do you think evil in your hearts?" He asked them. ⁵"Is it easier to say, 'Your sins are forgiven,' or to say, 'Get up and walk?' ⁶I want you to know the Son of Man has power on earth to forgive sins." Then He said to the paralyzed man, "Get up, take your bed, and go home."

⁷He got up and went home. ⁸When the crowd saw this, they were amazed, and they praised God for giving such authority to men.

Matthew — *Mark 2:13-17; Luke 5:27-32*

⁹When Jesus left that place, He saw a man by the name of Matthew sitting in the tax office. "Follow Me," He told him. He got up and went with Him.

¹⁰As Jesus was lying down to eat at the house, many tax collectors and sinners came and ate with Jesus and His disciples. ¹¹When the Pharisees saw this, they asked His disciples, "Why does your Teacher eat with tax collectors and sinners?"

¹²Jesus heard them and said, "Those who are healthy don't need a doctor, but those who are sick. ¹³Go and learn what this means: *'I want mercy and not* mere *sacrifice.'* I didn't come to call righteous people but sinners."

---

29 I Kings 17:18

The Bridegroom — *Mark 2:18-22; Luke 5:33-39*

[14]Then John's disciples came to Jesus. "We and the Pharisees fast often," they said. "Why don't Your disciples fast?"

[15]Jesus asked them, "Can the bridegroom's friends mourn while the bridegroom is with them? The time will come when the bridegroom will be taken away from them; then they'll fast.

[16]"No one sews a piece of new cloth on an old garment. The patch will tear away some of the garment, and the hole will get worse. [17]No one pours new wine into old wineskins. If you do, the skins burst, the wine runs out, and the skins are ruined. No, you pour new wine into fresh skins; then both are preserved."

The Daughter of Jairus — *Mark 5:21-43; Luke 8:40-56*

[18]While He was talking to the people, a leader came to Him and bowed down to the ground before Him. "My daughter just died," he said, "but come, lay Your hand on her, and she will live."

[19]Jesus and His disciples got up and followed him.

[20]Now there was a woman who had a flow of blood for twelve years. She came to Him from behind and touched the tassel of His garment. [21]"If I only touch His garment," she said to herself, "I'll get well."

[22]Jesus turned and saw her. "Cheer up, daughter," He said, "your faith made you well." At that moment the woman was well.

[23]When Jesus came to the leader's home, He saw the flute players and the noisy crowd. [24]"Go away," He said. "The little girl isn't dead; she's sleeping." But they laughed at Him.

[25]When the crowd had been put outside, He went in and took her hand, and the little girl got up.

[26]The news about this spread all over that part of the country.

Two Blind Men

[27]When Jesus left that place, two blind men followed Him and called, "Have pity on us, Son of David."

[28]He went into a house, and there the blind men came to Him. "Do you believe I can do this?" Jesus asked them.

"Yes, Lord," they told Him.

[29]Then He touched their eyes and said, "As you believed, so let it be done to you!" [30]Then they could see again.

"See that no one finds out about this!" He sternly ordered them. [31]But they went out and spread the news about Him all over that part of the country.

A Man Who Could Not Talk

[32]As they were going out, some people brought to Him a man unable

to talk, who was demon-possessed. [33]But as soon as the demon was forced out, the man who was unable to talk began to speak.

The crowds were amazed and said, "We've never seen anything like this in Israel."

[34]But the Pharisees declared, "The ruler of the demons helps Him drive out the demons."

Pray for Workers

[35]Then Jesus traveled through all the towns and villages, teaching in their synagogues, preaching the good news of the kingdom, and healing every disease and sickness.

[36]As He saw the crowds, He felt sorry for them, because they were troubled and helpless *like sheep without a shepherd.* [37]Then He said to His disciples, "There's much grain to be harvested, but there are only a few workers. [38]Ask the Owner of the harvest to send out workers to bring in His grain."

Twelve Apostles — *Mark 3:13-19; Luke 6:13-16*

10 Jesus called His twelve disciples and gave them authority to drive out unclean spirits and to heal every disease and sickness.

[2]These are the names of the twelve apostles: first, Simon, called Peter, and his brother Andrew; James, Zebedee's son, and his brother John; [3]Philip and Bartholomew, Thomas and Matthew, the tax collector; James, the son of Alphaeus, and Thaddaeus; [4]Simon the Zealot, and Judas Iscariot, who betrayed Him.

Jesus Sends Out the Twelve — *Mark 6:7-13; Luke 9:1-6*

[5]Jesus sent these twelve out with the following instructions: "Don't go among the Gentiles or into any town of the Samaritans. [6]But go to the lost sheep of Israel. [7]As you go, preach, 'The kingdom of heaven is here.' [8]Heal the sick, raise the dead, cleanse lepers, drive out demons. Give these things as you received them — without pay.

[9]"Don't take any gold, silver, or copper money along in your pockets, [10]and no traveling bag for the way. Don't take two tunics, or sandals, or a stick — a worker earns his keep.

[11]"When you go into any town or village, look for a person there who is deserving, and stay with him until you leave. [12]When you go into a home, greet the family. [13]If the home is deserving, let your peace come on it. But if it's unworthy, let your peace come back to you. [14]If anyone doesn't welcome you or listen to what you say, leave that house or town, and shake the dust off your feet. [15]I tell you the truth, on Judgment Day it will be easier for the land of Sodom and Gomorrah than for that town.

[16]"You see, I'm sending you like sheep among wolves. So be shrewd as

36 *Num 27:17; I Kings 22:17; Ezek 34:5; Zech 10:2*

snakes and innocent as doves. [17]Be on your guard against men, because they'll hand you over to their courts and whip you in their places of worship. [18]On My account you'll be dragged before governors and kings to testify to them and to the nations. [19]But when they hand you over to the authorities, don't worry how you'll speak or what you'll say. When the time comes, you'll be told what to say. [20]It isn't you speaking but the Spirit of your Father speaking through you.

[21]"A brother will betray his brother to death, and a father his child. Children will *turn against* their parents and kill them. [22]Everyone will hate you because of My name. But be faithful to the end, and you will be saved. [23]When they persecute you in one town, flee to another. I tell you the truth, before you have gone through all the towns of Israel, the Son of Man will come.

[24]"A pupil isn't above his teacher, nor a slave above his master. [25]A pupil should be satisfied to share his teacher's lot and a slave to share his master's. If the master of the house was called Beelzebul, how much more certainly the members of his household! [26]So, don't be afraid of them.

"All that's covered will be uncovered, and all that's hidden will be known. [27]What I say to you in the dark, tell in the daylight; and what you hear whispered in your ear, preach from the housetops. [28]Don't be afraid of those who kill the body and can't kill the soul, but *fear Him* who can destroy soul and body in hell. [29]Aren't two sparrows sold for a cent? And not one of them will fall to the ground without your Father's permission. [30]As for you, even the hairs on your head are all counted. [31]So don't be afraid. You're worth more than many sparrows. [32]Whoever will confess Me before other people, him will I confess before My Father in heaven. [33]Whoever will deny Me before others, him will I deny before My Father in heaven.

[34]"Don't think that I came to bring peace to the earth. I didn't come to bring peace but a sword. [35]I came to set *a man against his father, a daughter against her mother, a daughter-in-law against her mother-in-law.* [36]*A man's enemies will be those in his own home.* [37]If you love father or mother more than Me, you're not worthy of Me; and if you love son or daughter more than Me, you're not worthy of Me. [38]If you don't take your cross and follow Me, you're not worthy of Me. [39]If you find your life, you'll lose it, but if you lose your life for Me, you'll find it.

[40]"Anyone who welcomes you welcomes Me; and anyone who welcomes Me welcomes Him who sent Me. [41]Anyone who welcomes a prophet because he is a prophet will get a prophet's reward. Anyone who welcomes a righteous man because he is righteous will get a righteous man's reward. [42]Anyone who will give one of these little ones just a cup of cold water because he is My disciple, I tell you the truth, he will certainly not lose his reward."

11 After Jesus finished giving His twelve disciples these instructions, He went on from there to teach and preach in their towns.

---

21 Mic 7:6   28 Prov 3:7   35-36 Mic 7:6

About John — *Luke 7:18-35*

[2]When John, who was in prison, heard about the things Christ was doing, he sent his disciples [3]to ask Him, "Are You the One Who is coming, or should we look for someone else?"

"Go," Jesus answered them, "tell John what you hear and see: [5]*The blind see*, the lame walk, lepers are made clean, *the deaf hear,* the dead are raised, and *the poor hear the good news,* [6]and happy is anyone who doesn't turn against Me."

[7]When they were leaving, Jesus began to talk to the crowds about John:

"What did you go out into the wilderness to see — a reed shaken by the wind?

[8]What, then, did you go out to see — a man dressed in soft robes? Those who wear soft robes you'll find in the palaces of kings.

[9]"What, then, did you go out for — to see a prophet? I tell you, he's even more than a prophet. [10]This is the one of whom it is written: '*I will send My messenger ahead of You to prepare* Your *way before* You.' [11]I tell you the truth, there never has appeared a woman's son greater than John the Baptizer. Yet the least in the kingdom of heaven is greater than John. [12]From the time of John the Baptizer until now the kingdom of heaven has been suffering violence, and violent men are trying to take it by force. [13]All the prophets and the Law prophesied up to the time of John, [14]but he (are you willing to accept it?) is the Elijah who has to come. [15]If you have ears, listen!

[16]"How should I picture the people of this generation? They're like little children sitting in the marketplaces and calling to others: [17]'We played a tune on the flute for you, but you didn't dance. We sang a funeral song, but you didn't mourn.' [18]John the Baptizer has come; he doesn't eat or drink, and people say, 'There's a demon in him!' [19]The Son of Man has come; He eats and drinks, and people say, 'Look at the glutton and drunkard, the friend of tax collectors and sinners!' And yet, wisdom is proven correct by her actions."

Woe!

[20]Then He began to denounce the cities where He had done most of His miracles, because they had not repented: [21]"Woe to you, Chorazin! Woe to you, Bethsaida! If the miracles done in you had been done in Tyre and Sidon, they would have repented long ago in sackcloth and ashes. [22]I tell you, on Judgment Day it will be easier for Tyre and Sidon than for you. [23]And you, Capernaum, will you be *lifted up to heaven? No, you will go down to hell!* If the miracles that have been done in you had been done in Sodom, it would still be there today. [24]I tell you, on Judgment Day it will be easier for the country of Sodom than for you."

---

5 Is 29:18; 35:5; 61:1   *10 Ex 23:20; Mal 3:1*

"Come to Me!"

²⁵At that time Jesus said, "I praise You, Father, Lord of heaven and earth, for hiding these things from wise and intelligent people and uncovering them for little children. ²⁶Yes, Father, I praise You for wanting it to be that way.

²⁷"My Father put everything in My hands. Only the Father knows the Son. And only the Son — and anyone to whom the Son wants to reveal Him — knows the Father.

²⁸"Come to Me, all you who are working hard and carrying a heavy load, and I will give you rest. ²⁹Take My yoke upon you, and learn from Me — I am gentle and humble-minded — then *you will find your rest.* ³⁰My yoke is easy, and My load is light."

Lord of the Sabbath — *Mark 2:23-28; Luke 6:1-5*

12 At that time Jesus walked through the grain fields on a Sabbath. His disciples were hungry and began to pick the heads of grain and eat them.

²When the Pharisees saw this, they said to Him, "Look, Your disciples are doing something they shouldn't do on a day of rest."

³"Haven't you read what David did," Jesus asked them, "when he and his men got hungry — ⁴how he went into God's house and ate the *loaves set out before God,* which he and his men had no right to eat, but only the priests? ⁵Or haven't you read in the Law that the priests in the temple work on a Sabbath as on other days and yet do no wrong? ⁶I tell you, here is something greater than the temple. ⁷If you knew what this means: *'I want mercy and not* mere *sacrifice',* you would not have condemned the innocent. ⁸The Son of Man is Lord of the Sabbath."

The Shriveled Hand — *Mark 3:1-6; Luke 6:6-11*

⁹He went on to another place and went into their synagogue, ¹⁰and there was a man with a shriveled hand.

"Is it right to heal on a Sabbath?" they asked Him. They wanted to accuse Him of something.

¹¹"If anyone of you has only one sheep," Jesus asked them, "and it falls into a hole on a Sabbath, won't you take hold of it and lift it out? ¹²Now, isn't a man much more valuable than a sheep? It is right, then, to do good on a day of rest!"

¹³Then He told the man, "Stretch out your hand." He stretched it out and it was made healthy again like the other hand.

¹⁴But the Pharisees left and plotted against Him to kill Him. ¹⁵Jesus knew about this, and so He left.

---

23 *Is 14:13,15*   **29** *Jer 6:16*   **4** *Lev 24:5-8; I Sam 21:6*   **7** *Hos 6:6*

The Servant

Many followed Him, and He healed them all, [16]but He ordered them not to tell people Who He was. [17]In this way what was said through the prophet Isaiah was to come true:

[18] *Here is My Servant Whom I have chosen,*
Whom I love and delight in.
I will put My Spirit on Him,
and He will announce justice to the nations.
[19] *He will not quarrel or shout.*
Nor will anyone hear His voice in the streets.
[20] *He will not crush a bruised reed nor put out a smoking wick*
until He has made justice victorious.
[21] *And His Name will be the hope of the nations.*

Power over a Demon — *Mark 3:20-30; Luke 11:14-23*

[22]At that time some people brought to Jesus a demon-possessed man who was blind and couldn't talk. He healed him so that he could talk and see.

[23]The people were all amazed. "Could this be the Son of David?" they asked. [24]When the Pharisees heard about it, they said, "He can drive out the demons only with the help of Beelzebul, who rules over the demons."

[25]Knowing what they were thinking, Jesus said to them, "If one part of any kingdom fights another, it loses its people. And if one part of any town or home fights another, it will not stand. [26]If Satan drives out Satan, he's fighting against himself. How then will his kingdom stand? [27]Now if Beelzebul helps Me drive out the demons, who helps your sons drive them out? That's why they'll be your judges. [28]But if the Spirit of God helps Me drive out the demons, then God's kingdom has come to you. [29]How can anyone go into a strong man's house and take away his goods without first tying the strong man up? After that he'll rob his house.

[30]"Anyone who's not with Me is against Me, and anyone who doesn't help Me gather, scatters. [31]So I tell you, any sin or slander will be forgiven, but slandering the Spirit will not be forgiven. [32]Anyone who talks against the Son of Man will be forgiven, but anyone who talks against the Holy Spirit will not be forgiven in this world or the next.

[33]"Either the tree is good, and then its fruit is good. Or the tree is bad, and then its fruit is bad. You can tell a tree by its fruit. [34]Brood of poisonous snakes, how can you who are so evil say anything good? What you say flows from your hearts. [35]A good man produces good things from the good stored in him, but an evil man produces evil from the evil stored in him. [36]But I tell you, on Judgment Day people will have to give an account of every useless word they say. [37]By your words you'll be acquitted, and by your words you'll be condemned."

18-21 Is 41:8-9; 42:1-4; Hab 1:4

The Sign of Jonah — *Luke 11:29-32*

[38]Then some Bible scholars and Pharisees said, "Teacher, we want You to show us a miraculous sign."

[39]"This wicked and unfaithful generation is looking for a miraculous sign," He answered them, "but the only sign they'll get is the prophet Jonah. [40]As *Jonah was in the belly of the big fish three days,* so the Son of Man will be in the heart of the earth three days. [41]*The men of Nineveh* will rise up in the Judgment with these people and condemn them, because they repented when *Jonah preached;* now look, One greater than Jonah is here. [42]The *queen* from the south will rise up in the Judgment with these people and condemn them, because she *came* from the ends of the earth to *hear Solomon's wisdom;* now look, One greater than Solomon is here.

[43]"When an unclean spirit comes out of a person, it goes through dry places looking for a place to rest but doesn't find any. [44]Then it says, 'I'll go back to the home I left.' He comes and finds it empty, swept, and decorated. [45]Then it goes and takes home with it seven other spirits worse than itself, and they go in and live there. In the end that man is worse than he was before. That's what will happen to this wicked generation."

The Mother and Brothers of Jesus — *Mark 3:31-35 Luke 8:19-21*

[46]He was still talking to the people when His mother and brothers were standing outside wanting to talk to Him. [47]"Your mother and Your brothers are standing outside," someone told Him, "and want to talk to You."

[48]"Who is My mother," He asked the man that told Him, "and who are My brothers?" [49]Pointing with His hand to His disciples, He said, "These are My mother and My brothers. [50]If you do what My Father in heaven wants, you are My brother and sister and mother."

The Sower — *Mark 4:1-20 Luke 8:4-15*

13 That same day Jesus left the house and sat down by the sea. [2]But so many people gathered around Him that He stepped into a boat and sat there while all the people stood on the shore. [3]Then He told them many things in parables.

[4]"A sower went out to sow," He said. "As he was sowing, some seed fell along the road, and the birds came and ate it. [5]Some seed fell on rocky ground, where it didn't have much soil. Because the soil wasn't deep, the seed came up quickly. [6]When the sun rose, it was scorched, and because it had not taken root, it withered. [7]Some seed fell on thorns, and the thorns grew up and choked it. [8]But some seed fell on good ground and produced grain, some a hundred, some sixty, and some thirty times as much as was sown. [9]If you have ears, listen!"

[10]The disciples came to Him. "Why are You talking to them in para-

---

40 Jonah 1:17   41 Jonah 3:4-5   42 II Chr 9:1-7

bles?" they asked Him.

[11]"You are given the privilege to know the mysteries of the kingdom of heaven,"

He answered, "but it isn't given to the others. [12]If you have something, you'll be given more, and so you'll get more and more. But if you don't have what you should have, even what you have will be taken away from you. [13]I talk to them in parables because they see and yet don't see, and hear and yet don't hear or understand. [14]In them more and more Isaiah's prophecy is coming true:

> *You will hear but never understand; you will look but never see.*
> [15] *These people have become dull at heart and hard of hearing*
>   *and have shut their eyes,*
>   *so that their eyes will never see, their ears never hear,*
>   *nor their hearts understand,*
>   *and they will never turn to Me and let Me heal them.*

[16]"Blessed are your eyes because they see and your ears because they hear. [17]I tell you the truth, many prophets and righteous people longed to see what you see and didn't see it, to hear what you hear and didn't hear it.

[18]"Listen to what the parable of the sower means. [19]When anyone hears the message of the kingdom but doesn't understand it, the evil one comes and takes away what was sown in his heart. That is what was sown along the road. [20]In another the seed falls on rocky ground. He's one who welcomes the Word with joy as soon as he hears it, [21]but it doesn't take root in him. He believes for a while, but as soon as the Word brings him trouble or persecution, he falls away. [22]In another the seed is sown among thorns. He's one who hears the Word, but the worry of the world and the deceitful pleasure of riches choke the Word, and it can't produce anything. [23]But in another the seed is sown on good ground. He's one who continues to hear and understand the Word and so goes on producing good things, one a hundred, another sixty, and another thirty times as much as was sown."

Weeds in the Wheat

[24]Jesus pictured it to them another way: "The kingdom of heaven is like a man who sowed good seed in his field. [25]But while people were sleeping, his enemy came and sowed weeds among the wheat and went away. [26]When the wheat came up and formed kernels, then the weeds showed up too.

[27]"The owner's slaves came to him and asked him, 'Master, didn't you sow good seed in your field? Where did the weeds come from?'

[28]" 'An enemy did that,' he told them.

" 'Do you want us to go and pull them out?' the slaves asked him.

[29]" 'No,' he said, 'if you pull out the weeds, you may pull up the wheat with them. [30]Let both grow together until the harvest. When the grain is cut, I will tell the reapers, "Gather the weeds first, and tie them in bundles

---

14-15 Is 6:9-10

to be burned, but bring the wheat into my barn.' ' "

A Mustard Seed and Yeast — *Mark 4:30-34; Luke 13:18-21*

³¹He pictured it to them another way: "The kingdom of heaven is like a mustard seed a man took and sowed in his field. ³²It's the smallest of all seeds, but when it has grown, it's the largest of the garden plants; it becomes a tree big enough for *the birds* to come and *nest in its branches."*

³³He pictured it to them another way: "The kingdom of heaven is like yeast a woman took and mixed into a bushel of flour until it was all fermented."

³⁴Jesus used parables to tell the crowds all these things. He didn't tell them anything without a parable, ³⁵so that what was said through the prophet would come true:

I will open My mouth to speak in parables;
I will tell what has been hidden since the world was made.

The Meaning of the Weeds in the Wheat

³⁶When Jesus had dismissed the people and gone into the house, His disciples came to Him and said, "Tell us what the parable of the weeds in the field means."

³⁷"The sower who sows the good seed," He answered, "is the Son of Man. ³⁸The field is the world. The good seed are the sons of the kingdom. The weeds are the sons of the evil one. ³⁹The enemy who sowed them is the devil. The harvest is the end of the world. The reapers are the angels. ⁴⁰As the weeds are gathered and burned, so it will be at the end of the world. ⁴¹The Son of Man will send His angels, and they will take out of His kingdom *those who do wrong and all who lead others to do wrong,* ⁴²and will throw them into the fiery furnace, where they will cry and grind their teeth. ⁴³Then *the righteous will shine like* the sun in their Father's kingdom. If you have ears, listen!"

The Treasure, the Pearl, and the Fish

⁴⁴"The kingdom of heaven is like a treasure buried in a field. When a man found it, he buried it again and was so delighted with it he went and sold everything he had and bought that field.

⁴⁵"Here's another picture of the kingdom of heaven: A dealer was looking for fine pearls. ⁴⁶When he found a very valuable pearl, he went and sold everything he had and bought it.

⁴⁷"Again, the kingdom of heaven is like a net that was let down into the sea, and it gathered all kinds of fish. ⁴⁸When it was full they pulled it onto the shore, sat down, and picked out the good fish and put them in containers but threw the bad ones away. ⁴⁹So it will be at the end of the world.

---

32 Ps 104:12; Ezek 17:23; 31:6; Dan 4:12,21   *35 Ps 78:2*
41 Zeph 1:2,3; Job 12:16   43 Dan 12:3

The angels will go out and separate the wicked from the righteous [50]and throw them into the fiery furnace, where they will cry and grind their teeth. [51]"Did you understand all this?" "Yes," they answered.

[52]"And so every Bible student trained for the kingdom of heaven," He told them, "is like the owner of a house who brings out of his storeroom new things and old."

[53]When Jesus had finished these parables, He left that place.

His Last Visit to Nazareth — *Mark 6:1-6 Luke 4:16-30*

[54]He went to His hometown and taught the people in their synagogue in such a way they were amazed. "Where did he get this wisdom and the power to do these miracles?" they asked. [55]"Isn't he the carpenter's son? Isn't his mother's name Mary, and aren't James, Joseph, Simon, and Judas his brothers? [56]And aren't all his sisters here with us? Where did he get all this?" [57]So they turned against Him.

"A prophet is without honor only in his hometown and in his family," Jesus told them. [58]He did not work many miracles there because of their unbelief.

Herod Kills John — *Mark 6:14-29; Luke 9:7-9*

14 At that time Herod, the governor, heard the news about Jesus. [2] "This is John the Baptizer!" he told his servants. "He's risen from the dead, and that's why these powers are working in Him."

[3]Herod had arrested John, bound him, and put him in prison on account of Herodias, the wife of his brother Philip, [4]because John was telling him, "It isn't right for you to have her." [5]Herod wanted to kill him but was afraid of the people because they considered John a prophet.

[6]When Herod's birthday was celebrated, the daughter of Herodias danced before the guests. Herod was so delighted with her [7]he swore to give her anything she might ask for.

[8]Urged on by her mother, she said, "Give me here on a platter the head of John the Baptizer."

[9]Then the king was sorry. But he had sworn to do it, and there were the guests— so he ordered it given to her. [10]He sent and had John's head cut off in prison. [11]And his head was brought on a platter and given to the girl, who took it to her mother.

[12]John's disciples came and took his body away and buried it. Then they went and told Jesus.

Jesus Feeds 5,000 — *Mark 6:30-44; Luke 9:10-17; John 6:1-14*

[13]When Jesus heard about John, He left in a boat and went to a deserted place to be alone. The people heard of it and followed Him on foot from the towns. [14]When Jesus stepped out of the boat, He saw a big crowd. He felt sorry for them and healed their sick.

¹⁵In the evening the disciples came to Him. "This is a deserted place," they said, "and it's late. Send the crowds away to the villages to buy themselves some food."

¹⁶"They don't need to go away," Jesus answered them. "You give them something to eat."

¹⁷ "All we have here are five loaves and two fish," they told Him.

¹⁸"Let Me have them," He said.

¹⁹He ordered the people to sit down on the grass. Then taking the five loaves and the two fish and looking up to heaven, He blessed them. Breaking the loaves, He gave them to the disciples, and they gave them to the people. ²⁰All of them ate and had enough. They picked up the pieces that were left — twelve baskets full.

²¹Some 5,000 men had eaten, not counting women and children.

Jesus Walks on Water — *Mark 6:45-52; John 6:15-21*

²²Jesus quickly made the disciples get into the boat and go on ahead to the other side while He dismissed the people. ²³After sending them away, He went up the hill to be alone and pray. When it got late, He was there alone.

²⁴The boat, now many hundred yards from the shore, was troubled by the waves because the wind was against them.

²⁵Toward morning He came to them, walking on the sea. ²⁶When the disciples saw Him walking on the sea, they were terrified. "It's a ghost," they said, and they cried out in terror.

²⁷Immediately He talked to them. "Have courage," He said. "It is I. Don't be afraid."

²⁸"Lord, if it's You," Peter answered Him, "order me to come to You on the water."

²⁹"Come," He said. So Peter got out of the boat, walked on the water, and went toward Jesus. ³⁰But when he saw the wind, he was frightened and started to sink. "Lord, save me!" he cried.

³¹Quickly Jesus stretched out His hand and caught him. "How little you trust Me!" He said to him. "Why did you doubt?"

³²When they stepped into the boat, the wind stopped. ³³And the men in the boat bowed down before Him and said, "You certainly are God's Son."

³⁴They crossed over and came to the shore at Gennesaret. ³⁵The men of that place recognized Jesus and sent messengers all around that part of the country, and the people brought Him all the sick ones, ³⁶and they begged Him just to let them touch the tassel of His garment. All who touched it were made well.

Unclean Hands — *Mark 7:1-23*

15 Then some Pharisees and Bible scholars came to Him from Jerusalem. ²"Why do Your disciples sin against the rules handed down by our fathers?" they asked. "They don't wash their hands when they eat."

[3]"Why do you sin against God's commandment for the sake of your own rules?" He asked them. [4]"For example, God has said: '*Honor father and mother*', and: '*Anyone who curses father or mother must die*'. [5]But you say, 'Whoever tells his father or mother, "I'm giving God anything I might have used to help you," doesn't have to honor his father.' [6]For the sake of your rules you have set aside God's Word. [7]Hypocrites, Isaiah was right when he prophesied about you: [8]'*These people honor Me with their lips, but their hearts are far away from Me.* [9]*They worship Me in vain, teaching for doctrines rules which are only human.'* "

[10]Then He called the people and told them: "Listen to Me and understand this: [11]What comes into his mouth doesn't make a person unclean, but what goes out of his mouth makes him unclean."

[12]Then the disciples came to Him. "Do you know the Pharisees were offended when they heard You say that?" they asked Him.

[13]"Any plant My Father in heaven didn't plant," He answered, "will be torn out by the roots. [14]Let them go; they are blind leaders. When one blind man leads another, both will fall into a ditch."

[15]"Tell us what You mean by this parable," Peter said to Him.

[16]"Are you still as dense as the others?" He asked. [17]"Don't you know that everything that goes into the mouth goes into the stomach and so passes through? [18]But what goes out of the mouth comes from the heart, and that makes a person unclean. [19]Yes, out of the heart come evil thoughts, murders, adulteries, sexual sins, stealing, lies, slanders. [20]These are the things that make a person unclean. But eating without washing your hands doesn't make you unclean."

A Non-Jewish Woman — *Mark 7:24-30*

[21]Leaving that place, Jesus went away to the neighborhood of Tyre and Sidon. [22]There was a Canaanite woman of that territory who came out and shouted, "Have pity on me, Lord, Son of David! A demon is severely tormenting my daughter."

[23]But He didn't answer her a word. Then His disciples came to Him and urged Him, "Send her away. She's yelling after us."

[24]"I was sent only to the lost sheep of Israel," He answered.

[25]She came and bowed down before Him. "Lord, help me!" she said.

[26]"It isn't good," He answered, "to take the children's bread and throw it to the puppies."

[27]"You're right, Lord," she said, "but even the puppies eat some of the crumbs that drop from their masters' table."

[28]Then Jesus answered her, "O woman, you have a strong faith! Let it be done for you as you wish." At that moment her daughter was made well.

[29]Jesus left that place and went along the shore of the Sea of Galilee. Then He went up a hill and sat there.

[30]Many people came to Him, bringing the lame, blind, crippled, those

---

4 Ex 20:12; Deut 5:16; Ex 21:17; Lev 20:9; Prov 20:20   *8-9 Is 29:13*

unable to talk, and many others and laid them at His feet. He made them well, [31]so that the crowds were amazed to find those unable to talk speaking, the crippled being cured, the lame walking, and the blind seeing. And they praised the God of Israel.

Jesus Feeds 4,000 — *Mark 8:1-9*

[32]Jesus called His disciples. "I feel sorry for the people," He said. "They've been with Me three days now and have nothing to eat. I don't want to let them go without eating; they may become exhausted on the way."

[33]"Where could we get enough bread in a wilderness to feed such a crowd?" His disciples asked Him.

[34]"How many loaves do you have?" Jesus asked them. "Seven," they said, "and a few small fish."

[35]He ordered the people to sit down on the ground. [36]Then He took the seven loaves and the fish, gave thanks, broke them, and gave them to the disciples, and they gave them to the people.

[37]All of them ate and had enough. They picked up the pieces that were left — seven baskets full. [38]Four thousand men had eaten, not counting women and children.

[39]Then He dismissed the people.

He stepped into the boat and came into the neighborhood of Magadan.

A Proof from Heaven — *Mark 8:10-12*

16 The Pharisees and Sadducees came and, to test Him, asked Him to show them a sign from heaven.

[2]He answered them, "In the evening you say, 'The weather will be fine, because the sky is red.' [3]And in the morning: 'There will be a storm today, because the sky is red and gloomy.' You know how to judge the appearance of the sky correctly but can't judge the signs of the times.[d]

[4]"A wicked and unfaithful generation demands a sign, and the only sign they'll get is that of Jonah."

Then He left them and went away.

The Yeast of the Pharisees — *Mark 8:13b-21*

[5]When the disciples started out for the other side, they forgot to take bread.

[6]Jesus said to them, "Beware of the yeast of the Pharisees and Sadducees!"

[7]As they were discussing about this, they mentioned, "We didn't take any bread."

[8]Aware of what was going on, Jesus asked, "Why are you discussing about not having any bread? You have so little faith! [9]Don't you understand yet, and don't you remember the five loaves for the five thousand and how many baskets full you picked up? [10]Or the seven loaves for the four thou-

---

d - 3   Jesus' words in vv 2-3 are lacking in some of our oldest manuscripts

sand and how many baskets full you picked up? [11]Why don't you see I wasn't talking to you about bread? But beware of the yeast of the Pharisees and Sadducees!"

[12]Then they understood He didn't warn them against the yeast in bread but against the teaching of the Pharisees and Sadducees.

"You Are the Christ [Messiah]" — *Mark 8:27-30; Luke 9:18-21*

[13]When Jesus came to the neighborhood of Caesarea Philippi, He asked His disciples, "Who do people say the Son of Man is?"

[14]"Some say John the Baptizer," they answered, "others Elijah, still others Jeremiah, or one of the prophets."

[15]"Who do you say I am?" He asked them.

[16]"You are the Christ," Simon Peter answered, "the Son of the living God!"

[17]"Blessed are you, Simon, son of John," Jesus answered him, "because no flesh and blood, but My Father in heaven has revealed this to you. [18]I tell you, you are Peter, and on this rock I will build My church, and the forces of hell will not overpower it. [19]I will give you the keys of the kingdom of heaven. Anything you bind on earth will be bound in heaven, and anything you free on earth will be freed in heaven."

[20]Then He warned the disciples not to tell anyone that He was the Christ.

"I Will Die and Rise" — *Mark 8:31-33; Luke 9:22*

[21]After this, Jesus Christ kept pointing out to His disciples He had to go to Jerusalem, suffer much from the elders, ruling priests, and Bible scholars, be killed, and then on the third day rise.

[22]But Peter took Him aside and started to correct Him, "God be merciful to You, Lord! This must never happen to You!"

[23]Turning, He said to Peter, "Get behind Me, Satan! You're tempting Me, because you're not thinking what God thinks but what men think."

Take Up Your Cross — *Mark 8:34-9:1; Luke 9:23-27*

[24]Then Jesus said to His disciples, "If you want to follow Me, deny yourself, take up your cross, and come with Me. [25]If you want to save your soul, you will lose it. But if you will lose your soul for Me, you will find it. [26]What good will it do you to win the whole world and lose your soul? Or what would you give to buy back your soul? [27]The Son of Man is going to come with His angels in His Father's glory, and then *He will give each one according to what he has done.* [28]I tell you the truth, there are some standing here who will never taste death until they see the Son of Man coming in His kingdom."

27 Ps 62:12; Prov 24:12

Jesus Shows His Glory (The Transfiguration) — *Mark 9:2-13;* Luke 9:28-36

17 After six days Jesus took with Him Peter, James, and John, the brother of James, and led them up a high mountain to be alone with them.

²He was transfigured before them, His face shone like the sun, and His clothes became as white as light. ³Suddenly, Moses and Elijah appeared to them and were talking with Him.

⁴"Lord," Peter said to Jesus, "it's good for us to be here. If You wish, I'll put up three shelters here, one for You, one for Moses, and one for Elijah."

⁵He was still speaking when a bright cloud suddenly overshadowed them, and a voice came out of the cloud: "This is *My Son* Whom I love and *delight in. Listen to Him!*"

⁶When the disciples heard this, they fell facedown; they were terrified. ⁷But Jesus came and touched them. "Get up," He said, "and don't be afraid." ⁸They looked up and saw no one but Jesus.

⁹On their way down the mountain Jesus ordered them, "Don't tell anyone what you have seen until the Son of Man has risen from the dead."

¹⁰So the disciples asked Him, "Why, then, do the Bible scholars say, 'First Elijah has to come?'"

¹¹"*Elijah* is coming," He answered, "and *will put* everything *in order again.*¹²But I tell you Elijah has already come, and people didn't know him but treated him as they pleased. In the same way they're going to make the Son of Man suffer."

¹³Then the disciples understood He was talking about John the Baptizer.

The Demon-Possessed Boy — *Mark 9:14-29; Luke 9:37-43a*

¹⁴When they came to the people, a man came to Jesus and knelt before Him.

¹⁵"Lord," he said, "have pity on my son. He's epileptic and very sick. Often he falls into fire or into water. ¹⁶I brought him to Your disciples, but they couldn't make him well."

¹⁷"O you unbelieving and perverted generation!" Jesus answered. "How long must I be with you? How long must I put up with you? Bring him here to Me."

¹⁸Jesus talked sharply to the demon, and it came out of the boy, and after that the boy was well.

¹⁹Afterwards, when Jesus was alone, the disciples came to Him. "Why couldn't we drive out the demon?" they asked.

²⁰"You have so little faith," He told them. "I tell you the truth, if you have faith no bigger than a mustard seed, you will say to this mountain, 'Move from here to there,' and it will move. Then nothing will be impossible for you."ᵉ

---

5 *Ps 2:7; Is 42:1; Deut 18:15*   11 *Mal 4:5-6*

e - 21   Our two oldest manuscripts lack v. 21: "This kind goes out only by prayer and fasting." See Mark 9:29

"I Will Die and Rise" — *Mark 9:30-32; Luke 9:43b-45*

²²While they were gathering together in a group in Galilee, Jesus told them, "The Son of Man is going to be betrayed into the hands of men, ²³and they will kill Him, but on the third day He will rise." Then they were very sad.

A Coin in a Fish's Mouth

²⁴When they came to Capernaum, the collectors of the temple tax came to Peter. "Doesn't your teacher pay the temple tax?" they asked.
²⁵"Certainly," he answered.
Peter went into the house, but before he could speak, Jesus asked him, "What do you think, Simon? From whom do the kings of the world collect tolls or taxes — from their children or from other people?"
²⁶"From other people," he answered.
"Then the children are exempt," Jesus told him. ²⁷"But we don't want to give them a reason to think wrong of us. So go to the sea and throw in a hook. Take the first fish that comes up, open its mouth, and you will find a coin. Take that and give it to them for Me and you."

Who Is the Greatest? — *Mark 9:33-37; Luke 9:46-48*

18 At that time the disciples came to Jesus and asked, "Who is the greatest in the kingdom of heaven?"
²He called a little child and had him stand in front of them. ³"I tell you the truth," He said to them, "if you aren't converted and become like little children, you will never get into the kingdom of heaven. ⁴If you become humble like this little child, you are the greatest in the kingdom of heaven. ⁵And if you welcome a child like this in My name, you welcome Me."

Do I Lead Others to Sin? — *Mark 9:42-48; Luke 17:1-2*

⁶"If anyone leads into sin one of these little ones who believe in Me, it would be better for him to have a big millstone hung around his neck and be drowned in the sea where it's deep. ⁷Woe to the world because it tempts people to sin! Temptations to sin must come, but woe to that man who tempts others to sin!
⁸"If your hand or your foot makes you sin, cut it off and throw it away. It is better for you to go into life without one hand or one foot than to have two hands or two feet and be thrown into the everlasting fire. ⁹If your eye makes you sin, tear it out and throw it away. It is better for you to go into life with one eye than to have two eyes and be thrown into hellfire.
¹⁰"Be careful not to despise one of these little ones. I tell you their angels in heaven always see the face of My Father in heaven.ᶠ

---

f - 10   Our two oldest manuscripts lack v. 11: "The Son of man came to save the lost."

The Lost Sheep — *Luke 15:1-7*

[12] "What do you think? If a man has a hundred sheep and one of them gets lost, will he not leave the ninety-nine in the hills and go and look for the sheep that's wandering away? [13]And if he finds it, I tell you the truth, he's certainly more delighted with it than with the ninety-nine that didn't get lost. [14]So your Father in heaven doesn't want one of these little ones to be lost."

Tell Him His Fault

[15]"If your brother sins against you, go and point out his sin to him when you're alone with him. If he listens to you, you have won your brother. [16]But if he won't listen, take one or two with you so that *you have two or three witnesses to establish every word.* [17]If he won't listen to them, tell it to the church. But if he won't even listen to the church, treat him like a pagan and a tax collector. [18]I tell you the truth, whatever you bind on earth will be bound in heaven, and whatever you set free on earth will be free in heaven.

[19]"Again I tell you, if two of you here on earth agree to ask for anything, My Father in heaven will do it for you. [20]Where two or three have been brought together in My name, there I am among them."

Forgive!

[21]Then Peter came to Jesus and asked Him, "Lord, how often do I have to forgive my brother who sins against me? Seven times?"

[22]"I tell you," Jesus answered him, "not seven times but seventy times seven times.

[23]"That is why the kingdom of heaven is like a king who wanted to settle accounts with his slaves. [24]When he began to do so, there was brought to him one who owed him ten thousand talents.[g] [25]But he couldn't pay it, and so the master ordered him, his wife, his children, and all he had to be sold to pay the debt. [26]Then the slave got down on his knees and, bowing low before him, begged: 'Be patient with me, and I'll pay you everything.'

[27]"The master felt sorry for his slave, released him, and canceled his debt. [28]But when that slave went away, he found one of his fellow slaves who owed him a hundred denarii.[h] He grabbed him and started to choke him. 'Pay what you owe,' he said.

[29]"Then his fellow slave got down on his knees and begged him, 'Be patient with me, and I'll pay you.' [30]But he refused and went and put him in prison until he would pay what he owed.

[31]"When his fellow slaves saw what had happened, they were very sad and went and told their master the whole story.

[32]"Then his master sent for him. 'You wicked slave!' he said to him. 'I

---

16 Deut 19:15

g - 24   One talent of silver weighed about as much as 1,500 silver dollars
h - 28   One denarius was a day's pay.

canceled all you owed me, because you begged me. [33]Shouldn't you also have treated your fellow slave as mercifully as I treated you?'

[34]"His master was so angry he handed him over to the torturers until he would pay all he owed him.

[35]"That is what My Father in heaven will do to you if each of you will not heartily forgive his brother."

Husband and Wife — *Mark 10:1-12*

19 When Jesus finished saying this, He left Galilee and went to the part of Judea on the other side of the Jordan. [2]Large crowds followed Him, and He healed them there.

[3]Some Pharisees, coming to Him to test Him, asked Him, "Is it right for a man to divorce his wife for any reason?"

[4] "Haven't you read," He asked them, "He Who created them from the beginning *made them a male and a female?"* [5]And He added: *"That is why a man will leave his father and mother and live with his wife, and the two will be one flesh.* [6]And so they are no more two but one flesh. Now, what God has joined together man must not separate."

[7] "Why, then, did Moses order a man *to make out a divorce paper and divorce his wife?"* they asked Him.

[8]He answered them, "Because your hearts are hard, Moses let you divorce your wives, but originally there was no such thing. [9]I tell you, if anyone divorces his wife, except for adultery, and marries another, he's living in adultery."

[10]"If a man has to have such grounds in dealing with his wife," the disciples told Him, "it's better not to marry."

[11] "Not all can do this," He told them, "only those to whom it has been given. [12]Some don't marry because they were born that way. Others, because they have been castrated by men. And still others have decided to do without marriage for the kingdom of heaven. If anyone can do it, let him do it."

Jesus Loves Children — *Mark 10:13-16; Luke 18:15-17*

[13]Then some people brought little children to Jesus to have Him lay His hands on them and pray. But the disciples sternly told them not to do it.

[14]"Let the little children come to Me," Jesus said, "and don't keep them away. The kingdom of heaven belongs to such as these." [15]He laid His hands on them and then went away.

The Rich Young Leader — *Mark 10:17-31; Luke 18:18-30*

[16]There was one who came and asked Him, "Teacher, what good thing should I do to get everlasting life?"

---

4 Gen 1:27; 5:2   *5 Gen 2:24*   *7 Deut 24:1,3*

¹⁷"Why do you ask Me about something good? Only One is good. If you want to go into life, keep the commandments."

¹⁸"Which commandments?" he asked Him.

Jesus said, "*Do not murder*. Do not commit adultery. *Do not steal. Do not give false testimony.*

¹⁹*Honor father and mother, and love your neighbor as yourself.*"

²⁰"I've kept all these," the young man told Him. "What else do I need?"

²¹"If you want to be perfect," Jesus told him, "go, sell what you have, give the money to the poor, and you'll have a treasure in heaven. Then come and follow Me."

²²When the young man heard this, he went away sad, because he was very rich.

²³"I tell you the truth," Jesus said to His disciples, "it is hard for a rich man to get into the kingdom of heaven. ²⁴Again I tell you it's easier for a camel to go through the eye of a needle than for a rich man to get into God's kingdom."

²⁵The disciples, hearing this, were astonished. "Who, then, can be saved?" they asked.

²⁶"Men can't do this," Jesus said as He looked at them, "but *for God all things are possible.*"

²⁷Then Peter spoke up: "Look! We gave up everything and followed You. So what will we get?"

²⁸"I tell you the truth," Jesus said to them, "in the new world, when the Son of Man sits on His throne of glory, you who followed Me will also sit on twelve thrones and rule the twelve tribes of Israel. ²⁹And everyone who gave up homes, brothers or sisters, father, mother, or children, or fields for Me will get many times as much, and then everlasting life. ³⁰But many who are first will be last, and many who are last will be first."

"The Last Will Be First"

20 "The kingdom of heaven is like the owner of a place who went out early in the morning to hire men to work in his vineyard. ²He agreed with the workers to pay them a denarius[i] a day and sent them into his vineyard. ³About nine o'clock he went out and saw others standing in the marketplace doing nothing. ⁴'You go into the vineyard too,' he told them, 'and I'll pay you what's right.' So they went.

⁵"He went out again about twelve o'clock and three o'clock and did the same thing. ⁶About five o'clock he went out and found some others standing around. 'Why are you standing here all day long doing nothing?' he asked them.

⁷" 'No one has hired us,' they answered him.

" 'You go into the vineyard, too,' he told them.

---

*18-19 Ex 20:12-16; Deut 5:16-20   **19** Lev 19:18*
*   **26** Gen 18:14; Job 42:2; Zech 8:6*

i - 2   A denarius was one day's pay

⁸"When evening came, the owner of the vineyard told his manager, 'Call the men and give them their pay. Start with the last and go on to the first.'

⁹"Those who started working around five o'clock came, and each got a denarius. ¹⁰When the first ones came, they expected to get more, but each of them, too, got a denarius. ¹¹They took it, but they grumbled against the owner: ¹²"These last men worked only one hour, and you've treated them exactly like us who have worked hard all day in the blazing sun.'

¹³" 'Friend, I'm doing you no wrong,' he answered one of them. 'You agreed with me on a denarius, didn't you? ¹⁴Take your money and go. I want to give this last man as much as I give you. ¹⁵Don't I have the right to do as I please with what is mine? Or are you jealous because I'm generous?'

¹⁶"In this way the last will be first and the first last."

The Cup of Suffering — *Mark 10:32-45*

¹⁷When Jesus was going up to Jerusalem, He took the twelve by themselves and said to them on the way: ¹⁸"Look, we're going up to Jerusalem, and the Son of Man will be betrayed to the ruling priests and Bible scholars, who will condemn Him to die ¹⁹and hand Him over to the Gentiles to be mocked, whipped, and crucified, but on the third day He will rise."

²⁰Then the mother of Zebedee's sons came to Jesus with her sons and bowed before Him to ask Him for a favor.

²¹"What do you want?" He asked her.

She told Him, "Promise that one of my two sons will sit at Your right and the other at Your left in Your kingdom."

²²"You don't know what you're asking," Jesus answered. "Can you drink the cup I'm going to drink?"

"We can," they told Him.

²³"You'll drink My cup," He told them. "But sitting at My right and left is something I can give only to those for whom My Father prepared it."

²⁴When the other ten heard about it, they became angry with the two brothers. ²⁵Jesus called them and said: "You know the rulers of the nations are lords over them, and their great men are tyrants over them. ²⁶But among you it's different. Anyone who wants to become great among you let him be your servant, ²⁷and anyone who wants to be first among you let him be your slave, ²⁸just as the Son of Man did not come to be served but to serve and give His life as a ransom for many."

Two Blind Men

²⁹As they were leaving Jericho, a large crowd followed Him. ³⁰And there were two blind men sitting by the road. When they heard, "Jesus is passing by," they called, "Lord, have pity on us, Son of David!"

³¹The crowd urged them to be quiet. But they called all the louder, "Lord, have pity on us, Son of David!"

³²Jesus stopped and called them. "What do you want Me to do for

you?" He asked.

³³"Lord, we want to see," they told Him.

³⁴Jesus felt sorry for them and touched their eyes, and immediately they could see. And they followed Him.

The King Comes to Jerusalem — *Mark 11:1-11; Luke 19:29-44; John 12:12-19*

21 When they came near Jerusalem and had reached Bethphage and the Mount of Olives, Jesus sent two disciples. ²"Go into the village ahead of you," He told them, "and right away you'll find a donkey tied up and a colt with her. Untie them and bring them to Me. ³If anyone says anything to you, say, 'The Lord needs them,' and immediately he will send them."

⁴This happened so that what was said through the prophet would come true:

⁵ *Tell the daughter of Zion,*

"Look! Your King is coming to you,

gentle, riding on a donkey, even on a colt of a donkey."

⁶The disciples went and did as Jesus had directed them. ⁷They brought the *donkey and the colt* and laid their garments on them; and Jesus sat on them. ⁸Most of the people spread their garments on the road. Others cut branches from the trees and spread them on the road. ⁹The people who went ahead of Him and followed Him were shouting:

"Our Savior, the Son of David!

Blessed is He Who is coming in the Lord's name!

Our Savior — in the highest heavens!"

¹⁰When He came into Jerusalem, the whole city was excited, asking, "Who is this?"

¹¹The crowds answered, "This is the Prophet Jesus from Nazareth in Galilee."

Cleansing the Temple — *Mark 11:15-19; Luke 19:45-48*

¹²*Jesus went into the temple* and put out all who were selling and buying in the temple and upset the tables of the money changers and the chairs of those who sold pigeons. ¹³"It is written," He told them, " '*My house should be called a house of prayer,*' but you're making it *a den of robbers!*"

¹⁴Blind and lame persons came to Him in the temple, and He made them well.

¹⁵When the ruling priests and the Bible scholars saw the wonderful things He did and the children shouting in the temple, "*Our Savior,* the Son of David!" they didn't like it at all. ¹⁶"Do You hear what they're saying?" they asked Him.

5,7 Is 62:11; Gen 49:11; Zech 9:9   9 Ps 118:25-26   12 Mal 3:1
13 Is 56:7; Jer 7:11   15 Ps 118:25-26   16 Ps 8:2

"Yes," Jesus answered them. "Haven't you ever read: *'You have made children and babies praise You'?"*

[17]He left them and went out of the city to Bethany and spent the night there.

Nothing but Leaves — *Mark 11:12-14, 20-25*

[18]In the morning as He went back to the city, Jesus was hungry, [19]and seeing a fig tree by the road, He went up to it and found nothing on it but leaves. "May no fruit ever grow on you again!" Jesus said to it. And immediately the fig tree dried up.

[20]The disciples were amazed to see this. "How did the fig tree dry up so quickly?" they asked.

[21]"I tell you the truth," Jesus answered them, "if you believe and don't doubt, you will not only do what I did to the fig tree, but if you will say to this mountain,[j] 'Be lifted up and be thrown into the sea,'[k] it will be done. [22]*Anything you ask for in prayer,* believe, and *you will get it.*"

From Heaven — *Mark 11:27-33; Luke 20:1-8*

[23]When He came to the temple and was teaching, the ruling priests and the elders of the people came to Him. "By what authority are you doing these things?" they asked. "And who gave you the authority to do them?"

[24]Jesus answered them, "I will ask you a question. And if you answer Me, I'll tell you by what authority I'm doing these things. [25]John's baptism — was it from heaven or from men?"

They argued among themselves, "If we say, 'From heaven,' he will ask us, 'Then why didn't you believe him?' [26]But if we say, 'From men,' we're afraid of the people; they all think John is a prophet." [27]So they answered Jesus, "We don't know."

Then Jesus also told them, "Neither will I tell you by what authority I'm doing these things."

Say and Do

[28]"Now, what do you think of this? A man had two sons. He went to the first and said, 'Son, go and work in the vineyard today.'

[29]"'I won't,' he answered. Later he changed his mind and went.

[30]"The father went to the other one and told him the same thing. He answered, 'I will, sir,' but didn't go.

[31]"Which of the two did what the father wanted?"

They answered, "The first."

Jesus said to them, "I tell you the truth, tax collectors and prostitutes

---

22 Ps 50:15; Is 30:19

j - 21   The Mount of Olives
k - 21   The Dead Sea, which can be seen from the Mount of Olives.

are going into God's kingdom ahead of you. [32]John came to you showing the way of righteousness, but you didn't believe him; the tax collectors and prostitutes believed him. But even when you had seen that, you didn't change your minds and believe him."

God's Vineyard — *Mark 12:1-12; Luke 20:9-19*

[33]"Listen to another parable:

"A man who owned property *planted a vineyard.* He *put a wall around it, cut a winepress into the rock, and built a watchtower.* Then he rented it out to workers and left home.

[34]"When the grapes were getting ripe, he sent his servants to the workers to get his share of the grapes. [35]The workers took his servants and beat one, killed another, and stoned a third. [36]Then he sent other servants, this time a larger number, and they treated these the same way.

[37]"Finally he sent his son to them, saying, 'They will respect my son.'

[38]"When the workers saw the son, they said to one another, 'This is the heir. Come, let's kill him and get his inheritance.' [39]So they took him, threw him out of the vineyard, and killed him.

[40]"Now, when the owner of the vineyard comes, what will he do to those workers?"

[41]They said to Him, "He will have those scoundrels die a miserable death and rent out the vineyard to other workers who will bring him the grapes when they're ripe."

[42]Jesus asked them, "Haven't you ever read in the Scriptures: *'The Stone the builders rejected has become the Cornerstone. The Lord has done it, and we think it is wonderful'?* [43]That is why I tell you, God's kingdom will be taken away from you and be given to a people who will do its works. [44]Anyone who *falls on* that *Stone* will be *smashed to pieces,* and if It falls on anyone, It will scatter him like dust."

[45]When the ruling priests and Pharisees heard His parables, they knew He was talking about them. [46]They wanted to grab Him but were afraid because the people thought He was a prophet.

Come to the Wedding!

22 Again Jesus used parables in talking to them. He said:

[2]"The kingdom of heaven is like a king who prepared a wedding for his son.

[3]He sent his slaves to call those who had been invited to the wedding, but they refused to come. [4]Then he sent other slaves and said to them, 'Tell the people who are invited, "Look ! I prepared my dinner. My bulls and fattened calves are killed, and everything is ready. Come to the wedding."'

[5]"But they paid no attention and went away, one to his farm, another to his business, [6]and the rest took his slaves, shamefully mistreated them,

---

33 Is 5:1-2   42 Ps 118:22-23; Is 28:16   44 Is 8:14-15

and murdered them.

[7]"The king became angry. He sent his soldiers and they killed those murderers and burned their city.

[8]"Then he said to his slaves: 'The wedding is ready, but the people who were invited didn't deserve the honor. [9]Now go where the roads leave the city, and call everyone you find there to the wedding.' [10]Those slaves went out on the roads and brought in all the people they found, both bad and good. And the wedding hall was filled with guests.

[11]"When the king came in to look at the guests, he saw there a man without a wedding garment. [12]'Friend,' he asked him, 'how did you get in here without a wedding garment?'

"The man couldn't say a thing. [13]Then the king told the servants, 'Tie him hand and foot, and throw him out into the dark. There he will cry and grind his teeth.'

[14]"Many are invited, but few are chosen."

Taxes — *Mark 12:13-17; Luke 20:20-26*

[15]Then the Pharisees went away and plotted to trap Him with a question.

[16]They sent their disciples with Herod's men to say to Him: "Teacher, we know You're honest and teach God's way and don't care what others think, because You don't favor any special persons. [17]Now tell us: What do You think? Is it right to pay a tax to Caesar or not?"

[18]Knowing their wickedness, Jesus asked, "Why do you test Me, you hypocrites? [19]Show Me the coin with which the tax is paid."

They brought Him a denarius. [20]"Whose head is this and whose inscription?" He asked them. [21]"Caesar's," they said.

"Give to Caesar what is Caesar's," He told them, "and to God what is God's."

[22]They were amazed to hear this. Then they let Him alone and went away.

The Dead Live — *Mark 12:18-27; Luke 20:27-40*

[23]On that day some Sadducees, who say there is no resurrection, came to Him with this question: [24]"Teacher, Moses said: *'If anyone dies childless, his brother should marry his widow and have children for his brother.'* [25]Now, there were seven brothers among us. The first married and died, and since he had no children, he left his widow to his brother. [26]The second brother did the same, and so did the third and the rest of the seven. [27]Last of all the woman died. [28]Now, when they rise from the dead, which of the seven will be her husband? For they all married her."

[29]"You're wrong," Jesus answered them. "You don't know the Scriptures or God's power. [30]When the dead rise, men and women don't marry

---

24 *Gen 38:8; Deut 25:5-6*

but are like angels in heaven. [31]About the dead rising — didn't you read what God told you: [32]*'I am the God of Abraham, the God of Isaac, and the God of Jacob'?* He's not the God of the dead but of the living."

[33]His teaching amazed the people who heard Him.

Love God and Your Neighbor — *Mark 12:28-34*

[34]When the Pharisees heard He had silenced the Sadducees, they got together. [35]One of them, an expert in the Law, tested Him by asking Him, [36]"Teacher, which is the greatest commandment in the Law?"

[37]Jesus answered him, " *'Love the Lord your God with all your heart, with all your soul, and with all your* mind.' [38]This is the greatest and most important commandment. [39]The next is like it: *'Love your neighbor as yourself.'* [40]All the Law and the prophets depend on these two commandments."

David's Son — *Mark 12:35-37a; Luke 20:41-44*

[41]While the Pharisees were still together, Jesus asked them, [42]"What do you think of the Christ? Whose Son is He?"

"David's," they answered Him.

[43]He asked them, "Then how can David by the Spirit call Him 'Lord'? He says: [44]*The Lord said to my Lord, 'Sit at My right until I put Your enemies under Your feet.'* [45]Now, if David calls Him 'Lord', how can He be his son?"

[46]No one could answer Him, and after that no one dared to ask Him another question.

Beware! — *Mark 12:37b-40; Luke 20:45-47*

23 Then Jesus said to the crowd and to His disciples:
[2]"The Bible scholars and the Pharisees sit in Moses' seat. [3]Do everything they tell you, and observe it; but don't do what they do, because they don't do what they say. [4]They tie together heavy loads that are hard to carry and lay them on the shoulders of others, but they won't lift a finger to move them.

[5]"They do everything in order to be seen by others. They make their phylacteries broad and the tassels of their garments long.[1] [6]They like the places of honor at dinners and the front seats in synagogues, [7]to be greeted in the marketplaces and have people call them rabbi. [8]But don't you let them call you rabbi, because you have only one Teacher, and you are all brothers. [9]And don't call anyone on earth your father; you have only one Father, and He is in heaven. [10]Don't have others call you teachers; you have

---

32 Ex 3:6   37 Deut 6:5   39 Lev 19:18   44 Ps 110:1

1 - 5   A phylactery was a small leather box fastened by a leather strap on the forehead or on the left arm. In the box were pieces of parchment on which were written the words of Ex 13:1-10, 11-16; Deut 6:4-9; 11:13-21. An Israelite wore a tassel on each of the four corners of his outer garment. (Num 15:37-40; Deut 22:12)

only one Teacher, and that is Christ. [11]The greatest among you will be one who serves you. [12]*If you honor yourself, you will be humbled, but if you humble yourself, you will be honored.*"

Woe! — *Luke 11:37-54*

[13]"Woe to you Bible scholars and Pharisees, you hypocrites! You lock people out of the kingdom of heaven. You won't come into it yourselves, and when others try to come in, you won't let them.[m]

[15]"Woe to you Bible scholars and Pharisees, you hypocrites! You cross sea and land to convert a single person, and when he's converted, you make him twice as fit for hell as you are.

[16]"Woe to you blind guides! You say, 'If anyone swears by the temple, that's nothing. But if anyone swears by the gold in the temple, he must keep his oath.' [17]Blind fools! Which is greater, the gold or the temple that made the gold holy? [18]Or again, 'If anyone swears by the altar, that's nothing. But if anyone swears by the gift that's on it, he must keep his oath.' [19]You blind men! Which is greater, the gift or the altar that makes the gift holy? [20]If you swear by the altar, you swear by it and by everything on it. [21]If you swear by the temple, you swear by it and by Him Who lives there. [22]And if you swear by *heaven,* you swear by *God's throne* and by Him Who is sitting on it.

[23]"Woe to you Bible scholars and Pharisees, you hypocrites! You give a tenth of mint and dill and cumin but have neglected the more important things of the Law: justice, mercy, and faithfulness. You should have done the one without neglecting the other. [24]Blind guides! You strain out the gnat but swallow the camel.

[25]"Woe to you Bible scholars and Pharisees, you hypocrites! You clean the outside of a cup and of a dish, but inside they're full of greed and uncontrolled desire. [26]You blind Pharisee! First clean the inside of the cup and of the dish in order to make also the outside of it clean. [27]Woe to you Bible scholars and Pharisees, you hypocrites! You're like white-washed graves that look beautiful on the outside but inside are full of dead men's bones and every kind of decay. [28]So on the outside you look good to people, but inside you're full of hypocrisy and lawlessness.

[29]"Woe to you Bible scholars and Pharisees, you hypocrites! You build the tombs of the prophets and decorate the graves of the righteous [30]and say, 'If we had lived at the time of our fathers, we wouldn't have helped them murder the prophets.'

[31]And so you testify against yourselves that you are the sons of those who murdered the prophets. [32]Go on, finish what your fathers started!

[33]"You snakes! Brood of vipers! How can you escape being condemned

---

12 Prov 29:23   22 Is 66:1

m - 13   Our oldest manuscripts do not have v. 14: "Woe to you Bible scholars and Pharisees, you hypocrites! You swallow the widows' houses and then, to cover up, make long prayers. For this you'll be punished all the more." See Mark 12:40; Luke 20:47

to hell?

³⁴That's why I'm sending you men to speak God's Word, men who are wise and know the Bible. Some of them you will kill and crucify. Others you will whip in your synagogues and hunt from town to town, ³⁵so that all the *innocent blood* poured on the ground will come on you, from the blood of righteous Abel to the blood of Zechariah, Barachiah's son, whom you murdered between the holy place and the altar. ³⁶I tell you, all this will certainly come upon this generation.

³⁷"Jerusalem, Jerusalem, you murder the prophets and stone those sent to you! How often I wanted to bring your children together *as a hen gathers her chicks under her wings*, but you didn't want to! ³⁸Now your *house will be left* to you *a deserted place.* ³⁹I tell you, you will not see Me again until you say, *'Blessed is He Who is coming in the Lord's name.'* "

Sorrow Ahead! — *Mark 13:1-13; Luke 21:5-19*

24 When Jesus walked out of the temple and was going away, His disciples came to show Him the buildings of the temple. ²"You see all these things?" Jesus asked them. "I tell you the truth, not one stone will be left on another here but will be torn down."

³When He was sitting on the Mount of Olives, His disciples came to Him alone, saying, "Tell us, when will this be and how can we tell when You're coming back and the world will come to an end?"

⁴"Be careful not to let anyone deceive you," Jesus answered them. ⁵"Many will come using My name, and saying, 'I am the Christ,' and will deceive many.

⁶"You will hear of wars and rumors of wars. See that you don't get alarmed. It *must happen*, but that's not the end yet. ⁷*Nation will fight against nation,* and *kingdom against kingdom,* and there will be famines and earthquakes in different places. ⁸But all these are only the first pains.ⁿ

⁹"Then they will hand you over to those who will make you suffer, and they will kill you, and all nations will hate you on account of My name. ¹⁰Then *many will fall away* and betray one another and hate one another. ¹¹Many false prophets will arise and lead many people astray. ¹²And because there will be more and more wickedness, the love of most people will turn cold. ¹³But endure to the end, and you will be saved.

¹⁴"This good news of the kingdom must be preached all over the world so that all nations hear the truth, and then the end will come."

Jerusalem Will Be Destroyed — *Mark 13:14-20; Luke 21:20-24*

¹⁵"When you see what the prophet Daniel told about, *the abomination laying waste the land* and standing *in the holy place* (anyone who reads this

---

35 *Prov 6:17*   **37** *Ps. 91:4*   **38** *Jer 12:7; 22:5-6*   **39** *Ps 118:26*
6 *Dan 2:28-29,45* **7** *II Chr 15:6; Is 19:2*   **10** *Dan 11:41* **15** *Dan 9:27; 11:31; 12:11*

---

n - 8   As in childbirth, sharper pains will follow before the Savior comes in glory.

should understand it), [16]then if you're in Judea, flee to the hills. [17]If you're on the roof, don't come down to get the things in your house. [18]If you're in the field, don't turn back to get your garment.

[19]"Woe to the women who in those days are expecting babies or nursing them. [20]Pray that it may not be winter or a Sabbath when you flee. [21]It will be a time of great *misery such as hasn't been from the beginning* of the world *until now* and never will be again. [22]And if that time had not been cut short, no one would be saved. But that time will be cut short for the sake of those whom He has chosen."

Jesus Is Coming — *Mark 13:21-31; Luke 21:25-33*

[23]"If anyone tells you then, 'Look, here is Christ!,' or, 'There He is!' *don't believe* it, [24]because false Christs and false *prophets* will *come and do* great *miracles and wonders* to deceive if possible even those whom God has chosen. [25]You see, I've told you this before it happens. [26]So when you're told, 'There He is in the wilderness,' don't go out; or, 'Here He is in the inner rooms,' don't believe it. [27]The Son of Man will come like the lightning that flashes from the east to the west. — [28]Where the dead body is, there the vultures will gather.

[29]"Right after the misery of that time *the sun will turn dark, the moon will stop shining, the stars will be falling from the sky,* and *the powers of heaven* will be shaken. [30]Then the sign announcing the Son of Man will appear in the sky, and then *all the people on earth will mourn* when they see *the Son of Man coming on the clouds in the sky* with *power and great glory.* [31]And *with a loud trumpet call* He will send out His angels, and they *will gather* His chosen ones *from the north, south, east, and west, from one end of the sky to the other.*

[32]"Learn this lesson from a fig tree: When its branch gets tender and grows leaves, you know summer is near. [33]So also when you see all these things, you know that He is near, at your door.

[34]"I tell you the truth, this generation will not pass away until all this happens. [35]Heaven and earth will pass away, but My words will never pass away."

Be Ready! — *Mark 13:32-37; Luke 21:34-36*

[36]"No one knows when that day or hour will come, not the angels in heaven, not even the Son, but only the Father.

[37]"When the Son of Man comes, it will be like the time of Noah. [38]In the days before the flood, they were eating and drinking, and men and women were marrying until the day *Noah went into the ark.* [39]They weren't aware of anything until *the flood came* and swept them all away. That's how it

---

*21 Dan 12:1   24 Deut 13:1-3   **29** Is 13:10; 34:4; Ezek 32:7-8; Joel 2:10,31; 3:15   **30** Zech 12:10,12; 14:5; Dan 7:13-14   **31** Is 27:13; Deut 30:4; Zech 2:6; 14:5 **38-39** Gen 7:6-7*

will be when the Son of Man comes.

⁴⁰"Then there will be two men in the field — one will be taken and the other left. ⁴¹Two women will be grinding at a mill — one will be taken and the other left.

⁴²"Watch, then, because you don't know which day your Lord is coming. ⁴³You know if the owner of a house had known what time of the night the burglar was coming, he would have stayed awake and not let anyone break into his house.

⁴⁴You, too, get ready, because the Son of Man is coming when you don't expect Him. ⁴⁵"Now, who is the *faithful and sensible slave* whom the master has put in charge of his servants to give them their food at the right time? ⁴⁶*Blessed is that slave* whom his master finds doing this when he comes. ⁴⁷I tell you, he will certainly put him in charge of all his property. ⁴⁸But if that slave is wicked and says to himself, 'My master is staying a long time,' ⁴⁹and starts to beat his fellow slaves and eats and drinks with the drunkards, ⁵⁰the master of that slave will come one day when he's not expecting him and at a time he doesn't know ⁵¹and will cut him in pieces and put him with the hypocrites. There they will cry and grind their teeth."

The Bridegroom Is Coming

25 "Then the kingdom of heaven will be like ten girls who took their lamps and went out to meet the bridegroom. ²Five of them were foolish, and five were wise. ³The foolish girls brought their lamps, but they took no extra oil. ⁴The wise took flasks of oil with their lamps. ⁵But the bridegroom delayed, and so they all dozed off to sleep.

⁶"At midnight there was a shout: 'The bridegroom is here! Come out and meet him!' ⁷Then all those girls woke up and got their lamps ready.

⁸"But the foolish said to the wise, 'Give us some of your oil. Our *lamps are going out.*'

⁹"The wise girls answered, 'There will never be enough for us and for you. Better go to the dealers and buy some for yourselves.'

¹⁰"While they were away buying it, the bridegroom came, and the girls who were ready went with him to the wedding, and the door was shut.

¹¹"Later the other girls also came and said, 'Lord, lord, open the door for us!'

¹²" 'I tell you the truth,' he answered them, 'I don't know you.'

¹³"Keep awake, then, because you don't know the day or the hour."

Three Kinds of Workers

¹⁴"It's like a man going on a trip. He called his slaves and put his money into their hands. ¹⁵He gave one man five talents,° another two talents, and another one talent, each according to his ability. Then he left.

45-46 Prov 14:35   *8* Prov 13:9; 24:20

o - 15   It is hard to estimate the real value of a "talent." It is here taken to be equal to $2,000

[16]"The one who got five talents immediately went and put it into business and made another five talents. [17]The one who had two talents did the same and made another two talents. [18]But the one who got one talent went and dug a hole in the ground and hid his master's money.

[19]"After a long time the master of those slaves came and had them give an account. [20]The one who got five talents came and brought another five talents. 'Master,' he said, 'you let me have five talents. See, I've made another five talents.'

[21]"'Well done, good and faithful slave!' his master answered him. 'You proved You could be trusted with a small amount. I will put you in charge of a large amount. Come and share your master's joy.'

[22]"The one who got two talents came and said, 'Master, you let me have two talents. See, I've made another two talents.'

[23]"'Well done, good and faithful slave!' his master answered him. 'You proved you could be trusted with a little. I will put you in charge of something big. Come and share your master's happiness.'

[24]"Then came also the one who got one talent. 'Master,' he said, 'I found out you're a hard man. You reap where you didn't sow, and you gather where you didn't scatter. [25]I was afraid, so I went and hid your talent in the ground. There's your money!'

[26]"'You wicked and lazy slave!' his master answered him. 'You knew I reap where I didn't sow and gather where I didn't scatter. [27]Then you should have invested my money with the bankers, and when I came back, I could have gotten my money back with interest. [28]Take the talent away from him, and give it to the one who has the ten talents. [29]Whoever has anything will receive, and so he will have more and more. And from him who doesn't have what he should have, even what he has will be taken away. [30]Throw this good-for-nothing slave out into the dark where there will be crying and grinding of teeth.'"

Jesus Will Judge the World

[31]"When the Son of man *comes* in His glory *and all the* angels *with Him,* then He will sit on His throne of glory. [32]And all nations will be gathered before Him, and He will separate them from one another, as a shepherd separates the sheep from the goats, [33]and He will have the sheep stand at His right but the goats at His left.

[34]"Then the King will say to those at His right, 'Come, you whom My Father blessed, inherit the kingdom prepared for you from the time the world was made. [35]I was hungry, and you gave Me something to eat; I was thirsty, and you gave Me a drink; I was a stranger, and you took Me into your homes; [36]naked, and you gave Me something to wear; sick, and you looked after Me; in prison, and you visited Me.'

[37]"Then the righteous will ask Him, 'Lord, when did we see You hungry and feed You, or thirsty and give You a drink? [38]When did we see You

---

31 Zech 14:5

a stranger and take You into our homes, or naked and give You something to wear? [39]When did we see You sick or in prison and visit You?'

[40]"And the King will answer them, 'I tell you the truth, *anything you did for one of My brothers* here, however humble, *you did for Me.*'

[41]"Then He will say to those at His left, 'Go away from Me, you cursed ones, into the everlasting fire prepared for the devil and his angels. [42]I was hungry, and you gave Me nothing to eat; thirsty, and you didn't give Me a drink; [43]a stranger, and you didn't take Me into your homes; naked, and you didn't give Me anything to wear; sick and in prison, and you didn't look after Me.'

[44]"Then they, too, will ask, 'Lord, when did we see You hungry or thirsty or a stranger or naked or sick or in prison and didn't help You?' [45]Then He will answer them, 'I tell you the truth, anything you didn't do for one of these, however humble, you didn't do for Me.' [46]Then *these* will go away *to everlasting* punishment, but the righteous *to everlasting life.*"

The Plot — *Mark 14:1-2; Luke 22:1-2; John 11:45-57*

26 When Jesus finished saying all this, He told His disciples, [2]"You know that in two days the Passover will be celebrated, and the Son of Man will be handed over to be crucified."

[3]Then the ruling priests and the elders of the people met in the palace of the high priest, whose name was Caiaphas. [4]They plotted in an underhanded way to arrest Jesus and put Him to death. [5]But they said, "Not during the festival, or there may be a riot among the people."

Mary Anoints Jesus — *Mark 14:3-9; John 12:1-8*

[6]Jesus came to Bethany and went into the home of Simon the leper. [7]There a woman came to Him with an alabaster jar of expensive perfume, and she poured it on His head while He was reclining at the table.

[8]The disciples saw it and didn't like it. "Why should there be such a waste?" they asked. [9]"This could have been sold for a big sum and the money given to the poor."

[10]Knowing what was going on, Jesus asked them, "Why do you trouble the woman? She has done a beautiful thing to Me. [11]*The poor you always have with you,* but you will not always have Me. [12]She poured this perfume on My body to prepare Me for My burial. [13]I tell you the truth, wherever this good news is preached in the whole world, certainly what she has done will also be told in memory of her."

Judas Plans to Betray Jesus — *Mark 14:10-11; Luke 22:3-6*

[14]Then one of the twelve, called Judas Iscariot, went to the ruling priests.

---

40 Prov 19:17   46 Dan 12:2   11 Deut 15:11

[15]"What will you give me?" he asked. "I will betray Him to you."

They *offered* him *30 pieces of silver*. [16]And from then on he was looking for a chance to betray Him.

The Passover — *Mark 14:12-17; Luke 22:7-17*

[17]On the first day of the Festival of Bread Without Yeast the disciples came to Jesus. "Where do You want us to get things ready for You to eat the Passover?" they asked.

[18]"Go into the city," He said, "to a certain man and tell him: 'The Teacher says, "My time is near. I'm going to celebrate the Passover with My disciples at your house." ' "

[19]The disciples did as Jesus directed them and got the Passover ready.

[20]In the evening He reclined with the twelve for the supper.

"Is it I?" — *Mark 14:18-21; Luke 22:21-23; John 13:21-30*

[21]While they were eating, He said: "I tell you the truth, one of you is going to betray Me!"

[22]Feeling deeply hurt, they asked Him one by one, "You don't mean me, Lord?" [23]"One who is dipping into the bowl with Me will betray Me!" He answered. [24]"The Son of Man is going away as it is written about Him, but woe to that man who betrays the Son of Man! It would be better for that man if he had never been born."

[25]"You don't mean me, Master?" asked Judas, who was going to betray Him. "I do!" He told him.

The Lord's Supper — *Mark 14:22-26; Luke 22:18-20; I Cor. 11:23-25*

[26]While they were eating, Jesus took bread and blessed it. He broke it and gave it to the disciples and said, "Take and eat. This is My body."

[27]Then He took a cup and gave thanks. He gave it to them, saying, "Drink of it, all of you. [28]For this is My *blood of the* New *Testament,* which is poured out for many for the forgiveness of sins.

[29]"I tell you, I will not drink again of this fruit of the vine until that day when I drink it with you in a new way in My Father's kingdom."

[30]Then they sang a hymn.[p]

"You Will Deny Me" — *Mark 14:27-31; Luke 22:31-34; John 13:36-38*

They started out for the Mount of Olives.

[31]Then Jesus said to them, "Tonight you will all turn against Me. It is written: 'I will *strike down the Shepherd, and the sheep of the flock will be scattered.'* [32]But after I have risen, I will go ahead of you to Galilee."

[33]"Even if they all turn against You," Peter answered Him, "I'll never turn against You."

---

15 Zech 11:12   28 Ex 24:8; Jer 31:31-32; Zech 9:11   31 Zech 13:7

p - 30   Perhaps Psalms 115 to 118

[34]"I tell you the truth," Jesus told him, "tonight before the rooster crows, you will deny Me three times."

[35]"Even if I have to die with You," Peter told Him, "I'll never deny You!" All the other disciples said the same thing.

Gethsemane — *Mark 14:32-42; Luke 22:39-46*

[36]Then Jesus went with the disciples to a place called Gethsemane and told them, "Sit down here while I go over there and pray."

[37]Taking Peter and Zebedee's two sons with Him, He started to feel sad and distressed. [38]Then He said to them,

"My soul is so full of sorrow that I am at the point of death. Stay here and keep awake with Me."

[39]Going ahead a little, He threw Himself face down on the ground and prayed, "My Father, if it is possible, let this cup pass away from Me. But let it not be as I want it but as You want it."

[40]When He came back to the disciples, He found them asleep. He said to Peter, "So you couldn't keep awake with Me one hour! [41]Stay awake and pray that you may not be tempted. The spirit is willing, but the flesh is weak."

[42]Then He went away a second time and prayed, "My Father, if this cannot pass by without My drinking it, Your will be done."

[43]He came again and found them asleep. They couldn't keep their eyes open. [44]Leaving them again, He went and prayed the same prayer a third time. [45]Then He came back to the disciples. "Are you going to sleep on now and rest?" He asked them. "Now the time has come, and the Son of Man will be betrayed into the hands of sinners. [46]Get up, let us go. Here comes the one who is betraying Me!"

The Arrest — *Mark 14:43-52; Luke 22:47-54a; John 18:1-14*

[47]While He was still talking, there came Judas, one of the twelve, and with him a large crowd with swords and clubs, from the ruling priests and elders of the people. [48]The traitor had given them a signal. "The One I kiss," he said, "is the Man. Grab Him."

[49]Then Judas quickly stepped up to Jesus and said, "Greetings, Rabbi!" and kissed Him.

[50]"Friend, why are you here?" Jesus asked him.

Then the others came forward, took hold of Jesus, and arrested Him. [51]One of the men with Jesus reached for his sword and drew it. He struck the high priest's slave and cut off his ear. [52]Then Jesus told him, "Put your sword back in its place. All who take the sword will die by the sword. [53]Or do you think I couldn't call on My Father to send right now more than 70,000 angels to help Me? [54]How, then, could the Bible be fulfilled when it says this must happen?"

---

38 *Ps 42:5-6,11; 43:5*

[55]Then Jesus said to the crowd, "You came out to arrest Me with swords and clubs as if I were a robber! Day after day I sat and taught in the temple, and you didn't arrest Me. [56]But all this has happened so that what the prophets have written would come true."

Then all the disciples left Him and ran away.

The First Trial Before the Jewish Council — Mark 14:53-65

[57]Those who arrested Jesus took Him to Caiaphas, the high priest, where the Bible scholars and the elders had been called together. [58]Peter followed Him at a distance until he came to the high priest's courtyard. Going inside, he sat with the attendants to see how this would end.

[59]The ruling priests and the whole Jewish council tried to get false testimony against Jesus in order to put Him to death [60]but didn't find any, although many came forward to give false testimony. At last two men came forward, [61]saying, "He said, 'I can tear down God's temple and rebuild it in three days.'"

[62]The high priest stood up and asked Him, "Don't you have any answer to what these men testify against you?"

[63]But Jesus was silent.

Then the high priest said to Him, "Swear by the living God, and tell us, are you the Christ, the Son of God?"

[64]"I am," Jesus answered him. "But I tell you, from now on you will all see *the Son of Man sitting at the right hand* of power and *coming on the clouds of heaven.*" [65]Then the high priest tore his robes. "He has blasphemed!" he declared. "Why do we need any more witnesses? You just heard the blasphemy. [66]What's your verdict?"

"He deserves to die!" they answered.

[67]Then they *spit* in His face, struck Him with their fists, and some slapped Him, [68]saying, "Prophesy, you Christ; tell us who hit you?"

Peter Denies Jesus — Mark 14:66-72; Luke 22:54b-62; John 18:15-18, 25-27

[69]Peter was sitting out in the courtyard. A maid came to him, saying, "You, too, were with Jesus, the Galilean."

[70]But he denied it in front of all of them: "I don't know what you're talking about."

[71]As he went out to the entrance, another maid saw him. "He was with Jesus from Nazareth," she told those who were there.

[72]Again Peter denied, and he swore, "I don't know the Man!"

[73]After a little while the men standing there approached Peter and said, "Sure, you're one of them. Anyone can tell by the way you talk."

[74]Then he started to curse and swear, "I don't know the Man!" Just

---

64 Ps 110:1; Dan 7:13   67 Is 50:6

then the rooster crowed, [75]and Peter remembered Jesus saying, "Before the rooster crows, you will deny Me three times." And he went outside and cried bitterly.

The End of Judas

27 Early in the morning all the ruling priests and the elders of the people decided to put Jesus to death. [2]They bound Him, led Him away, and handed Him over to Pilate, the governor.

[3]When Judas, who betrayed Him, saw that Jesus was condemned, he regretted what he had done and brought the 30 pieces of silver back to the ruling priests and elders. [4]"I have sinned," he said. "I have betrayed innocent blood."

"What do we care about that?" they asked. "That's your problem."

[5]Then he threw the money into the temple and left. He went away and hanged himself.

[6]The ruling priests took the money. "It isn't right to put this into the temple treasury," they said; "it's blood money." [7]So they decided to buy with it the potter's field for the burial of strangers. [8]That's why that field has been called the Field of Blood ever since. [9]Then what was said through the prophet Jeremiah came true: *I took the thirty pieces of silver, the price of Him on whom some men of Israel set a price,* [10]*and I gave them for the potter's field, as the Lord directed me.*"

Before Pilate — *Mark 15:1-5; Luke 23:1-4; John 18:28-38*

[11]Jesus stood before the governor. "Are you the King of the Jews?" the governor asked Him.

"Yes," Jesus answered.

[12]While the ruling priests and elders were accusing Him, He said nothing. [13]Then Pilate asked Him, "Don't you hear how many accusations they are bringing against you?"

[14]But Jesus didn't answer him in regard to anything that was said, so that the governor was very much surprised.

Barabbas — *Mark 15:6-15; Luke 23:17-25; John 18:39-40*

[15]Now, at every Passover festival the governor used to free one prisoner whom the crowd wanted. [16]At that time there was a well-known prisoner by the name of Barabbas. [17]When the people had gathered, Pilate asked them, "Whom do you want me to set free for you, Barabbas or Jesus, who is called Christ?" [18]He knew they had handed Jesus over to him because they were jealous.

[19]While he was sitting on the judge's seat, his wife sent someone to tell him, "Let that righteous Man alone. I suffered much in a dream last

---

9-10 Zech 11:12-13; Jer 32:6-9

night on account of Him."

²⁰But the ruling priests and elders persuaded the people to ask for Barabbas and to have Jesus killed.

²¹ "Which of the two," the governor asked them, "do you want me to set free for you?"

They said, "Barabbas."

²²"Then what should I do with Jesus, who is called Christ?" Pilate asked them.

"He must be crucified!" all of them said.

²³"Why, what wrong has he done?" he asked.

But they kept yelling all the louder, "He must be crucified!"

²⁴When he saw he wasn't getting anywhere, but a riot was breaking out instead, Pilate took water and washed his hands before the crowd. "I am innocent of this man's blood," he said. "It's your responsibility!"

²⁵And all the people answered, "His blood be on us and on our children."

²⁶Then he freed Barabbas for them, but Jesus he whipped and handed over to be crucified.

"Hail, King!" — Mark 15:16-19; John 19:1-3

²⁷Then the governor's soldiers took Jesus into the governor's palace and gathered the whole troop of soldiers around Him. ²⁸They took off His clothes and put a scarlet cloak on Him. ²⁹They twisted some thorns into a crown, placed it on His head, and put a stick in His right hand. Then they knelt before Him and mocked Him, saying, "Hail, King of the Jews!" ³⁰They *spit on* Him, took the stick, and kept hitting Him on the head with it.

"They Crucified Him" — Mark 15:20-32; Luke 23:26-38; John 19:16b-24

³¹After mocking Him, they took off the cloak and put His own clothes back on Him. Then they took Him away to crucify Him.

³²Going out, they found a man from Cyrene by the name of Simon. They forced him to carry His cross.

³³They came to a place called Golgotha, which means Skull Place. ³⁴*They offered Him a drink* of wine, mixed with *gall,* but when He tasted it, He refused to drink it. ³⁵ After they crucified Him, *they divided His clothes among them by throwing lots.* ³⁶Then they sat down there and kept watch over Him. ³⁷They put above His head a notice stating why He was being punished. It read: THIS IS JESUS, THE KING OF THE JEWS. ³⁸At that time they crucified two *robbers with Him,* one at His right and the other at His left.

³⁹Those who passed by *ridiculed* Him, *shaking their heads* ⁴⁰and saying, "You were going to tear down the temple and rebuild it in three days — save yourself, if you are God's Son, and come down from the cross." ⁴¹The

---

30 Is 50:6   34 Ps 69:21   35 Ps 22:18 38 Is 53:9

ruling priests, with the Bible scholars and elders, mocked Him in the same way, saying, [42]"He saved others, but he cannot save himself. He's King of Israel. He should come down from the cross now, and we'll believe him. [43]*He trusts God — Let God deliver him now, seeing He delights in him.* He said, 'I am God's Son.'" [44]In the same way also the robbers crucified with Him *insulted* Him.

Jesus Dies — *Mark 15:33-41; Luke 23:44-49; John 19:28-30*

[45]At twelve o'clock darkness came over the whole country and lasted until three in the afternoon. [46]About three o'clock Jesus called out with a loud voice, *"Eli, Eli, lema, sabachthani?"* which means, "My God, My God, why did You forsake Me?" [47]Hearing Him, some of those standing there said, "He's calling Elijah." [48]And just then one of the men ran, took a sponge, soaked it in *sour wine,* put it on a stick, and *gave Him a drink.* [49]The others said, "Let's see if Elijah comes to save him."

[50]But Jesus called out again with a loud voice and gave up His spirit. [51]Just then the curtain in the temple was torn in two from top to bottom, the earth was shaken, the rocks were split, [52]the graves were opened, and many bodies of the holy people asleep in death were brought back to life; [53]they came out of the graves and after He had risen went into the holy city, where many saw them. [54]Now, when the captain and those watching Jesus with him saw the earthquake and the other things happening, they were terrified. "He truly was the Son of God," they said.

[55]There were many women watching *from a distance.* They had followed Jesus from Galilee to help Him. [56]Among them were Mary from Magdala and Mary, the mother of James and Joseph, and the mother of Zebedee's sons.

Jesus Is Buried — *Mark 15:42-47; Luke 23:50-56; John 19:38-42*

[57]In the evening there came a rich man from Arimathea by the name of Joseph, who had also become a disciple of Jesus. [58]He went to Pilate and asked for Jesus' body. Then Pilate ordered it given to him.

[59]Joseph took the body, wrapped it in some clean linen cloth, [60]and laid it in his own unused grave that he had cut in the rock. After rolling a big stone against the door of the grave, he went away. [61]Mary from Magdala and the other Mary were there, sitting facing the grave.

The Guard

[62]The next day — the day after the day of preparation — the ruling priests and Pharisees met with Pilate. [63]"Sir," they said, "we remember how that deceiver said while he was still alive, 'On the third day I will rise.'

---

39 Ps 22:6-7; 109:25   43 Ps 22:8   44 Ps 22:6,7   46 Ps 22:1
48 Ps 69:21   55 Ps 38:11

[64]Now, order the grave to be made secure until the third day, or his disciples may come and steal him and tell the people, 'He rose from the dead.' Then the last deception will be worse than the first."

[65]"Take a guard," Pilate told them; "go and make it as secure as you know how."

[66]So they went and secured the grave by sealing the stone and setting the guard.

Jesus Rises — *Mark 16:1-8; Luke 24:1-12; John 20:1-10*

28 After the Sabbath, as the first day of the week was dawning, Mary from Magdala and the other Mary went to look at the grave.

[2]There was a great earthquake. An angel of the Lord came down from heaven, went and rolled the stone away, and sat on it. [3]He was as bright as lightning, and his clothes were as white as snow. [4]The guards were so afraid of him they shook and became like dead men.

[5]"Don't be afraid," the angel said to the women. "I know you're looking for Jesus, Who was crucified. [6]He is not here. He has risen as He said. Come, see the place where He was lying. [7]And go quickly, tell His disciples, 'He has risen from the dead. Remember, He is going ahead of you to Galilee. There you will see Him.' Now, I have told you."

[8]They hurried away from the grave with fear and great joy and ran to tell His disciples.

[9]And there — Jesus met them and said, "Good morning!" They went up to Him, took hold of His feet, and worshiped Him.

[10]Then Jesus said to them, "Don't be afraid. Go, tell My brothers to go to Galilee, and there they will see Me."

The Guards

[11]While the women were on their way, some of the guards went into the city and told the ruling priests everything that happened.

[12]These men met with the elders and agreed on a plan. They gave the soldiers a large sum of money [13]and told them, "Say, 'His disciples came at night and stole him while we were sleeping.' [14]And if this comes to a hearing before the governor, we'll persuade him and see that you have nothing to worry about."

[15]They took the money and did as they were told. And that story has been spread among the Jews to this day.

The Great Commission

[16]The eleven disciples went to the mountain in Galilee where Jesus had told them to go. [17]When they saw Him, they worshipped Him, but some doubted.

[18]And coming nearer, Jesus spoke to them, saying: *"To Me has been given all authority* in heaven and earth. [19]Therefore, wherever you go[q], disciple all nations, baptizing them in the name of the Father, and the Son, and of the Holy Spirit, [20]teaching them to observe everything as I have commanded you; and remember, I am with you always until the end of the age."

---

18 Dan 7:14

q - 19   Literally: "having gone".

THE GOOD NEWS AS IT WAS TOLD BY
MARK

John Prepares the Way — *Matthew 3:1-12; Luke 3:1-18; John 1:19-28*

1 BEGINNING THE GOOD NEWS about Jesus Christ, God's Son: [2]It is written in the prophet Isaiah:

> *Look! I will send My messenger ahead of You*
> *to prepare the way for You.*
> [3] *A voice will be calling in the wilderness:*
> *"Prepare the way for the Lord;*
> *make the paths straight for Him."*

[4]So John the Baptizer came into the wilderness, preaching that people repent and be baptized for the forgiveness of sins. [5]All Judea and all the people of Jerusalem were coming out to him. As they confessed their sins, he baptized them in the Jordan River.

[6]John was dressed in camel's hair with a leather belt around his waist. And he lived on grasshoppers and wild honey.

[7]He preached: "The One Who is mightier than I is coming after me. I'm not good enough to bend down and untie His sandal straps. [8]I have baptized you with water. He will baptize you with the Holy Spirit."

John Baptizes Jesus — *Matthew 3:13-17; Luke 3:21-22; Compare John 1:29-34*

[9]It was in those days that Jesus came from Nazareth in Galilee and was baptized by John in the Jordan. [10]Just as He stepped out of the water, He saw heaven torn open and the *Spirit* coming down as a dove *on Him*. [11]And a voice from heaven said, "You are *My Son,* Whom I love. *I am delighted* with You.

The Devil Tempts Jesus — *Matthew 4:1-11; Luke 4:1-13*

[12]Then the Spirit drove Him out into the wilderness, [13]and He was in the wilderness for 40 days while Satan tempted Him. He was there with the wild animals. And the angels took care of Him.

"Come with Me" — *Matthew 4:18-22; Luke 5:1-11; John 1:35-51*

[14]After John had been put in prison, Jesus went to Galilee and preached

---

2 Mal 3:1　　　3 Is 40:3　　　10 Is 42:1　　　11 Ps 2:7; Is 42:1

God's good news: [15] "The time has come, and God's kingdom is here. Repent, and believe the good news."

[16]As He was walking along the Sea of Galilee, He saw Simon and Simon's brother Andrew (who were fishermen) casting a net into the sea. [17]"Come, follow Me," Jesus told them, "and I will make you fishers of men." [18]Immediately they left their nets and went with Him.

[19]Going on a little further, He saw James, Zebedee's son, and his brother John in their boat mending the nets. [20]Then He called them, and they left their father Zebedee with the hired men in the boat and followed Him.

Jesus Drives Out a Demon — *Luke 4:31-37*

[21]Then they went to Capernaum. The next Sabbath Jesus went into the synagogue and began to teach. [22]His teaching amazed the people because He taught them as one who had authority and not like the Bible scholars. [23]There was in their synagogue just then a man with an unclean spirit. [24]And he screamed, "Leave us alone, Jesus from Nazareth! You've come to destroy us! I know Who You are — God's Holy One."

[25]Jesus talked sharply to him: "Be quiet, and come out of him." [26]The unclean spirit threw the man into convulsions and with a loud shriek came out of him.

[27]They were all so amazed they argued with one another: "What is this? A new teaching! With authority! He gives orders to the unclean spirits, and they obey Him."

[28]The news about Him quickly spread everywhere in all the surrounding country of Galilee.

Peter's Mother-in-Law — *Matthew 8:14-18; Luke 4:38-41*

[29]Right after leaving the synagogue, they went into the home of Simon and Andrew. James and John went with them. [30]Simon's mother-in-law was lying sick with a fever, and so the first thing they did was to tell Him about her. [31]He went to her, took her hand, and helped her get up. The fever left her, and she waited on them.

[32]In the evening when the sun had gone down, the people brought to Him all the sick and those who were demon-possessed. [33]The whole town had gathered at His door. [34]He healed many who were suffering from various sicknesses and drove out many demons and wouldn't let the demons talk, because they knew Him.

Preaching in Galilee — *Matthew 4:23-25; Luke 4:42-44*

[35]In the morning, long before daylight, Jesus got up and went out to a lonely place, and there He prayed. [36]Simon and those who were with him searched for Jesus. [37]When they found Him, they told Him, "Everyone's looking for You."

[38]"Let us go somewhere else," He told them, "to the small towns that are near, so that I may preach there, too. That's why I've come."

[39]He went and preached in their synagogues everywhere in Galilee and drove out the demons.

Jesus Heals a Leper — *Matthew 8:1-4; Luke 5:12-14*

[40]A leper came to Him and begged Him on his knees, "If You want to, You can make me clean."

[41]Jesus felt sorry for him, stretched out His hand, and touched him. "I want to," He said. "Be clean!" [42]Immediately the leprosy left him, and he was made clean. [43]Jesus sent him away with a stern warning: [44]"Be careful not to say anything to anyone, but go, *let the priest examine* you, and for your cleansing offer the sacrifices Moses ordered, to show them you're well."

[45]But when he had left, he talked so much and spread the news until Jesus could no longer openly go into a town. He stayed out in lonely places, and still the people kept coming to Him from everywhere.

Jesus Forgives Sins — *Matthew 9:1-8; Luke 5:17-26*

2 Some days later Jesus came again to Capernaum, and people heard, "He's home." [2]So many gathered that there was no room even in front of the door. He was speaking the Word to them.

[3]Then some people came and brought Him a paralyzed man, carried by four men. [4]But when they couldn't bring him to Jesus because of the crowd, they opened up the roof over the place where Jesus was. Through the opening they had dug they let down the bed on which the paralytic was lying. [5]Seeing their faith, Jesus said to the paralytic, "Son, your sins are forgiven."

[6]There were some Bible scholars sitting there, and they questioned within themselves: [7]"Why does He say this? He's blaspheming. Who but God alone can forgive sins?"

[8]Immediately Jesus knew in His spirit what they were thinking. "Why do you have these thoughts in your hearts?" He asked them. [9]"Is it easier to say to this paralyzed man, 'Your sins are forgiven,' or to say, 'Get up, take your bed, and walk'? [10]I want you to know the Son of Man has power on earth to forgive sins" — then He said to the paralyzed man, [11]"I tell you, get up, take your bed, and go home."

[12]The man got up, immediately took his bed, and walked out before all of them, so that all were amazed and praised God. "Never have we seen anything like this," they said.

Matthew (Levi) — *Matthew 9:9-13; Luke 5:27-32*

[13]Again Jesus went out along the seashore. All the people were coming

---

44 Lev 13:7,49

to Him, and He taught them.

¹⁴As He passed by, He saw Levi, the son of Alphaeus, sitting in the tax office. "Come with Me," He told him. He got up and went with Him.

¹⁵As Jesus was reclining to eat at his home, many tax collectors and sinners were eating with Jesus and His disciples, because there were many who followed Him. ¹⁶When the Bible scholars, who were Pharisees, saw Him eating with sinners and tax collectors, they asked His disciples, "Why does He eat with tax collectors and sinners?"

¹⁷Jesus heard them and answered them: "Those who are healthy don't need a doctor, but those who are sick. I didn't come to call righteous people but sinners."

The Bridegroom — *Matthew 9:14-17; Luke 5:33-39*

¹⁸John's disciples and the Pharisees, who were fasting, came to Jesus. "John's disciples and the disciples of the Pharisees fast," they told Him. "Why don't Your disciples fast?"

¹⁹Jesus asked them, "Can the bridegroom's friends fast while the bridegroom is with them? As long as they have the bridegroom with them, they can't fast. ²⁰The time will come when the bridegroom will be taken away from them, and on that day they'll fast.

²¹"No one sews a piece of new cloth on an old garment. If you do, the new patch will tear away some of the old cloth, and the hole will get worse. ²²No one pours new wine into old wineskins. If you do, the wine will burst the skins, and the wine and the skins will be lost. Rather, new wine has to be poured into fresh skins."

Lord of the Sabbath — *Matthew 12:1-8; Luke 6:1-5*

²³Jesus was going through the grain fields on a Sabbath. As the disciples walked along, they were picking the heads of grain.

²⁴The Pharisees asked Him, "Look, why are they doing something they shouldn't do on a day of rest?"

²⁵"Haven't you ever read what David did," Jesus asked them, "when he and his men were in need and got hungry — ²⁶how he went into God's house when Abiathar was high priest, and he ate the *loaves laid before God,* which only the priests had the right to eat? And he gave his men some too."

²⁷Then He added, "The Sabbath was made for man, not man for the Sabbath. ²⁸The Son of Man is Lord also of the Sabbath."

The Shriveled Hand — *Matthew 12:9-15a; Luke 6:6-11*

3 He went again into a synagogue, and there was a man with a shriveled hand. ²They were watching Jesus to see if He would heal him on a Sabbath; they wanted to accuse Him of something.

³"Get up," He told the man with the shriveled hand, "and come for-

---

26 Lev 24:5-8; I Sam 21:6

ward." [4]Then He asked them, "Is it right on a day of rest to do good or to do evil, to save a life or to kill?"

But they were silent. [5]Looking around at them, He was angry as well as sorry because their hearts were hard. Then He told the man, "Stretch out your hand." He stretched it out, and his hand was made healthy again.

[6]Then the Pharisees left and immediately started plotting with Herod's men how they might destroy Him.

Many Are Healed — *Luke 6:17-19*

[7]Jesus went away with His disciples to the sea. A large crowd from Galilee followed Him; and also from Judea, [8]Jerusalem, Idumea, the other side of the Jordan, and the neighborhood of Tyre and Sidon there were many people who heard about everything He was doing and came to Him. [9]To keep the crowd from crushing Him, He told His disciples to have a small boat ready for Him. [10]He healed many so that all who had diseases rushed up to Him in order to touch Him. [11]Whenever the unclean spirits saw Him, they would fall down before Him and yell, "You're God's Son!" [12]But He strictly ordered them not to tell Who He was.

Twelve Apostles — *Matthew 10:1-4; Luke 6:13-16*

[13]He went up the hill and called those whom He wanted, and they came to Him. [14]He appointed twelve to be with Him and be sent out by Him to preach [15]and have power to drive out demons.

[16]He appointed the twelve and gave Simon the name Peter; [17]James, Zebedee's son, and John, the brother of James — He also gave these the name Boanerges, which means "thunderbolts"; [18]Andrew, Philip, Bartholomew, Matthew, and Thomas; James, the son of Alphaeus, and Thaddaeus; Simon the Zealot; [19]and Judas Iscariot, who betrayed Him.

Power over a Demon — *Matthew 12:22-32; Luke 11:14-23*

[20]Then Jesus came home. Again such a crowd gathered that Jesus and those with Him couldn't eat. [21]When His family heard about it, they went to take charge of Him, because they were saying, "He's out of His mind!"

[22]The Bible scholars who had come down from Jerusalem said, "Beelzebul is in Him," and, "The ruler of the demons helps Him drive out the demons."

[23]He called them to Him and pictured it to them in this way: "How can Satan drive out Satan? [24]If one part of a kingdom fights another, that kingdom can't stand. [25]And if one part of a home fights against the other, it can never stand. [26]And so if Satan rebels and fights against himself, he can't stand, but his end has come. [27]"No one can go into a strong man's house and take away his goods without first tying up the strong man. After that he will rob his house.

[28]"I tell you the truth, anything that people do will be forgiven, their

sins and their slanders, though they slander ever so much. ²⁹But anyone who slanders the Holy Spirit will never be forgiven. Yes, he is guilty of an everlasting sin." ³⁰He said this because they had said, "He has an unclean spirit."

The Mother and Brothers of Jesus — *Matthew 12:46-50; Luke 8:18-21*

³¹His mother and His brothers came. They stood outside and sent someone to Him to ask Him to come out. ³²The crowd sitting around Jesus told Him, "Your mother and Your brothers are outside looking for You."

³³"Who are My mother and My brothers?" He asked them. ³⁴Then looking around at those who sat in a circle around Him, He said, "Here are My mother and My brothers. ³⁵If you do what God wants, you are My brother and sister and mother."

The Sower — *Matthew 13:1-23; Luke 8:4-15*

4 Again Jesus began to teach by the seashore. The crowd that gathered around Him was so very large that He stepped into a boat and sat in it on the sea, while all the people were on the shore, facing the sea. ²Then He used parables to teach them many things.

³"Listen!" He said as He taught them. "A sower went out to sow. ⁴As he was sowing, some seed fell along the road, and the birds came and ate it. ⁵Some seed fell on rocky ground, where it didn't have much soil. Because the soil wasn't deep, the seed came up quickly. ⁶When the sun rose, it was scorched, and because it had not taken root, it withered. ⁷Some seed fell among thorns. The thorns grew up and choked it, and it produced no grain. ⁸But some seed fell on good ground. It came up, grew, and produced grain, thirty, sixty, and a hundred times as much as was sown." ⁹He added, "You have ears to hear; then listen."

¹⁰When He was alone, the twelve and the others around Him asked Him about the parables.

¹¹"You are given the privilege of knowing the mystery of God's kingdom," He answered them, "but to those on the outside everything comes in parables

¹² *that they may*
  see and yet not see,
  hear and yet not understand,
  and so may never turn to Me and be forgiven.

¹³"You don't understand this parable," He said to them. "Then how will you understand any parables?

¹⁴"The sower sows the Word. ¹⁵And these are the ones along the road where the Word is sown: as soon as they hear it, Satan comes and takes away the Word that was sown into them. ¹⁶It is the same with those in whom the seed falls on rocky ground. As soon as they hear the Word, they

12 Is 6:9-10

welcome it with joy, [17]but it doesn't take root in them. They believe for a while. But when the Word brings them trouble or persecution, they immediately fall away. [18]In others the seed falls among thorns. They hear the Word, [19]but the worries of the world, the deceitful pleasure of riches, and the desires for other things come in and choke the Word, and it produces nothing. [20]The ones in whom the seed falls on good ground are those who continue to hear the Word, welcome it, and go on producing good things, thirty, sixty, and a hundred times as much as was sown.

A Lamp — *Matthew 5:14-16; Luke 11:33*

[21]"Do you get out a lamp," He asked them, "to put it under a bucket or under a bed? Shouldn't it be put on a lampstand? [22]Something is secret only to be told, and hidden only to come to light. [23]If you have ears to hear, listen!

[24]"Be careful what you hear!" He told them. "The measure you measure with will be used for you. Yes, you will get even more. [25]If you have something, you will be given more. But if you don't have what you should have, even what you have will be taken away from you."

Seed Growing by Itself

[26]"God's kingdom," He said, "is like this: A man will sow seed on the ground. [27]He will sleep through the night and get up for the day, and the seed will come up and grow, although he doesn't know how. [28]The ground by itself produces grain, first the green blade, then the head, then the full wheat in the head. [29]When the grain is ready, he *swings the sickle, because it is time to cut the grain.*"

The Mustard Seed — *Matthew 13:31-32; Luke 13:18-19*

[30] "What should we say God's kingdom is like," He asked, "or how should we picture it? [31]It's like a mustard seed, which when sown on the ground is the smallest of all the seeds on earth. [32]But when it's sown, it comes up and becomes the largest of all the garden plants. It grows such large branches that *the birds in the air* can *nest in its shade.*"

[33]He used many parables like these to speak the Word as they were able to hear it. [34]He wouldn't speak to them without a parable. But when He was alone with His disciples, He would explain everything to them.

Wind and Water Obey Him — *Matthew 8:23-27; Luke 8:22-25*

[35]In the evening of that day Jesus said to His disciples, "Let us cross over to the other side."

[36]Leaving the crowd behind, they took Jesus, just as He was, with them in the boat. There were other boats with Him.

---

29 Joel 3:13   *32 Ps 104:12; Ezek 17:23; 31:6; Dan 4:12,21*

³⁷Then a violent storm came up, and the waves dashed into the boat so that it was filling up fast. ³⁸Meanwhile, in the back of the boat, He was sleeping on the cushion.

They woke Him up. "Teacher, we're going to drown," they told Him. "Don't You care?"

³⁹He got up and ordered the wind to stop. "Hush!" He said to the sea. "Be still!" And the wind quieted down, and it became very calm.

⁴⁰"Why are you so afraid?" He asked them. "Haven't you learned to trust yet?"

⁴¹Struck with awe, they asked one another, "Who is He? Even the wind and the sea obey Him."

The Gerasenes — *Matthew 8:28-34; Luke 8:26-39*

5 They went to the country of the Gerasenes on the other side of the sea. ²Just as He stepped out of the boat, a man with an unclean spirit came out of the burial caves and met Him. ³He lived in these burial caves. No one could bind him any more, not even with a chain. ⁴He had often been bound with chains on hands and feet, but he had torn the chains and shattered the shackels on his feet, and no one was strong enough to control him. ⁵Always, day and night, he was shrieking in the burial caves and in the hills and bruising himself with stones.

⁶When he saw Jesus at a distance, he ran, bowed down before Him, ⁷and yelled at the top of his voice, "Let me alone, Jesus, Son of the Most High God! Swear to me by God that You won't torture me." ⁸Jesus had told him, "You unclean spirit, get out of the man."

⁹"What is your name?" Jesus asked him.

"My name is Legion [Six Thousand]," he told Him, "because we are many." ¹⁰They begged Him earnestly not to send them out of the country. ¹¹There was a large herd of hogs feeding on the hillside. ¹²"Send us to the hogs," they begged Him; "We want to go into them."

¹³He let them do this. The unclean spirits came out and went into the hogs, and the herd, about 2,000 hogs, stampeded down the cliff into the sea and was drowned.

¹⁴Those who had taken care of them ran away and told about it in the town and in the country, and the people came to see what had happened. ¹⁵They came to Jesus and looked at the man who had been demon-possessed, but now was sitting there dressed and in his right mind; and they were frightened. ¹⁶Those who had seen it told them what had happened to the man plagued by demons and about the hogs. ¹⁷Then the people begged Jesus to leave their country.

¹⁸As He was stepping into the boat, the man who had been demon-possessed begged Jesus to let him go with Him. ¹⁹But Jesus didn't let him. "Go home to your people," He told him, "and tell them how much the Lord has done for you and how merciful He has been to you."

²⁰So the man left and began to tell publicly in the Decapolis [Ten-

Towns] how much Jesus had done for him. And all were amazed.

The Daughter of Jairus — *Matthew 9:18-26; Luke 8:40-56*

[21]When Jesus had again crossed over in the boat to the other side of the sea, a large crowd gathered around Him by the seashore.

[22]A synagogue leader by the name of Jairus came, and when he saw Jesus, he knelt at His feet [23]and earnestly pleaded with Him: "My little daughter is dying. Come and lay your hands on her so she will get well and live."

[24]He went with him. A large crowd followed Him and pressed Him on all sides. [25]There was a woman who had a flow of blood for twelve years. [26]She had suffered much under many doctors and had spent all she had. And she had not been helped at all but had actually gotten worse. [27]Since she heard about Jesus, she came from behind in the crowd and touched His garment. [28]"If I touch His clothes," she said, "I'll get well." [29]Immediately her blood stopped flowing, and she felt in her body that she had been healed from her suffering.

[30]At that moment Jesus felt power had gone from Him. Turning around in the crowd, He asked, "Who touched My clothes?"

[31]"You see how the crowd is pressing you on all sides," His disciples said to Him, "and You ask, 'Who touched me?'"

[32]But He was looking around to see her who had done this. [33]The woman, trembling with fear because she knew what had been done to her, came, bowed down before Him, and told Him the whole truth.

[34]"Daughter," He told her, "your faith made you well. Go in peace, be healed from your suffering."

[35]While He was still talking, some men came from the home of the synagogue leader. "Your daughter died," they said. "Why trouble the Teacher any more?"

[36]Having heard what they said, Jesus told the synagogue leader, "Don't be afraid! Only believe!"

[37]He let only Peter, James, and John, the brother of James, go with Him. [38]So they came to the home of the synagogue leader. There He saw the noisy crowd, crying and wailing aloud. [39]"Why do you make a noise and cry?" He asked them when He came into the house. "The child isn't dead; she's sleeping."

[40]They laughed at Him. But He put them all outside, took the child's father and mother and those who were with Him, and went in where the child was. [41]He took the child's hand and said to her, "Talitha, koom!" which means, "Little girl, I tell you, get up!"

[42]Immediately the girl got up and walked around. She was twelve years old.

Then the others were utterly amazed.

[43]He gave them strict orders not to let anyone know about this. And He told them to give her something to eat.

His Last Visit to Nazareth — *Matthew 13:54-58; Luke 4:16-30*

6 Leaving that place, Jesus went to His hometown, and His disciples went with Him. ²When the Sabbath came, He taught in the synagogue. Many who heard Him were amazed. "Where did he get this?" they asked. "What is this wisdom given to him?" and, "Such miracles his hands are doing! ³Isn't he the carpenter, Mary's son, and a brother of James, Joseph, Judas, and Simon? And aren't his sisters here with us?" So they turned against Him.

⁴But Jesus told them, "A prophet is without honor only in his hometown, among his relatives, and in his family." ⁵He couldn't do any miracle there except to lay His hands on a few sick people and make them well. ⁶Their unbelief amazed Him.

Then He went around in the villages and taught.

Jesus Sends Out the Twelve — *Matthew 10:1-42; Luke 9:1-6*

⁷Jesus called the twelve and sent them out in pairs, giving them authority over the unclean spirits. ⁸He gave them these instructions: "Don't take anything with you on the way except a staff — no bread, no bag, and no copper money in your belt. ⁹But have sandals strapped on your feet. And don't wear two tunics.

¹⁰"Wherever you go into a home," He told them, "stay there until you leave the place. ¹¹If the people of any place don't welcome you or listen to you, leave that place, and shake the dust off the soles of your feet as a warning to them."

¹²They left and preached that people should repent. ¹³They also drove out many demons and poured oil on many who were sick and made them well.

Herod Kills John — *Matthew 14:1-12; Luke 9:7-9*

¹⁴King Herod heard about Jesus, because His name was now well known. "John the Baptizer has risen from the dead," he said, "and that's why these powers are working in him." ¹⁵Others said, "He is Elijah." Still others, "He is a prophet like one of the other prophets." ¹⁶But when Herod heard about it, he said, "John, whose head I cut off, has risen!"

¹⁷Herod had sent men who arrested John, bound him, and put him in prison, because Herod had married Herodias, the wife of his brother Philip. ¹⁸"It isn't right for you to have your brother's wife," John had told Herod.

¹⁹Herodias had a grudge against John and wanted to kill him, but she couldn't do it. ²⁰Herod was afraid of John because he knew John was a just and holy man. So he protected him. When he listened to John, he was very much disturbed, and yet he liked to hear him.

²¹An opportunity came on Herod's birthday, when he gave a dinner for his noblemen, the tribunes, and the leading men of Galilee. ²²His daughter, that is, the daughter of Herodias, came in and danced, and Herod and

his guests were delighted with her. "Ask me for anything you want," the king told the girl, "and I'll give it to you." [23]And he solemnly swore to her: *"I'll give you anything you ask, up to half of my kingdom."*

[24] She went out and asked her mother, "What should I ask for?"

"The head of John the Baptizer," her mother told her.

[25] She hurried right back to the king. "I want you to give me right now," she demanded, "on a platter the head of John the Baptizer."

[26] The king was very sorry. But because of the oaths and because of the guests, he didn't want to refuse her. [27] The king quickly sent a guard and ordered him to bring John's head. He went and cut off John's head in prison. [28] Then he brought the head on a platter and gave it to the girl, and the girl gave it to her mother.

[29] When John's disciples heard about it, they came and took his body and laid it in a grave.

Jesus Feeds 5,000 — *Matthew 14:13-21; Luke 9:10-17; John 6:1-14*

[30]The apostles gathered around Jesus and reported to Him everything they had done and taught. [31] "Now you come away to some deserted place," He told them, "where you can be alone, and rest a little." So many were coming and going there wasn't even time to eat.

[32]So they went away in the boat to a deserted place to be alone . [33]But many saw them leave and recognized them. And they ran there from all the towns and got there ahead of them. [34]When Jesus stepped out of the boat, He saw a big crowd and felt sorry for them because they were *like sheep without a shepherd.* He began to teach them many things.

[35]When it was quite late, His disciples came to Him. "This is a deserted place," they said, "and it's late. [36]Send them away to the farms and villages around us to buy themselves something to eat."

[37]"You give them something to eat," Jesus answered them.

"Should we go and buy bread for two hundred denarii,[a]" they asked Him, "and give it to them to eat?"

[38]"How many loaves do you have?" He asked them. "Go and see." They found out and said, "Five, and two fish."

[39]He ordered them all to sit down in groups on the green grass. [40]They sat down in groups of hundreds and fifties.

[41]Taking the five loaves and the two fish and looking up to heaven, He blessed them. He broke the loaves and gave them to the disciples to give to the people. He also gave pieces of the two fish to everyone. [42]All of them ate and had enough.

[43]They picked up pieces of bread and of the fish — twelve baskets full. [44]There were 5,000 men who had eaten the bread.

---

23 *Esth 5:3; 7:2*   **34** *Num 27:17; I Kings 22:17; Ezek 34:5; Zech 10:2*

a - 37   one denarius was one day's pay.

Jesus Walks on Water — *Matthew 14:22-33; John 6:15-21*

[45]He quickly made His disciples get into the boat and cross over to Bethsaida ahead of Him; meanwhile He would send the people away. [46]After saying good-bye to them, He went up the hill to pray. [47]When it got late, the boat was in the middle of the sea, and He was alone on the land.

[48]Jesus saw they were in great trouble as they rowed, because the wind was against them. Toward morning He came to them, walking on the sea. He wanted to pass by them. [49]They saw Him walking on the sea, and thinking He was a ghost, they cried out, [50]because they had all seen Him and were terrified.

Immediately He talked to them. "Have courage!" He said. "It is I. Don't be afraid." [51]He came into the boat with them, and the wind died down. The disciples were completely dumbfounded. [52]They hadn't understood about the loaves. Their minds were dull.

[53]They crossed over and came to the shore at Gennesaret and anchored there. [54]As soon as they stepped out of the boat, the people recognized Him. [55]They ran all over that part of the country and started to carry the sick on their beds to any place where they heard He was. [56]And wherever He came — to villages, towns, or farms — they would lay down the sick in the public places and beg Him just to let them touch the tassel of His garment. And all who touched it were made well.

Unclean Hands — *Matthew 15:1-20*

7 The Pharisees and some Bible scholars who had come from Jerusalem gathered around Jesus. [2]They saw some of His disciples eat with unclean hands, that is, without washing them. [3](Now the Pharisees, like all other Jews, don't eat without washing their hands up to the wrist — to keep the rules handed down by their fathers. [4]Coming from the marketplace, they don't eat without first washing; and there are many other rules they've learned to keep — baptizing cups, huge wine jars, and brass pans).[b]

[5]"Why don't your disciples live according to the rules handed down by our fathers?" the Pharisees and the Bible scholars were asking Him. "They eat with unclean hands!"

[6]He told them, "Isaiah was right when he prophesied about you hypocrites as it is written: *'These people honor Me with their lips, but their hearts are far away from Me. [7]They worship Me in vain because they teach men's rules.'* [8]You give up God's commandment and keep men's rules." [9]He added: "You have a fine way of setting aside God's commandment in order to keep your rules! [10]For example, Moses said: *'Honor your father and your mother,'* and: *'Anyone who curses father or mother must die.'* [11]But you say, 'If anyone says to his father or mother, "Anything by which I might help you is Korban (that is, a gift to God)," ' [12]then you don't let him do anything for

---

6-7 Is 29:13   **10** Ex 20:12; Deut 5:16; Ex 21:17; Lev 20:9

b - 4   Some early manuscripts add "and dinner tables."

his father or his mother anymore. [13]In this way, by the rules you have taught, you set aside what God has said. And you're doing many things like that."

[14]Then He called the people again and said to them, "Listen to Me, all of you, and understand this: [15]Nothing that comes from the outside into a person can make him unclean, but what comes out of a person makes him unclean."[c]

[17]When He had left the people and gone home, His disciples asked Him about the illustration.

[18]"Are you just as dense as the rest?" He asked them. "Don't you know that nothing coming from the outside into a person can make him unclean, [19]because it doesn't go into his heart but into his stomach and so passes through?" (Here Jesus made all foods clean). [20]He added: "What comes out of a person makes him unclean. [21]Instead, from the inside of men's hearts come out evil thoughts, sexual sins, stealing, murders, adulteries, [22]greed, wickedness, cheating, lust, a jealous eye, slander, pride, foolishness. [23]All these evils come from within and make a person unclean."

A Non-Jewish Woman — *Matthew 15:21-31*

[24]Leaving that place, Jesus went away to the neighborhood of Tyre. He went into a house and didn't want anyone to know it, but it couldn't be kept a secret.

[25]There was a woman in whose little daughter there was an unclean spirit. As soon as she heard about Him, she came and bowed down at His feet. [26]The woman wasn't Jewish but was born a Phoenician in Syria. She was asking Him to drive the demon out of her daughter.

[27]"First let the children eat all they want," He answered her. "It isn't good to take the children's bread and throw it to the puppies."

[28]"You're right, Lord," she answered Him, "but even the puppies under the table eat some of the children's crumbs."

[29]"Because you said this, go!" Jesus told her. "The demon has gone out of your daughter."

[30]The woman went home and found the little child lying on the bed and the demon gone.

Jesus Heals a Deaf Man

[31]Jesus again left the country of Tyre and went through Sidon and the country of the Decapolis [Ten-Towns] to the Sea of Galilee.

[32]Some people brought Him a man who was deaf and had a speech defect, and they urged Jesus to lay His hand on him. [33]Taking him away from the crowd to be alone with him, He put His fingers into the man's ears. He spit and touched his tongue [34]and looked up to heaven and sighed. Then He said to him, "Ephphatha!" which means, "Be opened!" [35]His ears were

---

c - 15   Our two oldest manuscripts lack v. 16: "If you have ears to hear, listen!" See 4:23.

opened, his tongue was set free to speak, and he talked naturally.

[36]Jesus ordered the people not to tell anyone. But the more He forbade them, the more widely they spread the news. [37]They were dumbfounded. "He has done everything well," they said. "He even makes the deaf hear and the speechless speak."

Jesus Feeds 4,000 — *Matthew 15:32-39*

8 At that time there were again many people who had nothing to eat. So He called the disciples. [2]"I feel sorry for the people," He said to them. "They've been with Me three days now and have nothing to eat. [3]If I let them go home without eating, they will become exhausted on the road. Some of them have come a long way."

[4]"Where could anyone get enough bread here in the wilderness to feed these?" His disciples asked Him.

[5]"How many loaves do you have?" Jesus asked them.

"Seven," they answered.

[6]He ordered the people to sit down on the ground. Then He took the seven loaves, gave thanks, broke them, and gave them to His disciples to hand out, and they handed them to the people. [7]They also had a few small fish. He blessed them and asked that these too be handed out. [8]They ate and had enough. And they picked up the pieces that were left — seven baskets. [9]There were about 4,000 people.

Then He dismissed them.

A Proof from Heaven — *Matthew 16:1-4*

[10]Then Jesus and His disciples got into the boat and came into the neighborhood of Dalmanutha.

[11]The Pharisees came and started to argue with Him. To test Him, they asked Him for some sign from heaven.

[12]With a deep sigh from His spirit He asked, "Why does this generation want a sign? Surely, I tell you, these people will get no sign!"

[13]Then He left them.

The Yeast of the Pharisees — *Matthew 16:5-12*

He got into the boat again and started to cross to the other side. [14]They forgot to take bread and had only one loaf with them in the boat.

[15]Then Jesus definitely warned them: "Beware of the yeast of the Pharisees and of Herod!"

[16]Discussing about this with one another, they mentioned that they had no bread. [17]Aware of what was going on, Jesus asked, "Why are you discussing about not having any bread? Don't you know or understand yet? Are your hearts hardened? [18]*You have eyes — don't you see? You have ears — don't you hear?* And don't you remember? [19]When I broke the five loaves

---

18 *Jer 5:21; Ezek 12:2*

for the five thousand, how many baskets full of pieces did you pick up?"

"Twelve," they told Him.

[20]"And the seven loaves for the four thousand — how many baskets full of pieces did you pick up?"

"Seven," they answered Him.

[21]"Don't you understand yet?" He asked them.

A Blind Man

[22]So they came to Bethsaida. There people brought a blind man to Jesus and begged Him to touch him. [23]He took the blind man's hand and led him out of the village. Then He spit on his eyes and laid His hands on him. "Can you see anything?" He asked him.

[24]He looked up. "I see the people," he said. "They look to me like trees walking around."

[25]When Jesus again laid His hands on his eyes, he saw distinctly; sight came back, and he saw everything clearly. [26]Jesus sent him home, saying, "But don't go into the village."

"You Are the Christ [Messiah]" — *Matthew 16:13-20; Luke 9:18-21*

[27]Then Jesus and His disciples went to the villages around Caesarea Philippi.

On the way He asked His disciples, "Who do people say I am?"

[28]"John the Baptizer," they answered Him. "Others say Elijah, and still others, one of the prophets."

[29]"But who do you say I am?" He asked them. "You are the Christ!" Peter answered Him.

[30]He warned them not to tell anyone about Him.

"I Will Die and Rise" — *Matthew 16:21-23; Luke 9:22*

[31]Then He was teaching them: "The Son of Man has to suffer much, be rejected

by the elders, the ruling priests, and the Bible scholars, be killed, and then rise on the third day." [32]He was speaking quite frankly.

But Peter took Him aside and started to correct Him. [33]Turning, He looked at His disciples and corrected Peter. "Get behind Me, Satan!" He said. "You're not thinking what God thinks but what men think."

Take Up Your Cross — *Matthew 16:24-28; Luke 9:23-27*

[34]He called the people as well as His disciples. "If you want to follow Me," He told them, "deny yourself, take up your cross, and come with Me. [35]If you want to save your soul, you will lose it. But if you will lose your soul for Me and for the good news, you will save it. [36]What good does it do you to win the whole world and lose your soul? [37]Or what would you give to buy back your soul? [38]If in this unfaithful and sinful generation you're

ashamed of Me and what I say, then the Son of Man will be ashamed of you when He comes with the holy angels in His Father's glory.

9 "I tell you the truth," He told them, "there are some standing here who will never taste death until they see that the kingdom of God has come with power."

Jesus Shows His Glory (The Transfiguration) —
Matthew 17:1-8; Luke 9:28-36

²After six days Jesus took Peter, James, and John with Him and led them up a high mountain to be alone with them.

He was transfigured before them, ³and His clothes became dazzling white — no one on earth could bleach them so white. ⁴Elijah and Moses appeared to them and were talking with Jesus.

⁵"Master," Peter said to Jesus, "it's good for us to be here. Let's put up three shelters, one for You, one for Moses, and one for Elijah." ⁶He didn't know what he was saying; they were so terrified.

⁷A cloud came and overshadowed them, and a voice came out of the cloud: "This is *My Son* Whom I love. *Listen to Him.*"

⁸Suddenly, as they looked around, they no longer saw anyone but Jesus with them.

⁹On their way down the mountain Jesus ordered them not to tell anyone what they had seen, until the Son of Man had risen from the dead. ¹⁰They kept in mind what He said and argued with one another, asking, "What is this rising from the dead?" ¹¹So they asked Him, "Why do the Bible scholars say, 'First Elijah has to come?'"

¹²"First *Elijah* does come," He told them, "and *puts* everything *in order again.* And what is written about the Son of Man? That He must suffer much and be treated shamefully. ¹³Yes, I tell you, Elijah has come, and people treated him as they pleased, as it is written about him."

The Demon-Possessed Boy — *Matthew 17:14-20; Luke 9:37-43a*

¹⁴When they got back to the other disciples, they saw a big crowd around them and some Bible scholars arguing with them. ¹⁵Then the whole crowd was amazed to see Jesus, and they ran and welcomed Him.

¹⁶"What is this argument about?" He asked them.

¹⁷"Teacher," someone in the crowd answered, "I brought You my son. There's a speechless spirit in him. ¹⁸Wherever the spirit takes hold of him, it throws him down; he foams at the mouth and grinds his teeth and gets rigid. I asked Your disciples to drive out the spirit, but they couldn't do it."

¹⁹"O you unbelieving generation!" Jesus answered. "How long must I be with you? How long must I put up with you? Bring him to Me."

²⁰They brought the boy to Him. As soon as the spirit saw Jesus, it threw the boy into convulsions. He fell on the ground and rolled around

7 Ps 2:7; Is 42:1; Deut 18:15   12 Mal 4:5-6

and foamed at the mouth.

[21]Jesus asked his father, "How long has he been like this?"

"Since he was a child," he said. [22]"It often threw him into fire or into water to kill him. Oh, if You can do anything, have pity on us and help us."

[23]"You say, 'If you can!'" Jesus answered him. "Anything can be done if you believe."

[24]Immediately the child's father cried out, "I do believe; help me with my unbelief."

[25]When Jesus saw a crowd quickly gather around Him, He talked sharply to the unclean spirit: "You deaf and speechless spirit, I order you, 'Come out of him, and don't go into him again.'"

[26]It screamed and wrenched him violently and came out. The boy became like a corpse, so that everyone said, "He's dead."

[27]Jesus took his hand, helped him get up, and he stood up.

[28]When He went into a house and His disciples were alone with Him, they asked Him, "Why couldn't we drive out the spirit?"

[29]"This kind can be driven out only by prayer," He told them.

"I Will Die and Rise" — *Matthew 17:22-23; Luke 9:43b-45*

[30]Leaving that place, they started to go on byways through Galilee. Jesus didn't want anyone to know about it, [31]because He was teaching His disciples and telling them: "The Son of Man is going to be betrayed into the hands of men, and they will kill Him, but on the third day after He's killed He will rise."

[32]They didn't understand what He said and were afraid to ask Him.

Who Is the Greatest? — *Matthew 18:1-5; Luke 9:46-48*

[33]They went to Capernaum. When He came home, He asked the disciples, "What were you discussing on the way?" [34]They were silent because they had on the way discussed who was the greatest.

[35]He sat down and called the twelve. "If anyone wants to be first," He told them, "he will have to be last of all and serve everyone." [36]He took a little child, had him stand in front of them, put His arms around him, and said to them, [37]"If you welcome a child like this in My name, you welcome Me. And if you welcome Me, you welcome not only Me but Him Who sent Me."

"He Is for Us" — *Luke 9:49-50*

[38]"Teacher," John said to Jesus, "we saw a man drive out demons in Your name, and we tried to stop him because he hasn't been with us."

[39]"Don't try to stop him," Jesus said. "Anyone who does a miracle in My name cannot turn around and speak evil of Me. [40]Anyone who isn't against us is for us. [41]I tell you, anyone who gives you a cup of water to drink because you belong to Christ will certainly not lose his reward."

Do I Lead Others to Sin? — *Matthew 18:6-10; Luke 17:1-2*

[42]"If anyone leads one of these little ones who believe in Me into sin, it would be better for him to have a large millstone hung around his neck and be thrown into the sea. [43]"If your hand makes you sin, cut it off. It is better for you to go into life crippled than to have two hands and go to hell, where the fire can't be put out.[d] [45]If your foot makes you sin, cut it off. It is better for you to go into life with only one foot than to have two feet and be thrown into hell. [47]If your eye makes you sin throw it away. It is better for you to go into God's kingdom with one eye than to have two eyes and be thrown into hell, [48]where *the worm that consumes them doesn't die and the fire isn't put out.*

[49]"Everyone will be salted with fire. [50]Salt is good. But if salt loses its taste, how will you make it taste salty again? Keep salt within you, and so live in peace with one another."

Husband and Wife — *Matthew 19:1-12*

10 Jesus left that place and went into the country of Judea, which was on the other side of the Jordan, and again the crowds gathered around Him. And again He taught them as He used to do.

[2]Some Pharisees came to Him. "Is it right for a man to divorce his wife?" they asked Him in order to test Him.

[3]"What did Moses order you to do?" He asked them.

[4]"Moses let a man *make out a divorce paper and divorce his wife,*" they said.

[5]"He wrote this law for you on account of your hard hearts," Jesus told them. [6] "But when God made the world, He in the beginning *made them a male and a female.* [7]*That's why a man will leave his father and mother* [8]*and the two will be one flesh.* And so they are no more two but one flesh. [9]Now, what God has joined together man must not separate."

[10]In the house the disciples also asked Him about this. "If anyone divorces his wife," He answered them, [11]"and marries another, he's living in adultery with her. [12]And if a wife divorces her husband and marries another man, she's living in adultery."

Jesus Loves Children — *Matthew 19:13-15; Luke 18:15-17*

[13]Some people brought little children to Jesus to have Him touch them, but the disciples sternly told them not to do it. [14]But when Jesus saw this, He became angry. "Let the little children come to Me," He told them. "Don't keep them away. God's kingdom belongs to such as these. [15]I tell you the truth, if you don't receive God's kingdom like a little child, you will not get into it."

---

48 Is 66:24   4 Deut 24:1,3 6 Gen 1:27; 5:2   7-8 Gen 2:24

d - 43   Our two oldest manuscripts lack vv. 44 and 46, which both say: "where their worm doesn't die and the fire isn't put out." See v. 48.

[16]He took them in His arms, laid His hands on them, and blessed them.

The Rich Young Leader — *Matthew 19:16-30; Luke 18:18-30*

[17]As Jesus was coming out to the road, a man came running to Him and knelt before Him. "Good Teacher," he asked Him, "what should I do to inherit everlasting life?"

[18]"Why do you call Me good?" Jesus asked him. [19]No one is good except One — God. "You know the commandments: *Do not murder. Do not commit adultery. Do not steal. Do not give false testimony.* Do not cheat. *Honor your father and mother.*"

[20]"Teacher," he told Him, "I've kept all these since I was a child."

[21]Jesus looked at him and loved him. "You lack one thing," Jesus told him. "Go, sell everything you have, and give the money to the poor, and you'll have a treasure in heaven. Then come and follow Me."

[22]When he heard that, he looked gloomy and went away sad, because he was very rich. [23]Jesus looked around and said to His disciples, "How hard it is for rich people to get into God's kingdom!"

[24]The disciples were surprised He said that. But Jesus said to them again, "Children, how hard it is to get into God's kingdom! [25]It's easier for a camel to go through the eye of a needle's than for a rich man to get into God's kingdom."

[26]They were more amazed than ever. "Who can be saved?" they asked one another.

[27]As he looked at them, Jesus said, "For men it is impossible, but not for God, because *everything is possible for God.*"

[28]Then Peter spoke up: "Look! We gave up everything and followed You."

[29]"I tell you the truth," Jesus said, "everyone who gave up his home, brothers or sisters, mother, father, or children, or fields for Me and for the good news, [30]will certainly get a hundred times as much here in this life: houses, brothers and sisters, mothers and children and fields, with persecutions, and in the coming world everlasting life. [31]But many who are first will be last, and the last first."

The Cup of Suffering — *Matthew 20:17-28*

[32]As they were on their way up to Jerusalem, Jesus walked ahead of them. They were amazed, and the others who were following Him were afraid. So once again He took the twelve with Him and told them what was going to happen to Him: [33]"Look, we're going up to Jerusalem, and the Son of Man will be betrayed to the ruling priests and the Bible scholars, who will condemn Him to die and hand Him over to the Gentiles . [34]They'll mock Him and *spit on* Him, whip Him and kill Him. But on the third day He will rise."

---

19 *Ex 20:12-16; Deut 5:16-20*   **27** *Gen 18:14; Job 42:2; Zech 8:6*   **34** *Is 50:6*

[35]James and John, the sons of Zebedee, came to Him. "Teacher," they said to Him, "we want You to do for us what we ask."

[36]"What do you want Me to do for You?" He asked them.

[37]"Let one of us sit at Your right," they told Him, "and the other at Your left in Your glory."

[38]"You don't know what you're asking," Jesus answered them. "Can you drink the cup I'm drinking or be baptized with the baptism with which I'm being baptized?"

[39]"We can," they told Him.

"You'll drink the cup I'm drinking," Jesus told them, "and be baptized with the baptism with which I'm being baptized. [40]But sitting at My right or left is something I can give only to those for whom it is prepared." [41]When the other ten heard about it, they became angry with James and John. [42]Then Jesus called them and told them, "You know that those who are considered rulers of the nations are lords over them, and their great men are tyrants over them. [43]But among you it's different. Anyone who wants to become great among you will have to serve you, [44]and anyone who wants to be first among you will have to be everyone's slave. [45]Why, even the Son of Man didn't come to be served but to serve and give His life as a ransom for many people."

Blind Bartimaeus — *Luke 18:35-43*

[46]Then they came to Jericho. As Jesus and His disciples and many people were leaving Jericho, Bartimaeus, the son of Timaeus, a blind beggar, was sitting by the road. [47]When he heard it was Jesus from Nazareth, he began to call, "Son of David, Jesus, have pity on me!"

[48]Many were urging him to be quiet. But he called all the louder, "Son of David, have pity on me!"

[49]Jesus stopped and said, "Call him!" They called the blind man and told him, "Cheer up! Get up! He's calling you." [50]He laid aside his garment, jumped up, and went to Jesus.

[51]"What do you want Me to do for you?" Jesus asked him. "Rabboni [Teacher], I want to see again," the blind man told Him. [52]"Go," Jesus told him; "your faith has made you well." Immediately he could see, and he followed Him on the road.

The King Comes to Jerusalem — *Matthew 21:1-11; Luke 19:29-44; John 12:12-19*

11 When they were getting near Jerusalem and came to Bethphage and Bethany, at the Mount of Olives, Jesus sent two of His disciples. [2]"Go into the village ahead of you," He told them, "and just as you go into it, you'll find a young donkey tied up that no one ever sat on. Untie it and bring it to Me. [3]And if anyone asks you, 'Why are you doing that?' say, 'The Lord needs it, and He will promptly send it back here.'"

[4]They went and found the colt tied to the gate, outside in the street, and they started to untie it.

⁵"What are you doing, untying the colt?" some of the men standing there asked them. ⁶They answered them just as Jesus had told them, and the men let them go. ⁷So they brought the colt to Jesus, put their garments on it, and He sat on it.

⁸Many spread their garments on the road, and others spread leafy branches that they cut in the fields. ⁹Those who went ahead and those who followed Him were shouting:

"Our Savior!

Blessed is He Who is coming in the Lord's name!
¹⁰ Blessed is the coming kingdom of our father David! Our Savior — in the highest heavens!"

¹¹ He came into Jerusalem and into the temple and looked around at everything. Since it was late now, He went with the twelve out to Bethany.

Nothing but Leaves — *Matthew 21:18-22*

¹²The next day when they left Bethany, Jesus was hungry. ¹³In the distance He saw a fig tree with leaves, and He went to see if He could find anything on it. When He came to it, He found nothing but leaves, because it wasn't the season for figs. ¹⁴Then He said to the tree, and His disciples heard Him: "May no one ever eat fruit from you again!"

He Cleanses the Temple Again — *Matthew 21:12-17; Luke 19:45-48*

¹⁵When they came to Jerusalem, He went into the temple and proceeded to drive out those who were selling and buying in the temple, and He upset the tables of the money changers and the chairs of those who sold pigeons. ¹⁶He would not let anyone carry a vessel across the temple courtyard. ¹⁷Then He taught: "Isn't it written: 'My house should be called a house of prayer for all the nations?' But you made it a den of robbers."

¹⁸When the ruling priests and Bible scholars heard Him, they tried to find a way to destroy Him. They were afraid of Him, because He amazed all the people by His teaching.

¹⁹When evening came, He would leave the city.

The Fig Tree Is Withered — *Matthew 21:18-22; Mark 11:12-14*

²⁰When they walked by early in the morning, they saw the fig tree withered from the roots up. ²¹Peter, remembering, said to Him, "Rabbi, look! The fig tree You cursed is dried up."

²²"Believe in God!" Jesus answered them. ²³ "I tell you the truth, if you will say to this mountain, 'Be lifted up and be thrown into the sea,'ᵉ and have no doubt in your mind but believe what you say will be done, it will

---

9 Ps 118:25-26   17 Is 56:7; Jer 7:11

---

e - 23   By this mount Jesus means the Mount of Olives; by the sea He means the Dead Sea, which can be seen from the Mount of Olives.

be done for you. ²⁴That's why I tell you, anything you ask for in prayer, believe that you received it, and you will have it. ²⁵When you stand and pray, if you have anything against anyone, forgive him, so that your Father in heaven will forgive you your sins." ^f

From Heaven — *Matthew 21:23-27; Luke 20:1-8*

²⁷They came again to Jerusalem. As He was walking in the temple, the ruling priests, the Bible scholars, and the elders came to Him. ²⁸ "By what authority are you doing these things?" they asked Him. "Or who gave you the authority to do them?"

²⁹Jesus answered them, "I will ask you a question. You answer Me, and then I'll tell you by what authority I'm doing these things. ³⁰John's baptism — was it from heaven or from men? Answer Me."

³¹They argued among themselves, "If we say, 'From Heaven,' he will ask, 'Then why didn't you believe him?' ³²But should we say, 'From men?' " They were afraid of the people. Everyone thought John certainly was a prophet. ³³So they answered Jesus, "We don't know."

Then Jesus told them, "Neither will I tell you by what authority I'm doing these things."

God's Vineyard — *Matthew 21:33-46; Luke 20:9-19*

12 Then He used parables in talking to them:

"A man *planted a vineyard*. He *put a wall around it, cut a vat into the rock, and built a watchtower*. Then he rented it out to workers and left home.

²"At the right time he sent a slave to the workers to get from them a share of the products of the vineyard. ³But they took him, beat him, and sent him back empty-handed. ⁴He sent another slave to them. They hit him on the head and treated him shamefully. ⁵He sent another, and that one they killed. Then many others: some of these they beat, and others they killed.

⁶"He had one more, a son, whom he loved. Finally he sent him to them saying, 'They will respect my son.'

⁷"But those workers said to one another, 'This is the heir. Come, let's kill him, and then we'll get the inheritance.' ⁸They took him, killed him, and threw him out of the vineyard.

⁹"What will the owner of the vineyard do? He will come and kill the workers and give the vineyard to others. ¹⁰Haven't you read this in your Bible:

---

1 Is 5:1-2

f - 26   Our two oldest manuscripts lack v. 26: "But if you don't forgive, your Father in heaven will not forgive your sins." See Matt. 6:14-15

The Stone
the builders rejected
has become the Cornerstone.
[11] *The Lord has done it, and we think it is wonderful?"*

[12]They wanted to arrest Him, because they knew His parable was aimed at them, but they were afraid of the crowd. So they let Him alone and went away.

Taxes — *Matthew 22:15-22; Luke 20:20-26*

[13]They sent some Pharisees and some of Herod's men to Him in order to trap Him with a question. [14]When they came to Him, they said, "Teacher, we know you're honest and don't care what others think, because you don't favor any special persons but you really teach God's way. Is it right to pay a tax to Caesar or not?

[15]Should we pay it or not?"

Seeing through their hypocritical way, Jesus asked them, "Why do you test Me? Bring Me a denarius; I want to see it."

[16]They brought it. "Whose head is this and whose inscription?" He asked them. "Caesar's," they told Him.

[17]"Give to Caesar what is Caesar's," Jesus told them, "and to God what is God's." He amazed them.

The Dead Live — *Mathew 22:23-33; Luke 20:27-40*

[18]The Sadducees, who say there is no resurrection, came to Him with this question: [19]"Teacher, Moses wrote for us: '*If anyone dies and leaves* a wife but *no child, his brother should marry his widow and have children for his brother.*' [20]Now, there were seven brothers. The first took a wife, died, and left no children. [21]The second married her, died, and left no children. So did the third. [22]None of the seven left any children. Last of all the woman died, too. [23]When the dead rise, whose wife will she be? You know, the seven had her as wife."

[24]Jesus asked them, "Aren't you wrong because you don't know your Bible or God's power? [25]When they rise from the dead, men and women don't marry but are like angels in heaven. [26]About the dead rising, didn't you read in the book of Moses, in the passage about the bush, how God told him: '*I am the God of Abraham, the God of Isaac, and the God of Jacob*'? [27]He's not the God of the dead but of the living. You're badly mistaken!"

Love God and Your Neighbor — *Matthew 22:34-40*

[28]One of the Bible scholars came to Him. Hearing the others argue with Him and seeing how well Jesus answered them, he asked Him, "Which is the most important of all the commandments?"

[29]Jesus answered, "The most important is: '*Listen, Israel, the Lord our God alone is Lord.* [30]*Then love the Lord your God with all your heart, with*

10-11 Ps 118:22-23   19 Gen 38:8; Deut 25:5-6   26 Ex 3:6   29-30 Deut 6:4-5

all your soul, with all your mind, and with all your strength.' [31]The next is: *'Love your neighbor as yourself.'* No other commandment is greater than these."

[32]"Right, Teacher!" the Bible scholar said to Him. "You told the truth: *'He is the only One, and there is no other beside Him,* [33]and *loving Him with all your heart,* with all your understanding, *and with all Your strength,* and *loving your neighbor as yourself* is more than all the *burnt offerings and sacrifices.'* "

[34]When Jesus saw how sensibly he answered, He told him, "You're not far from God's kingdom."

No one dared to ask Him another question.

David's Son — *Matthew 22:41-46; Luke 20:41-44*

[35]While Jesus was teaching in the temple, He asked, "How can the Bible scholars say the Christ is David's son? [36]David himself by the Holy Spirit said: *The Lord said to my Lord, 'Sit at My right until I put Your enemies under Your feet.'* [37]David himself calls Him 'Lord'. Then how can He be his son?"

Beware! — *Matthew 23:1-12; Luke 20:45-47*

The large crowd liked to hear Him. [38]As He taught, He said, "Beware of the Bible scholars who like to go around in long robes, be greeted in the marketplaces, [39]sit in the front seats in synagogues, and have the places of honor at dinners. [40]They swallow the houses of widows, and then, to cover up, make long prayers. They will be punished all the more."

A Cent — *Luke 21:1-4*

[41]As Jesus sat facing the contribution boxes, He was watching how people put money into them. Many rich people put in much. [42]A poor widow came and dropped in two small coins, worth about a cent.

[43]He called His disciples. "I tell you," He said to them, "this poor widow certainly put in more than all the others who put in money. [44]All the others took some of what they had left over and dropped it in, but she put in what she needed herself, all she had — all she had to live on."

Sorrow Ahead! — *Matthew 24:1-14; Luke 21:5-19*

13 As He was going out of the temple, one of His disciples said to Him, "Teacher, look at those wonderful stones and buildings!"

[2]"You see these large buildings?" Jesus asked him. "Not one stone will be left on another here but will be torn down."

[3]When He was sitting on the Mount of Olives, facing the temple, Peter, James, John, and Andrew asked Him privately: [4]"Tell us, when will this

---

31 Lev 19:18   *32-33* Deut 4:35; 6:4-5   *33* Lev 19:18; I Sam 15:22   *36* Ps 110:1

be, and how can we tell when all this is going to happen?"

[5]"Be careful not to let anyone deceive you," Jesus told them. [6]"Many will come using My name and saying, 'I am He,' and will deceive many.

[7]"When you hear of wars and rumors of wars, don't get alarmed. *It must happen,* but that's not the end yet. [8]*Nation will fight against nation,* and *kingdom against kingdom.* There will be earthquakes in different places, and famines. These are only the first pains.[g]

[9]"Be on your guard! Men will hand you over to their courts and whip you in their synagogues. You will be brought before governors and kings for My sake to tell them the truth. [10]The good news must be preached to all nations before the end comes. [11]When they are taking you away to hand you over to the authorities, don't worry beforehand what you will say. But say whatever is given you to say when the time comes; you see, it isn't you speaking but the Holy Spirit.

[12]"A brother will betray his brother to death, and a father his child. *Children will rebel against their parents* and kill them. [13]Everyone will hate you because of My name. But endure to the end, and you'll be saved."

Jerusalem Will Be Destroyed — *Matthew 24:15-22; Luke 21:20-24*

[14]"When you see *the devastating abomination* standing where it should not be (anyone who reads this should understand it), then if you're in Judea, flee to the hills. [15]If you're on the roof, don't come down and go into your house to get anything. [16]If you're in the field, don't turn back to get your garment.

[18]"Woe to the women who in those days are expecting babies or nursing them. [18]Pray that it won't happen in winter. [19]*It will be a time of misery such as never has been from the beginning* of the world that God made *until now* and never will be. [20]And if the Lord had not cut short that time, no one would be saved. But for the sake of the elect whom He has chosen, God has cut short the time."

Jesus Is Coming — *Matthew 24:23-35; Luke 21:25-33*

[21]"If anyone tells you then, 'Look, here is Christ!' or, 'There He is!' *don't believe* it. [22]False christs and false prophets will *come and do signs and wonders* to deceive if possible those whom God has chosen. [23]Be on your guard. You see, I've told you everything before it happens.

[24]"Now, after the misery of that time *the sun will turn dark, the moon will stop shining,* [25]and *the stars will be falling from the sky.* And *the powers of heaven* will be shaken. [26]Then people will see *the Son of Man coming in the clouds* with great power and glory. [27]And then He will send the angels

---

7 *Dan 2:28 -29,45*   8 *II Chr 15:6; Is 19:2*   12 *Mic 7:6*
14 *Dan 9:27; 11:31; 12:11*   19 *Dan 12:1*   21-22 *Deut 13:1-3*
24-25 *Is 13:10; 34:4; Ezek 32:7-8; Joel 2:10,31; 3:15*   26 *Dan 7:13*

g - 8   As in childbirth, sharper pains will follow before the Savior comes in glory.

and *gather* His chosen ones *from the north, south, east, and west, and from one end of the world to the other.*

[28]"Learn this lesson from a fig tree: When its branch gets tender and grows leaves, you know summer is near. [29]So also when you see those things happen, you know He is near, at your door.

[30]"I tell you the truth, these people will not pass away until all this happens.

[31]Heaven and earth will pass away, but My words will not pass away.'"

Be Ready! — *Matthew 24:36-51; Luke 21:34-36*

[32]"No one knows when that day or hour will come, not the angels in heaven, not the Son, only the Father. [33]Be careful and watch, because you don't know when it will happen. [34]It's like a man who went on a trip. As he left home, he put his slaves in charge, assigned work to every one, and ordered the doorkeeper to watch. [35]Watch, then, because you don't know when the master of the house is coming, whether in the evening, at midnight, at the time when the rooster crows, or early in the morning. [36]Make sure he doesn't come suddenly and find you asleep. [37]What I tell you, I tell everyone: 'Watch!' "

The Plot — *Matthew 26:1-5; Luke 22:1-2; John 11:45-57*

14 It was two days before the Festival of the Passover and of Bread Without Yeast. The ruling priests and the Bible scholars were looking for some treacherous way to arrest Jesus and put Him to death. [2]They said, "Not during the festival, or there will be a riot among the people."

Mary Anoints Jesus — *Matthew 26:6-13; John 12:1-8*

[3]While Jesus was in Bethany in the home of Simon the leper and was reclining at the table, a woman came with an alabaster jar of perfume, real nard and very expensive. She broke the jar and poured the perfume on His head.

[4]Some who were there were annoyed and said to one another, "Why was the perfume wasted like this? [5]This perfume could have been sold for more than three hundred denarii and the money given to the poor." And they were grumbling at her.

[6]"Let her alone," Jesus said. "Why should you trouble her? She has done a beautiful thing to Me. [7]*The poor you always have with you,* and you can help them whenever you want to, but you will not always have Me. [8]She has done what she could. She came ahead of time to pour the perfume on My body to prepare it for burial. [9]I tell you, wherever the good news is preached in the whole world, certainly what she has done will also be told in memory of her."

---

27 *Deut 30:4; Zech 2:6*   7 *Deut 15:11*

Judas Plans to Betray Jesus — *Matthew 26:14-16; Luke 22:3-6*

[10]Judas Iscariot, one of the twelve, went to the ruling priests to betray Jesus to them. [11]They were delighted to hear it and promised to give him money. So he was looking for a chance to betray Him.

The Passover — *Matthew 26:17-20; Luke 22:7-17*

[12]On the first of the Passover days of Bread Without Yeast, when it was customary to kill the Passover lamb, the disciples asked Jesus, "Where do You want us to go and get things ready for You to eat the Passover?"

[13]He sent two of His disciples and told them: "Go into the city, and you will meet a man carrying a jar of water. Follow him, [14]and when he goes into a house, tell the owner: 'The Teacher asks, "Where is My room in which I can eat the Passover with My disciples?" ' [15]Then he will show you a large room upstairs, furnished and ready. Get the things ready for us there."

[16]The disciples left, went into the city, and found everything as He had told them. And so they got the Passover ready.

[17]In the evening He came there with the twelve.

"Is it I?" — *Matthew 26:21-25; Luke 22:21-23; John 13:21-30*

[18]While they were still reclining and eating, Jesus said, "I tell you the truth, one of you is going to betray Me, one who is *eating with Me!*"

[19]They felt hurt and asked Him one after another, "You don't mean me?"

[20]"One of the twelve," He told them, "one who is dipping into the bowl with Me. [21]The Son of Man is going away as it is written about Him, but woe to that man who betrays the Son of Man! It would be better for that man if he had never been born."

The Lord's Supper — *Matthew 26:26-30; Luke 22:18-20; I Corinthians 11:23-25*

[22]While they were eating, Jesus took bread and blessed it. He broke it and gave it to them and said, "Take it. This is My body."

[23]Then He took a cup, gave thanks, and gave it to them. And they all drank of it. [24]He told them, "This is My *blood of the* new *testament,* which is poured out for many.

[25]"I tell you the truth, I will not drink again of the fruit of the vine until that day when I drink it in a new way in God's kingdom."

[26]Then they sang a hymn.[h]

---

18 Ps 41:9   24 Ex 24:8; Jer 31:31-32; Zech 9:11

h - 26   Perhaps Psalms 115 through 118

"You Will Deny Me" — *Matthew 26:31-35; Luke 22:31-34; John 13:36-38*

They started out for the Mount of Olives.

[27]Then Jesus told them, "You will all turn against Me, because it is written: 'I will *strike down the Shepherd, and the sheep will be scattered.*' [28]But after I have risen, I will go ahead of you to Galilee."

[29]"Even if they all turn against You," Peter answered Him, "I will not."

[30]"I tell you the truth," Jesus told him, "tonight, before the rooster crows twice, you will deny Me three times."

[31]But he kept insisting all the more, "If I have to die with You, I'll never deny You." All the others said the same thing.

Gethsemane — *Matthew 26:36-46; Luke 22:39-46*

[32]They came to a place called Gethsemane, and He said to His disciples, "Sit down here while I pray."

[33]He took Peter, James, and John with Him, and He started to be very distressed and troubled. [34]He told them, "*My soul is so full of sorrow* that I am at the point of death. Stay here and keep awake."

[35]Going ahead a little, He bowed down to the ground and prayed that, if it were possible, He might not have to suffer what was ahead of Him. [36]"My Father," He said, "You can do anything. Take this cup away from Me. But let it not be as I want it but as You want it."

[37]He came and found them asleep. "Simon, are you sleeping?" He asked Peter. "So you couldn't keep awake one hour! [38]Stay awake and pray that you may not be tempted. The spirit is willing, but the flesh is weak."

[39]He went away again and prayed the same as before. [40]He came again and found them asleep — they couldn't keep their eyes open and didn't know what to say to Him.

[41]He came back a third time. "Are you going to sleep on now and rest?" He asked them. "It's enough. The time has come. Now the Son of Man will be betrayed into the hands of sinners . [42]Get up, let us go. Here comes the man to betray Me!"

The Arrest — *Matthew 26:47-56; Luke 22:47-54a; John 18:1-14*

[43]Just then, while Jesus was still talking, Judas, one of the twelve, came with a crowd of men with swords and clubs from the ruling priests, the Bible scholars, and the elders. [44]The traitor had given them a signal. "The One I kiss is the Man," he said. "Grab Him, take Him away, and don't let Him escape."

[45]When he came there, he quickly stepped up to Jesus and said, "Master!" and kissed Him.

[46]Then the men took hold of Jesus and arrested Him. [47]One of those who were standing near Him drew his sword, struck the high priest's slave, and cut off his ear.

---

27 Zech 13:7   34 Ps 42:5-6,11; 43:5

⁴⁸"Did you come out to arrest Me," Jesus asked them, "with swords and clubs as if I were a robber? ⁴⁹Day after day I was with you as I taught in the temple, and you didn't arrest Me. But what the Bible says has to come true."

⁵⁰Then all the disciples left Him and ran away. ⁵¹A certain young man who also was following Him had nothing on but a linen cloth. They tried to grab him, ⁵²but he left the linen cloth and ran away naked.

The First Trial Before the Jewish Council — Matthew 26:57-68

⁵³The men took Jesus to the high priest, and all the ruling priests, elders, and Bible scholars were coming together. ⁵⁴Peter followed Him at a distance and even went into the high priest's courtyard. And he was sitting with the attendants, warming himself at the fire.

⁵⁵The ruling priests and the whole Jewish court tried to get some testimony against Jesus in order to put Him to death but couldn't find any. ⁵⁶While many gave false testimony against Him, their statements didn't agree.

⁵⁷Then some got up and gave this false testimony against Him: ⁵⁸"We heard him say, 'I will tear down this temple made by human hands, and in three days build another not made by human hands.' " ⁵⁹But even on this point their statements didn't agree.

⁶⁰Then the high priest stepped forward. He asked Jesus, "Don't you have any answer to what these men testify against you?"

⁶¹But He was silent and didn't answer.

Again the high priest asked Him, "Are you the Christ, the Son of the Blessed?"

⁶²"I am," Jesus said. "And you will all see *the Son of Man sitting at the right hand* of power and *coming in the clouds of heaven.*"

⁶³Then the high priest tore his clothes, saying, "Why do we need any more witnesses? ⁶⁴You've heard the blasphemy. What do you think?"

Then all condemned Him, saying He must die. ⁶⁵Some of them started to *spit* at Him. They covered His face, hit Him with their fists, and told Him, "Prophesy!" The attendants also slapped Him when they took charge of Him.

Peter Denies Jesus — Matthew 26:69-75; Luke 22:54b-62; John 18:15-18, 25-27

⁶⁶While Peter was down in the courtyard, one of the high priest's maids came, ⁶⁷and seeing Peter warming himself, she looked at him and said, "You also were with this Jesus from Nazareth!"

⁶⁸But he denied it: "I don't know Him, and I don't know what you're talking about."

He went out to the entrance. Then a rooster crowed.

⁶⁹The maid saw him. "He's one of them," she also told those who were

62 Ps 110:1; Dan 7:13   65 Is 50:6

standing around. [70]Again he denied.

After a little while those who stood near him also told Peter, "Sure, you're one of them, because you're a Galilean!"

[71]Then he started to curse and swear: "I don't know this Man you're talking about." [72]Just then a rooster crowed a second time, and Peter remembered Jesus telling him: "Before the rooster crows twice, you will deny Me three times." And he started to cry.

Before Pilate — *Matthew 27:11-14; Luke 23:1-4; John 18:28-38*

15 As soon as it was morning, the ruling priests, the elders, and the Bible scholars, that is, the whole Jewish council, came to a decision. They bound Jesus, took Him away, and handed Him over to Pilate.

[2]Pilate asked Him, "Are you the King of the Jews?" "Yes," Jesus answered him.

[3]The ruling priests were accusing Him of many things.

[4]"Don't you have anything to say to this?" Pilate asked Him again. "See how many accusations they're bringing against you!"

[5]But Jesus didn't answer him anymore, so that Pilate was surprised.

Barabbas — *Matthew 27:15-26; Luke 23:17-25; John 18:39-40*

[6]Now, at every festival Pilate used to free a prisoner whom the people asked for. [7]There was a man by the name of Barabbas. He was in prison with the rebels who in their revolt had committed a murder. [8]And the crowd came up and asked Pilate to do for them as he had done before. [9]Pilate answered them by asking, "Do you want me to free the King of the Jews for you?" [10]He knew the ruling priests had handed Jesus over to him because they were jealous.

[11]The ruling priests stirred up the people to get him to free Barabbas for them instead.

[12]"Now, what should I do with him you call the King of the Jews?" Pilate again asked them.

[13]Then they yelled, "Crucify him!"

[14]"Why, what wrong has he done?" Pilate asked them. But they yelled all the louder, "Crucify him!"

[15]Then Pilate, wanting to satisfy the people, freed Barabbas for them, but Jesus he whipped and handed over to be crucified.

[16]The soldiers took Him into the courtyard of the governor's palace and called together the whole troop of soldiers. [17]They put a purple cloak on Him, twisted some thorns into a crown and placed it on His head, [18]and started to greet Him: "Hail, King of the Jews!" [19]They kept hitting Him on the head with a stick, *spit* on Him, knelt, and worshiped Him. [20]After mocking Him, the soldiers took off the purple cloak and put His own clothes back on Him. Then they took Him out to crucify Him.

---

[19] Is 50:6

"They Crucified Him" — *Matthew 27:31-44 Luke 23:26-38; John 19:16b-24*

[21]A certain Simon from Cyrene, the father of Alexander and Rufus, was on his way in from the country, and as he was going to pass by, they forced him to carry the cross of Jesus.

[22]They took Him to the Golgotha place, which means Skull Place. [23]They tried to give Him wine mixed with myrrh, but He didn't take it. [24]After they crucified Him, *they divided His clothes among them by throwing lots for them* to see what each one should get. [25]It was nine in the morning when they crucified Him. [26]There was a notice stating why Jesus was being punished; it read: THE KING OF THE JEWS. [27]With Him they crucified two robbers, one at His right hand and the other at His left.[i]

[29]Those who passed by were *ridiculing* Him, *shaking their heads* and saying, "Ha! You were going to tear down the temple and rebuild it in three days — [30]come down from the cross, and save yourself!" [31]In the same way the ruling priests and the Bible scholars *made fun of* Him among themselves and said, "He saved others — he cannot save himself. [32]The Christ, the King of Israel, should now come down from the cross. He should let us see that, and we'll believe him." Those crucified with Him also were *insulting* Him.

Jesus Dies — *Matthew 27:45-46; Luke 23:44-49; John 19:28-30*

[33]When twelve o'clock came, darkness came over the whole country and lasted until three in the afternoon. [34]At three o'clock Jesus called out aloud, *"Eloi, Eloi, lama sabachthani?"* which means, "My God, My God, why did You forsake Me?"

[35]Hearing Him, some of those standing near said, "Listen! He's calling Elijah." [36]Someone ran, soaked a sponge in *sour wine,* put it on a stick, and *gave Him a drink.* "Let's see," he said, "if Elijah comes to take him down."

[37]Then Jesus called out with a loud voice and died. [38]And the curtain in the temple was torn in two from top to bottom.

[39]When the captain who stood facing Jesus saw how He gave up His spirit, he said, "This Man certainly was the Son of God!"

[40]There were women watching *from a distance.* Among them were Mary from Magdala and Mary, the mother of James the Less and of Joseph, and Salome.

[41]While He was in Galilee, they had followed Him and supported Him. There were also many other women who had come up to Jerusalem with Him.

---

24 *Ps 22:18*   **29** *Ps 22:6-7; 109:25*   **31-32** *Ps 22:6-8*   **34** *Ps 22:1*
                    36 *Ps 69:21*   **40** *Ps 38:11*

---

i - 28   Our oldest manuscripts lack v. 28: "And what the Bible said came true, He will be counted among criminals." See Luke 22:37. The prophetic source of these words is Isaiah 53:9,12.

Jesus Is Buried — *Matthew 27:57-61; Luke 23:50-56; John 19:38-42*

[42]In the evening, since it was the day of preparation, that is, Friday, [43]Joseph from Arimathea, an important member of the Jewish council who also was waiting for God's kingdom, dared to go to Pilate and ask for Jesus' body.

[44]Pilate was surprised He was already dead. He called the captain and asked him, "Has he died already?" [45]When the captain told him, Pilate let Joseph have the body. [46]Joseph bought some linen, took the body down, wrapped it in the linen, and laid it in a grave that had been cut in the rock, and rolled a stone against the door of the grave.

[47]Mary from Magdala and Mary the mother of Jesus watched where He was laid.

Jesus Rises — *Matthew 28:1-10; Luke 24:1-12; John 20:1-10*

16 When the Sabbath was over, Mary from Magdala, Mary the mother of James, and Salome bought spices to go and anoint Jesus.

[2]On Sunday they were coming to the grave very early when the sun was up. [3]"Who is going to roll away the stone for us from the door of the grave?" they asked one another; [4]it was very large. But when they looked up, they saw the stone had been rolled back. [5]As they went into the grave, they saw a young man, dressed in a white robe, sitting at the right. And they were amazed.

[6]"Don't be amazed," he told them. "You're looking for Jesus from Nazareth, Who was crucified. He has risen. He is not here. See the place where He was laid. [7]But go and tell His disciples and Peter, 'He is going ahead of you to Galilee. There you will see Him, as He told you.'"

[8]They went out and hurried away from the grave, because they were trembling and bewildered. They were so frightened they didn't tell anyone anything.[j]

The Living Savior

[9]After Jesus rose early on Sunday, He showed Himself first to Mary from Magdala, out of whom He had driven seven demons. [10]She went and told the news to those who had been with Him and were now mourning and crying. [11]When they heard He was alive and had been seen by her, they didn't believe it.

[12]Later He appeared in a different form to two of them as they were walking into the country. [13]They went back and told the others, but these didn't believe them either.

[14]Still later He showed Himself to the eleven while they were reclining at the table, and He scolded them because their minds were closed and they didn't believe those who had seen Him after He had risen.

[15]Then He told them, "Go everywhere in the world and preach the good news to the whole world. [16]He who believes and is baptized will be saved,

j - 8   The two oldest manuscripts lack Mark 16:9-20 but end Mark's Gospel with v. 8.

but he who doesn't believe will be damned.

[17]"The believers will have these miraculous signs: In My name they will drive out demons. They will speak new languages. [18]They will pick up snakes. If they drink any deadly poison, it will not hurt them. They will lay their hands on the sick, and these will get well."

[19]After talking with them, the Lord was *taken up to heaven and sat down at the right of God.*

[20]They went out and preached everywhere, and the Lord worked with them and confirmed the Word by the miraculous signs that went with it.

---

19 II Kings 2:11; Ps 110:1

THE GOOD NEWS AS IT WAS TOLD BY
LUKE

1 MANY HAVE UNDERTAKEN to plan and write a story of what has been done among us, [2]just as we heard it from those who from the first became eyewitnesses and servants of the Word. [3]For this reason I, too, decided to check everything carefully from the beginning and to write it down in the proper order for you, excellent Theophilus, [4]so that you will be sure what you have heard is true.

An Angel Comes to Zacharias

[5]When Herod was king in the country of the Jews, there was a priest by the name of Zacharias. He belonged to the division of priests named after Abijah. His wife was a descendant of Aaron, and her name was Elizabeth. [6]Both were righteous before God as they lived blamelessly according to all the rules and regulations of the Lord.

[7]But they had no children, because Elizabeth was barren and both were old.

[8]Once Zacharias was on duty with his division and serving as priest before God. [9]According to the custom of the priests he was chosen by lot to go into the Lord's temple to burn incense. [10]All the people were praying outside while he was burning incense.

[11]Then he saw an angel of the Lord standing at the right side of the altar of incense. [12]Zacharias was startled to see him and was terrified.

[13]*"Don't be afraid,* Zacharias," the angel told him. *"Your prayer has been heard. You and your wife* Elizabeth *will have a son, and you will call him* John. [14]He will be your joy and delight, and many will be glad he was born.

[15]"He will be a great man before the Lord. *He will drink no wine or liquor.* He will be filled with the Holy Spirit even before he is born. [16]And he will bring many in Israel back to the Lord their God. [17]He will go ahead of Him with the spirit and power of *Elijah, to turn the hearts of the fathers to the children*, and the disobedient to think as righteous men — and so *to get a people thoroughly prepared for the Lord."*

[18]"How can I be sure of this?" Zacharias asked the angel. "I'm an old man, and my wife is old."

[19]"I am Gabriel!" the angel answered him. "I stand before God and was sent to speak to you and tell you this good news. [20]And now, you will be

---

13 Dan 10:12; Gen 17:19 15 Num 6:3; Judg 13:4   17 Mal 3:1; 4:5-6

silent and not able to talk until the day this happens, because you didn't believe what I said. But it will come true at the right time."

²¹Meanwhile the people were waiting for Zacharias and were surprised he was staying so long in the holy place. ²²When he did come out, he couldn't speak to them. Then they realized he had seen a vision in the holy place. He kept motioning to them and wasn't able to talk.

²³When the days of his service were over, he went home. ²⁴After this, his wife Elizabeth conceived and for five months she didn't show herself in public. ²⁵"The Lord did this for me," she said. "I was feeling ashamed among people, but He was kind and helped me, and I don't have to be ashamed any more."

The Angel Comes to Mary

²⁶In the sixth month God sent the angel Gabriel to a town in Galilee called Nazareth, ²⁷to a virgin engaged to a man by the name of Joseph, a descendant of David. The virgin's name was Mary.

²⁸Coming into her home, the angel said, "Greetings, you blessed one. The Lord is with you."

²⁹Startled by what he said, she tried to figure out what such a greeting might mean.

³⁰"Don't be afraid, Mary," the angel told her. "God has chosen to bless you. ³¹*You see, you will conceive and have a son, and you will call Him* JESUS. ³²He will be great and will be called *the Son of* the Most High *God.* And the Lord will give Him *the throne of* His ancestor *David.* ³³*He will be King over* the people of Jacob *forever, and His kingdom will never end."*

³⁴"How can this be?" Mary asked the angel. "I've had no relations with a husband."

³⁵"The Holy Spirit will come over you," the angel answered her, "and a power of the Most High God will overshadow you. And for that reason the Holy One to be born will be called the Son of God. ³⁶Now there is also Elizabeth, your relative. She is old, but she too conceived. People call her childless, but she's now in her sixth month. ³⁷*There is nothing that God will not be able to do."*

³⁸"I am the Lord's servant" Mary answered. "Let it happen to me as you said."

Then the angel left her.

Mary Visits Elizabeth

³⁹Then Mary hurried away to the hill country to a town of Judah. ⁴⁰There she went into the home of Zacharias and greeted Elizabeth.

⁴¹When Elizabeth heard Mary's greeting, the baby leaped in her womb. Then Elizabeth was filled with the Holy Spirit, ⁴²and she shouted, "Blessed are you among women, and blessed is the Child in your womb. ⁴³But how

31 Is 7:14   32-33 II Sam 7:12-14,16; Is 9:7; Mic 4:7; I Chr 17:12-14; Dan 2:44
37 Gen 18:14

does this happen to me that the mother of my Lord comes to me? [44]The moment I heard your greeting, the baby leaped with delight in my womb. [45]And blessed is she who believed that the Lord will accomplish what He promised to do for her."

[46]Mary said:

"*My soul* magnifies *the Lord,*

[47]and my spirit *delights in God, my Savior,*

[48]because *He has looked kindly at His humble servant.*

Yes, from now on the people in all generations *will call me blessed.*

[49]He has done great things to me —

He Who is mighty   and *Whose name is holy*

[50]and *Who is always merciful to those who fear Him.*

[51]"Mighty are the deeds He has done *with His arm.*

He has scattered those who think so proudly in their hearts.

[52]*He has pushed strong rulers down* from their thrones

and *lifted up lowly people.*

[53]*Those who were hungry He has filled with good things*, and the rich

He has sent away empty-handed.

[54]"*He has come to help His servant Israel*, because He wants to *remember His mercy*

[55](*as He promised our fathers*),

the mercy He has for Abraham and his descendants forever."

[56]Mary stayed with Elizabeth about three months and then went back home.

John Is Born

[57]The time came for Elizabeth to give birth, and she had a baby boy. [58]Her neighbors and relatives heard how the Lord had been unusually kind to her, and they shared her joy.

[59]On the eighth day they came to circumcise the baby. They were going to call him Zacharias because that was his father's name. [60]But his mother spoke up. "No!" she said. "He's going to be called John."

[61]"But there's no one among your relatives who has that name," they told her. [62]Then they motioned to his father to see what name he might want him to have. [63]He asked for a writing tablet and wrote, saying, "His name is John." They were all surprised.

[64]Just then he got his speech back and could talk again. He began to speak, praising God.

[65]All who lived around them were overawed. And all over the hills of Judea people kept talking about all these things. [66]All who heard of them kept them in mind. "What is this child going to be?" they asked. It was clear — the Lord's hand was with him.

[67]His father Zacharias was filled with the Holy Spirit, and he prophesied:

46-47 *I Sam 2:1; Hab 3:18*   **48** *I Sam 1:11; Gen 30:13*   **49** *Ps 111:9; Is 57:15*
50 *Ps 103:11,17*   **51** *Ps 89:10*   **52** *Job 12:19; 5:11; Ezk 21:26*
53 *Ps 107:9*   **54** *Is 41:8-9; Ps 98:3*   **55** *Gen 17:7; Mic 7:20*   **59** *Lev. 12:3*

[68]*"Praise the Lord, the God of Israel,*
because He has visited *His people*
and prepared *a ransom for them*.
[69]And He has *raised* up a *Horn of salvation* for us in the family of His
servant David,
[70] as He said long ago through His holy prophets
[71] that *He would save* us *from* our *enemies,*
from the power of all *who hate* us.
[72] He wanted to be *merciful to our fathers*
and *keep in mind His* holy *covenant,*
[73]*the oath He swore to* our father *Abraham*
[74]to rescue us from our *enemies*
and let us serve Him without fear
[75]in holiness and righteousness before Him all our life.
[76]"And you, child, will be called a prophet of the Most High God.
You will go *ahead of the Lord to prepare the ways for Him,*
[77]to make known to His people that they can be saved
by the forgiveness of their sins,
[78]because our God is merciful
and will let a heavenly *Sun rise* among us,
[79]*to shine on those who sit in the dark*
and in the shadow of death
and to guide our feet into *the way of peace.*"
[80]The child John grew and became strong in spirit. He lived in the
wilderness until he appeared publicly before Israel.

Jesus Is Born

2 In those days Caesar Augustus ordered a census taken of the whole
world. [2]This census took place while Quirinius was ruling Syria. [3]Everyone
went to register, each to his own town.

[4]Joseph also went up from the town of Nazareth in Galilee to David's
town, called Bethlehem, in Judea, because he was of the house and family
of David, [5]to register with Mary, his fiancee, who was going to have a child.

[6]And while they were there, the time came for her to have her child.
[7]She had her first son, and she wrapped Him in strips of cloth and laid Him
in a manger because there was no room for them in the inn.

The Shepherds

[8]There were shepherds not far away, living in the field and taking
turns watching their flock during the night.

[9]Then an angel of the Lord stood by them, and the Lord's glory shone
around them. They were terrified. [10]"Don't be afraid," the angel said to

---

68 *Ps 41:13; 72:18; 89:52; 106:48; 111:9*   **69** *I Sam 2:10; Ps 18:2; 132:17*
71 *Ps 106:10*   **72** *Mic 7:20*   **72-74** *Gen 22:16-17; Lev 26:42; Ps 105:8-9; 106:45*
76 *Mal 3:1*   **78** *Mal 4:2*   **79** *Ps 107:10; Is 9:2; 59:8*

them. "I have good news for you. A great joy will come to all the people: ¹¹the Savior, Who is Christ the Lord, was born for you today in David's town. ¹²And this is how you will know Him: you will find a baby all wrapped up and lying in a manger."

¹³Suddenly there was with the angel a large crowd of the angels of heaven, who were praising God and saying: ¹⁴"Glory to God in the highest heavens, and on earth *peace* among people who have His good will!"

¹⁵When the angels had left them and gone to heaven, the shepherds said to one another, "The Lord has told us what has happened. Let's go to Bethlehem and see it."

¹⁶They hurried over there and searched until they found Mary and Joseph with the Baby, Who was lying in the manger. ¹⁷When they had seen Him, they told others what they had been told about this Child. ¹⁸And everyone was surprised to hear the story the shepherds told.

¹⁹But Mary treasured all these things in her heart and kept thinking about them.

²⁰The shepherds went back, glorifying and praising God for everything they had heard and seen. It was just as they had been told.

In the Temple

²¹*On the eighth day the time came to circumcise the Child*, and He was called Jesus, the name the angel gave Him before He was conceived.

²²When *the time came* for them *to be purified* according to the Law of Moses, Joseph and Mary took Jesus up to Jerusalem to present Him to the Lord ²³(as it is written in the Law of the Lord: *"Every first born boy should be* called *'the Lord's holy one'* ") ²⁴and to offer a sacrifice according to the Law of the Lord, *a pair of turtledoves or two young pigeons.*

²⁵Now, there was in Jerusalem a man by the name of Simeon. He was a righteous man, fearing God and waiting for the One Who would comfort Israel. The Holy Spirit was on him. ²⁶The Holy Spirit had told him that before he would die he would see the Christ sent by the Lord.

²⁷Moved by the Spirit, he went into the temple. When the parents brought in the Child Jesus to do for Him what was customary according to the Law, ²⁸Simeon took Him in his arms, praised God, and said:

²⁹ "Lord, now You are letting Your servant go in peace as You promised,
³⁰ because my eyes have *seen Your salvation*
³¹ that You prepared for all people to see,
³² *a light to shine on the Gentiles*,
   and the *glory of* Your people *Israel*."

³³His mother and Joseph were surprised such things were said about Him. ³⁴Then Simeon blessed them and said to His mother Mary, "Here is what this Child is appointed for: *Many in Israel will fall* and rise again *because of Him*; and He'll be a sign that many will talk against, ³⁵to show

14 Is . 9:6   21 Lev 12:3   22 Lev 12:6   23 Ex. 13:2,12   24 Lev 5:7,11; 12:8, Num 6:10
30 Is 40:5; 52:10   32 Is 42:6; 46:13; 49:6   34 Is 8:14-15

what they're thinking in their hearts. And a sword will pierce your own soul, too."

³⁶Anna, a prophetess, was also there. She was a daughter of Phanuel, of the tribe of Asher. She was now very old. When she was a girl, she had married a man and lived with him seven years.

³⁷After that she was a widow until she was 84. She never left the temple but worshiped day and night, fasting and praying. ³⁸She too came forward just then, thanked God, and talked about the Child to all who were looking for Jerusalem to be set free.

³⁹When Joseph and Mary had done everything the Law of the Lord told them to do, they went back to Galilee to their town of Nazareth.

The Boy Jesus

⁴⁰The little Child grew big and strong and full of wisdom, and God's favor was with Him.

⁴¹Every year His parents would go to Jerusalem to celebrate the Passover. ⁴²And so when He was twelve, they went up for the festival as usual.

⁴³When the festival days were over and they started for home, the boy Jesus stayed behind in Jerusalem. But His mother and Joseph didn't know about it. ⁴⁴They thought He was with the others who were traveling with them. After traveling a day, they started to look for Him among their relatives and friends. ⁴⁵When they didn't find Him, they went back to Jerusalem, looking for Him.

⁴⁶Two days later they found Him in the temple, sitting among the teachers, listening to them and asking them questions. ⁴⁷His understanding and His answers surprised all who heard Him.

⁴⁸They were amazed to see Him there. "Son, why did You do this to us?" His mother asked Him. "See how anxiously Your father and I have been looking for You!"

⁴⁹"Why were you looking for Me?" He asked them. "Didn't you realize I must be in My Father's house?" ⁵⁰But they didn't understand what He told them.

⁵¹Then He went back with them to Nazareth. And He obeyed them.

His mother kept all these things in her heart. ⁵²And Jesus grew wiser and taller and *won the approval of God and of people.*

John Prepares the Way — *Matthew 3:1-12; Mark 1:1-8;*
John 1:19-28

3 In the fifteenth year of the rule of Emperor Tiberius, Pontius Pilate was governor of Judea, Herod ruled Galilee, his brother Philip ruled Iturea and Trachonitis, Lysanias ruled Abilene, ²and Annas and Caiaphas were the high priests. Then God spoke to John, the son of Zacharias, in the wilderness. ³He went into the whole Jordan valley and preached: "Repent

---

52 I Sam 2:26; Prov 3:4

and be baptized to have your sins forgiven." [4]This was what the prophet Isaiah had said in his book:

> A voice will be calling in the wilderness:
> "Prepare the way for the Lord;
> make the paths straight for Him.
> [5] Every ravine will be filled;
> every mountain and hill will be cut down.
> The crooked will be made straight and the rough roads smooth.
> [6] All people will see the salvation of God."

[7] So he would say to the crowds who were coming out to be baptized by him, "Brood of poisonous snakes, who warned you to run away from the punishment waiting for you? [8]Do the works that show you have repented. And don't start telling yourselves, 'Abraham is our father.' I tell you, God can raise up children for Abraham from these stones. [9]The ax is now ready to strike at the roots of the trees, and any tree that doesn't produce good fruit will be cut down and thrown into the fire."

[10] "What should we do?" the crowds asked him.

[11] "If you have two garments," he answered them, "share them with him who has none, and if you have food, do the same."

[12] Some tax collectors also came to be baptized. "Teacher," they asked him, "what should we do?"

[13] "Don't collect more money than you're ordered to collect," he told them.

[14] Some soldiers also asked him, "And what should we do?"

"Don't use threats or blackmail to get money from anyone," he told them, "but be satisfied with your pay."

[15] The people were expecting something and all were wondering if John was perhaps the Christ. [16]John answered them all: "I baptize you with water. But the One Who is mightier than I is coming. I'm not worthy to untie His sandal straps. He will baptize you with the Holy Spirit and fire. [17]He has the winnowing shovel in His hand to clean up His threshing floor and gather the wheat into His barn, but the chaff He'll burn in a fire that can't be put out."

[18]And so with many other challenging words he was telling the people the good news.

In Prison—

[19] When John was showing Herod, the governor, how wrong he was in regard to his brother's wife Herodias and all the other wicked things Herod did, [20] he, on top of everything, locked John up in prison.

John Baptizes Jesus— *Matthew 3:13-17; Mark 1:9-11; Compare John 1:29-34*

[21]When all the people were being baptized, Jesus was baptized too.

4-6 Is 40:3-5

While He was praying, heaven opened, ²²and the Holy Spirit came down on Him in the bodily form of a dove. And a voice from heaven said, "You are *My Son*, Whom I love. *I am delighted* with You."

²³Jesus was about 30 years old when He began His work.

The Son of Man — *Matthew 1:1-17*

Jesus, so people thought, was a son of Joseph, of Eli, ²⁴of Matthat, of Levi, of Melchi, of Jannai, of Joseph, ²⁵of Mattathias, of Amos, of Nahum, of Esli, of Naggai, ²⁶of Maath, of Mattathias, of Semein, of Josech, of Joda, ²⁷of Joanan, of Rhesa, of Zerubbabel, of Shealtiel, of Neri, ²⁸of Melchi, of Addi, of Cosam, of Elmadam, of Er, ²⁹of Jesus, of Eliezer, of Jorim, of Matthat, of Levi, ³⁰of Simeon, of Judas, of Joseph,of Jonam, of Eliakim, ³¹of Melea, of Menna, of Mattatha, of Nathan, of David, ³²of Jesse, of Obed, of Boaz, of Salmon, of Nahshon, ³³of Amminadab, of Ram, of Admin, of Arni, of Hezron, of Perez, of Judah, ³⁴of Jacob, of Isaac, of Abraham, of Terah, of Nahor, ³⁵of Serug, of Reu, of Peleg, of Eber, of Shelah, ³⁶of Cainan, of Arphaxad, of Shem, of Noah, of Lamech, ³⁷of Methuselah, of Enoch, of Jared, of Mahalaleel, of Cainan, ³⁸of Enos, of Seth, of Adam, of God.

The Devil Tempts Jesus — *Matthew 4:1-11; Mark 1:12-13*

4 Jesus, full of the Holy Spirit, left the Jordan and was led by the Spirit into the wilderness ²where the devil continued to tempt Him for 40 days. He ate nothing during those days, and when they were over, He was hungry.

³The devil said to Him, "If You're God's Son, tell this stone to become a loaf of bread."

⁴"It is written," Jesus answered him, " '*A man doesn't live on bread alone.*' "

⁵The devil took Him up and in a moment showed Him all the kingdoms of the world. ⁶"I'll give You all this power and glory," the devil told Him, "because it was given to me and I give it to anyone I please. ⁷So, if You'll worship me, all this will be Yours."

⁸"It is written," Jesus answered him, " '*Worship the Lord, your God, and serve Him* only.' "

⁹The devil took Him into Jerusalem and had Him stand on the edge of the temple. "If You're God's Son," he told Him, "jump down from here. ¹⁰It is written: '*He will order His angels to watch carefully over you.* ¹¹*They will carry you in their hands* and *never let you stub your foot against a stone.*' "

¹² "It is written," Jesus answered him, " '*Don't test the Lord your God.*' "
¹³When the devil had finished every way of tempting Him, he left Him until another opportunity would come.

---

22 *Ps 2:7; Is 42:1,7*   4 *Deut 8:3*   8 *Deut 6:13*   **10-11** *Ps 91:11-12*
         12 *Deut 6:16*

Nazareth Rejects Jesus — *Matthew 13:54-58; Mark 6:1-6*

[14]With the power of the Spirit Jesus went back to Galilee. The news about Him spread all over the surrounding country. [15]He taught in their synagogues, and everyone praised Him.

[16]Then Jesus came to Nazareth, where He had been raised. On the Sabbath He went into the synagogue as He used to do. He got up to read [17]and was given the scroll of the prophet Isaiah. Unrolling the scroll, He found the place where it says:

[18]*The Spirit of the Lord is on Me because —*
He anointed Me
To tell the poor the good news.
He sent Me
To announce to prisoners, "You are free,"
to the blind, "You will see again,"
To free those who are oppressed,
[19] *To announce a season when the Lord welcomes people.*

[20] He rolled up the scroll, gave it back to the attendant, and sat down. Everyone in the synagogue was watching Him closely [21]as He said, "Today, while you're listening, what is written here has come true."

[22]All spoke well of Him and were amazed to hear the gracious words flowing from His lips. "Isn't this Joseph's son?" they were asking.

[23]He answered them: "You will undoubtedly quote to Me the proverb 'Doctor, heal yourself!' and say, 'We've heard about everything You did in Capernaum. Do the same here in Your hometown.' [24]I tell you," He added, "it is true no prophet is accepted in his hometown.

[25]"Let Me tell you this truth: There were many widows in Israel in the days of Elijah, when it didn't rain for three years and six months and there was a big famine all over the country. [26]But Elijah wasn't sent to anyone except *a widow at Zarephath in the territory of Sidon.* [27]And there were lepers in Israel at the time of the prophet Elisha. But no one except *Naaman* from Syria *was made clean.*"

[28]As they were listening, all in the synagogue became furious. [29]They got up, pushed Him out of the town, and took Him to a brow of the hill on which their town was built, to throw Him over the cliff. [30]But He walked right through them and went away.

Jesus Drives Out a Devil — *Mark 1:21-28*

[31]He went down to Capernaum, a town in Galilee, and was teaching people on a Sabbath. [32]His teaching amazed them because He spoke with authority.

[33]In the synagogue there was a man with a spirit of an unclean demon. He screamed out loud, [34]"Oh, leave us alone, Jesus from Nazareth! You've come to destroy us! I know Who You are — God's Holy One."

18-19 Is 42:7; 58:6; 61:1-2   *26 I Kings 17:9*   *27 II Kings 5:14*

[35]Jesus talked sharply to him: "Be quiet, and come out of him." The demon threw him down in the middle of the crowd, then came out of him without doing him any harm.

[36]They were all amazed and said to one another, "What kind of speaking is this? With authority and power He gives orders to the unclean spirits, and out they go."

[37]So the news about Him spread to every place in the surrounding country.

Peter's Mother-in-Law — *Matthew 8:14-18; Mark 1:29-34*

[38]Leaving the synagogue, Jesus went to Simon's home. Simon's mother-in-law was sick with a high fever, and they asked Him to help her. [39]He went to her and, bending over her, ordered the fever to leave, and it left. She got up immediately and waited on them.

[40]When the sun was going down, all who had sick ones suffering from various diseases brought them to Him. He laid His hands on each of them and made them well. [41]The demons went out of many, screaming, "You're God's Son." He talked sharply to them and wouldn't let them go on talking, because they knew He was the Christ.

[42]In the morning He went out to a lonely place. The crowds were looking for Him. When they came to Him, they tried to keep Him from leaving them. [43]But He said to them, "I have to tell the good news of God's kingdom also in other towns. That's what I was sent to do."

[44]Then He kept on preaching in the synagogues of the country of the Jews.

Fishers of Men — *Matthew 4:18-22; Mark 1:14-20; John 11:35-51*

5 One day Jesus was standing by the Sea of Galilee, and the people were crowding Him as they were listening to God's Word. [2]He saw two boats on the shore of the sea. The fishermen had stepped out of them and were washing their nets. [3]So Jesus got into one of the boats (it belonged to Simon) and asked him to go out a little way from the shore. Then He sat down and taught the people from the boat.

[4]When He had stopped speaking, He told Simon, "Take the boat out where the water is deep, and let down your nets for a catch."

[5]"Master," Simon answered, "we've worked hard all night and caught nothing. But if You say so, I'll let down the nets."

[6]When the men had done this, they caught a very large number of fish, and their nets started to tear. [7]So they waved to their partners in the other boat to come and help them. They came, and now they filled both boats so that they started to sink

[8]When Simon Peter saw this, he fell down at Jesus' knees. "Leave me, Lord," he said. "I'm a sinful man." [9]He and all who were with him were amazed to see the fish they had caught, [10]and so were James and John, Zebedee's sons, who were Simon's partners.

"Don't be afraid," Jesus told Simon. "From now on you're going to catch men."

[11]So when they had brought the boats to the shore, they left everything and followed Him.

Jesus Heals a Leper — *Matthew 8:1-4; Mark 1:40-44*

[12]One day Jesus was in a town where there was a man who had leprosy all over his body. When he saw Jesus, he bowed down to the ground. "Lord," he begged Him, "if You want to, You can make me clean."

[13]Jesus stretched out His hand and touched him. "I want to," He said. "Be clean!" Immediately the leprosy left him.

[14]"Don't tell anyone," Jesus ordered him, "but go, *let the priest examine you*, and for your cleansing offer the sacrifice Moses ordered, to show them you're well." [15]But the news about Jesus spread all the more, and large crowds were gathering to hear Him and have their diseases healed. [16]And He would go away to lonely places and pray.

Jesus Forgives Sins — *Matthew 9:1-8; Mark 2:1-12*

[17]One day as He was teaching, Pharisees and Bible scholars were sitting there.

They had come from every village in Galilee and Judea and from Jerusalem. And Jesus had the Lord's power to heal.

[18]Then some men brought a paralyzed man on a bed and tried to take him in and lay him in front of Jesus. [19]But when they couldn't find a way to get him in on account of the crowd, they went up on the roof and through the tiles let him and the bed down among the people, right in front of Jesus.

[20]When Jesus saw their faith, He said, "Man, your sins are forgiven." [21]Then the Bible scholars and the Pharisees began to argue, saying, "Who is this fellow, talking such blasphemies? Who but God alone can forgive sins?"

[22]Jesus knew what they were thinking. "Why do you have such thoughts in your hearts?" He asked them. [23]"Is it easier to say, 'Your sins are forgiven,' or to say, 'Get up and walk?' [24]I want you to know the Son of Man has power on earth to forgive sins" — then He said to the paralyzed man, "I tell you, get up, take your bed, and go home."

[25]Immediately the man got up in front of them, took the bed he had been lying on, and went home, praising God.

[26]All were amazed and praised God. Fearfully they declared, "You wouldn't believe what we've seen today!"

Matthew (Levi) — *Matthew 9:9-13; Mark 2:13-17*

[27]After that He went out and saw a tax collector by the name of Levi sitting in the tax office. "Come with Me," He told him. [28]He got up, left

14 Lev 13:7,49

everything, and went with Him.

²⁹Then Levi gave a big dinner for Him at his home, and there was a big crowd of tax collectors and others who were eating with them.

³⁰The Pharisees and their Bible scholars complained to His disciples: "Why do you eat and drink with tax collectors and sinners?"

³¹"Those who are healthy don't need a doctor," Jesus answered them, "but those who are sick. ³²I didn't come to call righteous people, but sinners to repent."

The Bridegroom — *Matthew 9:14-17; Mark 2:18-22*

³³"John's disciples as well as the disciples of the Pharisees often fast and say prayers," they said to Him. "Why do Yours eat and drink?"

³⁴Jesus asked them, "Can you make the bridegroom's friends fast while the bridegroom is with them? ³⁵The time will come when the bridegroom will be taken away from them, and in those days they will fast."

³⁶He pictured it to them in this way: "No one tears a piece of cloth from a new garment and sews it on an old garment. If you do, you'll tear the new cloth, and the patch from the new won't match the old. ³⁷No one pours new wine into old wine skins. If you do, the new wine will burst the skins and run out, and the skins will be ruined. ³⁸New wine has to be poured into fresh skins.

³⁹"No one who has drunk old wine wants the new. 'The old is better,' he says."

Lord of the Sabbath — *Matthew 12:1-8; Mark 2:23-28*

6 While Jesus was walking through grain fields on a Sabbath, His disciples were picking the heads of grain, rubbing them in their hands, and eating them.

²Some of the Pharisees asked, "Why are you doing something you shouldn't do on a day of rest?"

³"Haven't you read what David did," Jesus asked them, "when he and his men were hungry — ⁴how he went into God's house and took the *loaves laid before God*, and ate them and gave his men some? Only the priests had the right to eat them." ⁵Then He added, "The Son of Man is Lord of the Sabbath."

The Shriveled Hand — *Matthew 12:9-15a; Mark 3:1-6*

⁶On another Sabbath Jesus went into a synagogue and taught. And there was a man whose right hand was shriveled. ⁷But the Bible scholars and the Pharisees were watching Jesus to see if He would heal him on a Sabbath. They wanted to find something to accuse Him of.

⁸But He knew what they were thinking; so He said to the man with the shriveled hand, "Get up and come forward." The man got up and stood

---

4 Lev 24:5-8; I Sam 21:6

there. [9]Then Jesus said to them, "I ask you, is it right on a Sabbath to do good or to do evil, to save a life or to kill?" [10]After looking around at all of them, He told the man, "Stretch out your hand." He did, and his hand was made healthy again.

[11]They were furious and began to discuss with one another what they could do to Jesus.

Twelve Apostles — *Matthew 10:1-4; Mark 3:13-19*

[12]In those days Jesus went out to the hill to pray, and He prayed to God all night.

[13]When it was day, He called His disciples. He chose twelve of them and called them apostles: [14]Simon, whom He also gave the name Peter, and his brother Andrew; James and John, Philip and Bartholomew, [15]Matthew and Thomas; James, the son of Alphaeus; Simon, called Zealot; [16]Judas, the son of James; and Judas Iscariot, who became a traitor.

Many Are Healed — *Mark 3:7-12*

[17]He went down with them and stood on a level place with a big crowd of His disciples and very many people from the whole country of the Jews, from Jerusalem, and from the seacoast of Tyre and Sidon. They had come to hear Him and have their diseases healed. [18]And those who were plagued by unclean spirits were made well. [19]All the people were trying to touch Him, because power came from Him and made them all well.

Blessing and Woe

[20]Jesus looked at His disciples and said:
>   "Blessed are you who are *poor* —
>   you have God's kingdom.
> [21]Blessed are you who are hungry now —
>   you will be satisfied.
>   Blessed are you who are crying now —
>   you will laugh.
> [22]Blessed are you when people hate you, exclude you from their company, insult you, reject your name as evil because you believe in the Son of Man. [23]In that day rejoice and leap for joy, because you have a great reward in heaven. You see, that's how their fathers treated the prophets. [24]But —
>   Woe to you who are rich —
>   you've had your comfort.
> [25] Woe to you who are well fed now —
>   you will be hungry.
>   Woe to you who are laughing now —
>   you will mourn and cry aloud.

20 Is 57:15

²⁶Woe to you when everyone speaks well of you —
   that is how their fathers treated the false prophets."

Love Your Enemies — *Matthew 5:38-48*

²⁷"But I tell you who are listening, love your enemies, be kind to those who hate you, ²⁸bless those who curse you, and pray for those who insult you. ²⁹If anyone hits you on your cheek, offer him the other cheek also. If anyone takes your coat, don't stop him from taking your shirt. ³⁰If anyone asks you for anything, give it to him. And if anyone takes what is yours, don't insist on getting it back.

³¹"Treat others just as you want them to treat you.

³²"If you love those who love you, how should anyone be especially pleased with you? Even sinners love those who love them. ³³If you help those who help you, how should anyone be especially pleased with you? Sinners do that, too. ³⁴If you lend anything to those from whom you expect to get something, how should anyone be especially pleased with you? Sinners also lend to sinners to get back what they lend. ³⁵No, love your enemies, help them, and lend to them without expecting to get anything back. Then you will have a great reward and will be the sons of the Most High God, since He is kind to unthankful and wicked people. ³⁶Be merciful as your Father is merciful."

Criticize Yourself — *Matthew 7:1-5*

³⁷"Don't judge, and you will not be judged. Don't condemn, and you will not be condemned. Forgive, and you will be forgiven. ³⁸Give, and it will be given you. A good measure, pressed together, shaken down, and running over, will be put into your lap. You see, the measure you use will be used for you."

³⁹He pictured it to them in this way: "Can a blind man lead another blind man? Won't they both fall into a ditch? ⁴⁰A pupil is not above his teacher. But anyone who is well trained will be like his teacher.

⁴¹"And why do you look at the speck in your brother's eye and don't notice the log in your own eye? ⁴²How can you say to your brother, 'Brother, let me take the speck out of your eye,' as long as you don't see the log in your own eye? You hypocrite, first throw the log out of your own eye. Then you'll see clearly enough to take the speck out of your brother's eye."

Hear and Do! — *Matthew 7:15-23*

⁴³"A good tree doesn't bear bad fruit, or a bad tree good fruit. ⁴⁴Every tree is known by its fruit. You don't pick figs from thornbushes, or grapes from brambles. ⁴⁵A good man produces good things from the good stored in his heart, and an evil man produces evil from his evil stored there. What a person says with his mouth flows from his heart.

⁴⁶"Why do you call Me 'Lord, Lord,' but don't do what I tell you?

⁴⁷"I will show you what kind of man anyone is who comes to Me and

hears and does what I say. [48]He's like a man who built a house. He dug deep and laid the foundation on a rock. When there was a flood, the torrent dashed against that house. But it couldn't move it, because it was built right. [49]Anyone who hears My words but doesn't follow them is like a man who built a house on the ground without a foundation. When the torrent dashed against it, that house immediately collapsed and went down with a big crash."

A Believing Captain — *Matthew 8:5-13*

7When Jesus had finished all He had to say to the people who heard Him, He went to Capernaum. [2]There a certain captain's servant was sick. He was dear to him and now he was dying. [3]The captain heard about Jesus and sent some Jewish elders to ask Him to come and save his servant's life. [4]They came to Jesus and earnestly pleaded with Him, "He deserves to have You do this for him, [5]because he loves our people and built the synagogue for us."

[6]So Jesus went with them. He wasn't far from the house when the captain sent friends to tell Him, "Lord, don't bother. I'm not worthy for You to come under my roof. [7]And so I didn't think I was fit to come to You either. But just say a word, and my servant will be made well. [8]I'm only a man who has to obey others, but I have soldiers under me. I tell one, 'Go', and he goes. And another, 'Come', and he comes. And my servant, 'Do this', and he does it."

[9]Amazed to hear him say this, Jesus turned to the crowd following Him. "I tell you," He said, "not even in Israel have I found such faith."

[10]When the men who had been sent went back to the house, they found the servant well again.

Jesus Raises a Widow's Son

[11]Soon after this, Jesus went to a town called Nain, and His disciples and a large crowd went with Him. [12]As He came near the gate of the town, a dead man was carried out. He was his mother's only son, and she was a widow. A large crowd from the town was with her.

[13]When the Lord saw her, He felt sorry for her. "Don't cry," He told her.

[14]He went up to the open coffin and touched it, and the men who were carrying it stood still. "Young man," He said, "I tell you, wake up." [15]The dead man sat up and started to talk. And Jesus *gave him to his mother*.

[16]They were all overawed and praised God. "A great prophet has risen among us," they said, and, "God has come to help His people." [17]This story about Jesus spread all over the country of the Jews and in all the surrounding territory.

---

15 *I Kings 17:23*

John Sends Two Disciples — *Matthew 11:2-6*

[18]John's disciples told him about all these things. [19]Then John called two of his disciples and sent them to ask the Lord, "Are You the One Who is coming, or should we look for someone else?"

[20]The men came to Jesus and said, "John the Baptizer sent us to ask You, 'Are You the One Who is coming, or should we look for someone else?' "

[21]Just then He had healed many people of their diseases, ailments, and evil spirits and had given sight to many who were blind.

[22]"Go," Jesus answered, "tell John what you've seen and heard: *The blind see*, the lame walk, lepers are made clean, *the deaf hear*, the dead are raised, and *the poor hear the good news* — [23]and blessed is anyone who doesn't turn against Me."

About John — *Matthew 11:7-19*

[24]When John's messengers had left, Jesus talked to the crowds about John:

"What did you go out into the wilderness to see — a reed shaken by the wind? [25]What, then, did you go out to see — a man dressed in soft robes? Those who wear fine clothes and live in luxury you'll find in the palaces of kings.

[26]"What, then, did you go out to see — a prophet? Let Me assure you, far more than a prophet. [27]This is the one of whom it is written: '*I will send My messenger ahead of You to prepare* Your *way before* You.' [28]I tell you, no woman's son is greater than John, and yet the least in God's kingdom is greater than he.

[29]"By letting John baptize them, all the people who heard him, even the tax collectors, admitted that God was right. [30]But the Pharisees and the learned men of the Law, by not letting John baptize them, *rejected what God had planned* for them.

[31]"How should I picture the people of this generation? What are they like? [32]They're like little children sitting in the marketplace and calling to one another, 'We played a tune on the flute for you, but you didn't dance. We sang a funeral song, but you didn't weep.' [33]John the Baptizer has come; he doesn't eat bread or drink wine, and you say, 'There's a demon in him!' [34]The Son of Man has come; He eats and drinks, and you say, 'Look at the glutton and drunkard, the friend of tax collectors and sinners!' [35]And yet wisdom is shown to be right by all her children."

"She Loved Much"

[36]One of the Pharisees invited Jesus to eat with him. He went into the Pharisee's home and reclined for the meal.

[37]In the town there was a sinful woman. When she found out He was eating at the Pharisee's home, she brought a flask of perfume [38]and stood

---

22 *Is 29:18; 35:5; 61:1*   ***27*** *Ex 23:20; Mal 3:1*   ***30*** *Prov 1:25*

behind Him at His feet. She was weeping and started to wet His feet with her tears. Then with the hair of her head she dried His feet, kissed them, and poured perfume on them.

[39]The Pharisee who had invited Jesus saw this and said to himself, "If He were a prophet, He would know who is touching Him and what kind of woman she is. She's a sinner."

[40]"Simon," Jesus answered him, "I have something to tell you."

"Say it, Teacher," he said.

[41]"Two men owed a moneylender some money: One owed him five hundred denarii, and the other fifty. [42]When they couldn't pay it back, he was kind enough to cancel the debt for both of them. Now, which of them will love him more?"

[43]"I suppose," Simon answered, "the one who had the bigger debt canceled."

"You're right," Jesus told him. [44]Then, turning to the woman, He said to Simon, "You see this woman? I came into your home, and you gave Me no water for My feet, but she wet My feet with her tears and dried them with her hair. [45]You gave Me no kiss, but ever since I came in, she hasn't stopped kissing My feet. [46]You poured no oil on My head, but she poured perfume on My feet. [47]That's why I tell you her sins are forgiven, many as they are. You see, she has loved much. Of course, he to whom little is forgiven loves only a little."

[48]Then He said to her, "Your sins are forgiven." [49]His fellow guests began to ask among themselves, "Who is this that he should even forgive sins?"

[50]Jesus said to the woman, "Your faith saved you. Go in peace!"

Through Galilee

8 After this Jesus traveled from one town and village to another, preaching and telling the good news of God's kingdom. The twelve were with Him. [2]Also some women who had been healed of evil spirits and diseases: Mary, also called the woman from Magdala (seven demons had gone out of her); [3]Johanna, the wife of Herod's manager Chusa; Susanna; and many other women. They supported Jesus and His disciples with their property.

The Sower — *Matthew 13:1-23; Mark 4:1-20*

[4]When a large crowd was gathering and people were coming to Him from every town, He told them a parable:

[5]"A sower went out to sow his seed. As he was sowing, some seed fell along the road and was trampled on, and the birds in the air ate it. [6]Some fell on a rock. It came up and withered because it had no moisture. [7]Some seed fell among thorns, and the thorns grew up with it and choked it. [8]But some seed fell on good ground, and it came up and produced a hundred times as much as was sown."

When He had said this, He called out, "You have ears to hear. Then listen!"

⁹His disciples asked Him what this parable meant. ¹⁰"You are given the privilege to know the mysteries of God's kingdom," He answered, "but to the others they come in parables that *they may see and yet not see, and hear and yet not understand.*

¹¹"This is what the parable means: ¹²The seed is God's Word. The people along the road are those who hear it. Then the devil comes and takes the Word out of their hearts to keep them from believing and being saved. ¹³In others it falls on a rock. As soon as they hear it, they welcome the Word with joy, but it doesn't take root in them. They believe for a while, but when they're tempted, they desert. ¹⁴In others the seed falls among thorns. They hear the Word, but as they go along, worries, riches, and pleasures of life choke them, and they don't produce anything good.

¹⁵But in others the seed falls on good ground. They are the ones who hear the Word and keep it in a good and honest heart and go on faithfully producing good things.

¹⁶"No one lights a lamp and hides it under a jar or puts it under a bed. No, you put it on a lamp stand so that those who come in will see the light. ¹⁷Everything hidden will be uncovered, and every secret will be known and come to the light.

¹⁸"Be careful, then, how you listen! If you have something, you'll be given more. But if you don't have what you should have, even what you think you have will be taken away from you."

The Mother and Brothers of Jesus — *Matthew 12:46-50; Mark 3:31-35*

¹⁹His mother and His brothers came to Him but couldn't get near Him on account of the crowd. ²⁰Jesus was told, "Your mother and Your brothers are standing outside and want to see You."

²¹"My mother and My brothers are these," He answered them, "who hear and do what God says."

Wind and Water Obey Him — *Matthew 8:23-27; Mark 4:35-41*

²²One day He and His disciples stepped into a boat. "Let us cross over to the other side of the sea," He said to them. They started out. ²³And as they were sailing along, He fell asleep.

A violent storm hit the sea, the boat was filling with water, and they were in danger. ²⁴So they went to Him and woke Him up. "Master, Master!" they called, "we're going to drown."

He got up and ordered the winds and the *waves* to stop. They stopped and it became calm. ²⁵"Where is your faith?" He asked them.

Frightened and amazed, they asked one another, "Who is He? He orders even the winds and the water, and they obey Him!"

---

10 Is 6:9   24 Ps 65:7

The Gerasenes — *Matthew 8:28-34; Mark 5:1-20*

²⁶They landed in the country of the Gerasenes, which is opposite Galilee. ²⁷When He stepped out on the shore, a man from the town who had demons in him met Him. He had worn no clothes for a long time. He wouldn't stay in a house but in the burial places. ²⁸When he saw Jesus, he screamed and bowed down before Him. "Let me alone, Jesus, Son of the Most High God," he shouted. "I beg You, don't torture me." ²⁹Jesus had been ordering the unclean spirit to come out of the man. For a long time it had a firm hold on him. He had been bound with chains on hands and feet and had been kept under guard, but he would tear the chains and be driven by the demon into lonely places.

³⁰"What is your name?" Jesus asked him.

"Six Thousand," he answered, because many demons had gone into him. ³¹They begged Him not to order them to go into the bottomless pit.

³²There was a herd of many hogs feeding on the hillside. So they begged Him to let them go into these. He let them. ³³The demons came out of the man and went into the hogs, and the herd stampeded down the cliff into the sea and was drowned.

³⁴But when those who had taken care of the hogs saw what had happened, they ran away and told about it in the town and in the country. ³⁵The people went out to see what had happened. They came to Jesus and found the man from whom the demons had gone out, now sitting dressed and in his right mind at Jesus' feet; and they were frightened. ³⁶Those who had seen it told them how the man plagued by demons had been made well.

³⁷Then all the people of the surrounding country of the Gerasenes asked Jesus to leave them, because terror had gripped them.

He got into a boat and started back. ³⁸Now, the man from whom the demons had gone out begged Jesus to let him be with Him. But He sent him away and told him, ³⁹"Go home and tell how much God has done for you." So the man left and made known all over the town how much Jesus had done for him.

The Daughter of Jairus — *Matthew 9:18-26; Mark 5:21-43*

⁴⁰When Jesus came back, the people welcomed Him, because they were all expecting Him.

⁴¹A synagogue leader by the name of Jairus came and, kneeling at Jesus' feet, begged Him to come to his home, ⁴²because his only daughter, about twelve years old, was dying. As he went, the crowd almost crushed Him.

⁴³There was a woman who had a flow of blood for twelve years. No one could cure her. ⁴⁴She came to Him from behind and touched the tassel of His garment, and immediately her blood stopped flowing.

⁴⁵"Who touched Me?" Jesus asked.

When everyone denied having touched Him, Peter said, "Master, the people are crowding You and pressing against You."

⁴⁶"Someone did touch Me," Jesus said. "I noticed that power went from Me."

⁴⁷When the woman saw she was discovered, she came trembling, bowed down before Him, and in front of all the people told why she touched Him and how she was made well immediately.

⁴⁸"Daughter," He told her, "your faith made you well. Go in peace!"

⁴⁹While He was still speaking, someone came from the synagogue leader. "Your daughter is dead," he said. "Don't trouble the Teacher any more."

⁵⁰Hearing this, Jesus told him, "Don't be afraid! Only believe, and she'll get well."

⁵¹Coming into the house, He let only Peter, John, James, and the child's father and mother go in with him. ⁵²Everyone was crying and beating their chests, mourning her. "Don't cry," He said. "She isn't dead; she's sleeping."

⁵³They laughed at Him, because they knew she had died. ⁵⁴He took her hand and called, "Girl, wake up!" ⁵⁵Her spirit returned, and she got up immediately. Jesus ordered that she be given something to eat. ⁵⁶And her parents were amazed. But He ordered them not to tell anyone what had happened.

Jesus Sends Out the Twelve — *Matthew 10:1-42; Mark 6:7-13*

9 Jesus called the twelve together and gave them power and authority over all demons and to heal diseases. ²He sent them to preach God's kingdom and heal the sick.

³"Don't take anything with you on the way," He told them, "no stick or bag or bread or money. Don't take two tunics. ⁴When you go into a home, stay there, and from there go out. ⁵If people don't welcome you, leave that town, and shake the dust off your feet as a warning to them."

⁶They left and went from village to village, telling the good news everywhere and healing the sick.

Has John Come Back? — *Matthew 14:1-12; Mark 6:14-29*

⁷Herod, the governor, heard about everything Jesus was doing and didn't know what to make of it, because some people said, "John has risen from the dead"; ⁸others, "Elijah has appeared"; still others, "One of the old prophets has risen."

⁹"I cut off John's head," Herod said. "Now who is this about whom I hear such things?" And he wanted to see Jesus.

Jesus Feeds 5,000 — *Matthew 14:13-21; Mark 6:30-44; John 6:1-14*

¹⁰The apostles came back and told Jesus all they had done. He took them away with Him near a town called Bethsaida in order to be alone. ¹¹But the crowds found out about it and followed Him. He welcomed them,

talked to them about God's kingdom, and healed those who needed healing.

¹²Toward the end of the day the twelve came to Him and told Him, "Send the crowd away to the villages and farms around us to get shelter and find food. We're here in a deserted place."

¹³"You give them something to eat," He told them.

"All we have is five loaves and two fish," they answered, "unless perhaps we go and buy food for all these people." ¹⁴There were about 5,000 men.

Then He told His disciples, "Have them sit down in groups of about fifty."

¹⁵They did this and got them all seated.

¹⁶He took the five loaves and the two fish, looked up to heaven, blessed them and broke them, and gave them to the disciples to give to the people. ¹⁷All of them ate and had enough. And they picked up the pieces that were left — twelve baskets full.

"You Are the Christ [Messiah]" — *Matthew 16:13-20; Mark 8:27-30*

¹⁸Once when He was praying and only His disciples were with Him, He asked them, "Who do people say I am?"

¹⁹"John the Baptizer," they answered Him; "others say Elijah, and still others that one of the old prophets has come back to life."

²⁰"And you," He asked them, "who do you say I am?" "The Christ Whom God has sent," Peter answered.

²¹But He gave them strict orders not to tell anyone about this.

Take Up Your Cross — *Matthew 16:24-28; Mark 8:34-9:1*

²²"The Son of Man has to suffer much," He said, "be rejected by the elders, ruling priests, and Bible scholars, be killed, and then rise on the third day."

²³And He told all of them, "If you want to follow Me, deny yourself, take up your cross every day, and come with Me. ²⁴If you want to save your life, you will lose it. But if you will lose your life for Me, you will save it. ²⁵What good does it do you to win the whole world and destroy or lose yourself? ²⁶If you're ashamed of Me and what I say, then the Son of Man will be ashamed of you when He comes in His glory and the glory of the Father and the holy angels.

²⁷"I tell you the truth, there are some standing here who will never taste death until they see God's kingdom."

Jesus Shows His Glory (The Transfiguration) — *Matthew 17:1-8; Mark 9:2-13*

²⁸About a week after He said this, Jesus took Peter, James, and John

with Him and went up the mountain to pray. ²⁹While He was praying, His face changed and looked different, and His clothes became dazzling white. ³⁰Suddenly there were two men talking with Him; they were Moses and Elijah. ³¹They appeared in glory and were talking about His leaving this world, which was to happen at Jerusalem. ³²But Peter and the men with him had been overcome by sleep. Waking up, they saw *His glory* and the two men standing with Him.

³³When these were leaving Him, Peter said to Jesus, "Master, it's good for us to be here. Let's put up three shelters, one for You, one for Moses, and one for Elijah." He didn't know what he was saying.

³⁴While he was saying this, a cloud came and overshadowed them. They were frightened as they went into the cloud. ³⁵Then a voice came out of the cloud: "This is *My Son Whom I have chosen. Listen to Him.*" ³⁶When the voice had spoken, they saw Jesus was alone.

They kept silent and in those days told no one anything of what they had seen.

The Demon-Possessed Boy — *Matthew 17:14-20; Mark 9:14-29*

³⁷The next day, when they had come down from the mountain, He met a large crowd. ³⁸Then a man in the crowd called, "Teacher, I beg You, look at my son, he is my only child. ³⁹A spirit takes hold of him, and suddenly he shrieks. It throws him into convulsions, and he foams at the mouth. It will hardly stop mistreating him. ⁴⁰I asked Your disciples to drive out the spirit, but they couldn't do it."

⁴¹"O you unbelieving and perverted generation!" Jesus answered. "How long must I be with you and put up with you! Bring your son here."

⁴²While the boy was coming, the demon dashed him on the ground and threw him into convulsions.

Jesus talked sharply to the unclean spirit, made the boy well, and gave him back to his father. ⁴³All were amazed to see God's wonderful power.

"The Son of Man Will Be Betrayed" — *Matthew 17:22-23; 18:1-5; Mark 9:30-37*

While everyone thought how wonderful everything was that Jesus was doing, He said to His disciples, ⁴⁴"Listen carefully to what I say. The Son of Man is going to be betrayed into the hands of men."

⁴⁵But they didn't know what He meant. It was hidden from them so that they didn't understand it. And they were afraid to ask Him about it.

⁴⁶A discussion got started among them as to which of them was the greatest. ⁴⁷But Jesus knew what they were thinking. He took a little child, had him stand by Him, ⁴⁸and said to them, "If you welcome this little child in My name, you welcome Me. And if you welcome Me, you welcome Him Who sent Me. You see, if anyone is the least of all of you, he is great."

32 Ex 16:7,10   35 Ps 2:7; Is 42:1; Deut 18:15

"He Is for Us" — *Mark 9:38-41*

[49]"Master," John said, "we saw a man driving out demons in Your name, and we tried to stop him, because he's not one of us."

[50]"Don't stop him," Jesus told him; "anyone who is not against you is for you."

To Jerusalem

[51]As the time was coming nearer for Him to be taken up to heaven, He showed He was determined to go to Jerusalem. [52]He sent messengers ahead of Him. They went and stopped in a village of the Samaritans to arrange a place for Him to stay. [53]But the people didn't welcome Him, because He was going to Jerusalem. [54]When His disciples James and John saw this, they asked, "Lord, do You want us to order *fire to come down from heaven and burn* them up?"

[55]But He turned and sternly corrected them. [56]So they went on to another village.

"I Will Follow, but ..." — *Matthew 8:19-22*

[57]As they were walking along the road, a man said to Him, "I will follow You anywhere You go."

[58] "Foxes have holes," Jesus told him, "and birds in the air have nests, but the Son of Man doesn't have a place to lay His head."

[59]He told another man, "Follow Me."

"Lord, first let me go and bury my father," he said.

[60]But Jesus told him, "Let the dead bury their own dead. But you go and tell about God's kingdom."

[61]"I will follow You, Lord," said another, "but first let me say goodby to my people at home."

[62]"Anyone who lays his hand on a plow," Jesus answered him, "and keeps looking back isn't fit for God's kingdom."

72 Missionaries

10 After this the Lord appointed 72 others and sent them out in pairs to go ahead of Him to every town and place where He intended to go. [2]"There's much grain to be harvested, but there are only a few workers," He told them. "Ask the Owner of the crop to send out workers to bring in His grain. [3]Go! I'm sending you like lambs among wolves. [4]Don't carry a purse, a bag, or shoes, and don't stop to greet anyone on the way. [5]When you go into a house, say first, 'May there be peace in this house.' [6]If a man of peace lives there, your peace will rest on him; but if not, it will come back to you. [7]Stay in that house and eat and drink whatever they have, since a worker earns his pay. Don't move from one house to another. [8]When you go into any town and the people welcome you, eat what they serve you. ⁹Heal the sick that are there, and tell people, 'God's kingdom has come close to you!'

¹⁰"But if you go into a town and they don't welcome you, go out on its streets and say, ¹¹"The dust of your town has clung to our feet — we're wiping it off in protest against you! But realize this: God's kingdom has come near you!' ¹²I tell you, on that Day it will be easier for Sodom than for that town.

¹³"Woe to you, Chorazin! Woe to you, Bethsaida! If the miracles done in you had been done in Tyre and Sidon, they would long ago have repented, sitting in sackcloth and ashes. ¹⁴In the judgment it will be easier for Tyre and Sidon than for you. ¹⁵And you, Capernaum, will you be *lifted up to heaven? You will go down to hell.*

¹⁶"Anyone who hears you hears Me, and anyone who rejects you rejects Me. But anyone who rejects Me rejects Him Who sent Me."

¹⁷The 72 came back delighted. "Lord," they said, "even the demons do what we tell them in Your name."

¹⁸"I watched Satan fall from heaven like lightning," He told them. ¹⁹"You know, I've given you the power to *step on snakes* and scorpions and to trample on all the enemy's power, and nothing will hurt you. ²⁰Only don't be glad that the spirits obey you but that your names are written in heaven."

²¹In that hour the Holy Spirit filled Jesus with joy. "I praise You, Father, Lord of heaven and earth," He said, "for hiding these things from wise and intelligent people and revealing them to little children. Yes, Father, I praise You for wanting it to be that way.

²²"My Father has put everything in My hands. Only the Father knows the Son. And only the Son — and anyone to whom the Son wants to reveal Him —knows the Father."

²³Turning to His disciples, He said to them alone, "Blessed are the eyes that see what you see. ²⁴I tell you, many prophets and kings longed to see what you see but didn't see it, and hear what you hear but didn't hear it."

The Good Samaritan

²⁵Then an expert in the Law came forward to test Jesus. "Teacher," he asked, "what do I do to inherit everlasting life?"

²⁶"What is written in the Law?" Jesus asked him. "What do you read there?"

²⁷"*Love the Lord your God with all your heart,*" he answered, "*and with all your soul and with all your strength* and with all your mind, and *your neighbor as yourself.*"

²⁸"You're right," Jesus told him. "*Do that and you will live.*"

²⁹But he wanted to justify himself. So he asked Jesus, "And who is my

15 Is 14:13,15   19 Ps 91:13   27 Deut 6:5; Lev 19:18   28 Lev 18:5

neighbor?"

³⁰In reply, Jesus said: "A man going from Jerusalem down to Jericho fell into the hands of robbers. They stripped him, struck him blow after blow, and went away leaving him half dead.

³¹"Just at that time a priest happened to go along that road, but when he saw him, he passed by on the other side. ³²So did also a Levite who came to the place: he looked at him and passed by on the other side.

³³"Then a Samaritan, as he was traveling, came near him, and when he saw him, he felt sorry for him. ³⁴He went to him and bandaged his wounds, pouring on oil and wine. Then he put him on his own animal, brought him to an inn, and took care of him. ³⁵The next day he took out two denarii and gave them to the innkeeper. 'Take care of him,' he said, 'and anything else you spend on him I'll repay you when I come back.'

³⁶"Which of those three, do you think, was a neighbor to the man who had fallen into the hands of the robbers?"

³⁷"The one who was kind enough to help him," he said.

"Go and do as he did," Jesus told him.

Mary Listens to Jesus

³⁸As they were walking along, Jesus came to a village where a woman by the name of Martha welcomed Him to her home. ³⁹She had a sister by the name of Mary. She sat down at Jesus' feet and listened to what He said.

⁴⁰But Martha was worried about all she had to do for them. So she came and asked, "Lord, don't You care that my sister has left me and I have to do the work alone? Now tell her to help me."

⁴¹"Martha, Martha," the Lord answered her, "you worry and fuss about a lot of things. ⁴²But there's only one thing you need. Mary has made the right choice, and it must not be taken away from her."

The Lord's Prayer — *Matthew 6:9-13*

11 Once Jesus was praying in a certain place. When He stopped, one of His disciples asked Him, "Lord, teach us to pray as John taught his disciples."

²He told them, "When you pray, say:

'Father, may Your name be kept holy, Your kingdom come,
Your will be done on earth as it is in heaven.
³Give us every day our daily bread.
⁴Forgive us our sins, as we, too, forgive everyone who sins against us.
And don't bring us into temptation.' "

Pray! — *Matthew 7:7-11*

⁵ "Suppose one of you has a friend," Jesus said to His disciples, "and you go to him at midnight and ask him, 'Friend, lend me three loaves. ⁶A friend of mine on a trip has dropped in on me, and I have nothing to serve

him.' [7]Will he answer from within, 'Don't bother me. The door is already locked, and my children are with me in bed. I can't get up and give you anything?' [8]I tell you, although he won't get up and give you anything even though he's your friend, yet because you persist, he'll get up and give you anything you need.

[9]"So I tell you: Ask and it will be given to you. Search and you will find. Knock and the door will be opened for you. [10]Anyone who continues to ask receives; anyone who continues to search finds; and anyone who continues to knock, the door will be opened for him.

[11]"If your son asks you, his father, for a fish, will any of you give him a snake instead of a fish? [12]Or if he asks for an egg, will you give him a scorpion? [13]Now if you, wicked as you are, know enough to give your children good gifts, how much more will your Father in heaven give the Holy Spirit to those who ask Him?"

Power over a Demon — *Matthew 12:22-32; Mark 3:20-30*

[14]He was driving out a demon who was speechless. When the demon had gone out, the speechless man spoke.

The people were amazed. [15]But some of them said, "He drives out the demons with the help of Beelzebul, who rules over the demons." [16]Others, meaning to test Him, demanded that He show them some miraculous sign from heaven.

[17]Knowing what they were thinking, He said to them, "If one part of any kingdom fights against another part, it loses its people, and one house falls on another. [18]If Satan fights against himself, how can his kingdom stand? I say this because you say Beelzebul helps Me drive out the demons. [19]But if Beelzebul helps Me drive out the demons, who helps your sons drive them out? That's why they'll be your judges. [20]But if God's finger helps Me drive out the demons, then God's kingdom has come to you.

[21]"When a strong man, completely armed, guards his palace, his property is not disturbed. [22]But when someone stronger than he attacks him and defeats him, he'll take away his whole armor, in which he trusted, and divide the plunder.

[23]"Anyone who is not with Me is against Me, and anyone who doesn't help Me gather, scatters.

[24]"When an unclean spirit comes out of a man, he goes through dry places looking for rest but doesn't find any. Then he says, 'I'll go back to the home I left.' [25]He comes and finds it swept and decorated. [26]Then he goes and takes home with him seven other spirits worse than himself, and they go in and live there. In the end that man is worse than he was before."

[27]When Jesus said this, a woman in the crowd raised her voice and called out, "Blessed is the mother who bore You and nursed You."

[28]"Yes," He said, "but *blessed are those who* continue to *listen to God's Word and keep it.*"

---

28 *Prov 8:32*

"The Sign of Jonah" — *Matthew 12:38-42*

[29]As the people were crowding around Him, He said, "This is a wicked generation. They're looking for a miraculous sign, but the only sign they'll get is Jonah. [30]As Jonah became a miraculous sign to the people of Nineveh, so the Son of Man will be a miraculous sign to these people. [31]The *queen* of the south will rise up in the Judgment with the men of this generation and condemn them, because she *came* from the ends of the earth to *hear Solomon's wisdom*; and here you see more than Solomon. [32]*The men of Nineveh* will rise up in the Judgment with the people of this generation and condemn them, because they repented when *Jonah preached*; and here you see more than Jonah."

Your Light — *Matthew 5:14-16; Mark 4:21-23*

[33]"You don't light a lamp and put it in a cellar or under a bucket but on the lampstand so that those who come in will see it shine. [34]"Your eye is the lamp of your body. When your eye is healthy, you have light for your whole body. But when your eye is bad, your body is dark! [35]Then see to it that the light in you isn't dark. [36]Now if you have light for your whole body and no part of it is dark, it will all have light just as when a lamp shines brightly on you."

Warnings — *Matthew 23:13-39*

[37]Jesus had been speaking, when a Pharisee invited Him to eat at his home. So He went in and reclined to eat. [38]But the Pharisee was surprised to see He didn't wash before the meal.

[39]The Lord said to him, "You Pharisees keep cleaning the outside of the cup and of the dish, but inside you're full of greed and wickedness. [40]You fools, didn't He Who made the outside make the inside too? [4]Give what is inside as a gift to help the poor, and you'll find everything clean.

[42]"But woe to you Pharisees! You give a tenth of mint, rue, and every vegetable, and you fail to be just and to love God. You should have done these without neglecting the others.

[43]"And woe to you Pharisees! You like to have the seats of honor in the synagogues and to be greeted in the marketplaces. [44]Woe to you! You're like the unmarked graves people walk over without knowing what they are."

[45]"Teacher," one of the experts in the Law said to Him, "when You say that, You insult us too."

[46]"Woe also to you experts in the Law!" He said. "You load people with burdens they can hardly carry, but not with one finger will you touch these burdens yourselves. [47]Woe to you! You build monuments for the prophets your fathers murdered. [48]So you are witnesses and approve of what your fathers did. They murdered them, and you just build something. [49]That's why

---

31 II Chron 9:1-7   *32 Jonah 3:4-5*

God's wisdom has said: I will send them prophets and apostles, and they will murder or persecute some of them [50]so that the people of this generation may be punished for the blood of all the prophets poured out since the world was made, [51]from the blood of Abel to the blood of Zachariah, who was killed between the altar and the temple. Yes, I tell you, the people of today will be punished for it.

[52]"Woe to you experts in the Law! You've taken away the key to knowledge.

You didn't go in yourselves and kept out those who tried to go in."

[53]When Jesus went outside, the Bible scholars and the Pharisees fiercely opposed Him and cross-examined Him about many things, [54]watching Him closely to trap Him in something He might say.

Don't Be Afraid of Men

12 When so many thousands of people came together that they trampled on one another, Jesus began to speak first to His disciples: "Beware of the yeast of the Pharisees — I mean, their hypocrisy. [2]Everything that's covered will be uncovered, and every secret will be known. [3]Everything you said in the dark will be heard in the light, and what you whispered in the ear in the inner rooms will be announced from the roofs. [4]But I tell you, My friends, don't be afraid of those who kill the body and then can't do any more. [5]I will point out the One you must fear. *Fear Him* Who after killing you has the power to throw you into hell. Yes, I tell you, fear Him!

[6]"Aren't five sparrows sold for two cents? And God doesn't forget any one of them. [7]Why, even the hairs on your heads are all counted! Don't be afraid — you're worth more than many sparrows! [8]I tell you, whoever will confess Me before other people, him the Son of Man will confess before God's angels. [9]Anyone who denies Me before other people will be denied before God's angels. [10]Anyone who will speak against the Son of Man will be forgiven. But he who slanders the Holy Spirit will not be forgiven.

[11]"When they bring you before synagogues, rulers, and authorities, don't worry how you will defend yourselves or what you will say. [12]When that time comes, the Holy Spirit will teach you what to say."

Don't Be Greedy

[13]"Teacher," someone in the crowd said to Him, "tell my brother to give me my share of the property our father left us."

[14]"Man," He asked him, "who appointed Me to be your judge or to divide your property?

[15]"Be careful," He told the people. "Guard against every kind of greed. Even if you have more than enough, your property doesn't give you life."

[16]Then He told them a story:

"A rich man had good crops on his land. [17]What am I going to do?' he said to himself. 'I have no place to store my crops.' [18]Finally he said, 'This is what I'll do: I'll tear down my barns and build bigger ones and store all my grain and goods in them. [19]Then I'll say to myself, "You have a lot of good things stored up for many years. Take life easy, eat, drink, and enjoy yourself." '

[20] "But God said to him, 'You fool, tonight you die. And what you've prepared— who will get it?' [21]That's how it is when you store up goods for yourself and aren't rich toward God.

Stop Worrying — *Matthew 6:25-34*

[22]"That is why I tell you," He said to His disciples: "Don't worry about what you'll eat to keep alive or what you'll wear on your bodies. [23]Life is more than food, and the body more than clothes. [24]Look at the crows. They don't sow or cut grain, they have no storeroom or barn; and yet God feeds them. You're worth much more than birds. [25]And can any of you by worrying add anything to your life? [26]If you can't do even the smallest thing, why worry about the rest? [27]See how the flowers grow. They don't work or spin. Yet I tell you, even Solomon in all his glory didn't dress like one of them. [28]If that's how God dresses the grass, which lives in the field today and tomorrow is thrown into a stove, how much more certainly will He put clothes on you — who trust Him so little? [29]So don't just think of what you'll eat or drink, and don't worry. [30]The people in the world run after all these things, but your Father knows you need them. [31]Only seek God's kingdom, and you'll get these things, too. [32]Don't be afraid, little flock, for your Father is pleased to give you the kingdom.

[33]"Sell what you have and give the money to the poor. Make yourselves purses that don't wear out and a treasure that will never be used up — in heaven, where no thief gets near it and no moth destroys it. [34]Where your treasure is, there your heart will be."

Be Ready — *Matthew 24:36-51; Mark 13:32-37*

[35]"Be ready for action with belts fastened and lamps burning, [36]like men waiting for their master when he comes back from a wedding, so that they can open the door for him the moment he comes and knocks. [37]Blessed are those slaves whom the master finds watching when he comes. I tell you he'll certainly fasten his belt, have them lie down for a meal, and come and serve them. [38]Even if he comes in the middle of the night or toward morning and finds them that way, blessed are they.

[39]"You know if the owner of a house had known just when the burglar was coming, he would not have let anyone break into his house. [40]You, too, get ready, because the Son of Man is coming when you don't expect Him."

[41]"Lord," Peter asked, "by this illustration do you mean to warn us — or everyone else too?"

[42]The Lord asked, "Who do you suppose is the *manager that can be trusted and has good sense*, whom the master will put in charge of his ser-

vants to give them their share of food at the right time? ⁴³Blessed is that slave whom his master will find doing just this when he comes. ⁴⁴I tell you he certainly will make him manager of all his property. ⁴⁵But if that slave says to himself, 'My master isn't coming back for some time,' and starts to beat the other slaves, men and women, and eats, drinks, and gets drunk, ⁴⁶the master of that slave will come one day when he's not expecting him and at a time he doesn't know and will cut him in pieces and put him with the unfaithful.

⁴⁷"That slave who knew what his master wanted and didn't prepare himself or do what he wanted will get many blows. ⁴⁸But he who didn't know and did things for which he deserved to be beaten will get few blows. If you were given much, much will be expected of you, and if much was entrusted to you, all the more will be demanded of you."

Sorrow Ahead

⁴⁹"I have come to bring fire on earth, and how glad I would be if it were already started! ⁵⁰I must be baptized with a baptism, and how I am troubled until it is done!

⁵¹"Do you think I came to bring peace on earth? No, I tell you — to bring division. ⁵²From now on five in one family will be divided, three against two and two against three. ⁵³A father will be against a son and a *son against a father*, a mother against a daughter and *a daughter against her mother*, a mother-in-law against her daughter-in-law and *a daughter-in-law against her mother-in-law*."

This Is Your Opportunity

⁵⁴"When you see a cloud coming up in the west," Jesus said to the people, "you immediately say, 'There's going to be a heavy rain,' and so it rains. ⁵⁵And when you see a wind blowing from the south, you say, 'It's going to be hot,' and so it is. ⁵⁶You hypocrites! You can tell what the appearance of the earth and of the sky means. How is it that you can't interpret this present time? ⁵⁷Why don't you yourselves decide what is right?

⁵⁸"When you go with your opponent to be tried before a ruler, do your best to settle with him on the way, or he may drag you before the judge, and the judge will hand you over to the officer, and the officer will put you in prison. ⁵⁹I tell you, you will never get out until you pay the last cent."

Repent

13At that time some men were there to tell Him about the Galileans whose blood Pilate had mixed with their sacrifices. ²Jesus asked them, "Do you think, because this happened to them, those Galileans must have been worse sinners than all the other Galileans? ³I tell you, no. And if you don't repent, you will all perish as they did. ⁴Or those eighteen the tower at

Siloam fell on and killed — do you think they must have been worse transgressors than all the other people living in Jerusalem? [5]I tell you, no. And if you don't repent, you will all perish as they did."

Another Year

[6]He told them this parable:

"A man had a fig tree growing in his vineyard. He came looking for fruit on it but didn't find any. [7]So he said to the man who worked the vineyard, 'Look here! For the last three years I've come looking for figs on this fig tree and haven't found any. Cut it down. Why should it use up the ground?'

[8]" 'Master,' he answered him, 'let it stand one more year, and I'll dig around it and fertilize it; [9]it may have figs next year. If not, cut it down.' "

Sick for Eighteen Years

[10]Jesus was teaching in one of the synagogues on a Sabbath, [11]and there was a woman whom a spirit had crippled for eighteen years. She was bent over and couldn't stand up straight. [12]When Jesus saw her, He called her and said, "Woman, you're rid of your trouble." [13]He laid His hands on her, and immediately she stood up straight and praised God.

[14]But the synagogue leader was annoyed with Jesus for healing on a Sabbath."There are six days to do your work," he told the people. "Come on those days and get healed, but not on the day of rest."

[15]"You hypocrites!" the Lord answered him. "Doesn't every one of you on a Sabbath untie his ox or donkey from the manger and take it out to water? [16]And this woman a daughter of Abraham, whom Satan has bound these eighteen years, shouldn't she on the day of rest be freed from what bound her?"

[17]As He said this, all His enemies had to be ashamed, but all the common people were happy over the wonderful things He was doing.

Mustard Seed and Yeast — *Matthew 13:31-33; Mark 4:30-32*

[18]"What is God's kingdom like," He asked, "and what will I compare it with? [19]It's like a mustard seed a man took and planted in his garden. It grew to be a tree, and the *birds in the air nested in its branches.*

[20]"With what should I compare God's kingdom?" He asked again. [21]"It's like yeast a woman mixed into a bushel of flour until it was all fermented."

The Narrow Door

[22]Then Jesus went and taught in one town and village after another on His way to Jerusalem.

[23]Someone asked Him, "Lord, are only a few people saved?"

19 Ps 104:12; Ezek 17:23; 31:6; Dan 4:12,21

[24]"Struggle to get in through the narrow door," He told them. "I tell you, many will try to get in and not succeed. [25]After the Owner of the house gets up and closes the door, you'll be standing outside and knocking at the door. 'Lord, open up for us!' you'll say. But He'll answer you, 'I don't know where you're from.' [26]Then you'll say, 'We ate and drank with You, and You taught in our streets.' [27]But He'll tell you, 'I don't know where you're from. *Get away from Me, all you who do wrong.*' [28]Then you will cry and grind your teeth when you see Abraham, Isaac, Jacob, and all the prophets in God's kingdom but you yourselves thrown out. [29]People will come *from the east and the west*, the north and the south, and will eat in God's kingdom. [30]You see, some who are last will be first, and some who are first will be last."

Jesus Warns Jerusalem

[31]Just then some Pharisees came and told Him, "Leave and get away from here; Herod wants to kill You."

[32]"Go," He answered them, "and tell that fox, 'Listen, today and tomorrow I will drive out demons and do healings, and on the third day I will finish.' [33]But I must be on My way today, tomorrow, and the next day, because a prophet just can't be killed outside Jerusalem.

[34]"Jerusalem, Jerusalem, you murder the prophets and stone those sent to you! How often I wanted to gather your children the way a hen gathers her chicks under her wings, but you didn't want to! [35]Look, now your *house is left* to you. I tell you, you will not see Me until you say, '*Blessed is He Who is coming in the Lord's name.*'"

Dinner Is Ready!

14 Once on a Sabbath Jesus went to the home of a leader of the Pharisees to eat a meal, and they were watching Him carefully.

[2]In front of Him was a man who had dropsy. [3]This led Jesus to ask the experts in the Law and the Pharisees, "Is it right to heal on a day of rest or not?" [4]But they didn't say anything.

So Jesus took hold of the man, made him well, and sent him away. [5]"If your son or your ox falls into a well," He asked them, "won't anyone of you pull him out immediately on a Sabbath?" [6]They couldn't answer this.

[7]He noticed how the guests were trying to get the places of honor, and so He used the scene to teach them: [8]"When anyone invites you to a wedding, don't take the place of honor. He may have invited someone more important than you. [9]And he who invited both of you will come and tell you, 'Give this man your place,' and then you'll feel ashamed when you have to take the lowest place. [10]No, when you're invited, go and take the lowest place, so that when your host comes *he'll tell you*, 'Friend, *move up higher*.' Then all your fellow guests will see how you're honored. [11]If you honor your-

---

27 Ps 6:8   *29 Is 49:12; 59:19; Mal 1:11* *35 Jer 12:7; 22:5-6; Ps 118:26*
10 Prov 25:7

self, you'll be humbled, but if you humble yourself, you'll be honored."

¹²Then He told the man who had invited Him, "When you give a dinner or a supper, don't invite your friends, your brothers, your relatives, or rich neighbors. Otherwise they'll invite you, too, and pay you back. ¹³No, when you give a banquet, invite the poor, crippled, lame, and blind. ¹⁴Then you'll be happy because they can't pay you back. You'll be paid back when the righteous rise from the dead."

¹⁵When one of those eating with Him heard this, he said to Jesus, "Blessed is he who will eat bread in God's kingdom."

¹⁶Jesus said to him:

"A man once gave a big dinner and invited many. ¹⁷When it was time for the dinner, he sent his slave to tell those who were invited, 'Come, it's ready now!'

¹⁸"Then they all alike began to excuse themselves. 'I bought a field,' the first told him, 'and I have to go out and see it. Please excuse me.' ¹⁹Another said, 'I bought five teams of oxen, and I'm on my way to try them out. Please excuse me.' ²⁰And another said, 'I just got married, and that's why I can't come.'

²¹"The slave went back and reported this to his master. Then the master of the house became angry. 'Go out quickly into the streets and alleys of the city,' he told his slave, 'and bring in here the poor, crippled, blind, and lame.'

²²"And the slave said, 'Master, it's done as you ordered, and there's still room.'

²³"Then the master told the slave, 'Go out to the roads and stone fences, and make them come in! I want my house to be full. ²⁴I tell you, none of those men who were invited will taste my dinner.'"

Leave Everything

²⁵Large crowds were going with Jesus. Turning to them, He said, ²⁶"If you come to Me and don't hate your father, mother, wife, children, brothers, and sisters and even your own life, you can't be My disciple. ²⁷Whoever doesn't carry his cross and follow Me can't be My disciple.

²⁸"If anyone of you wants to build a tower, won't you first sit down and figure out what it costs, to see if you have enough to finish it? ²⁹Otherwise, when you've laid a foundation but can't finish the building, all who watch you will make fun of you ³⁰and say, 'This fellow started to build but couldn't finish it.'

³¹"Or suppose a king is going into battle against another king. Won't he first sit down and consider if with ten thousand men he can oppose the other coming against him with twenty thousand? ³²If he can't, then, while the other is still far away, he sends ambassadors to ask for terms of peace. ³³Just so, anyone of you who doesn't give up everything he has can't be My disciple.

³⁴"Now, salt is good. But if the salt loses its taste, how will it be made salty again? ³⁵It is no good for the ground or for the manure pile. People

throw it away.

"If you have ears to hear, listen!"

Lost — a Sheep — *Matthew 18:12-14*

15 All the tax collectors and sinners were coming to Jesus to hear Him. [2]But the Pharisees and the Bible scholars grumbled and said, "This man welcomes sinners and eats with them."

[3]So He told them this story: [4]"If anyone of you has a hundred sheep and loses one of them, don't you leave the ninety-nine in the wilderness and go after the lost one until you find it? [5]When you find it, you lay it on your shoulders and are glad. [6]You go home and call your friends and neighbors together and say to them, 'Be happy with me. I found my lost sheep!' [7]So, I tell you, there will be more joy in heaven over one sinner who repents than over ninety-nine good people who don't need to repent."

Lost — a Coin

[8]"Or suppose a woman has ten coins and loses one. Won't she light a lamp and sweep the house and look for it carefully until she finds it? [9]When she finds it, she calls her women friends and neighbors together and says, 'Be happy with me. I found the coin I lost.' [10]So, I tell you, God's angels will be happy over one sinner who repents."

Lost — a Son

[11]Then Jesus said: "A man had two sons. [12]The younger of them said to his father, 'Father, give me my share of the property.' So he divided his property between them.

[13]"A few days later the younger son gathered his possessions, left home for a distant country, and there squandered his property by wild living. [14]When he had spent it all, a severe famine came over that country, and he started to be in need. [15]So he went and hired himself out to a citizen of that country, who sent him to his fields to feed hogs. [16]And he would have been glad to fill up on the pods the hogs were eating. But no one would give him anything.

[17]"Then he came to his senses and said, 'How many of my father's hired men have more food than they can eat, and here I'm starving to death! [18]I'll start out and go to my father and tell him, "Father, I've sinned against heaven and against you. [19]I don't deserve to be called your son anymore. Make me one of your hired men." '

[20]"So he started out and went to his father. While he was still far away, his father saw him and felt sorry for him. He ran and put his arms around him and kissed him. [21]Father,' the son told him, 'I've sinned against heaven and against you. I don't deserve to be called your son anymore.[a]

[22]" 'Hurry,' the father told his slaves, 'bring out a robe — the best —

a - 21   Some of the older manuscripts and early translations add "Make me one of your hired men".

and put it on him; put a ring on his finger and shoes on his feet. [23]And bring the fattened calf, kill it, and let's eat and celebrate. [24]This son of mine was dead and is alive. He was lost and is found.' And they started to celebrate.

[25]"Now, his older son was out in the field. As he was coming in, he got near the house — he heard music and dancing! [26]Calling one of the servants, he asked what was going on.

[27]" 'Your brother's home,' he was told, 'and your father has killed the fattened calf because he got him back safe and sound.'

[28]"Then he became angry and wouldn't go in. So his father came out and begged him. [29]But he answered his father. 'All these years I've been working like a slave for you and have never disobeyed your order, and you never gave me even a little goat to celebrate with my friends. [30]But as soon as this son of yours came back, who devoured your property with prostitutes, you killed the fattened calf for him.'

[31]" 'Son,' the father said to him, 'you're always with me, and everything I have is yours. [32]But we had to celebrate and be glad. This brother of yours was dead and is alive. He was lost and is found.' "

The Dishonest Manager

16 Then Jesus said to His disciples:

"There was a rich man whose manager was accused of squandering the man's property. [2]He called the manager. 'What's this I hear about you?' he asked him.'Give an account of your management, because you can't manage my property any longer.'

[3]" 'What will I do?' the manager said to himself. 'My master is taking my job away from me. I'm not strong enough to dig; I'm ashamed to beg. [4]I know what I'll do so that when I've lost my job people will welcome me into their homes.'

[5]So he called everyone who owed his master anything. 'How much do you owe my master?' he asked the first.

[6]" 'Eight hundred gallons of oil,' he answered.

" 'Take your note,' he said, 'sit down quickly and write "four hundred." '

[7]"Then he asked another, 'How much do you owe?' " 'A thousand bushels of wheat,' he answered.

" 'Take your note,' he told him, 'and write "eight hundred." '

[8]"And the master praised the dishonest manager for acting so shrewdly.

"In dealing with their own kind of people, the men of this world are shrewder than those who are in the light.

[9]"And I tell you, with the money that's often used in wrong ways win friends for yourselves so that when it's gone, you'll be welcomed into the everlasting homes. [10]If you can be trusted with very little, you can be trusted with much. And if you're dishonest with very little, you're dishonest with much. [11]If you couldn't be trusted with wicked money, who will trust you with that which is really good? [12]And if you couldn't be trusted with

someone else's things, who will give you your own?

[13]"No servant can be the slave of two masters. Either he will hate the one and love the other, or he'll be loyal to the one and despise the other. You can't serve God and money [mammon]."

[14]The money-loving Pharisees heard all this and turned up their noses at Him. [15]Then He said to them, "*You try to make people think you're good,* but God knows your hearts. What people consider great is detested by God.

[16]"The Law and the prophets were until John. Since then the good news of God's kingdom is told, and everyone tries to force his way into it. [17]It is easier for heaven and earth to disappear than for the Law to drop one dot of an i.

[18]"Anyone who divorces his wife and marries another is living in adultery. And the man who marries a woman divorced from her husband is living in adultery."

The Rich Man and Lazarus

[19]"There was a rich man who dressed in purple and fine linen and lived in luxury every day. [20]A beggar by the name of Lazarus was laid at his gate. He was covered with sores [21]and longed to satisfy his hunger with anything that might fall from the rich man's table. And the dogs would even come and lick his sores.

[22]"One day the beggar died, and the angels carried him to Abraham's side. The rich man also died and was buried. [23]Being tormented in hell, he looked up, and though far away, he saw Abraham, and Lazarus at his side. [24]'Father Abraham,' he called, 'have pity on me and send Lazarus to dip the tip of his finger in water and cool off my tongue, because I'm suffering in this fire.'

[25]"But Abraham said, 'Remember, son, you had your good things in your life, while Lazarus had his misery. Now he is comforted here, while you're suffering. [26]And besides all these things, there's a wide chasm fixed between us and you, so that those who might want to cross from here over to you can't do it, nor do any from there come over to us.'

[27]" 'Then I ask you, father,' he said, 'send him to my father's home — [28]I have five brothers — to warn them not to get into this place of torture.'

[29]" 'They have Moses and the prophets,' Abraham said. 'They should listen to them.'

[30]" 'No, Father Abraham,' he said, 'but if someone comes to them from the dead, they'll repent.'

[31]" 'If they don't listen to Moses and the prophets,' he answered him, 'they won't be convinced even if someone rose from the dead.' "

When Others Sin — *Matthew 18:6-10; Mark 9:42-48*

17 "Temptations to sin are sure to come," Jesus told His disciples, "but woe to him through whom they come. [2]It would be better for him to

---

15 *Prov 21:2*

have a big millstone hung around his neck and to be thrown into the sea than to lead one of these little ones into sin. ³Watch yourselves.

"If your brother sins, correct him; and if he repents, forgive him. ⁴Even if he sins against you seven times in one day and seven times comes back to you and says, 'I'm sorry,' forgive him."

Faith and Duty

⁵Then the apostles said to the Lord, "Give us more faith."

⁶"If you have a faith like a mustard seed," the Lord said, "you could say to this mulberry tree, 'Be pulled up by the roots, and be planted in the sea,' and it would obey you.

⁷"If your slave is plowing or watching sheep and comes in from the field, will any of you say to him, 'Come quickly and eat?' ⁸Or won't you rather tell him, 'Prepare something for me to eat, fasten your belt, and serve me while I eat and drink, and afterwards you eat and drink?' ⁹You won't thank the slave for doing what he was ordered to do, will you? ¹⁰So you, too, when you've done all you were ordered to do, say 'We are slaves who claim no credit. We've only done our duty.'"

The Ten Lepers — Only One Thanks God

¹¹On His way to Jerusalem, Jesus traveled along the border between Samaria and Galilee. ¹²As He came to a village, ten lepers came toward Him. They stopped at a distance ¹³and called out, "Jesus, Master, have pity on us!"

¹⁴When He saw them, He told them, "Go and *let the priests examine you*." And this is what happened: As they went, they were cleansed of their leprosy.

¹⁵One of them, seeing he was healed, turned back and loudly praised God. ¹⁶He bowed to the ground at His feet and thanked Him. And he was a Samaritan.

¹⁷"Weren't there ten cleansed?" Jesus asked. "But the nine — where are they? ¹⁸Weren't there any who came back to give God glory except this foreigner?"

¹⁹And He told him, "Get up and go! Your faith made you well."

Where Is God's Kingdom?

²⁰"When will God's kingdom come?" the Pharisees asked Jesus.

People can't see the coming of God's kingdom," He answered them. ²¹"They will not say, 'Look, here it is!' or, 'There it is!' You see, God's kingdom is within you."

Jesus Is Coming

²²"The time will come," He told the disciples, "when you will long to see

---

14 Lev 13:7,49

one of the days of the Son of Man and will not see it. [23]People will say, 'Look, there He is!' or, 'Here He is!' Don't go off and run after them.

[24]"The Son of Man will be like the lightning that flashes and lights up the sky from one end to the other. [25]But first He must suffer much and be rejected by this generation.

[26]"When the Son of Man comes, it will be like the time of Noah: [27]They were eating and drinking, and men and women were marrying until the day *Noah went into the ark,* and *the flood came* and destroyed them all.

[28]"Or like the time of Lot: They were eating and drinking, buying and selling, planting and building. [29]But the day Lot left Sodom, *fire and sulfur rained from heaven and destroyed* them all. [30]That is how it will be on the day the Son of Man is revealed.

[31]"On that day, if you're on the roof and have your goods in the house, don't go down to get them. If you're in the field, *don't turn back.* [32]Remember *Lot's wife!* [33]If you try to save your life, you'll lose it; but if you'll lose it, you'll save it.

[34]"I tell you, that night there will be two in one bed. One will be taken and the other left. [35]Two women will be grinding together. One will be taken and the other left."[b] [37]They asked Him, "Where, Lord?"

"Where there's a dead body," He told them, "there the vultures will gather."

God Hears

18 Jesus told them a parable to show that they should always pray and not get tired of it:

[2]"In a town there was a judge who didn't fear God or care what people thought. [3]In that town there was also a widow who kept coming to him and saying, 'Get me justice and defend me against my enemy!'

[4]"For a while he refused to do anything, but then he said to himself, 'Even though I don't fear God or care what people think, [5]yet because this widow keeps bothering me, I'll have to see that she gets justice, or she'll keep coming until she wears me out.' "

[6]The Lord added, "Listen to what the unjust judge says. [7]And won't God get justice for His chosen ones who cry to Him day and night? Is He slow to help them? [8]I tell you, He will quickly get justice for them. But when the Son of Man comes, will He find faith on earth?"

The Pharisee and the Tax Collector

[9]Jesus told this parable to some who were sure they were righteous and so looked down on everyone else:

[10]"Two men went up to the temple to pray. One was a Pharisee and the other a tax collector. [11]The Pharisee stood and prayed by himself: 'God, I

---

27 Gen 7:6-7   **29** Gen 19:24-25   **31-32** Gen 19:17,26

---

b - 35   Our three oldest manuscripts, including P[75] lack v. 36: "Two will be in a field — one will be taken and the other left." See Mt. 24:40.

thank You I'm not like the other people: robbers, wrongdoers, adulterers, or even like that tax collector. [12]I fast twice a week and give a tenth of all my income.'

[13]"But the tax collector, standing a distance away, wouldn't even look up to heaven but was beating his chest and saying, 'God, forgive me, a sinner!'

[14]"I tell you, this man, and not the other, went home justified [declared free from his sin]. *Everyone who honors himself will be humbled; but if you humble yourself, you will be honored.*"

Jesus Loves Children — *Matthew 19:13-15; Mark 10:13-16*

[15]Some people brought babies to Jesus to have Him touch them. When the disciples saw them, they sternly told them not to do it.

[16]But Jesus called the children to Him and said, "Let the little children come to Me, and don't keep them away. God's kingdom belongs to such as these. [17]I tell you the truth, if you don't receive God's kingdom like a little child, you will not get into it."

The Rich Young Leader — *Matthew 19:16-30; Mark 10:17-31*

[18]An official asked Him, "Good Teacher, what do I do to inherit everlasting life?"

[19]"Why do you call Me good?" Jesus asked him. "No one is good except One — God. [20]You know the commandments: *Do not commit adultery. Do not murder. Do not steal. Do not give false testimony. Honor your father and mother.*"

[21]"I've kept all these since I was a child," he said.

[22]When Jesus heard this, He told him, "You still lack one thing: Sell everything you have, distribute the money among the poor, and you'll have a treasure in heaven. Then come and follow Me."

[23]When he heard this, he became very sad, because he was very rich. [24]Jesus watched him and said, "How hard it is for rich people to get into God's kingdom! [25]It's easier for a camel to go through the eye of a needle than for a rich man to get into God's kingdom."

[26]Those who heard Him asked, "Who then can be saved?"

[27]"What men can't do God can do," He answered.

[28]Then Peter said, "Look, we've left our things and followed You."

[29]"I tell you the truth," He answered them, "everyone who gave up his home or wife, brothers, parents, or children for God's kingdom [30]will certainly get a hundred times as much in this life, and in the coming world everlasting life."

---

14 Prov 29:23   *20 Ex 20:12-16; Deut 5:16-20*

The Shadow of the Cross

[31]He took the twelve aside and said to them: "Look, we're going up to Jerusalem, and everything the Prophets wrote about the Son of Man will be done: [32]He'll be handed over to the non-Jews. They'll mock and insult Him, *spit on* Him, [33]whip Him and put Him to death. And on the third day He will rise."

[34]But they understood none of this. It was a mystery to them, and they didn't know what He meant.

A Blind Man — *Mark 10:46-52*

[35]As He came near Jericho, there was a blind man sitting by the road, begging.

[36]Hearing a crowd go by, he tried to find out what it was all about.

[37]"Jesus from Nazareth is passing by," they told him.

[38]He called, "Jesus, Son of David, have pity on me!" [39]Those who went ahead were urging him to be quiet. But he called all the louder, "Son of David, have pity on me!"

[40]Jesus stopped and ordered the man brought to Him. When he came near, Jesus asked him, [41]"What do you want Me to do for you?"

"Lord, I want to see," he said.

[42]"See!" Jesus told him. "Your faith has made you well." [43]Immediately he could see, and he followed Jesus, praising God. And all the people praised God for what they had seen.

Zacchaeus

19 He went into Jericho and was passing through it. [2]Here there was a man by the name of Zacchaeus. He was an overseer of tax collectors and was rich. [3]He was trying to see what kind of person Jesus was, but being a small man, he couldn't see Him on account of the crowd. [4]So he ran ahead and climbed up a fig-mulberry tree to see Him, because Jesus was coming that way.

[5]When Jesus came to the place, He looked up. "Zacchaeus, hurry down," He told him. "Today I must stay at your home."

[6]He hurried down and was happy to welcome Him. [7]But all who saw them started to grumble: "He went to be the guest of a sinful man."

[8]Zacchaeus stood there and said to the Lord, "Look, Lord, half of my property I'm giving to the poor, and if I've cheated anyone, I'm paying him back four times as much."

[9]"Today salvation has come to this home," Jesus told him, "since he too is a son of Abraham. [10]The Son of Man came to *seek* and save *the lost.*"

---

32 Is 50:6   10 Ezek 34:16

Use God's Gifts

[11]While they were listening to this, Jesus went on to tell them a parable, because He was near Jerusalem and they thought God's kingdom was to appear immediately.

[12]"A nobleman," He said, "went to a distant country to be made a king and then come back. [13]He called ten of his slaves, gave them ten minas,[c] and told them, 'Trade with these until I come.'

[14]"But the men of his own country hated him and sent representatives after him to say, 'We don't want this man to be our king.'

[15]"But he was made king. When he came back, he said, 'Call those slaves to whom I gave the money. I want to see what each one has made by his trading.'

[16]"The first came and said, 'Master, your mina has made ten more minas.'

[17]" 'Well done, my good slave!' he told him. 'You proved you could be trusted in a very small matter. Take charge of ten cities.'

[18]"The second came and said, 'Your mina, master, made five minas.'

[19]" 'You be in charge of five cities,' he told this one.

[20]"Then the one who was different came and said, 'Master, here is your mina.

I put it away in a cloth and kept it there. [21]I was afraid of you. You're a hard man. You take what you didn't deposit, and you harvest what you didn't sow.'

[22]" 'I'll judge you by what you say, you wicked slave!' he told him. 'You knew I'm a hard man, taking what I didn't deposit and harvesting what I didn't sow? [23]Why didn't you put my money in the bank? Then, when I came back, I could have collected it with interest.' [24]So he told his men, 'Take his mina away and give it to the man who has ten.'

[25]" 'Master,' they answered him, 'he has ten minas.'

[26]" 'I tell you, everyone who has something will be given more, and anyone who doesn't have what he should have, even what he has will be taken away. [27]But those enemies of mine who didn't want me to be their king — bring them here and kill them in front of me.' "

[28]After Jesus had said this, He continued on His way up to Jerusalem.

The King Is Coming — Matthew 21:1-11; Mark 11:1-11; John 12:12-19

[29]When He came near Bethphage and Bethany at the Mount of Olives, as it was called, He sent two of His disciples. [30]"Go into the village ahead of you," He said, "and as you go in, you'll find a colt tied up that no one ever sat on. Untie it and bring it to Me. [31]And if anyone asks you, 'Why are you untying it?' say, 'The Lord needs it.' "

[32]The men whom He sent went and found it as He had told them.

---

c - 13   A mina is equal to about 100 days' wages.

[33]While they were untying the colt, its owners asked them, "Why are you untying the colt?"

[34]"The Lord needs it," they said.

[35]So they brought it to Jesus, put their garments on the colt, and set Jesus on it. [36]As He was riding along, people spread their garments on the road. [37]And as He was coming near the place where the road goes down the Mount of Olives, the whole crowd of the disciples began to praise God joyfully and loudly for all the miracles they had seen. [38]They said,

"Blessed is the King *Who is coming in the Lord's name!*
In heaven peace, and glory in the highest heavens."

[39]Some of the Pharisees in the crowd said to Him, "Teacher, urge your disciples to be quiet."

[40]"I tell you," He answered them, "if these are quiet, the stones will cry out."

[41]When He came near and saw the city, He wept over it [42]and said, "If today you only knew — yes, you — the way to peace! But now it's hidden so that you can't see it. [43]The time will come for you when your enemies will put up ramparts against you and surround you and press against you from every side. [44]They'll *dash* you and *your children* to the *ground* and not leave one stone on another in you, because you didn't know the time your help came to you."

He Cleanses the Temple — *Matthew 21:12-17; Mark 11:15-19*

[45]Jesus went into the temple and proceeded to drive out the men who were selling things there. [46]He said to them, "It is written, '*My house should be a house of prayer*, but you have made it *a den of robbers*.'"

[47]Every day He was teaching in the temple. The ruling priests, the Bible scholars, and the leaders of the people were trying to kill Him, [48]but they couldn't find a way to do it, because the people were all eager to hear Him.

From Heaven — *Matthew 21:23-27; Mark 11:27-33*

20 One day, as He was teaching the people in the temple and telling them the good news, the ruling priests, Bible scholars, and elders came to Him. [2]"Tell us," they asked Him, "by what authority are you doing these things? Or who gives you the authority to do them?"

[3]Jesus answered them, "I will ask you a question. Tell Me, [4]John's baptism — was it from heaven or from men?"

[5]They argued among themselves, "If we say, 'From heaven,' he will ask, 'Why didn't you believe him?' [6]But if we say, 'From men,' all the people will stone us. They're convinced John was a prophet." [7]So they answered that they didn't know where it was from.

[8]Then Jesus told them, "Neither will I tell you by what authority I'm doing these things."

38 Ps 118:26   44 Ps 137:9   46 Is 56:7; Jer 7:11

God's Vineyard — *Matthew 21:33-46; Mark 12:1-12*

[9]Then He told the people this parable:
"A man *planted a vineyard*, rented it out to workers, and left to be gone a long time.

[10]"At the right time he sent a servant[d] to the workers to get from them a share of the products of the vineyard. But the workers beat him and sent him back empty-handed. [11]He sent another servant; they beat him, too, treated him shamefully, and sent him back empty-handed. [12]Then he sent a third; they wounded him and threw him out.

[13]"Then the owner of the vineyard said, 'What should I do? I'll send my son whom I love. Maybe they'll respect him.'

[14]"When the workers saw him, they talked it over among themselves, saying, 'This is the heir. Let's kill him and get the inheritance.' [15]So they threw him out of the vineyard and killed him.

"Now, what will the owner of the vineyard do to them? [16]He will come and kill those workers and give the vineyard to others."

"That must never happen!" said those who heard Him.

[17]Jesus looked at them and asked, "What does this mean in your Bible: *The Stone the builders rejected has become the Cornerstone*? [18]Everyone who falls on that Stone will be dashed in pieces, and if that Stone falls on anyone, it will scatter him like dust."

[19]The Bible scholars and the ruling priests wanted to grab Him then and there, because they knew He had aimed this story at them, but they were afraid of the people.

Taxes — *Matthew 22:15-22; Mark 12:13-17*

[20]They watched for an opportunity and sent spies to act holy in order to catch Him in what He would say. They wanted to hand Him over to the governor's control and authority. [21]They had a question for Him. "Teacher," they said, "we know You're right in what You say and teach, and You don't favor any special persons but really teach God's way. [22]Is it right for us to pay a tax to Caesar or not?"

[23]Seeing through their trickery, He told them, [24]"Show Me a denarius. Whose head is on it and whose inscription?"

"Caesar's," they answered.

[25]"Well, then, give to Caesar what is Caesar's," He told them, "and to God what is God's."

[26]So they couldn't catch Him before the people in anything He said. His answer surprised them so much they didn't say anything.

The Dead Live — *Matthew 22:23-33; Mark 12:18-27*

[27]Some of the Sadducees, who say there is no resurrection, came to

---

9 Is 5:2   17 Ps 118:22

d - 10   Literally: "slave," which in Greek reflects total subjection (also in v. 11).

Him with this question: [28]"Teacher, Moses wrote for us, '*If any* married *man dies and has no children, his brother should marry the widow and have children for his brother.*' [29]Now, there were seven brothers. The first married and died childless. [30]Then the second brother married the widow, [31]and so did the third. In the same way all seven died and left no children. [32]Finally the woman died, too. [33]Now, when they rise from the dead, whose wife will she be? You know, the seven had her as wife."

[34]"In this world men and women marry," Jesus told them; [35]"but those who are considered worthy to rise from the dead and live in the other world don't marry. [36]Nor can they die anymore, because they're like the angels. They're God's children and share in the resurrection.

[37]"That the dead rise, Moses showed in the story about the bush when he called the Lord *the God of Abraham, the God of Isaac, and the God of Jacob.* [38]He's not the God of the dead but of the living. All who are with Him are alive."

[39]"Teacher," some Bible scholars told Him, "You have told the truth." [40]No one dared to ask Him another question.

David's Son — *Matthew 22:41-46; Mark 12:35-37a*

[41]"How can people say the Christ is David's son?" He asked them. [42]"David himself says in the book of Psalms: *The Lord said to my Lord, 'Sit at My right* [43]*until I make Your enemies Your footstool.*' [44]So David calls Him 'Lord.' Then how can He be his son?"

Beware! — *Matthew 23:1-12; Mark 12:37b-40*

[45]While all the people were listening, He said to the disciples: [46]Beware of the Bible scholars! They like to go around in long robes and love to be greeted in the marketplaces, to sit in the front seats in the synagogues, and to have the places of honor at dinners. [47]They swallow the widows' houses and then, to cover up, make long prayers. They'll be punished all the more."

A Cent — *Mark 12:41-44*

21 Looking up, He saw rich people dropping their gifts into the contribution boxes. [2]And He saw a poor widow drop in two small coins. [3]He said, "I tell you, this poor widow certainly put in more than all the others. [4]All the others took some of what they had left over and dropped it in among the gifts. But she put in what she needed for herself, all she had to live on."

Sorrow Ahead! — *Matthew 24:1-14; Mark 13:1-13*

[5]Some were saying about the temple, "It is beautifully constructed with fine stones and gifts."

---

28 *Gen 38:8; Deut 25:5-6*   37 *Ex 3:6*   42-43 *Ps 110:1*

[6]"About these things that you see," He said, "the time will come when not one stone will be left on another here but will be torn down."

[7]"Teacher," they asked Him, "when will this be, and how can we tell when this will happen?"

[8]"Be careful not to let anyone deceive you," Jesus said. "Many will come using My name and saying, 'I am He!' and, 'The time has come.' Don't follow them.

[9]"When you hear of wars and revolutions, don't get alarmed. These things *must happen* first, but the end won't come right away."

[10]Then He told them, "*Nation will fight against nation*, and *kingdom against kingdom*. [11]There will be great earthquakes and famines and plagues in different places, terrible sights and great signs coming from heaven.

[12]"Before all these things happen, men will arrest you and persecute you, hand you over to church councils, and put you in prisons. They'll bring you before kings and governors on account of My name. [13]It will be your chance to tell them the truth. [14]So make up your minds not to worry beforehand how you'll defend yourselves. [15]I'll give you such speech and wisdom none of your enemies will be able to oppose it or talk against it.

[16]"Even parents, brothers, relatives, and friends will betray you and kill some of you, [17]and everyone will hate you because of My name. [18]But not a hair on your head will be lost. [19]Endure patiently, and you'll win your lives."

Jerusalem Will Be Destroyed — *Matthew 24:15-22; Mark 13:14-20*

[20]"When you see Jerusalem surrounded by an army, then know the time has come for her to be destroyed. [21]Then if you're in Judea, flee to the hills. If you're in Jerusalem, leave it. If you're in the country, don't go into the city. [22]Those will be *days of vengeance* when everything must happen as it is written.

[23]"Woe to the women who in those days are expecting babies or nursing them. There will be great distress in this country, and God will punish this nation. [24]The sword will cut them down, they'll be taken away as prisoners among all nations, and *the Gentiles will trample on Jerusalem* until the time for the Gentiles has passed."

Jesus Is Coming — *Matthew 24:23-35; Mark 13:21-31*

[25]"There will be signs in *the sun, the moon, and the stars*, and on the earth *nations* will be in distress, not knowing which way to turn from *the roaring and tossing of the sea*. [26]People will faint as they fearfully wait for what will happen to the world. *The powers of the heavens* will be shaken.

[27]"Then they will see *the Son of Man coming in a cloud* with power and great glory.

---

9 *Dan 2:28-29,45*   **10** *2 Chr 15:6; Is 19:2;*   **22** *Deut 32:35; Hos 9:7*
24 *Is 63:18; Zech 12:3*   **25** *Is 13:10; Ps 65:7; Ezek 32:7-8*   **26** *Is 34:4*

[28]"When these things begin to happen, stand ready and look forward cheerfully because you will soon be set free."

[29]Then He pictured it this way: "Look at a fig tree, or any of the trees. [30]As soon as leaves grow on it, you see and know without being told that summer is near. [31]So also when you see those things happen, you know God's kingdom is near.

[32]"I tell you the truth: these people will not pass away until everything happens. [33]Heaven and earth will pass away, but My words will not pass away.

Watch and Pray! — *Compare Matthew 24:36-51; Mark 13:32-37*

[34]"Be careful never to get your hearts burdened with drunkenness and its nausea and with worries about this life, or that day will take you by surprise like *a trap*. [35]It will surprise all people wherever they *live on the earth*. [36]But always watch and pray to be considered worthy to escape all these things that are going to happen and to stand before the Son of Man."

[37]During the day He would teach in the temple, but at night He would go out to the Mount of Olives, as it was called, and stay there for the night. [38]All the people used to get up early to go to Him in the temple and hear Him.

The Plot — *Matthew 26:1-5; Mark 14:1-2; John 11:45-57*

22 The Festival of Bread Without Yeast, called the Passover, was near. [2]Then the ruling priests and the Bible scholars were looking for a way to kill Him. They were afraid of the people.

[3]Satan entered Judas, called Iscariot, one of the twelve. [4]He went to the ruling priests and the captains of the temple and discussed with them how he might betray Jesus to them. [5]They were delighted and agreed to give him some money. [6]He promised to do it and so was looking for a chance to betray Him when He was away from the crowd.

The Passover — *Matthew 26:17-20; Mark 14:12-17*

[7]Then came the day of the Festival of Bread Without Yeast, when the Passover lamb had to be killed. [8]Jesus sent Peter and John, saying, "Go, get the Passover ready for us to eat."

[9]"Where do You want us to get it ready?" they asked Him.

[10]"Go into the city," He told them, "and you'll meet a man carrying a jar of water. [11]Follow him into the house he enters, and tell the owner of the house: 'The Teacher asks you, "Where is the room in which I can eat the Passover with My disciples?" ' [12]He will show you a large furnished room upstairs. Get things ready there."

[13]They went and found it as He had told them, and they got the Passover ready.

---

27 Dan 7:13   34-35 Is 24:17

¹⁴When the hour had come, He and the apostles reclined for the meal. ¹⁵"I have very much longed to eat this Passover with you before I suffer," He said to them. ¹⁶"I tell you, I will not eat it again until it is fulfilled in God's kingdom." ¹⁷Then He was handed a cup, and He gave thanks. "Take this," He said, "and share it."

The Lord's Supper — *Matthew 26:26-30; Mark 14:22-26;*
I Cor. 11:23-25

¹⁸"I tell you, from now on I will not drink of the fruit of the vine until God's kingdom comes."

¹⁹Jesus took bread, gave thanks, broke it, and gave it to them, saying, "This is My body, which is given for you. Do this to remember Me."

²⁰He did the same with the cup when the supper was over, saying, "This cup is *the* new *testament* in My *blood*, poured out for you."

"Is it I?" — *Matthew 26:21-25; Mark 14:18-21; John 13:21-30*

²¹"Look, the hand of him who is betraying Me is with Me on the table. ²²The Son of Man is going as it is decreed, but woe to that man who is betraying Him."

²³They started to discuss with one another which of them was going to do this.

"Who Is the Greatest?"

²⁴The disciples also started to quarrel among themselves as to which of them was considered the greatest.

²⁵"The kings of the nations lord it over them," He told them, "and their rulers call themselves benefactors. ²⁶With you it's different. The greatest among you should become like the youngest, and one who leads should be like one who serves. ²⁷Who is greater, the one who reclines to eat or the one who serves? Isn't it the one who reclines to eat? But I am among you as one who serves.

²⁸"You have stood by Me in the troubles that have tested Me. ²⁹As My Father has appointed Me to be King, so I appoint you ³⁰to eat and drink at My table in My kingdom and to sit on thrones and rule the twelve tribes of Israel."

You Will Be Tested — *Matthew 26:31-35; Mark 14:27-31;*
John 13:36-38

³¹"Simon, Simon," said the Lord, "you know Satan has begged to have all of you to sift you like wheat. ³²But I prayed for you, Simon, that your faith will not fail. And when you come back, strengthen your fellow disciples."

20 Ex 24:8; Jer 31:31-32; Zech 9:11

[33]"Lord," he told Him, "I'm ready to go to prison and to die with You."

[34]"I tell you, Peter," He said, "the rooster will not crow tonight until you deny three times that you know Me."

[35]Then He asked them, "When I sent you out without purse, bag, or shoes, you didn't lack anything, did you?"

"Not a thing!" they answered.

[36]"But now," He told them, "if you have a purse, take it, and also a bag. And if you don't have a sword, sell your garment and buy one. [37]It is written: *'He will be counted among criminals,'* and I tell you, that must happen to Me. Whatever is written about Me must happen!"

[38]"Lord, look, here are two swords!" they said.

"It is enough," He told them.

Gethsemane — *Matthew 26:36-46; Mark 14:32-42*

[39]Jesus went out and as usual came to the Mount of Olives. The disciples went with Him. [40]When He came to the place, He told them, "Pray that you may not be tempted."

[41]He withdrew from them about as far as you'd throw a stone, knelt, and prayed, [42]"Father, if it is Your will, take this cup away from Me; but let it not be as I want it but as You want it."

[43]An angel from heaven appeared to Him and gave Him strength. [44]And as He began to struggle inwardly, He prayed more earnestly, and His sweat became like thick drops of blood falling on the ground.[e]

[45]After praying, He got up, went to the disciples, and found them sleeping because they were overcome with sadness. [46]"Why are you sleeping?" He asked them. "Get up and pray that you may not be tempted."

The Arrest — *Matthew 26:47-56; Mark 14:43-52; John 18:1-14*

[47]While He was still talking, the crowd came. The one called Judas, one of the twelve, was leading them, and he came close to Jesus to kiss Him.

[48]"Judas," Jesus asked him, "are you betraying the Son of Man with a kiss?"

[49]The men around Jesus, seeing what was going to happen, asked, "Lord, should we strike with our swords?" [50]And one of them struck the high priest's slave and cut off his right ear.

[51]But Jesus said, "Let them do it. No more of this!" And, touching the ear, He healed him.

[52]Then Jesus said to the ruling priests, captains of the temple, and elders who had come for Him, "You came out for Me with swords and clubs as if I were a robber! [53]Day after day I was with you in the temple, and you laid no hands on Me. But this is your time when darkness rules."

---

37 Is 53:9,12

---

e - 44   p[75] and other old manuscripts lack vv. 43-44

⁵⁴They arrested Him, led Him away, and took Him to the high priest's palace.

Peter Denies Jesus — *Matthew 26:69-75; Mark 14:66-72; John 18:15-18, 25-27*

Peter followed at a distance.
⁵⁵The men had lit a fire in the middle of the courtyard, and as they sat together, Peter sat among them. ⁵⁶A maid saw him sitting in the light of the fire, and looking straight at him, she said, "He, too, was with him."
⁵⁷But he denied and said, "I don't know Him, woman."
⁵⁸A little later someone else looked at him and said, "You're one of them." "Man, I'm not!" Peter said.
⁵⁹About an hour later another insisted: "Certainly he was with him. Why, he's a Galilean!"
⁶⁰"Man, I don't know what you're talking about," Peter said.
Just then, while he was still speaking, a rooster crowed. ⁶¹Then the Lord turned and looked at Peter, and Peter remembered the Lord telling him, "Before the rooster crows today, you will deny Me three times." ⁶²So he went outside and cried bitterly.

The Jewish Council Condemns Jesus

⁶³The men who were holding Him were *making fun of* Him as they struck Him. ⁶⁴They covered His face and kept asking Him: "Prophesy! Who hit you?" ⁶⁵And so they went on *insulting* Him in many other ways.
⁶⁶In the morning all the elders of the people, ruling priests, and Bible scholars had a meeting. They brought Jesus before their court and asked, ⁶⁷"Are you the Christ? Tell us."
"If I tell you, you won't believe Me," He said to them. ⁶⁸"And if I ask you a question, you won't answer. ⁶⁹But from now on *the Son of Man* will be *sitting at the right of God's* power."
⁷⁰"Are you, then, the Son of God?" all of them asked. He answered them, "As you say: I am He."
⁷¹"Why do we need any more testimony?" they asked. "We've heard him say it ourselves."

23 Then the whole crowd of them got up and took Him to Pilate.

Before Pilate — *Matthew 27:11-14; Mark 15:1-5; John 18:28-38*

²Then they started to accuse Him: "We found that he makes our people disloyal, keeps them from paying taxes to the emperor, and says he is Christ, a king."
³Pilate asked Him, "Are you the King of the Jews?"
"Yes," He answered him.

---

63 Ps 22:7   65 Ps 22:7; Is 50:6   69 Dan 7:13; Ps 110:1

[4]Pilate told the ruling priests and the crowd, "I don't find this man guilty of anything."

Before Herod

[5]The priests and the crowd kept urging him: "He stirs up the people by teaching all over the country of the Jews, beginning in Galilee and coming here."

[6]When Pilate heard that, he asked, "Is the man from Galilee?" [7]And when he found out Jesus came from the country governed by Herod, he sent Him to Herod, who also was in Jerusalem at that time.

[8]Herod was very glad to see Jesus. For a long time he wanted to see Him because he was hearing about Him, and he was expecting to see Jesus do some miracle. [9]He asked Him a lot of questions, but Jesus didn't answer him. [10]The ruling priests and the Bible scholars were standing there and accusing Him vehemently.

[11]So Herod and his soldiers treated Him with contempt and made fun of Him. They put a splendid garment on Him and then sent Him back to Pilate. [12]On that day Herod and Pilate became friends. Before this they had been enemies.

[13]Then Pilate called the ruling priests, the other leaders, and the people together. [14]"You brought me this man as one who turns the people against the government," he told them. "And now look, I've examined this man before you and found him innocent of the things you accuse him of. [15]And Herod did, too, because he sent him back to us. You see, he hasn't done anything to deserve death. [16]So I'm going to teach him a lesson and let him go."[f]

Barabbas — *Matthew 27:15-26; Mark 15:6-15; John 18:39-40*

[18]Then the whole crowd yelled: "Away with him. Free Barabbas for us." [19]He had been put in prison for a revolt that had taken place in the city and for murder.

[20]But Pilate wanted to let Jesus go, so he called to them again.

[21]But they kept yelling: "Crucify, crucify him!"

[22]And Pilate spoke to them a third time: "Why, what wrong has he done? I haven't found anything in him that deserves death. So I will have him whipped and let him go."

[23]But they kept pressing him with loud shouts, demanding that He be crucified, and their shouts were overpowering Pilate. [24]Then Pilate decided what they demanded should be done: [25]he let them have Barabbas, who had been put in prison for revolt and murder, but whom they were asking for, and he handed Jesus over to them to do what they wanted.

---

f - 16   Our oldest papyrus, P[75], and our oldest parchment, Codex Vaticanus, lack v. 17 "At every festival he had to set someone free for them." See Mt. 27:15; Mk 15:6; Jn 18:39.

On the Way

²⁶As they led Jesus away, they took hold of Simon, a man from Cyrene, who was coming in from the country, and they laid the cross on him, to carry it behind Jesus.

²⁷A large crowd of the people followed Him. The women in the crowd were beating their chests and weeping over Him. ²⁸Turning to them, Jesus said, "Daughters of Jerusalem, don't cry over Me, but cry over yourselves and your children, ²⁹because the time is coming when people will say:

> 'Happy are —
> the women who couldn't have children,
> the wombs that didn't bear,
> and the breasts that didn't nurse.'
> ³⁰ *Then people will say —*
> *to the mountains: 'Fall on us!'*
> *and to the hills: 'Cover us!'*

³¹If this is done to the *green tree*, what will be done to a *dry one?*"

³²Two others, who were *criminals*, were also taken away to be put to death *with Him*.

"They Crucified Him" — *Matthew 27:31-44; Mark 15:20-32; John 19:16b-24*

³³When they came to the place called Skull, they crucified Him there with the criminals, one at His right and the other at His left.

³⁴Then Jesus said, "*Father, forgive them*; they don't know what they are doing."ᵍ

They divided His clothes among them by throwing lots for them.

³⁵The people stood there *watching*. The rulers were *sneering*, "He saved others. Let him save himself if he's the Christ, God's chosen One." ³⁶The soldiers also made fun of Him by going up to Him and *offering Him sour wine*. ³⁷"If you're the King of the Jews," they said, "save yourself."

³⁸There was a notice placed above Him: THIS IS THE KING OF THE JEWS.

A Robber Turns to Jesus

³⁹One of the crucified criminals was mocking Him, "Aren't you the Christ? Save yourself and us!"

⁴⁰But the other warned him, "Aren't you afraid of God?" he asked him. "You're condemned just as He is. ⁴¹Our punishment is just. We're getting what we deserve for what we've done. But this One has done nothing wrong."

⁴²Then he said, "Jesus, remember me when You come into Your kingdom."

---

30 Hos 10:8   **31** Ezek 20:47 32 Is 53:9   **34** Is 53:12; Ps 22:18   **35** Ps 22:7
36 Ps 69:21

---

g - 34   P75 and some other old manuscripts lack the first word from the cross.

⁴³"I tell you the truth," Jesus said to him, "today you will be with Me in Paradise."

Jesus Dies — *Matthew 27:45-56; Mark 15:33-41; John 19:28-30*

⁴⁴It was about twelve o'clock when darkness came over the whole country, because the sun stopped shining, and the darkness lasted until three in the afternoon. ⁴⁵The curtain in the temple was torn in two.

⁴⁶Then Jesus called out with a loud voice, "Father, *into Your hands I entrust My spirit.*" After He said this, He died.

⁴⁷When the captain saw what had happened, he praised God and said, "This Man certainly was righteous." ⁴⁸When all the people who had come there to see this saw what happened, they beat their chests and turned back. ⁴⁹All *His friends were standing at a distance*, also the women who had followed Him from Galilee and now were watching these things.

Jesus Is Buried — *Matthew 27:57-61; Mark 15:42-47; John 19:38-42*

⁵⁰There was a man by the name of Joseph, a member of the Jewish council, a good and righteous man ⁵¹who had not voted for their plan and action. He was from Arimathea, a Jewish town, and was looking forward to God's kingdom.

⁵²He went to Pilate and asked for Jesus' body. ⁵³He took it down, wrapped it in some linen, and laid it in a grave cut in the rock, in which no one had yet been laid. ⁵⁴It was the day of preparation, and the day of rest was just starting.

⁵⁵The women who had come with Him from Galilee, following close behind, saw the grave and how His body was laid. ⁵⁶Then they went back and prepared spices and perfumes. But *on Saturday they rested according to the commandment.*

Jesus Rises — *Matthew 28:1-10; Mark 16:1-8; John 20:1-10*

24 Very early on Sunday morning the women came to the grave bringing the spices they had prepared. ²They found the stone rolled back from the grave, ³but when they went in, they didn't find the body of the Lord Jesus. ⁴While they were troubled about this, suddenly two men stood beside them in clothes that flashed like lightning. ⁵The women were terrified, and they bowed down to the ground.

"Why do you look among the dead for Him Who is alive?" they asked the women. ⁶"He is not here; He has risen! Remember what He told you while He was still in Galilee, ⁷'The Son of Man must be handed over to sinful men, be crucified, and rise on the third day.'"

⁸They remembered what He said. ⁹They left the grave, went back, and reported all this to the eleven and all the others. ¹⁰It was Mary from Magdala, Johanna, Mary the mother of James, and the other women with them

46 Ps 31:5   *49 Ps 38:11*   *56 Ex 20:10; Deut 5:14*

that told the apostles about it.

¹¹The apostles thought it was nonsense and wouldn't believe them.

¹²But Peter started out and ran to the grave. He bent down and saw only the linen cloths. Then he went home, amazed at what had happened.

On the Way to Emmaus

¹³On the same day, two of them were going to a village called Emmaus, about seven miles from Jerusalem. ¹⁴They were talking about everything that had happened.

¹⁵While they were talking and discussing, Jesus Himself joined them and walked with them. ¹⁶They saw Him but were kept from knowing Who He was.

¹⁷"What are you discussing as you're walking along?" He asked them.

They stood still and looked gloomy. ¹⁸"Are you the only stranger living in Jerusalem," the one by the name of Cleopas asked Him, "who doesn't know what happened there these days?"

¹⁹"What do you mean?" He asked.

"All about Jesus from Nazareth," they told Him, "Who was a prophet, mighty in what He did and said before God and all the people, ²⁰and how our high priests and rulers handed Him over to be condemned to death and crucified Him. ²¹But we were hoping He would be the One to free Israel. What is more, this is now the third day since it happened. ²²And then some of our women startled us. They went to the grave early this morning ²³and didn't find His body. They came and told us they had even seen a vision of angels who said He is alive. ²⁴Some of our men went to the grave and found it as the women had said; and they didn't see Him."

²⁵"How foolish you are," He told them, "and how slow to believe everything the prophets said! ²⁶Didn't the Christ have to suffer this and so go to His glory?" ²⁷Then He explained to them, starting with Moses and all the prophets, what they said about Him in all their writings.

²⁸And so they came near the village where they were going, and He acted as if He were going farther. ²⁹"Stay with us," they urged Him. "It's getting late, and the day is almost gone." So He went in to stay with them.

³⁰While He was at the table with them, He took the bread, blessed and broke it, and gave it to them. ³¹Then their eyes were opened, and they knew Who He was. But He vanished from them.

³²"Didn't our hearts glow," they said to each other, "as He was talking to us on the way and explaining the Bible to us?"

³³That same hour they started out, went back to Jerusalem, and found the eleven and those who were with them all together. ³⁴These said, "The Lord really did rise, and Simon saw Him."

³⁵Then the two men told what had happened on the way and how they had recognized Him while He was breaking the bread.

Behind Locked Doors — *John 20:19-23*

[36]While they were talking about what had happened, Jesus stood among them. "Peace to you!" He said to them. [37]They were startled and terrified and thought they were seeing a ghost.

[38]"Why are you troubled?" He asked them. "And why do doubts come into your minds? [39]Look at My hands and My feet: it is I Myself. Touch Me and see. A ghost doesn't have flesh and bones as you see I have." [40]As He said this, He showed them His hands and His feet.

[41]They were overcome with joy and amazement because they thought it was too good to be true. "Do you have anything here to eat?" He asked them. [42]They gave Him a piece of broiled fish. [43]He took it and ate it while they watched Him.

[44]"While I was still with you," He said to them, "I told you that everything written about Me in the Law of Moses, the Prophets, and the Psalms must come true." [45]Then He opened their minds to understand the Bible. [46]"This," He told them, "is what is written: The Christ will suffer and will rise from the dead on the third day; [47]and that repentance and the forgiveness of sins will be preached in His name to all people, beginning at Jerusalem. [48]You will testify of these things."

Jesus Goes Up to Heaven

[49] "I am *sending you Him Whom My Father promised.* Wait here in the city until you are armed with power from above."

[50]He took them out to a place where Bethany lay ahead of them. Then He raised His hands and blessed them. [51]While He was blessing them, He parted from them and was taken up to heaven.

[52]They knelt and worshiped Jesus. And then they went back to Jerusalem filled with joy. [53]And they were always in the temple praising God.

THE GOOD NEWS AS IT WAS TOLD BY
JOHN

1 *IN THE BEGINNING WAS THE WORD, and the Word was with God, and the Word was God.* ²*He was in the beginning with God.*

³Everything was made by Him, and not one thing that was made was made without Him.

⁴In Him was life, and the Life was the Light of men. ⁵The Light is shining in the dark, and the darkness has not put it out.

⁶A man came — God sent him — his name was John. ⁷He came to tell the truth about the Light so that through him everyone might believe. ⁸He was not the Light but came to tell the truth about the Light.

⁹The true Light that gives light to everyone was coming into the world. ¹⁰He was in the world, and He made the world, and the world didn't know Him. ¹¹He came to His own, and His own people didn't welcome Him. ¹²But to all who welcomed Him, who believe in His name, He gave the right to become God's children. ¹³They have been born, not of the blood of parents, nor of a sexual desire, nor of a man's desire, but of God.

¹⁴And the Word became flesh and lived among us for a time and we saw His glory, the glory of the only-begotten of the Father, full of grace and truth.

¹⁵John told the truth about Him when he called: "This is the One of Whom I said, He Who is coming after me is ahead of me because He was before me."

¹⁶All of us have taken from all that is in Him — gift after gift of His love. ¹⁷*The Law was given through Moses*, but Jesus Christ brought grace and truth. ¹⁸No one has ever seen God. The one-and-only Son Who is God, Who is close to the Father's heart, has made Him known.

John Prepares the Way — *Matthew 3:1-12; Mark 1:1-8; Luke 3:1-18*

¹⁹When the Jews in Jerusalem sent priests and Levites to John to ask him, "Who are you?" this was John's testimony. ²⁰He confessed and didn't deny. He confessed: "I'm not the Christ."

²¹ "Who are you, then?" they asked him. "Are you Elijah?" "I am not," he said.

"Are you the Prophet?" "No," he answered.

²² Then they asked him, "Who are you? We want to bring an answer to those who sent us. What do you say about yourself?"

1-2 Prov 8:22-23,30   *17 Deut 33:4*

[23]He said: "I am *a voice calling in the wilderness: 'Make straight the way for the Lord,'* as the prophet Isaiah said."

[24]Some who had been sent belonged to the Pharisees. [25]They asked him, "Why, then, do you baptize if you're not the Christ or Elijah or the Prophet?"

[26]"I baptize with water," John answered them. "There is standing among you Someone you don't know, [27]the One Who is coming after me. I'm not good enough to untie His sandal strap."

[28]This happened at Bethany on the other side of the Jordan, where John was baptizing.

The Lamb of God — *Compare Matthew 3:13-17; Mark 1:9-11; Luke 3:21-22*

[29]The next day John saw Jesus coming toward him. And he said, "Look at the Lamb of God Who takes away the sin of the world. [30]He is the One I meant when I said, 'A Man is coming after me but is ahead of me, because He was before me.'

[31]Even I didn't know Who He was, but I came and baptized with water to show Him to Israel." [32]John testified: "I saw the Spirit come down from heaven as a dove and stay on Him. [33]I didn't know Who He was, but He Who sent me to baptize with water told me, 'When you see the Spirit come down on Someone and stay on Him, He is the One Who baptizes with the Holy Spirit.' [34]I saw it and testified, 'This is the Son of God.' "

The First Disciples — *Matthew 4:18-22; Mark 1:14-20; Luke 5:1-11*

[35]The next day, while John was again standing with two of his disciples, [36]he saw Jesus passing by. "Look at the Lamb of God!" he said. [37]When the two disciples heard him say this, they followed Jesus.

[38]Jesus turned around and saw them following. "What are you looking for?" He asked them.

"Rabbi" (which means Teacher), "where are You staying?" they asked Him.

[39]"Come and you'll see," He told them. So they came and saw where He was staying, and they stayed with Him that day. It was about ten in the morning.

[40]One of the two who heard John and then followed Jesus was Andrew, Simon Peter's brother. [41]He first found his own brother Simon and told him, "We have found the Messiah." (The Greek word for Him is Christ.) [42]He brought him to Jesus.

Looking at him, Jesus said, "You are Simon, John's son. Your name will be Cephas" (which means Peter[a]).

[43]The next day Jesus wanted to go to Galilee. He found Philip. "Follow Me!" Jesus told him. [44]Philip was from Bethsaida, the home town of Andrew and Peter.

---

23 Is 40:3

a - 42   "Cephas" in Aramaic and "Peter" in Greek both mean "rock."

⁴⁵Philip found Nathanael and told him, "The One Moses wrote about in the Law, and the prophets, too — we've found Him, Jesus, Joseph's son from Nazareth."

⁴⁶"Nazareth — can anything good come from there?" Nathanael asked him.

"Come and see!" Philip told him.

⁴⁷Jesus saw Nathanael coming toward Him. "Here's a true Israelite in whom there is no deceit," He said of him.

⁴⁸"Where did You get to know me?" Nathanael asked Him.

"Before Philip called you," Jesus answered him, "when you were under the fig tree, I saw you."

⁴⁹"Master," Nathanael answered Him, "You are God's Son! You are Israel's King!"

⁵⁰"You believe because I told you I saw you under the fig tree," Jesus answered him. ⁵¹"You will see greater things than that." And He said to him, "I tell you people the truth, You will see *heaven* opened *and God's angels going up and coming down* on the Son of Man."

Jesus Changes Water to Wine

2 Two days later there was a wedding in Cana in Galilee, and Jesus' mother was there. ²Jesus and His disciples had also been invited to the wedding.

³When the people were out of wine, Jesus' mother said to Him, "They don't have any wine."

⁴ "Will you leave that to Me, woman?" Jesus asked her. "It isn't the right time yet."

⁵His mother told the waiters, *"Do anything He tells you."*

⁶Six stone water jars were standing there for the religious washings of the Jews. Each jar held 18 to 27 gallons.

⁷"Fill the jars with water," Jesus told them. And they filled them to the top. ⁸"Now take some of it," He told them, "and take it to the manager of the dinner." So they took it to him.

⁹When the manager tasted the water that had been changed to wine, he didn't know where it was from; only the waiters who had dipped the water knew. So the manager called the groom. ¹⁰"Everyone serves his good wine first," he told him, "and when people have drunk much, then the poorer wine. You've kept the good wine until now."

¹¹Jesus did this, the first of His miracles, in Cana in Galilee. He showed His glory, and His disciples believed in Him.

¹²After this He, His mother, His brothers, and His disciples went down to Capernaum and stayed there a few days.

---

51 Gen 28:12   5 Gen 41:55

Jesus Cleans the Temple

[13]The Jewish Passover was near, so Jesus went up to Jerusalem.

[14]In the temple He found men selling cattle, sheep, and pigeons, and the money changers were sitting there. [15]So He made a whip of small ropes and with their sheep and cattle drove them all out of the temple. He scattered the coins of the money changers and upset their tables.

[16]"Take these away!" He told those who sold pigeons. "Don't make My Father's house a place for business."

[17]His disciples had to think of what the Bible said: *"The zeal for Your house will consume Me."*

[18]Then the Jews came back at Him by asking, "By what miracle can you prove to us you may do this?"

[19]"Tear down this Temple," Jesus answered them, "and I will raise it in three days."

[20]"It took forty-six years to build this temple," said the Jews, "and you'll raise it in three days?"

[21]But the Temple He spoke of was His own body. [22]After He rose from the dead, His disciples remembered He had said this, and they believed the Bible and this statement which Jesus had made.

[23]Now, while He was in the crowd at the Passover in Jerusalem, many believed in His name when they saw the miracles He was doing. [24]Jesus, however, did not take them entirely into His confidence, because He knew everyone. [25]He didn't need to be told about anyone, because He knew what was in him.

Nicodemus

3 Now, there was a Pharisee by the name of Nicodemus, a member of the Jewish council. [2]He came to Jesus one night. "Rabbi," he said to Him, "we know You're a teacher Who has come from God. No one can do these miracles You do unless God is with him."

[3]"I tell you the truth," Jesus answered him, "if anyone isn't born from above, he can't see God's kingdom."

[4]"How can anyone be born when he's old?" Nicodemus asked Him. "He can't go back into his mother's womb and be born again, can he?"

[5]"I tell you the truth," Jesus answered him, "if anyone isn't born of water and the Spirit, he can't get into God's kingdom. [6]Anything born of the flesh is flesh, but anything born of the Spirit is spirit. [7]Don't be surprised when I tell you you must all be born from above. [8]The wind blows where it pleases and you hear the sound of it, but you don't know where it's coming from or where it's going. So it is with everyone born of the Spirit."

[9]"How can that be?" Nicodemus asked Him.

[10]"You are the teacher in Israel," Jesus said to him, "and don't know this? [11]I tell you the truth, We tell what We know, and We testify to what

17 Ps 69:9

We have seen. But you people don't accept Our testimony. [12]If you don't believe the earthly things I told you, how will you believe Me if I tell you heavenly things? [13]*No one has gone up to heaven except the One Who came down from heaven* — the Son of Man.[b]

[14]"As *Moses lifted up the snake* in the desert, so the Son of Man must be lifted up [15]so that everyone who believes in Him has everlasting life. [16]God so loved the world that He gave His only-begotten Son so that whoever believes in Him would not perish but have everlasting life. [17]You see, God didn't send His Son into the world to condemn the world but to save the world through Him. [18]If you believe in Him, you're not condemned. But if you don't believe, you're already condemned because you don't believe in the name of God's only-begotten Son. [19]This is why people are condemned: The Light came into the world, but people have loved darkness instead of the Light because they have been doing wrong. [20]Everyone who does wrong hates the Light and will not come to the Light — he doesn't want his works to be seen in the light. [21]But anyone who lives in the truth comes to the Light so that his works may be seen to have been done in God."

John the Baptizer Talks About the Christ

[22]After this, Jesus and His disciples went into the country of Judea, and there He spent some time with them and baptized.

[23]John, too, was baptizing in Aenon, near Salim, because there was much water there. So people came and were baptized. [24]John had not yet been put in prison.

[25]John's disciples started a discussion with a Jew about religious cleansing, [26]and they came to John. "Rabbi," they told him, "He who was with you on the other side of the Jordan and to whom you gave your testimony — He's here. He's baptizing, and everyone's going to Him."

[27]"A man can get only what Heaven has given him," John answered. [28]"You yourselves are witnesses that I said I'm not the Christ but am sent ahead of Him.

[29]"The One Who has the bride is the Bridegroom. The Bridegroom's friend stands and listens to Him. And when the Bridegroom speaks, He makes His friend very happy. Now, this is my happiness, and it's complete. [30]He must grow while I must become less. [31]The One Who comes from above is above all others.

"Anyone who comes from the earth is earthly and talks about earthly things. The One who comes from heaven is above all others. [32]He tells the truth of what He has seen and heard, and no one accepts the truth He tells. [33]But anyone who has accepted the truth He tells has stamped with his seal of approval that God tells the truth. [34]The One Whom God has sent says what God says because God gives Him His Spirit without limit. [35]The Fa-

---

13 Prov 30:4   *14 Num 21:9*

b - 13   Later manuscripts add, "Who is in heaven" while older manuscripts and translations omit it.

ther loves the Son and has put everything in His hands. [36]Anyone who believes in the Son has everlasting life. But anyone who will not listen to the Son will not see life, but God's wrath rests on him."

The Samaritan Woman

4 The Lord found out that the Pharisees had heard, "Jesus is making and baptizing more disciples than John," [2]although it wasn't Jesus but His disciples who baptized. [3]Then He left Judea and started back on the way to Galilee, [4]and He had to go through Samaria. [5]He came to a town in Samaria by the name of Sychar, near the piece of land Jacob gave his son Joseph. [6]Jacob's Well was there. So Jesus, tired as He was from traveling, sat down by the well. It was about six in the evening.

[7]A woman of Samaria came to draw water. "Give Me a drink," Jesus said to her. [8]His disciples had gone into the town to buy food.

[9]The Samaritan woman asked Him: "How can you, a Jew, ask me, a Samaritan woman, for a drink?" Jews, you see, don't drink from the same jar with Samaritans.

[10]"If you knew what God is giving," Jesus answered her, "and Who it is that says to you, 'Give Me a drink,' you would have asked Him, and He would have given you *living water.*"

[11]"Sir, you have nothing to draw water with," she told Him, "and the well is deep. Where can you get living water from a spring? [12]Are you greater than Jacob, our ancestor, who gave us the well? He himself drank from it, and also his sons and his animals."

[13]"Everyone who drinks this water," Jesus answered her, "will get thirsty again. [14]Anyone who drinks the water I'll give him will never get thirsty again. But the water I'll give him will be in him *a spring of water bubbling up to everlasting life.*"

[15]"Sir, give me this water," the woman told Him. "Then I won't get thirsty or have to come out here to draw water."

[16]"Go, call your husband," Jesus told her, "and come back here."

[17]"I don't have a husband," the woman answered Him.

"You're right when you say, 'I don't have a husband,' " Jesus told her. [18]"You've had five husbands, and the man you have now isn't your husband. You've told the truth!"

[19]"Sir," the woman said to Him, "I see you're a prophet! [20]Our ancestors worshiped on this mountain, but you say, 'The place where people must worship is in Jerusalem.' "

[21]"Believe Me, woman," Jesus told her, "the time is coming when you will not be worshiping the Father on this mountain or in Jerusalem. [22]You don't know what you're worshiping. We know what we're worshiping, because salvation comes from the Jews. [23]But the time is coming, and it is here now, when genuine worshipers will worship the Father in spirit and

---

10,14 *Prov 10:11; 13:14; 14:27; 16:22; Jer 2:13; Zech 14:8*

in truth. You see, the Father is looking for such people to worship Him. [24]God is a spirit, and those who worship Him must worship in spirit and in truth."

[25]The woman said to Him, "I know that the Messiah" (Who is called Christ) "is coming. When He comes, He'll tell us everything."[c]

[26]"I am He — I Who am talking to you," Jesus told her.

[27]Just then His disciples came and were surprised to find Him talking to a woman. But none of them asked, "What do You want?" or, "Why are You talking to her?"

[28]Then the woman left her water jar and went back into the town. [29]"Come," she told the people, "see a man Who told me everything I've done. Could He be the Christ?" [30]They left the town and were coming to Him.

[31]Meanwhile the disciples were urging Him, "Master, eat."

[32]He told them, "I have food to eat which you don't know about."

[33]"Could anyone have brought Him something to eat?" the disciples asked one another.

[34]"My food is to do what He wants Who sent Me," Jesus told them "and to finish His work.

[35]"Don't you say, 'Four more months and we'll cut the grain?' I tell you, look and see how the fields are white and ready to be cut. [36]Already the reaper is getting paid and is gathering grain for everlasting life, so that the sower is happy with the reaper. [37]Here the saying is true, 'One man sows, and another reaps.' [38]I sent you to reap where you had not worked before. Others have done the hard work, and you have succeeded them in their work."

[39]Many Samaritans in that town believed in Him because the woman had declared, "He told me everything I've done." [40]When the Samaritans came to Him, they asked Him to stay with them. And He stayed there two days. [41]Then many more believed because of what He said. [42]"We no longer believe on account of what you said," they told the woman. "Now we heard Him ourselves and know He certainly is the Savior of the world."

[43]After two days He left and went to Galilee.

An Officer's Son

[44]Jesus Himself declared a prophet is not honored in his own country. [45]Now, when He came to Galilee, the people in Galilee welcomed Him. They had seen all He did at the festival in Jerusalem, since they, too, had gone to the festival.

[46]Then Jesus went again to Cana in Galilee, where He had changed water to wine.

One of the king's officers lived at Capernaum. Now, his son was sick. [47]When he heard Jesus had come from Judea to Galilee, he went to Him and asked Him to come down and heal his son, who was dying.

[48]"If you don't see wonderful proofs and miracles," Jesus told him, "you

---

c - 25   Probably referring to Deut 18:18.

won't believe."

⁴⁹"Lord, come down," the officer asked Him, "before my little boy dies."

⁵⁰"Go," Jesus told him, "your boy is well." The man believed what Jesus told him and left.

⁵¹On his way back his slaves met him and told him his boy was well. ⁵²So he asked them what time he got better. They told him, "Yesterday at seven in the evening the fever left him." ⁵³Then the father knew it was the same hour when Jesus had told him, "Your boy is well." And he and everyone at his house believed.

⁵⁴This was the second miracle Jesus did after He had come from Judea to Galilee.

Sick for 38 Years

5 After this there was a Jewish festival, and Jesus went up to Jerusalem.

²Near the Sheep Gate in Jerusalem there's a pool that the Jews call Bethesda. It has five porches. ³In them there used to lie a crowd of people who were sick, blind, lame, and paralyzed.ᵈ ⁵One man who was there had been sick 38 years. ⁶Jesus saw him lying there and found out he had been sick a long time. "Would you like to get well?" He asked him.

⁷"Lord," the sick man answered Him, "I don't have anyone to put me into the pool when the water is stirred. And while I'm trying to get there, someone else steps in ahead of me."

⁸"Get up," Jesus told him, "pick up your bed, and walk." ⁹Immediately the man got well, picked up his bed, and walked.

That day was a Sabbath. ¹⁰"Today is the day of rest," the Jews told the man who had been healed. "It's wrong for you to carry your bed."

¹¹He answered them, "The One Who made me well told me, 'Pick up your bed and walk.'"

¹²They asked him, "Who is the man who told you, 'Pick up your bed and walk?'" ¹³But the man who had been healed didn't know Who He was, because Jesus had disappeared in the crowd that was there.

¹⁴Later Jesus found him in the temple and said to him, "Look, you're well now. Don't sin any more, or something worse may happen to you." ¹⁵The man went back and told the Jews it was Jesus Who made him well.

God's Son

¹⁶Because Jesus was doing such things on a Sabbath, the Jews started to persecute Him. ¹⁷But Jesus answered them, "My Father has been working until now, and so I am working."

---

d - 3   Our oldest manuscripts, including P⁷⁵ and P⁶⁶, lack vv. 3b-4: "waiting for the water to be stirred. At a certain time an angel of the Lord would come down into the pool and stir the water. After the stirring of the water, the first to step in got well, whatever disease he was suffering from."

[18]Then the Jews were all the more eager to kill Him, because He wasn't only abolishing the Sabbath but even calling God His own Father, making Himself equal to God.

[19]"I tell you the truth," Jesus answered them, "the Son can do nothing by Himself but only what He sees the Father doing. You see, the Son does exactly what the Father does. [20]The Father loves the Son and shows Him everything He is doing. And He will show Him even greater works than these so that you'll be amazed. [21]As the Father wakes up the dead and makes them live, so the Son makes alive whom He wants to make alive.

[22]"The Father doesn't judge anyone but has entrusted the judgment entirely to the Son [23]so that all should honor the Son as they honor the Father. Anyone who doesn't honor the Son doesn't honor the Father Who sent Him. [24]I tell you the truth, if you listen to what I say and believe Him Who sent Me, you have everlasting life, and you will not be judged, but you have come from death to life.

[25]"I tell you the truth, the hour is coming and is here now when the dead will hear God's Son calling them, and those who hear Him will live. [26]As the Father has life in Himself, so He has given the Son the power of having life in Himself.

[27]"He has also given Him power to judge because He is the Son of Man. [28]This should not surprise you, because the hour is coming when all who are in their graves will hear Him calling [29]and will come out. Those who have done good will rise to live; those who have done evil will rise to be condemned. [30]I can do nothing by Myself. I judge only as I'm told to do, and so *My judgment is just*, because I'm not trying to do what I want but what He wants Who sent Me.

[31]"If I alone testify about Myself, My testimony isn't dependable. [32]There's Someone else testifying about Me, and I know what He testifies about Me is true. [33]You sent to John, and he testified to the Truth. [34]Not that I get My testimony from a man, but I say this to save you. [35]John was a lighted lamp that shone, and for a while you wanted to enjoy his light. [36]But I have a greater testimony than John had. The works the Father gave Me to finish, these works that I do testify the Father sent Me. [37]The Father Who sent Me — He testified about Me. You never heard His voice or saw His form. [38]You don't keep His Word within you, because you don't believe Him Whom He sent. [39]You search the Scriptures since you think you have everlasting life in them; and still they testify about Me! [40]But you don't want to come to Me to have life.

[41]"I don't get glory from men. [42]But I know in your hearts you don't love God. [43]I have come in My Father's name, and you don't accept Me. If someone else comes in his own name, you'll accept him. [44]How can you believe while you accept honor from one another but are not eager to have the honor that comes from the only God?

[45]"Don't think that I will accuse you before the Father. There is already one who accuses you — Moses, whom you trust. [46]If you really be-

---

30 *Is 11:4*

lieved Moses, you would believe Me, because he wrote about Me. [47]But if you don't believe what he wrote, how will you believe what I say?"

Jesus Feeds 5,000 — *Matthew 14:13-21; Mark 6:30-44; Luke 9:10-17*

6 Some time later Jesus crossed over to the other side of the Sea of Galilee, which is the Sea of Tiberias. [2]A large crowd was following Him because they saw the miracles He did on the sick. [3]Jesus went up the hill and sat down there with His disciples. [4]The Jewish Festival of the Passover was near.

[5]As Jesus looked up, He saw a large crowd coming to Him. He turned to Philip: "Where should we buy bread for these people to eat?" [6]He asked this only to test him, since He knew what He was going to do.

[7]"Two hundred denarii,"[e] Philip answered, "wouldn't buy enough bread for each of them to get just a little."

[8]One of His disciples, Andrew, Simon Peter's brother, told Him, [9]"There's a boy here who has five barley loaves and two fish. But what is that among so many?" [10]"Have the people sit down," Jesus said. There was much grass at the place. So they sat down. There were about 5,000 men.

[11]Then Jesus took the loaves, gave thanks, and distributed them to the people who were sitting down, and in the same way as much of the fish as they wanted.

[12]When they had enough, He told His disciples, "Gather the pieces that are left so that nothing will be wasted." [13]They gathered them and filled twelve baskets with pieces of the five barley loaves left by those who had eaten.

[14]Seeing the miracle He did, the people said, "This certainly is the *Prophet* Who is coming into the world."

Jesus Walks on Water — *Matthew 14:22-33; Mark 6:45-52*

[15]When Jesus learned that the people meant to come and take Him by force and make Him king, He went back again to the hill by Himself. [16]Meanwhile, as it got late, His disciples went down to the sea, [17]stepped into a boat, and were on their way across the sea to Capernaum. By this time it was dark, and Jesus hadn't come to them yet. [18]A strong wind started to blow and stir up the sea.

[19]After they had rowed three or four miles, they saw Jesus walking on the sea and coming near the boat, and they were terrified.

[20]"It is I," He told them. "Don't be afraid."

[21]They wanted to take Him into the boat. And in a moment the boat came to the shore where they were going.

---

14 Deut 18:15,18

e - 7   A denarius was one day's pay.

Bread from Heaven

²²The next day the people were still lingering on the other side of the sea. They had noticed only one boat was there and Jesus had not stepped into that boat with His disciples but they had gone away without Him. ²³Other boats came from Tiberias near the place where they had eaten the bread after the Lord gave thanks. ²⁴When the people saw that neither Jesus nor His disciples were there, they stepped into these boats and came to Capernaum, looking for Jesus. ²⁵They found Him on the other side of the sea and asked Him, "Rabbi, when did You get here?"

²⁶"I tell you the truth," Jesus answered them, "you're not looking for Me because you've seen miracles but because you've eaten some of the bread and been well fed. ²⁷Don't work for the food that spoils but for the food that keeps for everlasting life, which the Son of Man will give you because God the Father has sealed in Him the power to give it."

²⁸"What are the works God wants us to do?" they asked Him.

²⁹"What God wants you to do," Jesus answered them, "is to believe in Him Whom He sent."

³⁰"What miracle can You do?" they asked Him. "Let us see it, and we'll believe You. What can You do? ³¹Our fathers ate the manna in the desert, as it is written: *'He gave them bread from heaven to eat.'*"

³²"I tell you the truth," Jesus said to them, "Moses didn't give you the bread from heaven, but My Father gives you the real bread from heaven. ³³God's bread is coming down from heaven and giving life to the world."

³⁴"Lord," they said to Him, "always give us this bread."

³⁵"I am the Bread of Life," Jesus told them. "Come to Me, and you will never be hungry. Believe in Me, and you will never be thirsty. ³⁶But I have told you, 'You have seen Me, and you don't believe!' ³⁷All the Father gives Me will come to Me, and anyone who comes to Me I will never turn away, ³⁸because I came down from heaven, not to do what I want but what He wants Who sent Me; ³⁹and He Who sent Me doesn't want Me to lose any of those He gave Me but to raise them on the last day. ⁴⁰Yes, My Father wants everyone who sees the Son and believes in Him to have everlasting life, and He wants Me to raise him on the last day."

⁴¹Then the Jews grumbled because He said, "I am the Bread that came down from heaven." ⁴²"Isn't this Jesus, Joseph's son," they asked, "whose father and mother we know? Then how can He say, 'I came down from heaven?'"

⁴³"Don't grumble among yourselves," Jesus answered them. ⁴⁴"A person can come to Me only if the Father Who sent Me draws him. Then I will raise him on the last day. ⁴⁵The prophets wrote: *'God will teach everyone'*. Everyone who listens to the Father and learns from Him comes to Me. ⁴⁶Not that anyone has seen the Father; only He Who comes from God has seen the Father. ⁴⁷I tell you the truth, anyone who believes has everlasting life.

⁴⁸"I am the Bread of Life. ⁴⁹Your fathers ate the manna in the desert,

---

31 Ex 16:4,15,32; Neh 9:15; Ps 78:24   45 Is 54:13

and they died. [50]But this is the Bread coming down from heaven so that anyone may eat it and not die. [51]I am the living Bread that came down from heaven. If anyone eats this Bread, he will live forever. The bread I'll give to bring life to the world is My flesh."

[52]Then the Jews argued with one another: "How can He give us His flesh to eat?"

[53]"I tell you the truth," Jesus answered them, "unless you eat the flesh of the Son of Man and drink His blood, you don't have any life in you. [54]If you eat My flesh and drink My blood, you have everlasting life, and I will raise you on the last day. [55]My flesh is a true food, and My blood is a true drink. [56]If you eat My flesh and drink My blood, you stay in Me and I in you. [57]As the living Father sent Me and I live because of the Father, so if you feed on Me, you will live because of Me. [58]This is the Bread that came down from heaven. It isn't like the bread the fathers ate. They died. Eat this Bread, and you will live forever."

[59]He said this while He was teaching in a synagogue in Capernaum. [60]When they heard it, many of His disciples said, "This is hard to understand. Who can listen to Him?"

[61]Inwardly aware that His disciples were complaining about this, Jesus asked them, "Does this upset you? [62]What if you see the Son of Man go up where He was before? [63]The Spirit makes alive; the flesh doesn't help. The words I spoke to you are Spirit, and they are life. [64]But some of you don't believe." Jesus knew from the beginning who wouldn't believe and who would betray Him. [65]So He added, "That is why I told you a person can come to Me only if the Father gives him the power."

[66]As a result many of His disciples went back to their old life and wouldn't go with Him anymore. [67]Then Jesus asked the twelve, "Do you want to leave Me too?" [68]"Lord, to whom should we go?" Simon Peter answered Him, "You have words of everlasting life. [69]And we have come to believe and know You are God's Holy One."

[70]"Didn't I choose the twelve of you," Jesus asked, "and one of you is a devil?" [71]He meant Judas, the son of Simon, Iscariot. He was going to betray Him — one of the twelve.

To Jerusalem

7Later Jesus went around in Galilee. He didn't want to travel in Judea because the Jews were trying to kill Him.

[2]The Jewish Festival of Booths was near. [3]So His brothers told Jesus, "Leave this place, go to Judea, and there let your disciples see the works you're doing. [4]No one goes on doing things secretly when he wants to be known publicly. If you do these things, let the world see you." [5]Not even His brothers believed in Him.

[6]"It isn't the right time for Me yet," Jesus told them, "but any time is right for you. [7]The world can't hate you, but it hates Me because I tell the truth about it that it is doing wrong. [8]You go up to the festival. I'm not going up to this festival right now, because it isn't the right time for Me

yet."

⁹After telling them this, He did stay in Galilee. ¹⁰But after His brothers had gone up to the festival, He went up too, not publicly but without being seen.

At the Festival of Booths

¹¹So the Jews were looking for Jesus in the crowd at the festival. "Where is he?" they kept asking. ¹²And there was much whispering about Him in the crowds. "He's a good man," some said; but others, "No, he deceives the people." ¹³Yet no one would talk about Him in public because everyone was afraid of the Jews.

¹⁴But when the festival was already half over, Jesus went up to the temple and started to teach. ¹⁵The Jews were surprised. "How can he know so much," they asked, "when he hasn't been in the schools?"

¹⁶"What I teach doesn't come from Me," Jesus answered them, "but from Him Who sent Me. ¹⁷If anyone wants to do His will, he'll know whether My teaching is from God or I speak My own thoughts. ¹⁸Anyone who speaks his own thoughts tries to glorify himself. But He Who wants to glorify the One Who sent Him tells the truth, and there's nothing wrong in Him. ¹⁹Didn't Moses give you the Law? Yet none of you does what the Law tells you. Why do you want to kill Me?"

²⁰"There's a demon in you," the crowd answered. "Who wants to kill you?"

²¹"I did one thing," Jesus answered them, "and you're all surprised about it. ²²Moses gave you circumcision (not that it came from Moses but from our ancestors), and you circumcise a person on a Sabbath. ²³If a child is circumcised on a day of rest to keep the Law of Moses, are you angry with Me because I made all of a man well on a Sabbath? ²⁴Don't judge by what you see, but be fair when you judge."

²⁵Then some of the men from Jerusalem said, "Isn't he the man they want to kill? ²⁶But here he speaks in public, and they don't say a thing to him! Surely the rulers haven't found out he's the Christ, have they? ²⁷Now, we know where this one comes from. But when the Christ comes, no one knows where He's from."

²⁸"You know Me," Jesus called aloud as He was teaching in the temple, "and you know where I come from. I didn't by Myself decide to come, but there's One who is true Who sent Me. You don't know Him, ²⁹but I know Him because I come from Him and He sent Me."

³⁰Then they tried to arrest Him, but no one laid a hand on Him, because the right time hadn't come yet for Him.

³¹But many in the crowd believed in Him. "When the Christ comes," they asked, "will He do more miracles than this One has done?"

³²The Pharisees heard the people muttering such things about Him. So the ruling priests as well as the Pharisees sent their men to arrest Him.

---

34 Prov 1:28

[33]"I'll be with you just a little longer," said Jesus; "then I go to Him Who sent Me. [34]You'll be *looking for Me and won't find Me*; and where I am, you can't come."

[35]The Jews asked one another, "Where's He intending to go, saying we won't find Him? He doesn't intend to go to our people scattered among the non-Jews and teach the non-Jews, does He? [36]What does He[f] mean by saying, 'You'll be looking for Me and won't find Me,' and, 'Where I am, you can't come?'"

[37]On the last day, the great day of the festival, as Jesus was standing there, He called out loudly, *"If you're thirsty, come to Me and drink. [38]If you believe in Me, streams of living water will flow from you,* as the Bible has said." [39]By this He meant the Spirit, Whom those who believed in Him were to receive. The Spirit had not come yet, because Jesus hadn't been glorified yet.

[40]After they heard Him say this, some of the people said, "This is certainly the *Prophet*." [41]Others said, "This is the Christ." Still others asked, "What! Does the Christ come from Galilee? [42]Doesn't the Bible say: 'The Christ *will come from the descendants of David* and *from* the little town of *Bethlehem*, where David lived'?" [43]So the people were divided over Him. [44]Some of them wanted to arrest Him, but no one laid hands on Him.

[45]When the men who had been sent went back to the ruling priests and Pharisees, these asked them, "Why didn't you bring him?"

[46]"No one ever spoke like this man," the men answered.

[47]"You haven't been deceived, too, have you?" the Pharisees asked them. [48]"No ruler or Pharisee has believed in him, has he? [49]But this crowd, which doesn't know the Bible, is cursed."

[50]One of them, Nicodemus, who had once come to Jesus, asked them, [51]"Does our Law condemn anyone without first hearing what he has to say and finding out what he's doing?"

[52]"Are you from Galilee, too?" they asked him. "Search and see; the Prophet doesn't come from Galilee."[g]

[53]Then everyone went home.

The Adulteress

8 But Jesus went to the Mount of Olives. [2]Early in the morning He came back into the temple. All the people came to Him, and He sat down and taught them.

[3]The Bible scholars and the Pharisees brought to Him a woman who

---

37 Is 55:1   38 Ezek 47:1-2,7-8,12; Zech 14:8   40 Deut 18:18
42 II Sam 7:12; Mic 5:2,4

---

f - 36   This quote, according to the context, seems to be coming from a mixture of believers and non-believers. Pronouns referring to Jesus could be capitalized (believers) or not capitalized (non-believers).

g - 52   Our best manuscripts, including the two oldest papyri (P[66] and P[75], dated about A.D. 200) lack 7:53-8:11, the story of the adulteress.

had been caught in adultery and had her stand in the middle. ⁴"Teacher," they told Him, "this woman was caught in the act of adultery. ⁵In the Law, Moses ordered us to stone such women. Now, what do you say?" ⁶They asked this to test Him. They wanted to find something to accuse Him of.

Jesus bent down and with His finger wrote on the ground. ⁷But when they kept on asking Him, He got up. "Anyone that's without sin among you," He said, "should be the first to throw a stone at her." ⁸Then He bent down again and wrote on the ground.

⁹Convicted by their conscience as they heard Him, they went out one by one, beginning with the older men, until all had gone and Jesus was left alone with the woman in the middle of the place. ¹⁰Jesus got up. "Woman, where are they?" He asked her. "Didn't anyone condemn you?"

¹¹"No one, Lord," she said.

"I don't condemn you either," Jesus said. "Go! From now on don't sin anymore."

Jesus Argues with the Jews

¹²Jesus spoke to them again. "I am the Light of the world. Follow Me, and you will never wander in the dark but will have the Light of Life."

¹³"You testify about yourself," the Pharisees said to Him. "Your testimony is not true."

¹⁴"Even if I testify about Myself," Jesus answered them, "My testimony is true, because I know where I came from and where I'm going; but you don't know where I came from or where I'm going. ¹⁵You judge in a human way, a way in which I don't judge anyone. ¹⁶But whenever I judge, My judgment is valid because I am not alone, but I'm with the Father Who sent Me. ¹⁷In your own Law it is written that the testimony of two men is valid. ¹⁸I testify about Myself, and the Father Who sent Me testifies about Me."

¹⁹"Where is your father?" they asked Him.

"You don't know Me or My Father," Jesus answered. "If you knew Me, you would know My Father."

²⁰He said this in the room of the treasury while He was teaching in the temple; no one arrested Him, because the right time hadn't come yet for Him.

²¹"I'm going away," He said to them again, "and you'll be looking for Me, but you will die in your sin. Where I'm going, you can't come."

²²"Is he going to kill himself?" the Jews asked. "Is that what he means when he says, 'Where I'm going, you can't come'?"

²³"You're from below," He told them. "I'm from above. Your home is in this world. My home is not in this world. ²⁴That's why I told you, 'You will die in your sins'; if you don't believe I'm the One, you will die in your sins."

²⁵"Who are you?" they asked Him.

"What should I tell you first?" Jesus asked them. ²⁶"I have much to say about you and to condemn. But I tell the world only what I heard from Him Who sent Me, and He tells the truth." ²⁷They didn't understand He was talking to them about the Father.

²⁸So Jesus told them, "When you have lifted up the Son of Man, you will know I am the One and I do nothing by Myself, but I speak as My Father taught Me. ²⁹And He Who sent Me is with Me and has not left Me alone, because I always do what pleases Him."

³⁰As He was saying this, many believed in Him. ³¹Then Jesus said to those Jews who believed in Him, "If you live in My Word, you are truly My disciples, ³²and you will know the truth, and the truth will free you."

³³"We are Abraham's descendants," they answered Him, "and have never been anyone's slaves. How can you say, 'You'll be freed?'"

³⁴"I tell you the truth," Jesus answered them, "everyone who lives in sin is a slave to sin. ³⁵A slave doesn't stay in the home forever. A son stays forever. ³⁶If, then, the Son frees you, you will really be free. ³⁷I know you're Abraham's descendants. But you want to kill Me because there is no room for My Word in you. ³⁸I'm telling what I've seen, being with My Father, and you do what you've heard from your father."

³⁹"Abraham is our father," they answered Him.

"If you were Abraham's children," Jesus told them, "you would do what Abraham did. ⁴⁰But now you want to kill Me, a Man Who told you the truth, which I heard from God. Abraham didn't do that. ⁴¹You're doing what your father does."

"We weren't born outside of marriage," they said. "God alone is our Father."

⁴²"If God were your Father," Jesus told them, "you would love Me because I came from God, and as such I am here. I did not by Myself decide to come, but He sent Me. ⁴³Why don't you understand what I say? Because you can't listen to what I tell you. ⁴⁴Your father is the devil, and you want to do what your father wants. From the beginning he has been murdering people and hasn't stood in the truth, because there's no truth in him. When he tells a lie, he's telling it from his heart, because he's a liar and the father of lies. ⁴⁵Now, because I tell the truth, you don't believe Me. ⁴⁶Which of you can prove Me guilty of a sin? If I tell the truth, why don't you believe Me? ⁴⁷A child of God listens to what God says. You don't listen to Him because you're not God's children."

⁴⁸"Aren't we right," the Jews answered Him, "when we say you're a Samaritan and there's a demon in you?"

⁴⁹"There's no demon in Me," Jesus answered. "No, I honor My Father, but you dishonor Me. ⁵⁰I'm not trying to get glory for Myself. There's One Who wants Me to have it, and He's the judge. ⁵¹I tell you the truth, if you keep My Word, you will never see death."

⁵²"Now we know there's a demon in you," the Jews told Him. "Abraham died, and so did the prophets, but you say, 'If you keep My Word, you will never taste death.' ⁵³Are you greater than our father Abraham? He died, and the prophets died. Who do you think you are?"

⁵⁴"If I glorify Myself," Jesus said, "My glory is nothing. It is My Father Who glorifies Me, He of Whom you say, 'He's our God.' ⁵⁵You don't know Him, but I know Him. And if I would say I don't know Him, I'd be a liar like

you. But I do know Him, and I observe His Word. ⁵⁶Your father Abraham was delighted to know of My day; he saw it and was glad."

⁵⁷"You're not fifty years old yet," the Jews said to Him, "and Abraham has seen you?"

⁵⁸"I tell you the truth," Jesus told them, "before Abraham ever was born, *I am.*"

⁵⁹Then they picked up stones to throw at Him. But Jesus hid Himself and left the temple.

A Blind Man Sees

9As Jesus was passing by, He saw a man who had been blind from his birth.

²"Master," His disciples asked Him, "why was he born blind? Did he sin or his parents?"

³"Neither he nor his parents," Jesus answered. "He is blind to show what God can do with him. ⁴We must do the works of Him Who sent Me while it is day. The night is coming when no one can work. ⁵As long as I'm in the world, I'm the Light of the world."

⁶After He said this, He spit on the ground and with the spit made some mud and put the mud on the man's eyes. ⁷"Go," He told him, "wash in the pool of Siloam" (the name means "sent"). He went and washed. And as he walked away, he could see.

⁸Now, his neighbors and others who used to see him as a beggar asked, "Isn't this the man who used to sit and beg?"

⁹"It is he," some said. Others said, "No, but he looks like him." But he himself said, "I'm the one."

¹⁰Then they asked him, "How did you get your sight?"

¹¹"The Man they call Jesus made some mud," he answered, "and put it on my eyes and told me, 'Go to Siloam and wash.' So I went and washed, and then I could see."

¹²"Where is he?" they asked him. "I don't know," he answered.

¹³They brought him who had been blind to the Pharisees. ¹⁴Now, it was a Sabbath when Jesus made the mud and gave him his sight. ¹⁵So the Pharisees also asked him how he got his sight.

"He put mud on my eyes," the man told them, "and I washed them, and now I can see."

¹⁶"This man is not from God," said some of the Pharisees, "because he doesn't observe the Sabbath." Others asked, "How can a sinful man do such miracles?" So they disagreed.

¹⁷Then they asked the blind man again, "What do you say about him, since he gave you your sight?"

"He's a prophet," he answered.

¹⁸The Jews didn't believe the man had been blind and got his sight until they called the parents of the man who could see now. ¹⁹"Is this your

58 Ex 3:14; Is 43:10-13,15

son who you say was born blind?" they asked them. "How does it happen he can see now?"

²⁰"We know he's our son," his parents answered, "and was born blind. ²¹But we don't know how it is he can see now or who gave him his sight. Ask him; he's of age. He'll tell you about himself." ²²His parents said this because they were afraid of the Jews. The Jews had already agreed to put out of the synagogue anyone who confessed Jesus was the Christ. ²³That is why his parents said, "He's of age; ask him."

²⁴So once again they called the man who had been blind. "Give glory to God," they told him. "We know this man is a sinner."

²⁵"I don't know if He's a sinner," he answered. "I know only one thing — I used to be blind, and now I can see."

²⁶"What did he do to you?" they asked him. "How did he give you your sight?"

²⁷"I've already told you," he answered them, "and you heard it. Why do you want to hear it again? You don't want to be his disciples, too, do you?"

²⁸"You're his disciple," they answered him scornfully, "but we're Moses' disciples. ²⁹We know God spoke to Moses, but this fellow — we don't know where he's from."

³⁰"Well, that's strange!" the man answered them. "You don't know where He's from, and yet He gave me my sight. ³¹We know that God doesn't hear sinners but hears anyone who worships God and does what He wants. ³²No one has ever heard of anyone giving sight to a man born blind. ³³If this One were not from God, He couldn't do anything."

³⁴"You were altogether born in sins," they answered him, "and are you trying to teach us?" Then they put him out of the synagogue.

³⁵Jesus heard they had put him out. Finding him, He asked him, "Do you believe in the Son of Man?"

³⁶"Who is He, sir?" he asked. "I want to believe in Him."

³⁷"You've seen Him," Jesus told him. "It is He Who is now talking to you."

³⁸"I do believe, Lord," he said and bowed down to worship Him.

³⁹Then Jesus said, "I've come into this world to judge men, so that those who don't see may see and those who see may become blind."

⁴⁰Some Pharisees who were near Him heard this. "We aren't blind, are we?" they asked Him.

⁴¹"If you were blind," Jesus told them, "you wouldn't be sinning. But now you say, 'We see,' and you go on sinning."

The Good Shepherd

10 "I tell you the truth, the man who doesn't come into the sheepfold through the door but climbs over somewhere else, is a thief and a robber. ²But the one who comes in through the door is the shepherd of the sheep. ³The doorkeeper opens the door for him, and the sheep listen to his voice. He calls his own sheep by their names and leads them out. ⁴When he has brought out all his own sheep, he walks ahead of them, and the sheep follow him because they know his voice. ⁵They will not follow a stranger but will run away from him because they don't know the voice of strangers."

⁶This was the illustration Jesus used in talking to them, but they didn't know what He meant. ⁷So Jesus spoke again: "I tell you the truth, I am the Door for the sheep. ⁸All who came before Me were thieves and robbers, but the sheep didn't listen to them. ⁹I am the Door. If anyone comes in through Me, he will be saved and will go in and out and find pasture.

¹⁰"A thief comes only to steal and kill and destroy. I came so that they will have life and have it overflowing in them. ¹¹I am the Good Shepherd. The Good Shepherd gives His life for the sheep. ¹²When a hired man, who isn't a shepherd and doesn't own the sheep, sees a wolf coming, he leaves the sheep and runs away — and the wolf carries them off and scatters them — ¹³because he works for money and doesn't care about the sheep. ¹⁴I am the Good Shepherd, and I know My own and My own know Me, ¹⁵as the Father knows Me and I know the Father. And I give My life for the sheep. ¹⁶I have other sheep, too, that are not in this fold. I must lead those, too, and they will listen to My voice, and so they will become one flock with *one Shepherd*. ¹⁷The Father loves Me because I give My life in order to take it back again. ¹⁸No one takes it from Me. No, of My own free will I am giving it. I have the power to give it, and I have the power to take it back again. This is what My Father ordered Me to do."

¹⁹These words again caused a split among the Jews. ²⁰Many of them said, "There's a demon in Him and He's crazy. Why do you listen to Him?" ²¹Others said, "No one talks like this when there's a demon in him. Can a demon give sight to the blind?"

"I and the Father Are One"

²²Then came the Festival of Dedication in Jerusalem. It was winter, ²³and Jesus was walking in Solomon's porch in the temple. ²⁴There the Jews surrounded Him. "How long will You keep us in suspense?" they asked Him. "If you're the Christ, tell us frankly."

²⁵"I did tell you," Jesus answered them, "but you don't believe it. The works I do in My Father's name tell the truth about Me. ²⁶But you don't believe, because you're not My sheep. ²⁷My sheep listen to My voice, and I know them, and they follow Me, ²⁸and I give them everlasting life. They will never be lost, and no one will tear them out of My hand. ²⁹My Father, Who gave them to Me, is greater than all others, and no one can tear them out of My Father's hand. ³⁰I and the Father are one."

³¹Again the Jews picked up stones to stone Him. ³²Jesus answered them, "I have shown you many good works that come from the Father. For which of these works are you trying to stone Me?"

³³"We're stoning you," the Jews answered Him, "not for a good work but for blasphemy because you, a man, claim to be God."

³⁴Jesus said to them, "Isn't it written in your Bible: *'I said, "You are*

---

16 Ezek 34:23   *34 Ps 82:6*

gods" '? [35]If it called them gods to whom God's Word came — and the Bible can't be set aside — [36]do you say to Me, Whom the Father appointed for His holy purpose and sent into the world, 'You're blaspheming,' because I said, 'I'm God's Son?' [37]If I'm not doing My Father's works, don't trust Me. [38]But if I do them, even if you don't trust Me, trust My works so as to learn and understand the Father is in Me and I am in the Father."

[39]Again they tried to arrest Him, but He escaped from their hands. [40]He went back across the Jordan to the place where John had been baptizing earlier, and He stayed there.

[41]Many came to Him. "John did no miracle," they said, "but everything John said about this One is true." [42]And many believed in Him there.

Jesus Raises Lazarus

11 Then Lazarus was sick. He was in Bethany, the village where Mary and her sister Martha were living. [2]Mary was the one who poured perfume on the Lord and wiped His feet with her hair. It was her brother Lazarus who was sick.

[3]So the sisters sent someone to tell Jesus, "Lord, the one You love is sick."

[4]When Jesus heard it, He said, "The purpose of this sickness isn't death but to show God's glory: it is to glorify God's Son."

[5]Jesus loved Martha and her sister and Lazarus. [6]Now, when He heard Lazarus was sick, He stayed two days where He was. [7]After that He said to His disciples, "Let us go back to Judea."

[8]"Master," the disciples said to Him, "the Jews have just been wanting to stone You, and You're going back there?"

[9]"Aren't there twelve hours in a day?" Jesus answered. "If you walk during the day, you don't stumble, because you see the light of this world. [10]But if you walk at night, you stumble, because you have no light."

[11]After He said this, He told them, "Our friend Lazarus has gone to sleep, but I'm going there to wake him up."

[12]"Lord, if he has gone to sleep," His disciples said to Him, "he'll get well."

[13]Jesus meant he was dead, but they thought He meant he was only sleeping. [14]Then Jesus told them in plain words, "Lazarus died. [15]And I'm glad I wasn't there, so that you will believe. But let us go to him."

[16]Then Thomas, who was called Twin, said to his fellow disciples, "Let us go too and die with Him."

[17]When Jesus got there, He found that Lazarus had been in the grave four days already.

[18]Bethany was near Jerusalem, not quite two miles away, [19]and many Jews had come to Martha and Mary to comfort them about their brother.

[20]Now, when Martha heard, "Jesus is coming," she went to meet Him, while Mary stayed at home. [21]"Lord, if You had been here," Martha told Jesus, "my brother wouldn't have died. [22]But even now I know God will give You anything You ask Him."

[23]"Your brother will rise again," Jesus told her.

[24]"I know he'll rise again," Martha answered Him, "in the resurrection on the last day."

[25]"I am the Resurrection and the Life," Jesus said to her. "Anyone who believes in Me will live even if he dies. [26]Yes, anyone who lives and believes in Me will never die. Do you believe that?"

[27]"Yes, Lord," she told Him, "I believe You are the Christ, God's Son, Who is coming into the world."

[28]After she said this, she went to call her sister Mary. "The Teacher is here," she whispered, "and is calling for you."

[29]When Mary heard it, she got up quickly to go to Him. [30]Jesus hadn't come to the village yet but was still where Martha had met Him. [31]Now, the Jews who were in the house with Mary to comfort her saw her get up quickly and leave. So they followed her, thinking she was going to the grave to weep there. [32]When Mary came where Jesus was and saw Him, she bowed down at His feet and said, "Lord, if You had been here, my brother wouldn't have died."

[33]When Jesus saw her weeping, and the Jews weeping who came with her, He groaned deeply and was troubled.

[34]"Where did you lay him?" He asked. "Lord, come and see," they answered Him.

[35]Jesus burst into tears. [36]"See how He loved him," the Jews said. [37]But some of them asked, "He gave sight to the blind man — couldn't He have kept this man from dying?"

[38]Groaning deeply again, Jesus went to the grave. It was a cave, and a stone was laid against it. [39]"Move the stone away," said Jesus.

Martha, the dead man's sister, told Him, "Lord, by this time there will be a terrible odor. He's been dead four days."

[40]Jesus said to her, "Didn't I tell you, 'If you believe, you will see God's glory?'" [41]So they moved the stone away.

Jesus looked up and said, "Father, I thank You for hearing Me. [42]I knew You always hear Me. But I spoke so that the people standing around Me will believe You sent Me." [43]After He had said this, He called out with a loud voice, "Lazarus, come out!"

[44]The man who had been dead came out, his feet and hands wrapped in bandages and his face wrapped in a cloth. "Unwrap him," Jesus told them, "and let him go."

The Plot — *Matthew 26:1-5; Mark 14:1-2; Luke 22:1-6*

[45]Then many of the Jews who had come to Mary and had seen what He did believed in Him. [46]But some of them went to the Pharisees and told them what Jesus had done. [47]Then the ruling priests and the Pharisees called a meeting of the council. "What are we doing?" they asked. "This man is doing many miracles. [48]If we let him go on like this, everyone will believe in him, and then the Romans will come and take away our place and our nation."

[49]But one of them, Caiaphas, who was high priest that year, told them, "You don't know anything, [50]and you don't consider it is better for you that one man dies instead of the people and the whole nation doesn't perish." [51]He didn't think of this himself, but being high priest that year, he prophesied Jesus was going to die for the nation, [52]and not only for this nation but also to bring God's scattered children together and make them one.

[53]From that day on they plotted to put Him to death. [54]So Jesus no longer walked in public among the Jews but left and went into the country near the wilderness, to a town called Ephraim, and He stayed there with His disciples.

[55]The Jewish Passover was near, and many came from the country to Jerusalem before the Passover to purify themselves. [56]They were looking for Jesus and asking one another as they stood in the temple, "What do you think? He isn't coming to the festival, is He?" [57]The ruling priests and the Pharisees had given orders if anyone found out where He was he should report it so that they might arrest Him.

Mary Anoints Jesus — *Matthew 26:6-13; Mark 14:3-9*

12 Six days before the Passover, Jesus came to Bethany, where Lazarus was, whom Jesus had raised from the dead. [2]There a dinner was prepared for Him. Martha served, and Lazarus was one of those eating with Him.

[3]Then Mary took a pound of perfume, pure nard and very expensive, and poured it on Jesus' feet and dried His feet with her hair. The fragrance of the perfume filled the house.

[4]Judas (Iscariot, one of His disciples, who was going to betray Him) asked. [5]"Why wasn't this perfume sold for three hundred denarii[h] and the money given to the poor?" [6]He didn't say this because he cared about the poor but because he was a thief and used to steal what was put in the money box he carried.

[7]"Let her do it for the day of My burial," Jesus said. [8]*"The poor you always have with you,* but you don't always have Me."

[9]A large crowd of the Jews found out He was there, and they came, not only on account of Jesus but also to see Lazarus, whom He had raised from the dead. [10]But the ruling priests decided to kill Lazarus, too, [11]because he was the reason many Jews were going over to Jesus and believing in Him.

The King Comes to Jerusalem – *Matthew 21:1-11; Mark 11:1-11; Luke 19:29-44*

[12]The next day the large crowd that had come to the festival and heard, "Jesus is coming to Jerusalem," [13]took branches from the palm trees and went out to meet Him, shouting:

---

8 Deut 15:11   *13 Ps 118:25-26*   *15 Is 40:9; 62:11; Zech 9:9*

---

h - 5   A denarius was one day's pay.

"Our Savior!
Blessed is He Who is coming in the Lord's name,
the King of Israel!"

[14]Jesus found a donkey and sat on it, as it is written:
[15]*"Don't be afraid, daughter of Zion!*
Look! Your King is coming, riding on a donkey's colt!"

[16]At the time His disciples didn't know what it meant, but after Jesus was glorified, they remembered that these things had been written about Him and were done to Him.

[17]The people who had been with Him when He called Lazarus out of the grave and raised him from the dead were telling what they had seen. [18]Because the crowd heard He had done this miracle, it came to meet Him.

[19]Then the Pharisees said to one another, "You see, you're not getting anywhere. Look! The world is running after him."

Death and Glory

[20]Among those who came up to worship at the festival were some Greeks. [21]They went to Philip (who was from Bethsada in Galilee) and told him, "Sir, we want to see Jesus. [22]Philip went and told Andrew. Andrew and Philip went and told Jesus.

[23]Jesus answered them, "The *time* has come *for the Son of Man to be glorified.* [24]Surely, I tell you, if a kernel of wheat doesn't fall into the ground and die, it will be just one kernel. But if it dies, it produces much grain. [25]Love your life and lose it, but hate your life in this world, and you will keep it for an everlasting life. [26]If you serve Me, follow Me; and where I am, there My servant will be. If you serve Me, the Father will honor you.

[27]*"I am deeply troubled* now. But what should I say? Father, save Me from what is going to happen? No! I came to suffer this now. [28]Father, glorify Your name."

Then a voice came from heaven: "I have glorified My name and will glorify it again."

[29]The crowd, which stood there and heard it, said it had thundered. Others said, "An angel talked to Him." [30]Jesus explained: "That voice did not come for My benefit but for yours.

[31]"Now this world is being judged: now the ruler of this world will be thrown out. [32]And once I have been lifted up from the earth, I will draw all people to Me." [33]He said this to indicate how He was going to die.

[34]Then the crowd answered Him. "We've heard from the Bible *the Christ remains forever.* How, then, can You say the Son of Man must be lifted up? Who is this Son of Man?"

[35]"The Light will be with you just a little longer." Jesus answered them. *"Walk while you have the Light,* or darkness will overtake you. If you walk *in the dark, you don't know where you're going.* [36]While you have the Light,

---

23 Is 40:527 *Ps* 6:3   *32 Is* 52:13   *34 Ps* 89:29,36
    35 Is 2:5; *Prov* 4:19   *38 Is* 53:1

believe in the Light in order to become enlightened people."

After Jesus had said this, He went away and hid from them.

[37]Although they had seen Him do so many miracles, they wouldn't believe in Him — [38]what the prophet Isaiah said had to come true:

> "Lord, who has believed what we preach?
> And to whom has the Lord's arm been uncovered?"

[39]And so they couldn't believe, because Isaiah also said:

> [40]"He blinded their eyes
>   and dulled their hearts, so that their eyes don't see,
>   their hearts don't understand,
>   and they don't turn and let Me heal them."

[41]Isaiah said this because he saw His glory and spoke of Him. [42]And yet even many of the rulers believed in Him but wouldn't say so publicly, because the Pharisees would have put them out of the synagogue. [43]Yes, they loved to be praised by men more than God.

[44]Then Jesus called out, "If you believe in Me, you don't believe only in Me but in Him Who sent Me. [45]And if you see Me, you see Him Who sent Me. [46]I have come as a light into the world so that anyone who believes in Me will not have to stay in the dark. [47]If anyone hears My words but doesn't keep them, I don't condemn him, because I didn't come to condemn the world but to save the world. [48]*If anyone rejects* Me and doesn't take to heart *what I say*, he has one that is condemning him. The Word that I spoke will condemn him on the last day, [49]because what I said didn't come from Me, but *the Father Who sent Me ordered Me to say and tell it.* [50]I know what He orders is everlasting life. And so, whatever I say, I say it just as the Father told Me."

Jesus Washes the Disciples' Feet

13 Before the Passover Festival Jesus knew the time had come for Him to leave this world and go to the Father. He had loved His own who were in the world, and now He loved them to the end.

[2]It was during the supper. The devil had already put the idea of betraying Jesus into the mind of Judas Iscariot, the son of Simon.

[3]Jesus knew the Father put everything in His hands and He had come from God and was going back to God.

[4]So Jesus rose from supper, laid aside His outer garment, took a towel, and tied it around Him. [5]Then He poured water into a basin and started to wash the disciples' feet and to dry them with the towel that was tied around Him.

[6]And so He came to Simon Peter. "Lord," Peter asked Him, "are You going to wash my feet?"

[7]"You don't know now what I'm doing," Jesus answered him. "But later you will understand."

[8]"No!" Peter told Him. "You'll never wash my feet."

---

40 Is 6:10   *48-49 Deut 18:18-19*

"If I don't wash you," Jesus answered him, "you have no share in Me."
[9]"Lord," Simon Peter told Him, "not only my feet but also my hands and my head."
[10]"Anyone who has bathed needs only to have his feet washed," Jesus told him. "He's clean all over. You're clean, but not every one of you." [11]He knew who was betraying Him. That's why He said, "Not all of you are clean."

[12]After He had washed their feet and put on His garment, He lay down again. "Do you know what I've done to you?" He asked them. [13]"You call Me 'Teacher' and 'Lord', and you're right because I am that. [14]Now if I, the Lord and the Teacher, have washed your feet, you, too, should wash one another's feet. [15]I've given you an example so that you will do as I did to you. [16]Surely, I tell you, a slave is no greater than his Master, and if you're sent, you're no greater than the One Who sent you. [17]If you know this, you're happy if you do it.

[18]"I'm not talking about all of you. I know whom I've chosen. But what the Bible says has to come true: *'He who eats My bread kicks Me'*. [19]From now on I'm telling you these things before they happen so that when they happen you will believe I am the One.

[20]"I tell you the truth, if you receive anyone I send, you receive Me, and if you receive Me, you receive Him Who sent Me."

"Is it I?" — *Matthew 26:21-25; Mark 14:18-21; Luke 22:21-23*

[21]After saying this, Jesus was deeply troubled. "I tell you the truth," He declared, "one of you is going to betray Me!"
[22]The disciples started to look at one another, wondering whom He meant.
[23]One of His disciples, the one Jesus loved, was reclining close to Him. [24]Simon Peter motioned to him to ask whom He meant.
[25]Leaning back, where he was, against Jesus' chest, he asked Him, "Lord, who is it?"
[26]"I'll dip this piece of bread and give it to him," Jesus answered. "He's the one." Then he dipped it and gave it to Judas Iscariot, the son of Simon.
[27]After Judas took the piece of bread, Satan entered into him. So Jesus told him, "What you're doing, do quickly." [28]What He meant by telling him this, no one at the table knew. [29]Some thought, since Judas had the money box, Jesus was telling him, "Buy what we need for the festival," or that he should give something to the poor.
[30]Right after taking the piece of bread, Judas went outside. And it was night.
[31]When Judas had gone out, Jesus said, "Now the Son of Man is glorified, and in Him God is glorified. [32]God will also glorify Him in Himself; yes, He will glorify Him now."

---

18 Ps 41:9

Jesus Warns Peter — *Matthew 26:31-35; Mark 14:27-31; Luke 22:31-38*

[33] "Children," Jesus said, "I'm with you just a little longer. You will look for Me. but as I told the Jews, so I tell you now: Where I'm going, you can't come.

[34] "I'm giving you a new commandment: Love one another! Love one another as I have loved you. [35]By your loving one another everyone will know you're My disciples."

[36] "Lord, where are You going?" Simon Peter asked Him.

"Where I'm going you can't follow Me now," Jesus answered him; "but you will follow Me later."

[37]"Lord, why can't I follow You now?" Peter asked Him. "I'll give my life for You."

[38]"You'll give your life for Me?" Jesus asked. "I tell you the truth, the rooster will not crow until you've denied Me three times."

"I Am Going Away"

14"Don't be troubled. Believe in God, and believe in Me. [2]In My Father's house there are many rooms. If it were not so, I would have told you, because I go to prepare a place for you. [3]And when I have gone and prepared a place for you, I'll come again and take you home with Me so you'll be where I am. [4]You know the way to the place where I'm going."

[5]"Lord, we don't know where You're going," Thomas said to Him. "So how can we know the way?"

[6]"I am the Way, the Truth, and the Life," Jesus answered him. "No one comes to the Father except by Me. [7]If you have learned to know Me, you'll know My Father, too. From now on you know Him and have seen Him."

[8]Philip said to Him, "Lord, show us the Father; that's enough for us."

[9]"I've been with all of you so long," Jesus answered him, "and you don't know Me, Philip? If you have seen Me, you have seen the Father. How can you say, 'Show us the Father?' [10]Don't you believe I am in the Father and the Father is in Me? What I tell you doesn't come from Me, but the Father, Who lives in Me, is doing His works. [11]Believe Me, I am in the Father, and the Father is in Me. Or else believe Me because of My works.

[12]"I tell you the truth, if you believe in Me, you'll do the works I'm doing, and you'll do greater works than these, because I'm going to the Father, [13]and I will do anything you ask in My name in order that the Son may glorify the Father. [14]If you *ask* Me for anything *in My name*, I'll do it.

[15]"If you love Me, you will keep My commandments. [16]And I will ask the Father, and He will give you another Comforter to be with you forever. [17]He is the Spirit of truth, Whom the world cannot receive, because it doesn't see or know Him. You know Him, because He lives with you and

---

14 Zech 13:9

will be in you.

[18]"I will not leave you orphans; I'm coming back to you. [19]Only a little while and the world won't see Me anymore. But you will see Me. Because I live, you too will live. [20]On that day you will know I'm in My Father and you in Me and I in you. [21]If you have My commandments and obey them, you love Me. And if you love Me, My Father will love you, and I will love you and show Myself to you."

[22]Judas (not Iscariot) asked Him, "Lord, what has happened that You're going to show Yourself to us and not to the world?"

[23]Jesus answered him, "If you love Me, you'll keep My word, and My Father will love you, and We will come to you and live with you. [24]Anyone who doesn't love Me doesn't keep My words. And you are hearing, not what I say, but what the Father says Who sent Me.

[25]"I've told you this while I'm still with you. [26]But *the Comforter*, the Holy Spirit, *Whom the Father will send* in My name, will teach you everything and remind you of everything I told you.

[27]"*I leave peace with you; I give you My peace.* I don't give it to you as the world gives it. Don't be troubled or afraid. [28]You heard Me tell you, 'I'm going away, but I'm coming back to you.' If you loved Me, you'd be glad I'm going to the Father, because the Father is greater than I.

[29]"I've told you this now before it happens, so that when it happens, you believe. [30]I won't say much to you anymore, because the ruler of the world is coming. He has no claim on Me. [31]But I want the world to know I love the Father and am doing just what the Father ordered Me to do.

"Come, let us go."

The Vine and the Branch

15 "I am the true Vine, and My Father takes care of the vineyard. [2]He cuts away any branch of Mine that bears no fruit, and He trims any branch that bears fruit to make it bear more fruit.

[3]"What I have said to you has already made you clean. [4]Stay in Me, and I will stay in you. A branch can't bear any fruit by itself unless it remains on the vine. Neither can you if you don't stay in Me. [5]I am the Vine; you are the branches. If you stay in Me and I in you, you will bear much fruit, for without Me you can do nothing. [6]If anyone doesn't stay in Me, he's thrown away like a branch and dries up. Such branches are gathered, thrown into the fire, and burned. [7]If you stay in Me and My words stay in you, ask for anything you want, and it will be done for you. [8]You glorify My Father when you bear much fruit and show yourselves to be My disciples. [9]As the Father has loved Me, so I have loved you. Stay in My love. [10]If you obey My commandments, you'll stay in My love, as I have obeyed My Father's commandments and stay in His love. [11]I told you this so that My joy will be in you and your joy will be complete. [12]This is what I order you to

---

26 Is 66:13 27 Is 26:12

do: Love one another as I have loved you. [13]No one has a greater love than he who gives his life for his friends. [14]You're My friends if you do what I order you to do. [15]I don't call you servants anymore, because a servant doesn't know what his master is doing. But I've called you friends because I've told you everything I heard from My Father. [16]You didn't choose Me, but I chose you and appointed you to go and bear fruit that doesn't pass away and to have the Father give you anything you ask Him in My name. [17]This is what I order you to do: Love one another.

[18]"If the world hates you, you know it hated Me first. [19]If you belonged to the world, the world would love you as its own. But you don't belong to the world; I took you away from the world; that's why the world hates you. [20]Remember what I told you: 'A slave is no greater than his Master.' If they persecuted Me, they'll persecute you. If they keep My word, they'll also keep yours. [21]Now they will do all this to you on account of Me, because they don't know Him Who sent Me. [22]If I hadn't come and spoken to them, they wouldn't be sinning, but now they have no excuse for their sin. [23]Anyone who hates Me hates My Father. [24]If I hadn't done among them the works no one else has done, they wouldn't be sinning. But now they have seen and hated Me and My Father. [25]What is written in their Bible has to come true: *'They will hate Me without any reason.'*

[26]"When the Comforter comes, Whom I'll send you from the Father, the Spirit of truth, Who proceeds from the Father, He'll tell the truth about Me. [27]And you, too, tell the truth, because you've been with Me from the beginning."

Sorrow Will Turn to Joy

16"I told you this so that nothing will upset your faith. [2]You will be put out of the synagogue. Yes, the time will come when anyone who murders you will think he's serving God. [3]Men will do these things because they didn't get to know the Father or Me. [4]But I told you this so that when it happens you'll remember I told you about it. I didn't tell you this at first, because I was with you.

[5]"Now I'm going to Him Who sent Me, and none of you asks Me, 'Where are You going?' [6]But because I told you this, you are very sad. [7]But I tell you the truth, it's good for you that I go away. If I don't go away, the Comforter will not come to you. But if I go, I'll send Him to you. [8]He will come and convict the world of sin, righteousness, and judgment: [9]of sin because they don't believe in Me; [10]of righteousness because I'm going to the Father and you won't see Me anymore; [11]of judgment because the ruler of this world is judged.

[12]"I have much more to tell you, but it would be too much for you now. [13]When the Spirit of truth comes, He will lead you into the whole truth. What He will say will not come from Himself, but He'll speak what He hears and tell you what is coming. [14]He will glorify Me, because He'll take

25 *Ps 35:19; 69:4*

from what is Mine and tell it to you. [15]Everything the Father has is Mine. That is why I said, 'He takes from what is Mine and will tell it to you.'

[16]"A little while and you'll not see Me anymore; and again a little while and you'll see Me."

[17]Then some of His disciples asked one another, "What does He mean when He tells us, 'a little while and you'll not see Me; and again a little while and you'll see Me,' and 'I'm going to the Father'? " [18]So they were asking, "What does He mean when He says, 'A little while'? We don't know what He means."

[19]Jesus knew they wanted to ask Him something. "Are you trying to find out from one another," He asked them, "what I meant by saying, 'A little while and you'll not see Me; and again a little while and you'll see Me?' [20]I tell you the truth, you will cry and mourn, but the world will be glad. You will have sorrow, but your sorrow will turn to joy. [21]When a woman is going to have a child, she has pains because her time has come. But after the child is born, she's so happy a child was brought into the world she doesn't remember her pains any more. [22]You, too, are sad now; but I'll see you again, *and then you'll be filled with joy*, and no one will take your joy away from you. [23]Then you won't ask Me any questions. I tell you the truth, if you ask the Father for anything in My name, He will give it to you. [24]So far you haven't asked for anything in My name. Ask and you will receive and your joy will be complete.

[25]"I used veiled speech in telling you these things. The time is coming when I won't use veiled speech any more in talking to you, but I'll tell you about the Father in plain words. [26]Then you will ask in My name, and I don't tell you that I'll ask the Father for you. [27]The Father Himself loves you because you have loved Me and believe that I came from the Father. [28]I left the Father and came into the world; and now I'm leaving the world again and going to the Father."

[29]"Yes, now You're talking in plain words," His disciples said, "and using no veiled speech. [30]Now we know You know everything and don't need to have anyone ask You anything. That's why we believe You've come from God."

[31]"Now you believe," Jesus answered them. [32]"The hour is coming, in fact, it's here now, when you'll be scattered, everyone to his home, and you'll leave Me alone. But I'm not alone, because the Father is with Me. [33]I told you this so you will have peace in Me. In the world you have trouble. But have courage; I have conquered the world."

"Jesus' High Priestly Prayer"

17 After saying this, Jesus looked up to heaven and said: "Father, the time has come. Glorify Your Son so that Your Son will glorify You, [2]since You have given Him authority over all men, to give everlasting life to all

---

22 Is 66:14

whom You gave Him. [3]This is everlasting life — to know You, the only true God, and Jesus Christ, Whom You sent. [4]I have glorified You on earth by finishing the work You gave Me to do. [5]And now, Father, glorify Me at Your side with the glory I had with You before the world began.

[6]*"I made Your name known to the people You gave Me* out of the world. They were Yours, and You gave them to Me, and they have kept Your Word. [7]Now they know everything You gave Me comes from You, [8]because I gave them the message You gave Me. And they have accepted it and learned the truth that I came from You, and have believed You sent Me.

[9]"I pray for them. I don't pray for the world but for those You gave Me, because they are Yours. [10]All that is Mine is Yours, and what is Yours is Mine. And I am glorified in them. [11]I am no longer in the world, but they are in the world, and I am coming to You. Holy Father, keep them in Your name, which You gave Me, so that they will be one as We are one. [12]While I was with them, I kept them safe in Your name, which You gave Me. I watched over them, and none of them was lost except that lost one — what the Bible says had to come true.

[13]"But now I am coming to You, and I say this while I am in the world so that they will have all My joy in their hearts. [14]I gave them Your Word. But the world has hated them because they don't belong to the world any more than I belong to the world. [15]I'm not asking You to take them out of the world, but to keep them from the evil one. [16]They don't belong to the world any more than I belong to the world.

[17]"Make them holy by the truth; Your Word is truth. [18]As You sent Me into the world, I sent them into the world. [19]In this holy way I give Myself for them to make them holy, too, by the truth. [20]I'm not asking for them only but also for those who through their word believe in Me [21]that they all be one. As You, Father, are in Me and I in You, let them be in Us so that the world may believe You sent Me. [22]I gave them the glory You gave Me to make them one as We are one. [23]I am in them, and You are in Me to make them perfectly one that the world may know You sent Me and loved them as You loved Me.

[24]"Father, I want those You gave Me to be with Me where I am and to see My glory that You gave Me because You loved Me before the world was made. [25]Righteous Father, the world didn't know You, but I knew You, and these have learned to know You sent Me. [26]I told them and I am going to tell them Your name, so that the love You have for Me will be in them and I will be in them."

The Arrest — *Matthew 26:47-56; Mark 14:43-52; Luke 22:47-54a*

18After Jesus said this, He took His disciples to the other side of the Kidron valley where there was a garden. He and His disciples went into it.

[2]Judas, who was betraying Him, also knew the place because Jesus and His disciples often got together there. [3]So Judas took the troop of soldiers and servants from the ruling priests and Pharisees and came there

6 Ps 22:22

with lanterns and torches and weapons.

[4]Then Jesus went out, knowing exactly what was going to happen to Him. "Whom are you looking for?" He asked them.

[5] "Jesus from Nazareth," they answered Him. "I am He," Jesus told them.

Judas, ready to betray Him, was standing with them. [6]When Jesus told them, "I am He," they went backward and fell to the ground.

[7]He asked them again, "Whom are you looking for?"

"Jesus from Nazareth," they said.

[8]"I told you I am He," Jesus answered. "So if I'm the One you want, let these others go." [9]This was to make good what He had said: "I lost none of those You gave Me."[i]

[10]Then Simon Peter, who had a sword, drew it, struck the high priest's slave, and cut off his right ear. The slave's name was Malchus.

[11]"Put your sword into its scabbard," Jesus told Peter. "The cup My Father gave Me — shouldn't I drink it?"

[12]So the troop of soldiers, the tribune, and the attendants of the Jews arrested Jesus, bound Him, [13]and took Him first to Annas, because he was the father-in-law of Caiaphas, who was high priest that year. [14]It was Caiaphas who advised the Jews, "It is better that one man dies instead of the people."

PeterDeniesJesus – *Matthew 26:69-75; Mark 14:66-72; Luke 22:54b-62; John 18:25-27*

[15]Now, Simon Peter and another disciple were following Jesus. The other disciple was known to the high priest and went with Jesus into the high priest's courtyard. [16]But Peter was standing outside the door. So the other disciple, whom the high priest knew, went out and talked to the girl watching the door and brought Peter in.

[17]This doorkeeper asked Peter, "You aren't one of this man's disciples, too, are you?"

"I'm not," he answered.

[18]The slaves and the attendants were standing around and had made a heap of burning coals because it was cold. As they warmed themselves, Peter was standing with them warming himself.

Before Annas

[19]Then the high priest asked Jesus about His disciples and His teaching.

[20] "I have spoken publicly to the world," Jesus answered him. "I have always taught in a synagogue or in the temple, where all the Jews gather, and I haven't said anything in secret. [21]Why do you ask Me? Ask those who heard Me what I said to them; they know what I said."

[22]When He said this, one of the attendants standing near Jesus

slapped His face. "Is that how you answer the high priest?" he asked.

²³"If I said anything wrong," Jesus answered him, "tell us what was wrong. But if I told the truth, why do you hit Me?"

²⁴Then Annas sent Him, still bound, to Caiaphas, the high priest.

Peter Denies Again — *Matthew 26:69-75; Mark 14:66-72; Luke 22:54b-62; John 18:15-18*

²⁵Simon Peter continued to stand and warm himself. So the men asked him, "You aren't one of his disciples, too, are you?"

He denied, saying, "I'm not!"

²⁶One of the high priest's slaves, a relative of the man whose ear Peter had cut off, asked, "Didn't I see you with him in the garden?"

²⁷Again, Peter denied, and just then a rooster crowed.

Before Pilate — *Matthew 27:11-14; Mark 15:1-5; Luke 23:1-4*

²⁸The Jews took Jesus from Caiaphas to the governor's palace. It was early in the morning.

To keep from getting unclean (they wanted to celebrate the Passover), the Jews themselves didn't go into the governor's palace. ²⁹So Pilate came out to them. "What accusation are you bringing against this man?" he asked.

³⁰"If he weren't a criminal," they answered him, "we wouldn't have handed him over to you."

³¹"Take him yourselves," Pilate therefore told them, "and judge him according to your law."

"We're not allowed to kill anyone," the Jews answered him. ³²And so what Jesus said when He predicted how He would die was to come true.

³³Pilate went back into the palace and called for Jesus. "Are you the King of the Jews?" he asked Him.

³⁴"Did you think of that yourself," Jesus asked, "or did others tell you about Me?"

³⁵"Am I a Jew?" Pilate asked. "Your own people and the ruling priests handed you over to me. What did you do?"

³⁶"My kingdom is not of this world," Jesus answered. "if My kingdom were of this world, My servants would fight to keep Me from being handed over to the Jews. But now My kingdom is not of this world."

³⁷"Then you are a king?" Pilate asked Him.

"Yes, I am a king!" Jesus answered. "I was born and came into the world to testify to the truth. Everyone who lives in the truth listens to Me."

³⁸Pilate said to Him, "What is truth?" After saying this, he went out to the Jews again and told them, "I don't find this man guilty of anything.

³⁹"You have a custom that I set someone free for you at the Passover. So would you like me to set the King of the Jews free for you?"

⁴⁰Then they yelled: "Not this one but Barabbas!" Now, Barabbas was a robber.

"Look at the Man!" — *Matthew 27:27-30; Mark 15:16-19*

19Then Pilate took Jesus and had Him whipped. [2]The soldiers twisted some thorns into a crown and placed it on His head and put a purple garment on Him. [3]They went up to Him and said, "Hail, King of the Jews!" and slapped His face.

[4]Pilate went outside again. "I'm bringing him out to you," he told them, "to let you know I don't find him guilty of anything." [5]Jesus came outside wearing the crown of thorns and the purple cloak. "Look at the man!" Pilate said to them.

[6]When the ruling priests and the servants saw Him, they shouted, "Crucify, crucify him!"

"Take him yourselves," Pilate told them, "and crucify him. I don't find him guilty of anything."

[7]"We have a law," the Jews answered him, "and according to the law he must die. He has claimed to be God's Son."

[8]When Pilate heard them say that, he was frightened more than ever. [9]He went into the palace again. "Where are you from?" he asked Jesus. But Jesus didn't answer him.

[10]"Don't you speak to me?" Pilate then asked Him. "Don't you know I have the power to free you or to crucify you?"

[11]"You wouldn't have any power over Me," Jesus answered him, "if it hadn't been given to you from above. That is why the man who handed Me over to you is guilty of a greater sin."

[12]This made Pilate anxious to let Him go, but the Jews shouted, "If you let him go, you're no friend of Caesar. Anyone who makes himself a king is against Caesar."

[13]When Pilate heard this, he took Jesus outside and sat in the judge's seat at a place called Stone Pavement, or Gabbatha in the Jewish language. [14]It was the Friday of the Passover and about six o'clock.

"Look at your king!" he said to the Jews.

[15]Then they shouted, "Take him away! Take him away! Crucify him!"

"Should I crucify your king?" Pilate asked them.

"We don't have any king but Caesar," the ruling priests answered.

[16]Then Pilate handed Jesus over to them to be crucified.

"They Crucified Him" — *Matthew 27:31-44; Mark 15:20-32*
Luke 23:26-38

So they took Jesus, [17]and He, carrying His cross, went out to what was called Skull Place, which the Jews call Golgotha. [18]There they crucified Him with two others, one on each side and Jesus in the middle.

[19]Pilate also wrote a notice and put it on the cross. It read: JESUS FROM NAZARETH, THE KING OF THE JEWS. [20]Many Jews read this notice, because the place where Jesus was crucified was near the city, and it was written in Aramaic, Latin, and Greek.

[21]Then the ruling priests of the Jews told Pilate, "Don't write: 'The

King of the Jews,' but: 'He said, "I am the King of the Jews." ' "

[22]Pilate answered, "What I've written I've written."

[23]When the soldiers had crucified Jesus, they took His clothes and divided them into four parts, one for each soldier, and the tunic was left over. The tunic was without a seam, woven in one piece from top to bottom. [24]"Let's not tear it," they said to one another, "but let's throw lots and see who gets it" — what the Bible said had to come true: *They divided My clothes among them, and for My garment they threw lots.*" So that's what the soldiers did.

Mary

[25]Now, His mother and her sister, Mary the wife of Clopas, and Mary from Magdala were standing near Jesus' cross.

[26]Jesus saw His mother and the disciple He loved standing near. "Woman," He said to His mother, "there is your son!" [27]Then He said to the disciple, "There is your mother!"

The disciple took her and from that time on had her in his home.

Jesus Dies — *Matthew 27:45-56; Mark 15:33-41; Luke 23:44-49*

[28]After this, knowing everything had now been done, and to have the words of the Bible come true, Jesus said, "*I am thirsty.*"

[29]A jar full of *sour wine* was standing there. So they put a sponge soaked in the wine on a hyssop stem and held it to His mouth.

[30]When Jesus had taken the wine, He said, "*It is finished.*"

Then He bowed His head and gave up His spirit.

No Bone Broken

[31]Since it was Friday and the Jews didn't want the bodies to stay on the crosses on Saturday, because that Sabbath was an important day, they asked Pilate to have the legs of the men broken and the bodies taken away. [32]So the soldiers came and broke the legs of the first man and then of the other who had been crucified with Him.

[33]But when they came to Jesus and saw He was dead already, they didn't break His legs, [34]but one of the soldiers stuck a spear into His side, and immediately blood and water came out. [35]He who saw it has testified about it, and his testimony is true, and he knows he is telling the truth so that you, too, will believe.

[36]In this way what the Bible said had to come true: "*None of His bones will be broken.*" [37]And it says in another place: "*They will look at Him Whom they pierced.*"

---

24 Ps 22:18   *28-29* Ps 69:21   *30* Ps 22:31

Jesus Is Buried — *Matthew 27:57-61; Mark 15:42-47; Luke 23:50-56*

[38]Later Joseph from Arimathea — who was a disciple of Jesus, but secretly because he was afraid of the Jews — asked Pilate to let him take Jesus' body away. Pilate let him have it. So he came and took His body away. [39]Then came also Nicodemus, who had first come to Jesus at night. He brought a mixture of myrrh and aloes, about 75 pounds.

[40]They took Jesus' body and wrapped it with the spices in linen according to the Jewish custom of burying the dead.

[41]There was a garden at the place where Jesus was crucified, and in the garden was a new grave, in which no one had yet been laid. [42]Here, then — because it was Friday (when the Jews got ready for the Sabbath) and the grave was near — they placed Jesus.

Peter and John — *Matthew 28:1-10; Mark 16:1-8; Luke 24:1-12*

20 Early on Sunday morning while it was still dark Mary from Magdala went to the grave and saw the stone had been taken away from the grave. [2]So she ran and came to Simon Peter and the other disciple, whom Jesus loved. "They've taken the Lord out of the grave," she told them, "and we don't know where they laid Him."

[3]So Peter and the other disciple started out for the grave. [4]The two were running side by side, but the other disciple ran faster than Peter and got to the grave first. [5]He looked in and saw the linen wrappings lying there but didn't go in.

[6]When Simon Peter got there after him, he went into the grave. He saw the linen wrappings lying there, [7]also the cloth that had been on Jesus' head, not lying with the linen wrappings but rolled up in a place by itself. [8]Then the other disciple, who got to the grave first, also went in, saw it, and believed. [9]They didn't know yet what the Bible meant when it said He had to rise from the dead.

[10]So the disciples went home again.

"Mary!"

[11]Mary stood outside, facing the grave and crying. As she cried, she looked into the grave [12]and saw two angels in white clothes sitting where Jesus' body had been lying, one at the head and the other at the feet. [13]"Woman, why are you crying?" they asked her.

"They've taken my Lord away," she told them, "and I don't know where they laid Him." [14]After she said this, she turned around and saw Jesus standing there but didn't know it was Jesus. [15]"Woman, why are you crying?" Jesus asked her. "Whom are you looking for?"

"Sir," she said to Him, thinking He was the gardener, "if you carried Him away, tell me where you laid Him, and I will take Him away."

---

36 Ex 12:46; Num 9:12; Ps 34:20   *37 Zech 12:10*

¹⁶Jesus said to her, "Mary!"

She turned. "Rabboni!" she said to Him in the Jewish language. (The word means "Teacher.")

¹⁷"Don't hold on to Me," Jesus told her. "I didn't go up to the Father yet. But go to My brothers and tell them, 'I am going up to My Father and your Father, to My God and your God.'"

¹⁸Mary from Magdala went and told the disciples, "I saw the Lord," and that He said this to her.

Behind Locked Doors — *Luke 24:36-48*

¹⁹That Sunday evening the doors were locked where the disciples were, because they were afraid of the Jews. Then Jesus came and stood among them and said to them, "Peace to you!" ²⁰When He said this, He showed them His hands and His side. Then the disciples were delighted to see the Lord.

²¹"Peace to you!" Jesus said to them again. "As the Father sent Me, so I send you." ²²When He had said this, He breathed on them and said, "Receive the Holy Spirit. ²³Whenever you forgive people's sins, they are forgiven; whenever you do not forgive them, they are not forgiven."ʲ

Thomas Sees Jesus

²⁴But Thomas, one of the twelve, who was called Twin, was not with them when Jesus came. ²⁵So the other disciples told him, "We saw the Lord."

"Unless I see the marks of the nails in His hands," he told them, "and put my finger in the marks of the nails and put my hand in His side, I won't believe it."

²⁶A week later His disciples were again in the house, and Thomas was with them. The doors were locked, but Jesus came and stood among them. "Peace to you!" He said. ²⁷Then He told Thomas, "Put your finger here, and look at My hands— and take your hand and put it in My side. And don't doubt but believe."

²⁸"My Lord and my God!" Thomas answered Him.

²⁹"Do you believe because you've seen Me?" Jesus asked him. "Blessed are those who have not seen and yet have believed."

Much More

³⁰His disciples saw Jesus do many other miracles that are not written in this book. ³¹But these things are written so that you believe Jesus is the Christ, God's Son, and by believing have life in His name.

---

j - 23   Literally: "they have not been forgiven"; the Greek uses a perfect tense here to indicate action which is completed with continuing results.

Breakfast with Jesus

21 After this, Jesus showed Himself again to the disciples at the Sea of Tiberias.[k] This is how He showed Himself.

[2]Simon Peter, Thomas (called Twin), Nathanael from Cana in Galilee, Zebedee's sons, and two other disciples of Jesus were together. [3]Simon Peter said to the others, "I'm going fishing."

"We're going with you," they told him.

They went out and got into the boat. But that night they caught nothing. [4]When morning came, Jesus stood on the shore. But the disciples didn't know it was Jesus.

[5]"Lads, you don't have any fish, do you?" Jesus asked them. They answered Him, "No."

[6]"Drop the net on the right side of the boat," He told them, "and you will find some." So they dropped it. And now they couldn't pull it in, there were so many fish.

[7]The disciple whom Jesus loved said to Peter, "It is the Lord." When Simon Peter heard him say, "It is the Lord," he put on the coat he had taken off, fastened it with his belt, and jumped into the lake. [8]But the other disciples, who were not far from the shore, only about 100 yards, came in the small boat, dragging the net full of fish.

[9]As they stepped out on the shore, they saw burning coals there with fish lying on them, and bread.

[10]"Bring some of the fish you just caught," Jesus told them. [11]Simon Peter got into the small boat and pulled the net on the shore. It was filled with 153 big fish. Although there were so many, the net wasn't torn.

[12]"Come, have breakfast," Jesus told them. None of the disciples dared to ask Him, "Who are You?" They knew it was the Lord. [13]Jesus came, took the bread, and gave it to them, and also the fish.

[14]This was the third time Jesus showed Himself to the disciples after He rose from the dead.

"Do You Love Me?"

[15]When they had eaten breakfast, Jesus asked Simon Peter, "Simon, son of John, do you love Me more than these do?"

"Yes, Lord," he answered Him, "You know I love You."

"Feed My lambs," Jesus told him.

[16]"Simon, son of John," He asked him a second time, "do you love Me?"

"Yes, Lord," he answered Him, "You know I love You."

"Be a shepherd of My sheep," Jesus told him.

[17]"Simon, son of John," He asked him a third time, "do you love Me?"

Peter felt sad because He asked him a third time, "Do you love Me?"

"Lord, You know everything," he answered Him, "You know I love You."

"Feed My sheep," Jesus told him. [18]"I tell you the truth, when you

---

k - 1   Alternate name for the Sea of Galilee.

were younger, you used to fasten your belt and go where you wanted to. But when you're old, you'll stretch out your hands, and someone else will tie you and take you where you don't want to go." [19]He said this to show by what kind of death Peter would glorify God. After saying this, He told him, "Follow Me."

[20]Peter turned and saw the disciple whom Jesus loved following them. He was the one who at the supper leaned against Jesus' chest and asked, "Lord, who is going to betray You?" [21]When Peter saw him, he asked Jesus, "Lord, what about him?"

[22]"If I want him to stay until I come," Jesus asked him, "what is that to you? You follow Me." [23]And so it was said among the Christians, "That disciple will not die." But Jesus didn't say, "He will not die," but, "If I want him to stay until I come, what is that to you?"

[24]This is the disciple who testified about these things and wrote this. And we know what he testifies is true.

Much More

[25]Jesus also did many other things. If every one of these were written down, I suppose the world would not have room for the books that would be written.

LUKE WRITES
THE ACTS OF THE APOSTLES
ACTS

1 IN MY FIRST BOOK, Theophilus, I wrote about everything Jesus did and taught [2]until the day He was taken up to heaven after giving orders by the Holy Spirit to the apostles He had chosen.

Jesus Goes Up to Heaven

[3]After His suffering Jesus proved to the apostles in many convincing ways that He was alive as He showed Himself to them for forty days and talked about God's kingdom.

[4]When He met with them, He ordered them not to leave Jerusalem but to wait for what the Father had promised: "You heard Me tell about Him: [5]John baptized with water, but in a few days you will be baptized with the Holy Spirit."

[6]When they came together, they asked Him, "Lord, are You now going to reestablish the kingdom of Israel?"

[7]"It isn't for you to know," He told them, "what times or periods the Father has set by His own authority. [8]But when the Holy Spirit comes on you, you will receive power and will testify of Me in Jerusalem, in all Judea and Samaria, and to the farthest parts of the world."

[9]When He had said this and while they were watching Him, He was lifted up, and a cloud took Him away so they couldn't see Him anymore.

[10]As He was going and they were gazing up into the sky, two men in white clothes were standing right beside them. [11]"Men of Galilee," they asked, "why are you standing here looking up to heaven? This Jesus, Who was taken away from you to heaven, will come back the same way you saw Him go to heaven."

[12]Then they went back to Jerusalem from the Mount of Olives, as it was called (it's near Jerusalem, only half a mile away).

There Must Be Twelve

[13]When they came into the city, they went to the second-floor room where they were staying — Peter, John, James, and Andrew; Philip and Thomas; Bartholomew and Matthew; James, the son of Alphaeus, Simon the Zealot, and Judas, the son of James.

[14]With one mind these all kept praying together. With them were the women, including Jesus' mother Mary, and His brothers.

[15]In those days Peter got up among the disciples (a crowd of them was there, about 120), and he said, [16]"Brothers, long ago the Holy Spirit spoke through David about Judas, who led the men that arrested Jesus. And what He wrote had to come true. [17]Judas was one of us and was given a share in the work we're doing. [18]With the money he got for his crime he bought a piece of land; and falling headfirst, he burst in the middle, and all his intestines poured out. [19]Everyone living in Jerusalem heard about it. And so that piece of land is called Akeldama in their language; the word means 'Place of Blood'. [20]It is written in the book of Psalms: *'His home should be deserted, and no one should live there'*, and *'Someone else should take over his office'*. Then someone should be added to our number as a witness of His resurrection. [21]He should be one of these men who went with us all the time the Lord Jesus went in and out among us, [22]from John's baptism to the day He was taken up from us."

[23]The disciples named two: Joseph (called Barsabbas; he was also called Justus) and Matthias. [24]Then they prayed, "Lord, You know the hearts of all. Show us which of these two You have chosen [25]to serve in this office of apostle, which Judas left to go where he belonged."

[26]They provided lots for them, and so Matthias was chosen and added to the eleven apostles.

The Holy Spirit Comes

2 The day of Pentecost[a] came, and they were all together in one place. [2]Suddenly a sound like a violent blast of wind came from heaven and filled the whole house where they were sitting. [3]They saw tongues like flames that separated, and one rested on each of them. [4]They were all filled with the Holy Spirit and started to speak in other languages as the Spirit gave them the ability to speak.

[5]Jews who feared God had come from every nation under heaven to live in Jerusalem. [6]When that sound came, the crowd gathered and was dumbfounded because each one heard the disciples speak his own language. [7]Amazed and wondering, they asked, "Don't all these who are speaking come from Galilee? [8]And how does every one of us hear his own language he was born in — [9]Parthians, Medes, Elamites, and people living in Mesopotamia, Judea and Cappadocia, Pontus and the province of Asia, [10]Phrygia and Pamphilia, Egypt and the country near Cyrene in Libya, the visitors from Rome, Jews and those who have accepted the Jewish religion, [11]people from Crete and Arabia? In our own languages we hear them tell about God's wonderful things." [12]They were all amazed and puzzled. "What can this mean?" they asked one another. [13]Others sneered: "They're full of new wine."

---

20 *Ps 69:25; Ps 109:8*

---

a - 1   A festival on the fiftieth day after Passover.

Peter's Pentecost Sermon

¹⁴Then Peter got up with the eleven, raised his voice, and addressed them: "Jews and all you who live in Jerusalem, understand this, and listen to what I say. ¹⁵These men are not drunk, as you suppose. Why, it's only nine in the morning. ¹⁶No, this is what the prophet Joel spoke about:

¹⁷'In the last days,' *God says,*

> *'I will pour out My Spirit on all people.*
> *Then your sons and your daughters will speak God's Word,*
> *your young men will have visions*
> *and your old men will have dreams.*

¹⁸*In those days*

> *I will pour out My Spirit on My servants, both men and women,*
> *and they will speak God's Word.*

¹⁹*I will give you startling wonders in the sky* above

> *and* marvelous signs *on the earth* below;
> *blood and fire and a cloud of smoke;*

²⁰*the sun will turn dark and the moon to blood*

> *before the coming of the Lord's great and splendid day.*

²¹*Then everyone who calls on the Lord's name will be saved.'*

²²"Men of Israel, listen to what I have to say: Jesus from Nazareth — God showed you Who the Man is by doing miracles, startling wonders, and miraculous signs through Him among you, as you know. ²³God definitely planned and intended to have Him betrayed, and so you had wicked men nail Him to a cross, and you killed Him. ²⁴But God set aside the pains of death and raised Him — death could not hold Him. ²⁵David says of Him:

> *'I always see the Lord before Me.*
> *He is at My right hand*
> *so that I will not be shaken.*

²⁶*And so My heart is glad, and My tongue rejoices,*

> *yes, even My body will rest hopefully,*

²⁷*because You will not leave Me in the grave*

> *or let Your Loved One experience decay.*

²⁸*You show Me ways of life.*

> *You will fill Me with joy by being with Me.'*

²⁹"Fellow Jews, I can tell you frankly our ancestor David died and was buried, and his grave is here to this day. ³⁰He was a prophet and knew *God had sworn to him to put One of his descendants on his throne.* ³¹David saw what was ahead and said the Christ would rise again: *He was not deserted when He was dead,* and His body *did not experience decay.* ³²God has raised this Jesus — we're all witnesses of that. ³³Lifted up to God's right hand and receiving from the Father the promised Holy Spirit, He has poured out what you see and hear. ³⁴David didn't go up to heaven, but he says: *'The Lord says to my Lord, "Sit at My right* ³⁵*until I make Your enemies Your*

17-21 Joel 2:28-32   *25-28* Ps 16:8-11   *30* Ps 89:3-4; 132:11
31 Ps 16:10   *34-35* Ps 110:1

footstool." ' "

36"Then all the people of Israel should know it's true that God made Him Lord and Christ — this Jesus Whom you crucified."

37When the people heard this, they were cut to the heart. They asked Peter and the other apostles, "Fellow Jews, what should we do?"

38Peter answered them, "Repent and be baptized, every one of you, in the name of Jesus Christ for the forgiveness of your sins, and you will be given the Holy Spirit. 39What is promised belongs to you, to your children, and to all *who are far away*, all *whom the Lord* our God *will call*."

40He said much more to warn them. "Be saved from these crooked people," he urged them. 41Those who accepted what he said were baptized. And that day about 3,000 persons were added.

How Christians Lived

42They were loyal to what the apostles taught in their fellowship, in breaking of bread, and in the prayers. 43Awe came on everyone — the apostles were doing many wonders and miracles. 44All who believed were together and shared everything with one another. 45They would sell their lands and other property and distribute the money to anyone as he needed it. 46All were one at heart as they went to the temple regularly every day. They had their meals in their homes and ate their food with glad and simple hearts, 47praising God and having the good will of all the people. And every day the Lord added to their number those who were being saved.

Crippled From Birth

3 Peter and John were going up to the temple for the hour of prayer at three in the afternoon. 2Now there was a man who had been crippled from his birth. Men would carry him and put him down every day at the temple gate called Beautiful so he could beg the people for gifts as they went into the temple. 3When he saw Peter and John were going into the temple, he asked them for a gift.

4Peter and John looked at him. "Look at us!" Peter said. 5He looked at them, expecting to get something from them. 6"I don't have any silver or gold," Peter said, "but I'll give you what I have. In the name of Jesus Christ from Nazareth, walk!" 7He took hold of his right hand and raised him up. Immediately his feet and ankles were made strong. 8He jumped up, stood, and started to walk. And he went with them into the temple, walking, jumping, and praising God.

9When all the people saw him walking and praising God, 10they knew he was the man who used to sit and beg at the Beautiful gate of the temple, and they were very much surprised and amazed to see what had happened to him. 11As he clung to Peter and John, all the people came running together to them in Solomon's Porch, as it was called. They were dumbfounded.

39 Is 57:19; Joel 2:32

[12]When Peter saw the people, he said to them, "Men of Israel, why are you wondering about this, or why are you staring at us as if by our own power or piety we had made him walk? [13]*The God of Abraham, Isaac, and Jacob*, the God of our fathers, has *glorified His Servant* Jesus, Whom you delivered and denied before Pilate when he had decided to let Him go. [14]You denied the holy and righteous One and asked to have a murderer given to you. [15]You killed the Author of life. But God raised Him from the dead — we're witnesses of that. [16]Through faith in His name, His name made this man strong whom you see and know. The faith that Jesus works has given him this perfect health right in front of all of you.

[17]"And now, fellow Jews, I know that like your rulers you didn't know what you were doing, [18]but in this way God did what He predicted by all the prophets — His Christ had to suffer. [19]Repent then, and turn, to have your sins wiped out that a time may come when the Lord refreshes you [20]and sends Jesus, Whom He appointed to be your Savior [21]and Whom heaven had to receive until the time when everything will be restored, as God said long ago by His holy prophets.

[22]"Moses said: *'The Lord* our *God will raise One of your people to be a Prophet to you like me. Listen to everything He tells* you. [23]*And destroy anyone among the people who will not listen to that Prophet.'* [24]Samuel and all the other prophets after him, as many as have spoken, told about these days. [25]You are the heirs of the prophets and of the covenant God made with our fathers when He said to Abraham: *'And in your Descendant all the people on earth will be blessed.'* [26]Now that God has given *His Servant*, He sent Him first to you to bless you by *turning* every one of you *from* your *wicked ways.*"

In Court

4 While they were talking to the people, the priests, the captain of the temple, and the Sadducees stepped up to them, [2]much annoyed because they were teaching the people and preaching that in Jesus the dead rise. [3]They arrested them, and since it was already evening, they put them in prison until the next day.

[4]But many of those who had heard the Word believed, and the number of the men grew to about 5,000.

[5]The next day their rulers, elders, and Bible scholars met in Jerusalem [6]with Annas the high priest, Caiaphas, John, Alexander, and all the others of the high priest's family. [7]And they had the two men stand before them. "By what power or name did you do this?" they asked.

[8]Then Peter was filled with the Holy Spirit. "Rulers of the people and elders," he said to them. [9]"if we're questioned today about helping a crippled man, how he was made well, [10]all of you and all the people of Israel should know this man stands healthy before you by the name of Jesus Christ from

---

13 Ex 3:6; Is 42:1; 52:13   22 Deut 18:15, 18-19   23 Lev 23:29; Deut 18:19
25 Gen 12:3; 18:18; 22:18; 26:4; 28:14; Ps 72:17   26 Is 42:1

Nazareth, Whom you crucified but God raised from the dead. ¹¹He is *the Stone rejected* by you *builders and has become the Cornerstone.* ¹²No one else can save us, because in all the world there is *only one name* given us *by which we must be saved.*"

¹³When they found out Peter and John had no education or training, they were surprised to see how boldly they spoke. Then they realized these men had been with Jesus. ¹⁴And seeing the healed man standing with them, they couldn't say anything against them. ¹⁵So they ordered them to leave the court and talked the matter over among themselves: ¹⁶"What should we do with these men? They've done a miracle; everyone living in Jerusalem can see it clearly, and we can't deny it. ¹⁷But to keep this from spreading any more among the people, let's warn them never again to speak to anyone in this name."

¹⁸They called Peter and John and ordered them not to say or teach anything in the name of Jesus.

¹⁹Peter and John answered them, "Does God consider it right to listen to you and not to God? Judge for yourselves. ²⁰We can't stop telling what we've seen and heard."

²¹Once more they threatened them and then let them go. They couldn't find any way to punish them, because all the people were praising God for what had happened; ²²the man who had been healed by this miracle was over 40 years old.

The Church Prays

²³When Peter and John were free again, they went to their friends and told them everything the ruling priests and spiritual leaders had said. ²⁴When they heard it, they all raised their voices together to God and said, "Lord, You *made heaven and earth, the sea, and everything in them.* ²⁵You said by the Holy Spirit through our ancestor, Your servant David:

> *Why do the nations rage*
> *and the people plan in vain*
> ²⁶*The kings of the earth stand ready,*
> *and the rulers get together*
> *against the Lord and His Anointed.*

²⁷"Herod and Pontius Pilate *certainly got together* with *non-Jews and the people* of Israel in this city against *Your* holy *Servant* Jesus, *Whom You anointed,* ²⁸to do everything You by Your will and power long ago decided should be done.

²⁹"And now, Lord, see how they're threatening, and grant that Your servants speak Your Word very boldly ³⁰as You stretch out Your hand to heal and do miracles and wonders by the name of *Your* holy *Servant* Jesus."

³¹When they had prayed, the place where they were meeting was shaken, and they were all filled with the Holy Spirit and boldly spoke God's Word.

---

11 Ps 118:22   12 Hos 13:4   24 Ex 20:11; Ps 146:6; Neh 9:6
25-27 Ps 2:1-2   27,30 Is 42:1

Sharing

³²The whole group of believers was one in heart and soul. And no one called anything he had his own, but they shared everything.

³³With great power the apostles told the truth that the Lord Jesus had risen, and much good will rested on all of them.

³⁴None of them was in need, because all who had land or houses would sell them and bring the money they got for them ³⁵and lay it at the apostles' feet. Then it was distributed to each one as he needed it. ³⁶There was Joseph, for example, a descendant of Levi, born on Cyprus. The apostles called him Barnabas, which means "a man of comfort". ³⁷He had some land and sold it and brought the money and laid it at the apostles' feet.

Ananias and Sapphira

5 But a man by the name of Ananias and his wife Sapphira sold some property; ²he kept some of the money for himself — and his wife knew about it — and some of it he brought and laid at the apostles' feet.

³"Ananias," Peter asked, "why did Satan fill your heart so that you should lie to the Holy Spirit and keep back some of the money you got for the land? ⁴While you had the land, wasn't it your own? And after it was sold, couldn't you have done as you pleased with the money? How could you think of doing such a thing? You didn't lie to men but to God!"

⁵When Ananias heard him say this, he fell down and died. And all who heard of it were terrified. ⁶The young men got up, wrapped him up, carried him out, and buried him.

⁷About three hours later his wife came in. She didn't know what had happened. ⁸"Tell me," Peter asked her, "did you sell the land for that price?"

"Yes, that was the price," she answered.

⁹"Why did you two agree to put the Lord's Spirit to a test?" Peter asked her. "There at the door are the feet of those who buried your husband, and they'll carry you out."

¹⁰Immediately she fell down at his feet and died. When the young men came in, they found her dead and carried her out and buried her beside her husband. ¹¹The whole church and all others who heard about it were terrified.

Many Miracles

¹²Many miracles and startling wonders were done among the people by the apostles' hands. And they were all together in Solomon's Porch. ¹³None of the others dared to come too near them. But the people thought very highly of them, ¹⁴and still more believers, a large number of men and women, were added to the Lord. ¹⁵As a result people carried their sick out into the streets and laid them down on cots and mats, to have at least Peter's shadow fall on any one of them when he went by. ¹⁶Even from the towns around Jerusalem crowds would gather, bringing their sick and those who

were troubled by unclean spirits, and they were all made well.

In the Jewish Council

[17]The high priest and all who were with him, that is, the party of the Sadducees, became very jealous. [18]They arrested the apostles and put them in the public prison.

[19]But at night an angel of the Lord opened the prison doors and brought them out. [20]"Go," he said, "stand in the temple, and keep on telling the people everything about this life." [21]After they had heard him, they went into the temple early in the morning and started to teach.

The high priest and those who were with him came and called the council and all the elders of Israel together and sent men to the prison to get the apostles. [22]But when the men got there, they didn't find them in prison. They came back and reported, [23]"We found the prison very securely locked and the guards standing at the doors, but when we opened them, we found no one inside." [24]When the captain of the temple and the ruling priests heard this, they were puzzled as to what could have happened to them.

[25]Then someone came and told them, "The men you put in prison are standing in the temple teaching the people."

[26]Then the captain and his men went and got them, but without using force, because they were afraid the people would stone them. [27]They brought them and had them stand before the council.

The high priest questioned them and said, [28]"We gave you strict orders not to teach in this name, and here you have filled Jerusalem with your teaching. And you want to get us punished for killing this man."

[29]Peter and the other apostles answered, "We must obey God rather than men. [30]*You hanged* Jesus *on a cross* and murdered Him. But the God of our fathers raised Him [31]and took Him up to His right hand as Leader and Savior in order to give the people of Israel repentance and forgiveness of sins. [32]We are witnesses of these things — we and the Holy Spirit, Whom God has given those who obey Him."

[33]When they heard this, they became furious and wanted to kill them. [34]But a Pharisee in the court by the name of Gamaliel, a teacher of the Law, highly respected by all the people, got up and ordered the men taken outside for a little while.

[35]"Men of Israel," he said to them, "consider carefully what you're going to do   with these men. [36]Sometime ago Theudas appeared, claiming to be somebody, and about four hundred men joined him. He was killed, and all who followed him were scattered, and they disappeared.

[37]"After him, at the time of the census, came Judas from Galilee and got people to follow him in a revolt. He perished, too, and all who followed him were scattered.

[38]"And now I tell you, keep away from these men and let them alone. If it's only men planning or doing this, it will break down, [39]but if it's God,

_____

30 Deut 21:22

you won't be able to stop them. You may even be fighting against God."

⁴⁰They took his advice. They called the apostles, beat them, ordered them not to speak in the name of Jesus, and let them go. ⁴¹The apostles left the court, happy to have been thought worthy to suffer shame for Jesus. ⁴²And every day, in the temple and from house to house, they kept right on teaching and telling the good news that Jesus is the Christ.

Seven Helpers

6 In those days, as the number of the disciples grew larger and larger, a complaint was brought against those who spoke Aramaic by those who spoke Greek that every day, when the food was handed out, their widows were being neglected.

²The twelve called the whole group of disciples together and said, "No one likes it if we give up teaching God's Word and serve at tables. ³Now, fellow disciples, appoint seven men among you whom people speak well of, who are full of the Spirit and wisdom, and we'll put them in charge of this work. ⁴Then we'll devote ourselves to praying and to serving by speaking the Word."

⁵The whole group liked the idea. So they chose Stephen, a man full of faith and of the Holy Spirit, Philip, Prochorus, Nicanor, Timon, Parmenas, and Nicolaus (who had become a Jew in Antioch). ⁶They had these men stand before the apostles, who prayed and laid their hands on them.

⁷God's Word kept on spreading, and the number of disciples in Jerusalem was getting very large. Even a large crowd of the priests were coming to faith's obedience."

Stephen Is Arrested

⁸Stephen, full of God's gifts and power, was doing great wonders and miracles among the people. ⁹Some men of the Synagogue of the Freedmen, as it was called, and of men from Cyrene and Alexandria, and men from Cilicia and Asia got up to argue with Stephen. ¹⁰But they couldn't resist the wisdom and the Spirit by Whom he spoke.

¹¹Then they secretly got some men to say, "We heard him slander Moses and God." ¹²They stirred up the people, the elders, and the men of the Law, and rushing at him, took him by force and brought him before the Jewish council. ¹³There they had *witnesses* stand up and lie, "This man won't stop talking against the holy place and the Law. ¹⁴We heard him say, 'This Jesus from Nazareth will tear this place down and change the customs Moses gave us.'"

¹⁵All who sat in the council stared at him and saw his face — it was like an angel's face.

13 Prov 14:5

Stephen Defends Himself

7 Then the high priest asked, "Is this so?"

[2] He answered, "Fellow Jews and fathers, listen. *The God of glory* appeared to our father Abraham while he was in Mesopotamia before he lived in Haran. [3] *'Leave your country and your relatives,' God told him, 'and come to the country I will show you.'*

[4] "Then Abraham left the country of the Chaldeans and lived in Haran. After his father died, God had him move from there to this country where you live now. [5] He *gave* him nothing to call his own, *not even enough to set his foot on*, but promised *to give it to him as his own and to his descendants after him*, although he had no child. [6] And God spoke in this way — that *his descendants would be strangers in a foreign country, and its people would make slaves of them and mistreat them four hundred years.* [7] *'But I will punish the people whom they will serve,'* God said, *'and after that they will leave and worship Me in this* place.' [8] He gave him a *covenant* of *circumcision.* And so, when his son Isaac was born, *he circumcised him on the eighth day.* Isaac did the same to his son Jacob, and Jacob to his twelve sons, the ancestors of our tribes.

[9] "These ancestors *were jealous of Joseph and sold him into Egypt,* but *God was with him.* [10] He rescued him from all his troubles *and gave him the good will of Pharaoh, the king of Egypt, and wisdom as he stood before him — Pharaoh made him ruler of Egypt and of his whole palace.* [11] But a *famine* with much misery *came over all Egypt* and *Canaan*, and our ancestors couldn't find any food. [12] When *Jacob heard there was grain in Egypt,* he sent our ancestors on their first trip. [13] On the second, *Joseph told his brothers who he was,* and Pharaoh learned about the family from which Joseph came. [14] Joseph sent and had his father Jacob come to him, and *all* his *relatives — seventy-five persons.* [15] And so *Jacob went down to Egypt.* Then *he and our ancestors died* [16] and *were brought to Shechem* and *laid* in the tomb *Abraham bought* for a sum of money *from Hamor's sons at Shechem.*

[17] "When the time that God set in His promise to Abraham had almost come, the people *had grown and their number had become very large* in Egypt. [18] And now *a different king who knew nothing of Joseph became ruler of Egypt.* [19] He *was shrewd in scheming against* our people, and he *mistreated* our fathers by making them abandon their babies so they wouldn't live.

[20] "At that time Moses was born, and he was a *beautiful* child before God. For *three months* he was cared for in his father's home. [21] When he

---

2 *Ps 29:3*   **3** *Gen 12:1*   **5** *Deut 2:5; Gen 12:7; 13:15; 17:8; 48:4*
  6-7 *Gen 15:13-14; Ex 2:22; 12:40-41; Ex 3:12*   **8** *Gen 17:10-12; 21:4*
9 *Gen 37:11,28; 45:4; Gen 39:2-3,21-23*   **10** *Gen 39:21; 41:46; Gen 41:40-41,43; Ps 105:21*
11 *Gen 41:54-56; 42:5*   **12** *Gen 42:2*   **13** *Gen 45:1*
14-15 *Gen 46:6,27; 49:33; Ex 1:5-6; Deut 10:22*   **16** *Gen 50:13; Josh 24:32*
   17-19 *Ex 1:7-8,10-11,22*   **20** *Ex 2:2*

was set out, *Pharaoh's daughter took him up* and raised him *as her son.* [22]Moses was educated in all the wisdom of the Egyptians and became a great man in what he said and did. [23]When he was forty years old, he thought he would *visit his own people, the Israelites.* [24]There he saw a man wronged and defended him. He avenged the man who was mistreated, by *striking down the Egyptian.* [25]He thought his own people would understand he was the one by whom God was freeing them, but they didn't understand. [26]*The next day he came* to them *as they were fighting*, and he tried to make peace between them. 'Men, you are brothers,' he said. 'Why are you doing wrong to one another?'

[27]"But *the man who was doing wrong to his neighbor* pushed Moses away. *'Who made you ruler and judge over us?'* he asked. [28]*'Do you want to kill me as you killed the Egyptian yesterday?'* [29]When he said that, *Moses fled and became a stranger in the land of Midian.* There he had *two sons.*

[30]"And so forty years passed. Then *an Angel appeared to him in the wilderness* of Mount Sinai *in the flames of a burning thornbush.* [31]Moses was amazed to see this. As *he went closer to examine it, the Lord said,* [32]*'I am the God of your fathers, the God of Abraham, Isaac, and Jacob.'* Moses started to tremble and *didn't dare to look.* [33]*The Lord told him, 'Take your sandals off; the place where you're standing is holy ground.* [34]*I have seen how my people are mistreated in Egypt. I have heard their groaning and have come down to rescue them. And now come, I will send you to Egypt.'*

[35]"This Moses whom they rejected by saying, *'Who made you ruler and judge?'* this one God sent to rule and free them with the help of the Angel he saw in the thornbush. [36]He led them out, doing *startling wonders and miracles in Egypt*, at the Red Sea, and *for forty years in the desert.* [37]It was this Moses who told the Israelites: *'God will raise One of your people to be a Prophet to you like me.'* [38]Moses was in the congregation in the wilderness with the Angel Who spoke to him on Mount Sinai and with our fathers. He received living truths to give you, [39]but our fathers refused to obey him. Yes, they rejected him, and their hearts *turned away to Egypt.* [40]*'Make gods for us who will lead us,'* they told Aaron. *'This Moses who took us out of Egypt — we don't know what happened to him.'* [41]That was the time *they made a calf, brought a sacrifice* to the idol, *and delighted* in what their hands had made.

[42]"So God turned away from them and abandoned them to worship *the sun, the moon, and the stars*, as it is written in the book of the prophets: *'People of Israel, you didn't offer Me slaughtered animals and sacrifices during the forty years in the desert, did you? [43]You even took along the tent of Moloch, the star of the god Rompha, and the images you made* in order to worship them. *And so I will send you away to live on the other side* of Babylon.'

---

21 *Ex 2:5,10*   23-26 *Ex 2:11-12*   27-29 *Ex 2:13-15,22; 18:3*
30-34 *Ex 2:24; 3:1-8,10; 4:19*   35 *Ex 2:14*   36 *Ex 7:3; Num 14:33-34*
37 *Deut 18:15,18* 3   39 *Num 14:3-4*
40 *Ex 32:1,23*   41 *Ex 32:4,6,35*   42 *Jer 7:18; 19:13*   42-43 *Amos 5:25-27*

[44]"In the desert our fathers had *the tabernacle in which God spoke to His people*. It was built *like the model Moses had seen*, just as He Who *spoke to Moses* had ordered him *to make* it. [45]From him our fathers received it, and they brought it here under Joshua when they took the country from the nations God drove out before our fathers, and here it was until the time of David. [46]He found God was kind to him and asked that *he might find a home for the God of Jacob*. [47]And *Solomon built Him a temple*.

[48]"But the Most High God doesn't live in anything made by human hands, as the prophet says: [49]*Heaven is My throne, and the earth My footstool. What kind of temple will you build Me, the Lord asks, or what place is there where I can rest?* [50]*Didn't My hand make all this?*'

[51]"*How stubborn you are and pagan at heart and deaf to the truth!* You're always *opposing the Holy Spirit*. Your fathers did it, and so do you! [52]Was there ever a prophet your fathers didn't persecute? They killed those who announced, 'The Righteous One will come!' and now you betrayed and murdered Him. [53]Angels were ordered to give you the Law, but you didn't keep it!"

Stoning Stephen

[54]While they were listening, the men of the council became furious and ground their teeth at him. [55]But he, full of the Holy Spirit, gazed up to heaven and saw God's glory and Jesus standing at God's right hand. [56]"Look!" he said, "I see heaven opened and the Son of Man standing at God's right hand."

[57]But they yelled at the top of their voices, held their ears shut, and all together rushed at him. [58]They threw him out of the city and started to stone him. The witnesses had laid their outer clothes at the feet of a young man — his name was Saul.

[59]While they were stoning Stephen, he called, "Lord Jesus, receive my spirit." [60]Then, kneeling, he called out loud, "Lord, don't hold this sin against them." When he had said this, he fell asleep.

8 And Saul also approved of their killing him.

That day a great persecution broke out against the church in Jerusalem, and all except the apostles were scattered over the open country of Judea and Samaria.

[2]God-fearing men buried Stephen and mourned loudly over him.

The Samaritans Believe

[3]Saul was trying to destroy the church. Going into one house after another and dragging off men and women, he put them in prison.

---

44 *Ex 25:9,40; 26:30; 27:8*   **46** *Ps 132:5*   **47** *I Kings 6:1*
48-50 *Is 66:1-2*   **51** *Ex 32:9; 33:3,5; Lev 26:41; Jer 9:26; 6:10; Num 27:14; Is 63:10*

⁴So the people who were scattered went from place to place telling the good news. ⁵Philip went down to the city of Samaria and preached Christ to the people. ⁶When they heard him, all listened eagerly to what Philip had to say, especially when they saw the miracles he did. ⁷There were those who were plagued by unclean spirits; many came screaming out of them. And many who were paralyzed and lame were made well. ⁸So there was great joy in that city.

⁹There was in the city a man by the name of Simon who was practicing witchcraft and amazing the people of Samaria, claiming to be a great man. ¹⁰Everyone from the least to the greatest listened eagerly to him, saying, "He's God's power; people call it great." ¹¹They were so interested in him because he had for a long time amazed them by his witchcraft. ¹²But when Philip told the good news of God's kingdom and of the name of Jesus Christ, men and women believed him and were baptized. ¹³Even Simon believed, and when he was baptized, he stayed with Philip. He was amazed to see the miracles and wonderful works that were done.

¹⁴When the apostles in Jerusalem heard Samaria had accepted God's Word, they sent Peter and John to them. ¹⁵These two went down and prayed that the people would receive the Holy Spirit. ¹⁶He had not come on any of them yet; but they had only been baptized into the name of the Lord Jesus. ¹⁷Then Peter and John laid their hands on them, and they received the Holy Spirit.

¹⁸Simon saw the Spirit was given when the apostles laid their hands on anyone. So he offered them money. ¹⁹"Give me this power," he said, "that anyone I lay my hands on receives the Holy Spirit."

²⁰"Your money perish with you," Peter told him, "because you meant to buy God's gift with money. ²¹You have no part or share in this because your *heart isn't right with God.* ²²Now repent of this wickedness of yours, and ask the Lord if He will perhaps forgive you for thinking such a thing. ²³I see you're turning to *bitter poison* and being *chained by wickedness.*"

²⁴"You ask the Lord for me," Simon answered, "that none of the things you said may happen to me."

²⁵After they had testified and spoken the Lord's Word, they also brought the good news to many Samaritan villages on their way back to Jerusalem.

The Treasurer from Ethiopia

²⁶An angel of the Lord said to Philip, "Get up and go south to the road going from Jerusalem down to Gaza." It is a deserted road.

²⁷He got up and went. Here there was a man from Ethiopia, a eunuch and high official of Candace, queen of the Ethiopians, in charge of all her treasures. He had come to Jerusalem to worship ²⁸and was on his way home, sitting in his chariot and reading the prophet Isaiah.

²⁹The Spirit said to Philip, "Go over to that chariot and keep close to it."

[30]Philip ran up to it and there heard him reading the prophet Isaiah. "Do you understand what you're reading?" he asked.

[31]"Why, how can I without someone to guide me?" he asked, and he urged Philip to come up and sit with him.

[32]This was the part of the Bible he was reading:
He will be led away like a sheep to be slaughtered,
and as a lamb is dumb before the man who cut off her wool,
so He will not open His mouth.
[33]*When He humbles Himself,*
His condemnation will be taken away.
Who will describe the people of His time?
His life will be cut off from the earth.

[34]"I ask you," the eunuch said to Philip, "about whom is the prophet talking — himself or someone else?"

[35]Then Philip spoke. Starting with this statement of the Bible, he told him the good news of Jesus. [36]As they were going along the road, they came to some water. "Here is water," the eunuch said. "What keeps me from being baptized?"[b]

[38]He ordered the chariot to stop, and both Philip and the eunuch stepped down into the water, and Philip baptized him. [39]When they had stepped out of the water, the Spirit of God suddenly took Philip away, and the eunuch, going happily on his way, didn't see him again.

[40]But Philip found himself in Ashdod. He went through all the towns, bringing them the good news.

Jesus Changes Saul [Paul]

9 And Saul, still breathing threats and murder against the Lord's disciples, went to the high priest [2]and asked him for letters to the synagogues in Damascus, in order to bring any of the followers of Jesus he might find there, men or women, back to Jerusalem in chains.

[3]On his way, as he was coming near Damascus, suddenly a light from heaven flashed around him. [4]He fell to the ground and heard a voice saying to him, "Saul! Saul! Why are you persecuting Me?"

[5]"Who are You, Lord?" he asked.

"I am Jesus," He said, "Whom you are persecuting. [6]But get up, go into the city, and you will be told what you should do."

[7]Meanwhile the men traveling with him were standing speechless. They heard the voice but didn't see anyone.

[8]Saul got up from the ground. When he opened his eyes, he couldn't see anything. So they took him by the hand and led him into Damascus. [9]For three days he couldn't see and didn't eat or drink.

32-33 *Is 53:7-8*

b - 36   Our oldest manuscripts lack v. 37: " 'If you believe with all your heart,' Philip said, 'you may.' He answered, 'I believe Jesus Christ is God's Son.' "

Ananias Comes to Saul [Paul]

[10]In Damascus there was a disciple by the name of Ananias. The Lord said to him in a vision: "Ananias!"

"Yes, Lord," he answered.

[11]"Get up," the Lord told him, "go to the street called Straight, and in the home of Judas look for a man from Tarsus by the name of Saul. You see, he's praying. [12]And in a vision he has seen a man by the name of Ananias come in and lay his hands on him so that he will see again."

[13]"Lord," Ananias answered, "I've heard many tell how much wrong this man has done to Your holy people in Jerusalem, [14]and he's here with authority from the ruling priests to put in chains all who call on Your name."

[15]"Go," the Lord told him, "he's an instrument I have chosen to bring My name before the Gentiles, before kings, and the people of Israel. [16]I will show him how much he has to suffer for Me."

[17]Ananias went. When he came into the house, he laid his hands on Saul. "Brother Saul," he said, "the Lord sent me — Jesus, Whom you saw on your way here — so that you will see again and be filled with the Holy Spirit."

[18]Immediately something like scales fell from his eyes, and he saw again. He got up and was baptized. [19]Then he had something to eat and was strengthened.

Saul [Paul] Preaches Jesus

While Saul was with the disciples in Damascus several days, [20]he immediately started to preach in the synagogues: "Jesus is God's Son." [21]All who heard him were amazed. "Isn't this the man," they asked, "who in Jerusalem destroyed those who call on this name, and didn't he come here to bring them in chains to the ruling priests?"

[22]But Saul grew more and more powerful and bewildered the Jews living in Damascus by proving "He is the Christ." [23]After some time the Jews plotted to murder him, [24]but Saul was told about their plot. When they were even watching the gates day and night to murder him, [25]his disciples took him one night and let him down through an opening in the wall by lowering him in a basket.

[26]He went to Jerusalem and there tried to join the disciples. But they were all afraid of him because they wouldn't believe he was a disciple.

[27]Then Barnabas took him, brought him to the apostles, and told them how Saul saw the Lord on the road and the Lord spoke to him and how in Damascus Saul boldly preached in Jesus' name. [28]Then he went in and out among them in Jerusalem, [29]preaching boldly in the Lord's name.

He was talking and arguing with the Greek-speaking Jews. But they were trying to kill him. [30]As soon as the other disciples found out about it, they took him down to Caesarea and sent him away to Tarsus.

[31]So the church all over Judea, Galilee, and Samaria had peace and

was built up. Living in the fear of the Lord and in the comfort of the Holy Spirit, it grew larger and larger.

Aeneas — Tabitha

³²Now when Peter was going around among all the disciples, he also came down to the holy people living in Lydda. ³³There he found a man by the name of Aeneas who was paralyzed and had been lying on a mat for eight years.

³⁴"Aeneas," Peter said to him, "Jesus Christ makes you well. Get up and make your bed." And immediately he got up.

³⁵All who lived in Lydda and Sharon saw him and turned to the Lord.

³⁶In Joppa there was a disciple by the name of Tabitha, which in Greek is Dorcas.ᶜ She was always doing good works and giving things to the poor. ³⁷Just at that time she got sick and died; so she was washed and laid in a room upstairs.

³⁸Lydda is near Joppa. When the disciples heard Peter was in Lydda, they sent two men to him and urged him: "Come to us without delay!"

³⁹Peter went with them. When he came there, they took him upstairs. There all the widows stood around him; they were crying and showing all the inner and outer garments Dorcas made while she was still with them.

⁴⁰But Peter made them all leave the room.

He knelt and prayed. Then, turning toward the body, he said, "Tabitha, get up!"

She opened her eyes, and seeing Peter, she sat up. ⁴¹He gave her his hand and helped her stand up. Then he called the holy people, and especially the widows, and gave her back to them alive.

⁴²The news spread all over Joppa, and many believed in the Lord.

⁴³Peter stayed for some time with Simon, a tanner, in Joppa.

Cornelius Sees a Vision

10 Now, there was a man in Caesarea by the name of Cornelius, a captain in the troop called Italian. ²He was a religious man, who with all those in his home *feared God*. He gave much to the poor among the people and was always praying to God.

³One day about three in the afternoon he had a vision in which he clearly saw an angel of God come to him and say to him, "Cornelius!"

⁴He stared at the angel and was terrified, "What is it, Lord?" he asked him. "Your prayers and your gifts to the poor," the angel answered him, "have come up before God as an offering He remembers. ⁵And now send men to Joppa, and get Simon, who is also called Peter. ⁶He is a guest of Simon, a tanner, whose house is by the sea."

⁷When the angel who was speaking to him had left, he called two of his

---

2 Prov 3:7

c - 36   Both names mean "gazelle."

servants and a God-fearing soldier, one of those who served him regularly. [8]After telling them everything he sent them to Joppa.

Peter Sees a Vision

[9]The next day about noon, while they were on their way and getting near the town, Peter went up on the roof to pray. [10]But he got hungry and wanted to eat. While the food was being prepared, he fell into a trance. [11]He saw heaven opened and something like a large linen sheet coming down, being let down by its four corners to the ground. [12]In it were all kinds of four-footed animals, reptiles that crawled along the ground, and birds of the air.

[13]"Get up, Peter," a voice told him, "kill and eat."

[14]"Oh, no, Lord!" Peter answered, "I've never eaten anything common or unclean."

[15]A voice spoke to him a second time: "Don't make unclean what God has made clean."

[16]This happened three times, then the sheet was quickly taken up to the sky.

[17]While Peter was still puzzling over the meaning of the vision he had seen, the men sent by Cornelius asked for Simon's house and came to the gate. [18]They called and asked, "Is Simon, who is called Peter, staying here?" [19]Peter was still thinking about the vision when the Spirit said, "There are three men looking for you. [20]Now get up, go down, and do not hesitate to go with them, for I have sent them."

[21]So Peter went down to the men. "I'm the man you're looking for," he said. "What brings you here?"

[22]They answered, "Cornelius is a captain, a righteous man who *fears God*, and all the Jewish people speak well of him. A holy angel told him to bring you to his home and hear what you have to say."

[23]Peter asked them to come in, and they were his guests.

Peter and Cornelius

The next day he left with them, and some fellow disciples from Joppa went along. [24]The following day he came to Caesarea. Cornelius was expecting them and had called his relatives and close friends together.

[25]When Peter was about to go in, Cornelius met him, bowed down at his feet, and worshiped him. [26]But Peter made him stand up. "Get up," he said. "I'm only a man."

[27]Talking with him, he went in and found many people had gathered. [28]"You understand," he said to them, "how wrong it is for a Jew to live with or visit anyone who's not a Jew. But God has taught me not to call anyone common or unclean. [29]That's why I didn't object to coming here when you

---

22 Prov 3:7

sent for me. Now I want to know: Why did you send for me?"

[30]"Three days ago," Cornelius answered, "I was at home praying at this very time, at three in the afternoon, when a man in shining clothes stood in front of me. [31]'Cornelius,' he said, 'God has heard your prayer and remembers your gifts to the poor. [32]Now send to Joppa and ask Simon, who is called Peter, to come to you. He's a guest in the home of Simon, a tanner, by the sea.' [33]So I sent to you immediately, and it was good of you to come. We're all here before God now, ready to hear everything the Lord has ordered you to say."

[34]Then Peter spoke: "Now I really understand that *God doesn't favor one person over another.* [35]It doesn't matter what people you belong to; if you *fear Him* and do what's right, He accepts you. [36]*He sent His Word* to the people of Israel to *bring the news of peace* in Jesus Christ — He is Lord of all!

[37]"You know what happened in the whole country of the Jews, how after the baptism that John preached, [38]*God anointed* Jesus from Nazareth *with the* Holy *Spirit* and power, and Jesus, beginning in Galilee, went around doing good and healing all who were under the tyranny of the devil, because God was with Him. [39]We have seen everything He did in the land of the Jews and in Jerusalem, and we can tell about it. Men *hanged Him on a cross* and killed Him. [40]But God raised Him on the third day and showed Him to us — [41]not to all our people but to us whom God has chosen to be witnesses and who ate and drank with Him after He rose from the dead. [42]He ordered us to preach to the people and warn them that God has appointed Him to judge the living and the dead. [43]All the prophets declare that through His name everyone who believes in Him receives forgiveness for his sins."

[44]While Peter was still speaking, the Holy Spirit came down on all who heard the Word. [45]All the Jewish believers who had come with Peter were surprised the gift of the Holy Spirit had been poured out also on people who were not Jews. [46]They heard them speaking in other languages and praising God.

[47]Then Peter asked, "Surely no one can refuse water and keep them from being baptized, can he? They have received the Holy Spirit just as we did." [48]And he ordered them to be baptized in the name of Jesus Christ.

Then they asked him to stay several days.

Peter Defends Himself

11 The apostles and other disciples in all Judea heard: "The non-Jewish people too have accepted God's Word." [2]But when Peter went up to Jerusalem, those who still believed in circumcision disagreed with him. [3]"You went to visit uncircumcised men," they said, "and you ate with them."

[4]Then Peter explained to them point by point what had happened. [5]"I

---

34 Deut 10:17   *35* Prov 3:7
36 Ps 107:20; 147:15,18; Is 52:7; Nah 1:15 *38* Is 61:1   *39* Deut 21:22-23

was in the town of Joppa praying," he said, "when in a trance I saw a vision: Something like a large linen sheet was coming down. It was lowered by its four corners from the sky, and came down to me. ⁶Looking in, I examined it and saw four-footed animals of the earth, wild animals, reptiles, and birds of the air. ⁷I also heard a voice telling me, 'Get up, Peter, kill and eat.'

⁸"But I answered, 'Oh, no, Lord. Nothing common or unclean has ever come into my mouth.'

⁹"A voice spoke from heaven a second time, 'Don't make unclean what God has made clean.' ¹⁰This happened three times. Then all of it was pulled up to the sky again.

¹¹"At that moment three men, sent to me from Caesarea, came to the house we were in. ¹²The Spirit told me to go with them without any hesitation. These six fellow disciples went with me, and we came into the man's home.

¹³"He told us how he had seen the angel standing in his home and saying, 'Send to Joppa and get Simon, who is called Peter. ¹⁴What he will tell you will save you and everyone in your home.'

¹⁵"While I was speaking, the Holy Spirit came down on these people as He originally came on us, ¹⁶and I had to think of what the Lord had said: 'John baptized with water, but you will be baptized with the Holy Spirit.' ¹⁷Now if God gave them the same gift He gave us after believing in the Lord Jesus Christ, who was I — could I stop God?"

¹⁸When the others heard this, they kept quiet. And they praised God, saying, "Then God has given repentance also to the non-Jewish people so that they will live."

The New Church in Antioch

¹⁹The people scattered by the persecution that broke out over Stephen went as far as Phoenicia, Cyprus, and Antioch, and they spoke the Word only to the Jews. ²⁰But among them were some men from Cyprus and Cyrene who came to Antioch and started talking also to the non-Jews, telling them the good news of the Lord Jesus. ²¹The Lord's hand was with them, and a large number believed and turned to the Lord.

²²The church in Jerusalem heard the news about them, and they sent Barnabas to Antioch. ²³When he came there, he was delighted to see what God's grace had done, and he urged them all with a hearty determination to be faithful to the Lord. ²⁴He was a good man, full of the Holy Spirit and faith. And a large crowd was brought to the Lord.

²⁵Then Barnabas left for Tarsus to look for Saul. ²⁶He found him and brought him to Antioch. And they were guests of the church for a whole year and taught a large crowd. It was in Antioch the disciples were first called Christians.

²⁷At that time some prophets came from Jerusalem down to Antioch. ²⁸One of them by the name of Agabus got up and by the Spirit predicted there would be a big famine all over the world (it came while Claudius was emperor). ²⁹Every one of the disciples decided, as he was able, to send relief

to the fellow Christians living in Judea. [30]They did this by sending Barnabas and Saul to bring it to the spiritual leaders.

An Angel Frees Peter

12 At that time King Herod[d] arrested some members of the church in order to mistreat them. [2]He killed John's brother James with a sword. [3]When he saw how the Jews liked that, he arrested Peter, too. It happened during the Passover days of Bread Without Yeast. [4]When he arrested Peter, he put him in prison and had sixteen soldiers in squads of four guard him. He wanted to bring him before the people after the Passover. [5]So Peter was kept in prison.

But the church was earnestly praying to God for him. [6]The night before Herod was going to bring him before the people, Peter, bound with two chains, was sleeping between two soldiers, and guards in front of the door were watching the prison. [7]Suddenly an angel of the Lord stood near him, and a light shone in his cell. He struck Peter on his side, woke him, and said, "Get up! Quick!" Peter's chains dropped from his wrists.

[8]"Fasten your belt," the angel told him, "and tie on your sandals!" He did this. "Put on your garment," the angel told him, "and follow me."

[9]Peter followed him outside, not realizing the angel was actually doing this. He thought he was seeing a vision. [10]They passed through the first guards and the second guards and came to the iron gate leading into the city. It opened by itself before them, and they went outside and up the street. There the angel suddenly left him.

[11]"Now I'm sure the Lord sent His angel," Peter said when he was himself again, "and He rescued me from Herod and from everything the Jewish people were expecting."

Peter Comes to His Friends

[12]When he realized what had happened, He went to the home of Mary (the mother of John — the one called Mark), where many had gathered and were praying. [13]He knocked at the entrance gate, and a maid by the name of Rhoda came to answer. [14]Recognizing Peter's voice, she was so happy she didn't open the gate but ran in and announced, "Peter is standing at the gate!"

[15]"You're crazy!" they told her. But she insisted it was so. "It's his angel," they said. [16]But Peter kept on knocking. When they opened the gate, they were surprised to see him. [17]He waved his hand to quiet them down and told them how the Lord had taken him out of the prison. "Tell James and the other Christians about this," he said. Then he left and went to another place.

[18]In the morning the soldiers were very much upset as they asked, "What happened to Peter?" [19]Herod searched for him but didn't find him. So

---

d - 1   Herod, Agrippa I, grandson of Herod the Great who tried to kill the baby Jesus.

he examined the guards and ordered them executed.

Herod Dies

Then Herod left Judea, went down to Caesarea, and stayed there awhile.

²⁰He had a violent quarrel with the people of Tyre and Sidon. So they came to him in a body. After they had won over Blastus, who took care of the king's bedroom, they asked for peace because the king's country provided food for their country.

²¹On a day that was set, Herod put on his royal robe, sat on the platform, and made a speech to them. ²²The people shouted, "It's a god speaking, not a man!"

²³Immediately an angel of the Lord struck him because he didn't give glory to God. He was eaten by worms, and he died.

²⁴But God's Word continued to spread and win many followers.

On Cyprus

²⁵After Barnabas and Saul delivered the offering for relief, they came back from Jerusalem, bringing with them John, also called Mark.

13 The following were prophets and teachers in the church at Antioch: Barnabas, Symeon, called Black, Lucius from Cyrene, Manaen, who had been raised with Herod the governor, and Saul.

²While the Christians were worshiping the Lord and fasting, the Holy Spirit said, "Set Barnabas and Saul apart for Me to do the work I called them for."

³Then they fasted and prayed, laid their hands on them, and let them go. ⁴And so they, sent by the Holy Spirit, went down to Seleucia and from there sailed to Cyprus. ⁵They came to Salamis and there started to preach God's Word in the synagogues of the Jews. They also had John to help them. ⁶They went through the whole island as far as Paphos. There they found a Jewish sorcerer and false prophet by the name of Barjesus, ⁷who was with the proconsul Sergius Paulus, an intelligent man. He sent for Barnabas and Saul and wanted to hear God's Word. ⁸But Elymas, the sorcerer (that was what his name meant), opposed them and tried to turn the proconsul away from the faith.

⁹Then Saul (who was Paul), filled with the Holy Spirit, looked steadily at him ¹⁰and said, "O you who are full of every treachery and villainy, you son of the devil, enemy of all that is right! Won't you stop twisting *the Lord's right ways*? ¹¹And now the Lord's hand is on you: You'll be blind and not see the sun for a while."

At that moment a mist and a darkness came over him, and he went around looking for people to take his hand and lead him. ¹²When the pro-

---

10 Hos 14:9

consul saw what had happened, he believed. The Lord's teaching amazed him.

At Antioch near Pisidia

[13]Paul and his men took a ship from Paphos and came to Perga in Pamphylia. There John[e] left them and went back to Jerusalem. [14]But they went on from Perga and came to Antioch near Pisidia. On the Sabbath they went into the synagogue and sat down.

[15]After the reading of the Law and the prophets, the synagogue leaders had a man go and tell them, "Fellow Jews, if you have anything to say to encourage the people, speak."

[16]Paul got up and motioned with his hand. "Men of Israel," he said, "and you others who *fear God*, listen to me. [17]The God of this people Israel chose our fathers and made them a great people while they lived as strangers in Egypt, and *with an uplifted arm He led them out of it*. [18]About forty years *He put up with them in the desert*. [19]Then He *destroyed seven nations in Canaan and gave* their *country* to His people *as an inheritance*. [20]He did all this in about four hundred and fifty years. After that He gave them judges until the time of the prophet Samuel.

[21]"Then the people demanded a king, and God gave them Saul for forty years. He was a son of Kish, a man of the tribe of Benjamin. [22]But God took the throne away from him again and made David their king. In regard to him He declared: '*I found David*, Jesse's son, *to be a man after My own heart*, who *will do everything I want him to do*.'

[23]"As He had promised, God had a Savior — Jesus — come from David's descendants to Israel. [24]When He came into the world, John went ahead of Him as herald to tell all the people of Israel to repent and be baptized. [25]As John was finishing his work, he said, 'Who do you think I am? I'm not the One. No, there's Someone coming after me, and I don't deserve to untie the sandals on His feet.'

[26]"Fellow Jews, Abraham's descendants, and you others who *fear God*, *the message* of this salvation *was sent* to us. [27]Not knowing who Jesus was or understanding the messages of the prophets that are read every Sabbath, the people in Jerusalem and their rulers by condemning Jesus did what their prophets predicted. [28]Although they found no good reason to kill Him, they asked Pilate to have Him killed. [29]When they had done everything that was written about Him, they took Him down from the cross and laid Him in a grave. [30]But God raised Him from the dead, [31]and for many days He was seen by those who had come with Him from Galilee up to Jerusalem. They are now telling the people the truth about Him. [32]And we are bringing you the good news: [33]What God promised the fathers He did for

---

16 Prov 3:7   *17 Ex 6:1,6; 12:51; 14:8*   *18 Deut 1:31*
19 Deut 7:1; Josh 14:1   *20 Judg 2:16*   *22 I Sam 13:14; Ps 89:20; Is 44:28*

e - 13   That is Mark, also called John Mark

us, their children, by raising Jesus, as it is written in the second Psalm: *'You are My Son; today I have begotten You.'*

[34]"He raised Him from the dead, never to suffer *decay*, as He said: 'I will give *you what I gave David — mercies that one can trust.'* [35]Another Psalm says: *'You will not let Your Loved One experience decay.'* [36]When *David* had served the people of his time, he by God's will *went to his rest* and was laid away *with his fathers*. His body decayed, [37]but the body of Him Whom God raised did not decay.

[38]"And so you should know, my friends and brothers — we are announcing to you that this *Jesus forgives your sins* [39]and declares everyone who believes righteous and free from everything from which Moses' Law couldn't free you.

[40]"Now be careful, or what the prophets said will happen to you: [41]*Look, you scorners, then wonder and perish, because I'm doing something in your days that you would never believe if anyone told you.*"

[42]As Paul and Barnabas were going out, the people urged them to tell them the same things the next Sabbath. [43]When the meeting of the synagogue broke up, many Jews and others who feared God followed Paul and Barnabas, who talked to them and urged them to stay in God's grace.

[44]The next Sabbath almost the whole town was there to hear God's Word. [45]When the Jews saw the crowds, they got very jealous. They contradicted what Paul said and slandered him.

[46]Paul and Barnabas boldly declared: "We had to speak God's Word to you first, but since you reject it and judge yourselves unworthy of everlasting life, we are now turning to the non-Jews. [47]That is what the Lord has ordered us to do: *'I have made you a light for the non-Jews, to save people all over the earth.'*"

[48]The non-Jews were delighted to hear what the Lord had said and praised Him for it, and all who had been appointed for everlasting life believed. [49]The Lord's Word spread all over the country. [50]But the Jews stirred up the noble women who worshiped with them, and the leaders of the town. These started a persecution against Paul and Barnabas and drove them out of their territory.

[51]In protest against them, Paul and Barnabas shook the dust off their feet and went to Iconium. [52]Meanwhile the disciples continued to be full of joy and of the Holy Spirit.

In Iconium

14 The same thing happened in Iconium. Paul and Barnabas went into the synagogue of the Jews and spoke in such a way that a large crowd of Jews and non-Jews believed. [2]But the Jews who refused to believe stirred up the non-Jews and poisoned their minds against the Christians. [3]For a long time Paul and Barnabas continued to speak boldly, trusting in the

26 *Prov 3:7; Ps 107:20; 147:15,18*
33 *Ps 2:7*   **34** *Is 55:3*   **35** *Ps 16:10*

Lord, Who gave His approval to the words of His grace by letting their hands do miracles and wonders. [4]But the people of the town were divided — some were with the Jews, others with the apostles.

[5]But when non-Jews and Jews with their rulers planned to mistreat and stone them, [6]they found out about it and escaped to Lystra and Derbe, towns of Lycaonia, and to the surrounding territory. [7]There they kept on telling the good news.

In Lystra

[8]In Lystra there was a man sitting who couldn't use his feet. He had been lame from his birth and had never walked. [9]He was listening to Paul as he spoke. Paul watched him, and when he saw the man believed he would be made well, [10]he called out loud, "*Stand up* straight *on your feet.*" The man jumped up and walked around.

[11]The people who saw what Paul had done shouted in the language of Lycaonia, "The gods have become like men and have come down to us." [12]And they called Barnabas Zeus, and Paul Hermes, because he was the main speaker. [13]The priest of the temple of Zeus in front of the town brought bulls and garlands to the gates. He and the crowd wanted to offer sacrifices.

[14]When the apostles Barnabas and Paul heard of it, they tore their clothes and rushed out into the crowd. [15]"You men, why are you doing this?" they shouted. "We're just human beings, too, with experiences like yours and are telling you the good news to turn you from these empty things to the living God, *Who made heaven and earth, the sea, and everything in them.* [16]In the ages that have gone by He let all people go their own ways; [17]yet He didn't fail to give evidence of Himself by doing good, giving you rains from heaven and crops in their seasons, filling you with food, and making you happy."

[18]Even by saying this they could hardly keep the crowd from sacrificing to them. [19]But then some Jews came from Antioch and Iconium and won the people over. So they stoned Paul and dragged him out of the town, thinking he was dead. [20]But when the disciples came and stood around him, he got up and went into the town.

Derbe and Back Home

The next day he and Barnabas left for Derbe. [21]As they were telling the good news in that town, they won many disciples. Then they went back to Lystra, Iconium, and Antioch, [22]strengthening the disciples and encouraging them to be loyal to the faith, saying, "We must suffer much to enter into God's kingdom." [23]They had spiritual leaders elected for them in each church. And with prayer and fasting they entrusted them to the Lord in Whom they believed.

---

10 Ezek 2:1-2   15 Ex 20:11; Ps 146:6

²⁴When they had gone through Pisidia, they came to Pamphylia. ²⁵They spoke the Word in Perga and went down to Attalia. ²⁶From there they took a boat to Antioch, where they had been entrusted to God's love for the work they now had finished. ²⁷When they arrived, they called the church together and told them everything God had done with them and how He had opened the door for the people who were not Jews so that they, too, might believe. ²⁸Then they spent a long time with the disciples.ᶠ

Must Non-Jews Be Circumcised?

15 Some men came down from Judea and started to teach the Christians: "If you're not circumcised according to the custom taught by Moses, you can't be saved." ²When Paul and Barnabas had no small conflict and argument with them, Paul and Barnabas and some of the others were appointed to go up to Jerusalem and see the apostles and spiritual leaders about this question.

³The church sent them on their way. As they were going through Phoenicia and Samaria, they told the whole story of how the non-Jews were turning to God, and they brought great joy to all the Christians.

⁴When they came to Jerusalem, they were welcomed by the church, the apostles, and the spiritual leaders. They reported everything God had done with them. ⁵But some believers of the party of the Pharisees got up and said, "We must circumcise people and order them to keep the Law of Moses."

⁶The apostles and spiritual leaders met to look into this matter. ⁷After much discussion Peter got up. "Fellow Christians," he said to the others, "you know in the early days God chose me to be the one among you to tell the good news to the non- Jews so that they would hear it and believe. ⁸And God, Who knows our hearts, showed them He approved by giving them the Holy Spirit as He gave Him to us. ⁹And by cleansing their hearts by faith He has declared we are not different from them. ¹⁰Now then, why do you test God by putting on the disciples' neck a yoke neither our fathers nor we could bear? ¹¹No, we believe that we are saved by the grace of the Lord Jesus, in the same way as they are."

¹²The whole crowd was silent. Then they heard Barnabas and Paul tell about all the miracles and wonders God had done among the non-Jews through them.

¹³After they finished speaking, James said, "Fellow Christians, listen to me. ¹⁴Simon has explained how God first came to the non-Jews to get a people for Himself. ¹⁵This agrees with what the prophets said. It is written: ¹⁶*Afterwards I will come back and rebuild the tent of David that has fallen*

---

f - 28   At this time, late in A.D. 48, Paul wrote his letter to the Galatians. They were the people he had been with on his first journey.

down; and its ruins I will rebuild and set up again, [17]so that the rest of the people, yes, all the nations who are called by My name, may search for the Lord. [18]The Lord says this and does this which was known long ago.' [19]So it is my judgment that we should not trouble these non-Jews who are turning to God [20]but write them to keep away from the unclean things of idols and from sexual sin and not eat anything strangled or any blood. [21]Ever since the earliest days there are in each town those who preach Moses when he is read in the synagogues every Sabbath."

[22]Then the apostles, the spiritual leaders, and the whole church decided to choose some of their men and send them with Paul and Barnabas to Antioch: Judas, called Barsabas, and Silas — leaders among the Christians. [23]And they wrote this letter for them to deliver:

"The apostles and spiritual leaders, your brothers, send greetings to their non-Jewish fellow Christians in Antioch, Syria, and Cilicia.

[24]"Since we heard that some men, coming from us without instructions from us, have said things to trouble you, and they continue to upset you, [25]we have unanimously decided to choose men and send them to you with our dear Barnabas and Paul, [26]who have devoted their lives to the name of our Lord Jesus Christ. [27]So we are sending Judas and Silas to talk to you and tell you the same things.

[28]"The Holy Spirit and we have decided not to burden you more than is necessary: [29]Keep away from food sacrificed to idols, from blood, from the meat of strangled animals, and from sexual sin. Be careful to avoid these and you will be doing right. Farewell!"

[30]So they were sent on their way and came to Antioch, where they got the church together and delivered the letter. [31]The people read it and were delighted with the encouragement it brought them. [32]And Judas and Silas, who also were prophets, said much to encourage and strengthen the Christians.

[33]After they had stayed for some time, the Christians let Judas and Silas go back with a friendly greeting to those who had sent them.[g] [35]But Paul and Barnabas stayed in Antioch and with the help of many others taught and told the Lord's good news.

Paul Takes Silas with Him

[36]After a while Paul said to Barnabas, "Let's go back and visit our fellow Christians in every town where we told them the Lord's Word, and let's see how they are."

[37]Barnabas wanted to take along John, who was called Mark. [38]But Paul thought it best not to take the man who had deserted them in Pamphylia and had not gone with them into the work. [39]They disagreed so sharply that they separated, and Barnabas, taking Mark along, sailed away

---

16 Jer 12:15   *16-18* Amos 9:11-12; Is 45:21

---

g - 33   Our two oldest manuscripts lack v. 34: "But Silas decided to stay there, and Judas left alone."

to Cyprus. ⁴⁰But Paul chose Silas and started out, his fellow Christians entrusting him to the Lord's grace.

Timothy Joins Paul in Lystra

⁴¹He went through Syria and Cilicia, strengthening the churches.

16 He came down to Derbe, then to Lystra. Here there was a disciple by the name of Timothy. His mother was a Jewish Christian, but his father was a Greek. ²The Christians in Lystra and Iconium spoke well of him. ³Paul wanted him to go with him, so he took him and circumcised him on account of the Jews who were in those places, because everybody knew his father was a Greek.

⁴As they went through the towns, they delivered the decisions the apostles and spiritual leaders in Jerusalem had made and the people were to keep. ⁵So the churches were strengthened in the faith and grew in number more and more every day.

The Call to Europe

⁶They went through the region of Phrygia and Galatia because the Holy Spirit kept them from speaking the Word in the province of Asia. ⁷They came as far as Mysia and tried to get into Bithynia, but the Spirit of Jesus did not let them. ⁸So they passed through Mysia and went down to Troas.

⁹One night Paul saw a vision — a man from Macedonia was standing there and urging him, "Come over to Macedonia and help us!"

¹⁰As soon as he had seen the vision, we looked for a way to get to Macedonia since we concluded God had called us to tell them the good news.

At Philippi

¹¹Sailing from Troas, we went straight to Samothrace, the next day to Neapolis, ¹²and from there to Philippi, a leading city in that part of Macedonia and a colony of Rome. We stayed in that city for some days.

¹³On the Sabbath, we went out of the gate and along the river, where we thought there was a place for prayer. We sat down and started to talk to the women gathered there. ¹⁴There was a woman by the name of Lydia, a dealer in purple goods, who came from the town of Thyatira. She worshiped God. As she listened, the Lord opened her heart to be interested in what Paul said. ¹⁵When she and her family were baptized, she urged us, "If you're convinced I believe in the Lord, come and stay at my home." And she made us come.

¹⁶One day when we were going to the place of prayer, we met a slave girl with a spirit of fortune-telling in her; she made much money for her owners by telling the unknown. ¹⁷She would follow Paul and us and shout, "These men are servants of the Most High God and are telling you how to

be saved." [18]She kept on doing this for many days until Paul, very much annoyed, turned to the spirit and said, "In the name of Jesus Christ I order you to go out of her!"

Then and there the spirit went out of her, [19]and with it, as her owners realized, went their chance of making money. So they grabbed Paul and Silas, dragged them before the officers in the marketplace, [20]and brought them before the highest Roman officials. "These men are stirring up a lot of trouble in our city," they said. "They're Jews, [21]and they're teaching religious ways that we as Romans aren't allowed to adopt or practice."

[22]The crowd also joined in attacking them. Then the officials tore the clothes off Paul and Silas and ordered them beaten with rods. [23]After striking them many times, the men put them in prison and ordered the jailer to watch them and not let them escape. [24]He did as he was ordered and put them in the inner cell and fastened their feet in the stocks.

[25]About midnight Paul and Silas were praying and singing hymns of praise to God, and the other prisoners were listening to them. [26]Suddenly the earth quaked so violently the foundations of the prison were shaken, all the doors flew open, and everyone's chains were unfastened. [27]The jailer woke up and saw the prison doors open. Thinking the prisoners had escaped, he drew his sword and was going to kill himself. [28]But Paul called out in a loud voice, "Don't harm yourself! We're all here!"

[29]The jailer asked for lights, rushed in, and fell down trembling before Paul and Silas. [30]Then he took them outside and asked, "Sirs, what do I have to do to be saved?"

[31]"Believe in the Lord Jesus," they answered, "and you and your family will be saved." [32]They spoke the Lord's Word to him and everyone in his home.

[33]At that hour of the night he took them with him and washed their wounds. And he and all who were with him were baptized immediately. [34]He took them up into his home and gave them a meal. He and everyone in his home were very happy to have found faith in God.

[35]In the morning the officials sent attendants and said, "Let those men go."

[36]The jailer reported the message to Paul. "The officials sent word to let you go," he said. "Come out now, and *go in peace*."

[37]But Paul told them, "They have beaten us publicly without a trial and have thrown us into prison, even though we are Roman citizens. And now they're trying to put us out secretly? I should say not! They should come themselves and take us out."

[38]The attendants reported to the officials what Paul said. Hearing that Paul and Silas were Roman citizens, they were frightened. [39]So they came and pleaded with them, took them out, and asked them to leave the city.

[40]Leaving the prison, they went to Lydia, saw and encouraged the Christians there, and then left.

---

36 Judg 18:6

In Thessalonica

17 Paul and Silas traveled through Amphipolis and Apollonia and came to Thessalonica. Here the Jews had a synagogue. ²Paul went in as usual and on three Sabbaths had Bible discussions with them. ³He explained and showed them: "The Christ had to suffer and rise from the dead, and this Christ is the Jesus I'm telling you about."

⁴He convinced some of the Jews, and they joined Paul and Silas, as did a large crowd of the God-fearing Greeks, and many of the wives of the leaders.

⁵Then the Jews got jealous, took some wicked men in the marketplace, formed a mob, and started a riot in the city. They attacked Jason's home and searched for Paul and Silas to bring them out to the people. ⁶When they didn't find them, they dragged Jason and some other Christians before the city officials, shouting, "Those men who have made trouble all over the world are here now ⁷and are Jason's guests. They're all going against the emperor's decrees by saying there's another king — Jesus!"

⁸Hearing this, the crowd and the officials were upset. ⁹But after they had taken security from Jason and the others, they let them go.

¹⁰That same night the Christians sent Paul and Silas away to Berea.

At Berea

When they came there, they went into the synagogue of the Jews. ¹¹These people were nobler than those at Thessalonica — they were very eager to get the Word and every day studied the Bible to see if those things were so. ¹²And many of them believed, also many noble Greeks, women as well as men.

¹³But when the Jews at Thessalonica found out Paul had now preached God's Word also in Berea, they came there to stir up trouble among the people. ¹⁴Immediately the Christians sent Paul away to the sea, but Silas and Timothy stayed there.

In Athens

¹⁵Those who escorted Paul took him all the way to Athens. When they left, they took instructions to Silas and Timothy to come to him as soon as possible.

¹⁶While Paul was waiting for them in Athens, he was inwardly stirred up when he saw how many idols there were in the city. ¹⁷Then he had discussions in the synagogue with Jews and others who feared God, and every day in the marketplace with those who happened to be there. ¹⁸Some Epicurean and Stoic philosophers also debated with him, but some asked, "What is this fellow with his scraps of learning trying to say?" Others said, "He seems to be telling about foreign gods" — because he was telling the good news of Jesus and the resurrection.

¹⁹Then they took him and brought him before the court of Mars' Hill and asked, "Could we know, what is this new thing you teach? ²⁰You bring

some things that sound strange to us, and we want to know what they mean."

²¹Now everyone in Athens, also the visitors staying there, used their time only to tell or hear something new.

²²Paul stood before the court of Mars' Hill and said, "Men of Athens, I see how very religious you are in every way. ²³As I went through your city and saw the things you worship, I found an altar with the inscription TO AN UNKNOWN GOD. Now I'm telling you about what you don't know and yet worship. ²⁴*The God Who made* the world and everything in it is the Lord of *heaven and earth* and doesn't live in temples made by human hands, ²⁵and He isn't served by human hands as if He needed anything. He Himself *gives* everyone *life* and *breath* and everything. ²⁶From one man He made every nation to have the people live all over the earth, *setting* the times allotted to them and the *boundaries* they live in, ²⁷that they should look for God and perhaps feel their way to Him and find Him. He is never far from any one of us, ²⁸because we live and move and are in Him; as some of your poets[h] have said, 'You see, we are His children.' ²⁹Now, if we're God's children, we shouldn't think God is like gold, silver, or stone, carved by man's art and imagination.

³⁰"While God overlooked the times when people were ignorant, He now tells all of them everywhere to repent, ³¹because He has set a day when *He is going to judge the world with justice* by the Man He has appointed for this. And by raising Him from the dead He has given everyone a good reason to believe."

³²When they heard about a resurrection of the dead, some started to mock, while others said, "We'll hear you again about this."

³³And so Paul left the meeting. ³⁴Some men joined him and believed. Among them were Dionysius, a member of the court, and a woman by the name of Damaris, and some others with them.

In Corinth

18 After that he left Athens and came to Corinth. ²There he found a Jew by the name of Aquila, born in Pontus, and his wife Priscilla. They had recently come from Italy because Claudius had ordered all Jews to leave Rome. Paul went to them, ³and because they made tents for a living just as he did, he stayed with them, and they worked together.

⁴Every Sabbath he would discuss Scripture in the synagogue and try to win Jews and Greeks. ⁵But when Silas and Timothy came down from Macedonia, Paul devoted himself entirely to teaching the Word as he solemnly assured the Jews, "Jesus is the Christ!" ⁶But they opposed him and slandered him. In protest he shook the dust from his clothes and told them, "Your blood be on your own heads. I am innocent. From now on I'll

---

24-25 Is 42:5   26 Deut 32:8   31 Ps 9:8; 96:13; 98:9; Is 11:4

h - 28   Aratus and Cleanthes wrote this about 270 B.C.

go to the non-Jews."

⁷Then he left the place and went to the home of a man by the name of Titius Justus, who worshiped God. His house was right beside the synagogue. ⁸Now Crispus, the synagogue leader, and all who were in his home believed in the Lord. And many other people in Corinth who heard Paul believed and were baptized.

⁹One night the Lord spoke to Paul in a vision, *"Don't be afraid!* But speak, and don't be silent — ¹⁰ *I am with you,* and *no one will* attack you so as to harm you, because I have many people in this city."

¹¹He stayed there a year and six months and taught God's Word among them.ⁱ ¹²But when Gallio was proconsul of Greece, the Jews united in an attack on Paul and brought him before Gallio as judge. ¹³"This man," they said, "is persuading people to worship God in ways that are against the Law."

¹⁴Just as Paul was going to answer, Gallio said to the Jews, "if this were a crime or vicious wrong, it would be only fair that I listen to you Jews. ¹⁵But since we have questions here about words, names, and your own Law, see to it yourselves. I don't want to be a judge of those things." ¹⁶And he drove them away from the judgment seat.

¹⁷Then all of them took Sosthenes, the synagogue leader, and beat him in front of the judgment seat. But Gallio paid no attention to it.

Home

¹⁸After staying there quite a while longer, Paul said goodbye to the Christians. Priscilla and Aquila went with him. At Cenchrea he had his hair cut, since he had been under a vow. They took a boat for Syria ¹⁹and came to Ephesus, where Paul left Priscilla and Aquila. There he went into the synagogue and had a discussion with the Jews. ²⁰They asked him to stay longer, but he refused. ²¹As he said goodbye to them, he told them, "I will come back to you if God wants me to."

He sailed from Ephesus ²²and landed at Caesarea. He went up, greeted the church, and then went down to Antioch.

Apollos

²³After staying there for some time, Paul left and went from place to place through the Galatian country and through Phrygia, strengthening all the disciples.

²⁴A Jew by the name of Apollos, who was born in Alexandria, came to Ephesus. He was a learned man and mighty in the Bible. ²⁵After he had been instructed in the Lord's way, he spoke with a glowing enthusiasm and taught correctly about Jesus but knew only John's baptism. ²⁶He started to speak boldly in the synagogue. When Priscilla and Aquila heard him, they

---

9-10 *Ex 3:12; Josh 1:5; Is 41:10; 43:5; Jer 1:8*

---

i - 11   In A.D. 50 Paul wrote the two letters to the Thessalonians.

took him with them and explained God's way to him more accurately.

27As he wanted to cross over to Greece, the Christians wrote to the disciples there urging them to welcome him. When he got there, he gave much help to those who by God's grace were now believers. 28Publicly and vigorously he proved the Jews were wrong as he showed from the Scriptures that Jesus is the Christ.

Paul in Ephesus

19 While Apollos was in Corinth, Paul traveled over the hills to get to Ephesus. Meeting some disciples there, 2he asked them, "Did you receive the Holy Spirit when You became believers?"

"No," they answered him, "we haven't even heard there is a Holy Spirit."

3"Into what then were you baptized?" he asked them. "Into John's baptism," they answered.

4Paul said, "John baptized with the baptism of repentance and told the people to believe in the One coming after him, that is, Jesus."

5When they heard this, they were baptized into the name of the Lord Jesus. 6And as Paul laid his hands on them, the Holy Spirit came on them, and they started to talk in other languages and to speak God's Word. 7There were about twelve men in the group.

8He went into the synagogue and spoke there boldly for three months, discussing and trying to convince people about God's kingdom. 9When some got stubborn, refused to believe, and slandered the Christian religion before the crowd, he left them, took his disciples away from them, and had daily discussions in the lecture hall of Tyrannus. 10This went on for two years so that all who lived in the province of Asia, Jews and Greeks, heard the Lord's Word.

11God did extraordinary miracles by Paul's hands. 12When handkerchiefs and aprons that had touched his skin were taken to the sick, their sicknesses left them, and the evil spirits went out of them.

13Some Jews who made it their business to go around and drive out evil spirits tried to use the name of the Lord Jesus over those having the evil spirits. "I order you by that Jesus whom Paul preaches," they said. 14Seven sons of Sceva, a Jewish ruling priest, were doing this.

15But the evil spirit answered them, "I know Jesus, and I know Paul, but who are you?" 16Then the man with the evil spirit jumped on them, got the better of them, and overpowered them all so that they ran naked and bruised out of that house.

17All the Jews and Greeks living in Ephesus heard about it. They were all frightened and started to think very highly of the name of the Lord Jesus. 18Many believers came to confess and tell about their magic spells.

[19]Many of those who had practiced magic gathered their books and burned them in front of everyone. They added up the cost of these books and found they were worth 50,000 denarii.[j] [20]In that way the Lord's Word grew mightily and triumphed.[k]

[21]After all these things had happened, Paul decided to go through Macedonia and Greece and then to Jerusalem. "After I have been there," he said, "I must also see Rome." [22]But he sent two of his helpers, Timothy and Erastus, to Macedonia, while he himself stayed in the province of Asia a while longer.

The Riot

[23]During that time there was a big disturbance over the Christian religion.

[24]A silversmith by the name of Demetrius provided a big income for the skilled workers by making silver shrines of Artemis. [25]He called a meeting of these and others who did similar work. "Men," he said, "you know we're getting a fine income from this business, [26]and you see and hear how this Paul has won and taken away a large crowd not only in Ephesus but almost all over the province of Asia by telling them, 'Gods made by human hands are no gods.' [27]There is a danger people will not only reject our line of business but will also think nothing of the temple of the great goddess Artemis, and then she whom all Asia and the world worship will be robbed of her glory."

[28]When they heard this, they became furious and shouted, "Great is Artemis of the Ephesians!" [29]The confusion spread all over the city. And they all rushed into the theater together, dragging with them Gaius and Aristarchus, Paul's fellow travelers from Macedonia.

[30]Paul wanted to go into the crowd, but the disciples wouldn't let him. [31]Even some officials of the province of Asia who were his friends sent men to him and urged him not to risk going into the theater.

[32]Some were shouting one thing, some another. The crowd was confused, and most of them didn't know why they had come together. [33]Then the Jews pushed Alexander to the front, and some of the crowd told him what to do. Alexander waved his hand to quiet them and wanted to make a defense before the people. [34]But when they found out he was a Jew, they all started to shout in unison and kept it up for about two hours, "Great is Artemis of the Ephesians!"

[35]Then the city secretary quieted the crowd. "Men of Ephesus," he said, "who in the world doesn't know that this city of the Ephesians is the keeper of the temple of the great Artemis and of the statue that fell down from Zeus? [36]Since no one can deny this, you must be quiet and not do anything

---

j - 19   A denarius was one day's pay.

k - 20   From Ephesus, during the time of A.D. 54 to 55, Paul wrote his first letter to the Corinthians. There are good reasons to believe that here he also wrote the letters to the Philippians, Philemon, Colossians, and Ephesians.

reckless. [37]The men you brought here don't rob temples or insult our goddess. [38]Now if Demetrius and his workers have something against anyone, we have special days and proconsuls to hold court; there they should accuse one another. [39]And if you want anything else, it must be settled in a legal meeting. [40]We're in danger of being accused of a riot today for which there is no good reason. We'll not be able to explain this mob." [41]After saying this, he dismissed the assembly.

20 When the uproar had died down, Paul sent for the disciples, encouraged them, and saying goodbye to them, left to go to Macedonia.[l] [2]He went through those parts of the country and spoke much to encourage the people and then went to Greece [3]and stayed there three months.[m]

At Troas

Just as Paul was going to sail for Syria, the Jews plotted against him, so he decided to go back through Macedonia. [4]Sopater from Berea, the son of Pyrrhus, went with him; also Aristarchus and Secundus from Thessalonica, and Gaius from Derbe, and Timothy, but Tychicus and Trophimus were from the province of Asia; [5]they came and were waiting for us in Troas. [6]After the Passover days of Bread Without Yeast we sailed from Philippi and in five days came to them in Troas and stayed there seven days.

[7]On Sunday, when we met for a meal, Paul spoke to the people. Since he intended to leave the next day, he went on talking until midnight. [8]There were many lamps in the upstairs room where we were meeting.

[9]A young man by the name of Eutychus, sitting in the window, was dropping off into a deep sleep as Paul talked on and on. Finally, overcome by sleep, he fell down from the third story and was picked up dead. [10]But Paul went down, lay on him, and took him into his arms. "Don't get excited," he said. "He's alive!" [11]Then he went upstairs again, broke the bread, and ate. And after a long talk that lasted until the sun rose, he left.

[12]The people took the young man away alive and were very much comforted.

From Troas to Miletus

[13]We went ahead to the boat and sailed to Assos. There we were going to take Paul into the boat; he had arranged it that way, planning himself to go there on foot. [14]When we met him in Assos, we took him on board and went on to Mitylene. [15]We sailed from there and on the following day came opposite Chios. The next day we crossed over to Samos and on the next came to Miletus. [16]Paul had decided to sail past Ephesus to avoid spending time in the province of Asia; he was in a hurry to get to Jerusalem for the

---

l - 1   From Macedonia in A.D. 55 Paul wrote his second letter to the Corinthians.
m - 3   From Corinth in A.D. 56 Paul wrote his letter to the Romans.

day of Pentecost if possible.

With the Spiritual Leaders of Ephesus

[17]From Miletus he sent men to Ephesus to get the spiritual leaders of the church. [18]When they came to him, he said to them: "You know how I lived with you all the time from the first day I came into the province of Asia; [19]how I served the Lord very humbly, with tears, and in trials I endured as the Jews plotted against me; [20]how I didn't shrink from telling you anything that would help you or from teaching you publicly and from house to house; [21]and how I earnestly warned Jews and non-Jews to turn from sin to God and to believe in our Lord Jesus. [22]And now, you see, the spirit compels me to go to Jerusalem. I don't know what will happen to me there, [23]except that the Holy Spirit keeps warning me from town to town that chains and troubles are waiting for me. [24]I don't count my life worth anything. I just want to finish running my race and doing the work the Lord Jesus entrusted to me, declaring the good news of God's grace.

[25]"I went around among you preaching the kingdom, and now I know none of you will see me again. [26]That is why I declare to you today I am innocent of the blood of any of you, [27]because I didn't shrink from telling you God's whole plan.

[28]"Take care of yourselves and the whole *flock* in which the Holy Spirit has made you spiritual overseers to be shepherds of *God's church that He bought* with His own blood. [29]I know when I'm gone fierce wolves will come among you and not spare the flock. [30]And even some of your own men will start to tell perversions of the truth to get the disciples to leave and follow them. [31]So watch and remember how for three years, day and night, I didn't stop warning everyone with tears. [32]And now I entrust you to God and to the Word of His grace, which can build you up and give you *the salvation to be shared by all who are made holy.*

[33]"I didn't want anyone's silver or gold or clothes. [34]You know these hands worked for what I needed and for the men with me. [35]In every way I showed you that by working hard as I do we should help the weak and remember what the Lord Jesus said: 'We are more blessed when we give than when we receive.' "

[36]When he had said this, he knelt down with all of them and prayed. [37]They wept very much, put their arms around Paul, and kissed him. [38]It hurt them most of all that he had said they wouldn't see him again. Then they took him to the ship.

At Tyre

21 When we had broken away from them, we sailed and followed a straight course to Cos and the next day to Rhodes and from there to Patara. [2]We found a ship going across to Phoenicia, went on board, and sailed. [3]We

---

28 *Ps 74:1-2*   32 *Deut 33:3-4*

came in sight of Cyprus, and leaving it on our left, sailed on to Syria and landed at Tyre because the ship was to unload its cargo there.

⁴We looked up the disciples and stayed there seven days. By the Spirit they told Paul not to go up to Jerusalem. ⁵When our time was up, we started on our way. All of them with their wives and children accompanied us out of the city. There we knelt on the beach and prayed ⁶and said good-bye to one another. Then we went on board the ship, and they went back home.

At Caesarea

⁷We continued our sailing, going from Tyre to Ptolemais. There we greeted our fellow Christians and spent a day with them. ⁸The next day we left and came to Caesarea. We went into the home of Philip the evangelist, one of the seven, and stayed with him. ⁹He had four unmarried daughters who prophesied.

¹⁰While we were staying there longer than we had expected, a prophet by the name of Agabus came down from Judea. ¹¹He came to us, took Paul's belt, tied his own feet and hands, and said, "The Holy Spirit says, 'This is how the Jews in Jerusalem will tie the man this belt belongs to and hand him over to the non-Jews.'"

¹²When we heard this, we and those living there urged him not to go up to Jerusalem.

¹³Then Paul answered, "What are you doing — crying and making me weak in my purpose? I'm ready not only to be bound but even to die in Jerusalem for the name of the Lord Jesus."

¹⁴When he would not be persuaded, we were silent and could only say, "The Lord's will be done."

In Jerusalem

¹⁵After those days we got ready and started for Jerusalem. ¹⁶Some of the disciples from Caesarea came with us and took us to the home of Mnason to be his guests. He was from Cyprus and was one of the first disciples. ¹⁷When we came to Jerusalem, our fellow Christians eagerly welcomed us.

¹⁸The next day we went with Paul to James, and all the spiritual leaders came there, too. ¹⁹After greeting them, Paul told them everything God had done through his work among the non-Jews.

²⁰When they heard about it, they praised God. They told him, "You see, brother, how many tens of thousands among the Jews now believe, and all are zealous for the Law. ²¹They've been told you teach all the Jews living among the non-Jews to turn away from Moses and tell them not to circumcise their children or follow the customs. ²²What should we do about it? They will certainly hear you have come. ²³So do what we tell you. We have four men who are under a vow. ²⁴Take them, purify yourself with them,

and pay their expenses so that they may *shave their heads*. Then everyone will know there's nothing in what they've told about you but you live strictly according to the Law. 25About the non-Jews who now believe, we wrote in a letter we decided they should keep away from food sacrificed to idols, from blood, from the meat of strangled animals, and from sexual sin."

26Then Paul took the men and the next day purified himself with them and went to the temple to announce when, with the bringing of the sacrifice for each of them, *the days* of purification *would be over*.

27When the seven days were almost over, the Jews from the province of Asia, seeing him in the temple, stirred up the whole crowd. They grabbed him, 28yelling, "Men of Israel, help! This is the man who in his teaching everyone everywhere is against our people, the Law, and this place. And now he has even brought non-Jews into the temple and made this holy place unclean." 29They had seen Trophimus from Ephesus with him in the city and thought Paul had taken him into the temple.

30The whole city was aroused and the people rushed together. They took Paul, dragged him out of the temple, and immediately the doors were shut.

31They were trying to kill him when it was reported to the tribune who was in charge of about 600 soldiers: "All Jerusalem is stirred up!" 32Immediately he took soldiers and captains and ran down to them. When they saw the tribune and the soldiers, they stopped hitting Paul. 33Then the tribune went to him, arrested him, and ordered him bound with two chains.

He asked who he was and what he had done. 34Some in the crowd shouted this and some that. There was such a noisy confusion that he couldn't get the facts, so he ordered Paul to be taken to the barracks. 35When Paul came to the stairs, the crowd was so violent the soldiers had to carry him. 36The mob was right behind them, yelling, "Kill him!"

Paul Defends Himself

37Just as he was going to be taken into the barracks, Paul asked the tribune, "May I say something to you?"

"Can you talk Greek?" he asked. 38"Aren't you the Egyptian who some time ago got four thousand daggermen to rebel and follow him into the wilderness?"

39"I'm a Jew," Paul answered, "from Tarsus in Cilicia, a citizen of an important city. Now I'm asking you, let me talk to the people."

40And he let him. Then Paul, standing on the stairs, waved his hand to quiet the people. When there was a hush all around, he spoke to them in Aramaic:

22 "Brothers and fathers, listen as I now defend myself before you."
²When they heard him call to them in their own language, they quieted down still more.

³Then he said: "I'm a Jew, born in Tarsus in Cilicia but raised in this city, trained at the feet of Gamaliel in the strict ways of the Law of our fathers, as zealous for God as all of you are today. ⁴I hunted to their death men and women who believed as I do now, tying them up and putting them in prisons, ⁵as the high priest and the whole council of elders can tell about me. From them I got letters to our fellow Jews in Damascus and was going there to bind those who were there and bring them to Jerusalem to be punished. ⁶But as I was on my way and coming near Damascus, suddenly about noon a bright light from heaven flashed around me. ⁷I fell to the ground and heard a voice asking me, 'Saul! Saul! Why are you persecuting Me?'

⁸"I asked, 'Who are You, Lord?'

" 'I am Jesus from Nazareth,' He told me, 'Whom you are persecuting.' ⁹The men who were with me saw the light but didn't understand the voice of Him Who was talking to me.

¹⁰"Then I asked, 'What should I do, Lord?'

"The Lord told me, 'Get up, go into Damascus, and there you will be told everything you are ordered to do.'

¹¹"That light was so bright I couldn't see anything. So the men who were with me took me by the hand and led me into Damascus.

¹²"There was Ananias, a man who feared God according to the Law, and all the Jews living there spoke well of him. ¹³He came to me and stood by me. 'Brother Saul,' he said to me, 'see again!' Immediately I could see him.

¹⁴"He said, 'The God of our fathers chose you to know His will, to see the Righteous One and hear Him speak to you, ¹⁵because you must be His witness and tell everyone what you've seen and heard. ¹⁶And now, what are you waiting for? Get up, and calling on His name, have yourself baptized and your sins washed away.'

¹⁷"I came back to Jerusalem. While I was praying in the temple, I fell into a trance ¹⁸and saw Him. 'Hurry,' He told me, 'and get out of Jerusalem quickly because they will not accept the truth you tell about Me.'

¹⁹" 'Lord,' I said, 'they know I went from synagogue to synagogue and put in prison and beat those who believe in You. ²⁰And when the blood of Your witness Stephen was being poured out, I was standing by, approving, and watching the clothes of those who were murdering him.'

²¹" 'Go,' He told me. 'I will send you far away to people who are not Jews.' "

²²They listened to him until he said that. Then they shouted, "Kill him! Rid the world of such a fellow! He's not fit to live!"

²³While they were yelling, tossing their clothes around, and throwing dust in the air, ²⁴the tribune ordered him taken to the barracks and told his men to get information from Paul by whipping him. He wanted to find

out why the people were yelling at him like this. ²⁵But when his men had stretched him out with the straps, Paul asked the captain standing nearby, "Is it right for you to whip a Roman citizen who hasn't been condemned?"

²⁶When the captain heard this, he went and told the tribune about it. "What are you going to do?" he asked. "This man is a Roman citizen."

²⁷The tribune went and asked Paul, "Tell me, are you a Roman citizen?"

"Yes," he said.

²⁸The tribune declared, "I had to pay a lot of money to be a citizen."

"But I was born a citizen," Paul said.

²⁹Immediately those who were going to examine him withdrew from him. When the tribune found out Paul was a Roman citizen, he was frightened because he had tied him up.

Paul Before the Council

³⁰The next day, since he wanted to find out exactly what the Jews were accusing Paul of, he untied him and ordered the ruling priests and the whole council to meet. Then he brought Paul down and had him stand before them.

23 Paul looked earnestly at the council and said, "Fellow Jews, I have lived before God with a very good conscience to this very day."

²The high priest Ananias ordered the men standing near him to strike him on the mouth. ³Then Paul said to him, "God will strike you, you whitewashed wall! Do you sit there to judge me according to the Law and yet break the Law by ordering them to strike me?"

⁴The men standing near him asked, "Do you insult God's high priest?"

⁵"Fellow Jews," Paul answered, "I didn't know he's the high priest. The Bible does say: *'Don't speak evil of a ruler of your people.'*"

⁶When Paul saw that some of them were Sadducees and others Pharisees, he called out in the council, "Fellow Jews, I'm a Pharisee and a son of Pharisees. I'm on trial for my hope that the dead will rise."

⁷When he said that, the Pharisees and Sadducees started to quarrel, and the men in the meeting were divided. ⁸The Sadducees say the dead don't rise and there is no angel or spirit, while the Pharisees believe in all these things. ⁹So there was some loud shouting. Some of the Bible scholars who belonged to the party of the Pharisees got up and argued vehemently: "We find nothing wrong with this man. Suppose a spirit spoke to him, or an angel —."

¹⁰The quarrel was getting violent, and the tribune was afraid they would tear Paul to pieces. So he ordered the soldiers to go down, take him away from them by force, and bring him to the soldiers' quarters.

¹¹That night the Lord stood near him and said, "Keep up your courage!

5 *Ex 22:28*

As you have told the truth about Me in Jerusalem, so you must tell it in Rome."

The Plot to Kill Paul

¹²In the morning the Jews banded together and vowed that God should punish them if they ate or drank anything before they had killed Paul. ¹³There were more than forty who swore to carry out this plot.

¹⁴They went to the ruling priests and elders and said, "We have vowed that God should punish us if we taste any food before we have killed Paul. ¹⁵Now then, you and the council tell the tribune to bring him down to you as if you meant to get more exact information about him. We're ready to kill him before he gets to you."

¹⁶But the son of Paul's sister heard about the ambush. He came and entered the barracks and told Paul. ¹⁷Then Paul called one of the captains and told him, "Take this young man to the tribune. He has something to tell him."

¹⁸He took him to the tribune and said, "The prisoner Paul called me and asked me to bring this young man to you. He has something to tell you."

¹⁹The tribune took him by the arm and stepping aside to be alone with him, he asked him, "What do you have to tell me?"

²⁰"The Jews," he answered, "have agreed to ask you to bring Paul down to the council tomorrow as if they meant to get more information about him. ²¹Now, don't you listen to them. More than forty of them are planning to ambush him. They have vowed that God should punish them if they eat or drink anything before they have murdered him. They're ready now, just waiting for you to promise them."

²²The tribune dismissed the young man. "Don't tell anyone you reported this to me," he ordered.

²³Then he called two of his captains and said, "Get two hundred soldiers to go to Caesarea, and seventy on horses, and two hundred with spears, and have them ready to start at nine tonight." ²⁴They were also to provide animals for Paul to ride on and so to take him safely to Governor Felix. ²⁵The tribune wrote a letter with this message:

²⁶"Claudius Lysias sends greetings to the excellent Governor Felix.

²⁷"The Jews had seized this man and were going to murder him, but when I found out he was a Roman citizen, I came with the soldiers and rescued him. ²⁸I wanted to know what they had against him; so I took him down to their council ²⁹and found their accusations had to do with questions about their Law, but there was none for which he deserved to die or to be in chains. ³⁰Since I'm informed that they're plotting against the man, I'm quickly sending him to you and also ordering his accusers to state before you what they have against him."

³¹So the foot soldiers, as they were ordered, took Paul and brought him to Antipatris during the night. ³²The next day they returned to their barracks, letting the men on horses ride on with him. ³³When these came to

Caesarea, they delivered the letter to the governor and handed Paul over to him. [34]After he read the letter, he asked which province he was from and found out he was from Cilicia. [35]"I will hear your case," he said, "when your accusers come." And he ordered him kept in Herod's palace.

Before Felix

24 Five days later the high priest Ananias came down with some elders and Tertullus, an attorney, and they reported to the governor what they had against Paul. [2]When Paul had been called, Tertullus started to accuse him, saying, "Excellent Felix, you have brought us much peace, and your foresight has given these people reforms [3]in every way and in every place. We appreciate them and thank you very much. [4]Not to keep you too long — I ask you to listen in your kindly way to what we briefly have to say. [5]We have found this man a pest who starts quarrels among all the Jews in the world, and he is a ringleader of the sect of the Nazarenes. [6]He even tried to pollute the temple, and so we arrested him.[n] When you examine him yourself, you will be able to find out from him everything of which we accuse him."

[9]The Jews supported his attack by declaring these things were so.

[10]The governor nodded to Paul to speak, and he answered, "For many years you have been a judge of this nation. Knowing that, I'm glad to defend myself. [11]Only eleven days ago, as you can find out for yourself, I went up to Jerusalem to worship. [12]They didn't find me arguing with anyone in the temple or stirring up a crowd in the synagogues or in the city; [13]and they can't prove to you the things they're now accusing me of. [14]But I confess to you that according to the Christian religion, which they call a sect, I worship *the God of our fathers*. I believe everything written in the Law and the prophets [15]and trust God for the same thing they're looking for, that the dead will rise, the righteous and the wicked. [16]That's why I'm doing my best always to have a clear conscience before God and men. [17]After some years I came to my people to bring gifts for the poor and offerings. [18]They found me busy with these and purified in the temple, but there was no crowd or noisy mob. [19]There were some Jews from the province of Asia, who should be here before you to accuse me if they have anything against me. [20]Or these men should tell what wrong they found in me as I stood before their council, [21]unless it's the one thing I shouted when I stood among them: 'I'm on trial before you today in regard to the resurrection of the dead.'"

[22]But Felix, who knew the Christian religion rather well, told them to wait for a decision. "When Tribune Lysias comes down," he said, "I will decide your case." [23]He ordered the captain to guard him but to let him have some liberty and not keep any of his friends from helping him.

[24]Some days later Felix came again. His wife Drusilla, who was a Jew, was with him. He sent for Paul and heard him tell about faith in Christ Jesus. [25]As he spoke of righteousness, self-control, and the coming judg-

ment, Felix was frightened and answered, "Go now. When I get a chance, I'll send for you." ²⁶At the same time he expected Paul to give him money. And so he used to send for him often and talk with him.

²⁷Two whole years passed. Then Porcius Festus succeeded Felix. Since Felix wanted to do the Jews a favor, he left Paul in prison.

Paul Appeals to the Emperor

25 Three days after Festus took over his duties in the province of Judea, he went from Caesarea up to Jerusalem. ²The ruling priests and the leaders of the Jews reported to Festus what they had against Paul. They urged ³and begged him to do them a favor and have Paul brought to Jerusalem. They were laying an ambush to kill him on the way.

⁴But Festus answered that Paul would be kept in Caesarea and he himself would be going there soon. ⁵"Those of you who have the authority," he said, "come down with me, and if the man has done anything wrong, accuse him." ⁶He stayed with them no more than eight or ten days and then went down to Caesarea. The next day he sat on the judge's chair and ordered Paul brought in.

⁷When Paul came in, the Jews who had come down from Jerusalem surrounded him and were accusing him of many serious wrongs that they couldn't prove. ⁸Paul defended himself: "I have in no way sinned against the Law of the Jews or the temple or the emperor."

⁹But Festus wanted to do the Jews a favor. So he asked Paul, "Do you want to go up to Jerusalem to be tried there before me in regard to these things?"

¹⁰"I'm standing before the emperor's judgment seat," Paul said, "and there I must be tried. I haven't done the Jews any wrong, as you, too, know very well. ¹¹Now if I'm guilty and have done something to deserve to die, I don't refuse to die. But if their accusations are nothing, no one can hand me over to them. I appeal to the emperor!"

¹²Festus talked it over with his council and then answered, "You appealed to the emperor; you will go to the emperor!"

¹³Some time later King Agrippa and Bernice came down to Caesarea to welcome Festus. ¹⁴When they stayed there a number of days, Festus laid Paul's case before the king.

"There's a man here whom Felix left in prison," he said. ¹⁵"When I went up to Jerusalem, the ruling priests and elders of the Jews informed me about him and asked me to condemn him.

¹⁶"I answered them, 'It isn't customary for Romans to hand over a man before he has faced his accusers and had a chance to defend himself against their accusation.'

---

14 Ex 3:6

---

n - 6 Our oldest manuscripts lack vv. 6b-8a: "And we wanted to try him under our Law. But Tribune Lysias came along and with much force took him out of our hands, ordering his accusers to come before you."

[17]"They came here with me, and the next day without any delay I sat down in the judge's chair and ordered the man to be brought. [18]When his accusers got up, they didn't accuse him of the crimes I was suspecting. [19]But they disagreed with him about their own religion and about a certain Jesus who died; Paul claimed he is alive. [20]I was puzzled how I should look into this and asked if he would like to go to Jerusalem and be tried there in regard to these things. [21]But Paul appealed. He wanted to be held and have Augustus° decide his case. So I ordered him to be kept in prison until I send him to the emperor."

[22]Agrippa told Festus, "I myself would like to hear the man." "Tomorrow," he answered, "you will hear him."

Before Agrippa

[23]The next day Agrippa and Bernice came with great pomp and went with the tribunes and leading men of the city into the hall. Then Festus gave the order, and Paul was brought in.

[24]"King Agrippa and all you men here with us," Festus said, "You see this man about whom all the Jewish people in Jerusalem and here have appealed to me, shouting he mustn't live any longer. [25]I found he hasn't done anything to deserve to die, but when he appealed to Augustus, I decided to send him. [26]I don't have anything reliable to write our lord about him. So I have brought him before you, and especially before you, King Agrippa, so we could examine him and I'll have something to write. [27]It makes no sense to me to send a prisoner without reporting what he's accused of."

26 Agrippa said to Paul, "You may speak for yourself."

Then Paul, stretching out his hand, began to defend himself:

[2]"King Agrippa, I think I am fortunate in that I am going to defend myself today before you in regard to everything the Jews accuse me of, [3]because you are so very familiar with all the Jewish customs and problems. So I ask you to listen to me patiently.

[4]"The Jews all know how I lived from my youth, from my earliest days, among my people in Jerusalem. [5]They have known long ago, if they want to tell the truth, that I lived the life of a Pharisee, the strictest party of our religion.

[6]"And now I'm on trial here because I trust the promise God made to our fathers. [7]Our twelve tribes, worshiping zealously day and night, expect to see this promise come true. This is the hope, O King, in regard to which some Jews accuse me. [8]Why do you think it incredible that God raises the dead?

[9]"Once I believed I had to work hard against the name of Jesus from Nazareth. [10]I did that in Jerusalem. By the authority I received from the ruling priests I locked up many of the holy people in prison, and when they

---

o - 21   Another title for Nero

were to be killed, I voted against them. [11]And many a time in every synagogue I would punish them to make them blaspheme, and raging furiously against them, I hunted them down even to foreign cities.

[12]"That is how I came to be traveling to Damascus, authorized and appointed by the ruling priests, [13]when on the way, O King, at noon I saw a light brighter than the sun, flashing from heaven around me and those who were going with me. [14]All of us fell to the ground, and I heard a voice asking me in the Jewish language, 'Saul, Saul! Why are you persecuting Me? You're only hurting yourself by kicking against the goads.'

[15]"I asked, 'Who are you, Lord?'

" 'I am Jesus,' the Lord answered, 'Whom you are persecuting. [16]But get up and *stand on your feet*. I showed Myself to you to appoint you to serve Me and tell the truth of what you have seen and what you will see whenever I appear to you. [17]*I will rescue you* from your people and *from the non-Jews to whom I'm sending you*, [18]*to open their eyes* and turn them *from darkness to light* and from Satan's control to God so that they receive the forgiveness of sins and the inheritance of those who are made holy through faith in Me.'

[19]"And so, King Agrippa, I didn't disobey what I saw from heaven, [20]but first I told the people in Damascus and Jerusalem, then the whole country of the Jews, and the other nations to turn from sin to God and do the works that show they have repented. [21]For this the Jews grabbed me in the temple and tried to murder me.

[22]"God has helped me to this day, and so I have been standing and telling the truth to high and low, stating only what the prophets and Moses said would happen, [23]that Christ had to suffer and by being the first to rise from the dead would announce *light to* our people and the other *nations*."

[24]As he was defending himself in this way, Festus shouted, "You're insane, Paul! Your great learning is driving you out of your mind."

[25]"I'm not insane, excellent Festus," Paul said, "but I'm telling the sober truth. [26]The king knows about these things, and I'm talking boldly to him. I'm sure he hasn't missed any of them, since this wasn't done in a corner. [27]King Agrippa, do you believe the prophets? I know you believe them!"

[28]"You're trying to persuade me," Agrippa said to Paul, "that with a little effort you've made me a Christian!"

[29]"I wish to God," Paul said, "that with little or much effort not only you but all who hear me today would become what I am — except for these chains!"

[30]The king, the governor, Bernice, and those who sat with them got up [31]and left and said to one another, "This man isn't doing anything to deserve to die or be in chains."

[32]"This man could be free," Agrippa told Festus, "if he hadn't appealed to the emperor."

16 Ezek 2:1-2   17 Chr 16:35; Jer 1:7-8   18 Is 35:5; 42:7,16

Paul Sails for Rome

27 When it was decided we should sail to Italy, Paul and some other prisoners were turned over to a captain by the name of Julius, of the troop of Augustus. [2]We boarded a ship from Adramyttium that was going to sail to the ports on the coast of the province of Asia, and we started out. Aristarchus, a Macedonian from Thessalonica, went with us.

[3]The next day we landed at Sidon, where Julius treated Paul kindly and let him go to his friends to get any care he needed. [4]Leaving Sidon, we sailed on the sheltered side of Cyprus because the winds were against us. [5]We crossed the sea off Cilicia and Pamphylia and landed at Myra in Lycia. [6]There the captain of the soldiers found a ship from Alexandria sailing to Italy and put us on it. [7]We were sailing slowly for a number of days and had some difficulty getting near Cnidus. The wind wouldn't let us go on, and so, starting at Cape Salmone, we sailed on the sheltered side of Crete. [8]Hugging the coast, we struggled on to a place called Fair Havens, near the town of Lasea.

[9]We had lost a lot of time. Even the day of fasting[p] had already gone by, and sailing was now dangerous. [10]So Paul advised them: "Men, I see that in this sailing we're going to suffer hardship and a heavy loss not only of the cargo and ship but also of our lives." [11]But the captain of the soldiers listened to the pilot and the captain of the ship and not to what Paul said. [12]Since that harbor was not a good place to spend the winter, the majority decided to sail away, hoping they could somehow reach Phoenix to spend the winter there. It is a harbor of Crete facing southwest and northwest. [13]When a gentle breeze blew from the south, they felt they could easily make it. They took up the anchor and sailed close to the shore of Crete.

[14]But after a little while a hurricane, called Northeaster, dashed down from Crete. [15]It caught the ship so that it couldn't face the wind, and we gave up and were swept along. [16]As we ran into the shelter of a small island called Clauda, we managed with a struggle to get hold of the lifeboat. [17]They pulled it up on deck. Then they passed ropes around the ship to reinforce it. Fearing they would run on the great sandbank near Africa, they lowered the sail and so drifted along. [18]We continued to be tossed by the storm so violently that the next day the men started to throw the cargo overboard, [19]and on the third with their own hands they threw the ship's equipment overboard. [20]For a number of days we couldn't see any sun or stars and were in a great storm until at last we were giving up all hope of coming through alive.

[21]Since hardly anyone wanted to eat, Paul stepped before them and said, "Men, you should have listened to me and not have sailed from Crete. You would have avoided this hardship and damage. [22]But now I urge you to cheer up because you will lose no lives but only the ship. [23]I am God's

own and serve Him. Last night His angel stood by me. ²⁴'Don't be afraid, Paul!' he said, 'You must stand before the emperor, and now God has given you all who are sailing with you.' ²⁵So, cheer up, men, because I trust God it will be just as He told me. ²⁶But we must run on some island."

The Shipwreck

²⁷It was the fourteenth night and we were drifting through the Adriatic Sea^q when about midnight the sailors suspected land was coming closer. ²⁸They dropped the lead and found the water 120 feet deep. A little farther they dropped it again and found it was 90 feet. ²⁹Fearing we might run on rocks, they dropped four anchors from the back of the ship and prayed for morning to come.

³⁰Then the sailors tried to escape from the ship. They let the lifeboat down into the sea, pretending they were going to take out the anchors from the front of the ship and let them down. ³¹But Paul told the captain of the soldiers and his men, "If these don't stay on the ship, you can't be rescued." ³²Then the soldiers cut the ropes that held the boat and let it drift away.

³³Just before daybreak Paul was urging them all to eat something. "This is the fourteenth day you've waited and gone hungry and not eaten a thing. ³⁴So I urge you to eat something. It will help you come through this safely. None of you will lose a hair of his head." ³⁵After saying this, he took some bread, thanked God in front of everyone, broke it, and started to eat. ³⁶They were all cheered up, and they too had something to eat. ³⁷There were 276 of us in the ship. ³⁸After they had eaten all they wanted, they lightened the ship by dumping the wheat into the sea.

³⁹In the morning they couldn't tell what land it was but gradually could see a bay with a beach on which they planned, if possible, to run the ship ashore. ⁴⁰They cut off the anchors and left them in the sea. At the same time they untied the ropes that held up the steering oars, spread out the foresail to catch the wind, and steered the ship to the shore. ⁴¹They struck a bank in the water and ran the ship aground. The front of the ship stuck and couldn't be moved, while the back was being pounded to pieces by the sea.

⁴²To keep any of the prisoners from swimming away and escaping, the soldiers planned to kill them, ⁴³but the captain of the soldiers wanted to save Paul; so he kept them from doing this. He ordered those who could swim to jump out first and get to the shore, ⁴⁴and the rest to follow, some on planks and some on other pieces from the ship. In this way all of them came safely to the shore.

---

23 Is 42:6

q - 27　　At that time the "Adriatic" Sea included the present Adriatic plus a large part of the Mediterranean Sea south of it.

Safe on Malta

28 Once we were safe on the shore, we found out that the island was called Malta. [2]The natives were unusually kind to us. It had started to rain and was cold, and so they made a fire and welcomed all of us around it.

[3]Paul gathered an armful of dry branches and put them on the fire. The heat made a viper come out, and it bit his hand. [4]When the natives saw the snake hanging from his hand, they said to one another, "This man certainly is a murderer! He did escape from the sea, but justice didn't let him live."

[5]So he shook the snake into the fire and suffered no harm. [6]They were waiting for him to swell up or suddenly fall down dead. But they waited long and saw nothing unusual happen to him. Then they changed their minds and said he was a god. [7]The governor of the island, whose name was Publius, had land around that place. He welcomed us and treated us kindly while we were his guests for three days. [8]The father of Publius happened to be sick in bed with fever and dysentery.

Paul went to him, prayed, and laid his hands on him, and made him well.

[9]After that had happened, the other sick people on the island also came to him and were made well. [10]They honored us in many ways, and when we were going to sail, they put on board whatever we needed.

From Malta to Rome

[11]After three months we sailed on a ship from Alexandria that had stopped at the island for the winter. It had in front a figure of the Twin Sons of Zeus.[r] [12]We stopped at Syracuse and stayed there three days. [13]From there we sailed around and came to Rhegium. After a day a south wind started blowing, and on the second day we came to Puteoli. [14]There we found fellow Christians who urged us to stay seven days with them.

And so we came to Rome. [15]The fellow Christians in Rome, who had heard about us, came as far as the Market Town of Appius and the Three Shops to meet us. When Paul saw them, he thanked God and was encouraged.

In Rome

[16]When we came into Rome, Paul was allowed to live by himself with the soldier guarding him. [17]After three days he called the leaders of the Jews together. When they came, he said to them, "Fellow Jews, although I haven't done anything against our people or the customs of our fathers, I'm a prisoner from Jerusalem who was handed over to the Romans. [18]They examined me and wanted to let me go because I had done no wrong to deserve

---

r - 11   Castor and Pollux, the guardian gods of sailors.

to die. [19]But the Jews objected and forced me to appeal to the emperor —
not that I'm accusing my people of anything. [20]That's why I asked to see
you and talk to you, since it is for the hope of Israel I wear this chain."

[21]"We have had no letters from Judea about you," they told him, "and
no Jew coming here has reported or said anything bad about you. [22]We
would like to hear from you what you think, because we know that everywhere people are talking against this sect."

[23]They set a day to meet with him, and more of them came to him
where he was staying. From morning until evening he explained the matter to them, earnestly telling the truth about God's kingdom and trying to
convince them about Jesus from the Law of Moses and the prophets. [24]Some
of them were convinced by what he said, but others wouldn't believe.

[25]They disagreed with one another as they were leaving, and Paul
added a statement: "The Holy Spirit spoke the truth to your fathers
through the prophet Isaiah [26]when he said: *'Go to these people and say*:

> *You will hear and never understand, look and never see,*
> [27] *because these people have become dull at heart*
> *and hard of hearing*
> *and have shut their eyes,*
> *so that their eyes don't see,*
> *their ears don't hear,*
> *their hearts don't understand,*
> *and they never turn to Me for healing.'*

[28]"You should know that *God's salvation* has been sent *to the non-
Jews*, and they will listen."[s]

[30]For two whole years he lived in his own rented place and welcomed
all who came to him. [31]He preached God's kingdom and very boldly taught
the truth about the Lord Jesus Christ, and no one stopped him.

26-27 Is 6:9-10   *28 Ps 67:2; 98:2-3*

s - 28   Our oldest manuscripts lack v. 29: "And after he said this, the Jews left, arguing
vigorously among themselves."

PAUL
WRITES TO THE
ROMANS

1 PAUL, SERVANT OF JESUS CHRIST, called to be an apostle and appointed to tell God's good news—
²He promised it long ago through His prophets in the Holy Bible. ³It is about His Son, Who was born a descendant of David, in terms of human descent; ⁴but according to His spirit of holiness, He was declared to be the mighty Son of God by His resurrection. And He is our Lord Jesus Christ, ⁵through Whom we have received God's grace and the privilege of being apostles for faith's obedience and so glorify Him among all nations. ⁶This includes you who have been called to belong to Jesus Christ — ⁷to all in Rome whom God loves and has called to be His holy people: Grace to you and peace from God our Father and the Lord Jesus Christ.

I Want to See You

⁸First, I thank my God through Jesus Christ for all of you because the news of your faith is spreading all over the world. ⁹God, Whom I serve in my spirit by telling the good news of His Son, knows how I never fail to mention you ¹⁰whenever I pray and to ask that somehow by God's will I will now at last succeed in coming to you. ¹¹I long to see you, to share a spiritual gift with you to strengthen you. ¹²I mean when I'm with you I'll be encouraged by your faith and you by mine. ¹³I want you to know, fellow Christians, so far I have been kept from coming to you, but I often planned to come in order to enjoy some results of working among you as I do among the other non-Jewish people. ¹⁴I must help Greeks and non-Greeks, the wise and the foolish. ¹⁵So I'm eager to bring the good news also to you in Rome.

¹⁶I am not ashamed of the Gospel. It is God's power to save everyone who believes it, the Jew first and also the Greek. ¹⁷For it reveals the righteousness which comes from God by faith to bring people to faith, as the Bible says: *"The righteous will live by faith."*

God Is Angry

¹⁸God in heaven shows He is angry at all the ungodliness and wickedness of people who by their wickedness hold back the truth. ¹⁹What can be known about God is clear to them because God has made it clear to them. ²⁰Ever since He made the world, they have seen the unseen things of God

---

17 Hab 2:4

— from the things He made they can tell He has everlasting power and is God. Then they have no excuse. [21]They knew God and didn't honor Him as God or thank Him, but their thoughts turned to worthless things, and their ignorant hearts were darkened. [22]Claiming to be wise, they showed how foolish they are [23]when *for the glory* of God, who cannot die, *they substituted images* of man, who dies, and of birds, four-footed animals, and reptiles. [24]And so God, letting them follow the lusts of their hearts, gave them up to live immorally and dishonor their bodies [25]because they traded the true God for a lie, worshiped and served what was created instead of the Creator, Who is blessed forever. Amen! [26]That is why God gave them up to shameful lusts. Women have changed their natural way to an unnatural one. [27]And men likewise have given up the natural relation with a woman and burned with lust for one another, men doing shameful acts with men and for their error getting punished in themselves as they must. [28]As they refused to know God any longer, God gave them up so that their minds were degraded and they lived immorally. [29]Their lives are full of all kinds of wrongdoing, wickedness, greed, malice. They are full of envy, murder, quarreling, treachery, viciousness. They gossip and slander. [30]They hate God. They are insulting, proud, boasting. They invent new evils. They disobey parents. [31]They are foolish. They break their promises. They have no love or mercy. [32]Knowing God's righteous decree that those who do such things deserve to die, they not only do them but approve when others do them.

God Will Judge the Jews

2 So, whoever you are, if you condemn anyone, you have no excuse. What you condemn in anyone else you condemn in yourself, since you, the judge, are doing the same things. [2]We know God is right when He condemns people for doing such things. [3]When you condemn people for doing such things but do them yourself, do you think you will escape being condemned by God? [4]Or do you think lightly of God, Who is very kind to you, patiently puts up with you, and waits so long before He punishes you? Can't you see God is kind to you to move you to repent of your sins?

[5]But *because of your stubborn* and unrepentant *heart*, you are ensuring that *God will be* more and more *angry* with you on the Day of His Anger, when God will show how righteous His judgment is. [6]*He will give everyone according to what he has done*: [7]everlasting life to those who by patiently doing good look for glory, honor, and immortality, [8]but anger and fury to those who, because they are selfish and refuse to listen to the truth, follow wickedness. [9]There will be sorrow and anguish for every human being doing wrong, for the Jew first and also the Greek; [10]but glory, honor, and peace for everyone doing good, for the Jew first and also the Greek. [11]*God doesn't favor one person over another.*

[12]All who sin without having the Law will perish without the Law. And all who sin having the Law will be judged by the Law. [13]We aren't right-

23 Ps 106:20; Deut 4:16-18   5 Prov 28:14   6 Ps 62:12; Prov 24:12   11 Deut 10:17

eous before God if we only hear the Law, but if we do what the Law says, we'll be declared righteous. [14]When people who are not Jews and don't have the Law do by nature what the Law says, they who don't have the Law are a law to themselves. [15]They show that what the law wants them to do is written in their hearts. Their conscience tells the same truth, and their thoughts between themselves accuse them or defend them, [16]as we'll see on the day when God through Christ Jesus judges the secrets of people according to the good news I tell.

Who Is a Jew?

[17]Suppose you call yourself a Jew, rest comfortably in your Law, boast about your God, [18]know what He wants, and approve of the better things, being instructed in the Law, [19]and feel sure you're a guide to the blind and a light to those in the dark, [20]that you can train the foolish and teach children because you have in the Law the body of knowledge and truth. [21]You teach someone else — won't you teach yourself? You preach, *"Do not steal"* — are you stealing? [22]You say, *"Do not commit adultery"* — are you doing it yourself? You are disgusted with idols — are you robbing their temples? [23]You boast about the Law — are you breaking the Law and so dishonoring God? [24]*"You make the non-Jews slander God's name,"* as the Bible says.

[25]Circumcision helps you only if you do what the Law says. If you are breaking the Law, you have lost your circumcision. [26]If an uncircuised man does what the Law demands, will he not be considered circumcised? [27]If a man who has never been circumcised really does what the Law says, he will condemn you with your written Law and circumcision for breaking the Law. [28]He is no Jew who is one only outwardly, nor is that circumcision which is only outward and physical. [29]But he is a Jew who is one inwardly, and a man is circumcised in his heart by the Spirit, not just by doing what the words say. Such a person will not be praised by men but by God.

3 What is the advantage then of being a Jew? Or what good is there in being circumcised? [2]Much in every way! The most important advantage is that God entrusted His Word to the Jews.

God Is Faithful

[3]What if some were unfaithful? Will their unfaithfulness make God unfaithful? [4]Never! God must be true and *any man a liar*, as the Bible says:
> That You may be declared righteous when You speak
> and prove You are superior when You judge.

[5]But if our wrong shows how right God is, what will we say? Is God wrong (I'm talking like a man) when He's angry and He punishes? [6]Never! Otherwise how could God judge the world? [7]But if my lie honors God by showing how much truth there is in Him, why am I still condemned as a sin-

---

21-22 Ex 20:14-15   24 Is 52:5   4 Ps 116:11; Ps 51:4

ner? [8]And "shouldn't we do evil that good may come of it?" Some slander us and claim we say that. They are condemned as they deserve.

All Are Sinners

[9]What then? Do we have any advantage? Not at all. We have already accused everyone, Jews and Greeks, that they are under sin, [10]as the Bible says:

> No one is righteous, no, not one.
> [11] No one understands.
>   No one is searching for God.
> [12] All have turned away
>   and have one and all become worthless.
>   No one is doing anything good, not a single one.
> [13] Their throats are an open grave.
>   They have spoken to deceive.
>   Their lips hide the poison of snakes.
> [14] Their mouths are full of cursing and bitterness.
> [15] Their feet run fast to pour out blood.
> [16] Wherever they go, there is destruction and misery.
> [17] They have not learned the way of peace.
> [18] They have no fear of God.

[19]Now we know that whatever the Law says, it says to those who are under the Law, so that every mouth may be silenced and the whole world may stand guilty before God. [20]Therefore *not one person will be declared righteous*[a] *before God* by doing what the Law says, because the Law teaches us to recognize sin.

God Declares and Makes Us Righteous

[21]But now God has shown His righteousness apart from the Law. The Law and the Prophets tell about it. [22]This righteousness through faith in Jesus Christ comes from God to all who believe.

There is no difference. [23]All have sinned and come short of God's glory. [24]They are declared righteous freely by His grace through the ransom Christ Jesus paid to free them. [25]God publicly set Him up to be the *Atonement Cover*[b] through faith in His blood, to show His righteousness even though He had patiently passed by the sins done in the past. [26]Now He wanted to show His righteousness, to be righteous Himself and to declare righteous anyone who believes in Jesus.

10-12 Ps 14:1-3; 53:1-3; Eccl 7:20   13 Ps 5:9; Ps 140:3   14 Ps 10:7
15-17 Prov 1:16; Is 59:7-8 18 Ps 36:1   20 Ps 143:2   25 Ex 25:20; 37:9; Lev 16:2

a - 20   "Righteous" ["Justify"] is a court term. God, who gives us the righteousness of Christ (3:23- 24,28; 4:5; Phil. 3:9), as a judge declares us righteous and by His verdict makes us righteous in His sight.
b - 25   "Atonement Cover" here is applied to Christ, Who became our Covering or Atonement Cover for sin. As such, Christ's blood became the means or provided the "propitiatory power" by which our sins were forgiven.

²⁷What then becomes of our pride? It is excluded. How? By the way of works? No, by the way of faith. ²⁸We are convinced that anyone is declared righteous through faith without the works of the Law.

²⁹Or is God only the God of the Jews? Isn't He also the God of the non-Jews? Certainly also of the non-Jews. ³⁰There is only one God, and He will declare the circumcised man righteous by faith and the uncircumcised man righteous through the same faith.

³¹Do we then through faith cancel the Law? Never! We uphold the Law.

We Are Declared and Made Righteous By Faith

4 What should we say Abraham, our natural ancestor, found? ²If he was declared righteous by what he did, he had something to boast about. But he couldn't boast before God. ³What does the Bible say? *"Abraham believed God and so he was counted righteous."*

⁴If you work, your pay isn't considered a gift but a debt. ⁵But if instead of working you believe in Him Who declares the ungodly righteous, your faith is counted as righteousness. ⁶So David calls the man blessed whom God counts righteous apart from what he does: ⁷*"Blessed are you if your wrongs are forgiven and your sins are covered. ⁸Blessed are you if the Lord doesn't count sins against you."*

⁹Can only a circumcised person be blessed in this way or also an uncircumcised person? We say, *"Abraham's faith was counted as righteousness."* ¹⁰How was it counted? Was he circumcised then, or not? He wasn't circumcised but uncircumcised. ¹¹And he received *circumcision as a mark* to confirm the righteousness he received through faith *before he was circumcised.* He was to be the father of all who without being circumcised believe *and so are counted righteous* ¹²as well as the father of the Jews who are not only circumcised but also walk in the footsteps of our father Abraham by believing as he did before he was circumcised.

¹³It was not by the Law that Abraham or his descendants received the promise that he would inherit the world, but it was by the righteousness of faith. ¹⁴For if the Law is the way to inherit, then faith has been made worthless and the promise has been made powerless. ¹⁵No, the Law brings God's anger on us, and only where there is no Law there is no breaking of the Law. ¹⁶Therefore the promise is by faith that it might come to us by grace, so that the promise might be sure to all the descendants, not only to those who live by the Law but also to those who only believe as Abraham did. He is the father of all of us, ¹⁷as it is written: *"I have made you a father of many nations."* Standing before God, Abraham believed God makes the dead live and calls into being that which doesn't exist. ¹⁸Hoping contrary to what he could expect, he had the faith to become *a father of many nations,* as he had been told: *"That is how many descendants you will have."* ¹⁹He didn't get

---

3 Gen 15:6   *7-8* Ps 32:1-2   *9* Gen 15:6   *11* Gen 17:11; Gen 15:6
17-18 Gen 17:5-6; Gen 15:5; 26:24

weak in faith, although he realized that, being about a hundred years old, his body was as good as dead, and Sarah was unable to have children. [20]There was no unbelief to make him doubt what God promised, but by faith he got strong and gave glory to God. [21]He was fully convinced God could do what He promised. [22]That is why *he was counted righteous.* [23]But the words *"he was counted righteous"* were written not only for him [24]but also for us. He had in mind already then to *count* us *righteous* on the basis of our *believing* in Him Who raised our Lord Jesus from the dead. [25]It was He Who was *handed over to death* for our failures and then was raised for our justification.

Our Hope

5 Now that we have been declared righteous through faith, we have peace with God through our Lord Jesus Christ, [2]Who gave us access to God's grace, in which we stand. We boast in the hope of God's glory.

[3]More than that, we also boast of our sufferings, because we know that suffering produces patient endurance, [4]and patient endurance produces a genuine Christian character; and a genuine Christian character produces hope. [5]In this *hope we're not disappointed,* because the Holy Spirit, Who has been given to us, poured God's love into our hearts.

[6]At the right time, while we were still helpless, Christ died for the ungodly. [7]A man will hardly die for a righteous person; oh, for a kind person someone may dare to die. [8]But God shows how He loves us by this, that while we were still sinners Christ died for us.

[9]Now that His blood has declared us righteous, we are all the more certain He will save us from God's anger. [10]If while we were His enemies we were made God's friends by the death of His Son, now that we are His friends we are all the more certain He will save us by His life. [11]More than that, we rejoice in God through our Lord Jesus Christ, Who has now given us this friendship.

Adam and Christ

[12]One man brought sin into the world, and his sin brought death. And so because all have sinned, death spread to all people. [13]There was sin in the world before the Law was given, but where there is no Law, sin isn't counted. [14]Still death ruled from Adam to Moses even over those who, when they sinned, didn't break a law as Adam did.

He was a picture of Him Who was to come. [15]But the gift is more than the sin. If one man's sin brought death to all people, we are all the more certain God's grace and the gracious gift of the one Man, Jesus Christ, have been richly poured out on all people. [16]The gift also does more than that one man's sin. The sentence, due to one man, condemns us, but the gift, following many sins, declares us righteous. [17]Yes, if death ruled through one man

---

22-24 Gen 15:6   *25 Is 53:12*   *5 Ps 22:5; 25:3,20*

as a result of his sin, we who have received God's overflowing grace and His gift of righteousness, will live and rule even more through the one Man, Jesus Christ.

[18]Now then, as by one sin all people were condemned, so also through one righteous act, justification which brings life came to all people. [19]When one man disobeyed, the many were made sinners. So when One obeyed, the *many* will be *made righteous*. [20]The Law came to multiply sin, but where there was much sin, God's grace was so much greater [21]that, as sin ruled in its deadly way, so His grace is to rule, giving a righteousness by which we live forever through our Lord Jesus Christ.

Live for God

6 What shall we say? Shall we go on sinning so that God may be more gracious to us? [2]Certainly not! We died to sin. How can we live in it any longer?

[3]Or don't you know that all of us who were baptized into Christ Jesus were baptized into His death? [4]Now when we were baptized into His death, we were buried with Him so that as the Father's glory raised Christ from the dead we, too, will live a new life. [5]If we were united with Him in this likeness of His death, then we will be united with Him also in the likeness of His resurrection. [6]We know our old self was nailed with Him to the cross to stop our sinful body and keep us from serving sin any longer. [7]When we're dead, we're free from sin.

[8]But if we died with Christ, we believe we'll also live with Him [9]because we know that Christ, risen from the dead, will not die again. Death has no hold on Him anymore. [10]When He died, He died to sin once, never to die again, and the life He lives He lives for God. [11]So you, too, because you are in Christ Jesus, think of yourselves as dead to sin and living for God.

[12]Then sin should no longer rule in your dying bodies and make you do what they wish. [13]Don't let sin keep on using the parts of your body as tools for doing wrong. But as people who have come back from the dead and live, give yourselves to God, and let God use the parts of your body as tools for doing what is right. [14]Sin will never rule over you, because you are not under the Law but under grace.

[15]What then? Are we going to sin because we are not under the Law but under grace? Certainly not! [16]Don't you know if you give yourselves to anyone to obey him as slaves, you are his slaves? Either you are the slaves of sin and will die, or you obey God resulting in righteousness. [17]But thank God! Although you once were the slaves of sin, you have heartily obeyed the pattern of teaching to which you were entrusted. [18]Freed from sin, you were made the slaves of righteousness. [19]I talk in a human way because you are naturally weak. But just as you once let uncleanness and wickedness use the parts of your body as slaves to do wrong, so now let righteousness use the parts of your body as slaves in order to live holy. [20]When you were slaves

---

19 Is 53:11

of sin, you weren't free to serve righteousness as your master. ²¹What was your advantage then in doing the things that make you blush now? For they end in death. ²²But now that you've been made free from sin and have been made slaves of God, your advantage is that you live in a holy way and finally have everlasting life. ²³The wages paid by sin is death, but the gift given freely by God in Christ Jesus our Lord is everlasting life.

7 Or don't you know, my fellow Christians — I'm speaking to people who know the Law — that you have to obey the Law only as long as you live? ²The Law, for example, binds a married woman to her husband while he is living, but if her husband dies, the Law doesn't bind her to her husband any more. ³So, while her husband is living, she will be called an adulteress if she lives with another man. But if her husband dies, she is free and no longer bound by the Law, and so she's no adulteress if she marries another man.

⁴So you, too, my fellow Christians, have through Christ's body died to the Law to marry Another — Him Who rose from the dead so that we will produce fruit for God. ⁵While we were living in the flesh, the Law stirred into action the sinful lusts in parts of our bodies to produce fruit for death. ⁶But now that we have died to the Law which bound us, we are freed from it, not to serve in the old way under the Law but in the new way of the Spirit.

The Law Shows What Sin Is

⁷What does it mean? Is the Law sin? Certainly not! But only by the Law did I learn what sin is. For example, only when the Law said: "*Do not covet*," did I know how wrong it is to covet. ⁸Taking the commandment as a challenge, sin worked in me every kind of wrong desire. Without the Law sin is dead. ⁹Once I was alive without the Law, but when the commandment came, sin became alive, and I died. ¹⁰And the commandment which is to bring life actually brought me death. ¹¹Taking the commandment as a challenge, sin seduced me and with the commandment killed me.

¹²So the Law itself is holy, and the commandment is holy, right, and good. ¹³Now, did this good thing kill me? Certainly not! But sin, to be sin, clearly used this good thing to kill me so that sin would by the commandment become extremely sinful.

Struggling with Sin

¹⁴We know the Law is spiritual, but I am flesh, sold to be a slave of sin. ¹⁵I am doing something strange, because I don't do what I want to do, but I do what I hate. ¹⁶And if I do what I don't want to do, I agree that the Law is right. ¹⁷It is really no longer I who am doing it, but sin living in me. ¹⁸I know that nothing good lives in me, that is, in my flesh. I'm willing, but

---

7 Ex 20:17; Deut 5:21

I'm not doing what is right. [19]I don't do the good things I want to do, but I do the evil I don't want to do. [20]Now if I do what I don't want to do, it is no longer I who am doing it but sin living in me.

[21]So I find this to be a rule: When I want to do what is right, evil is there with me. [22]In my inner being I delight in God's Law, [23]but all through my body I see another law fighting against the Law in my mind and making me a prisoner to the sin ruling my body. [24]What a miserable man I am! Who will rescue me from the body that brings me to this death? [25]Thank God — He does it through our Lord Jesus Christ! So I serve the Law of God with my mind but the law of sin with my flesh.

The Spirit Gives Life

8 So those who are believers in Christ Jesus can no longer be condemned. [2]The rule of the Spirit, who gives life, has in Christ Jesus freed you from the rule of sin that kills. [3]What the Law, weakened by the flesh, could not do God has done by sending His Son to be like sinful flesh and to be a sacrifice for sin. He condemned sin in the flesh [4]so that we who don't follow the flesh but the spirit will be as righteous as the Law demands. [5]Those who follow the flesh have their minds on the things of the flesh, but those who follow the spirit have their minds on the things of the spirit. [6]What the flesh thinks kills; what the spirit thinks gives life and peace. [7]This is so because the fleshly mind hates God. It refuses to obey God's Law because it can't obey it. [8]Those who are in the flesh can't please God. [9]You are not in the flesh but in the spirit if the Spirit of God lives in you. But anyone who doesn't have the Spirit of Christ doesn't belong to Him. [10]But if Christ is in you, even though your bodies are dead because you were sinful, your spirits are alive because you are righteous. [11]And if the Spirit of Him Who raised Jesus from the dead lives in you, He Who raised Christ Jesus from the dead will also make your dying bodies alive by His Spirit living in you.

[12]And so, fellow Christians, we don't owe it to the flesh to live according to the flesh. [13]If you live according to the flesh, you will die. But if by the spirit you kill the activities of the body, you will live. [14]All who are moved by the Spirit of God are God's children. [15]You didn't receive the spirit of slaves to make you feel afraid again, but you received the Spirit who makes us God's adopted children and moves us to call "Abba, Father!" [16]This Spirit assures our spirit that we are God's children, [17]and if children, then heirs, God's heirs, and joint heirs with Christ since we share in His suffering in order that we may also share in His glory.

We Want to Be Free

[18]I think what we suffer now isn't important when I compare it with the glory to be revealed to us. [19]For the created world is waiting on tiptoe to see the unveiling of God's sons. [20]For this created world must waste away, not because it wants to but because its Master would have it so, but it does so with the hope [21]that this created world also will be freed from the slavery

of decay in order to share the freedom of glory with the children of God. [22]We know that all creation has been groaning with the pains of childbirth until now.

[23]And what is more, also we, who have the Spirit as our first taste of heaven, groan inwardly as we look forward to being adopted as His children; then our body will be set free. [24]We are saved, hoping for this. But if we hope for something we see, we really don't hope. Why should we hope for what we can see? [25]But if we hope for what we can't see, we wait for it patiently.

[26]In the same way the Spirit helps us in our weakness, because we don't know how we should pray, but the Spirit Himself pleads for us with yearnings that can't find any words. [27]He Who searches our hearts knows what the Spirit means to do, that in God's own way He's pleading for the holy people.

God Gives Us Glory

[28]We know that God works all things out for good for those who love God, who are called according to His plan. [29]Those whom He chose from the first He also appointed long ago to be thoroughly like His Son so He would be the firstborn among many brothers. [30]Those whom He appointed long ago He called. Those whom He called He declared righteous. And those whom He declared righteous He glorified.

[31]What does this mean? If God is for us, who can be against us? [32]He didn't spare His own Son but gave Him up for all of us — He will certainly with Him give us everything. [33]Who will accuse those whom God has chosen? It is God *Who declares* us *righteous.* [34]*Who will condemn?* Christ died, more than that, He rose, He is at the right hand of God, and He prays for us. [35]Who will separate us from God's love? Will sorrow, hardship or persecution, hunger or nakedness, danger or a sword? [36]So it is written: *"For You we are being killed all day long. We are considered sheep to be slaughtered."* [37]But in all this He Who loved us helps us win an overwhelming victory. [38]I'm convinced that neither death nor life, neither angels nor rulers, nothing now nor in the future, no powers, [39]nothing above or below, nor any other creature can ever separate us from the love God has for us in Christ Jesus our Lord.

God's People

9 I'm telling the truth in Christ; I'm not lying, as my conscience assures me by the Holy Spirit, [2]when I say I have a great sorrow and continuous pain in my heart. [3]I could wish myself cut off from Christ and damned for my fellow Jews, my own flesh and blood. [4]They are the people of Israel. They were made God's family. They have the glory, the covenant, the Law, the worship, and the promises. [5]They have the ancestors, and from them ac-

33-34 Is 50:8-9   *36* Ps 44:22

cording to His body came Christ, Who is God over everything, blessed forever. Amen.

[6]It doesn't mean God failed to do what He said. Not all who are descended from Israel are the real Israel, [7]and not all who are descended from Abraham are for that reason his real children. No, *Isaac's children will be called your descendants.* [8]This means children born in a natural way are not God's children. Only the children he had because God promised them are counted his descendants.

God's Right to Choose

[9]God promised: *"I will come back at the right time, and Sarah will have a son."* [10]The same thing happened to Rebekah. She was going to bear children for our ancestor Isaac. [11]They had not been born yet nor done anything good or bad. Even then — in order that God may carry out His purpose according to His choice, which doesn't depend on anything we do but on Him Who calls us — [12]she was told: *"The older will serve the younger."* [13]And so the Bible says: *"I loved Jacob, but I hated Esau."*

[14]Does this mean God is unjust? Never! [15]He says to Moses: *"I will be merciful to whom I want to be merciful; I will pity whom I want to pity."* [16]Then it doesn't depend on anyone wanting it or running hard after it but on God being merciful. [17]The Bible says to Pharaoh: *"I raised you to the throne to demonstrate My power on you and to make myself known all over the earth."* [18]So He pities whom He wants to pity and *makes stubborn* whom He wants to make stubborn.

[19]You will ask me, "Why does He still find fault with anyone? Who can resist His will?" [20]But now, who are you, man, to talk back to God? *Will the thing formed say to the one who formed it,* "Why did you make me like this?" [21]Doesn't *a potter* have the right over *his clay* to make out of the same mud one thing for a noble purpose and another for a lowly purpose?

[22]God wanted to show people His anger and let them know His power, but He waited very patiently before He would *punish those who deserved it* and had prepared themselves *for destruction,* [23]so as to show the riches of glory He has in store for those He's merciful to and long ago prepared for glory — [24]I mean us whom He called not only from the Jews but also from the non-Jews.

God Chooses Non-Jews

[25]So He says in Hosea: *"Those who are not My people I will call My people, and those who are not loved I will call My loved ones,* [26]and where they were told, 'You are not My people,' they will be called sons of the living God."*

---

7 Gen 21:12   9 Gen 18:10,14   12 Gen 25:23   13 Mal 1:2-3   15 Ex 33:19
17 Ex 9:1618 Ex 4:21; 7:3; 9:12; 10:20; 11:10; 14:4,8,17   20 Is 29:16; 45:9
21 Jer 18:6   22 Is 13:5; Jer 50:25   25-26 Hos 2:1,23; 1:10

²⁷Isaiah exclaims in regard to Israel: *"Though the people of Israel are as many as the sand by the sea, only a remnant will be saved.* ²⁸*The Lord will completely and decisively execute His sentence on the country."* ²⁹So Isaiah said long ago: *"If the Lord of armies hadn't left us some survivors, we would have become like Sodom and ended like Gomorrah."*

³⁰What does it mean? Non-Jewish people who didn't search for righteousness found a righteousness we receive through believing, ³¹while Israel, pursuing a Law with its righteousness, didn't find it. ³²Why? They didn't try to get it by faith but thought they could get it by works. They stumbled over *the stumbling block,* ³³as the Bible says: *"I'm putting in Zion a Stone they will stumble over and a Rock they will fall over. But if you believe in Him, you will not be disappointed."*

Jews Should Believe

10 Fellow Christians, my heart's desire and my prayer to God is to save the Israelites. ²I can testify they are zealous for God but don't understand. ³Not knowing the righteousness God gives, and trying to set up their own, they haven't submitted to God's righteousness. ⁴You see, Christ is the end of the Law to give righteousness to everyone who believes.

⁵Moses writes: *"If you have done* the righteous things demanded by the Law, *you will find life in them."* ⁶But the *righteousness you receive* by faith says this: *"Don't ask yourself, Who will go up to heaven?"* which means to bring Christ down, ⁷or, "Who will *go down into the depths?"* which means, to bring Christ up from the dead. ⁸But what does it say? *"The Word is near you, in your mouth and in your heart."* This is the Word of faith that we preach. ⁹If with your mouth you confess, "Jesus is the Lord," and in your heart you believe "God raised Him from the dead," you will be saved. ¹⁰With your heart you believe and become righteous; with your mouth you confess and are saved. ¹¹*"Anyone who believes in Him,"* the Bible says, *"will not be disappointed."* ¹²There is no difference between Jew and Greek, because they all have the same Lord, Who gives His riches to all who call on Him. ¹³*"Everyone who calls on the Lord's name will be saved."*

¹⁴But how can they call on Him if they haven't believed in Him? How can they believe in Him if they haven't heard of Him? How can they hear if no one preaches? ¹⁵How can men preach if they're not sent? Just as the Bible says: *"How beautiful are the feet of those who bring good news!"*

¹⁶But not all have obeyed the good news. Isaiah asks: *"Lord, who has believed what we told them?"*

¹⁷So then faith comes from hearing the message, and the message comes through the Word of Christ.

27-28 *Is 10:22-23; 28:22*   **29** *Is 1:9*   **32-33** *Is 8:14-15; 28:16*
5 *Lev 18:5*   6 *Deut 9:4; Prov 30:4*   6-8 *Deut 30:12,14; Ps 107:26*
11 *Is 28:16*   13 *Joel 2:32*   15 *Is 52:7; Nah 1:15*   16 *Is 53:1*

[18]But I ask, "didn't they hear it?" Of course they did.

> *Their voice has gone all over the earth*
> *and their words to the farthest parts of the world.*

[19]Again I ask, "didn't Israel know?" Moses was the first to say:

> *I will make you jealous of those who are not a nation,*
> *I will make you angry with a people who don't understand.*

[20]Then Isaiah boldly says:

> *I was found by those who were not looking for Me;*
> *I was revealed to those who were not asking for Me.*

[21]And He says about Israel: "*All day long I have stretched out My hands to a people who disobey Me and oppose Me.*"

The Remnant.

11 So I ask, "Has *God rejected His people?*" Certainly not — I'm an Israelite myself, a descendant of Abraham and of the tribe of Benjamin. [2]*God has not rejected His people* whom He chose long ago. Or don't you know what the Bible says in the passages about Elijah when he pleads with God against Israel: [3]"*Lord, they have killed Your prophets, they have torn down Your altars, I am the only one left, and they are trying to kill me.*" [4]But what did *God answer him?* "*I have kept for Myself seven thousand men who have not knelt to Baal.*" [5]So there is right now, too, a remnant God has chosen by His grace. [6]But if they were chosen by grace, it could not have been because of what they had done; otherwise grace would no longer be grace.

[7]What does it mean? Israel didn't find what it was looking for, but those whom God chose did find it.

God's Way of Winning Jews

[8]And the minds of the others were dulled, as the Bible says:

> *God has given them a spirit of deep sleep,*
> *eyes that should not see,*
> *and ears that should not hear,*
> *and so it has been until this day.*

[9]And David says:

> *Let their table be a snare and a trap,*
> *to make them fall and get what they deserve.*
> [10]*Let their eyes turn dark so they cannot see,*
> *and bend their backs forever.*

[11]"Did they stumble," I ask, "to be lost altogether?" Certainly not! By

---

18 Ps 19:4   *19 Deut 32:21*   ***20-21** Is 65:1-2; Prov 1:24*
***1-2** I Sam 12:22; Ps 94:14*   ***3-4** I Kings 19:10,14,15,18*
8 Deut 29:4; Is 29:10   ***9-10** Ps 69:22-23*

their error salvation has come to the non-Jews *to make the Jews jealous.*
[12]And if their error made the world rich and their loss made the non-Jews
rich, how much more certainly will that happen when their full number
comes in! [13]Now, I am speaking to you non-Jews. As I am sent to the non-
Jews, I glorify my work. [14]Perhaps I can *make* my fellow Jews *jealous* and
save some of them. [15]When God rejects them, the world is reconciled to God;
when God accepts them, what can it mean but that the dead will live?

[16]If the first handful of dough is holy, so is the whole dough. If the root
is holy, so are the branches. [17]But if some of the branches have been broken
off, and you, a wild olive, have been grafted in among them, and the rich sap
from the root of the olive tree nourishes you, too, [18]don't brag of being more
than the other branches. If you brag, remember you don't support the root,
but the root supports you. [19]"Branches were cut off," you will say, "to graft
me in." [20]Right! They were broken off because they didn't believe, but you
stand by believing. Don't feel proud but be afraid. [21]If God didn't spare the
natural branches, He will not spare you. [22]Now see how kind and how severe God can be — severe to those who fell but kind to you if you cling to
His kindness; otherwise you, too, will be cut off.

[23]And if the others do not continue in unbelief, they will be grafted in,
because God can graft them in again. [24]You have been cut from an olive
tree that grows wild and have been unnaturally grafted into a cultivated
olive; how much more likely it is that these natural branches will be grafted
back into their own olive tree! [25]To keep you from thinking too well of yourselves, my fellow Christians, I want you to know this secret truth: The
minds of a part of the Jews were dulled until the full number of the non-
Jews comes in. [26]And in this way all Israel will be saved, as the Bible says:
"The Savior will come from Zion. He will get rid of ungodliness in Jacob,
[27]*And this will be My covenant with them when I take away their sins."*

[28]God's rule in telling the good news is to treat them as His enemies
to help you. But He chose them, and so He loves them on account of their
fathers. [29]God never changes His mind when He gives anything or calls
anyone. [30]Once you disobeyed God, but now that the Jews have disobeyed,
He has been merciful to you. [31]So they also have disobeyed now that when
you enjoy His mercy, they may have it, too. [32]You see, God has put all people
in a prison of disobedience in order to be merciful to all.

[33]How deep are God's riches, wisdom, and knowledge; how impossible
it is to find out His decisions and trace His ways! [34]*"Who has found out how
the Lord thinks? Or who has become His adviser?"* [35]*Or who has first given
Him something* for which he must *be paid back?* [36]Everything is from Him,
by Him, and for Him. To Him be glory forever. Amen.

11,14 Deut 32:218 Deut 29:4; Is 29:10   *26-27 Is 59:20-21; 27:9*
34 Is 40:13   35 Job 35:7; 41:11

Live for God

12 I appeal to you, fellow Christians, by the mercies of God, to give your bodies as a living sacrifice, holy and pleasing to God, and so worship Him as thinking beings. [2]Don't live like this world, but let yourselves be transformed by a renewing of your minds so you can test and be sure what God wants, what is good and pleasing and perfect.

[3]As God gave me His gift of grace for every one of you, I tell you, don't think too highly of yourselves, but take a sane view of yourselves, everyone according to the measure of faith God gave you. [4]We have many parts in one body, and these parts don't all do the same thing. [5]In the same way, many as we are, we are one body in Christ and individually parts of one another. [6]We have gifts that are different according to what His grace gave us. If you can speak God's Word, do it according to the faith. [7]If you can serve, then serve. If you can teach, teach. [8]If you can encourage, encourage. If you share, be generous. If you manage anything, do it eagerly. If you help people in need, do it cheerfully.

Love

[9]Love sincerely. Hate evil; cling to what is good. [10]Love one another tenderly as fellow Christians. Outdo one another in showing respect. [11]Don't be backward in zeal. Let your spirit glow. Serve the Lord. [12]Be happy in your hope, patient in trouble, and keep busy praying. [13]Share what you have with the holy people who need it. Eagerly welcome strangers as guests.

[14]Bless those who persecute you; bless, and don't curse them. [15]Be happy with those who are happy; weep with those who weep. [16]Live in harmony with one another. Don't be too ambitious, but go along with the humble ways of others. *Don't think you are wise.*

[17]*Don't pay back evil for evil. Be concerned with things that everyone considers noble.* [18]As much as you can, live in peace with everyone. [19]Don't take revenge, dear friends, but let God punish, because the Bible says: "*I alone have the right to avenge. I will pay back,*" says the Lord. [20]But, "*if your enemy is hungry, feed him. If he is thirsty, give him a drink. If you do this, you'll heap burning coals on his head.*" [21]Don't let evil conquer you, but conquer evil with good.

Obey Your Government

13 Everyone should obey the government that is over him, because there is no government except that which is put there by God. God has ordered our government to be over us. [2]Then anyone who is against the government opposes what God has ordered, and those who oppose will be condemned.

---

16 Prov 3:7   17 Prov 3:4 (Greek); 20:22; 24:29   19 Deut 32:35; Prov 20:22
20 Prov 25:21-22

[3]If you do right, you don't have to be afraid of those who rule, but only if you do wrong. Would you like to live without being afraid of your government? Do what is right, and it will praise you. [4]It is God's servant to help you. If you do wrong, you should be afraid, because the government doesn't carry a sword without a purpose. It is God's servant, an avenger, who must punish anyone doing wrong. [5]You must obey, then, not only because God punishes wrong but also because your conscience tells you to obey.

[6]That is why you also pay taxes. Men in the government serve God and are busy doing their work. [7]Pay to all whatever you owe them. If you owe anyone tribute, pay tribute; if taxes, then taxes; if respect, then respect; if honor, then honor.

Love One Another

[8]Don't owe anyone anything but to love one another. If you love the other person, you have kept the Law. [9]The commandments: *"Do not commit adultery, do not murder, do not steal, do not covet,"* and any others are summed up in this: *"Love your neighbor as yourself."* [10]Love does no wrong to another person. Therefore love is the fulfillment of the Law.

[11]Do this especially since you know the time we're living in. It's time now for you to wake up from sleep because we are now nearer being rescued than when we first believed. [12]The night is almost over, and the day is dawning. Then let us put away the works of darkness and put on the armor of light. [13]Let us live nobly as in the daytime, not carousing or getting drunk, not sinning sexually or living wildly, not quarreling or being jealous. [14]But put on the Lord Jesus Christ, and don't plan to have your fleshly desires aroused.

Weak Christians

14Welcome a man who is weak in his faith and not just to argue about different opinions. [2]One person believes he can eat anything, but a weak Christian eats only vegetables. [3]If you eat, don't despise anyone who doesn't eat, and if you don't eat, don't criticize anyone who eats, because God has accepted him. [4]Who are you to criticize someone else's servant? He belongs to the Lord, Who is concerned whether he succeeds or fails. And he will succeed, because the Lord can make him succeed.

[5]One man thinks one day is better than the other; another thinks they're all alike. Everyone should be thoroughly convinced in his own mind. [6]He who has a special day means to honor the Lord. He who eats does it for the Lord since he thanks God. And he who keeps from eating does it for the Lord, and he thanks God. [7]None of us lives for himself, and none dies for himself. [8]If we live, we live for the Lord; and if we die, we die for the Lord. So whether we live or die, we belong to the Lord. [9]Christ died and became alive again to be Lord of the dead and the living.

---

9 *Ex 20:13-15,17; Deut 5:17-19,21; Lev 19:18*

¹⁰I ask one of you, "Why do you criticize your fellow Christian?" Or another, "Why do you despise your fellow Christian?" We must all stand before God to be judged. ¹¹It is written: *"As sure as I live," says the Lord,* *"everyone will kneel to Me, and every tongue will praise God."* ¹²So each of us will have to give an account of himself to God.

¹³Then let us stop criticizing one another. But instead decide not to lay any stumbling block or trap in the way of a fellow Christian. ¹⁴I know and am convinced in the Lord Jesus that nothing is unclean in itself. Anything is unclean only to him who thinks it is unclean. ¹⁵But if what you eat hurts your fellow Christian, you're not living according to love anymore. By what you eat don't ruin him for whom Christ died. ¹⁶You have something good that no one should say anything bad about. ¹⁷God's kingdom is not eating and drinking but righteousness, peace, and joy in the Holy Spirit. ¹⁸If you serve Christ in this way, God is pleased with you, and people approve of you.

¹⁹So we eagerly go after the things which mean peace and by which we help one another grow. ²⁰Don't ruin God's work just for food. Everything is clean, but it's wrong for you to eat if it makes someone stumble. ²¹It is good not to eat meat, drink wine, or do anything else that makes your fellow Christian stumble, sin, or be weak in faith. ²²The faith you have, have it between yourself and God. Happy are you if you never have to condemn yourself in regard to anything you approve. ²³If anyone doubts and still eats, he is condemned because he doesn't go by what he believes. Anything that is not an act of faith is sin.

15 But we who are strong must be patient with the weaknesses of the weak and not just please ourselves. ²Every one of us should please his neighbor for his good, to help him grow. ³Even Christ didn't please Himself, but it happened to Him as it is written: *"Those who insult You insult Me."*

Jews and Non-Jews

⁴All that was written long ago was written to teach us by the endurance and encouragement we get from the Bible to have hope. ⁵May God, Who helps you to endure and encourages you, give you such harmony with one another as you follow Christ Jesus ⁶that together with one voice you praise the God and Father of our Lord Jesus Christ.

⁷Then, as Christ has welcomed you, welcome one another in order to glorify God. ⁸I tell you Christ became a servant to the Jews to do what God promised the fathers — showing that He tells the truth — ⁹and to have the other nations praise God for His mercy, as it is written:

> For this I will praise You among the nations
> and sing to honor Your name.

---

11 *Is 49:18; Is 45:23-24*   3 *Ps 69:9*   9 *II Sam 22:50; Ps 18:49*

¹⁰And again:

> Be happy, you other nations, with His own people!

¹¹And again:

> All you nations, praise the Lord,
> and all the people should praise Him.

¹²Again, Isaiah says:

> Jesse will have the Descendant
> Who will rise to rule the nations,
> and He will be the Hope of the nations.

¹³The God of hope fill you with perfect happiness and peace as you believe, to make you overflow with hope by the power of the Holy Spirit.

New Fields

¹⁴I am convinced, my fellow Christians, you are full of kindness, fully equipped with every kind of knowledge, and able to correct one another. ¹⁵Just to remind you, I have written you a letter, part of which is rather bold because God has by a special gift of His grace ¹⁶made me a servant of Christ Jesus among the non-Jewish nations, to work for God's good news as a priest and bring the nations as an offering made holy by the Holy Spirit and accepted by God. ¹⁷So I can in Christ Jesus be proud of what I'm doing before God ¹⁸because I'll dare to tell only what Christ has done through me to make the nations obedient, by my speaking and working, ¹⁹by the power to do miracles and wonders, by the power of God's Spirit, so that I have finished telling the good news of Christ all the way from Jerusalem as far around as Illyricum.

²⁰But I was ambitious to tell the good news only where Christ's name wasn't known, so as not to build on any foundation others had laid, ²¹but as it is written:

> Those who were never told about Him will see,
> and those who never heard will understand.

I Hope to See You

²²That is why I have so often been kept from coming to you. ²³But now there is in this territory no more opportunity for me to work, and for many years I have longed to come to you ²⁴on my way to Spain. I hope to see you when I pass through and after I have enjoyed being with you for a while to have you send me on my way there.

²⁵Right now I am going to Jerusalem to bring help to the holy people there. ²⁶You see, Macedonia and Greece decided to share their goods with the poor among the holy people in Jerusalem. ²⁷So they decided, and they really owe something to the Jews. If the Jews have shared their spiritual goods with the non-Jews, the non-Jews owe it to them to serve them with their earthly goods. ²⁸When that is done and I've brought them this contri-

---

10 Deut 32:43   **11** Ps 117:1   **12** Is 11:1,10   **21** Is 52:15

bution with my seal on it, I will come to you on my way to Spain. [29]I know that when I come to you, I'll bring the full blessing of Christ.

[30]By our Lord Jesus Christ and the love we have from the Spirit, I urge you to join me in my struggle by praying for me to God [31]to rescue me from those in Judea who refuse to believe and to have the holy people in Jerusalem welcome the help I bring [32]so that by God's will I'll come to you with joy and be refreshed with you.

[33]The God of peace be with you all. Amen.

Farewell

16 I'm introducing Phoebe, our fellow Christian, to you. She is a worker in the church in Cenchreae. [2]Welcome her in the Lord as holy people should, and give her any help she may need from you, because she has become a protector of many, including me.

[3]Greet Prisca and Aquila, my fellow workers in Christ Jesus, [4]who risked their necks to save my life. Not only I but all the churches among the non-Jews are thanking them.

[5]Greet also the church that meets at their home.
Greet my dear Epaenetus, who was the first in the province of Asia to turn to Christ.

[6]Greet Mary, who has worked very hard for you.

[7]Greet Andronicus and Junias, my fellow Jews, who went to prison with me. They are outstanding among the apostles. They also came to Christ before I did.

[8]Greet Ampliatus, who is dear to me in the Lord.

[9]Greet Urban, our fellow worker in Christ, and my dear Stachys.

[10]Greet Apelles, a veteran in Christ.
Greet those who belong to the family of Aristobulus.

[11]Greet Herodian, my fellow Jew.
Greet those in the family of Narcissus who are in the Lord.

[12]Greet Tryphaena and Tryphosa, who have worked hard for the Lord. Greet dear Persis, who has worked very hard for the Lord.

[13]Greet Rufus, the chosen one in the Lord, and his mother — who has been a mother to me, too.

[14]Greet Asyncritus, Phlegon, Hermes, Patrobas, Hermas, and the fellow Christians who are with them.

[15]Greet Philologus, Julia, Nereus, and his sister, and Olympas, and all the holy people who are with them.

[16]Greet one another with a holy kiss. All the churches of Christ greet you.

[17]I urge you, fellow Christians, to watch those who cause disagreements and make people fall by going against the teaching you learned. Turn away from them. [18]Such men are not serving Christ, our Lord, but their own bellies and by their fine and flattering talk are deceiving innocent people. [19]Everyone has heard how you obey, and so I'm happy about you. I want you to be wise for anything good, and too innocent for anything bad. [20]The

God of peace will soon *crush* Satan under your feet.

May the grace of our Lord Jesus be with you!

²¹Timothy, my fellow worker, greets you; so do Lucius, Jason, and Sosipater, my fellow Jews.

²²I, Tertius, who wrote this letter, greet you in the Lord.

²³Gaius, my host and the host of the whole church, greets you. Erastus, the city treasurer, greets you, and Quartus, our fellow Christian.ᶜ

²⁵Now, to Him —

> Who can make you strong by the good news I bring and the preaching of Jesus Christ, by unveiling the mystery veiled in silence for long ages ²⁶but now brought to light and by the writings of the prophets, as the everlasting God ordered them, shown to all the nations to lead them to faith's obedience — ²⁷to the only wise God through Jesus Christ be glory forever. Amen.

20 Gen 3:15

c - 23 Our oldest manuscripts, including Papyrus⁴⁶ do not have verse 24: "The grace of our Lord Jesus (Christ) be with you all. Amen." They have most of these words at the end of verse 20.

PAUL
WRITES THE FIRST LETTER TO THE
CORINTHIANS

1 PAUL, APOSTLE OF CHRIST JESUS, called by God's will, and Sosthenes, my fellow Christian, [2]to God's church in Corinth, made holy by Christ Jesus and called to be holy, with all who anywhere call on the name of our Lord Jesus Christ, their Lord and ours — [3]may God our Father and the Lord Jesus Christ give you grace and peace.

[4]I am always thanking God for you because of His grace which was given to you in Christ Jesus. [5]For in Him you have been made rich in every way, in speech and knowledge of every kind, [6]as the truth of Christ we spoke was confirmed in you. [7]And so you don't lack any gift as you eagerly look for our Lord Jesus Christ to appear again. [8]He will strengthen you to the end so that no one can accuse you of anything on the day of our Lord Jesus Christ. [9]You can depend on God, Who called you to the fellowship of His Son Jesus Christ, our Lord.

Everyone for Christ

[10]Fellow Christians, by the name of our Lord Jesus Christ I urge you all to agree and not be divided but perfectly united in your understanding and judgment. [11]Chloe's people told me you are quarreling, my fellow Christians. [12]I mean that each of you says, "I belong to Paul," or "I belong to Apollos," or "I belong to Peter," or "I belong to Christ." [13]Is Christ divided? Was Paul crucified for you? Or were you baptized into Paul's name? [14]I thank God I didn't baptize any of you except Crispus and Gaius. [15]Then no one can say you were baptized into my name. [16]I also baptized the family of Stephanas. I don't know if I baptized anyone else. [17]Christ didn't send me to baptize but to tell the good news; nor to be a clever speaker, or the cross of Christ would lose its power.

God's Foolish Things

[18]The message of the cross is something foolish to those who perish, but it is God's power to us who are saved. [19]The Bible says: *"I will destroy the wisdom of the wise and defeat the intelligence of the intelligent."* [20]*Where is the wise man? Where is the Bible scholar?* Where is the debater of our time? Hasn't God *made foolish the wisdom* of the world? [21]Since by God's wisdom the world by its wisdom didn't get to know God, God decided to use the foolishness of our preaching to save those who believe. [22]Now that Jews ask for miraculous signs and Greeks look for wisdom, [23]we preach a cruci-

---

19 Is 29:14; Ps 33:10   *20 Is 19:11-12; 33:18; 44:25*

fied Christ. The Jews stumble over Him, the Greeks think He's something foolish, ²⁴but to those who are called, both Jews and Greeks, He is Christ, God's power and God's wisdom. ²⁵God's foolishness is wiser than men's wisdom, and God's weakness is stronger than men's strength.

²⁶You see what happened, fellow Christians, when God called you. Not many of you are wise as the world judges, not many in positions of power, not many born of noble parents. ²⁷No, God chose the foolish things in the world to make wise men ashamed. God chose the weak things in the world to make strong men ashamed. ²⁸God chose the lowly things in the world, what it despises, what is nothing, to make what is something nothing ²⁹and to keep anyone from bragging before God. ³⁰He gave you your life in Christ Jesus, Whom God made our wisdom, righteousness, holiness, and ransom from sin, ³¹so that it may be as the Bible says: "*Let the one who boasts, boast in the Lord.*"

2 When I came to you, fellow Christians, I didn't come to tell you God's truth with any extra fine speech or wisdom. ²While I was with you, I was determined to know only Jesus Christ and Him crucified. ³I came to you weak and afraid and with much trembling. ⁴When I spoke and preached, I didn't use clever talk to persuade you, but the Spirit and His power proved the truth to you ⁵so that your faith may not be based on men's wisdom but on God's power.

⁶But we do speak a wisdom to those who are ripe for it, a wisdom unknown to the world today and to its rulers who pass away. ⁷Yes, we tell about God's secret wisdom that was kept hidden but that God before the world began planned for our glory. ⁸None of those who rule this world knew it. If they had known it, they would not have crucified the Lord of glory. ⁹But it is as the Bible says:

> *No eye has seen,*
> *no ear has heard,*
> and *no mind has thought of*
> *what* God has prepared *for those who* love *Him.*

¹⁰God has revealed it to us by His Spirit. The Spirit finds out everything, even the deep things of God. ¹¹Who knows what a man thinks except his own spirit? In the same way only God's Spirit knows what God thinks. ¹²Now we were not given the spirit of the world but the Spirit Who comes from God so that we know the good things God gave us. ¹³And we tell about them in words not taught by human wisdom but taught by the Spirit as we explain the things of the Spirit to those who have the Spirit.

¹⁴But a natural man doesn't accept the things of God's Spirit. He thinks they are foolish and he can't understand them, because one must be spiritual to judge them correctly. ¹⁵The spiritual person judges everything, but no one judges him. ¹⁶*Who has known the mind of the Lord so as to teach Him*? But we have the mind of Christ.

---

31 Jer 9:24   *9 Is 64:4; Jer 3:16*   *16 Is 40:13*

We Plant and Build

3 Fellow Christians, I couldn't talk to you as spiritual people but had to treat you as living in your weak flesh, as babies in Christ. ²I gave you milk to drink, not solid food, because you weren't ready for it. Why, you aren't ready for it even now yet, ³because you still live in your weak flesh.

When you are jealous, quarreling, and forming different parties, aren't you following your flesh and acting like other people? ⁴When one of you says, "I belong to Paul," and another, "I belong to Apollos," aren't you just ordinary people? ⁵What is Apollos anyhow? Or what is Paul? They are servants by whose help you came to believe, and each helped only as the Lord gave him the ability. ⁶I planted, Apollos watered, but God made it grow. ⁷Now then, the one who plants isn't anything, nor the one who waters, but God, Who makes it grow. ⁸The man who plants and the one who waters are together, but each of us will get paid for his own work. ⁹We are God's men, working together. You are God's field.

You are God's building. ¹⁰In His grace God gave me a work to do, and so as an expert master builder I laid a foundation, and someone else is building on it. Everyone should be careful how he builds on it. ¹¹No one can lay any other foundation than the one that is already laid, and that is Jesus Christ. ¹²If on this foundation you build anything of gold, silver, fine stones, wood, hay, or straw, ¹³what each one does will be known. That day will show what it is because the fire will reveal it and test it to show what kind of work everyone has done. ¹⁴If what you built on the foundation stands the test, you will get paid. ¹⁵If your work is burned, you will lose something, but you will be saved, though it will be like going through a fire.

¹⁶Don't you know you are God's temple and God's Spirit lives in you? ¹⁷If anyone destroys God's temple, God will destroy him, because God's temple is holy. And you are that temple.

¹⁸Don't deceive yourself. If any one of you imagines he is wise in the ways of this world, he should become a fool to become really wise. ¹⁹God considers this world's wisdom to be foolish, as the Bible says: "*He catches the wise with their own trickery,*" ²⁰and again: "T*he Lord knows that the planning of* the wise *is useless.*"

²¹So don't boast about men. You see, everything is yours — ²²Paul, Apollos, Peter, the world, life or death, present or future things — everything is yours, ²³but you belong to Christ, and Christ to God.

We Are Managers

4 Think of us as servants of Christ and managers who distribute God's hidden truths. ²Now then, you demand of any manager that he be trustworthy.

³It means very little to me that you or any human judges should examine me. I don't even examine myself. ⁴I don't know of anything that is

---

19 Job 5:13   *20 Ps 94:11*

against me, but that does not justify me.[a] It is the Lord Who examines me. [5]So don't judge anything too early. Wait until the Lord comes. He will let the light shine on what is hidden in the dark and bring to the light the plans people have in their hearts. And then everyone will get his praise from God.

[6]Fellow Christians, in a special way of speaking I have referred only to myself and Apollos, but I want you to learn from us not to go beyond what Scripture says, in order that you might not boast about one man at the expense of another.

Not a King but a Father

[7]Does anyone see anything special in you? What do you have that wasn't given to you? And if it was given to you, why do you brag as if it hadn't been given to you?

[8]So you're already satisfied! You've already become rich! You've become kings without us! I only wish you had become kings so that we might be kings with you.

[9]I think God has had us apostles come last in the procession like men condemned to die because we have become a big show for the world, for angels and people to see. [10]We are fools for Christ's sake, but you are wise in Christ. We are weak, but you are strong. You are honored, but we are despised. [11]Up to this hour we are hungry, thirsty, poorly dressed, beaten, homeless, [12]and we wear ourselves out working with our hands. When we're insulted, we bless. When we're persecuted, we put up with it. [13]When slandered, we talk kindly. We have come to be the filth of the world, the scum of the earth, and we are that to this day.

[14]I'm not writing this to make you feel ashamed, but I'm warning you as my dear children. [15]You may have 10,000 to guide you in Christ, but not many fathers, because in Christ Jesus I became your father by telling you the good news. [16]So I urge you to become like me. [17]That is why I sent you Timothy, who is my dear and dependable son in the Lord. He will help you keep in mind my ways in Christ Jesus, just as I teach them everywhere in every church.

[18]Some of you are puffed up as though I were not coming to you. [19]But I'll come to you soon if the Lord wants me to, and then I will find out, not what these puffed-up fellows say but what they can do. [20]God's kingdom isn't just talk but power.

[21]Which would you like? Should I come to you with a stick or with love and a gentle spirit?

Remove the Wicked Man

5 We actually hear there is sexual sin among you, and such as isn't found even among the people of the world, that a man has his father's wife. [2]And you feel proud of yourselves! Shouldn't you rather have wept and re-

---

a - 4   See note at Rom 3:20.

moved from among you the man who did this? [3]Although I'm away from you, I am with you in spirit, and being with you, I have already decided in regard to the man who did this. [4]Call a meeting. My spirit and the power of our Lord Jesus will be with you. Then in the name of our Lord Jesus [5]hand such a person over to Satan, to destroy his sinful flesh in order to save his spirit on the Day of the Lord.

[6]It isn't good for you to feel proud. Don't you know a little yeast ferments the whole dough? [7]Get rid of the old yeast in order to be a new dough, as you are really free from the old yeast, because our *Passover Lamb* was *sacrificed*; it is Christ. [8]Let us, then, celebrate our festival, not with old yeast, not with any yeast of vice and wickedness, but with the bread of purity and truth that has no yeast.

[9]In my letter I wrote you not to associate with those who live in sexual sin. [10]I didn't mean that you should altogether keep away from people who live in sexual sin in this world, from those who are greedy, who rob, or worship idols; then you would have to get out of this world. [11]But now I write you: Don't associate with anyone who calls himself a Christian but lives in sexual sin or is greedy, worships idols, slanders, gets drunk, or robs. Don't even eat with such a person.

[12]Is it my business to judge those who are outside the church? [13]God judges those who are outside. Shouldn't you judge those who are inside the church? *Remove that wicked man from among you*.

Don't Sue One Another

6 When one of you has a case against another, do you dare to bring it before a court of unrighteous men and not before the holy people? [2]Or don't you know these holy people *will judge the world*? And if you judge the world, aren't you able to judge trifles? [3]Don't you know we'll judge angels? Shouldn't we then judge things of this life? [4]If then you are having things of this life decided, will you let men who count nothing in the church be your judges? [5]I say this to make you feel ashamed. Really, isn't any one of you wise enough to decide a matter between one Christian and another? [6]Instead, one Christian sues another — and in front of unbelievers!

[7]Without going any further, suing one another means you have utterly failed. Why don't you rather suffer wrong? Why don't you rather let yourself be robbed? [8]Instead, you do wrong, and you rob, and you do it to your own fellow Christians.

You Are God's Temple

[9]Or don't you know wicked people will have no share in God's kingdom? Don't be mistaken about this: No one who lives in sexual sin or worships idols, no adulterers or men who sin sexually with other men, [10]who steal, are greedy, are drunkards, slander, or rob will have a share in God's kingdom. [11]Some of you used to do these things. But you have been washed,

---

7 Ex 12:11-13; 12:21

you have been made holy, you have been declared righteous by the name of the Lord Jesus Christ and by the Spirit of our God.

[12]It is permissible for me to do anything, but not everything is beneficial. It is permissible for me to do anything, but I will not allow anything to gain control over my life. [13]Food is for the stomach, and the stomach for food, but God will put an end to both of them. The body is not made for sexual sin but for the Lord; and the Lord is for the body. [14]And God, Who raised the Lord, will also raise us by His power.

[15]Don't you know your bodies are members of Christ? Now, should I take the members of Christ and make them members of a prostitute? Never! [16]Or don't you know he who gives himself to a prostitute is one body with her? The Bible says: *"The two will be one flesh."* [17]But if you give yourself to the Lord, you are one spirit with Him.

[18]Flee from sexual sin. Every other sin a man may do is outside his body. But if he sins sexually, he sins against his own body. [19]Or don't you know your body is a temple of the Holy Spirit, Whom God gives you and Who is in you? You don't belong to yourselves, [20]because you were bought for a price. Then glorify God with your bodies.

If You Are Married

7 Now about the things you wrote — it is good for a man not to have sexual relations with a woman. [2]But to avoid sexual sins, every man should have his own wife, and every woman her own husband.

[3]A husband should do for his wife what he owes her, and a wife should do the same for her husband. [4]A wife can't do as she likes with her body; her husband has a right to it. In the same way a husband can't do as he likes with his body; his wife has a right to it. [5]Don't deprive one another, unless you agree to do so for a while to take time to pray. And come together again, or Satan will tempt you because you cannot control yourselves. [6]But as I say this, I'm yielding to you, not ordering you.

[7]I would like everyone to be like myself, but each one has only the gift God gave him, one this and another that. [8]To those who aren't married and to widows I say, it is good for you to stay single like myself, [9]but if you can't control yourselves, get married; it is better to marry than to burn with desire.

[10]If you are married, I — that is, not I, but the Lord — order a wife not to leave her husband. [11]If she does leave him, she should stay single or make up with her husband. And a husband should not divorce his wife.

If You're Married to an Unchristian

[12]To the rest I say (not the Lord), if a Christian has a wife who doesn't believe and she agrees to live with him, he should not divorce her. [13]And if a wife has a husband who doesn't believe and he agrees to live with her,

---

13 Deut 17:7,12; 19:19; 21:21; 22:21-22,24; 24:7   2 Dan 7:18,22,27 16 Gen 2:24

she should not divorce her husband. ¹⁴An unbelieving man married to such a woman serves a holy purpose, and an unbelieving wife married to a Christian serves a holy purpose. Otherwise your children would be unclean, but now they are holy. ¹⁵But if the unbelieving person leaves, let him go. In such a case a Christian man or woman is not bound. But God called us to live in peace. ¹⁶You wife, what do you know — you may save your husband. Or you husband, what do you know — you may save your wife.

Stay as God Called You

¹⁷But everyone should live the life the Lord assigned to him just as God called him. This is the rule I lay down in all the churches. ¹⁸Were you circumcised when you were called? Don't try to get rid of your circumcision. Were you uncircumcised when you were called? Don't be circumcised. ¹⁹Circumcision is nothing, and the lack of it is nothing, but observing what God commands is everything. ²⁰Everyone should stay as he was called. ²¹Were you a slave when you were called? Don't let that trouble you. Of course, if you have a chance to get free, take it. ²²If you are a slave when you are called in the Lord, you are the Lord's free man. In the same way, if you are free when you are called, you are Christ's slave. ²³You were bought for a price; don't become slaves of men. ²⁴My fellow Christians, everyone should stay with God just as he was when he was called.

To Marry or Not to Marry

²⁵For the unmarried girls I have no order from the Lord, but the Lord's mercy made me one you can trust, and I'll tell you what I think. ²⁶Because of the troubles we're in I believe it is good for anyone to stay as he is. ²⁷Are you married? Don't look for a divorce. Are you separated from a wife? Don't look for a wife. ²⁸But if you get married, it's no sin, and if a girl gets married, it's no sin. But if you do, you'll have trouble in your life, and I'm trying to spare you.

²⁹I mean, my fellow Christians, the time has been shortened. While it lasts, if you have a wife, live as if you had none; ³⁰if you weep, as if you weren't weeping; if you're happy, as if you weren't happy; if you buy anything, act as if you didn't have it. ³¹While you use the world, don't try to get out of it all you can, since this world in its present form is passing away.

³²I don't want you to worry. An unmarried man is concerned about the Lord's things, how he can please the Lord. ³³But once he's married, he worries about earthly things, how he can please his wife. ³⁴He's interested in two different things. An unmarried woman or girl is concerned about the Lord's things, to be holy in body and in spirit. But once she's married, she worries about earthly things, how she can please her husband. ³⁵I'm saying this to help you, not to hold you by a rope but to show you how to live nobly for the Lord without being troubled about other things.

³⁶If a man thinks he's not acting properly toward his girl, if his passion is too strong and it must be so, he should do what he wants to — it's no sin

— they should get married. 37But suppose a man has a strong character and the willpower and feels no necessity but has made up his mind to keep his girl as she is, he'll be doing right. 38If, then, he marries his girl, he's doing right. But if he doesn't marry her, he'll be doing better.

39A wife is bound to her husband as long as he lives. If her husband dies, she's free to marry anyone she wants to, but it should be in the Lord. 40But she'll be happier if she stays as she is. That is my judgment, and I think I, too, have the Spirit of God.

Meat Sacrificed to Idols

8 About the meat sacrificed to idols:

We know that all of us have some knowledge. Knowledge puffs up, but love builds up. 2If anyone thinks he knows something, he still has something to learn. 3But if he loves God, God knows him.

4Now about eating meat that was sacrificed to idols, we know that an idol is nothing in the world and there is only one God. 5Even if there are so-called gods in heaven or on earth (as there are many gods and many lords), 6yet we have one God, the Father: from Him comes everything, and we live for Him. And there is one Lord, Jesus Christ: He made everything, and we live by Him.

7But not everyone knows this. Some are still so used to an idol they think of the meat they eat as sacrificed to the idol, and their conscience, being weak, is stained with guilt.

8Food will not bring us closer to God. We lose nothing by not eating and gain nothing by eating. 9But be careful, or weak Christians may fall into sin because you do as you please. 10If anyone sees you who have this knowledge lying down to eat in the temple of an idol, won't you be encouraging him who has a weak conscience to eat the meat sacrificed to idols? 11Then your knowledge is ruining the weak fellow Christian for whom Christ died. 12But when you sin against your fellow Christians in this way and wound their weak consciences, you sin against Christ.

13So if food makes my fellow Christian sin, I will never eat meat — I don't want to give him a reason for sinning.

A Pastor's Pay

9 Am I not free? Am I not an apostle? Didn't I see Jesus, our Lord? Aren't you my work in the Lord? 2If I'm not an apostle to others, I certainly am one to you. You are the Lord's seal that proves I'm an apostle. 3That's how I defend myself before those who examine me. 4Don't we have the right to eat and drink? 5Don't we have the right to take a Christian wife with us like the other apostles, the Lord's brothers, and Peter? 6Or do only Barnabas and I have no right to stop working for a living?

7Does a soldier ever pay his own expenses? Does anyone plant a vineyard and not eat its grapes? Or does anyone take care of a flock and not drink any milk from it? 8Am I stating only a human rule? Doesn't the Law say the same thing? [9]The Law of Moses says: *"Don't muzzle an ox when he's treading out grain."* Is God here interested in oxen? [10]Surely He has us in mind. This was written to show us when we plow or thresh we should expect to get a share of the crop. [11]If we have sown the spiritual life in you, is it too much if we'll reap your earthly goods? [12]If others have the right to expect this from you, don't we have a better claim? But we haven't made use of this right. No, we put up with anything in order not to hinder the preaching of Christ.

[13]Don't you know that the men who work at the temple get their food from the temple? That those who help at the altar get their share of what is on the altar? [14]In the same way the Lord has ordered that those who tell the good news should get their living from the good news.

[15]But I haven't used any of these rights. And I'm not writing this to get such things done for me. I'd rather die than let anyone take away my boast. [16]If I tell the good news, I have nothing to boast about. I must tell it. Woe to me if I don't tell the good news! [17]If I do it because I want to, I get a reward. But if I don't want to do it, I still have this work entrusted to me.

[18]What then is my reward? Just this: When I tell the good news, I won't let it cost anyone anything, and so I won't take advantage of my right in telling the good news.

Everything to Everyone

[19]Although I am free from all people, I made myself a slave of all of them to win more of them. [20]To the Jews I became like a Jew to win Jews; to those under the Law I became like a man under the Law — although I'm not under the Law — to win those under the Law. [21]To those who don't have the Law I became like a man without the Law — although I'm not outside the Law of God but under the law of Christ — to win those who don't have the Law. [22]To weak persons I became weak to win the weak. I've been everything to everyone so that in every way I might save some of them.

[23]I'm doing everything for the good news in order to have a share of what it gives. [24]Don't you know that all who are in a race run but only one wins the prize? Like them, run to win! [25]Anyone who enters a contest goes into strict training. Now, they do it to win a wreath that withers, but we do it to win one that never withers. [26]So I run with a clear goal ahead of me. I fight and don't just shadow box. [27]No, I beat my body and make it my slave so that, when I've called others to run the race, I myself will not somehow be disqualified.

A Warning

10 I want you to know, fellow Christians, our fathers were all under the cloud and all went through the sea, [2]and by baptism in the cloud and in the sea all were united with Moses, [3]all ate the same food of the Spirit, [4]and

---

9 Deut 25:4

all drank the same water of the Spirit, because they drank from the spiritual Rock that went with them, and that Rock was Christ. [5]Yet God wasn't pleased with most of them — *they were killed in the desert.*

[6]Now, this happened in order to warn us not to *long for* what is evil as they did. [7]Don't worship idols as some of them did, as the Bible says: *"The people sat down to eat and drink and got up to play."* [8]Let us not sin sexually as some of them did–23,000 died on one day. [9]Let us not go too far in testing the Lord's patience as some of them did — the snakes killed them. [10]Don't complain as some of them did–the angel of death killed them. [11]These things happened to them to make them a lesson to others and were written down to warn us who are living when the world is coming to an end. [12]So if you think you stand, be careful that you don't fall.

[13]You haven't been tempted more than you could expect. And you can trust God. He will not let you be tested more than you can stand. But when you are tested, He will also make a way out so that you can bear it.

Meat Sacrificed to Idols

[14]And so, my dear friends, keep away from the worship of idols.

[15]I'm talking to sensible people. Judge for yourselves what I say. [16]Is the cup of blessing which we bless not a communion of the blood of Christ? Is the bread which we break not a communion of the body of Christ? [17]All of us are one body, because there is one bread and all of us share that one bread.

[18]See how the Jews do it. Don't those who eat the sacrifices share the altar? [19]What do I mean by this? That a sacrifice made to an idol is something or that an idol really is something? [20]No, these *sacrifices* of the non-Jews *are made to demons and not to God.* I don't want you to be partners of demons. [21]You can't drink the Lord's cup and the cup of demons. You can't share *the Lord's table* and the table of demons. [22]Or are we *trying to make the Lord jealous*? Are we stronger than He?

[23]It is permissible for us to do anything, but not everything is beneficial. It is permissible for us to do anything, but not everything encourages growth. [24]No one should look for his own good, but rather for the good of the other person. [25]Eat anything sold in the market, and don't ask any questions or let your conscience trouble you, [26]because *the earth and everything in it belongs to the Lord.* [27]If any of the unbelievers invites you and you want to go, eat anything they serve you, and don't ask any questions or let your conscience trouble you. [28]But if someone tells you, "This was sacrificed," don't eat it, for the sake of him who told you, and for the sake of conscience — [29]I don't mean yours but the other one's conscience. Why should my freedom be judged by someone else's conscience? [30]If I give thanks for what I eat, why should I let myself be denounced for eating what I thank God for? [31]So, whether you eat or drink or do anything else, do everything

---

5 Num 14:16   *6 Num 11:4,34*   *7 Ex 32:6*   *20 Deut 32:17; Ps 106:37*
21 Mal 1:7,12   *22 Deut 32:21*   *26 Ps 24:1*

to glorify God. [32]Don't be the reason for others to sin, whether they are Jews, Greeks, or God's church. [33]So I try to please everyone in every way and don't look for my advantage but for that of many people so that they may be saved.

11 Imitate me as I imitate Christ.

Long Hair and Hats

[2]I praise you for thinking of me in every way and for keeping the truths as I delivered them to you.

[3]I want you to know that the head of every man is Christ, the head of a woman is her husband, and the head of Christ is God. [4]Any man who keeps his head covered when he prays or speaks God's Word dishonors his head. [5]But any woman who prays or speaks God's Word with nothing on her head dishonors her head. She's exactly like the woman whose head is shaved. [6]If a woman wears nothing on her head, she should also get her hair cut. But if it is a disgrace for a woman to get her hair cut or shaved off, she should keep her head covered. [7]A man shouldn't cover his head, because he is *God's image* and glory; but a woman is a man's glory. [8]The man wasn't made from the woman but the woman from the man, [9]and the man wasn't made for the woman but the woman for the man. [10]That's why a woman should wear something on her head to show she is under authority, out of respect for the angels.

[11]Yet in the Lord a woman needs a man, and a man needs a woman. [12]As the woman was made from the man, so a man is born of a woman, and it all comes from God.

[13]Judge for yourselves. Is it proper for a woman to pray to God with nothing on her head? [14]Doesn't nature itself teach you it's disgraceful for a man to have long hair [15]but that it's a woman's glory to wear her hair long? Her hair is given her as a covering. [16]But if anyone means to argue about it — we don't have such a custom, nor do God's churches.

How to Go to the Lord's Supper

[17]While I'm giving these instructions, I'm not praising you for doing harm instead of good at your meetings. [18]In the first place, I hear that when you meet as a church you are divided, and some of it I believe is true. [19]Of course, there must be divisions among you to show clearly which of you are approved.

[20]When you get together for a common purpose, it is not the Lord's Supper you are eating. [21]As a matter of fact, each of you eats his own supper ahead of time; and so one stays hungry and another gets drunk. [22]Don't you have homes where you can eat and drink? Or do you despise God's church and humiliate those who don't have anything? What should I say to you?

7 Gen 1:27

Should I praise you? I won't praise you for this.

²³The Lord gave me what I taught you, that the night He was betrayed the Lord Jesus took bread. ²⁴He gave thanks, broke it, and said, "This is My body, which is for you. Do this to remember Me." ²⁵He did the same with the cup after the supper. He said, "This cup is the new *testament* in My *blood*. Every time you drink it, do it to remember Me." ²⁶Every time you eat this bread and drink the cup, you are telling how the Lord died until He comes.

²⁷Then anyone who eats the bread or drinks the Lord's cup in an unworthy way is sinning against the Lord's body and blood. ²⁸Examine yourself and then eat some of the bread and drink from the cup. ²⁹Anyone who eats and drinks without seeing that the Lord's body is there is condemned for his eating and drinking.

³⁰That is why many of you are sick and ailing and a number are dead. ³¹If we would look at ourselves critically, we would not be judged. ³²But if the Lord judges us, He corrects us to keep us from being condemned with the world.

³³So then, my fellow Christians, when you get together to eat, wait for one another. ³⁴If you are hungry, eat at home, so you will not meet just to be condemned.

About the other things I'll give directions when I come.

The Spirit's Gifts

12 Fellow Christians, I want you to know about the gifts of the Spirit. ²You know that when you were unbelievers, you were led away in one way or another to idols that cannot talk. ³So I tell you that no one who is speaking by God's Spirit will say, "Jesus is cursed," and no one is able to say, "Jesus is the Lord", except by the Holy Spirit.

⁴Now gifts are given to different persons but by the same Spirit. ⁵Ways of serving are assigned to them but by the same Lord. ⁶Differing powers are given to them, but the same God works everything in all of them. ⁷Now, the Spirit shows Himself to each one to make him useful. ⁸The Spirit gives one person the ability to speak of wisdom. To another the same Spirit gives the ability to speak intelligently. ⁹To another the same Spirit gives faith. To another that same Spirit gives the ability to heal. ¹⁰Another can work miracles. Another can speak God's Word. Another can tell the true Spirit from evil spirits. Another can speak other languages. Another can tell the meaning of languages. ¹¹One and the same Spirit works all these things and gives as He wishes to each in his own way.

¹²As the body is one and yet has many parts, and all the parts of the body, many as they are, form one body, so is Christ. ¹³By one Spirit all of us — Jews or Greeks, slaves or free — were baptized to form one body, and that one Spirit was poured out for all of us to drink.

¹⁴Not one part but many make up the body. ¹⁵Suppose a foot says, "I'm not a hand, and so I'm not a part of the body"; it is still a part of the body.

25 Ex 24:8; Jer 31:31-32; Zech 9:11

¹⁶Or suppose an ear says, "I'm not an eye, and so I'm not a part of the body"; it is still a part of the body. ¹⁷If the whole body were an eye, how could we hear? If it were all hearing, how could we smell? ¹⁸As it is, God arranged the parts, fitting each of them into the body as He wanted it to be. ¹⁹If all of it were one part, how could there be a body? ²⁰As it is, there are many parts and one body.

²¹The eye cannot say to the hand, "I don't need you", or the head to the feet, "I don't need you". ²²No, we really can't do without the parts of the body that we think are weaker. ²³And the parts of the body that we think less honorable we dress with special honor so that our shameful parts have a special nobility, ²⁴which our noble parts don't need. But God has put the body together and given special honor to the part that lacks it, ²⁵so that the body may not be divided but rather that the parts might feel the same concern for one another. ²⁶If one member suffers, all the others suffer with it. If one is honored, all the others are happy with it.

²⁷Now, you are the body of Christ, and everyone has his place in it. ²⁸God has appointed in the church first apostles, next preachers, third teachers, then miracle workers, then healers, helpers, managers, and those who can speak (various) kinds of languages. ²⁹Are all apostles? Are all preachers? Are all teachers? Can all do miracles? ³⁰Can all heal? Can all speak in other languages? Can all tell what they mean? No, ³¹but try to have the better gifts.

Love

And now I'll show you the best way of all.

13 If I speak the languages of men and of angels but don't have any love, I've become a loud gong or a clashing cymbal. ²Even if I speak God's Word and know every kind of hidden truth and have every kind of knowledge, even if I have all the faith to move mountains but don't have any love, I'm nothing. ³Even if I give away all I have to feed the hungry and give up my body but only to boast and don't have any love, it doesn't help me.

⁴Love is patient. Love is kind. Love isn't jealous. It doesn't brag or get conceited. ⁵It isn't indecent. It isn't selfish. It doesn't get angry. It *doesn't plan to hurt anyone.* ⁶It doesn't delight in evil but is happy with the truth. ⁷It bears everything, believes everything, hopes for everything, endures everything.

⁸Love never dies. If there are prophecies, they will come to an end; or other languages, they will stop; or knowledge, it will vanish. ⁹We learn only a part of anything and prophesy only a part. ¹⁰But when that which is perfect comes, what is only a part will vanish. ¹¹When I was a child, I used to talk like a child, think like a child, plan like a child. Now that I'm a man, I've given up the ways of a child. ¹²Now we see a blurred image in a mirror, but then we'll see face to face. Now I learn only a part of anything, but then I'll know as He has known me.

5 Zech 7:10; 8:17

[13]And now these three, faith, hope, and love, go on, but the most important of these is love.

Speak to Be Understood

14 Pursue love, be eager to have the gifts of the Spirit, and especially to speak God's Word. [2]When a man speaks in another language, he doesn't speak to people but to God, because no one understands him; his spirit is speaking mysteries. [3]But when you speak God's Word, you speak to people to help them grow, to encourage and comfort them. [4]When you speak in another language, you encourage yourself. But when you speak God's Word, you help the church grow. [5]I want you all to speak in other languages, but I would rather have you speak God's Word. It is more important to speak God's Word than other languages, unless you explain what you say in order to help the church grow. [6]Now, my fellow Christians, if I come to you and speak other languages, how can I help you unless I tell you what God has told me and bring it as His Word or as something I know and teach?

[7]Lifeless instruments such as a flute or a lyre produce sounds, but if there's no difference in the sounds, how can you tell what is played on a flute or a lyre? [8]And if the trumpet doesn't sound a clear call, who will get ready for battle? [9]In the same way, if you don't speak with a clear meaning, how will anyone know what you're saying? You'll be talking into the air. [10]There are, I suppose, ever so many different languages in the world, and none is without meaning. [11]Now if I don't know what a language means, I'll be a foreigner to him who speaks it, and he'll be a foreigner to me. [12]So you, too, since you are eager to have the Spirit's gifts, try to be rich in them so as to build up the church. [13]If then you speak another language, pray to be able to explain it.

[14]If I pray in another language, my spirit prays, but my mind isn't helping anyone. [15]What then? I will pray in my spirit but also pray so as to be understood. I will sing praise in my spirit but also sing so as to be understood. [16]Otherwise, if you praise God only with your spirit, how can an ordinary person who is there say "Amen" to your prayer of thanks? He doesn't know what you mean. [17]It is good that you give thanks, but it doesn't help the other person. [18]I thank God I speak more in other languages than any of you, [19]but in a church I would rather say five words that can be understood, in order to teach others, than ten thousand words in a language no one understands.

[20]Fellow Christians, don't be childish in your understanding. In evil be babies, but grow up in your thinking. [21]It is written in the Bible: *"In strange languages and by the mouth* of foreigners *I will speak to these people, but even then they will not listen* to Me," says the Lord. [22]Then other languages are not meant to warn believers but unbelievers, while God's Word isn't meant for unbelievers but for believers. [23]Now if the whole congregation

---

21 Is 28:11-12

meets and all speak other languages and then some ordinary people or unbelievers come in, won't they say you're crazy? [24]But if all speak God's Word
and some unbeliever or ordinary person comes in, all convince him of his sin
and all examine him. [25]The secrets of his heart are shown, and so he bows
down with his face on the ground, worships God, and declares, *"God is certainly here among you."*

Keep Order in Worship Services

[26]What should you do, then, my fellow Christians? When you meet,
everyone is ready with a song, something to teach, some truth from God, another language, or an explanation. Do it all to help one another grow. [27]If
you speak another language, only two should speak, or three at the most,
and one at a time, and someone should explain. [28]If there's no one to explain
what you say, you shouldn't say anything in church but only speak to yourself and to God.

[29]Two or three should speak God's Word, and the others should decide
whether what is being said is right or wrong. [30]If God gives a truth to another person who is seated, the first speaker should be silent. [31]You can all
speak God's Word one after another so that everyone learns something and
is encouraged. [32]Men who speak God's Word control their own spirits. [33]You
see, God is not a God of disorder but of peace.

As in all the churches of the holy people, [34]the women should be silent
in church because they are not allowed to speak. They should submit, as
the Law says. [35]If there is something they want to know, they should ask
their husbands at home. It is a disgrace for a woman to speak in church.

[36]Did God's Word first come from you? Or were you the only ones to
whom it came? [37]If anyone thinks he speaks for God or has the Spirit, he
should know that what I write you is what the Lord orders. [38]But if anyone
ignores this, he should be ignored.

[39]So, my brothers, be eager to speak God's Word, and don't try to keep
anyone from speaking in other languages. [40]But everything should be done
in a proper and orderly way.

Jesus Rose

15 My brothers, I am telling you the good news I brought you and
you accepted. You stand in it [2]and are saved by it if you cling to the words
I used in telling it to you — unless you were trifling when you believed. [3]I
brought you what I received — something very important — that Christ
died for our sins as the Scriptures said He would, [4]He was buried, and He
rose on the third day as the Scriptures said He would. [5]Peter saw Him,
then the twelve, [6]then more than 500 Christians at one time; most of these
are still living, but some have gone to their rest. [7]Then James saw Him,
then all the apostles. [8]Last of all I saw Him, I who was like one prematurely

25 *Is 45:14*

born, [9]since I am the least of the apostles and not fit to be called an apostle because I persecuted God's church. [10]God's grace made me what I am, and His grace wasn't wasted on me. But I did far more work than all the others — not I but God's grace that was with me. [11]Now, whether I did it or they, this is what we preach, and this is what you believed.

We'll Rise

[12]If we preach that Christ rose from the dead, how can some of you say, "The dead don't rise?" [13]If the dead don't rise, Christ didn't rise. [14]And if Christ didn't rise, our preaching means nothing, and your faith means nothing. [15]Also, we are found to be men who lied about God because we testified about God that He raised Christ, Whom He did not raise if it is true that the dead are not raised. [16]You see, if the dead don't rise, Christ didn't rise. [17]But if Christ didn't rise, your faith can't help you, and you are still in your sins. [18]Then also those who have gone to their rest in Christ have perished. [19]If Christ is our hope only for this life, we should be pitied more than any other people.

[20]But now Christ did rise from the dead, the first in the harvest of those who are sleeping in their graves. [21]Since by man came death, by Man also came the resurrection of the dead. [22]As in Adam all die, so in Christ all will be made alive. [23]But everyone in his own group: first Christ, then, when He comes, those who belong to Christ.

[24]Then the end will come when He hands over the kingdom to God the Father after He has put an end to every other government, authority, and power, [25]since He must rule as King until *He puts* all *enemies under His feet.* [26]The last enemy He will get rid of is death. [27]You see, *He puts everything under His feet.* When He says *"everything is put under Him,"* this clearly doesn't include Him Who *puts everything under Him.* [28]But when *everything has been put under Him,* then the Son also will put Himself under Him Who *put everything under* the Son so that God will be everything in everything.

[29]Otherwise, what will they do who are baptized for the dead?[b] Why are they baptized for them if the dead don't actually rise?

[30]And why are we in danger every hour? [31]As I'm proud of you, my fellow Christians, in Christ Jesus, our Lord, I assure you I'm facing death every day. [32]If like other men I have fought with wild animals in Ephesus, what good is it to me? If the dead don't rise, *let us eat and drink — tomorrow we die!* [33]Don't let anyone deceive you. "Bad company ruins good habits."[c] [34]Come back to a sober and righteous life, and don't sin any more. Some people don't know God. I say this to make you feel ashamed.

---

25 Ps 110:1   27-28 Ps 8:6   32 Is 22:13

---

b - 29 The relative of a Christian who had died may wish to be baptized in order to see this Christian again in heaven. Or he may want to express the hope that a Christian friend who has died will rise.
c - 33   This saying is attributed to the Greek playwright Menander (342-291 B.C.) in his play "Thais".

Our Glorified Bodies

³⁵But someone will ask, "How do the dead rise? And what kind of body will they have when they come back?"

³⁶Just think a little! The seed you sow has to die before it is made alive. ³⁷And the seed you sow is not the body that it will be, but a bare kernel, maybe wheat or something else. ³⁸But God gives it the body He wanted it to have, and to each kind of seed its own body. ³⁹Not all flesh is the same. Human beings have one kind of flesh, animals have another, birds have another, and fish have another kind of flesh. ⁴⁰And so there are heavenly bodies and earthly bodies. But the splendor of the heavenly bodies is different from that of the earthly bodies. ⁴¹The shining of the sun is different from the shining of the moon, and the shining of the stars is different again. Even one star differs in splendor from another star.

⁴²That is how it will be when the dead rise. When the body is sown, it decays; when it rises, it can't decay. ⁴³When it is sown, it isn't wonderful; when it rises, it is wonderful. It is sown weak; it rises strong. ⁴⁴It is sown a natural body; it rises a spiritual body. Just as there is a natural body, so there is spiritual body. ⁴⁵That is what the Bible says: "*Adam, the first man, was made a natural living being*"; the last Adam became a life-giving spirit. ⁴⁶That which is spiritual doesn't come first, but the natural; then that which is spiritual. ⁴⁷The first *man is made of the soil of the ground*; the Second Man is from heaven. ⁴⁸The people of the ground are like the man from the ground; the people of heaven are like the Man from heaven. ⁴⁹Just as we have been like the man from the ground, we will be like the Man from heaven. ⁵⁰I tell you, fellow Christians, flesh and blood can't have a share in God's kingdom, or decay have what doesn't decay.

⁵¹Now I'll tell you a mystery. We're not all going to die, but we're all going to be changed — ⁵²in a moment, in the twinkling of an eye when the last trumpet sounds. It will sound, and the dead will rise immortal, and we'll be changed. ⁵³This decaying body must be made one that can't decay, and this dying body must be made one that can't die. ⁵⁴When this decaying body is made one that can't decay and this dying body is made one that *can't die*, then will happen what is written: "*Death is swallowed up in victory!*"

⁵⁵*Where, Death, is your victory?*
Where, Death, is your sting?

⁵⁶Sin gives death its sting, and the Law gives sin its power. ⁵⁷But thank God! He gives us the victory through our Lord Jesus Christ.

⁵⁸Stand firm, then, my dear fellow Christians, and let nothing move you. Always keep on doing a great work for the Lord since you know in the Lord your hard work isn't wasted.

45-47 Gen 2:7   54-55 Is 25:8; Hos 13:14

The Collection

16 About the collection for the holy people — do just as I ordered the churches in Galatia to do. [2]Every Sunday each of you should at home lay aside some money he makes and save it so that none will have to be collected when I come. [3]But when I come, I will send the men, whomever you approve, with letters to take your gift to Jerusalem. [4]If it is worthwhile for me to go, too, I'll go with them.

I Am Coming

[5]I will come to you when I go through Macedonia. I am going through Macedonia, [6]and probably will stay with you or even spend the winter with you so that you will send me on my way wherever I'm going. [7]I don't want to see you now just in passing, because I hope to stay with you for some time if the Lord will let me. [8]But I'll be staying in Ephesus until Pentecost, [9]because a door has opened wide for me to do effective work, and many are opposing me.

Timothy, Apollos, and Others

[10]If Timothy comes, see to it that he's not afraid when he's with you. He's doing the Lord's work just as I am. [11]No one should despise him. Send him on his way in peace so he will come to me, because I'm expecting him with the other Christians.

[12]As for Apollos, our fellow Christian — I tried hard to get him to go to you with the other Christians, but he really didn't want to go now. He will come when the time is right.

[13]Watch, stand firm in your faith, *be men, be strong.* [14]Do everything with love.

[15]You know that the family of Stephanas was the first to be won in Greece, and they gave themselves to the service of the holy people. I urge you, my fellow Christians, [16]let such people and anyone else who works hard with you lead you. [17]I'm glad Stephanas, Fortunatus, and Achaicus came here, because they have made up for your absence: [18]They have refreshed me — and you, too. You should appreciate men like that.

Greetings

[19]The churches in the province of Asia greet you. Aquila and Prisca and the church at their home send you hearty greetings in the Lord. [20]All the Christians greet you. Greet one another with a holy kiss. [21]Here is the greeting that I, Paul, write with my own hand.

[22]If anyone doesn't love the Lord, a curse on him! Our Lord, come!

[23]May the grace of the Lord Jesus be with you! [24]My love be with you all in Jesus. Amen.

---

13 Ps 27:14; 31:24

PAUL
WRITES THE SECOND LETTER TO THE
CORINTHIANS

1 PAUL, APOSTLE OF CHRIST JESUS by God's will, and Timothy, our fellow Christian, to God's church in Corinth and to all the holy people everywhere in Greece — [2]may God our Father and the Lord Jesus Christ give you grace and peace!

God Comforts and Rescues Us

[3]Let us praise the God and Father of our Lord Jesus Christ, the Father of mercy and the God of every comfort. [4]He comforts us in all our suffering to make us able to comfort others in all their suffering with the same comfort with which God comforts us. [5]As Christ's sufferings overflow to us, so Christ makes our comfort overflow. [6]If we suffer, it helps us to comfort and save you. If we are comforted, it helps us to comfort you effectively when you endure the same sufferings as we do. [7]Our hope for you is unshaken because we know as you share our sufferings you share our comfort.

[8]Fellow Christians, we want you to know our suffering in the province of Asia was so extreme, so much more than we could stand, we even despaired of living. [9]Yes, we felt sentenced to death. We were not to trust ourselves but God, Who raises the dead. [10]He rescued us from such a death, and He Who is our Hope will rescue us again. He will continue to rescue us [11]since you are also joining in helping us through your prayers for us. Then many people will thank God on our behalf for the gift which comes to us as the result of the prayers of many people.

We Were Sincere

[12]There is something of which we can boast (and our conscience will testify that it is true), namely, that we have conducted ourselves in the world, especially toward you, with God-given holiness and sincerity, without human cleverness but with God's grace. [13]We are writing you only what you can read and understand. And I hope you will understand until the end, [14]as you have to some extent understood us, that you can be proud of us as also we of you on the day of our Lord Jesus.

[15]Confident of this, I wanted you to have the benefit of a double visit. I planned to come to you first, [16]go from you to Macedonia, then come back again from Macedonia to you and let you send me on to Judea.

[17]When I wanted to do this, was I trifling? Or do I go on making my plans any way I please so that I can say "Yes, yes" and "No, no"? [18]You can trust God that what we tell you isn't "yes" and "no". [19]God's Son Jesus Christ, Whom I, Silas, and Timothy preached to you, wasn't "yes" and "no", but in Him there has come and is a "yes". [20]For all God's promises He is the "Yes" that makes them come true. And so He makes it possible for us to give glory to God by saying, "It is true."

[21]It is God Who makes us and you firm in Christ and also has anointed us. [22]He has put His seal on us and given us the Spirit as a guarantee in our hearts.

I Don't Want to Hurt You

[23]I call on God as a witness against me that I stayed away from Corinth in order not to hurt you. [24]I don't mean that we are lording it over your faith, but we're working with you to make you happy. For you stand on your own feet by faith.

2 I made up my mind not to come if I had to bring you grief again. [2]If I make you sad, who should make me happy but the person I'm making sad? [3]This is what I said in my letter. I didn't want to come and be made sad by those who should have made me happy. I am sure about all of you—that what makes me happy also makes all of you happy. [4]I was deeply troubled and in anguish when I wrote you with much weeping, not to make you sad but to have you realize how very much I love you.

Forgive the Man Who Did Wrong

[5]If someone caused grief, he didn't do it to me but to some extent (not to make it too strong) to all of you. [6]Most of you have punished him; that's enough for such a person. [7]Now you should turn around, forgive and comfort him, or too much grief may overwhelm such a person. [8]So I urge you to assure him of your love. [9]I wrote you to see if you would stand the test and obey in every way.

[10]When you forgive anyone, I do, too. If I forgave anything, I did it in the presence of Christ for your benefit [11]and to keep Satan from getting the best of us. We know what he has in mind.

The Aroma of Christ

[12]I went to Troas to tell the good news of Christ, and there a door to do the Lord's work stood wide open for me, [13]but my spirit couldn't get any relief because I didn't find Titus, my fellow Christian. So I said good-bye to the people and went to Macedonia.

[14]But thank God! He always leads us on triumphantly in Christ and everywhere through us spreads the aroma of knowing Him. [15]Yes, we are the aroma of Christ to God among those who are saved and among those who perish — [16]to some an aroma of death that kills, to others an aroma of

life that gives life.

And who is qualified for this? [17]At least we don't peddle an impure Word of God like many others, but in Christ we talk sincerely as men who come from God and stand before God.

3 Are we again recommending ourselves? Or do we, like some people, need letters of recommendation to you or from you? [2]You are our letter, written in our hearts, known and read by everyone. [3]Anyone can see you are Christ's letter, prepared by us, not written with ink but with the Spirit *of the living God*, not *on stone tablets* but on *tablets of human hearts.*

[4]That is how Christ gives us confidence in God. [5]We can't do anything by ourselves and so claim to produce it ourselves, but God gives us our ability. [6]He has made us able servants of a *new covenant*, not of a written Law but of the Spirit, because the written Law kills, but the Spirit makes alive.

The Glory of the New Covenant

[7]Now if that service, engraved in stone and bringing death, came with such glory the people of Israel couldn't look at *Moses' face* because it *shone with the glory* that was fading, [8]how much more certainly will the service of the Spirit have *glory*? [9]If the service that condemns has *glory*, the service that gives righteousness much more certainly overflows with *glory*. [10]That which had *glory* lost it because the other *glory* outshone it. [11]If that which fades away had its *glory*, that which is permanent much more certainly has *glory*.

[12]Because we expect this, we are very bold [13]and not like *Moses*, who *wore a veil over his face* to keep the people of Israel from seeing the last rays of the fading *glory*. [14]But their minds have been closed. To this day the same *veil* is still there on the reading of the old covenant and isn't taken away, because it is put away only in Christ. [15]Yes, to this day, when they read Moses, a *veil* lies on their hearts. [16]But *whenever anyone turns to the Lord, the veil is taken away.*

[17]The Lord is the Spirit, and where the Spirit of the Lord is, there is liberty. [18]And all of us, reflecting *the Lord's glory* in our unveiled faces, are changed from glory to glory to be like Him, as we expect it from the Lord, Who is the Spirit.

Treasure in Clay Jars

4 And so we who by God's mercy have this service don't get discouraged. [2]But we have renounced the secret ways that anyone should be ashamed of. We don't use trickery or falsify God's Word. But by clearly telling the truth we recommend ourselves to everyone's conscience before God.

[3]If the good news we tell is veiled, it is veiled to those who perish,

---

3 Ex 24:12; 31:18; Prov 3:3; 7:3; Ezek 11:19; 36:26

[4]whose minds the god of this world has blinded — they don't believe — to keep them from seeing the light of the good news of the glory of Christ, Who is God's image.

[5]You see, we don't preach ourselves but Jesus Christ as the Lord, and we are your servants for Jesus' sake. [6]God, Who said: *"Let light shine out of the dark,"* has shone in our hearts to bring you the light of knowing God's glory in the face of Jesus Christ.

[7]We have this treasure in clay jars to show that its extraordinary power comes from God and not from us. [8]In every way we are hard pressed but not crushed, in doubt but not in despair, [9]hunted but not forsaken, struck down but not destroyed. [10]We are always carrying around the death of Jesus in our bodies, so that you can see the life of Jesus in our bodies. [11]While we're living, we're always being given up to die for Jesus so that you can see in our dying bodies the life of Jesus. [12]So death is working in us, but life is working in you.

[13]It is written: *"I believed and so I spoke."* Having the same spirit of faith, we also believe and so we speak, [14]because we know that He Who raised the Lord Jesus will also raise us with Jesus and bring us with you before Him.

[15]All this is to help you so that God's grace, as it spreads, will move more and more people to overflow with thanks to God's glory. [16]That is why we are not discouraged. No, even if we outwardly perish, inwardly we're renewed from day to day. [17]The light trouble of this moment is preparing for us an everlasting weight of glory, greater than anything we can imagine. [18]We don't look at the things that are seen but at the things that are not seen. What we see lasts only a while, but what we don't see lasts forever.

We Long for a Heavenly Body

5 If the earthly tent we live in is torn down, we know we'll get one from God, not made by human hands but lasting forever in heaven. [2]In this body we sigh as we long to put on and live in the body we get from heaven. [3]Of course, if we put that on, we'll not be found without a body. [4]So while we are in this tent, we sigh, feeling distressed because we don't want to put off this body but put on the other and have life swallow up our death. [5]It is God Who has prepared us for this and given us His Spirit as a guarantee.

[6]And so we are always confident. We know that as long as we are living in this body we are living away from the Lord. [7]For we go through life by faith, not by sight. [8]We are confident and prefer to live away from this body and to live with the Lord. [9]Now, whether we live here or move out, we try hard to please Him. [10]We must all appear before the judgment seat of Christ, each to receive according to what he has done with his life, whether he has used it for good or evil.

---

6 Jer 31:31-32   **7-16 Ex 34:29-30,33-35**   *18 Ex 16:7,10; 24:17*
6 Gen 1:3

Christis Compels Us

Christ Compels Us

[11]Since we know the terror of the Lord, we're trying to persuade people. God already knows what we really are, and I hope you, too, are clearly conscious of it. [12]We are not recommending ourselves to you again but giving you a reason to be proud of us so that you can answer those who boast about outward things but nothing in the heart. [13]If we were crazy, it was for God. If we're sane, it is for you. [14]The love of Christ compels us because we're convinced One died for all and so all have died. [15]He died for all that those who live should no longer live for themselves but for Him Who died and rose for them.

[16]And so from now on we don't think of anyone only as a human being. Once we thought of Christ only as a man, but not now anymore. [17]So if anyone is in Christ, he is a new creation. The old things have passed away. They have become new.

Be God's Friends

Be God's Friends

[18]But God has done it all. He has restored our relationship with Him through Christ, and He has given us the task of proclaiming this restored relationship. [19]In Christ God restored the relationship of the world to Himself by not counting their sins against them, and He has put into our hands the message of this restored relationship. [20]Therefore we are ambassadors for Christ. God is pleading through us. We ask you for Christ, "Be reunited with God." [21]God made Him Who did not know sin to be sin for us, so that in Him we would have the righteousness of God.

6 As men who are working with God we plead with you: Don't let God's grace be wasted on you. [2]He says:

> At a favorable time I have heard you;
> On the day of salvation I have helped you.
> Look, now is *the favorable time*.
> Look, now is *the day of salvation*.

So We Endure

So We Endure

[3]We're not in any way giving people a reason to turn away, to keep them from finding fault with our work. [4]Instead we're in everything showing we're God's good workers by great endurance in suffering, in need, and in hardships; [5]when we're beaten or put in prison, when there are riots; when we're overworked and go without sleep and food; [6]by being pure, by knowledge, by patience and kindness; by the Holy Spirit; by sincere love; [7]by telling the truth; by God's power; with the weapons of righteousness in the right hand and the left; [8]when we're honored or dishonored, blamed or praised. Treated as deceivers, we are honest; [9]as unknown, we are well known; as *dying*, and you see, we go on *living*; as *corrected but not killed*;

---

13 Ps 116:10   2 Is 49:8   9 Ps 118:17-19

[10]as sad, we're always glad; as beggars, we're making many rich; as having nothing, we really have everything.

[11]We have talked frankly to you Corinthians. Our *hearts are wide open.* [12]There's plenty of room in them for you, but you're narrow in your attitude toward us. [13]I ask you as my children: Treat me as I treat you, and open your hearts wide, too.

Don't Touch Anything Unclean

[14]Don't be yoked with unbelievers. How can right and wrong be partners? Or how can light have anything to do with darkness? [15]How can Christ agree with the devil? Or what does a believer have in common with an unbeliever? [16]How can God's temple agree with idols? Now, we are the temple of the living God, as God said:

> *"I will live and walk among them,*
> *and I will be their God,*
> *and they will be My people.*
> [17]*So come out of them,*
> *and separate from them,"* says the Lord,
> *"and don't touch anything unclean.*
> *Then I will welcome you,*
> [18]*and I will be* your *Father,*
> *and* you will be My sons *and daughters,"*
> says *the Almighty Lord.*

7 Since we have such promises, dear friends, let us cleanse ourselves from everything that soils body and spirit, and let us continually do what is holy in the fear of God.

You Encouraged Us

[2]Make room in your hearts for us. We haven't wronged anyone, ruined anyone, gotten the best of anyone. [3]I'm not saying this to condemn you. I've told you before, you are in our hearts to die together and to live together. [4]I have much confidence in you. I'm very proud of you. I'm very much encouraged. I'm overjoyed in all our troubles.

[5]Even when we came to Macedonia, our bodies got no rest. We were in every kind of trouble, outwardly fighting and inwardly afraid. [6]But *God,* Who *comforts those who feel miserable, comforted* us by the coming of Titus, [7]and not only by his coming but also by the way you encouraged him. He told us how you long for me, how sorry you are, and how eager to take my side, and this made me happier still.

---

11 Ps 119:32
16-18 Gen 17:7-8; Ex 29:45-46; Lev 26:11-12; Deut 4:20; 26:18; 29:13; II Sam 7:7-8,14; Is 52:11; Jer 7:23; 11:4; 24:7; 30:22; 31:1,33; 32:28; 51:45; Ezek 11:20; 14:11; 20:34,41; 34:24; 36:28; 37:23,27; Amos 4:13; Zech 8:8; 13:9
6 Is 49:13

[8]I'm not sorry if my letter made you sad. Even if I did feel sorry when I saw   that letter make you sad, though only for a while, [9]I'm glad now, not that you were sad but because your sadness led you to repent of your sin. You were sad in a godly way. And so we haven't done you any harm. [10]In fact, godly sorrow produces repentance which leads to salvation, free from regret; but worldly sorrow produces death. [11]See how eager God's sorrow has made you, how ready to clear yourselves, how disgusted with wrong, how alarmed you were, what longing and zeal you felt, and how ready you were to punish! In every way you've shown you are innocent in this matter. [12]Although I wrote you, I didn't have in mind the man who did wrong or him who was wronged, but I wanted to show you before God how zealous you are for us. [13]This is what encouraged us.

While we were encouraged, we were much more delighted to see how happy Titus was because all of you had cheered him up. [14]If I boasted to him about you, you didn't disappoint me. But just as everything we told you was true, so our boast to Titus proved to be true. [15]And his heart goes out to you, all the more as he recalls how ready all of you were to do what he asked and how you welcomed him with respect and trembling. [16]I'm glad I can in every way feel confident about you.

Finish Your Collection

8 Fellow Christians, we want you to know what God's grace has done in the churches of Macedonia. [2]While they were severely tested by trouble, their overflowing joy and their deep poverty have yielded a richly overflowing generosity. [3]I assure you they have given all they could, yes, more than they could give, [4]of their own free will, and with much pleading they begged us for the privilege of sharing in the help given the holy people. [5]They did more than we expected: they gave themselves to the Lord first and then to us, doing just what God wanted.

[6]This led us to urge Titus, as he had started it, to finish in you, too, this work of God's kindness. [7]As you are rich in everything, in faith, speech, knowledge, every kind of zeal, and in the love which you have toward us, we want you also to be rich in this work of God's kindness.

[8]I'm not ordering you but testing you by the zeal of others to see how genuine your love is. [9]You know the grace of our Lord Jesus Christ — He was rich, but became poor for you to make you rich by His poverty.

[10]I'm telling you what I think you should do about this, because it is best for you. Last year you were the first not only to do something but to want to do something. [11]Now finish the job — you were eager to undertake it — in the same way finish it as well as you can. [12]If you're eager to give, God accepts it according to what you have, not according to what you don't have.

[13]We don't mean to bring relief to others and hardship to you but to be fair. [14]Right now what you don't need should relieve their need so that what

they will not need will relieve your need, and so it will be fair, [15]as it is written: *"Anyone who gathered much didn't have too much, and anyone who gathered little didn't have too little."*

[16]We thank God for making Titus just as eager to help you as I am. [17]He welcomed my request. He's very eager and is by his own choice coming to you.

[18]We're sending with him the fellow Christian whom all the churches praise for his telling the good news. [19]More than that, the churches appointed him to travel with us in this work of God's kindess we're doing to honor the Lord and to show we're willing to help.

[20]We're trying to avoid any criticism of the way we're handling this generous gift. [21]We *intend to do what's right not only before the Lord but also before other people.*

[22]We are also sending with them our fellow Christian whom we have often tested in many ways and found zealous and now more eager than ever because he has so much confidence in you.

[23]As for Titus, he is my partner and fellow worker among you. And our fellow Christians, the messengers of the churches, are the glory of Christ. [24]Show the churches how you love them and how right we were when we boasted to them about you.

How to Give

9 I really don't need to write you about helping the holy people, [2]because I know how eager you are. That's what I'm telling the people in Macedonia in boasting about you, "Greece has been ready since last year," and your enthusiasm has stirred up most of them. [3]Now I'm sending my fellow Christians so that we may not have been wrong in boasting about you on this point but that you may be ready as I said. [4]Otherwise, if any Macedonians come with me and find you aren't ready, you would make us (to say nothing of yourselves) feel ashamed of being so confident. [5]So I thought it necessary to urge these fellow Christians to go to you ahead of me, arrange in advance the gift you promised, and have it ready as money that was gladly given and not forced out of you.

[6]Remember this: *If you sow little, you* won't *harvest* much *grain. But if you sow* generously, *you will harvest* much *grain.* [7]Everyone should do what he has made up his mind to do, not with regret or being forced, because *God* loves *anyone who gives gladly.*

God Blesses You

[8]God can pour out every gift of His grace on you so you will always in every way have all you need and plenty to do any good work. [9]The Bible says of such a person: *He scatters his gifts to the poor. His righteousness*

---

15 Ex 16:18   *21 Prov 3:4*   *6-7 Prov 22:8*   *9 Ps 112:3,9 goes on forever.* [10]He Who gives *seed to the sower and bread to eat,* will give you seed and multiply it and make *your righteous grain* grow. [11]You will get rich in everything so you can give generously in every way; through us this will move people to thank God. [12]This work you do in serving others doesn't only supply the needs of the holy people; it makes them pour out many thanks to God. [13]As you prove by this service what you are, they praise God that you submit to the good news of Christ which you confess and that you freely share with them and with everyone. [14]While they pray for you, they long for you because they see the extraordinary grace of God that is given to you. [15]Thanks be to God for His gift that is more than we can tell.

I Am Bold

10 I myself, Paul, plead with you with the gentleness and kindliness of Christ — I who am humble when I'm face to face with you but get bold toward you when I'm away! [2]I beg you that when I come I don't have to be as confident and bold as I think I'll dare to be against some men who think we're living according to the flesh. [3]Of course, we're living in the flesh, but we're not fighting in a fleshly way. [4]The weapons we fight with are not those of the flesh but have the power before God to tear down fortresses. [5]With them we tear down arguments and everything raising its proud head against the knowledge of God and make every thought a prisoner and have it obey Christ. [6]We're ready to punish every disobedience when you are completely obedient.

[7]You see things as they are outwardly. If anyone feels sure he belongs to Christ, he should remind himself that we belong to Christ just as he does. [8]If I boast a little too much about our authority, which the Lord gave us to build you up and not to tear you down, I will not have to feel ashamed. [9]I don't want to seem to scare you with my letters. [10]"His letters are impressive and strong," someone says, "but when he's with us, he's weak, and people despise what he says." [11]Such a person should understand: When we come, we'll act exactly the way we express ourselves in letters when we're away.

We Are Proud of Our Work

[12]We don't dare to put ourselves in a class or compare ourselves with some of those who speak highly of themselves, but when they measure themselves by their own yardstick and compare themselves with themselves, they don't show good sense.

[13]Now we'll limit our boasting. Our limit is the field of work to which God has bound us. This includes coming to you. [14]It is not as though we were not coming to you and so we are reaching beyond our limit. We were the first to reach you with the good news of Christ. [15]We are not going be-

---

10 Is 55:10; Hos 10:12

yond our limit and boasting of work done by others, but we expect your faith to grow so as to enlarge the work in our field in your area until it goes beyond you, [16]and so we'll tell the good news in the countries beyond you without boasting of work already done in another man's field.

[17]*If anyone boasts, let him boast in the Lord.* [18]For it is not the man who approves of himself who is really approved but he of whom the Lord approves.

I Am Jealous

11 I wish you would put up with a little foolishness of mine. Yes, do put up with me. [2]I am jealous of you with godly jealousy. I promised you in marriage, to bring you as a pure bride to one husband — to Christ. [3]But I'm afraid that as *the snake* by its trickery *seduced* Eve, your minds may somehow be corrupted and you may lose your simple and pure loyalty to Christ. [4]When someone comes along and preaches a different Jesus whom we didn't preach or gives you a different spirit you didn't get before or a different gospel you didn't receive before, you put up with it well enough.

[5]I don't think I'm in any way less than your "super" apostles. [6]Even if I'm not a trained speaker, I know what I'm talking about. In every way we have shown you this before everyone.

[7]Did I do wrong when I humbled myself so you would be lifted up, when I charged you nothing for bringing you God's good news? [8]I robbed other churches, taking pay from them in order to serve you. [9]When I was with you and needed anything, I didn't bother anyone to help me, because our fellow Christians[a] who came from Macedonia supplied all I needed. I kept myself from being a burden to you in any way, and I'll continue to do so. [10]As the truth of Christ is in me, this boast of mine will not be silenced anywhere in Greece. [11]Why? Because I don't love you? God knows I do. [12]And I will go on doing as I do, to take away the opportunity of those who want an opportunity to get others to think they are like us in the work they're boasting about. [13]Such men are false apostles, deceitful workers masquerading as apostles of Christ. [14]And no wonder, when Satan himself masquerades as an angel of light. [15]So it isn't surprising if his servants also masquerade as servants of righteousness. In the end they'll get what they deserve for what they're doing.

I Will Boast

[16]Again I say no one should think I'm a fool. But if you do, then let me come to you as a fool and also boast a little. [17]What I say when I boast so confidently is not the Lord's way of speaking but a fool's. [18]Since many brag in a human way, I will, too, [19]because you, being wise, like to put up with fools. [20]You put up with anyone who makes you his slaves or devours what

---

17 Jer 9:24   3 Gen 3:4,13

a - 9   Silas and Timothy (Acts 18:5; 2 Cor 1:19)

you have or traps you or lords it over you or slaps your face. [21]I'm ashamed to admit it: As you say, we have been too weak.

But what anyone else dares to claim — I'm talking like a fool — I can claim, too. [22]Are they Jews? So am I! Do they belong to the people of Israel? So do I! Are they descended from Abraham? So am I! [23]Are they servants of Christ? I'm insane to talk like this, but I'm a better one! I've done much more hard work, been in prison much more, been beaten very much more, and often faced death. [24]Five times the Jews gave me thirty-nine lashes, three times I was beaten with a stick, once I was stoned, [25]three times I was in a shipwreck, a night and a day I drifted on the sea. [26]I've traveled much and faced dangers of flooded streams and of robbers, dangers from Jews and non-Jews, dangers in the city, in the wilderness, and on the sea, dangers from false friends. [27]I have toiled and struggled, often sleepless, hungry and thirsty, often starving, cold, and naked. [28]Besides everything else, I have a daily burden — I'm anxiously concerned about all the churches. [29]When anyone is weak, am I not weak, too? When anyone is led into sin, don't I burn with pain and grief? [30]If I have to boast, I'll boast of the things that show how weak I am. [31]The God and Father of the Lord Jesus, Who is blessed forever, knows I'm not lying. [32]In Damascus the governor under King Aretas had the city of Damascus watched to catch me, [33]but through an opening in the wall I was let down in a basket, and I escaped.

Caught Up to Paradise

12 I have to boast. It doesn't do any good, but I'll go on with what the Lord has shown and told me. [2]I know a man in Christ; fourteen years ago — whether in his body or outside it, I don't know, God knows — that man was caught up to the third heaven. [3]I know that such a man — whether in his body or outside it, I don't know, God knows — [4]was caught up to Paradise and heard what no human being can express or is allowed to talk about. [5]About such a man I will boast, but as to myself, I will boast only of my weaknesses.

[6]But if I would want to boast, I wouldn't be a fool, because I'd be telling the truth. But I'm not going to do it, in order to keep anyone from thinking more of me than he judges me to be by seeing me or hearing me. [7]To keep me from feeling proud because such wonderful things were revealed to me, a thorn was put into my flesh, Satan's messenger to plague me and keep me from feeling proud. [8]Three times I begged the Lord to have it leave me alone, [9]but He told me, "My grace is enough for you. When you are weak, My power is doing its best work." So I will delight all the more to boast of my weaknesses in order to have Christ's power rest on me. [10]That's why I'm glad to be weak and mistreated, to suffer hardships, to be persecuted and hard pressed for Christ. You see, when I'm weak, then I'm strong.

I Will Be No Burden

[11]I've become a fool. You forced me to it. Really, you should have spoken well of me. Even if I'm nothing, I wasn't in any way inferior to your "super" apostles. [12]The signs that prove I'm an apostle were very patiently done among you — miracles, wonders, and works of power.

[13]How were you treated worse than the other churches except that I didn't burden you? Forgive me this wrong! [14]Here I'm ready to come to you a third time, and I'm not going to be a burden, because I don't want your things but you. Children shouldn't save up for their parents but parents for their children. [15]And I'll be very glad to spend what I have and myself, too, to help you. Do you love me less because I love you so much?

[16]But granting I was no burden to you, was I a clever fellow who trapped you with some trick? [17]Did I take advantage of you through any of the men I sent you? [18]I urged Titus to go to you, and I sent the fellow Christian with him. Titus didn't take advantage of you, did he? Didn't both of us act in the same spirit and do things in the same way?

[19]Have you been thinking all along we're only defending ourselves before you? We are speaking before God in Christ, and everything, dear friends, is meant to help you.

Will There Be Trouble?

[20]I'm afraid I may come and find you different from what I want you to be, and you may find me different from what you want me to be. And there may be quarreling, jealousy, angry feelings, selfishness, slander, gossip, proud and disorderly behavior. [21]When I come, my God may again humble me before you, and I may have to weep over many who formerly lived in sin and haven't repented for the unclean, sexual, and lustful things they did.

13 This will be the third time I'm coming to you.
Everything must be proved by two or three witnesses. [2]When I was with you the second time as well as now when I'm not with you, I warned and I still warn you who formerly lived in sin and all you others: When I come again, I won't spare you— [3]seeing that you want proof that Christ is speaking through me. He's not weak in dealing with you but is powerful in you. [4]He died on a cross in weakness, but He lives by God's power. We too are weak in Him, but with Him we'll live by God's power as it comes to you.

[5]Examine yourselves to see if you really believe. Test yourselves. Don't you know Jesus Christ is in you — unless you fail in your test? [6]I hope you'll see we haven't failed in our test. [7]We pray God you will do no wrong — not to show we haven't failed, but we want you to do what is right even if we may seem to have failed. [8]We can't do anything against the truth but only work for it. [9]We are glad when we're weak and you're strong. And what we're praying for is this, that God may make you complete.

---

1 Deut 17:6; 19:15

[10]Here's the reason I'm writing this while I'm not with you: When I come, I don't want to be sharp in using the authority the Lord gave me to build you up and not to tear you down.

Farewell

[11]Finally, fellow Christians, farewell! Strive for perfection. Take encouragement from me. Agree with one another, live in peace, and the God of love and peace will be with you. [12]Greet one another with a holy kiss. [13]All the holy people greet you. [14]The grace of the Lord Jesus Christ, the love of God, and the fellowship of the Holy Spirit be with you all!

PAUL
WRITES TO THE
GALATIANS

1 PAUL, AN APOSTLE not sent from men or by any man but by Jesus Christ and by God the Father, Who raised Him from the dead, ²and all the Christians who are with me, to the churches in Galatia — ³grace and peace to you from God the Father and our Lord Jesus Christ, ⁴Who gave Himself for our sins to save us from this present wicked world according to the will of our God and Father. ⁵To Him be glory forever! Amen.

You Are Turning Away

⁶I am surprised you are so quickly leaving Him Who called you by the grace of Christ and are turning to a different kind of good news, ⁷which really is not good news at all. But there are some men who are troubling you and want to change the good news of Christ. ⁸But even if we or an angel from heaven would bring you any other good news than what we brought you, a curse be on him! ⁹I say again what we said before: If anyone brings you any other good news than the one you received, a curse be on him!

¹⁰Do I say this now to get the approval of men — or of God? Or am I trying to please men? If I were still trying to please men, I wouldn't be a servant of Christ.

Jesus Gave Me the Good News

¹¹I tell you, my fellow Christians, the good news I told is not a human idea, ¹²because no man gave it or taught it to me, but Jesus Christ revealed it to me.

¹³You have heard what I used to do when I still lived according to the Jewish religion, how violently I persecuted God's church and tried to destroy it ¹⁴and how in this Jewish religion I was ahead of many of my own age among my people, so extremely zealous was I for the traditions of my ancestors.

¹⁵But God *had appointed me before I was born*, and in His grace He called me. ¹⁶And when He kindly decided to show me His Son so that I would tell the good news of Him among the Gentiles, I didn't talk it over with other men ¹⁷or go up to Jerusalem to see those who were apostles before me, but I went immediately to Arabiaª and then came back to Damascus.

15 *Is 49:1; Jer 1:5*

a - 17   This part of Arabia may be near Damascus.

¹⁸After three years I went up to Jerusalem to get to know Peter, and I stayed with him fifteen days. ¹⁹But I didn't see any of the other apostles, only James, the Lord's brother. ²⁰(And I declare before God I'm writing you no lie.) ²¹Then I went to the regions of Syria and Cilicia. ²²In Judea the churches of Christ didn't know me personally. ²³They only heard people say: "The man who used to persecute us is now preaching the faith he once tried to destroy," ²⁴and they praised God for what they saw in me.

Fellowship with the Apostles

2 Fourteen years later I went up to Jerusalem again, this time with Barnabas, and I also took Titus with me. ²(God had told me to go.) Then I laid before the Christians, and privately before the leaders, the good news I preach among the non-Jewish people. I didn't in any way want to run or to have run in vain.

³Titus was with me, and he's a Greek. But no one forced him to be circumcised ⁴to please the false Christians who had come in secretly. They sneaked in to spy out the liberty we have in Christ Jesus and to make us slaves. ⁵Not for a moment did we let them dictate to us, so that you might always have the true good news.

⁶I don't care what those leaders once were – *God doesn't prefer one to another*. Those leaders didn't teach me anything new. ⁷On the contrary, they saw that I had been entrusted with bringing the good news to the non-Jews as Peter was to bring it to the Jews. ⁸He Who had worked in Peter to make him an apostle to the Jews had worked in me to make me an apostle to the non-Jews. ⁹When James, Peter, and John, who were considered pillars, saw what God's grace had given me, they gave Barnabas and me the right hand of fellowship with the understanding that we work among the non-Jews and they among the Jews. ¹⁰All they asked was that we remember the poor, and that I was eager to do.

I Criticized Peter

¹¹But when Peter came to Antioch, I opposed him to his face because he had shown how wrong he was. ¹²He had been eating with the non-Jews before certain men came from James. But when they came, he held back and kept away from non-Jews because he was afraid of those who believed in circumcision. ¹³And the other Jews acted just as insincerely as he did, so that even Barnabas was carried away to be a hypocrite with them.

¹⁴But when I saw they were not doing right according to the truth of the good news, I told Peter before everyone: "If you, a Jew, don't live like a Jew but like a non-Jew, how can you insist the non-Jews must live like Jews?

¹⁵"We were born Jews and not Gentile sinners; ¹⁶yet we know that a person cannot be declared righteousᵇ by doing what the Law says but only

---

6 Deut 10:17   *16 Ps 143:2*

b - 16   See note at Rom. 3:20.

through believing in Jesus Christ. So we also believed in Jesus Christ in order to be justified by faith in Christ and not by the works of the Law *because not one person will be declared righteous* by the works of the Law.

[17]"Now if we who want to be declared righteous in Christ are found to be sinners like the non-Jews, does Christ encourage us to sin? Never! [18]But if I build up again what I've torn down, I make myself a sinner. [19]By the Law I died to the Law, to live for God.[c] [20]I was crucified with Christ, and I don't live anymore, but Christ lives in me. The life I now live in my body I live by believing in the Son of God, Who loved me and gave Himself for me. [21]I don't reject God's grace. You see, if we could get righteousness through the Law, then Christ died for nothing."

The Believer Is Blessed

3 You foolish Galatians! Who has bewitched you – you who saw Jesus Christ publicly pictured as crucified? [2]I want you to tell me just one thing: Did you get the Spirit by doing what the Law says or by the truth you heard and believed? [3]Are you so foolish? You started with the Spirit; are you now going to finish with the flesh? [4]Did you experience so much for nothing? Perhaps it really was for nothing! [5]Does God give you the Spirit and make such powers active in you by your doing what the Law says or by the truth you hear and believe?

[6]It was the same way with *Abraham*. He *believed God, and so he was counted righteous*. [7]You see, then, that those who believe are Abraham's real descendants. [8]The Bible foresaw that God would declare the nations righteous by faith, and long ago He told Abraham the good news: *"Through you all nations will be blessed."* [9]So those who believe are blessed with Abraham, who believed.

[10]There is a curse on all who depend on doing what the Law says, because it is written: *"Cursed is everyone who doesn't follow and do everything written in the book of the Law."* [11]It is clear that no one is declared righteous before God by the Law, because *the righteous will live by faith*. [12]But the Law is not based on faith; on the contrary, it says: *"If you do these things, you will find life in them."* [13]Christ paid the price to free us from the curse of the Law when He was cursed for us (it is written: *"Cursed is everyone who hangs on a tree"*) [14]so that in Jesus Christ Abraham's blessing would come to the nations and we would receive the promised Spirit through faith.

---

6 Gen 15:6   **8** Gen 12:3; 18:18; 22:18; 26:4; 28:14   **10** Deut 27:26
11 Hab 2:4   **12** Lev 18:5   **13** Deut 21:22-23

c - 19   The meaning of vv. 17-19 is this: When we don't try to be righteous by doing what the Law demands, we "tear down" the Law, and the Jews may think we are just non-Jewish sinners. If, to please the Jews, we try again to do what the Law demands and so "build it up," the Law only condemns us as sinners. The Law condemned Jesus for our sins and killed Him, and us with Him. Now the Law can't demand any more from us than from a dead person.

The Promise Was First

[15]My fellow Christians, let me use an example from daily life. Once a will is ratified, even it it's only a man's will, no one sets it aside or adds to it. [16]Now the *promises* were *made to Abraham* and to his Descendant. He doesn't say: "and to the descendants," in the plural, but in the singular: "and *to your Descendant*, Who is Christ. [17]Now, I say this: First God confirmed His covenant; and the Law, which came 430 years later, doesn't set aside and cancel its promise. [18]If we get the inheritance by the Law, we don't get it by a promise; but God gave it to Abraham by a promise.

Our Guardian

[19]Why, then, was the Law given? It was added to arouse transgressions[d] until the Descendant would come to Whom the promise was made. And it was given through angels in the hands of a mediator. [20]A mediator deals with more than one, but God is one.[e] [21]Is the Law, then, opposed to God's promise? Never! If a law had been given that could make us alive, it certainly would have given us righteousness. [22]But the Scripture has said that everything is a prisoner of sin, so that the promised blessings might be given to believers through faith in Jesus Christ. [23]Before faith came, we were under the Law, guarded in prison for the faith that was to be revealed. [24]Then the Law has been our guardian so that we would come to Christ and be justified by faith. [25]But now that faith has come, we are no longer under a guardian. [26]You are all God's children through faith in Christ Jesus, [27]because all of you who were baptized into Christ have put on Christ. [28]There is no Jew or Greek, no slave or free person, no man or woman – you're all one in Christ Jesus. [29]If you belong to Christ, then you are Abraham's descendants and heirs of the blessing God promised.

God's Sons

4 Now, I say that as long as their heir is a child, he is no better than a slave, although he owns everything. [2]He is under guardians and managers until the day set by his father. [3]So it is with us. When we were children, we were slaves under the elementary ways of the world. [4]But when the right time came, God sent His Son, born of a woman, born under the Law, [5]to free those under the Law and make us His sons. [6]And because you are sons, God sent into our hearts the Spirit of His Son, Who cries, "Abba! Father!" [7]So you are no longer a slave but a son. And if you are His son, God has made you His heir.

16 Gen 12:3; 18:18; 22:18; 26:4; 28:14

d - 19   The Law was like a stick with which a trainer stirs up a sleeping wild animal to show how terrible it is.
e - 20   God gave the Law to Moses, who brought it to the people, but God gave His promise directly to Abraham.

[8]But when you didn't know God, you were slaves to gods who really don't exist. [9]Now that you know God – or rather, God knows you – how can you turn back to those elementary ways, so weak and beggarly, and want to be slaves to them again? [10]You keep days, months, seasons, and years! [11]I'm afraid the work I did on you may have been wasted.

You Welcomed Me

[12]I beg you, my fellow Christians, become like me, since I became like you. You did me no wrong. [13]You know I brought you the good news the first time because I was sick.[f] [14]Though my sick body was a test to you, you didn't despise or scorn me, but you welcomed me as if I were an angel of God or Christ Jesus Himself. [15]You thought you were happy – what has become of that? I tell you, if possible, you would have torn out your eyes and given them to me. [16]Can it be I have become your enemy by telling you the truth?

[17]These men are zealous for you, but not in your interest. They want to cut you off from me so that you will be zealous for them. [18]It is good to be zealous in a good cause always, and not only when I am present with you.

[19]My children, I am suffering birth pains for you again until Christ is formed in you. [20]I wish I were with you right now and could change my way of speaking to you, because I am puzzled about you.

We Are like Isaac

[21]Tell me, you who want to be under the Law, will you not listen to what the Law says? [22]It is written that Abraham had two sons; one was the son of the slave and the other the son of the free woman. [23]Now, the son of the slave was born like other children, but the son of the free woman by being promised.

[24]This has figurative meaning. The women are two covenants. The children of the covenant given on Mount Sinai are born to be slaves; this is Hagar. [25]"Hagar" in Arabia means Mount Sinai. She is like Jerusalem today, because she and her children are slaves. [26]But the Jerusalem that is above is free; and she is our mother.

[27]It is written:

> Be glad, barren woman, you who don't have any children;
> break into shouting, you who have no pains of childbirth,
> because the deserted woman has many more children
> than the one who has the husband.

[28]Now you, my fellow Christians, like Isaac, are children born by a promise.

[29]At that time the son born like other children persecuted the son born

---

f - 13   It may have been malaria that forced Paul to leave the swampy country of Pamphylia and go up into the mountains, 3,600 feet above sea level, and so come to the Galatians. (Acts 13:13-14)

by the Spirit. And so it is now. ³⁰But what does the Bible say? *"Put away the slave and her son, because the son of the slave must not get any of the inheritance of the son* of the free woman." ³¹Now, then, fellow Christians, we are not children of a slave but of a free woman.

Christ Freed Us

5 Christ has freed us so that we'll be free. Stand firm, then, and don't get caught again under a yoke of slavery.

²I, Paul, tell you, if you have yourself circumcised, Christ will do you no good. ³And again I warn everyone who has himself circumcised he must do everything the Law says. ⁴You who try to be declared righteous by the Law have cut yourselves off from Christ and have fallen from grace. ⁵But we who believe by the Spirit eagerly wait for the hope of the righteous. ⁶In Christ Jesus no circumcision or the lack of it counts for anything, but only faith that is active in love.

⁷You were running well. Who has kept you from obeying the truth? ⁸You were not persuaded by Him Who called you. ⁹A little yeast ferments the whole dough. ¹⁰I'm convinced in the Lord that you'll think as I do, but anyone who troubles you will have to take his punishment, whoever he may be. ¹¹My fellow Christians, if I'm "still preaching that people have to be circumcised," why am I still persecuted? If I were preaching that, the Jews would have no reason to oppose the cross. ¹²I could wish the men who upset you would castrate themselves.

¹³You were called to be free, my fellow Christians. Only don't use your freedom as a chance to sin as you like, but in love serve one another. ¹⁴You keep the whole Law when you do one thing: *"love your neighbor as yourself."* ¹⁵But if you continue to bite and devour one another, be careful, or you'll be destroyed by one another.

¹⁶I say, follow the Spirit, and you will not do what the flesh wants. ¹⁷What the flesh wants is against the Spirit, and what the Spirit wants is against the flesh, because they are opposed to each other and so keep you from doing what you want to do. ¹⁸But if the Spirit leads you, you are not under the Law.

¹⁹Now, you know the works of the flesh. They are: sexual sin, uncleanness, wild living, ²⁰worshiping of idols, witchcraft, hate, wrangling, jealousy, anger, selfishness, quarreling, divisions, ²¹envy, drunkenness, carousing, and the like. I warn you, as I did before, those who do such things will have no share in God's kingdom.

²²But the Spirit produces love, joy, peace. He makes us patient, kindly, good, faithful, ²³gentle, and gives us self-control. There's no law against such things. ²⁴But if we belong to Christ Jesus, we have crucified the flesh with its passions and desires. ²⁵If we live by the Spirit, let us also follow the Spirit. ²⁶Let us not become conceited, challenge one another and become jealous of one another.

---

27 Is 54:1   30 Gen 21:10   14 Lev 19:18

When Anyone Sins

6 My fellow Christians, if you find anyone doing wrong, you who are spiritual should set him right. But be gentle and keep an eye on yourself; you may be tempted, too. ²Help one another carry these burdens, and so do everything the Law of Christ demands.

³If anyone thinks he's something when he's nothing, he's fooling himself. ⁴Everyone should examine his own work. Then he will have something in himself that deserves praise, without comparing himself with anyone else. ⁵Everyone will have to carry his own burden.

We Reap What We Sow

⁶If someone teaches you the Word, share all your good things with your teacher. ⁷Don't make a mistake; you can't fool God. Whatever you sow, you'll reap. ⁸If you sow to please your own flesh, you will from your flesh reap destruction. If you sow to please the Spirit, you will from the Spirit reap everlasting life. ⁹Let us not get tired of doing good. At the right time we'll reap if we don't give up. ¹⁰So whenever we have a chance, let us do good to everyone but especially to the household of believers.

The World Is Crucified to Me

¹¹See what big letters I make when I write to you with my own hand. ¹²These men who want to be popular in a worldly way are insisting that you have yourselves circumcised only to keep themselves from being persecuted for the cross of Christ. ¹³Why, these who are circumcised don't keep the Law themselves, but they want you to have yourselves circumcised so that they can boast of that physical fact about you. ¹⁴May I never boast of anything but the cross of our Lord Jesus Christ, by Whom the world is crucified to me and I to the world. ¹⁵No circumcision or the lack of it is anything, but only the new life that is created. ¹⁶*Peace* and mercy on all who follow this rule, that is, *on* God's *Israel*.

¹⁷From now on no one should make trouble for me, because I have on my body the scars of Jesus.

¹⁸The grace of our Lord Jesus Christ be with your spirit, my fellow Christians. Amen.

---

16 Ps 125:5; 128:6

PAUL
WRITES TO THE
EPHESIANS

1 PAUL, APOSTLE OF CHRIST JESUS by God's will, to the people who are holy and faithful in Christ Jesus: [2]May God our Father and the Lord Jesus Christ give you grace and peace.

What God Has Done

[3]Let us praise the God and Father of our Lord Jesus Christ, Who in Christ has blessed us with every spiritual blessing in heaven.

[4]He has done what in His kindness He planned to do: Before He made the world, He Who loved us [5]appointed us to be made His sons by Jesus Christ. In Him He chose us to be holy and blameless before Him [6]in order to praise the glory of the love He gave us in His dear Son, [7]Who bought us with His blood to forgive our sins and set us free. So [8]He poured out the riches of His grace on us, giving us every kind of wisdom and understanding [9]as He told us the hidden meaning of His will.

It was His kindly purpose in Christ [10]to manage everything in heaven and on earth in such a way that when the right time would come it would all be organized under Christ as its Head.

[11]He Who accomplishes everything just as He wants to plan it, long ago appointed us in Christ and chose us according to His purpose [12]that we, the first to hope in Christ, should live to praise His glory. [13]When you heard the message of the truth, the good news that you were saved, and you believed in Him, you, too, were sealed in Him by the Holy Spirit — Whom He promised [14]and Who is now the Guarantee of our inheritance — that He might free you to be His people and to praise His glory.

I'm Praying for You

[15]That is why, since I heard how you believe in the Lord Jesus and love all the holy people, [16]I never stop thanking God for you as I remember you in my prayers. [17]I ask the God of our Lord Jesus Christ, the Father of glory, to give you His Spirit to make you wise and reveal the truth to you as you learn to know Him better [18]and to enlighten the eyes of your minds so that you know the hope He called you to, the riches of the glory of the *inheritance* He gives to *His holy people*, [19]and the vast resource of His power working in us who believe. It is the same mighty power [20]with which He worked in Christ, raised Him from the dead, and *made Him sit at His right* in heaven,

---

18 Deut 33:3-4   20 Ps 110:1

[21]above all rulers, authorities, powers, lords, and any name that can be mentioned, not only in this world but also in the next. [22]And *He put everything under His feet*, and gave Him as the Head of everything to the church, [23]which is His body, having all that is in Him who fills everything in every way.

God's Love Saved You

2 You, too, were dead in your transgressions and sins, [2]in which you once followed the ways of this present world and the ruler whose power is in the air, the spirit who is now working in the people who disobey. [3]Among them all of us once lived in our fleshly lusts, doing what our flesh and mind wanted to do, and by nature we, like the others, were people with whom God was angry.

[4]But God, Who is rich in mercy, loved us with such a great love. [5]He made us who were dead in sins alive with Christ. (You have been saved by grace.) [6]And since we are in Christ Jesus, He raised us with Him and had us sit with Him in heaven [7]to show in the coming ages the immeasurable riches of His grace by being kind to us in Christ Jesus. [8]Yes, by His grace you are saved through faith. It was not your own doing; it is God's gift. [9]It is not the result of anything you have done; and so no one may boast. [10]He has made us what we are, creating us in Christ Jesus to do good works, in which God long ago planned for us to live.

Jews and Non-Jews

[11]Remember, then, physically you once were Gentiles, and those who call themselves "circumcised" (which is physical and done by human hands) called you "uncircumcised." [12]You were then without Christ, excluded from being citizens of Israel and strangers to the covenants that had the promise. You had no hope and were without God in the world. [13]Once you were *far away*, but now in Christ Jesus the blood of Christ has brought you *near*. [14]He is our *Peace*: In His flesh He has made the Jew and the non-Jew one by breaking down the wall of hostility that kept them apart [15]and by putting away the Law with its rules and regulations, in order to make the Jew and the non-Jew in Himself one new man (so making peace) [16]and to make both in one body friends with God by His cross, on which He killed the hostility. [17]And He came with *the good news of peace to you who were far away and to those who were near*, [18]since by one Spirit he enables both of us to come to the Father.

[19]Then you are no longer foreigners or strangers but fellow citizens with the holy people and members of His household. [20]You are built on the *foundation* of the apostles and prophets, and Christ Jesus Himself is the *Cornerstone*. [21]In Him the whole building is fitted together and grows to be a holy temple in the Lord. [22]In Him you, too, are built up with the others to

---

22 Ps 8:6; 110:1   **13-14** Is 57:19   **17** Is 52:7; 57:19   **20** Is 28:16

be God's home in the Spirit.

God's Purpose in Me

3 For this reason I, Paul, whom Christ Jesus made a prisoner for you who are not Jews[a] – [2]surely you've heard how God gave me the responsibility of bringing His grace to you [3]and how He revealed to me the hidden truth, as I have briefly written. [4]When you read this, you can see I understand the hidden truth of Christ. [5]The people of other times weren't told about it as the Spirit now has revealed it to His holy apostles and prophets, [6]that in Christ Jesus the people who are not Jews have the same inheritance, belong to the same body, and have the same promise through the good news.

[7]I was made a servant of it by the gift of grace God gave me by the working of His power. [8]To me, the least of all His holy people, He gave this grace: to bring the news of the unsearchable riches of Christ to the non-Jews [9]and let everyone see clearly what God planned to do according to the truth hidden from the beginning in God, Who created everything, [10]so that through the church God's many-sided wisdom would now be shown to the rulers and authorities in heaven. [11]He planned it through the ages and then did it in Christ Jesus, our Lord. [12]In Him, by believing in Him, we have confidence and can boldly come to God. [13]So I ask you not to get discouraged by what I suffer for you. It brings you honor.

How Christ Loves Me

[14]For this reason I kneel before the "Father," [15]from Whom every group in heaven and on earth gets the name of "family,"[b] [16]and ask Him, as He is rich in glory, to give you this: that His Spirit will inwardly strengthen you with power, [17]Christ will live in your hearts by faith, and you will be firmly rooted and built up in love, [18]so that you and all the holy people can grasp how broad and long and high and deep His love is, [19]and know how Christ loves us – more than we can know – and so you will be filled with all that is in God.

[20]Now to Him Who by the power working in us can do far, far more than anything we ask or imagine, [21]to Him be glory in the church and in Christ Jesus to all ages forever. Amen.

We Are One

4 So I, a prisoner in the Lord, urge you to live as people whom God has called should live. [2]Be humble and gentle in every way, be patient, and lovingly bear with one another. [3]Do your best to keep the oneness of the

---

a - 1   Here Paul breaks off and doesn't take up the thought again until v. 14.

b - 15   "Family" (= clan) in Greek is the same word as "Father" with a special ending.

Spirit by living together in peace: [4]one body and one Spirit – even as you have been called to share one hope – [5]one Lord, one faith, one baptism, [6]one God and Father of all, Who rules over us all, works through us all, and lives in us all.

[7]But each of us has been given the gift measured out by Christ Who gave it. [8]So it says: "He *went up on high, took prisoners*, and gave *gifts to people*". [9]Now what can "He went up" mean but that He had gone down to the lower parts of the earth? [10]He Who went down also "went up" above all the heavens to fill everything. [11]And He gave us some men to be apostles, some to speak the Word, some to tell the good news, some to be pastors and teachers. [12]His purpose was to equip His holy people for service as workers to build up the body of Christ [13]until all of us get to be one as we believe and know God's Son, reach a mature manhood, and grow to the full height of Christ. [14]We shouldn't be babies any longer, tossed and driven by every windy thing that is taught, by the trickery of men and their clever scheming in error. [15]Let us tell the truth with love and in every way grow up into Him Who is the Head – Christ. [16]He makes the whole body fit together, unites it by every contact with its support, and to the extent that each and every part is doing its job, He makes the body grow and builds it up in love.

A New Life

[17]So I tell you and call on you in the Lord not to live any more like the people of the world. Their minds are set on worthless things. [18]Their understanding is darkened. Their ignorance and their closed minds have made them strangers to the life God gives. [19]Having lost their sense of right and wrong, they've given themselves up to a life of lust to practice every kind of vice with greed.

[20]But that is not what you learned when you got to know Christ, [21]if you have heard Him and in Him have been taught the truth as it is in Jesus. [22]Strip off your old self, which follows your former ways of living and ruins you as it follows the desires that deceive you. [23]Become new in the spirit of your minds, [24]and put on the new self, which is created to be like God, righteous and holy in the truth.

[25]So don't lie any more, but *tell one another the truth*, because we are members of one another. [26]*Be angry but don't sin.* Don't let the sun go down on your anger. [27]Don't give the devil a chance to work.

[28]Anyone who has been stealing should not steal any more, but instead work hard, doing something good with his own hands so that he has something to share with anyone in need. [29]Don't say anything harmful but only what is good, so that you help where there's a need and benefit those who hear it.

[30]And don't grieve God's Holy Spirit, by Whom you were sealed for the day when you will be set free.

[31]Get rid of all bitter feelings, temper, anger, yelling, slander, and

---

8 Ps 68:18   25 Zech 8:16   26 Ps 4:4

every way of hurting one another. ³²Be kind to one another and tender-hearted, and forgive one another as God in Christ has forgiven you.

You Are a light

5 As God's dear children try to be like Him ²and live in love as *Christ* loved us and *gave Himself* for us as a *fragrant offering and sacrifice* to God.

³Sexual sins, anything unclean, or greed shouldn't even be mentioned among you. This is the right attitude for holy people. ⁴No shameful things, foolish talk, or coarse jokes! These aren't proper. Instead give thanks. ⁵Be sure of this, that no one who is immoral, unclean, or greedy (a greedy person worships an idol) has any share in the kingdom of Christ, Who is God. ⁶Don't let anyone fool you with meaningless words. These things bring God's anger and punishment on those who don't obey the truth. ⁷So don't share their ways.

⁸Once you were darkness, but now you are light in the Lord. Live as children of light, ⁹since light produces everything good and righteous and true. ¹⁰And test things to see if they please the Lord. ¹¹Don't have anything to do with the works of darkness, from which no good can come. Instead show that they are wrong. ¹²We're ashamed even to mention what such people do secretly. ¹³When you show that anything is wrong, it is seen in the light; anything you can see is as clear as light. ¹⁴So it says: "Wake up, sleeper! Rise from the dead, and Christ will shine on you."

¹⁵Be very careful, then, as to how you live. Don't be unwise but wise. ¹⁶And make the most of your opportunities because these are evil days. ¹⁷So don't be foolish, but understand what the Lord wants. ¹⁸*Don't get drunk on wine*, which means wild living. But be filled with the Spirit ¹⁹as you speak psalms, hymns, and songs to one another and with your hearts sing and make music to the Lord, ²⁰always thanking God the Father for everything in the name of our Lord Jesus Christ.

Husband and Wife

²¹As you respect Christ, submit to one another. ²²You married women, obey your husbands as you obey the Lord, ²³because a husband is the head of his wife as Christ is the Head of the church, which is His body that He saves. ²⁴Yes, as the church obeys Christ, so wives should obey their husbands in everything.

²⁵You husbands, love your wives, as *Christ* loved the church and *gave Himself* for it ²⁶to make it holy by washing it clean with water by the Word, ²⁷to have the church stand before Him as something wonderful, without a spot or a wrinkle or anything like that; yes, it should be holy and without a fault. ²⁸This is how husbands should love their wives, like their own bodies. A man who loves his wife is loving himself. ²⁹No one ever hated his own body. Everyone feeds it and treats it tenderly, as Christ does the church

2 Is 53:12; Ex 29:18,25; Ezek 20:41; Ps 40:6   *18 Prov 23:31*
25 Is 53:12

[30]because we are parts of His body. [31]*This is why a man will leave his father and mother and live with his wife, and the two will be one flesh.* [32]There's a great truth hidden here — I mean that of Christ and the church. [33]But every one of you, too, love your wife as you love yourself. And a wife should respect her husband.

Children and Parents

6 Children, obey your parents in the Lord, because it is right.

[2]*Honor your father and mother* — this is an important commandment with a promise: [3]*it will be well with you, and you will live long on the earth.*

[4]And you fathers, don't make your children angry, but raise them in the *training* and instruction *of the Lord.*

Servants and Masters

[5]You servants, obey those who are your masters in this world, with respect and trembling and as sincerely as you obey Christ, [6]working not only while you are being watched, as if you merely wanted to please men, but as servants of Christ who are glad to do what God wants them to do. [7]Serve eagerly as you would serve the Lord and not merely men. [8]You know that if you do a good thing, the Lord will pay you back whether you are a slave or a free man.

[9]You masters, treat your slaves in the same way, and stop threatening them. You know that they and you have one Master in heaven, and *He doesn't prefer one to another.*

Put on the Whole Armor

[10]Finally, let the Lord and His mighty power make you strong. [11]Put on God's whole armor, and you will be able to stand against the devil's tricky ways. [12]You're not fighting against flesh and blood but against the rulers, authorities, and lords of this dark world, against the evil spirits that are above. [13]This is why you should take God's whole armor; then you can resist when things are at their worst and having done everything, you can hold your ground. [14]Stand, then, *with truth as a belt fastened around* your *waist, with righteousness covering you as a breastplate,* [15]and with shoes on your *feet,* ready to *bring the good news of peace.* [16]Besides all these, take faith as the shield with which you can put out all the flaming arrows of the evil one. [17]And take *salvation as your helmet,* and the Spirit's *sword,* which is God's Word.

[18]Pray at all times in the Spirit, using every kind of prayer. Be alert and keep at it continually as you pray for all the holy people. [19]Pray for me, too, that when I start to talk I'll be told what to say and will boldly tell the

31 Gen 2:24   *2-3* Ex 20:12; Deut 5:16   *4* Prov 3:11   *9* Deut 10:17
14 Is 11:5; 59:17   *15* Is 52:7; Nah 1:15   *17* Is 49:2; 59:17

hidden truth of the good news [20](for which I'm an ambassador in chains) just as boldly as I must tell it.

Farewell

[21]You should know what is happening to me and how I'm getting along. And so Tychicus, our dear fellow Christian and loyal helper in the Lord, will tell you everything. [22]I'm sending him to you to let you know about us and to encourage you.

[23]May God the Father and the Lord Jesus Christ give our fellow Christians peace and love with faith! [24]His grace be with all who have an undying love for our Lord Jesus Christ.

PAUL
WRITES TO THE
PHILIPPIANS

1 PAUL AND TIMOTHY, servants of Christ Jesus, to all the holy people in Christ Jesus in Philippi, especially to the spiritual overseers and deacons: [2]May God our Father and the Lord Jesus Christ give you grace and peace.

You Are in My Heart

[3]Every time I think of you, I thank my God. [4]Every time I pray for all of you, I always do it with joy [5]because of your partnership in telling the good news from the first day until now. [6]I'm sure that He Who started a good work in you will go on to finish it until the day of Christ Jesus. [7]And it is right for me to feel like this about all of you. Whether I'm in my chains or defending and confirming the good news, you're all in my heart as those who receive God's grace along with me. [8]God knows how I long for all of you with the tenderness of Christ Jesus.

[9]And I pray your love will still grow more and more in knowledge and in every kind of understanding. [10]Then you will approve the better things in order to be pure and without blame until the day of Christ, [11]as Jesus Christ has filled your life with righteous works by which you glorify and praise God.

If Only Christ Is Preached

[12]I want you to know, my fellow Christians, that what happened to me actually helped spread the good news [13]so that the whole palace guard and all the others have found out I'm in chains for Christ. [14]And so my chains have given most of our friends the confidence in the Lord to speak God's Word more boldly and fearlessly than ever.

[15]Some men are moved by jealousy and rivalry to preach Christ, but others by good will. [16]Those who love to preach Him know I'm appointed to defend the good news. [17]But the others preach Christ selfishly, without a pure motive, and mean to stir up trouble for me even while I am in chains. [18]But what does it mean? Only this, that in one way or another, whether their motive is false or real, they preach Christ — and I'm glad of that.

Live or Die?

Yes, and I'm also going to be happy [19]because I know that your prayer and the help of the Spirit of Jesus Christ will make *this turn out victoriously for me* [20]as I eagerly hope there will be nothing for me to be ashamed of. But by speaking very boldly I will now as always glorify Christ in my body by living or by dying [21]since for me to live is Christ, and to die is gain. [22]If I live here in my body, I'll enjoy the results of my work. And which would I choose? I don't know. [23]I find it hard to choose between the two. I want to leave and be with Christ; that is much better. [24]But for your sake it is more necessary that I remain in the body. [25]And since I am convinced of this, I know I'll live and be with all of you to help you grow and be happy in your faith. [26]And so by coming to you again I want to give you all the more reason to glory in Christ Jesus.

Fighting for the Faith

[27]But live as citizens worthy of the good news of Christ so that, whether I come and see you or stay away, I will hear you are standing firm, one in spirit, and fighting side by side like one man for the faith in the good news. [28]Don't let your enemies frighten you in any way. This is how you prove to them that they will be destroyed and you will be saved, and this proof is from God. [29]It is given to you to be for Christ, not only to believe in Him but also to suffer for Him [30]as you have the same struggle you once saw me have and now hear that I have.

Live in Harmony

2 Now if you are encouraged in Christ, moved by comforting words of love, if you and we have the same Spirit, if you are tender and sympathetic, [2]make me very happy – be one in thought and in love, live in harmony, keep one purpose in mind. [3]Don't be selfish or proud, but humbly treat others as better than yourselves. [4]Each of you, don't be interested in your own things, rather in the things of others.

Be like Jesus

[5]Think just as Christ Jesus thought: [6]Although He was God, He did not consider His being equal with God as a prize to be displayed, [7]but *He emptied Himself*, made Himself a slave, became like other human beings, [8]and was seen to have the ways of a man. He became obedient and *humbled Himself* until He died, yes, died on a cross. [9]That is why *God* also exalted Him up on high and *gave Him* the name above every other name [10]that at the name of JESUS *everyone* in heaven and on earth and under the earth *should kneel*, [11]and *everyone should confess*, "JESUS CHRIST IS *LORD!*" and so *glorify God* the Father.

---

19 Job 13:16   *7-9 Is 53:12*   *10-11 Is 45:23-24*

Work Out Your Salvation

[12]My dear friends, you have always obeyed, not only when I was with you but even more now that I'm away. And so work out your salvation with fear and trembling [13]since it is God Who continues to work in you, both to desire as well as to do what is pleasing to Him.

[14]Do everything without complaining or arguing, [15]so that you will be blameless and innocent, *God's children with whom no one can find a fault* in the middle of *a crooked and perverted people*, among whom you shine like stars in the world [16]as you cling to the Word of Life. Then I can boast on the day of Christ that I didn't run in vain or *work in vain*. [17]But even if my life is poured out while I bring your faith as a sacrifice and service to God, I'm glad, and I'm happy with all of you. [18]You, too, be glad and be happy with me.

Timothy and Epaphroditus

[19]I hope in the Lord Jesus to send Timothy to you soon to get news about you that will cheer me up, too. [20]You see, I don't have anyone who will take such a genuine interest in your welfare as he will. [21]All look after their own interests, not after those of Jesus Christ. [22]But you know how he has stood the test, how like a son helping his father he worked hard with me to tell the good news. [23]So I expect to send him as soon as I see what's going to happen to me. [24]And I trust the Lord that I'll be coming soon, too.

[25]I feel I must send you Epaphroditus, my fellow Christian, fellow worker, and fellow soldier, whom you sent to help me in my needs, [26]since he has been longing to see all of you and is troubled because you heard he was sick. [27]He was sick and almost died, but God had pity on him and helped him; not only him but me, to keep me from having one sorrow after another. [28]So I'm especially eager to send him and give you the joy of seeing him again and to feel more relief myself. [29]So give him a very happy welcome in the Lord, and value men like him. [30]For the work of Christ he risked his life and almost died, to make up for the service you couldn't give me.

Only Christ

3 Now, then my fellow Christians, be happy in the Lord. It is no trouble to write the same things to you, and it is necessary for your safety. [2]Look out for those dogs, look out for those who do wrong, look out for the men who circumcise only their bodies. [3]We are really the circumcised people, we who worship by God's Spirit, are proud of Christ Jesus, and don't trust anything human, [4]though I, too, would have something human to trust. If anyone else thinks he has anything human to trust, I have more. [5]I was circumcised on the eighth day, a descendant of Israel of the tribe of Benjamin, a Hebrew son of Hebrew parents; in regard to the Law, a Pharisee, [6]so zealous that I persecuted the church, and according to the Law so right-

---

15 Deut 32:5   16 Is 49:4; 65:23

eous no one could find any fault with me.

⁷But any advantages I had I considered a loss for Christ. ⁸Yes, I think it is all a loss because it is so much better to know Christ Jesus, my Lord. For Him I have lost everything and consider it garbage in order to win Christ ⁹and to be found in Him, not having my own righteousness which comes from keeping the Law but having the righteousness which is through faith in Christ and which comes from God on the basis of faith. ¹⁰I want to know Him and the power of His resurrection, to share His sufferings and be like Him in His death ¹¹if somehow I may join those who rise from the dead.

¹²I don't mean I have already reached this or am already at the goal, but I eagerly go after it to make it mine because Christ Jesus made me His own. ¹³Fellow Christians, I don't think I have it in my hands. But one thing I do: I forget what is behind, reach for what is ahead, ¹⁴and with my eyes on the mark I go after the heavenly prize to which God has called us in Christ Jesus. ¹⁵Let us all who are mature think this way. But if you think differently about anything, God will reveal this to you, too. ¹⁶Only be guided by what we have learned so far.

Citizens of Heaven

¹⁷My fellow Christians, all together imitate me more and more, and watch those who live according to the example we're giving you. ¹⁸As I have often told you and now tell you with tears, many live as the enemies of the cross of Christ. ¹⁹In the end they will be destroyed. Their god is their belly, they glory in their shame, and their mind is on earthly things. ²⁰But we are citizens of heaven and look for the Lord Jesus Christ to come from heaven as the Savior, ²¹Who will change our humble bodies and make them like His glorified body by the power by which He can make everything serve Him.

4 And so, my fellow Christians, whom I love and long for, my joy and crown, stand firm in the Lord, dear friends.

Two Women

²I urge Euodia and Syntyche to agree in the Lord. ³And I beg you, my true fellow worker, help them. They fought side by side with me in telling the good news, and with Clement and the rest of my fellow workers, whose names are in *the book of life*.

Be Happy

⁴*Be happy in the Lord* always! I'll say it again: Be happy! ⁵Everyone should know how gentle you can be. The Lord is near. ⁶Don't worry about anything, but in everything go to God, and pray to let Him know what you want, and give thanks. ⁷Then God's peace, better than all our thinking, will

---

3 Ps 69:28   4 Zech 10:7

guard your hearts and minds in Christ Jesus.

⁸Finally, my fellow Christians, keep your minds on all that is true or noble, right or pure, lovely or respectable, on anything that is excellent or that deserves praise. ⁹Do what you have learned, received, and heard from me and what you saw me do. Then the God of peace will be with you.

Your Gift

¹⁰It made me very happy in the Lord that now again you showed a fresh interest in me. You were interested but didn't have a chance to show it. ¹¹I'm not saying I need anything. I've learned to be content whatever my condition. ¹²I know how to live with too little or too much. In every way of life I've learned the secret of eating heartily and of being hungry, of having too much and too little. ¹³I can do everything through Him Who gives me the strength.

¹⁴But it was kind of you to share my trouble. ¹⁵You people at Philippi know, too, that when I first told you the good news and then left Macedonia, you were the only church to share with me in terms of giving and receiving. ¹⁶Even while I was in Thessalonica, you more than once sent help for my needs. ¹⁷It isn't the gift I want but to see the profits growing and credited to you. ¹⁸You have paid me in full, and I have more than enough. I am fully supplied, now that I received from Epaphroditus what you sent. It is a *sweet aroma, a sacrifice* that God accepts and *is pleased with*. ¹⁹And my God will give you all you need according to His riches, in His glory, and in Christ Jesus. ²⁰To our God and Father be glory forever. Amen.

²¹Greet all the holy people in Christ Jesus. The Christians who are with me greet you. ²²All the holy people greet you, especially those of the emperor's household. ²³The grace of our Lord Jesus Christ be with your spirits. Amen.

---

18 Ex 29:18,25; Ezek 20:41

PAUL
WRITES TO THE
COLOSSIANS

1 PAUL, APOSTLE OF CHRIST JESUS by God's will, and our fellow Christian Timothy, [2]to the holy and faithful fellow believers in Christ at Colossae: May God our Father give you grace and peace.

We're Praying for You

[3]In our prayers for you we are always thanking God, the Father of our Lord Jesus Christ, [4]because we have heard how you believe in Christ Jesus and love all the holy people [5]and what you hope for is stored up for you in heaven. You heard of it before when you were told the truth of the good news [6]that has come to you. As it is producing fruit and growing all over the world, so it did among you since the day you heard it and came to know what the grace of God truly means, [7]as you learned it from Epaphras, our dear fellow servant, who is loyally serving Christ in our place. [8]And he's the one who told us about your love in the Spirit.

[9]That is why, since the day we heard of it, we haven't stopped praying for you and asking God to fill you with a clear knowledge of His will by giving you every kind of spiritual wisdom and understanding [10]so that you live worthy of the Lord, aiming to please Him in every way as you produce every kind of good work and grow in the knowledge of God. [11]We ask Him according to His wonderful might to strengthen you with all the power you need to endure patiently whatever comes as you joyfully [12]thank the Father, Who made you fit to share the inheritance of the holy people in the light.

God's Son Brought Peace

[13]He rescued us from the tyranny of darkness and transferred us into the kingdom of the Son He loves, [14]who paid the ransom to forgive our sins and set us free. [15]He is the Image of the invisible God, *the Firstborn over all creation*, [16]since in Him was created everything visable and invisable in heaven and on earth — thrones, lords, rulers, or powers — everything was created by Him and for Him. [17]*He was before everything*, and He holds everything together. [18]He is the Head of the Church, which is His body. He is the Beginning, the Firstborn from the dead to become alive that He may be first in everything. [19]God decided to have His whole Being live in Him [20]and by Him to reconcile to Himself [a] everything on earth and in heaven in

15,17 Prov 8:22-23

a - 20   God and the world, who are enemies, become friends in Christ.

a peace made by the blood on His cross.

Our Work Among You

²¹Once you were strangers to God and in your hearts His enemies, doing wicked things, ²²but now by dying in His human body He has made you friends in order to have you stand before Him without sin or fault or blame ²³if, of course, you continue in your faith to stand firm on the foundation and are not moved from the hope of the good news you heard. This has been preached to every creature under heaven, and I, Paul, was made its servant.

²⁴I delight to suffer for you now and in my body am enduring what still needs to be endured of Christ's sorrows for His body, which is the church. ²⁵God made me its servant when He gave me this work among you in order to do everything God meant to do by His Word. ²⁶This was a mystery hidden from the people of all the ages but now shown to His holy people, ²⁷whom God wanted to tell how rich among the non-Jews is the glory of this hidden truth: Christ, the Hope of glory, is in you.

²⁸Him we preach, warning everyone and teaching everyone, using every kind of wisdom, in order to present everyone perfect in Christ. ²⁹This is what I'm working for, struggling like an athlete by His power that is working mightily in me.

2 I want you to know how much I'm struggling for you and the people of Laodicea and all who haven't seen me face to face, ²to encourage you, as you're bound together by love, to be ever so richly convinced in your understanding and to know well God's hidden truth, that is Christ, ³in Whom are *hidden* all the *treasures of wisdom and knowledge.* ⁴I say this so that no one will mislead you by fine-sounding arguments. ⁵Although I'm away from you, I'm with you in spirit and delight to see how orderly and firm you are in your faith in Christ.

You Live in Christ

⁶Just as you received Christ Jesus as your Lord, so live in Him. ⁷In Him be rooted, built up, and strengthened in your faith, as you were taught, and overflow with thanksgiving.

⁸Be careful or someone will capture you by his philosophy, tricking you with meaningless words, as he follows the traditions of men and the principles of this world rather than Christ.

⁹In Him, that is, in His body, lives all the fullness of the Deity. ¹⁰And in Him, Who is the Head of all rulers and powers, you are complete. ¹¹In Him you also were circumcised, not by human hands but by putting away the sinful body by the circumcision of Christ ¹²since in baptism you were buried with Him and raised with Him through faith produced by the power

---

3 Prov 2:3-4

of God, Who raised Him from the dead.

¹³Yes, you who were dead in sins and in your uncircumcised bodies He has made alive with Him when He forgave us all our sins, ¹⁴wiped out the Law's demands that were against us and took them out of the way by nailing them to the cross. ¹⁵He stripped rulers and powers of their armor and made a public show of them as He triumphed over them in Christ.

Rules Made by Man

¹⁶Then no one should say you are wrong in what you eat or drink or do on a festival, on the first of the month, or on a Sabbath. ¹⁷These have been a shadow of the coming things, but the reality is in Christ.

¹⁸No one who likes to be humble and worship angels should condemn you. Such a person goes on searching his visions and without a reason is puffed up by his fleshly mind. ¹⁹He doesn't cling to the Head, Who by being in touch with the whole body nourishes it and by its ligaments binds it together to make it grow as God gives it growth.

²⁰With Christ you have died to the basic principles of this world. Then why, as though you were living with the world, do you let others dictate to you: ²¹"Don't take hold, don't taste, and don't touch?" ²²These are rules about all such things as are meant to be used up and pass away. You are doing *what men order and teach*; ²³this looks like wisdom, with its self-imposed worship, humble way, and harsh treatment of the body. But it lacks honor — it serves the full enjoyment of the flesh.

In Christ We Put Away Sin

3 Now if you were raised with Christ, be eager for the things that are above, where Christ is *sitting at the right of God*. ²Keep your mind on things above, not on earthly things. ³You see, you have died, and your life is hidden with Christ in God. ⁴When Christ, your Life, appears, then you, too, will appear with Him in glory. ⁵Kill, then, what is earthly in you: sexual sin, uncleanness, passion, evil lust, and greed, which is idol worship; ⁶these are bringing down God's anger. ⁷Once you also practiced them when you lived in them. ⁸But now also get rid of all such things as anger, rage, malice, slander, and dirty talk. ⁹Don't lie to one another, seeing that you have put away your old self and its ways ¹⁰and have put on the new self, which is continually renewed in knowledge *to be like Him Who created him*. ¹¹Here there is no Greek or Jew, circumcised or uncircumcised, barbarian, Scythian, slave or free, but Christ is everything and in everything.

Live as God's People

¹²Then, as holy people whom God has chosen and loved, be tenderhearted, kind, humble, gentle, patient; ¹³bear with one another and forgive one another if you have a complaint against anyone. Forgive as the Lord

---

22 Is 29:13   1 Ps 110:1   10 Gen 1:26-27

forgave you. [14]With all this have love, which binds it all together to make it perfect.

[15]Let the peace of Christ, to which you were called as one body, be in your hearts to decide things for you. And be thankful. [16]Let Christ's Word live richly in you as you teach and warn one another, using every kind of wisdom. With thankful hearts sing psalms, hymns, and spiritual songs to God. [17]And everything you say or do, do it in the name of the Lord Jesus, and by Him give thanks to God the Father.

Parents, Children, and Slaves

[18]You married women, submit to your husbands as it is right in the Lord. [19]You husbands, love your wives, and don't be harsh with them.

[20]You children, obey your parents in everything. This is pleasing to the Lord. [21]Parents, don't irritate your children, or they will get discouraged.

[22]You slaves, obey your earthly masters in everything. Don't serve them only when they are watching you, as if you meant only to please them, but sincerely because you respect the Lord. [23]Whatever you do, work heartily as for the Lord and not for men, [24]because you know the Lord will give you the inheritance as your reward. Serve the Lord Christ. [25]The man who does wrong will get paid for the wrong he has done, and there will be no exceptions.

4 You masters, be just and fair to your slaves because you know you, too, have a Master in heaven.

Winning the Others

[2]Keep on praying, watch as you pray, and give thanks. [3]At the same time also pray for us that God will open a door for the Word and let us tell the hidden truth of Christ, for which I am in chains, [4]that I may make it as well known as I should.

[5]Be wise in the way you live with those who are outside, and make the most of your opportunities.

[6]Always talk pleasantly, season your talk with salt so you will know how you should answer everyone.

Tychicus and Onesimus

[7]Tychicus, a dear fellow Christian, loyal helper and fellow servant in the Lord, will tell you all about me. [8]I'm sending him to you to bring you the news about us and encourage you. [9]Onesimus, our loyal and dear fellow Christian who is one of you, is with him. They will tell you about everything that is happening here.

Greetings

[10]Aristarchus, my fellow prisoner, sends greetings. So does Mark, the cousin of Barnabas. You received instructions about him. If he comes to you, welcome him. [11]Jesus, called Justus, also greets you. They are the only Jews working with me for God's kingdom. They've been a comfort to me. [12]Epaphras, one of your men, a servant of Christ Jesus, greets you. He is always wrestling in prayer for you that you will stand mature and convinced in everything God wants. [13]I assure you he works hard for you and the people in Laodicea and Hierapolis. [14]Luke, the doctor and dear friend, and Demas greet you. [15]Greet the fellow Christians in Laodicea, and Nympha and the church that meets at her home.

[16]When this letter has been read to you, have it read also in the church at Laodicea, and see that you also read the letter from Laodicea.

[17]Tell Archippus, "See that you do all the work you were given to do as the Lord's servant."

[18]I, Paul, am writing this greeting with my own hand. Remember I'm in chains. Grace be with you.

PAUL
WRITES THE FIRST LETTER TO THE
THESSALONIANS

1 PAUL, SILAS, AND TIMOTHY to the church of the Thessalonians which is in God the Father and the Lord Jesus Christ: May grace and peace be yours!

The Good News

²We always thank God for all of you and mention you in our prayers, ³never forgetting before our God and Father how your faith is working, your love is toiling, and your hope in our Lord Jesus Christ is enduring. ⁴We know, fellow Christians, whom God has loved, that He has chosen you, ⁵because the good news we told did not come to you with mere words, but with power, with the Holy Spirit, and with conviction— just as you know what kind of men we proved to be among you for your good. ⁶And you became imitators of us and of the Lord as you welcomed the Word, which brought you much suffering, with such joy in the Holy Spirit ⁷that you became a model for all the believers in Macedonia and Greece. ⁸Not only has the Lord's Word spread from you through Macedonia and Greece, but everywhere people have heard of your faith in God so that we don't need to say anything. ⁹They tell how we came to you and you turned from the idols to God, to serve the living and true God ¹⁰and to wait for His Son to come from heaven — Whom He raised from the dead — Jesus, Who saves us from the punishment that is coming.

2 You know, my fellow Christians, our coming to you wasn't a waste of time. ²We had suffered and been shamefully mistreated in Philippi, as you know. But our God gave us the courage to tell you God's good news though it meant a hard struggle.

³Our appeal isn't based on error or an unclean desire, and we aren't tricking you. ⁴No, we have God's approval to be entrusted with the good news. And so we tell it, not to please people but God, *Who tests* our *hearts.* ⁵We never flattered, as you know, or found excuses to make money, as God knows, ⁶nor did we try to get you or other people to praise us, although we can claim respect as apostles of Christ.

You Are Dear to Us

⁷But we were gentle when we were with you — and like a mother tenderly caring for her children. ⁸So we longed for you and were determined to share with you not only God's good news but our own lives, so dear had you become to us. ⁹You remember, my fellow Christians, how hard we worked and struggled. Night and day working for our living, not to burden any of you, we preached God's good news to you. ¹⁰You are witnesses and God, too, how holy, righteous, and blameless we proved to be to you who believe. ¹¹As you know, like a father urging his children we used to urge, encourage, and warn every one of you ¹²to live worthy of God, Who is calling you into His kingdom and glory.

¹³We continually thank God also for this, that when you accepted God's Word, which you heard from us, you didn't accept it as the word of men but as the Word of God, which it really is. And it is working in you who believe.

¹⁴You, our fellow Christians, became just like God's churches in Christ Jesus that are in Judea, since you suffered the same things from your own people as they did from the Jews. ¹⁵These killed the Lord Jesus and the prophets and drove us out. They don't please God, are opposed to everyone, ¹⁶and try to keep us from talking to the non-Jews to save them, and so they always *fill up the cup of* their *sins.* Now God is angry with them forever.

¹⁷My fellow Christians, when we were separated from you for a little while — you were out of sight but not out of mind — we longed all the more eagerly and intensely to see you. ¹⁸We wanted to come to you — I, Paul, wanted to again and again — but Satan stopped us.

¹⁹After all, who is our hope or joy or crown of glory before our Lord Jesus when He comes? Isn't it you? ²⁰Yes, you are our glory and joy!

We Long to See You

3When we couldn't stand it any longer, we thought it best to be left alone in Athens, ²and we sent Timothy, our fellow Christian who works with God in telling the good news of Christ, to strengthen you and encourage you in your faith, ³so that these troubles will not disturb anyone, because you know they are planned for us. ⁴When we were with you, we warned you. "We're going to suffer." And so it happened, as you know. ⁵That's why I couldn't stand it any longer, and I sent to find out about your faith. I was afraid the Tempter had in some way tempted you and our work was wasted.

⁶But now Timothy came back to us from you and told us the good news of your faith and love, also that you always think kindly of us and long to see us as we long to see you. ⁷So you, fellow Christians, by your faith have encouraged us in all our distress and trouble. ⁸Now we live if you stand firm in the Lord.

⁹How can we thank God for all the joy you give us before our God ¹⁰as

---

16 Gen 15:16

day and night we are most ardently praying to see you face to face and to supply whatever is lacking in your faith? ¹¹May our God and Father Himself and the Lord Jesus lead us to you.

¹²The Lord make you grow in love and overflow with it for one another and for everyone else, just as we love you, ¹³and so may He give you inward strength to be holy and without a fault before our God and Father when our Lord Jesus comes with all His holy ones! Amen.

Live to Please God

4 And now, my fellow Christians, this is what we ask and urge you to do in the Lord Jesus. You learned from us how you are to live and please God, and that is how you are living. But now do so more and more. ²You know what instructions we gave you by the Lord Jesus. ³God wants you to be holy and keep away from sexual sin. ⁴Every one of you should know how to get a wife in a holy and honorable way ⁵and not in the way of passionate lust like *the people of the world who don't know God.* ⁶No one should wrong and cheat his fellow Christian in business, because *the Lord avenges* all these things, as we told you and warned you before. ⁷God didn't call us to be unclean, but holy. ⁸Now, if anyone rejects this, he doesn't reject a man but God, *Who gives you His* Holy *Spirit.*

⁹You don't need anyone to write you about brotherly love, because God has taught you to love one another, ¹⁰and you are practicing it toward all the Christians all over Macedonia. But we urge you, my fellow Christians, grow more and more, ¹¹do your best to live quietly, mind your own business, and work with your hands, as we ordered you to do, ¹²so that you live nobly with those who are not Christians — without needing anything.

Your Dead Will Rise

¹³We want you to know about those who go to their rest, my fellow Christians, so you don't grieve like the others, who have no hope. ¹⁴We believe that Jesus died and rose again; then God will in the same way through Jesus bring with Him those who went to their rest. ¹⁵We tell you only what the Lord has told us: We who are left behind and are still living when the Lord comes will not get ahead of those who went to their rest. ¹⁶When the order is given and the archangel calls and God's trumpet sounds, the Lord Himself will come down from heaven, and the dead who are in Christ will rise first. ¹⁷Then we who are still living and left behind will be caught up with them in the clouds to meet the Lord in the air, and so we'll always be with the Lord. ¹⁸Now, then, comfort one another with these words.

Watch!

5 You don't need anyone to write and tell you exactly when things will happen, my fellow Christians, ²because you know very well the Lord's

---

day will come just like a thief in the night. ³When people say, "All's well and safe!" then destruction will come on them suddenly like labor pains on a woman who is going to have a baby, and they will not escape. ⁴But you, my fellow Christians, are not in the dark that you should let that day take you by surprise like a thief. ⁵You are all the children of light and of the day. We have nothing to do with night and darkness. ⁶Let us not sleep, then, like the others, but be awake and sober. ⁷People sleep at night and get drunk at night. ⁸But let us who live in the daylight be sober and *put on* faith and love *as a breastplate* and the sure hope of *salvation as a helmet.* ⁹God didn't appoint us to be punished by His anger but to be saved by our Lord Jesus Christ, ¹⁰Who died for us so that, awake or asleep, we may live with Him. ¹¹Then encourage one another and strengthen one another just as you are doing.

Some Last Words

¹²We ask you, fellow Christians, to appreciate the men who work among you and lead you in the Lord and warn you. ¹³Love them and think very highly of them because of the work they're doing. Live in peace with one another.

¹⁴We urge you, fellow Christians, warn those who are disorderly, cheer up those who are discouraged, help the weak, be patient with every one. ¹⁵*Don't* let anyone *pay back wrong for wrong,* but always be eager to help one another and everyone.

¹⁶Always be happy. ¹⁷Never stop praying. ¹⁸Whatever happens, thank God, because that is what God in Christ Jesus wants you to do.

¹⁹Don't put out the fire of the Spirit. ²⁰Don't despise God's Word when anyone speaks it. ²¹But test everything and cling to what is good. ²²*Keep away from every* kind of *evil.*

²³The God of peace make you holy in every way and keep your spirit and soul and body sound and without a fault when our Lord Jesus Christ comes. ²⁴You can depend on Him Who calls you — He will do it.

²⁵My fellow Christians, pray for us.

²⁶Greet all the Christians with a holy kiss.

²⁷I order you by the Lord to read this letter to all the Christians.

²⁸The grace of our Lord Jesus Christ be with you. Amen.

PAUL
WRITES THE SECOND LETTER TO THE
THESSALONIANS

1 PAUL, SILAS, AND TIMOTHY to the church of the Thessalonians in God our Father and the Lord Jesus Christ: ²May God our Father and the Lord Jesus Christ give you grace and peace!

Look to God in Suffering

³We always have to thank God for you, my fellow Christians. It is the right thing to do because your faith is growing wonderfully and the love of every one of you for one another is increasing, ⁴so much so that we're boasting about you in God's churches how you endure and trust no matter how much you're persecuted and made to suffer. ⁵It shows how God judges righteously: He means to make you worthy of His kingdom, for which you are suffering; ⁶it really is just for God to pay back with suffering those who make you suffer ⁷and to give relief to you who suffer and to us when the Lord Jesus will be revealed from heaven with His mighty angels ⁸*in a blaze of fire, to take vengeance on those who don't know God and on those who will not obey* the good news of our Lord Jesus. ⁹They will be punished by being taken *away from the Lord and from the glory of His power* to be destroyed eternally ¹⁰when He comes *on that Day* to *be glorified in His holy people* and *admired* by all who believed (you did believe the truth we told you). ¹¹With this in mind we're always praying for you that our God will make you worthy of His calling and by His power accomplish every good thing you decide to do and every work of faith, ¹²*so as to glorify the name of our Lord* Jesus among you, and you in Him, according to the grace of our God and Lord Jesus Christ.

The Man of Sin

2 Our Lord Jesus Christ is coming, and we'll be gathered to meet Him. But we ask you, fellow Christians, ²not to lose your heads so quickly or get alarmed either by a "spirit" message or by any word or letter that seemed to come from us, saying "The day of the Lord has already come!" ³Don't let anyone deceive you in any way. First there must be a revolt, and

---

8 *Is 66:15; Ps 79:6; Jer 10:25; Is 66:4*   9 *Is 2:10,19,21*
  10 *Is 2:11,17, Is 49:3; Ps 68:35; 89:7*   12 *Is 66:5; Mal 1:11*

the man of sin must be revealed, who is doomed to destruction, [4]who opposes and *sets himself above anyone* who is called *God* or anything we worship, so that *he sits in God's temple* and proclaims *he is God*.

[5]Don't you remember I told you this when I was still with you? [6]And now you know what's holding him back so that he will be revealed when his time comes. [7]This wicked thing is already working secretly, but only until he who is now holding it back gets out of the way. [8]Then the wicked one will be revealed, and the Lord Jesus *will destroy him with the breath of His mouth* and wipe him out by coming and showing Himself. [9]The coming of this wicked one is the work of Satan, who uses every kind of fake miracle and false signs and wonders, [10]and every wicked way to deceive those who are perishing because they refused to love the truth and be saved. [11]That is why God sends them a power to deceive them so they will believe the lie [12]and all will be condemned who did not believe the truth but delighted in wrong.

God Has Chosen You

[13]But we always have to thank God for you, my fellow Christians, whom *the Lord loves*, because in the beginning God chose you to be made holy by the Spirit, to believe the truth, and so to be saved. [14]For this purpose He called you by the good news we tell; He wants you to have the glory of our Lord Jesus Christ.

[15]Stand then, fellow Christians, and cling to the instructions we gave you when we spoke to you or wrote to you.

[16]Now our Lord Jesus Christ Himself and God our Father, Who loved us and by His grace gave us an everlasting comfort and a good hope, [17]inwardly comfort and strengthen you to do and say everything that is good.

Pray for Us

3 Finally, my fellow Christians, pray for us that the Lord's Word will run well and win glory as it did among you [2]and we'll be rescued from wrong-minded and wicked people. Not everyone has faith.

[3]But the Lord is faithful. He will strengthen you and protect you against the evil one. [4]We are certain in the Lord you are doing and will be doing what we order you to do. [5]And may the Lord lead you to realize how God loves you and how patiently Christ suffered.

Work

[6]Now we order you, fellow Christians, in the name of our Lord Jesus Christ to keep away from any Christian who refuses to live and work as we instructed you. [7]You know how you should imitate us. We were not idle when we were with you [8]and took no free meals from anyone but worked hard and struggled day and night in order not to burden any of you. [9]Not

---

4 Dan 11:36; Ezek 28:2   8 Job 4:9; Is 11:4

as though we didn't have a right to get support. No, we wanted to give you an example to imitate. ¹⁰And while we were with you, we gave you the order, "If anyone doesn't want to work, he shouldn't eat."

¹¹We hear that some of you are living a lazy life, not doing any work, but being busybodies. ¹²Such people we order and encourage by the Lord Jesus Christ to work quietly and eat their own bread. ¹³And you, fellow Christians, don't get tired of doing good.

¹⁴If anyone will not listen to what we say in this letter, mark him, and don't have anything to do with him, so he will feel ashamed. ¹⁵Don't treat him like an enemy, but warn him like a brother.

Farewell

¹⁶The Lord of peace always give you peace in every way. The Lord be with you all.

¹⁷I, Paul, am writing this greeting with my own hand. By this you can recognize every letter; this is my handwriting.

¹⁸The grace of our Lord Jesus Christ be with all of you!

---

13 Deut 33:12

PAUL
WRITES THE FIRST LETTER TO
TIMOTHY

1 PAUL, APOSTLE OF CHRIST JESUS by the order of God, our Savior, and Christ Jesus, our Hope, [2]to Timothy, my real son in the faith: May God the Father and Christ Jesus our Lord, give you grace, mercy, and peace!

Teaching the Law

[3]When I was going to Macedonia, I urged you to stay in Ephesus. I wanted you to order certain men not to teach anything different [4]and not to busy themselves with myths and endless records of ancestors, that provide speculations but no divine training in faith.

[5]The goal of our instruction is love flowing from a pure heart, from a good conscience, and from a sincere faith. [6]Certain people have failed to find this and have turned to silly talk. [7]They want to be teachers of the Law but don't understand what they say or the things they so confidently express.

[8]But we know the Law is good if it is used as it was meant to be used, [9]if we keep in mind that the Law is not meant for a righteous man but for those who break the Law and rebel against it, the ungodly and sinners, those who live unholy lives and insult holy things, those who kill their fathers or mothers, murderers, [10]men who sin sexually with women or with other men, kidnappers, those who lie or swear to lies — and anything else that is contrary to sound teaching. [11]This is according to the good news of the glory of God, the Blessed, that was entrusted to me.

God Was Merciful to Me

[12]I thank Christ Jesus, our Lord, whose power has been in me. He thought I could be trusted and appointed me to do His work [13]although I used to slander, persecute, and shamefully mistreat Him. But He was merciful to me because, when I didn't believe, I didn't know what I was doing. [14]Our Lord poured His grace on me, bringing faith and love in Christ Jesus.

[15]This is a statement that can be trusted and deserves complete acceptance: Christ Jesus came into the world to save sinners. I am the worst of them, [16]but God was merciful to me so that Jesus Christ would first show

in me all His longsuffering and make me an example to those who are going to believe in Him and live forever. [17]To the everlasting King, the immortal, invisible, and only God, be honor and glory forever. Amen.

Fight and Pray

[18]I'm giving you these instructions, my son Timothy, according to the prophecies made earlier about you. In the spirit of those prophecies fight a good fight [19]with faith and a good conscience. Some refused to listen to their conscience and suffered shipwreck in their faith. [20]Among them are Hymenaeus and Alexander, whom I turned over to Satan to teach them not to slander holy things.

2 I urge you, as most important of all, to ask, pray, plead, and give thanks for all people, [2]for kings and all who are over us, so that we may live quietly and peacefully and be godly and noble in every way. [3]This is good and pleases God our Savior, [4]Who wants all people to be saved and to come to know the truth.

[5]There is one God, and One Who brings God and men together, the Man Christ Jesus, [6]Who gave Himself as a ransom to free all people, and this was announced at the right times. [7]For this purpose I was appointed a preacher and an apostle (I'm telling the truth and not lying) to teach the non-Jews to believe the truth.

[8]So I want the men to pray everywhere, lifting up holy hands, not in a mood of anger or argument.

Women

[9]Women should dress in decent clothes, modestly and properly, without braiding their hair, without gold, pearls or expensive dresses [10]but, as it is proper for women who promise to worship God, with good works.

[11]A woman should learn in silence, completely submitting herself. [12]I don't allow a woman to teach nor to have authority over a man; she should keep silent. [13]The reason is that Adam was formed first, then Eve. [14]And Adam wasn't deceived; the woman was deceived and so fell into sin. [15]But women, through the birth of the Child, will be saved if they live in faith, love, and holiness, and use good judgment.

Church Workers

3 This is a statement we can trust: If anyone sets his heart on being a spiritual overseer, he wants to do a noble work. [2]Now, a spiritual overseer must be blameless, the husband of one wife, not drinking too much wine, a man of good judgment and fine behavior, kind to guests, able to teach, [3]no drunkard, not violent but gentle, not quarrelsome, not one who loves money. [4]He should manage his own household well and have his children obey him as he treats them very seriously. [5]If anyone doesn't know how to manage his own family, how can he take care of God's church? [6]He should not be a new convert, or he may become proud and so be condemned with the devil. [7]The people outside the church must speak well of him, or he may fall into disgrace and the devil's snare.

[8]In the same way the deacons should be serious, sincere in speech, not drinking a lot of wine, not greedy. [9]With a clear conscience they should keep the hidden truth they believe. [10]They, too, should first be tested; then if no fault is found in them, they should serve. [11]In the same way the wives should be serious, not slandering, not drinking too much wine, but trustworthy in every way. [12]A deacon should be the husband of one wife and should manage his children and his home well.

[13]When they have served well, they gain a good standing and can talk very confidently of their faith in Christ Jesus.

We Bring the Truth

[14]I hope to come to you soon but am writing you this [15]so that if I'm delayed you know how people should behave in God's family, which is the church of the living God, a pillar and support of the truth.

[16]It must be admitted: Great is the mystery of our faith!

> He appeared in the flesh,
> was declared righteous in spirit,
> was seen by angels,
> was preached among nations,
> was believed on in the world,
> was taken up in glory.

Danger Ahead

4 The Spirit says clearly that in later times some will turn away from the faith as they listen to spirits who deceive and to what demons teach. [2]They are led astray by the hypocrisy of liars, whose consciences have been branded as with a red-hot iron, [3]who order people not to marry and to keep away from foods that God created to be eaten with thanks by those who believe and know the truth. [4]Everything God created is good. We shouldn't reject any of it but take it and thank God for it, [5]because the Word of God and prayer make it holy.

How to Serve Christ

[6]Point these things out to our fellow Christians, and you will be a good servant of Christ Jesus, nourished by the words of the faith and of the sound teaching you have followed. [7]Don't have anything to do with worldly fables such as old women tell. Train yourself for a godly life. [8]Training the body helps a little, but godliness helps in every way, having a promise of life here and hereafter. [9]That statement you can trust and accept absolutely. [10]That is what we work and struggle for, because our hope is in the living God, Who is the Savior of all people, especially of those who believe.

[11]Order them to do these things, and keep on teaching.

[12]Don't let anyone look down on you because you're young, but be an example to those who believe, in speech, behavior, love, faith, and purity. [13]Until I come, take care of the public reading, encouragement, and teaching. [14]Don't neglect the gift you have which was given you by prophecy when the spiritual leaders laid their hands on you. [15]Practice these things, continue in them, so that everyone can see your progress. [16]Watch yourself and your teaching. Continue in these things. If you do that, you will save yourself and those who hear you.

5 Don't be harsh with an older man, but encourage him like a father, young men like brothers, [2]older women like mothers, younger women like sisters, keeping yourself altogether pure.

Take Care of Widows

[3]Treat with respect widows who are all alone. [4]If any widow has children or grandchildren, these should learn as their first duty to respect their own family and repay their parents, because that pleases God. [5]A widow who is all alone and forsaken trusts the Lord and keeps on praying day and night. [6]But one who lives for pleasure is dead while she lives.

[7]Order them to do these things so that they can't be criticized. [8]If anyone doesn't take care of his own relatives, especially his family, he has denied the faith and is worse than an unbeliever. [9]Put a widow on your list if she isn't under 60, if she was faithful to her husband, [10]if people tell about the good she has done, if she raised children, welcomed strangers, washed the feet of holy people, helped the suffering, and was busy doing every kind of good work. [11]But don't put younger widows on the list. When they feel vigorous and turn against Christ, they want to marry [12]and so are guilty of breaking the pledge they made in the beginning. [13]At the same time they learn to be idle and go around from house to house. And they're not only idle but gossiping and meddling, saying things they shouldn't say.

[14]So I want younger women to marry, have children, manage their homes, and give the enemy no chance to slander them. [15]Some have already left us to follow Satan. [16]If any believing woman has relatives who are widows, she should help them and not let them be a burden to the church, so that the church may help those widows who are all alone.

[17]Spiritual leaders who lead well should be considered worthy of double honor, especially if their work is preaching and teaching, [18]because the Bible says: *"When an ox is treading out the grain, don't muzzle him,"* and "A worker deserves his pay."[a]

[19]Don't accept an accusation against a spiritual leader unless *it is supported by two or three witnesses.* [20]Those who keep on sinning, correct before everyone in order to make the others afraid.

[21]I solemnly call on you before God and Christ Jesus and the chosen

---

18 Deut 25:4   *19 Deut 17:6; 19:15*

a - See Matt. 10:10

angels to keep these things without a prejudice and without a preference for anyone in anything you do.

²²Don't be in a hurry to ordain anyone. Don't share in the sins of others. Keep yourself pure.

²³Don't drink water only, but use a little wine for your stomach because you are often sick.

²⁴The sins of some people are quite obvious, going ahead of them to judgment, but the sins of others follow them there. ²⁵And so anyone can also see good works, and even when they can't be seen, they can't stay hidden.

Slaves and Masters

6 All who are under the yoke of slavery should think of their masters as men who deserve every respect, so that God's name and what we teach isn't slandered. ²If you have masters who believe, don't think less of them because they are fellow Christians, but serve them all the better because those who get the benefit of your work are believers and dear to you.

Religion and Contentment

Teach and urge them to do these things. ³If anyone teaches anything else and will not agree with the sound words of our Lord Jesus Christ and godly teaching, ⁴he is proud and doesn't know anything; he has a morbid craving for debates and arguments, which produce jealousy, quarreling, insults, evil suspicions, ⁵continued wrangling of people whose minds are corrupt, who have lost the truth and think religion is a way to make money.

⁶Of course, there's a big profit in religion if we're satisfied. ⁷We didn't bring anything into the world, and we can't take anything out. ⁸If we have food and clothing, we should be satisfied.

⁹But people who want to get rich fall into temptation and a snare and many foolish and harmful desires that drown them in destruction and ruin. ¹⁰Love of money is a root of all kinds of evil, and some people, eager to get rich, have wandered away from the faith and pierced themselves with much pain.

Fight the Good Fight

¹¹But you, man of God, flee from these things. Be eager to be righteous, godly, full of faith and love, able to endure, gentle. ¹²Fight the good fight of faith, take hold of the everlasting life to which you were called and which you confessed so well before many witnesses.

¹³I order you before God, from Whom comes all life, and before Christ Jesus, Who testified before Pontius Pilate and made a good confession, ¹⁴that you keep the commandment without reproach, until our Lord Jesus

Christ appears. [15]At His own right time God will show Him to us — He, the blessed and only Ruler, *the* King of kings and *Lord of lords*, [16]Who alone cannot die, Who lives in a light to which no one can come near, Whom no one has ever seen or can see. To Him be honor and power forever. Amen.

[17]Tell those who are rich in this world not to feel proud and not to trust anything as uncertain as riches but to trust God, Who richly gives us everything to enjoy. [18]Tell them to do good, to be rich in good works, to be glad to give and share, [19]and so to store up for themselves a treasure, a good foundation for the future, and to take hold of the life that is real.

[20]Timothy, guard what has been entrusted to you. Turn away from empty, unholy talk and contradictory statements of what is falsely called knowledge. [21]Some claim to have it and have lost their faith.

Grace be with you all!

PAUL
WRITES THE SECOND LETTER TO
TIMOTHY

1 PAUL, APOSTLE OF CHRIST JESUS, by the will of God Who has promised life in Christ Jesus, [2]to Timothy, my dear son — God the Father and Christ Jesus, our Lord, give you grace, mercy, and peace!

[3]I thank God — whom I, like my fathers, serve with a clear conscience — when I remember you in my prayers, as I never fail to do day and night. [4]Remembering your tears, I long to see you and so to be filled with happiness. [5]I recall how sincere your faith was; just as it lived in your grandmother Lois and your mother Eunice before you, so I am convinced it is in you too.

Stir Up God's Gift

[6]That is why I remind you to stir into a flame God's gift that is in you through the laying on of my hands. [7]God didn't give us a cowardly spirit but a Spirit of power and love and good judgment. [8]So don't be ashamed to tell about our Lord, and don't be ashamed of me, His prisoner, but with God's power to back us, join me in suffering for the good news. [9]He saved us and called us to be holy, not because we did anything, but because He planned a gift of His grace and gave it to us in Christ Jesus before the world began; [10]it has now come to light by the coming of our Savior Christ Jesus. He took away the power of death and by the good news brought into the light the life that can't be destroyed. [11]To tell about it, I was appointed a preacher, apostle, and teacher.

[12]That is why I suffer as I do, but I'm not ashamed, because I know Him whom I trust, and I'm sure He can keep for that day what I have entrusted to Him.

[13]With a faith and a love in Christ Jesus keep what you heard me say as an example of sound teaching. [14]With the help of the Holy Spirit living in us, guard the good thing entrusted to you.

Onesiphorus

[15]You know how everyone in the province of Asia deserted me, including Phygelus and Hermogenes.

[16]The Lord be merciful to the family of Onesiphorus because he often cheered me up. He wasn't ashamed of my being a prisoner, [17]but coming to Rome, he searched hard for me and found me. [18]May the Lord let him find

mercy from the Lord on that day. And you know very well all he did to help me in Ephesus.

Be a Good Soldier

2 You, my son, let God's grace in Christ Jesus make you strong, ²and what you heard me say before many witnesses entrust to faithful people who will be able to teach others.

³Share hardships with me like a good soldier of Christ Jesus. ⁴If you're in the army, you don't get tangled up with the ways of making a living; you want to please him who made you a soldier. ⁵If you enter a contest, you win a prize only if you compete according to the rules. ⁶If you work the ground, you should be the first to get what grows on it. ⁷Try to understand what I say, because the Lord will give you understanding in everything.

⁸Keep in mind Jesus Christ risen from the dead, a descendant of David — this is the good news I tell. ⁹For this I'm suffering and am even chained like a criminal. But God's Word isn't chained. ¹⁰That's why I can endure anything for the chosen people so that they, too, may receive salvation in Christ Jesus and everlasting glory. ¹¹You can depend on this: If we have died with Him, we'll live with Him. ¹²If we endure, we'll rule with Him. If we disown Him, He'll disown us. ¹³If we're disloyal, He remains loyal because He cannot be untrue to Himself.

¹⁴Remind them of these things and warn them before the Lord not to fight about words; it doesn't do any good but only ruins those who are listening.

¹⁵Do your best to come before God as one whom He approves, a worker who doesn't have to feel ashamed because he teaches the Word of truth in the correct way. ¹⁶Keep away from empty, worldly talk, because such people become more and more ungodly, ¹⁷and their talk will spread like a cancer. Among them are Hymenaeus and Philetus, ¹⁸who have lost the truth by saying the resurrection has already taken place. They're upsetting the faith of some people.

¹⁹But there stands God's solid foundation, and it has this seal: *"The Lord knows those who are His own"*, and, "Let everyone who *calls on the name of the Lord* give up wrongdoing."

²⁰In a big house there are not only things of gold and silver but also of wood and clay. Some are used in a noble way and some in a dishonorable way. ²¹Now if anyone will cleanse himself from the latter, he'll be ready for a noble purpose, purified, useful to the owner, and prepared to do any good work.

²²Flee from the lusts of young people, try to be righteous, faithful, loving, peaceful with people who with pure hearts call on the Lord. ²³Don't have anything to do with foolish and unintelligent arguments; you know they breed quarrels. ²⁴A servant of the Lord must not quarrel but be kind

19 Num 16:5; Is 26:13

to everyone. He should be a good teacher, ready to suffer wrong, ²⁵and gentle in correcting those who oppose him. Perhaps God will change their hearts and lead them to know the truth. ²⁶Then they'll escape the snare of the devil, who trapped them to do what he wants, and they'll come to their senses.

The Last Days

3 Understand this, that in the last days there will come times of trouble. ²People will love themselves and money. They'll brag and be proud. They'll blaspheme. They'll disobey parents. They'll be ungrateful and unholy, ³without love, never forgiving an enemy, slandering. They'll be without control, wild, with no love for what is good. ⁴They'll be treacherous, reckless, proud. They'll love pleasure and not God. ⁵They'll have the form of godliness but reject it's power. Keep away from such people. ⁶Some of them get into homes and captivate weak women, loaded with sins, driven by all kinds of desires, ⁷always learning and never able to understand the truth. ⁸Just as Jannes and Jambres opposed Moses, so they oppose the truth. Their minds are corrupt, and their faith is no good. ⁹But they won't get very far; like Jannes and Jambres, they will be seen by everyone to be the plain fools they are.

Teach the Truth

¹⁰But you have followed closely my teachings, my way of life, my purpose, my faith, my patience, my love, my endurance, ¹¹my persecutions and sufferings — the things that happened to me in Antioch, Iconium, and Lystra — those persecutions which I endured. The Lord rescued me from everything. ¹²All who want to live a godly life in Christ Jesus will be persecuted.

¹³But evil men and swindlers will get worse as they cheat and are cheated. ¹⁴But you stay with what you've learned and found to be true. You know from whom you learned it ¹⁵and how, since you were a little child, you have known the Holy Scriptures, which are able to make you wise and save you through faith in Christ Jesus. ¹⁶All Scripture is inspired by God and is useful for teaching, showing what is wrong, correcting and training in right living ¹⁷so that a man of God is ready and equipped for every good work.

4 Before God and Christ Jesus, Who is going to judge the living and the dead, I solemnly call on you — in view of His coming and ruling over us — ²preach the Word, keep at it when convenient and when inconvenient, correct, rebuke, encourage, being very patient and thorough in your teaching.

³A time will come when people will not listen to sound teaching but, craving to hear something different, will get more and more teachers whom they like. ⁴They will refuse to listen to the truth and will turn to fiction.

⁵But you, keep a clear head in everything, endure hardship, do your work of telling the good news, and everything else you should do as a pastor.

The Lord Will Deliver Me

⁶I'm now being sacrificed, and it's time for me to leave. ⁷I fought the good fight, I ran the race, I kept the faith. ⁸Now there is waiting for me the crown of righteousness which the Lord, the righteous Judge, will give me on that day, and not only me but all who love to see Him come again.

⁹Do your best to come to me soon. ¹⁰Demas fell in love with this world, deserted me, and went to Thessalonica. Crescens went to Galatia, Titus to Dalmatia. ¹¹Only Luke is with me. Get Mark and bring him with you, because he's a good help to me in my work. ¹²I sent Tychicus to Ephesus.

¹³When you come, bring the warm coat I left with Carpus in Troas, and the scrolls, especially the parchments.

¹⁴Alexander the metalworker did me a lot of wrong. *The Lord will pay him back for what he did.* ¹⁵Be on your guard against him, because he was very much opposed to what we said.

¹⁶The first time I had to defend myself, no one came to help me, but everyone deserted me — may it not be held against them. ¹⁷But the Lord stood by me and gave me the strength to finish my preaching so that all the non-Jews would hear it. *I was rescued from the lion's mouth.* ¹⁸The Lord will rescue me from all the evil that is done and will save me and take me to His heavenly kingdom. To Him be glory forever. Amen.

Greetings

¹⁹Greet Prisca and Aquila and the family of Onesiphorus. ²⁰Erastus stayed in Corinth. I left Trophimus sick in Miletus. ²¹Do your best to get here before the winter. Eubulus and Pudens and Linus and Claudia and all the fellow Christians greet you.

²²The Lord Jesus Christ be with your spirit! Grace be with you all!

---

14 Ps 62:12; Prov 24:12   17 Ps 22:21; Dan 6:20,22,27

PAUL
WRITES TO
TITUS

1 PAUL, SERVANT OF GOD and apostle of Jesus Christ — sent to help God's chosen people to believe and to know the truth which promotes godliness, [2]hoping, as we do, for everlasting life, which God, Who never lies, promised ages ago [3]and at His own right times revealed in His Word by the preaching entrusted to me by an order of God our Savior — [4]to Titus, my real son by the faith we share: May God the Father and Christ Jesus our Savior give you grace and peace!

Appoint Good Pastors

[5]I left you behind in Crete to make the improvements still needed and to appoint spiritual leaders in every town as I directed you — [6]someone who is blameless, who has one wife, and believing children not accused of wild living or disobedient. [7]As a manager appointed by God, a spiritual overseer should be blameless. He shouldn't do as he pleases, get angry easily, drink too much, be quick to strike anyone, or be greedy. [8]He should welcome guests, love anything good, use good judgment, do what is right and God-pleasing. He should control himself. [9]He should cling to the Word, which he can depend on, just as he was taught, so that by sound teaching he can encourage people and correct those who oppose it.

Correct Your Opponents

[10]There are many who are rebellious, who talk foolishly and deceive, especially the Jews. [11]They must be silenced. They are ruining whole families by teaching what they must not teach, only to make money in such a shameful way.

[12]One of their own men, their own prophet, said, "Men of Crete are always liars, savage animals, lazy gluttons."[a] [13]That statement is true. For that reason correct them sharply so that they may be sound in their faith [14]instead of listening to Jewish myths or orders given by men who reject the truth. [15]Everything is pure to those who are pure. But nothing is pure to the evil-minded who don't believe — their minds and consciences are unclean. [16]They openly claim to know God but deny Him by what they do. They're detestable, disobedient, and not fit to do anything good.

---

a - 12   This may have been said by the Cretan poet Epimenides of Knossos (500 B.C.).

Special Instructions

2 But you tell people what is right according to sound teaching. [2]Tell older men: Be sober, serious, sensible, and sound in faith, love, and endurance.

[3]In the same way tell older women: Behave as holy women should behave. Don't slander. Don't be slaves to much wine. Teach what is good, [4]in order to train young women to love their husbands and their children, [5]to use good judgment and be pure, to keep house, to be good, to submit to their husbands, so that people don't slander God's Word.

[6]In the same way urge the young men to use good judgment. [7]In everything be an example of good works. Don't let anything corrupt your teaching. But be noble, [8]and give a sound message that can't be condemned, so that anyone who opposes us will be ashamed because he can't say anything bad about us.

[9]Tell slaves: Obey your masters in everything, please them, and don't talk back. [10]Don't steal, but show you can be trusted in every way, so that in everything you show the beauty of the teaching of God our Savior.

Jesus Is Coming

[11]God has shown His grace. It brings salvation to all people [12]and trains us to say no to ungodliness and worldly lusts, and to live sensible, law-abiding and godly lives in this world [13]as we look for the blessed One Who is our Hope, for our great God and Savior Christ Jesus to show Himself in glory. [14]He gave Himself as *a payment* for us *to free* us *from all wickedness* and cleanse us *to be His own people*, eager to do good works.

[15]Talk and urge these things, and correct with full authority — no one should ignore you.

3 Remind people to submit to governments and authorities, to obey, to be ready to do any good work, [2]not to insult anyone or fight, but to yield and show kindness to everyone.

What God Did for Us

[3]Once we, too, were foolish, disobedient, led astray, slaves to many kinds of passions and pleasures. We lived in wickedness and jealousy, being hated and hating one another.

[4]But when God our Savior showed how kind He is and how He loves us, [5]He saved us, not because of any good works we did but because He was merciful. He saved us by the washing in which the Holy Spirit gives us a new birth and a new life. [6]He poured a rich measure of this Spirit on us through Jesus Christ our Savior, [7]to declare us righteous by His grace so that we may be heirs according to the hope of everlasting life. [8]You can de-

---

14 Ps130:8; Ex 19:5; Deut 4:20; 14:2; 26:18; 29:13

pend on this statement.

And I want you to insist on these things so that those who believe in God have their minds on being busy with good works. This is good, and it helps other people.

[9]But keep away from foolish arguments, lists of ancestors, quarreling, and fighting about the Law. These help no one and are worthless. [10]A man who chooses to be different in his teaching warn once and a second time, and then don't have anything more to do with him [11]because you know such a man is set in his wrong way and is a sinner who condemns himself.

Farewell

[12]When I send Artemas or Tychicus to you, hurry to come to me at Nicopolis; I've decided to stay there for the winter. [13]Do your best to help Zenas the lawyer and Apollos to get on their way; they should have everything they need.

[14]Our people should learn to be busy with good works to help real needs and not waste their lives.

[15]All who are here with me send greetings. Greet those who love us as fellow believers.

Grace be with all of you!

PAUL WRITES TO
PHILEMON

PAUL, A PRISONER OF CHRIST JESUS, and our brother Timothy, to Philemon, our dear fellow worker, [2]Apphia, our fellow Christian, Archippus, our fellow soldier, and to the church that meets at your home: [3]May God our Father and the Lord Jesus Christ give you grace and peace!

[4]I'm always thanking my God when I mention you in my prayers, [5]because I hear how you believe in the Lord Jesus and love Him and all the holy people, [6]so that, knowing every good thing you have in Christ, the sharing of your faith may be effective. [7]Your love delighted and encouraged me very much because you, my fellow Christian, have refreshed the hearts of our holy people.

[8]For that reason, although I feel bold enough in Christ to order you to do what is right, [9]I am moved by love just to urge you. As Paul, an old man and now a prisoner of Christ Jesus, [10]I appeal to you for my son Onesimus, who became my son while I have been in chains. [11]Once he was useless to you, but now he's quite useful[a] to you and me.

[12]I'm sending him back to you — and my heart goes with him. [13]I would have liked to keep him with me and have him serve me in your place while I'm in chains for the good news, [14]but I don't want to do anything without your approval. I don't want you to be kind because you must but because you want to be. [15]Perhaps Onesimus left you for a while only to be yours again forever, [16]no longer a slave but more than a slave, a dear fellow Christian, especially to me, but how much more to you, as a man and as a Christian.

[17]Now if you think of me as your partner, welcome him as you would welcome me. [18]If he cheated you or owes you anything, charge it to me. [19]I Paul, am writing this with my own hand — I'll pay it back. I don't want to mention that you owe me more than that — your own self. [20]Yes, my fellow Christian, I want you to be useful to me in the Lord. Refresh my heart in Christ. [21]As I write to you, I'm sure you'll do this. I know you'll do even more than I ask.

[22]One thing more: Have a guest room ready for me, because I hope through the prayers of all of you to be given back to you.

[23]Greetings to you from Epaphras, my fellow prisoner in Christ Jesus, [24]and from my fellow workers: Mark, Aristarchus, Demas, and Luke.

[25]The love of the Lord Jesus Christ be with the spirit of all of you. Amen.

---

a - 11   Onesimus means "useful"

THE LETTER TO THE
HEBREWS

1 At many times and in many ways, God spoke to our fathers long ago by the prophets, [2]but in these last days He has spoken to us by His Son, Whom He made the heir of everything and by Whom He made the world. [3]He Who shines with God's glory and is the Expression of His Being sustains everything by His mighty Word. He made a cleansing from sins, *sat down at the right hand* of the Majesty in heaven, [4]and is as much superior than angels as the name He has is better than theirs.

[5]To which of the angels did God ever say:

> *You are My Son,*
> *today I have begotten You?*

Or again:

> *I will be His Father,*
> *and He will be My Son?*

[6]And when He again will bring the firstborn Son into the world, He says:

> *All of God's angels should worship Him.*

[7] He says of the angels:

> *He makes His angels winds and His servants fiery flames.*

[8]But to the Son He says:

> *Your throne, O God, is forever and ever,*
> and *You rule Your kingdom*
> *with a scepter of righteousness.*
> [9] *You have loved right and hated wrong.*
> *That is why God, Your God, has put You*
> *above Your companions*
> *by anointing You with the oil of joy.*

[10]And:

> *Lord, in the beginning You laid*
> *the foundation of the earth*
> *and Your hands made the heavens!*
> [11]*They will perish,*
> *but You continue.*
> *They will all become old like a garment.*
> [12]*You will roll them up like a blanket,*
> *and like a garment they will be changed.*
> *But You are the same,*

---

3 *Ps 110:1*   **5** *Ps 2:7; 2 Sam 7:14*   **6** *Deut 32:43; Ps 97:7*   **7** *Ps 104:4*
8-9 *Ps 45:6-7*   **10-12** *Gen 14:22; Ps 102:25-27; Is 50:9; 51:6*

and Your years will never end.

¹³To which of the angels did He ever say: "*Sit at My right hand until I make Your enemies a footstool for Your feet*"? ¹⁴Aren't all angels spirits that serve Him and are sent to help those who are going to inherit salvation?

Don't Neglect Your Salvation

2 That is why we should listen all the more carefully to what we have been told, or we may drift away. ²If what God said through angels was valid, and every transgression and disobedience got a just punishment, ³how can we escape if we neglect a salvation as great as this? First the Lord spoke of it, and then those who heard Him guaranteed its truth to us, ⁴while God added His testimony by both miraculous signs and wonders, by different kinds of miracles, and by distributing gifts of the Holy Spirit as He wished.

Lord of Everything

⁵He didn't put the coming world that we're talking about under the control of angels. ⁶But somewhere someone has declared:

What is man that You should think of him?
Or a son of man that You should come to help him?
⁷*You make Him lower than the angels for a little while*
then crown Him with glory and honor
and make Him Ruler over what Your hands have made
⁸*and put everything under His feet.*

Now, when *He put everything under His feet*, He left nothing outside His control.

Jesus Died for Us

As it is, we do not yet see *everything put under Him*. ⁹But we do see Jesus, Who *for a little while was made lower than the angels, now crowned with glory and honor* because He suffered death in order by God's grace to taste death for everyone. ¹⁰It fitted Him well, for Whom and by Whom everything exists, that in bringing many sons to glory He should make the One Who gives them salvation perfect through suffering.

¹¹He Who makes men holy and those who are made holy all have one Father.

That is why He is not ashamed to call them *brothers*. ¹²He says:

I will tell My brothers Your name,
in the congregation I will sing Your praise.

¹³And again: "*I will trust Him.*" And again: "*Here am I and the children God has given Me.*"

¹⁴Now since all these *children* have flesh and blood, He in the same

---

13 Ps 110:1　　*6-9 Ps 8:4-6*　　*11-12 Ps 22:22*
13 Ps 18:2; II Sam 22:3; Is 8:17-18　　*14-16 Is 41:8-9*

way took on flesh and blood in order to die and so take away all the powers of him who had the power of death, that is, the devil, [15]and to free those who, terrified by death, had to be slaves all their lives. [16]It is clear He didn't *come to help* angels but *Abraham's descendants.* [17]And so in every way He had to become like His brothers to be merciful and faithful as High Priest before God and to pay for the sins[a] of the people. [18]Because He Himself suffered when He was tested, He can help others when they're tested.

Greater than Moses

3 And so, fellow Christians — you're holy, and heaven called you as it called us — look at Jesus, the Apostle and High Priest Whom we confess, [2]being *faithful* to Him Who appointed Him, just as *Moses was faithful in God's whole house.* [3]He deserves greater glory than Moses, as the builder of a house is honored more than the house. [4]Every house is built by someone, but He Who built everything is God.

[5]Now, *Moses was faithful in God's household* as *a servant* who was to testify of what would be said later, [6]but Christ was faithful as the Son in charge of *God's household.* We are His household if to the end we continue unshaken in our courage and in the hope of which we boast.

Don't Harden Your Hearts

[7]And so, as the Holy Spirit says: *"Today, if you hear Him speak,* [8]*don't harden your hearts as it happened when the people provoked Me at the time they tested Me in the desert,* [9]*where your fathers put Me to a test when for forty years they saw what I could do.* [10]*That was why I was angry with those people, and I said: 'In their hearts they're always going astray and haven't learned My ways.'* [11]*So, because I was angry, I swore that they will never come to My place of rest!"*

[12]See to it, fellow Christians, that none of you has a wicked, unbelieving heart that turns away from the living God. [13]Yes, encourage one another every day, as long as you can say *today,* to keep sin from deceiving anyone of you with its pleasure and *hardening your heart* to the truth. [14]We share in Christ if we only keep our first confidence unshaken to the end.

[15]When it says: *"Today, if you hear Him speak, don't harden your hearts as it happened when the people provoked Me"* — [16]who were those that heard Him and yet *provoked* Him? Were they not all those Moses led out of Egypt? [17]With whom was He *angry for forty years?* Was it not with those who sinned and whose *bodies dropped dead in the desert?* [18]To whom did He *swear they would not come to His place of rest* if not to those who *disobeyed?* [19]So we see that they couldn't come there because they didn't believe.

4 We should be fearful then. While we still have the promise of com-

---

2,5-6 Num 12:7   **7-18** *Num 14:22; Ps 95:7-11; Num 14:29*

---

a - 17   Jesus wipes out our sins by His blood and so changes God's anger to love.

ing to His place of rest, someone of you may be judged to have missed it. [2]The good news came to us as it came to them, but the message they heard didn't help them because those who heard it didn't hear it with faith.

There Is a Rest for Us

[3]We who have believed *go to a rest*, since He has said: *"So I swore in My anger they will never come to My place of rest."* And yet God finished His work when He made the world, [4]because in one place He said about the seventh day: *"On the seventh day God rested from all He had done."* [5]And here, too, He says: *"They will never come to My place of rest."* [6]Now, it is still true that some *will go to His rest*, and those who once heard the good news didn't *go to* it because they disobeyed; [7]so He sets another day — *today* — when long afterwards He says in David's words, already quoted: *"Today if you hear Him speak, don't harden your hearts."* [8]If Joshua had given them rest, God wouldn't later have spoken of another day. [9]So there is still a Sabbath of rest for God's people, [10]since anyone who *goes to his rest finds rest from his work* as *God* did *from His.*

[11]Let us then be diligent to *come to* that *rest* so that no one may *disobey* and fall like those people.

The Living Word

[12]God's Word is living and active. It cuts better than any *two-edged sword.* It pierces until it divides soul and spirit, joints and marrow. And it can judge thoughts and purposes of the heart. [13]No creature can hide from Him. *Everything is uncovered and exposed before the eyes of Him* to Whom we must give account.

Our High Priest

[14]Now that we have a great High Priest Who has gone through the heavens, Jesus, God's Son, let us cling to what we confess. [15]We have a High Priest Who can sympathize with our weaknesses. He was tempted in every way just as we are, only without sin. [16]So let us come boldly to God's throne of grace to receive mercy and find grace to help us when we need it.

5 Any high priest selected from men is appointed to represent them before God and to bring gifts and sacrifices for sins. [2]He can be gentle with ignorant and erring people because he too is troubled with weakness [3]and for that reason must bring sacrifices for sins for himself just as he does for the people.

[4]No one takes the honor of this office, but God calls a man as He called Aaron. [5]So Christ didn't take the glory of being a high priest, but it was

---

3 Num 14:23; Ps 95:7-11   *4 Gen 2:2*   **5-10** *Num 14:23; Ps 95:7-11*
10 Gen 2:2   *11 Num 14:22; Ps 95:7-11*   *12 Is 49:2*   *13 Prov 5:21; 15:3*

given to Him by Him Who said:

> You are My Son,
> today I have begotten You.

[6]And so He said in another place: "*You are like Melchizedek, a priest forever.*"

[7]In His humble life on earth Jesus came to Him Who could save Him from death and prayed and pleaded, crying loud with tears, and because He feared God, He was heard. [8]Although Jesus is the Son, He learned from what He suffered what it means to obey. [9]And when He was finished, He became One Who gives *everlasting salvation* to all who obey Him, [10]being proclaimed by God a high *priest like Melchizedek.*

More than the ABC's

[11]We have much to say about this, but it's difficult to explain because you have become too dull to understand. [12]At a time when you should be teachers you need someone to teach you the ABC's[b] of God's Word again. It has come to this that you need milk again instead of solid food. [13]Anyone who lives on milk, being a baby, doesn't have enough experience to talk of what is right. [14]But solid food is for mature people, whose senses are trained by practice to tell good from evil.

6 Let us leave behind the ABC's of Christ and be moved along to be mature, not laying again a foundation of repentance from dead works, faith in God, [2]teaching about baptisms, laying on of hands, raising the dead, and everlasting judgment. [3]We will do this if God lets us.

[4]When those who once had the light and tasted the gift from heaven, who had the Holy Spirit just as others did [5]and tasted how good God's Word is and the powers of the coming world — [6]when those fall away, it is impossible to bring them back to a new repentance because they to their own undoing again crucify God's Son and hold Him up for mockery. [7]When *ground* drinks the rain that often falls on it and *produces plants* that can be used by those for whom it is worked, it is blessed by God. [8]But if *it produces thorns and thistles*, it is worthless. A *curse* hangs over it, and finally it will be burned.

[9]Although we say this, we are convinced that for you, dear friends, there are better things that mean salvation. [10]God is righteous to remember your work and the love you showed for Him as you helped His holy people and still help them. [11]But we want every one of you to show the same zeal to make certain of your hope until the end, [12]and not get lazy but be like those who by believing and being patient inherit what is promised.

[13]God promised Abraham, and since He had no one greater to swear

---

5 Ps 2:7   **6** Ps 110:4   **9** Is 45:17   **10** Ps 110:4
7 Gen 1:11-12   **8** Gen 3:17-18

b - 12   or "the elementary truths" (cf. 6:1).

by, He *swore by Himself* [14]and said: *I will certainly bless you and make you many people.* [15]And so, after waiting patiently, Abraham got what God promised.

[16]People swear by Someone greater to guarantee what they say and to silence anyone who opposes them. [17]So God, wanting to make it perfectly clear to those who would inherit His promise that He wouldn't change His plan, bound Himself with an oath [18]so that we who have fled to Him would have two unchangeable things, in which God cannot lie, to give us a strong encouragement to take hold of the hope set before us. [19]We have this hope like an anchor for our lives, sure and strong and *reaching behind the curtain,* [20]where Jesus has entered as a forerunner for us, having become *like Melchizedek a* high *priest forever.*

A Priest Forever

7 This *Melchizedek, king of Salem* and *priest of the Most High God, met Abraham coming back from defeating the kings, and he blessed Abraham.* [2]*And Abraham gave him a tenth of everything.* His name, in the first place, means *king of righteousness,* but then he is also *king of Salem,* that is, *king of peace.* [3]He is without father, mother, or line of ancestors. His life has no beginning or end. Like God's Son he continues *a priest forever.*

[4]See how great he was! *Abraham,* the father of the people, *gave him a tenth* from the best of the spoils. [5]And the Law orders those descendants of Levi who become priests to receive a tenth from the people, that is, from other Israelites, although they, too, have descended from Abraham. [6]But this man, who was outside their line of descent, received *a tenth* from *Abraham* and *blessed him* who had the promises. [7]No one can deny that the higher one blesses the lower one.

[8]And here those who receive a tenth are people who die, but there we are assured it is one who lives. [9]And we may say that Levi, who receives a tenth, in *Abraham gave a tenth,* [10]since he was in the body of his ancestor when *Melchizedek* met him.

[11]Levi's descendants were the priests; on this basis the people got the Law. Now, if the priests who descended from Levi could have given us something perfect, why did another *priest* still need to come who is *like Melchizedek* and said to be different from Aaron? [12]When a different person is made priest, the Law also has to be changed. [13]The One here spoken of belongs to a different tribe, which never had a priest serving at the altar. [14]Everyone knows our Lord came from Judah, but Moses said nothing about priests in this tribe. [15]That point is much clearer still when we see a different *priest* coming *like Melchizedek,* [16]not appointed according to a Law that says he must be someone's descendant but by the power of a life that can't be destroyed. [17]We are assured: *"You are like Melchizedek a priest forever."* [18]The earlier rule is canceled because it is weak and can't help us.

13-14 Gen 22:16-17   *19* Lev 16:2,12   *20* Ps 110:4   *1-2* Gen 14:17-20
3 Ps 110:4   *4-10* Gen 14:17-20   *11-28* Ps 2:7; 110:4

¹⁹The Law made nothing perfect, but the coming of a better hope did — it brings us close to God.

²⁰When those men were made priests, there was no oath. ²¹But when Jesus was appointed, God swore as He said to Him: *"The Lord has sworn and will not change His mind: 'You are a priest forever!'"* Swearing to it ²²made the agreement Jesus guarantees so much the better.

²³Once many were made priests because death didn't let them continue as priests. ²⁴But because Jesus lives forever, He will *always* be the *Priest*. ²⁵And so He can forever save those who come to God by Him, because He always lives to pray for them.

²⁶Here is the High Priest we needed — holy, innocent, spotless, separated from sinners, and risen higher than the heavens, ²⁷Who doesn't need to bring sacrifices every day like those high priests, first for His own sins, then for the sins of the people. He did this only once when He sacrificed Himself. ²⁸The Law appointed weak men to be high priests, but when God speaks with an oath later than the Law, He appoints the *Son*, Who was made perfect *forever*.

A Better Covenant

8 Now, this is my main point. We have such a High Priest, and He *sat down at the right* of the throne of the Majesty in heaven ²to serve as Priest in the holy place and in the true *tabernacle set up by the Lord* and not by men. ³As every high priest is appointed to offer gifts and sacrifices, this One, too, had to bring some sacrifice.

⁴If He were on earth, He wouldn't even be a priest, because there are priests who offer the gifts demanded by the Law. ⁵They serve a copy and a shadow of what is in heaven, as God told Moses when he was going to make the tabernacle: *"Be careful to make* all of *it like the pattern you were shown on the mountain."*

⁶Now, the priestly work that Jesus was given to do is more excellent, just as the covenant of which He is also the Mediator is a better one because God has based it on better promises. ⁷If that first covenant had been without a fault, no one would have wanted a second one. ⁸But God is finding fault with them when He says:

> *See! The time is coming, says the Lord, when I will set up a new testament [covenant] with the people of Israel and the people of Judah,* ⁹*not like the covenant I made with their fathers when I took them by the hand to lead them out of Egypt, because they have not been loyal to My covenant. And so I turned away from them, says the Lord.* ¹⁰ *The testament [covenant] I will make with the people of Israel after those days, says the Lord, is this: I will put My laws into their minds and write them on their hearts, and I will be their God, and they will be My people.* ¹¹*No more will anyone teach his*

---

1 Ps 110:1   2 Num 24:5-6   5 Ex 25:40; 25:9,40; 26:30; 27:8
8-13 Jer 31:31-34

fellow citizen *or his brother and say, "Know the Lord!" They will
all know Me from the least to the greatest of them,* [12]*because I will
forgive their wrongs and not remember their sins anymore.*

[13]By saying *"a new testament" [covenant],* He made the first one old.
When He treats it as old and it is getting old, it is ready to vanish.

The Tabernacle

9 The first covenant had its regulations for worship and the earthly
holy place. [2]A tabernacle was set up. In the first part were the lampstand,
the table, and the bread laid before God; this is called the holy place. [3]Be-
hind the second curtain was the part of the tabernacle called the most holy
place [4]with the gold altar of incense and the ark of the covenant, completely
covered with gold. In the ark were the gold jar containing the manna,
Aaron's rod that had budded, and the tablets on which the covenant was
written. [5]Above it were the *angels* of glory *overshadowing the "atonement
cover"* on which the blood was sprinkled. — I can't tell about these in detail
now.

[6]But that is how it was arranged. The priests are always going into the
first part of the tabernacle to serve God, [7]but only the high priest goes into
the second part once a year with blood he offers for himself and for the sins
the people have done in ignorance. [8]And so the Holy Spirit clearly tells us
that the way into the real holy place had not yet been shown as long as the
outer part of the tabernacle was still standing.

[9]This is a picture of the time we live in. Gifts and sacrifices are brought
which can't make the worshiper feel perfect in his conscience [10]but deal only
with gifts of food and drink and various baptisms, which are regulations for
the body imposed until the time when things would be set right.

Jesus' Blood

[11]But Christ came as High Priest of the good things that have come; He
went through that greater and more perfect tabernacle not made by human
hands (that is, not a part of this created world). [12]And He didn't use the
blood of goats and calves but through His own blood He entered only once
into the Holy of Holies and paid a price that frees us forever. [13]Now, sprin-
kling the blood of goats and bulls and the *ashes of a calf* on unclean people
makes them outwardly holy and clean. [14]How much more will the blood of
Christ, Who by the everlasting Spirit offered Himself without a spot to God,
wash our consciences clean from dead works to worship the living God?

[15]And He is the Mediator of a new testament [covenant]. By dying He
paid the ransom to free people from the sins under the first covenant, and
those who are called are to receive the everlasting inheritance promised
them. [16]Where there is a will, it must be shown that the one who made it
died, [17]since a will takes effect only when a person is dead. It is not in force

---

4 Num 17:8,10   *5 Ex 25:20; 37:9; Lev 16:2*   *13 Num 19:9-10*

as long as the one who made it is still living. ¹⁸That is why the first
covenant was also dedicated with blood. ¹⁹When *Moses* had told all the people every commandment of the Law, he *took the blood* of calves and goats
and some water, scarlet wool, and hyssop *and sprinkled* the scroll and *all
the people.* ²⁰*"This is the blood of the covenant,"* he said, *"that God has ordered you* to keep." ²¹In the same way he sprinkled blood on the tabernacle
and on everything used in the worship. ²²According to the Law almost
everything is cleansed by blood, and if no blood is poured out, no sins are
forgiven.

One Perfect Sacrifice

²³Now, the copies of the things in heaven had to be cleansed by these
sacrifices, but the heavenly things themselves needed better sacrifices.
²⁴Christ didn't go into a holy place made by human hands and just a copy
of the real thing but into heaven itself, now to appear before God for us.
²⁵And not to sacrifice Himself over and over again like that high priest going
every year into the holy place with blood that is not his own. ²⁶Otherwise He
would have had to suffer many times since the world was made. But as it
is, He appeared only once at the end of the ages to get rid of sin by His sacrifice. ²⁷And as people are appointed to die once and after that the judgment,
²⁸so Christ also was sacrificed once to *take away the sins of many people*, but
those who eagerly look for Him will see Him again, not to deal with sin, but
to bring salvation to them.

10 The Law, having only a dim outline of the good things in the future and not their substance, can never by the same sacrifices, repeated
endlessly year after year, make perfect those who come. ²Otherwise wouldn't
they have stopped bringing sacrifices? Once cleansed, the worshipers would
no longer be aware of any sins. ³No, year after year these sacrifices re-
minded people of their sins. ⁴The blood of bulls and goats can't take away
sins.
    ⁵That is why He says when He comes into the world:
        You didn't want sacrifice and offering,
            but You prepared a body for Me.
        ⁶ Burnt offerings and sacrifices for sin didn't
            please You.
        ⁷ Then I said: Look! I have come (the writing in the
            scroll of the book tells about Me).
        I'm here to do what You want, O God.
⁸First He says: *"You didn't want and weren't* pleased *with sacrifices, offerings, burnt offerings, and sacrifices for sin* which are offered according to
the Law." ⁹Then He says: *"Look! I have come and am here to do what You
want."* He takes away the first to set up the second. ¹⁰*Doing God's will,*

Jesus Christ *sacrificed* His *body* only once and so made us holy.

[11]Every other priest stands and serves day after day, and over and over again brings the same sacrifices, which can never take away sins. [12]But He made one sacrifice for sins, good forever, *sat down at the right hand of God,* [13]and since then is waiting *for His enemies to be made a footstool for His feet.* [14]By one sacrifice He forever made perfect those who are made holy.

[15]The Holy Spirit assures us of this. First He says: [16]*"This is the covenant I will make with them after those days," says the Lord: "I will put My laws on their hearts and write them on their minds."* [17]Then He adds: *"I will not remember their sins and their wrongs anymore."* [18]Now, where sins are forgiven, there is no more sacrificing for sin.

[19]Fellow Christians, with the blood of Jesus we can now boldly go into the holy place [20]by the new, living way He opened for us through the curtain, the way of His body, [21]and we have a *great Priest* in charge *of God's house.* [22]Let us then come near God, sincere in our hearts and convinced in our faith, because our hearts were *sprinkled to take away our guilty feelings,* and our bodies were washed *with clean water.* [23]Let us cling to the confession of our hope and not waver in it. He Who made the promise is faithful.

Give Up Sin

[24]And let us consider how we can stimulate one another to love and to do good works. [25]Let us not stay away from our worship services, as some are regularly doing, but let us encourage one another, all the more because you see the day coming nearer.

[26]If we willfully go on sinning after we have learned the truth, there is no more sacrifice for our sins, [27]only a terrible waiting for judgment and *a fire that will* be eager to *devour the enemies.* [28]Anyone who violates the Law of Moses *dies* without pity *on the testimony of two or three witnesses.* [29]How much worse a punishment do you think he will deserve who tramples on God's Son, treats as an unholy thing *the blood of the testament* that made him holy, and insults the Spirit of grace? [30]We know Him Who said: *"I have the right to punish: I will* pay *back,"* and again: *"The Lord will judge His people."* [31]It is terrifying to fall into the hands of the living God.

Endure

[32]Remember those early days, how after you received the light you patiently endured a hard and painful struggle. [33]Mocked and mistreated, you were made a public show, or you shared the life of those who were treated that way. [34]You sympathized with the prisoners, and when you were robbed of your property, you took it cheerfully because you knew you have something better that is permanent.

12-13 Ps 110:1   *16-17 Jer 31:33-34*   *21 Zech 6:11-13*   *22 Ezek 36:25*
        27 Is 26:11   *28 Deut 17:6; 19:15*   *29 Ex 24:8*
    30 Deut 32:35-36; Ps 135:14

³⁵Then don't lose your courage. There's a great reward for it. ³⁶You need endurance to do what God wants and so to receive what He promised. ³⁷*"Soon, very soon, He Who is coming will come and will not delay,* ³⁸*and by faith My righteous one will live. If he shrinks back, I will not be pleased with him."* ³⁹Now, we're not those who *shrink back* and so are lost, but we have *faith* and so are saved.

Faith

11 Faith is being sure of the things we hope for, being convinced of the things we can't see. ²The men of long ago were approved of in this faith.

³By faith we know God made the world by His Word so that what we see wasn't made of what can be seen. ⁴By faith *Abel brought* to God a better sacrifice than Cain and was declared to be righteous, when *God* approved *his offerings*. He died, but by his faith he is still speaking to us.

⁵By faith *Enoch* was taken away without dying *and couldn't be found, because God had taken him.* We are assured that *God was pleased with him* before he was taken. ⁶But it is impossible to *please* God without faith. If you come to God, you must believe He exists and will always reward those who search for Him.

⁷By faith Noah, when he was warned about the things no one could foresee, respected God and built an ark to save his family, and by such a faith he condemned the world and became an heir of the righteousness that comes by faith.

⁸By faith *Abraham* obeyed when he was called to *leave* home and go to a place he would receive as an inheritance, and he *left* without knowing where he was going. ⁹By faith he *lived as a stranger* in the promised land, as though it belonged to someone else, and lived in tents with Isaac and *Jacob*, who had the same promise he had. ¹⁰He was looking for the city with foundations, the one God built and made. ¹¹By faith Sarah, even though she was too old, got the strength to have a child because she believed she could trust Him Who had promised. ¹²And so, although he had become physically unable to have a child, one man had *many* descendants, *like the stars in the sky and the sand on the seashore that no one can count.*

¹³All these died in faith without having received what was promised. But they saw it far ahead and welcomed it, and they confessed they were *strangers and travelers* on earth. ¹⁴Those who talk that way show they're looking for a country of their own. ¹⁵If their hearts had been in the country they left, they could have found an opportunity to go back. ¹⁶Instead, they were longing for a better country — I mean heaven. That is why God is not ashamed to be called their God, because He has prepared a city for them.

---

37 Is 26:20   *37-39* Hab 2:3-4 *4* Gen 4:4   *5-6* Gen 5:22,24
8-9 Gen 12:1,4; 23:4; 47:9   *12* Gen 15:5; 22:17; 26:4; 32:12
13 Gen 12:1,4; 23:4; 47:9   *17* Gen 22:1-2,10,12

[17]By faith *Abraham*, when he was *tested, offered Isaac*. Yes, this man, who received the promises [18]and was told: *"Isaac's children will be called your descendants,"* was sacrificing *his only son*, [19]thinking, "God can even raise him from the dead." And so, figuratively speaking, he did.

[20]By faith Isaac blessed Jacob and Esau in regard to their future. [21]By faith a dying Jacob blessed each of Joseph's sons and *worshiped leaning on the top of his staff.* [22]By faith Joseph, when his end was near, remembered how the Israelites would leave Egypt and gave directions for his burial.

[23]By faith, when Moses was born, his parents *hid him three months* because *they saw he was a fine baby* and they were not afraid of the king's order. [24]By faith *Moses, when he grew up,* refused to be called a son of Pharaoh's daughter [25]and preferred being mistreated with God's people to enjoying the short-lived pleasures of sin. [26]He considered the *abuse suffered for Christ* greater riches than the treasures of Egypt, because he was looking ahead to the reward.

[27]By faith he left Egypt without fearing the king's anger. He persisted as one who was constantly seeing Him Who can't be seen. [28]By faith he celebrated the *Passover* and put the *blood* on the doorposts to keep him who *destroyed* the firstborn from touching his people. [29]By faith they went through the Red Sea as if it were dry land. The Egyptians tried it, too, but were drowned.

[30]By faith *the walls* of Jericho *fell* when the people marched around them seven days. [31]By faith the prostitute Rahab welcomed the spies as friends and didn't perish with her disobedient people.

[32]And what more should I say? There will not be time enough for me to tell about Gideon, Barak, Samson, Jephthah, David, Samuel, and the prophets, [33]who by faith conquered kingdoms, did righteous works, received what was promised, *shut the mouths of lions,* [34]put out raging fires, escaped death by the sword, found strength when weak, proved to be mighty in battle, put foreign armies to flight. [35]Women received their dead back alive. Some were tortured; they refused to be freed, in order to rise to a better life.

[36]Others suffered mocking and scourging and were even put in chains and in prison. [37]They were stoned, tempted, sawed in half, murdered with a sword. They went around in sheepskins and goatskins, needy, oppressed, mistreated. [38]The world wasn't worthy of them as they wandered around in deserts and in the hills, in caves and holes in the ground.

[39]By faith all these won approval but didn't receive what was promised. [40]God provided something better for us in order to have them reach their goal with us.

---

18 *Gen 21:12; 22:12*   21 *Gen 47:31*   23 *Ex 2:2*   24 *Ex 2:11*
26 *Ps 69:9; 89:50-51*   28 *Ex 12:11-13; 21-27*   30 *Josh 6:20*
33 *Dan 6:20,22*

Run the Race

12 Now then, with all these witnesses around us like a cloud, let us get rid of every burden and the sin we easily fall into and with endurance run the race laid out before us, [2]looking to Jesus, Who gives us our faith from start to finish. For the joy that was set before Him He endured the cross, thinking nothing of its shame, and *sat down at the right hand* of God's throne.

[3]Think of how sinners opposed Him and He endured it. It will help you not to get tired and give up. [4]In your struggle against sin you haven't yet resisted to the point where your blood has flowed. [5]And you have forgotten the encouragement spoken to you as sons:

My son, don't think lightly of the Lord's training
or give up when He corrects you.
[6]*The Lord corrects whom He loves,*
and He whips everyone He accepts as His son.

[7]What you endure is to *correct* you. God is treating you *as* His *sons.* Is there a *son* whom his father doesn't *correct*? [8]All sons are corrected; if you're not *corrected*, you're *not sons* but are illegitimate. [9]Furthermore, our natural fathers used to correct us, and we respected them. Shouldn't we much more be willing to put ourselves under the authority of the Father of spirits and live? [10]They corrected us for a short time as it seemed best to them. But He corrects us for our good, to have us share His holiness. [11]While we're being corrected, it always seems unpleasant and painful. But after we've been trained, correction gives us the peaceful fruit of righteousness.

[12]And so, *if your hands are letting go, take a firm hold; if you feel weak in your knees, stand firm*; [13]and *make straight paths for your feet.* Do this so that the crippled limb will not be dislocated but will be made well.

[14]*Try hard to live in peace* with everyone and to be holy. Without holiness no one will see the Lord. [15]See to it that no one loses God's grace, *that no root with bitter fruit grows up to trouble you* and so defiles many of you, [16]that no one lives in sexual sin or is unholy like *Esau,* who for one meal *sold his rights as the firstborn.* [17]You know that later, when he wanted to inherit the blessing, he was rejected. He had no chance to change his mind although he begged for it with tears.

You Have Come to God

[18]*You didn't come to anything you could touch*, to *a blazing fire, darkness, gloom, a storm*, [19]*the blast of a trumpet*, or the speaking of *a voice.* Those who heard that begged to be told no more, [20]because they couldn't endure the order that was given: *"Even an animal, if it touches the mountain, must be stoned."* [21]And the sight was so terrible Moses said, *"I am terrified and trembling."*

---

2 Ps 110:1   **5-8** Prov 3:11-12; Job 5:17   **12** Is 35:3   **13** Prov 4:26
14 Ps 34:14   **15** Deut 29:18   **16** Gen 25:33-34
18-20 Ex 19:12-13,16; 20:18; Deut 4:11   **21** Deut 9:19

²²No, you have come to Mount Zion, the city of the living God, the heavenly Jerusalem. Here are tens of thousands of angels, ²³the whole festival gathering and church of God's firstborn people with their names written in heaven. Here is the judge and God of all. Here are the spirits of the righteous who have been perfected. ²⁴And here is Jesus, the Mediator of a new testament, and the sprinkled blood that has better things to tell than Abel.

²⁵See that you don't refuse to listen to Him Who is speaking. If the others didn't escape when they refused to listen to Him warning them on earth, much less will we if we turn away from Him Who warns us from heaven. ²⁶Then His voice shook the earth. But now He has promised: *"Once more I will shake* not only the *earth* but also *heaven."* ²⁷The words *"once more"* show clearly He will take away what is *shaken*, seeing He made it, leaving what isn't *shaken as* permanent. ²⁸Since we have received *a kingdom that can't be shaken*, let us thank God and so worship in a way that pleases Him, with fear and awe, ²⁹because our *God is a consuming fire.*

Live as Christians

13 Christians, keep on loving one another. ²Don't neglect to welcome guests. This is how some without knowing it had angels as their guests. ³Remember those in prison as if you were in chains with them, and those who are mistreated as if you could feel it.

⁴Everyone should think highly of marriage and keep married life pure, because God will judge those who sin sexually whether single or married.

⁵Don't be greedy. Be satisfied with what you have, because He said: *"I will never leave you or desert you."* ⁶And so we have the courage to say: *"The Lord is my Help. I will not be afraid. What can man do to me?"*

Follow Your Teachers

⁷Remember your leaders who told you God's Word. Consider how their lives ended, and imitate their faith.

⁸Jesus Christ is the same yesterday, today, and forever.

⁹Don't get carried away with different kinds of strange teachings. It is good to be inwardly strengthened by God's grace, not by foods, which haven't helped those who make so much of them in their lives. ¹⁰We have an altar, and those who still worship at the Jewish tabernacle have no right to eat from this altar.

¹¹The high priest *brings the blood* of animals *into the holy place* for sin, but the bodies of those animals are *burned outside the camp.* ¹²And so Jesus suffered outside the gate to make the people holy by His own blood. ¹³Then let us go out to join Him *outside the camp* and bear the abuse He suffered. ¹⁴You see, we don't have a permanent city here but look for the one that's

---

26-28 Hag 2:6-7,21   **29** Deut 4:24; 9:3   **5** Deut 31:6,8; Josh 1:5; I Chr 28:20
6 Ps 56:4,11; 118:6-7   **11-13** Ex 29:14; Lev 4:12,21; 8:17; 9:11; 16:27; Num 19:3,5

coming. ¹⁵Through Jesus let us always *bring to God a sacrifice of praise*, that is, *the fruit of our lips*, praising His name. ¹⁶And don't forget to do good and to share; such sacrifices please God.

¹⁷Your leaders, who have to give an account, watch over you. Obey them and submit to them so that they may be happy in their work and not have to grieve, because that isn't good for you.

¹⁸Pray for us as we're sure we have a good conscience and want to live right in every way. ¹⁹I urge you the more earnestly to do this that I may be brought back to you sooner.

Farewell

²⁰The God of peace *brought back* from the dead our Lord Jesus, Who by His *blood made an everlasting testament* to become the great *Shepherd of the sheep* — ²¹may He give you every good thing you need, to do what He wants you to do, working in us through Jesus Christ what pleases Him. To Him be glory forever. Amen.

²²I urge you, fellow Christians, listen patiently to what I say to encourage you, because I've written you a short letter. ²³You should know that Timothy, our fellow Christian, is free again. If he comes here soon, he and I will see you.

²⁴Greet all your leaders and all the holy people. Those who are from Italy greet you.

²⁵Grace be with all of you.

---

20 Is 55:3; 63:11-12; Jer 32:40; 50:5; Ezek 16:60; 37:26; Zech 9:11
15 Ps 50:14,23; Hos 14:2

THE LETTER OF
JAMES

1 JAMES, SERVANT OF GOD and the Lord Jesus Christ, to the twelve tribes living scattered in the world: Greetings.

Cheer Up

[2]When you're tested in different ways, my fellow Christians, consider it a pure joy [3]because you know the testing of your faith produces endurance. [4]Then let endurance finish its work so that you may be perfect and complete, lacking nothing.

[5]If you lack *wisdom*, ask *God*, Who *gives* to everyone with an open hand and doesn't scold, and He will give it to you. [6]You should ask with faith and have no doubts. Anyone who doubts is like a wave of the sea, driven and tossed by the wind. [7]Such a man should not expect to get anything from the Lord. [8]He's indecisive — wavering in everything he does.

[9]A lowly Christian should be proud of his high position, [10]and a rich man of his lowliness, because he will pass away *like a flower in the grass.* [11]The sun comes up with a burning heat and *dries up the grass; the flower in it drops off,* and its beauty is gone. That's how the rich man will fade away in what he undertakes.

Our Desires Tempt Us

[12]*Blessed is* the man *who endures patiently* when he is tested. When he passes the test, *he will receive the crown of life* God promised those who love Him. [13]When you're tempted, don't say, "God is tempting me." God can't be tempted to do wrong, and He doesn't tempt anyone. [14]Everyone's own desire tempts him, draws him away, and tries to trap him. [15]When desire conceives, it gives birth to sin, and when sin grows up, it gives birth to death.

God's Children

[16]Don't make a mistake, my dear Christian friends. [17]Every good and perfect gift comes down from above, from the Father of lights, with Whom there is no variation or shifting shadow.

[18]As He wanted it, He gave birth to us by the Word of truth so we would be the first and best of His creatures.

---

5 Prov 2:6   **10-11 Is 40:6-8**   *12 Dan 12:12; Zech 6:14*

¹⁹My dear fellow Christians, you should know this. Everyone should be quick to listen, slow to talk, *slow to get angry*. ²⁰An angry man doesn't do what's right before God. ²¹So get rid of everything filthy and every breaking out of wickedness, and with a gentle spirit welcome the Word that's planted in you and can save your souls.

²²Always do what the Word says; don't merely listen to it and so deceive yourselves. ²³If anyone listens to the Word but doesn't do what it says, he's like a man who in a mirror sees the face he was born with. ²⁴He looks at himself, goes away, and immediately forgets what he looked like. ²⁵But if you look into God's perfect Word, which makes us free, and continue to do so — if you don't merely listen and forget but do what it says — you'll be happy as you do it. ²⁶Someone may think he's religious, but if he doesn't control his tongue, he's deceiving himself — his religion is worthless. ²⁷Your way of worshiping is pure and stainless before God the Father if you look after orphans and widows in their troubles and keep yourself unspotted by the world.

Don't Prefer the Rich

2 My fellow Christians, believing as you do in Jesus Christ, our Lord of glory, don't favor one person over another. ²If a man wearing gold rings and fine clothes comes into your meeting and a poor man in dirty clothes also comes in, ³and you give special attention to the one wearing fine clothes and say, "Please take this seat," but you say to the poor man, "Stand there," or "Sit here by my footstool," ⁴haven't you contradicted yourselves and become men who are wrong in their judgment? ⁵Listen, my dear fellow Christians, didn't God choose those who are poor in the world to be rich in faith and inherit the kingdom He promised those who love Him? ⁶But you have insulted the poor man. Don't the rich oppress you and drag you into court? ⁷Don't they slander the beautiful name by which you were called the Lord's own? ⁸If you really do everything the royal law demands, as it is written: "*Love your neighbor as yourself*," you're doing right. ⁹But if you favor one over another, you're sinning, and the Law convicts you of sin.

Keep the Whole Law

¹⁰If you keep the whole Law but fail in one point, you're guilty of breaking all of it. ¹¹The One who said: "*Do not commit adultery*," also said: "*Do not murder*." If you don't *commit adultery* but you *murder*, you're a lawbreaker. ¹²Talk and act as people who are going to be judged by the Law that brings liberty. ¹³Anyone who shows no mercy will be judged without mercy. Mercy triumphs over judgment.

---

19 Prov 14:29   8 Lev 19:18   11 Ex 20:13-14; Deut 5:17-18

Faith Is Active

[14]What good does it do, my fellow Christians, if you say you have faith but don't have any works? Can such a faith save you? [15]If a Christian man or woman doesn't have clothes or daily food [16]and one of you tells them, "Go in peace, keep warm, and eat heartily," but you don't give them what the body needs, what good does it do? [17]So faith by itself, if it doesn't have any works, is dead.

[18]But someone will say, "You have faith, and I have works." Prove to me you have faith without any works, and by my works I'll prove to you I have faith. [19]You believe there is *one God*. That's fine! The demons believe it, too — and shudder.

[20]Do you want proof, you foolish fellow, that faith without works is dead. [21]Wasn't our father *Abraham* considered justified[a] in what he did when he *offered his son Isaac on the altar*? [22]You see, his faith was active with works and by works reached its goal. [23]And what is written came true: *"Abraham believed God and so was counted righteous"* and was called *God's friend.* [24]You see, a person is considered righteous by what he does and not by faith alone. [25]The same is true of the prostitute Rahab. Was she not considered righteous because of what she did when she welcomed the messengers and sent them away on a different road? [26]Just as the body without the spirit is dead, so faith without works is dead.

Control Your Tongue

3 Not many of you should become teachers, my fellow Christians, because you know we who teach will be judged more severely.

[2]All of us sin much. If anyone doesn't sin in what he says, he's a perfect man who can control his whole body. [3]If we put bits into the mouths of horses to make them obey us, we direct their whole bodies. [4]Look at the ships — so big and driven by strong winds; but a very small rudder steers a ship anywhere the pilot wants it to go. [5]So the tongue is a small organ but can boast of big things.

You know how just a spark will set a large forest on fire. [6]The tongue is a fire, a world of wrong! Set among the parts of our body, the tongue soils the whole body and enflames the course of life as it gets its fire from hell. [7]A human being can tame and has tamed all kinds of animals, birds, reptiles, and creatures in the sea. [8]But no one can tame the tongue — a restless evil, full of deadly poison.

[9]We praise the Lord and Father with our tongue and with it curse other people, who once were *made like God.* [10]Praise and cursing come from the same mouth. We mustn't do that, my fellow Christians. [11]Does a spring from the same opening pour fresh and bitter water? [12]My fellow Christians,

---

19 Deut 6:4; Zech 14:9; Mal 2:10   *21* Gen 22:2,9   *23* Gen 15:6; Is 41:8; II Chr 20:7
9 Gen 1:26-27; 5:1

a - 21   See note on Rom 3:20

can a fig tree produce olives, or a grapevine figs? Neither can a salt spring produce fresh water.

Wisdom from Above

[13]Who among you is wise and intelligent? In a gentle spirit of wisdom show by a noble life what you can do. [14]But if you feel a bitter jealousy and a selfish ambition in your hearts, don't brag and lie against the truth. [15]Such wisdom doesn't come from above, but from this earth, from this life, and from the devil. [16]Where there is such jealousy and selfishness, there is confusion and every kind of evil.

[17]The wisdom that comes from above is first of all pure, then peaceful, gentle, willing to obey, full of mercy and good works, impartial, and without hypocrisy. [18]And the fruit of righteousness is sown in peace by those who make peace.

Don't Love the World

4 Why is there fighting and quarreling among you? Isn't it because your cravings for pleasure are fighting in your bodies? [2]You want something but don't get it, and so you murder. And you try to get something, but you can't lay your hands on it, and so you quarrel and fight. You don't get things, because you don't ask for them. [3]Or you ask for something but don't get it because you want it for a wrong purpose — to spend it on your pleasures.

[4]Adulterous people, don't you know that to love the world is to hate God? If you want to be a friend of the world, you make yourself an enemy of God. [5]Or do you think the statement means nothing: "The Spirit Whom He caused to live in us loves us in a jealous way?"

[6]But He *gives* a greater *blessing*. And so it says: "*God opposes the proud but is gracious to the humble.*" [7]Then submit to God. Resist the devil and he will run away from you. [8]Come close to God, and He will come close to you. Wash your hands, you sinners, and purify your hearts, you doubters. [9]Be miserable, mourn, and cry. Turn your laughter into mourning and your joy into gloom. [10]Humble yourselves before the Lord, and He will lift you up.

Don't Talk Against One Another

[11]Stop talking against one another, my fellow Christians. Anyone who talks against his fellow Christian or condemns him talks against the Law and condemns the Law. If you condemn the Law, you're not doing what it says, but you're being its judge. [12]There's only one Lawgiver and Judge. He can save and destroy. And who are you to judge your neighbor?

---

6 Prov 3:34

"If the Lord Is Willing"

[13]Come now, you who say, "Today or tomorrow we'll go into this city, stay there a year, do business, and make money." [14]You *don't* know about *tomorrow*. What is your life? You're a mist, seen for a little while, then vanishing. [15]You should say: "If the Lord is willing, we'll live and do this or that." [16]But instead you *brag and boast*. All such boasting is wrong.

[17]If you know what's right but don't do it, you're sinning.

Woe to the Rich

5 Come now, you rich people, cry and howl over the miseries that are coming to you. [2]Your riches are rotten, your clothes are eaten by moths, [3]your gold and silver are tarnished, and their tarnish will be evidence against you and will *eat* your flesh like *fire*. You have *piled up treasures* in these last days. [4]But now *the wages you never paid the men* who reaped your fields *cry out*. And the *groans* of those who cut the grain *have come to the ears of the Lord of armies*. [5]You have lived here on earth in luxuries and pleasures. You have fattened yourselves for *the day of slaughter*. [6]You have condemned and *murdered the righteous man* — he doesn't resist you.

Be Patient

[7]Be patient, fellow Christians, until the Lord comes. See how the farmer looks for the precious crop on the ground and waits patiently for it to get *the fall and the spring rains*. [8]You, too, be patient, and keep your courage, because the Lord will soon be here. [9]Don't blame your troubles on one another, fellow Christians, or you will be judged. You know, the Judge is standing at the door. [10]As an example of patiently suffering wrong, fellow Christians, take the prophets who spoke in the Lord's name. [11]Remember, *we call those happy who endured*. You heard how Job endured, and you saw how the Lord finally treated him because *the Lord is tenderhearted and merciful*.

Don't Swear

[12]Above all things, my fellow Christians, don't swear by heaven or by the earth or any other oath, but let your "yes" be just "yes" and your "no" be "no", so that you will not be condemned.

The Power of Prayer

[13]Is anyone of you suffering? Pray! Are you happy? Sing a song of

---

13-16 *Prov 27:1*   **3** *Ps 21:9; Prov 16:27*
4 *Lev 19:13; Mal 3:5; Gen 4:10; Ex 2:23; 3:9; Ps 18:6; 2 Sam 22:7; Is 5:9*
5 *Jer 12:3*   **6** *Prov 6:17*   **7** *Deut 11:14; Jer 5:24; Joel 2:23*
11 *Dan 12:12; Ex 34:6; Ps 86:15; 103:8; 111:4; 112:4; 145:8; Joel 2:13; Jon 4:3; Neh 9:17,31; 2 Chr 30:9*

praise! ¹⁴Is anyone among you sick? Let him call for the elders of the church and let them pray, anointing him with olive oil in the name of the Lord. ¹⁵And the prayer offered in faith will restore the sick person, and the Lord will heal him. And if he has committed sins, he will be forgiven. ¹⁶Confess your sins to one another, and pray for one another to be healed.

The earnest prayer of a righteous person accomplishes much. ¹⁷Elijah was a man just like us, and he prayed earnestly that there should be no rain, and no rain fell on the ground for three years and six months. ¹⁸Then he prayed again, and heaven sent rain, and the ground produced its crops.

Bring Back the Lost

¹⁹My fellow Christians, if one of you wanders away from the truth and someone brings him back, ²⁰you should know that whoever brings a sinner back from his wrong way will save his soul from death and *cover many sins*.

THE FIRST LETTER OF
PETER

1 PETER, APOSTLE OF JESUS CHRIST, to the chosen people living scattered as strangers in Pontus, Galatia, Cappadocia, the province of Asia, and Bithynia, [2]chosen long ago by God the Father to be made holy by the Spirit, to obey Jesus Christ and be *sprinkled with* His *blood*: God give *you more and more* grace and *peace*!

Christ Saves You

[3]Let us praise the God and Father of our Lord Jesus Christ, Who by raising Jesus Christ from the dead has in His great mercy given us a new birth so that we have a living hope [4]for an inheritance that isn't destroyed or defiled and never fades away, as it is kept for you in heaven. [5]And through faith you are protected by God's power until you come to the salvation that is waiting to be revealed at the end of time. [6]This delights you, although now for a little while you may have had to suffer various trials. [7]Gold is tested by fire, and your faith, when it is tested, should be found to be much more precious than gold, which perishes. This is how you will have praise and glory and honor when Jesus Christ appears again.

[8]You never saw Him, but you love Him. You don't see Him now, but you believe in Him. And a joy, unspeakable and wonderful, fills you with delight [9]as you receive by faith what you're looking for — your salvation.

[10]The prophets, who long ago wrote about what God's grace would do for you, made a thorough search to learn all about this salvation. [11]They tried to find out Whom and what time the Spirit of Christ in them was pointing out when He exactly predicted the sufferings of Christ and the glories that would follow. [12]God told them they were not serving themselves but you in these things. And now the Holy Spirit, sent from heaven, had men, telling you the good news, announcing to you these things the angels long to look into.

Be Holy

[13]Now, then, get mentally ready for action, keep a clear head, and be perfectly sure of what God's grace will give you when Jesus Christ appears. [14]Being children who know how to obey, don't live according to your lusts as you once did when you didn't know any better. [15]But be holy in all your

---

2 Ex 24:6,8; Lev 16:14-15; Dan 4:1; 6:25

ways, like the Holy One who called you. [16]It is written: *"Be holy, because I am holy."* [17]And if you *call on* Him as your *Father*, Who judges each one according to what he has done, without favoring one over another, live reverently as long as you are strangers here, [18]knowing that *you* were *freed* from the worthless life you inherited from your fathers, *not by a payment of silver or gold*, which perish, [19]but by the precious blood of Christ, the Lamb without a fault or a spot. [20]Appointed before the world was made, He was revealed in the last period of time to help you. [21]And through Him you believe in God, Who raised Him from the dead and gave Him glory; and so your faith and hope rest in God.

The Living Word

[22]Now that by obeying the truth you purified yourselves to love sincerely as brothers, love one another with a pure heart and intensely. [23]You were born again, not by a seed that perishes but by one that cannot perish, *God's ever-living* Word.

> [24]*All people are like grass,*
> *and all their glory like the flower in the grass.*
> *The grass withers,*
> *and the flower drops off,*
> [25] *but the Lord's Word lives forever.*

This *Word* is the *good news* you have been *told.*

2 Then get rid of every kind of wickedness and deceit, hypocrisy, jealousy, and every kind of slander, [2]and like newborn babies, thirst for the pure milk of the Word so that you'll grow and finally be saved. [3]Surely *you have tasted that the Lord is good.*

The Living Stone

[4]Come to Him. He is the living *Stone* Whom men rejected but God *selected* as *precious.* [5]You also are being built as living stones into a spiritual temple, to be holy priests who bring spiritual sacrifices that God gladly accepts through Jesus Christ.

[6]The Bible says: *"I am laying in Zion a Cornerstone, chosen and precious, and if you believe in Him, you'll never be disappointed."* [7]He is *precious* to you who believe, but to those who do not believe *"He is the Stone which, rejected by the builders, has become the Cornerstone, [8]the Stone they stumble over and the Rock they fall over."* When they disobey the Word, they stumble over it; that's the end appointed for them.

---

16 *Lev 11:44-45; 19:2; 20:7,26*   **17** *Ps 89:26*   **18** *Is 52:3*
23 *Dan 6:26; 12:7*   **24-25** *Is 40:6-9* **3** *Ps 34:8*   **4** *Is 28:16*
6-7 *Is 28:16* **7** *Ps 118:22* **8** *Is 8:14*

God's People

[9]But you are *a chosen people, priests of the King, a holy nation, a people saved to be His own and to tell of the wonderful deeds* of Him Who called you out of darkness into His marvelous light. [10]Once you were *not a people*, but now you are *God's people*. Once you had *received no mercy*, but now you have *received mercy*.

[11]Dear friends, I urge you, as *guests and strangers* in this world: Stay away from the desires of your body, because its appetites fight against the soul. [12]Live a noble life among the people of the world, so that instead of accusing you of doing wrong, they may see the good you do and glorify God *when He visits them*.

Submit to Authorities

[13]Submit to every human authority to please the Lord: to the emperor as one who is over you, [14]or to governors as men whom he sent to punish those who do wrong and to praise those who do right. [15]God wants you to silence ignorant and foolish people by doing right. [16]Act as free men, and don't use your freedom as an excuse to do wrong, but be God's slaves. [17]Honor everyone. Love your fellow Christians. *Fear God.* Honor the *emperor*.

[18]Servants, submit to your masters, showing every respect, not only when they're good and kind but also when they're unfair.

Suffer Patiently

[19]It is a fine thing if, moved by your conscience to please God, you suffer patiently when wronged. [20]What credit is it to you if you sin and patiently take a beating for it? But if you suffer for doing good and take it patiently, God is pleased with you.

[21]This is what you were called for, seeing that Christ also suffered for you and left you an example for you to follow in His steps. [22]He *never sinned nor was found to be deceiving when He spoke.* [23]When others abused Him, He didn't abuse them; when He suffered, He didn't threaten but left it in the hands of Him Who judges fairly. [24]*He carried our sins* in His body to the cross so that we'll die to sin and live for righteousness. *His wounds have healed you.* [25]You were *like lost sheep*, but now you've come back to the Shepherd Who takes care of you.

---

9 *Ex 19:5-6; Is 42:12; 43:20-21; 61:6; 62:12; Deut 4:20; 7:6; 14:2; 29:13*
10 *Hos 1:6,8-10; 2:1,23*   **11** *Gen 23:4; Lev 25:23; Ps 39:12; I Chr 29:15*
12 *Is 10:3*   **17** *Prov 3:7; 24:21*   **22** *Ps 32:2; Is 53:9; Zeph 3:13*
24 *Is 53:4,12*   **24-25** *Is 53:5-6; Ezek 34:5*

Wives and Husbands

3 Similarly, you married women, submit to your husbands. Then even if some of them refuse to listen to the Word, you will win them, without talking about it, by the way you live as wives, [2]when they see how you fear God and are pure in your lives.

[3]Your beauty should not be anything outward — braiding the hair, putting on gold ornaments and dresses — [4]but the person you are in your heart, with the imperishable quality of a gentle and quiet spirit; this is very precious to God. [5]And this is how the holy women in former times who trusted in God used to make themselves beautiful: They submitted to their husbands, [6]like *Sarah*, who obeyed Abraham and *called* him *"lord."* You are her daughters if you do good and *let nothing terrify you.*

[7]In the same way, you husbands, live with your wives with understanding; they are weaker than you are. Honor them as sharing the gift of life with you — so that nothing will interfere with your prayers.

When You Are Wronged

[8]Finally, all of you, live in harmony, be sympathetic, love your fellow Christians, be tenderhearted and humble. [9]*Don't pay back evil for evil*, insult for insult, but bless others instead, knowing that you were called for this, to inherit a blessing.

> [10]*If you want to love life*
> *and enjoy happy days,*
> *stop speaking evil*
> *or saying anything to deceive.*
> [11]*Turn away from wrong and do good.*
> *Be eager for peace and go after it.*
> [12]*The Lord watches the righteous and hears their prayer,*
> *but the Lord is against those who do wrong.*

[13]Who will harm you if you're eager to do good? [14]But even if you suffer because you're righteous, you are happy. *Never let others terrify or trouble you.* [15]*But give* your hearts *completely to* Christ *as Lord.* And always be ready to answer anyone who asks you to explain the hope you have, but be gentle and respectful. [16]Keep a good conscience so that those who slander your good life in Christ will feel ashamed of their slander. [17]It is better, if God wants it that way, to suffer for doing right than for doing wrong.

The Righteous One Died

[18]Christ died once for our sins, the Righteous One for the guilty, to bring us to God. He was killed in His body but made alive in His spirit. [19]In this spirit He also went and preached to the spirits kept in prison, [20]who disobeyed long ago in the days of Noah when God waited patiently while the

6 Gen 18:12; Prov 3:25   *9 Prov 20:22; 24:29*   *10-12 Ps 34:12-16*
14-15 Is 8:12-13

ark was being built, in which a few, that is, eight persons, were saved by water. [21]In the same way also, baptism now saves us, not by washing dirt from the body, but by guaranteeing us a good conscience before God by the resurrection of Jesus Christ, [22]Who has gone to heaven and is *at the right of God*, where angels, rulers, and powers have been put under Him.

You Have Given Up Sin

4 Now since Christ has suffered for us in His body, you, too, arm yourselves with the same way of thinking, that if you have suffered in your body, you have given up sin [2]and don't follow human desires anymore but do what God wants as long as you live in this world. [3]You spent enough time in the past doing what the world likes to do, when you lived in unbridled immorality, lusts, drunkenness, wild celebrations, drinking parties, and the detestable worship of idols. [4]They're surprised now that you don't plunge into the same flood of wild living with them, and they slander you. [5]They will have to give an account to Him Who is ready to judge the living and the dead. [6]The dead also once heard the good news, so that they will be judged as human beings in their earthly life, but then will live like God in their spiritual life.

Love Fervently

[7]The end of everything is near. So be sensible and keep your heads clear for your prayers. [8]Above all, continue to love one another fervently, because *love covers many sins.* [9]Welcome one another as guests without grumbling. [10]Serve one another, each with the gift he received, as good managers of the various gifts of God. [11]If you speak, say what God says. If you serve, do it with the strength God gives you so that in every way you glorify God through Jesus Christ. His is the glory and the power forever! Amen.

You Share Christ's Sufferings

[12]Dear friends, don't be surprised that you're being tested by a fiery trial as though something strange were happening to you. [13]But as you share Christ's sufferings, be happy so that you will also be full of joy when His glory will be revealed. [14]If you're insulted now for the name of Christ, you're happy because the Spirit of glory and power, *the Spirit of God, is resting* on you.

[15]Of course, none of you should suffer as a murderer, a thief, a criminal, or one who meddles in the affairs of others. [16]But if you suffer for being a Christian, don't feel ashamed, but praise God with that name. [17]It is time for the judgment *to start in God's temple.* But if it is starting with us, how will it end for those who refuse to listen to God's good news?

[18]*If it is hard for a righteous person to be saved,*

---

22 *Ps 110:1*   **8** *Prov 10:12*   **14** *Is 11:2*   **17** *Ezek 9:6*   **18** *Prov 11:31*

what will happen to the ungodly and the sinner?
[19]So you, too, who suffer as God wants you to suffer, entrust yourselves to your faithful Creator and keep on doing good.

To the Pastors

5 I appeal to you spiritual leaders, I who also am a spiritual leader. I saw Christ suffer, and I share in the glory that is to be revealed. [2]Be shepherds of God's flock that is with you, watching over it, not because you must but willingly, as God would have you do it; [3]not greedily but eagerly; not lording it over the people entrusted to you but being examples to the flock. [4]And when the Head Shepherd appears, you will receive the unfading garland of glory.

Humble Yourselves

[5]In a similar way, you young people, submit to those who are older.
All of you, be clothed with humility before one another because *God opposes the proud but is gracious to the humble.* [6]Humble yourselves, then, under God's mighty hand so that He may honor you at the right time.

Watch

[7]*Turn all your worry over to Him* because *He* cares for *you.* [8]Keep a clear head and watch! Your enemy, the devil, is prowling around like a roaring lion, looking for someone to devour. [9]Be strong in your faith and resist him, knowing that your fellow Christians in the world are going through the same kind of suffering. [10]After you have suffered a little while, the God of all grace, Who called you in Christ Jesus to share His everlasting glory, will make you perfect, firm, and strong. [11]He has the power forever. Amen.

Farewell!

[12]With the help of Silvanus, whom I consider a faithful fellow Christian, I'm writing you this short letter to encourage you and testify that this is the true grace of God. Stand firm in it.
[13]Your sister church in Babylon,[a] chosen by God, greets you; and so does Mark, my son. Greet one another with a kiss of love. [14]Peace to all of you who are in Christ!

---

5 *Prov 3:34*   **7** *Ps 55:22*

a - 13   By "Babylon" Peter seems to mean Rome.

THE SECOND LETTER OF
PETER

1 SIMON PETER, SERVANT AND APOSTLE OF JESUS CHRIST, to the people who by the righteousness of our God and Savior Jesus Christ were given a faith as precious as ours: [2]As you know God and our Lord Jesus, *may you enjoy more and more* of His grace and *peace*.

Grow

[3]His divine power has given us everything needed for life and godliness through knowing Him Who called us to His own glory and excellence. [4]Thus He has given us His precious and very great promises, so that after you have escaped the corruption that lust brought into the world, you might by these promises share in the divine nature.

[5]In view of that, try very hard to add to your faith moral excellence, to moral excellence knowledge, [6]to knowledge self-control, to self-control endurance, to endurance godliness, [7]to godliness brotherly kindness, to brotherly kindness love. [8]If you have these and they grow more and more, they keep you from being useless and unproductive in the knowledge of our Lord Jesus Christ. [9]But if anyone doesn't have these, he's blind, shortsighted, and has forgotten that his old sins were washed away.

[10]Be all the more eager, then, fellow Christians, to make sure your calling and choosing are secure. If you do this, you will never fail. [11]Then you will be welcomed richly into the everlasting kingdom of our Lord and Savior Jesus Christ. [12]And so I'm always going to remind you of this, although you already know it   and are well grounded in the truth you have. [13]I think it's right, as long as I'm in the tent of this body, to refresh your memory [14]because I know I'm soon going to lay aside my tent; our Lord Jesus Christ has told me. [15]And I will do my best to see to it that you will have a constant reminder of these things after I'm gone.

God's Word

[16]We didn't follow any clever myths when we told you about the power of our Lord Jesus Christ and His coming. No, with our own eyes we saw His majesty. [17]God the Father gave Him honor and glory when from His wonderful glory He said to Him: *"This is My Son* Whom I love and *with Whom I am delighted."* [18]We heard that voice speak to Him from heaven when we were with Him on the holy mountain.

---

2 Dan 4:1; 6:25   17 Ps 2:7; II Sam 7:14; Is 42:1

[19]And we have, as something more sure, the prophetic Word. Please look to it as to a light shining in a dark place until the day dawns and the *Morning Star rises* in your hearts. [20]Understand this first, that no prophecy of Scripture came as some private explanation. [21]For no prophecy was ever spoken because a man decided to prophecy, but men said what God gave them to say as they were directed by the Holy Spirit.

Men Who Teach Lies

2 But there were also false prophets among the people, just as there will also be false teachers among you. They will secretly bring in their own destructive teachings. Denying the Lord Who has bought them, they quickly destroy themselves. [2]And many will follow their immoral ways and *cause* people *to slander* the way of truth. [3]In their greed they will talk dishonestly to you to make a profit. A just punishment has long been getting ready for them, and destruction has been watching for them.

[4]God didn't spare angels who sinned but put them into the gloomy dungeons of hell to be kept for judgment. [5]And He didn't spare the ancient world but protected Noah, who preached righteousness, and seven others when He brought a flood on a world of ungodly people. [6]And He condemned the towns of Sodom and Gomorrah, destroyed them by burning them to ashes, and made them a warning to those who are going to be ungodly, [7]but He rescued righteous Lot, whom the wicked people vexed with their immoral life. [8](Seeing and hearing the wicked things they did, this righteous man tortured his righteous soul day after day as he lived among them.) [9]The Lord knows how to rescue godly people when they are tested and to keep the wicked under punishment for the day of judgment, [10]especially those who go lusting after sinful flesh to defile themselves and who despise the Lord.

Being bold and headstrong, they do not tremble when they slander beings of glory, [11]whereas angels, although they're greater in strength and power, don't condemn and abuse them before the Lord. [12]But like unthinking animals that are born to be physical, to be caught and killed, they slander what they don't understand, and like animals they will be destroyed — [13]and so lose what they hoped to gain by their wrongdoing.

Their idea of pleasure is to have a wild party in broad daylight. They are spots and blemishes! They enjoy deceiving you while they feast with you. [14]They have eyes only for an adulterous woman and are restlessly looking for sin. They try to trap weak souls.

Their hearts are trained to be greedy. Cursed people! [15]Leaving the right way, they've gone wrong. They've gone the way of Balaam, Beor's son, who loved the reward he would get for doing wrong. [16]But he was shown how wrong he was: A speechless donkey spoke with a human voice and didn't let the prophet go on in his insane way.

---

19 Is 14:12   2 Is 52:5

¹⁷They are dried-up springs, fogs driven by a storm. Dark gloom is reserved for them. ¹⁸By talking high-sounding nonsense and using physical cravings, they set traps baited with lusts for the people who are just escaping from those who live in error. ¹⁹Promising them freedom, they are themselves slaves of corruption — anyone is a slave of that which defeated him.

²⁰If by knowing the Lord and Savior Jesus Christ they escaped the world's corruptions but are again entangled and conquered by them, these people are worse off in the end than they were before. ²¹It would have been better for them never to have known the way of righteousness than to learn it and then turn their backs on the holy commandment that was given them. ²²The proverb is true that tells what happened to them: "A *dog goes back to what he has vomited up*," and "a sow that has washed goes back to roll around in the mud."

The World Will Be Destroyed

3 Dear friends, this is now the second letter I'm writing you. In both of them I stir up your pure minds by reminding you to think of ²the words spoken in the past by the holy prophets and of what the Lord and Savior commanded through your apostles.

³First of all you should know that in the last days mockers, following their own desires, will come mocking: ⁴"He promised to come. What has happened? From the time the fathers fell asleep everything has stayed as it was since the world was first created."

⁵They deliberately forget that long ago God's Word made the sky and formed the earth out of water and with water. ⁶Then this water also flooded the world and destroyed it. ⁷And the same Word has preserved the present heavens and the earth for the fire and keeps them for the day when the ungodly will be judged and destroyed.

⁸Don't forget, dear friends, with the Lord one day is like a thousand years, and *a thousand years are like one day*. ⁹The Lord isn't slow to do what He promised, as some people think. He is patient with you and doesn't want any to perish but wants them all to come to repentance.

¹⁰The Lord's day will come like a thief. On that day the heavens will pass away with a roar, the elements will be destroyed by heat, and the earth and what was done on it will be exposed.

¹¹Since all these things will be destroyed in this way, think how holy and godly you should live, ¹²waiting for and earnestly desiring the coming of God's day that will destroy the heavens with fire and melt the elements with heat. ¹³But according to His promise we expect *new heavens and a new earth* where righteousness lives. ¹⁴With this to look forward to, dear friends, do your best to have Him find you without a spot or blemish and at peace.

¹⁵Believe that our Lord's patience means salvation, just as our dear brother Paul wrote you according to the wisdom given him. ¹⁶He talks about

22 Prov 26:11   8 Ps 90:4   13 Is 65:17; 66:22

this in all his letters. Some things in them are hard to understand, and those who are ignorant and not well grounded twist their meaning as they do the rest of the Bible, and so they destroy themselves.

[17]Now you, dear friends, are warned. Be on your guard, and don't let men without principles lead you away with their error so that you fall from your position. [18]But grow in God's grace and in knowing our Lord and Savior Jesus Christ. To Him be glory now and forever. Amen.

THE FIRST LETTER OF
JOHN

IT WAS THERE FROM THE BEGINNING, we heard It, we saw It with our eyes, we looked at It, and our hands touched It — we're writing about the Word of Life. [2]That Life showed Itself and we saw It, and now we testify and tell you about the everlasting Life that was with the Father and showed Itself to us. [3]We saw and heard It, and we tell you about It so that you, too, will have It in fellowship with us. Our fellowship is with the Father and with His Son Jesus Christ. [4]We're writing this so that our joy may be complete.

[5]This is what we heard Him tell us and we're telling you: God is Light, and there is nothing dark in Him. [6]If we say we share what He has but live in the dark, we're lying and not living the truth.

The Blood of Jesus

[7]If we live in the light as He is in the light, we have it in fellowship with one another, and the blood of Jesus, His Son, washes us clean from every sin. [8]If we say we don't have any sin, we deceive ourselves, and the truth isn't in us. [9]If we confess our sins, He is faithful and just, to forgive our sins and wash us clean from all unrighteousness. [10]If we say we haven't sinned, we make Him a liar, and His Word is not in us.

2 My children, I'm writing this to you to keep you from sinning. If anyone sins, we have One to plead for us with the Father — Jesus Christ, Who is righteous. [2]He is the payment[a] for our sins, and not for ours only but for the whole world.

Live and Love

[3]We're sure we know Him if we keep His commandments. [4]Anyone who says, "I know Him," but doesn't keep His commandments is a liar and doesn't have the truth. [5]But if you keep His word, God's love has really accomplished in you what He wants. That's how we know we're in Him. [6]If you say, "I live in Him," you should live just as He lived.

[7]Dear friends, I'm not writing you a new commandment but an old one that you had from the beginning. This old commandment is the Word you've heard. [8]On the other hand, I'm writing you a new commandment. It's a truth that exists in Him and in you. I know this because the darkness

---

a - 2   Literally: "the atoning sacrifice." By His sacrifice Jesus wipes out our sins and changes God's anger to grace.

is passing away and the genuine light is already shining.

⁹Anyone who says, "I am in the light," but hates his brother is still in the dark. ¹⁰If you love your brother, you live in the light, and there's nothing in you to offend anyone. ¹¹Anyone who hates his brother is in the dark and walks in the dark and doesn't know where he's going, because the darkness has blinded his eyes.

Don't Love the World

¹²I'm writing you, children, because your sins are forgiven for His sake. ¹³I'm writing you, fathers, because you know Him Who has been from the beginning. I'm writing you, young men, because you have conquered the evil one. I'm writing you, children, because you know the Father. ¹⁴I'm writing you, fathers, because you know Him Who has been from the beginning. I'm writing you, young men, because you're strong, God's Word lives in you, and you have conquered the evil one.

¹⁵Don't love the world or anything in the world. If anyone loves the world, he doesn't love the Father, ¹⁶because everything in the world — the lust of the flesh, the lust of the eyes, and the vain display of property — doesn't come from the Father but from the world. ¹⁷And the world with its lust is passing away. But if you do what God wants, you live forever.

¹⁸Children, it is the last hour. You heard an antichrist is coming, and now many antichrists have come. That is how we know it is the last hour. ¹⁹They left us, but they never really belonged to us. If they had been a part of us, they would have stayed with us. But they left, to show that not all belong to us.

You Have the Son

²⁰The Holy One has anointed you, and now all of you know. ²¹I'm writing you, not as though you don't know the truth but because you know it and no lie comes from the truth.

²²Who is such a liar as he who denies Jesus is the Christ? He is the antichrist because he denies the Father and the Son. ²³Anyone who denies the Son doesn't have the Father. If you confess the Son, you also have the Father. ²⁴Keep in you what you have heard from the beginning. If what you have heard from the beginning stays in you, you will live in the Son and in the Father. ²⁵And this is what He promised us — everlasting life!

²⁶I'm writing you about those who are trying to lead you astray. ²⁷He anointed you, and that anointing stays in you, and you don't need anyone to teach you. But as His anointing teaches you everything — and it is true and no lie — as He has taught you, live in Him.

²⁸And now, children, live in Him so that when He appears we may be bold and not shrink from Him in shame when He comes.

God's Children

²⁹If you know He is righteous, you know that everyone who does right is His child.

3 See how the Father has loved us — we are called God's children, and that's what we are. The world doesn't know us, because it didn't know Him. ²Dear friends, we are now God's children, but it hasn't yet been shown what we're going to be. We know that when it will be shown, we'll be like Him because we'll see Him as He is. ³And everyone who trusts Him for this purifies himself as He is pure.

⁴Everyone who sins breaks the Law. Sin is breaking the Law. ⁵And you know He appeared in order to take away our sins. *There is no sin in Him.* ⁶Anyone who stays in Him doesn't sin. Anyone who sins hasn't seen or known Him. ⁷Children, don't let anyone deceive you. Whoever does right is righteous as He is righteous.

⁸Anyone who lives in sin is the devil's child because the devil has been sinning from the beginning. God's Son appeared in order to undo the devil's works. ⁹Everyone who is God's child refuses to sin, because God's new life is in him, and he cannot sin, because he is God's child. ¹⁰You can see who are God's children and who are the devil's children: Anyone who doesn't do right or love his brother isn't God's child.

Love One Another

¹¹This is the message you have heard from the beginning: Love one another. ¹²Don't be like Cain. He was a son of the evil one and murdered his brother. And why did he murder him? Because he did wrong and his brother did right. ¹³Don't be surprised, fellow Christians, if the world hates you.

¹⁴We know we have come from death into life, because we love our fellow Christians. Anyone who doesn't love stays dead. ¹⁵Everyone who hates his brother is a murderer, and you know that no murderer has everlasting life remaining in him.

¹⁶This is how we learned what love is: He gave His life for us. We, too, should give our lives for our fellow Christians. ¹⁷If anyone has this world's goods and sees his fellow Christian is in need but shuts his heart against him, how can he still be loving God? ¹⁸Children, let us not love only in words or in talk, but let us put our love into action and make it real.

¹⁹This is how we'll know we're born of the truth and will reassure ourselves before Him: ²⁰Whenever our conscience condemns us, God is greater than our conscience and knows everything. ²¹Dear friends, if our conscience doesn't condemn us, we can talk boldly to God ²²and get from Him anything we ask because we keep His commandments and do what pleases Him. ²³He orders us to believe in the name of His Son Jesus Christ and to love one another as He has ordered us to do. ²⁴Anyone who keeps His commandments

5 Is 53:9

lives in God and God in him. And this is how we know He lives in us: by the Spirit Whom He has given us.

False Prophets

4 Dear friends, don't believe every spirit, but test the spirits to see if they are from God. Many false prophets have gone out into the world. ²This is how you can recognize God's Spirit: Every spirit who confesses that Jesus Christ has come in the flesh is from God. ³And any spirit who doesn't confess this Jesus isn't from God. This is the spirit of the antichrist which you heard is coming, and here it is already in the world.

⁴Children, you are God's family, and you have won a victory over these men because He Who is in you is greater than he who is in the world. ⁵These men belong to the world. That is why they speak the thoughts of the world, and the world listens to them. ⁶We are God's children. Anyone who knows God listens to us. Anyone who is not God's child will not listen to us. In this way we can tell what is the spirit of truth and what is the spirit of error.

God's Love in Us

⁷Dear friends, let us love one another because love comes from God and everyone who loves is God's child and knows God. ⁸He who doesn't love hasn't learned to know God, because God is Love. ⁹God has shown us His love by sending His only-begotten Son into the world for us to live through Him. ¹⁰This is love, not that we loved God but that He loved us and sent His Son to be the payment for our sins. ¹¹Dear friends, if that's how God loved us, then we should love one another. ¹²No one has ever seen God. If we love one another, God lives in us, and His love has accomplished in us what He wants. ¹³This is how we know we live in Him and He in us: He has given us His Spirit.

¹⁴We have seen and can tell the truth that the Father sent His Son to save the world. ¹⁵If you confess Jesus is God's Son, God lives in you and you in God. ¹⁶And we have come to know and believe the love God has for us. God is Love, and if you live in love, you live in God, and God lives in you.

¹⁷His love has accomplished what He wants when we can look ahead confidently to the day of judgment because we are what He is in this world. ¹⁸Such love isn't terrified, but the finest love throws out terror. We are terrified by punishment, and if we're terrified, our love isn't at its best.

¹⁹We love because He first loved us. ²⁰If anyone says, "I love God," but hates his brother, he's a liar. If anyone doesn't love his brother whom he has seen, he can't love God Whom he hasn't seen. ²¹And this is the order He gave us: If you love God, love your brother.

5 Everyone who believes Jesus is the Christ is God's child. And everyone who loves the Father loves the Father's child. ²We know we love God's children when we love God and do what He orders us to do. ³Loving God means we keep His commandments. And what He orders is no burden.

God's Life in Us

[4]Every child of God conquers the world. Our faith is the victory over the world. [5]Who conquers the world but he who believes Jesus is God's Son?

[6]This is He Who came by water and blood — Jesus Christ; not by water only, but by water and blood. And the Spirit is telling the truth because the Spirit is the Truth. [7]There are three who bring us the truth:[b] [8]the Spirit, the water, and the blood, and these three have one purpose.

[9]If we accept the testimony of men, God's testimony is greater because God's testimony is the truth He told about His Son. [10]If you believe in God's Son, you have in you the testimony of the truth. Anyone who will not believe God has made Him a liar because he hasn't believed the truth God told about His Son.

[11]He told us this truth that God has given us everlasting life and this life is in His Son. [12]If you have the Son, you have life. If you don't have God's Son, you don't have life. [13]I'm writing you this so that you who believe in the name of God's Son will know you have everlasting life.

[14]We have confidence in God that if we ask for anything according to His will, He listens to us. [15]And if we know that He listens to us whatever we ask, we know that we will get what we ask Him for. [16]If anyone sees His brother sinning but the sin isn't deadly, he should pray, and God will give him life for those who sin if the sin isn't deadly. There is a sin that's deadly; I don't tell you to pray for it. [17]Every kind of wrong is sin, but there is a sin that isn't deadly.

[18]We know that no child of God goes on sinning, but God's Son protects him, and the evil one doesn't touch him. [19]We know we're God's children, and the whole world is in the power of the evil one.

[20]We know that God's Son came and gave us the understanding to know Him who is true, and we are in Him Who is true, in His Son Jesus Christ. He is the true God and everlasting life. [21]Children, keep away from idols.

---

b - 7   Our oldest manuscripts lack vv. 7b-8a: "in heaven: the Father, the Word, and the Holy Spirit, and these Three are One. And there are three testifying on earth." Early in the 16th century an editor translated these words from Latin manuscripts and inserted them in his Greek New Testament. Erasmus took them from the Greek New Testament and inserted them in the third edition (1522) of his Greek New Testament. Luther used the text prepared by Erasmus. But even though the inserted words taught the Trinity, Luther ruled them out and never had them in his translation. In 1550 Bugenhagen objected to these words "on account of the truth." In 1574 Feyerabend, a printer, added them to Luther's text, and in 1596 they appeared in the Wittenberg copies.

THE SECOND LETTER OF
JOHN

THE SPIRITUAL LEADER TO THE CHOSEN LADY and her children, whom I love in the truth, and not I alone but all who know the truth, [2]because the truth lives in us and will be with us forever — [3]God the Father and Jesus Christ, the Father's Son, will give us grace, mercy, and peace as we are in the truth and in love.

[4]I was very happy to find some of your children living in the truth as the Father has ordered us. [5]And now I ask you, dear lady — I'm not writing you a new commandment but one we've had from the beginning— that we love one another. [6]And Christian love means that we live according to His commandments. The commandment as you have heard it from the beginning is: Live in love.

[7]Many deceivers have gone out into the world. They don't confess Jesus Christ as One Who comes in the flesh. That is the mark of the deceiver and the antichrist. [8]Watch yourselves so you will not lose what you worked for but will get your full reward.

[9]Anyone who goes too far and doesn't stay with what Christ has taught doesn't have God. If you stay with what He taught, you have the Father and the Son. [10]If anyone comes to you and doesn't teach this, don't take him into your home or greet him. [11]If you greet him, you share the wicked things he does.

[12]While I have much to write you, I don't want to do it with paper and ink, but I hope to come to you and tell you face to face so that you may be very happy.

[13]The children of your sister, whom God has chosen, greet you.

THE THIRD LETTER OF
JOHN

THE SPIRITUAL LEADER TO MY DEAR GAIUS, whom I love in truth.

²Dear friend, I pray that you're doing well in every way and are also healthy, just as your soul is doing well. ³I was delighted when some Christians came and told me about the truth you have — how you live in it. ⁴Nothing gives me greater joy than to hear that my children live in the truth.

⁵Dear friend, you're faithful in whatever you do for the fellow Christians even though they're strangers. ⁶They have publicly told the church about your love. Please help them on their way as it is right before God, ⁷because they went out for Jesus, taking no help from unbelievers. ⁸We should help such people in order to work with them for the truth.

⁹I wrote something to the church, but Diotrephes, who likes to be their leader, won't listen to us. ¹⁰So, if I come, I'll bring up what he's doing when he talks such wicked nonsense about us. Not satisfied with that, he also will not welcome the fellow Christians as guests and stops those who want to welcome them and tries to put them out of the church.

¹¹Dear friend, don't imitate what is wrong but what is right. If you do right, you're God's child. Anyone who does wrong hasn't seen God.

¹²Everyone speaks well of Demetrius, and so does the truth itself. We also speak well of him, and you know we tell the truth.

¹³I have much to write you, but I don't want to do it with pen and ink. ¹⁴I hope to see you very soon and talk to you face to face.

¹⁵Peace to you! The friends here send you their greetings. Greet each of our friends by name.

THE LETTER OF
JUDE

JUDE, SERVANT OF JESUS CHRIST and brother of James, to you who have been called, who are loved in God the Father and kept for Jesus Christ: ²*May more and more* mercy, *peace*, and love *be yours.*

Fight for the Faith

³While I've been very eager to write you, dear friends, about the salvation we share, it's now necessary that I write you and urge you to fight for the faith once entrusted to the holy people.

⁴There are some men who have sneaked in among you — some time ago it was written that they were headed for this condemnation— ungodly persons who turn the grace our God has for us into unbridled lust and disown our only Master and Lord Jesus Christ.

⁵You already know all this, but I want to remind you how the Lord saved His people from Egypt but afterwards destroyed those who didn't believe. ⁶And the angels who didn't keep their position of authority but left their home He put in everlasting chains and gloom to be kept for the judgment of the great day — ⁷just like Sodom and Gomorrah and the towns around them, who for their sexual sins and unnatural vice have suffered their punishment and lie before us as a warning of everlasting fire.

⁸Yet in the same way these men with their dreams defile the body, reject the Lord, and slander beings of glory. ⁹When *the archangel Michael* was debating with the devil and arguing about Moses' body, he didn't dare to accuse him of slander but said, *"The Lord rebuke you!"* ¹⁰But whatever beings these men don't understand they slander, and whatever they know by instinct like unthinking animals they use to destroy themselves. ¹¹Woe to them! They've gone the way of Cain. For a profit they've rushed into the error of Balaam. They've rebelled like Korah and perished.

¹²They're a blot on your love meals, where they banquet together without fear. They're shepherds who take care of themselves; clouds driven along by the winds without giving rain, trees that in late fall have no fruit but are torn up by the roots and so are twice dead; ¹³wild waves of the sea, foaming out their own shame; wandering stars for whom dark gloom is reserved forever.

---

2 Dan 4:1; 6:25   *9 Dan 10:13,21; 12:1; Zech 3:2*

[14]Enoch, the sixth after Adam, prophesied about them. "The Lord has come with ten thousands of His holy ones," he said, [15]"to bring judgment on all of them and to convict all the ungodly of all the ungodliness they've done and of all the defiant things ungodly sinners have said against Him."

[16]They grumble, complain about their lot, follow their lusts, brag, and flatter people to take advantage of them.

[17]But you, dear friends, remember what the apostles of our Lord Jesus Christ predicted. [18]"In the last time," they told you, "there will be scoffers, following their own ungodly lusts." [19]They're causing divisions. They're worldly because they don't have the Spirit.

Build Yourselves Up

[20]But you, dear friends, building yourselves up on your most holy faith and praying in the Holy Spirit, [21]keep yourselves in God's love, as you look for the mercy of our Lord Jesus Christ to give you everlasting life.

[22]Some people are in doubt — pity them, [23]*snatch them from the fire*, and save them. Pity others with fear as you hate even their clothes stained by their flesh.

[24]To Him who is able to keep you from falling and have you stand without a fault and with great joy before His glory, [25]to the only God, Who saves us through Jesus Christ our Lord — to Him be glory, majesty, power, and authority — as it was from everlasting, so be it now and forever. Amen.

---

23 *Amos 4:11; Zech 3:2*

JOHN WRITES
REVELATION

1 THIS IS A REVELATION FROM JESUS CHRIST which God gave Him to show His servants *what must soon happen*; and by way of symbols sent the message through His angel to His servant John. ²And so John tells the truth about everything he saw, of what God said and to which Jesus Christ testified. ³*Blessed* are you who read and you who hear this prophecy *as you keep what is written* here because the time is near.

To the Seven Churches

⁴John to the seven churches in the province of Asia: Grace and peace to you from Him *Who is* and was and *is coming*, from the seven spirits who are before His throne, ⁵and from Jesus Christ, *the faithful Witness, the First* of the dead *to live* again, and *the One Who rules over the kings of the world*.

To Him Who loves us and by His blood has *freed* us *from* our *sins* ⁶and has made us *a kingdom* and *priests* serving His God and Father — to Him be glory and power forever. Amen. ⁷*Look, He is coming in the clouds*, and every eye *will see Him, even the men who pierced Him*, and all *the people on earth will mourn over Him*. So it will be. Amen. ⁸"*I am* the Alpha and the Omega [the A and the Z]," *says the Lord God, Who is* and was and *is coming, the Almighty*.ᵃ

⁹I, John, your fellow Christian, who in Jesus share with you suffering and ruling and enduring, was on the island called Patmos for speaking God's Word and the truth told by Jesus. ¹⁰I came under the Spirit's power on the Lord's Day, and I heard behind me a loud voice like a trumpet ¹¹saying: "What you see write on a scroll and send it to the seven churches in Ephesus, Smyrna, Pergamum, Thyatira, Sardis, Philadelphia, and Laodicea."

---

1 Is 48:6; Dan 2:28-30,45 **3** *Prov 3:18*
4 Ex 3:14; Ps 118:26; Is 40:10; Hab 2:3; Zech 14:5; Mal 3:1; Dan 7:13
5 Ps 89:37; Pr 14:5; Jer 42:5; Ps 89:27; 130:8; Is 40:2
6 Ex 19:6; Is 61:6; Dan 7:18,22,27 **7** *Dan 7:13; Ps 22:16; Zech 12:10-12,14*
8 Ex 3:14; Ps 118:26; Is 40:10; Hab 2:3; Mal 3:1; Dan 7:13; Amos 3:13

---

a - 8   The Septuagint, the ancient Greek translation of the Old Testament, translates "the Lord of armies" with "the Lord Almighty" exactly 100 times.

[12]I turned to see who was talking to me. And when I turned, *I saw seven gold lampstands* [13]and among the lampstands *Someone like the Son of Man.* He *wore a robe reaching down to His feet, with a gold belt* around His chest. [14]*His head and hair were white like white wool, like snow. His eyes were like flames of fire.* [15]*His feet were like glowing bronze* refined in a furnace, and *His voice was like the sound of many waters.* [16]In His right hand He held seven stars, and out of His *mouth* came a *sharp, double-edged sword,* and His face was *like the sun* when it shines *in all its brightness.*

[17]When I saw Him, I fell down at His feet like a dead man. Then He laid His right hand on me. *"Don't be afraid,"* He said, *"I am the First and the Last,* [18]and the One Who is living. I died, but now you see I am living forever and have the keys of death and hell. [19]Write what you have seen, what is now, and *what is going to happen later.* [20]*The hidden meaning* of the seven stars you saw in My right hand and of the seven gold lampstands is this: The seven stars are the messengers of the seven churches, and the seven lampstands are the seven churches."

2 "Write to the messenger of the church in Ephesus:

" 'He Who holds the seven stars in His right hand and walks among the seven gold lampstands says:

[2]" 'I know what you have done, how hard you have worked, how you have endured, and that you can't tolerate wicked people, and you have tested those who call themselves apostles but are none and found them to be liars. [3]You have endurance; you have borne trouble for Me and aren't tired out.

[4]" 'But I hold it against you that your love isn't what it was at first. [5]Remember from what you have fallen, and repent, and do as you did at first, or else if you don't repent, I will come to you and take your lampstand from its place.

[6]" 'But you have one thing. You hate what the Nicolaitans are doing, and I hate it, too.

[7]" 'You have ears; then listen to what the Spirit says to the churches. Be victorious, and I will let you eat from *the tree of life that stands in* God's *Paradise.'*

[8]"And write to the messenger of the church in Smyrna:

" '*The First and the Last,* Who died and became alive, says:

[9]" 'I know how you have to suffer and how poor you are (but you're rich!) and the slander of those who say they are Jews when they're not but are Satan's synagogue. [10]Don't be afraid of what you're going to suffer. You see, the devil is going to put some of you in prison. This is to *test* you, and you will have to suffer for *ten days.* Be faithful until you die, and I will give you the crown of life.

12-15 *Ezek 1:24; 43:2; Dan 7:9,13; 10:5-6*   **16** *Isa 49:2; Judg 5:31*
17 *Is 44:2,6; 48:12; 56:5; 62:2; 65:15*   **19-20** *Dan 2:28-29,45; Is 48:6*
7 *Gen 2:9; 3:22,24; Prov 3:18; 13:12; 15:4; Ezek 31:8* **8** *Is 41:4; 44:6; 48:12*
10 *Dan 1:12,14*

¹¹" 'You have ears; then listen to what the Spirit says to the churches. Be victorious, and the second death will not hurt you.'

¹²"And write to the messenger of the Church in Pergamum: " 'He Who holds the sharp, double-edged sword says:

¹³" 'I know where you live. Satan is there on his throne. But you cling to My name and didn't deny your faith in Me even in the days of Antipas, My loyal witness, who was killed among you — you have Satan living there!

¹⁴" 'But I have a few things against you because you have men there who hold what *Balaam* taught. He taught Balak how to trap *the people of Israel* to get them *to eat food sacrificed to idols* and *to sin sexually*. ¹⁵So you, too, have some who hold what the Nicolaitans teach. ¹⁶Repent, then, or else I will come to you quickly and fight them with the sword in My mouth.

¹⁷" 'You have ears; then listen to what the Spirit says to the churches. Be vic torious, and I will give you some of the hidden manna, and *I will give you* a white stone, and on the white stone is written *a new name* that is known only to him who gets it.'

¹⁸"And write to the messenger of the church at Thyatira:

" 'God's Son, Whose *eyes are like flames of fire and* Whose feet *are like glowing bronze*, says:

¹⁹" 'I know what you're doing and your love and faith and service and endurance and that lately you've done more than at first.

²⁰" 'But I hold it against you that you let the woman Jezebel, who calls herself a prophetess, teach My servants and mislead them to *sin sexually* and *to eat food sacrificed to idols*. ²¹And I gave her time to repent, but she refuses to repent of her sexual sins. ²²Now I'm throwing her on a bed and will make those who live in sexual sin with her suffer much unless they repent of what she is doing. ²³And I will kill her children. Then all the churches will know I am the One Who searches *minds and hearts*, and *I will give each* of you *according to what you have done*.

²⁴" 'But I say to the rest of you in Thyatira, all who don't hold this teaching and haven't learned "Satan's deep things," as they call them: I'm putting no other burden on you. ²⁵Only cling to what you have until I come.

²⁶" 'Be victorious and continue to observe My works until the end, and *I will give* you power over *the nations*, ²⁷just as I received it from My Father, and you *will rule them with an iron rod, shattering them like pottery*. ²⁸And I will give you the Morning Star.

²⁹" 'You have ears; then listen to what the Spirit says to the churches.'

3 "And write to the messenger of the church in Sardis:

" 'He Who has God's seven spirits and the seven stars says:

" 'I know what you're doing, that people say you're living — but you're dead. ²Wake up and strengthen the rest that are dying. I have found that

---

14 *Num 25:1-2; 31:16*   17 *Is 56:5; 62:2; 65:15*   18 *Dan 10:6*
20 *Num 25:1-2; 31:16*   23 *Ps 7:9; 26:2; Jer 11:20; 17:10; 20:12; Ps 62:12; Prov 24:12*
26-27 *Ps 2:8-9*

your works are not finished before My God. ³So remember how you once accepted and listened to the truth. Take it to heart and repent. If you don't wake up, I will come like a thief, and you will not know when I'm coming to you.

⁴" 'But you have a few people in Sardis who have not soiled their clothes, and they will walk with me in white garments because they are worthy. ⁵Be victorious and that's how you will be dressed — in white garments — and I will not *erase* your *name from the book of life* but will confess your name before My Father and before His angels.

⁶" 'You have ears; then listen to what the Spirit says to the churches.'

⁷"And write to the messenger of the church in Philadelphia:

" 'This is He Who is holy and true, Who has *the key of David. When He opens a door, no one will shut it; when He shuts a door, no one will open it.* He says: ⁸I know what you're doing. See, I have opened before you a door no one can shut. Although you have only a little strength, you have kept My Word and not denied Me.

⁹" 'There are those of Satan's synagogue who say they're Jews when they're not but are lying. I'll make them *come and bow down* at your feet and learn that *I have loved you.* ¹⁰Because you have waited patiently for Me as you were told, I will keep you safe when the time of testing comes for the whole world, to test those living on the earth. ¹¹I am coming soon. Cling to what you have and don't let anyone take your crown.

¹²" 'Be victorious, and I will make you a pillar in the temple of My God, and you will never leave it again. I will write on you the name of My God and *the name of the city* of My God — the new Jerusalem coming down from My God in heaven — and My *new name.*

¹³" 'You have ears; then listen to what the Spirit says to the churches.'

¹⁴"And write to the messenger of the church in Laodicea:

" 'The Amen, *the Witness Who is faithful* and true, the *Origin of God's creation,* says:

¹⁵" 'I know what you're doing, that you aren't cold or hot. I wish you were cold or hot. ¹⁶But now that you are lukewarm and not hot or cold, I am going to spit you out of My mouth.

¹⁷" 'You say, "*I am rich* and *wealthy* and don't need anything," and you don't know you're miserable, pitiful, poor, blind, and naked. ¹⁸So I advise you to buy from Me — gold, purified in fire, to make you rich; white clothes to put on, to keep your shameful nakedness from showing; salve to put on your eyes to help you see. ¹⁹*I correct and discipline all whom I love.* Be eagerly concerned then, and repent.

²⁰" 'See, I'm standing *at the door* and *knocking.* If you will listen to My voice and *open* the door, I will come in to you and eat with you, and you with Me.

---

5 *Ex 32:32-33; Ps 69:28*   7 *Job 12:14; Is 22:22*
9 *Ps 22:27; 86:9; Is 45:14; 49:23; 60:14; 66:23; Jer 16:19; Is 43:4*
12 *Ezek 48:35; Is 56:5; 62:2; 65:15*   14 *Ps 89:37; Prov 14:5; Jer 42:5; Prov 8:22-23*
17 *Hos 12:8*   19 *Prov 3:12*

²¹" 'Be victorious, and I will have you sit with Me on My throne, as I have won the victory and have sat down with My Father on His throne.

²²" 'You have ears; then listen to what the Spirit says to the churches.'"

Around the Throne

4 After this I saw a door opened in heaven, and there was the *voice* I had heard at first speaking to me like *a trumpet*. It said, "*Come up* here, and I will show you *what must happen* after this."

²Just then I came under the Spirit's power. *I saw* a throne standing in heaven and *Someone sitting on the throne.* ³The *One Who sat* there looked like jasper and carnelian, and *a rainbow around* the throne looked like an emerald. ⁴Around the throne I saw 24 other thrones, and on these thrones sat 24 elders dressed in white clothes, with gold crowns on their heads. ⁵From the throne *came flashes of lightning, rumblings*, and peals of thunder. Seven flaming torches were burning in front of the throne; these are God's seven spirits. ⁶In front of the throne there was also something like a sea of glass, *like crystal.* Around the throne, *in the middle* of each side of the throne, *were four living beings. They had eyes everywhere*, in front and behind. ⁷*The first living being was like a lion, the second like a young bull, the third had a human face*, and *the fourth was like a* flying *eagle.* ⁸And *each of the four living beings had six wings*, and *everywhere, all around* and under, *they had eyes.* And day and night without stopping they were saying: "*Holy, holy, holy is the Lord God Almighty, Who* was and *is* and *is coming.*" ⁹And whenever the living beings *give glory* and honor and thanks to *Him Who is sitting on the throne* and *living forever*, ¹⁰the 24 elders *bow down before Him* Who is *sitting on the throne* and *worship Him Who lives forever*, throwing down their crowns before the throne and saying: ¹¹"Our Lord and God, You deserve to receive glory and honor and power because You created everything and Your will caused them to be created and to be."

The Scroll with Seven Seals

5 In the right hand of *Him Who sat on the throne* I saw *a scroll, written on both sides and sealed* with seven seals. ²And I saw a mighty angel, calling out with a loud voice, "Who can open the scroll and break the seals on it?"

³But no one in heaven, on earth, or under the earth could open the

---

20 Song 5:2   *1* Ex 19:16,24; Is 48:6; Dan 2:28-29,45

2-3 I Kings 22:19; Ps 47:8; Is 6:1; II Chr 18:18; Ezek 1:26-28 *5* Ex 19:16; Ezek 1:13

6 Ezek 1:4-5,18,22; 10:12   *7* Ezek 1:10; 10:14

8 Is 6:2-3; Ezek 1:4-5,18; 10-12; Ex 3:14; Ps 118:26; Is 40:10; Hab 2:3; Mal 3:1; Dan 7:13

9 Dan 4:34; 6:26; 12:7; I Kings 22:19; Ps 47:8; Is 6:1; II Chr 18:18

10 Ps 22:27; 86:9; Is 45:14; 49:23; 60:14; 66:23; Jer 16:19; I Kings 22:19; Ps 47:8; Is 6:1; II Chr 18:18; Dan 4:34; 6:26; 12:7

1 I Kings 22:19; Ps 47:8; Is 6:1; II Chr 18:18; Is 29:11-12; Ezek 2:9-10

scroll and look into it. [4]And I cried bitterly because no one was found who could open the scroll and look into it.

[5]Then one of the elders said to me, "Don't cry! You see the *Lion* from the tribe of *Judah, the Root of David*, has won a victory, and He can open the scroll and its seven seals."

[6]Between the throne (with the four living beings) and the elders I saw a *Lamb* standing as though He had been *slaughtered*. He had seven horns and *seven eyes*, which are God's seven spirits that are sent *all over the world*. [7]He went and took the scroll from the right hand of Him Who sat *on the throne*. [8]When He had taken the scroll, the four living beings and the 24 elders bowed down before the Lamb, each holding a lyre and all had gold bowls full of *incense* (which are the *prayers* of the holy people). [9]And they *sang a new song*: "You are worthy to take the scroll and open the seals on it because You were sacrificed and with Your blood You bought them from every *tribe, language, people* and *nation* to be God's own [10]and, made them a *kingdom* and *priests* of our God, and they will rule as *kings over the earth*."

[11]As I saw this, I heard around the throne (with the four living beings and the elders) the voices of many angels, numbering *ten thousand times ten thousand and thousands of thousands*, [12]who called out loud: "The *Lamb* Who was *sacrificed* is worthy to receive power and wealth, wisdom and strength, honor, glory, and praise."

[13]Then I heard every creature in heaven, on earth, under the earth, and on the sea, and all that are in them saying: "To *Him Who sits on the throne* and to the Lamb be praise and honor, glory and might forever!"

[14]The four living beings said, "Amen!" And the elders *bowed down and worshiped*.

6 I saw when the Lamb opened the first of the seven seals, and I heard one of the four living beings call with a voice like thunder: "Come!" [2]And there *I saw a white horse*, and its rider had a bow. He was given a crown and rode off as a conqueror to conquer.

[3]When He opened the second seal, I heard the second living being call, "Come!" [4]And another *horse* came out, fiery *red*, and its rider was given the power to take away peace from the earth and to have people slaughter one another, and he was given a large sword.

[5]When He opened the third seal, I heard the third living being call, "Come!" And there I saw a *black horse*, and its rider had a scale in his hand. [6]I heard a voice that seemed to come from the middle of the four living beings saying: "A quart of wheat for a day's pay, and three quarts of barley for

---

5 Gen 49:9-10; Is 11:1,10; Jer 23:5   *6 Is 53:7; Zech 4:10*
7 I Kings 22:19; Ps 47:8; Is 6:1; II Chr 18:18   *8 Ps 141:2*
9 Ps 33:3; 40:3; 96:1; 98:1; 144:9; 149:1; Is 42:10; Dan 3:4; 7:14
10 Ex 19:6; Is 61:6; Dan 7:18,22,27   *11 Dan 7:10*   *12 Is 53:7*
13 I Kings 22:19; Ps 47:8; Is 6:1; II Chr 18:18
14 Ps 22:27; 86:9; Is 45:14; 49:23; 60:14; 66:23; Jer 16:19   *2-5 Zech 1:8; 6:1-3*

a day's pay, but don't damage the oil and the wine."

⁷When He opened the fourth seal, I heard the fourth living being call, "Come!" ⁸And there I saw a pale green horse, and its rider's name was *Death*, and *Hell* came close behind, and they were given power over a fourth of the earth, to kill *people with sword, famine,* and *plague,* and by the *wild animals* on the earth.

⁹When He opened the fifth seal, I saw under the altar the souls of those who had been killed for God's Word and the truth they were telling. ¹⁰They called out loud: "*Master,* holy and true, *how long* will You wait before You judge the people on the earth and *punish* them *for killing* us?" ¹¹Then each of them was given a white robe, and they were told to wait quietly a little longer until all their fellow servants and fellow Christians were present who were to be killed as they had been.

¹²When He opened the sixth seal, I saw a great earthquake, and the *sun turned black* like coarse cloth made of hair, *the* full *moon became* like *blood,* ¹³*the stars fell from the sky* to the earth like figs dropping from *a fig tree* shaken by a strong wind, ¹⁴*the sky* vanished *like a scroll being rolled up,* and every mountain and island was moved from its place. ¹⁵*The kings of the earth,* the great men, the tribunes, the rich, the powerful, and every slave and free man *hid in the caves and among the rocks* of the mountains, ¹⁶*calling to the mountains and rocks, "Fall on us and hide us from Him Who sits on the throne* and from the anger of the Lamb, ¹⁷because *the great day of* their *anger has come, and who can stand before it?"*

Saved!

7 After that I saw four angels standing at the *four corners* of the earth, holding back the *four winds of the earth* to keep any of them from blowing on land or sea or against any tree.

²Then I saw another angel coming up from the east with the seal of the living God, and he called out loud to the four angels who had been given power to damage land and sea. ³"Don't damage land, sea, or trees," he said, "until we have put the *seal on the foreheads* of the servants of our God." ⁴And I heard the number of those who were sealed: "144,000." They were from every tribe of the people of Israel. ⁵There were sealed:

12,000 from the tribe of Judah,
12,000 from the tribe of Reuben,
12,000 from the tribe of Gad,
⁶12,000 from the tribe of Asher,

8 Jer 14:12; 15:2; 21:7; Ezek 5:12,16-17; 6:11-12; 14:21; Hos 13:14
10 Ps 79:5; Deut 32:43; II Kings 9:7
12-14 Is 13:10; 34:4; Ezek 32:7-8; Joel 2:10,30-31; 3:15
15 Ps 2:2   15-16 Is 2:10,19,21; Jer 4:29; Hos 10:8
16 I Kings 22:19; Ps 47:8; Is 6:1; II Chr 18:18
17 Ps 76:8; Joel 2:11,31; Nah 1:6; Zeph 1:14-15; Mal 3:2; 4:5-6
1 Jer 49:36; Ezek 7:3; 37:9; Dan 7:2; Zech 6:5   3 Ezek 9:4,6

> 12,000 from the tribe of Naphtali,
> 12,000 from the tribe of Manasseh,
> ⁷12,000 from the tribe of Simeon,
> 12,000 from the tribe of Levi,
> 12,000 from the tribe of Issachar,
> ⁸12,000 from the tribe of Zebulun,
> 12,000 from the tribe of Joseph,
> 12,000 from the tribe of Benjamin.

⁹After that I saw a large crowd that no one could count, from every *nation, tribe, people, and language* standing before the throne and before the Lamb, wearing white robes, with palms in their hands. ¹⁰And they called out loud: "We are saved by our *God Who sits on the throne* and by the Lamb!"

¹¹All the angels stood around the throne, around the elders and *the four living beings*, and *bowed down* before the throne, with their faces to the ground, *worshiped God*, ¹²and said: "Amen! Praise, glory, wisdom, thanks, honor, power, strength be to our God forever! Amen."

¹³Then one of the elders turned to me and asked, "These people dressed in white robes — who are they and where did they come from?"

¹⁴And I answered him, "Sir, you know."

Then he told me, "They are the people who have come through great suffering, who have *washed* their *robes* and made them white in *the blood of the Lamb*. ¹⁵That is why they are before the throne of God and serve Him day and night in His temple, and *He Who sits on the throne* will spread His tent over them. ¹⁶*They will never be hungry or thirsty again,* and *the sun or any heat will never burn them,* ¹⁷because the *Lamb before the throne will be their Shepherd,* and He *will lead them to springs of the water of life.* And *God will wipe every tear from their eyes.*"

Prayer like Incense

8 When He opened the seventh seal, there was silence in heaven for about half an hour.

²And I saw the seven angels standing before God, and they were given seven trumpets.

³Another angel, with a gold censer, came and *stood at the altar,* and He was given much *incense* to offer with the *prayers* of all the holy people as he put it on the gold altar in front of the throne. ⁴From the angel's hand the smoke of the *incense* went up before God with the *prayers* of the holy people.

---

9 Dan 3:4; 7:14   *10 I Kings 22:19; Ps 47:8; Is 6:1; II Chr 18:18*   *11 Ezek 1:13*
14 Gen 49:11; Ex 12:5,7   *15 I Kings 22:19; Ps 47:8; Is 6:1; II Chr 18:18*
16-17 Ps 23:2; 121:6; Is 49:10; Jer 2:13; Ezek 34:23
17 Is 6:1; Prov 10:11; 13:14; 14:27; 16:22; Is 25:8   *3 Amos 9:1*   *3-4 Ps 141:2*

Fire and Death

[5]Then the angel took *the censer* and *filled it with fire from the altar* and poured it on the earth, and there came peals of thunder, *rumblings, flashes of lightning*, and an earthquake.

[6]The seven angels who had the seven trumpets got ready to blow them.

[7]The first blew his trumpet, and there came *hail and fire* mixed with *blood* which were poured *on the earth*. And a third of the earth was burned up, a third of the trees, and all the green grass.

[8]The second angel blew his trumpet, and something like a big *burning mountain* was thrown into the sea, and a third of the sea *turned to blood*, [9]a third of the creatures living in the sea *died*, and a third of the ships were destroyed.

[10]Then the third angel blew his trumpet, and a big *star*, flaming like a torch, *fell from the sky*, and it fell on a third of the rivers and on the springs of water. [11]That star was called Wormwood. Then a third of the waters turned to wormwood, and many people died from the water because it had turned bitter.

[12]Then the fourth angel blew his trumpet, and a third of *the sun* was struck, a third of *the moon*, and a third of the stars, so that a third of them turned dark, and there was *no light* for a third of the day and for a third of the night.

[13]Then I saw and heard an eagle flying in the middle of the sky. He called out with a loud voice: "Woe, woe, woe to those living on earth, because the other three angels are still going to blow their trumpets."

The First Woe

9 Then the fifth angel blew his trumpet, and I saw *a star that had fallen from the sky to the earth*. He was given the key to the shaft of the bottomless pit. [2]He opened the shaft of the bottomless pit, and *smoke went up from the shaft like the smoke from a big furnace*, and it *darkened the sun* and the air.

[3]Out of the smoke *came locusts on the earth*, and they were given power like the power of earthly scorpions. [4]But they were told not to harm the grass on the earth or any green plant or tree, only the people who don't have God's *seal on their foreheads*. [5]They were not allowed to kill these, only to torture them for five months, and the torture was like that of a scorpion when it stings a person. [6]In those days people will *look for death and not find it*, they will long to die, and death will flee from them. [7]The locusts were *like horses* armed *for battle*. On their heads there seemed to be crowns that looked like gold. Their faces were like human faces. [8]They had

---

5 Lev 16:12; Ezek 10:2; Ex 19:16   7 Ex 9:18,22-25; Ezek 38:22; Joel 2:31

8-9 Jer 51:25; Ex 7:17-21   10 Is 14:12; Dan 8:10   12 Ezek 32:7-8; Joel 2:10; 3:15

1 Is 14:12; Dan 8:10   2 Gen 19:28; Ex 19:18; Joel 2:10; 3:15   3 Ex 10:12

4 Ezek 9:4,6   6 Job 3:21   7-9 Joel 2:4-5; 1:6

hair like women and *teeth like lions.* [9]Their breasts were like iron breast-plates, and the noise of their wings was *like the roar of chariots* with many horses *rushing into battle.* [10]They had tails like scorpions, with stings, and their tails had the power to hurt people for five months. [11]The king who was over them was the angel of the bottomless pit. The Jews call him Abad-don,[b] but in Greek he is called Apollyon.[b]

[12]The first woe is past. There are two more woes still coming.

The Second Woe

[13]The sixth angel blew his trumpet, and I heard a voice from the four horns of the gold altar before God [14]say to the sixth angel who had the trum-pet: "Free the four angels who are held bound at *the big river Euphrates.*" [15]And the four angels who had been held ready for that hour, day, month, and year were set free to kill a third of the people.

[16]I heard how many soldiers there were on horses; there were 200,000,000. [17]In my vision I saw how the horses and their riders looked. Their breastplates were red like fire, blue like bluebells, and yellow like sulfur. The horses had heads like lions, and out of their mouths came fire, smoke, and sulfur. [18]These three plagues — the fire, smoke, and sulfur com-ing out of their mouths — killed a third of the people. [19]The power of the horses was in their mouths and in their tails. Their tails were like snakes, having heads with which they wounded people.

[20]But the rest of the people, whom these plagues hadn't killed, didn't repent by turning from *what their hands had made.* They did not give up worshiping demons and *idols of gold, silver, bronze, stone, and wood, that can't see or hear or walk.* [21]And they did not repent of their murders, their *magic arts,* their *sexual vice,* and their stealing.

The Scroll

10 I saw another mighty angel come down from heaven. He was robed in a cloud, and there was a rainbow over his head. His face was like the sun, and his feet were like pillars of fire. [2]In his hand he held a little scroll unrolled. He set his right foot on the sea, and his left on the land. [3]Then he shouted with a loud voice like a lion roaring. When he shouted, the seven thunders spoke with voices of their own. [4]When the seven thunders had spoken, I was going to write it down. But I heard someone say from heaven: "*Keep secret* what the seven thunders have said, and don't write it down."

[5]Then the angel whom I saw standing on the sea and on the land

---

14 Gen 15:18; Deut 1:7; 11:24; Josh 1:4
20 Deut 4:28; Ps 115:4-7; 135:15-17; Is 2:8,20; 17:8; Jer 1:16; Dan 5:4,23
21 II Kings 9:22 *4* Dan 8:26; 12:4,9

---

b- 11   The Destroyer

raised his right hand to heaven ⁶*and swore by Him Who lives forever, Who created heaven* and *what's in it, the earth and what's in it, and the sea and what's in it:* "There will be no more delay, ⁷but the time comes for the seventh angel to blow his trumpet, and *God's secret* purpose *as He told it to His servants, the prophets,* is carried out."

⁸Then he who had spoken to me from heaven spoke to me again. "Go," he said, "take the scroll that lies unrolled in the hand of the angel standing on the sea and on the land."

⁹I went to the angel and told him, "Give me the little *scroll.*"

"Take it," *he said to me,* "and *eat* all of *it,* and it will be bitter *in your stomach,* but in your mouth it will be *sweet as honey.*"

¹⁰I took the little scroll from the angel's hand and *ate it, and it was sweet as honey in my mouth.* But when *I had eaten it,* it was bitter *in my stomach.*

¹¹Then they told me, "You must prophesy again about many *peoples, nations, languages,* and kings."

Two Preachers

11 Then I was given *a measuring stick* like a *rod.* "Go," he said, "and measure God's temple and the altar, and count those who worship there. ²Omit the temple courtyard, and don't measure it, because it is given to *the non-Jewish people,* who will *trample on the holy* city for 42 months. ³I will let my two witnesses, dressed in sackcloth, speak God's Word for 1,260 days.

⁴"*These are the two olive trees* and the two lampstands *standing before the Lord of the earth.* ⁵And if anyone wants to hurt them, *fire comes out of* their *mouths* and *consumes* their *enemies,* that is how anyone who wants to hurt them must be killed. ⁶They have the power to shut up the sky and keep *rain* from falling during the days when they are speaking God's Word and the power over *waters* to *turn them into blood* and to *strike* the earth *with any plague* as often as they want to.

⁷"When they finish testifying, *the beast coming up* out of the bottomless pit *will fight with* them, *conquer them,* and kill them. ⁸And their dead bodies will lie on the street of the great city, which is called *Sodom* and Egypt, to show what kind of city it is. Here their Lord also was crucified. ⁹And some of the *peoples, tribes, languages,* and *nations* will look at their dead bodies for three and a half days and not let anyone bury them. ¹⁰The people living on the earth will be delighted over them and will celebrate and send gifts to one another because these two prophets tormented the people living on the earth.

¹¹"After three and a half days a *breath of life* from God *went into them,*

---

7 Deut 29:27; Amos 3:7; Zech 1:6   **9-10** Ezek 2:8-9; 3:1-3   **11** Dan 3:4,7; 7:14
1 Ezek 40:35   **2** Is 63:18; Zech 12:3   **4** Zech 4:3,11-12,14
5 II Sam 22:9; II Kings 1:10,12; Ps18:8; Is 26:11; Jer 5:14
6 Ex 7:17,21; I Sam 4:8; I Kings 17:1   **7** Dan 7:3,21   **8** Is 1:9-10   **9** Dan 3:4; 7:14

and they got up on their feet, and those who watched them *were terrified.* [12]They heard someone calling in a loud voice to them from heaven, 'Come up here.' And they went up to heaven in a cloud while their enemies watched them. [13]*Just then there* was *a big earthquake*, a tenth of the city *fell*, and 7,000 people were killed by the earthquake. The rest were terrified and gave glory to *the God of heaven."*

[14]The second woe is past. The third woe will soon be here.

The Third Woe

[15]The seventh angel blew his trumpet. Then there were loud voices in heaven, saying: *"The kingdom of* the world has become the kingdom of our *Lord and of His Christ*, and *He will be King forever."*

[16]Then the 24 elders who were sitting on their thrones before God *bowed down* on their faces *and worshiped God*, [17]saying: *"Lord God Almighty, You are* now, and You were. We thank You for taking Your great power and *becoming King.* [18]*The nations were angry*, but Your anger has come, and so has the time to judge the dead, to reward *Your servants, the prophets*, and the holy people, *little and great, who fear* Your name, and to destroy those who are destroying the earth."

[19]Then God's temple in heaven was opened, and *the ark of His covenant* was seen *in* His *temple*, and there were *flashes of lightning, rumblings*, peals of thunder, an earthquake, and *heavy hail.*

The Woman's Son and the Dragon

12 A great sign was seen in the sky: a woman with the sun for her garment, the moon under her feet, and a crown of twelve stars on her head. [2]She was pregnant, and she cried out *in pain* and agony *to give birth.*

[3]Another sign was seen in the sky: There was a large fiery dragon *with* seven heads and *ten horns* and with seven crowns on his heads. [4]His tail swept away a third of *the stars in the sky* and *hurled them to the earth.* Then the dragon stood in front of the woman who was going to have the Child, to devour her Child as soon as it was born.

[5]She *gave birth* to *a son, a boy, Who is to rule* all *the nations with an iron rod.* Her Child was snatched away and brought to God and to His throne. [6]The woman fled into the desert, where God has prepared a place for her and she is to be fed for 1,260 days.

[7]Then war broke out in heaven: Michael and his angels fought with the dragon. And the dragon and his angels fought, [8]but they *couldn't win,*

---

11 Ezek 36:27; 37:5,10; Gen 15:12   *13 Ezek 38:19-20; Dan 2:19*
15 Ex 15:18; Ps 2:2; 10:16; 22:28; 1 Sam 12:3; Obad 21; Mic 4:7; Dan 2:44
16 Ps 22:27; 86:9; Is 45:14; 49:23; 60:14; 66:23; Jer 16:19   *17 Ex 3:14*
17-18 Ps 99:1   *18 Amos 3:7; Zech 1:6; Dan 9:6,10; Ps 115:13*
19 I Kings 8:1,6; Ex 9:23; 19:16   *2 Is 66:7; Mic 4:10*   *3 Dan 7:7,20,24*
4 Dan 8:10   *5 Is 66:7; Ps 2:8-9*

and couldn't be found anywhere in heaven anymore. ⁹So the great dragon was thrown out. The old *snake,* called *Devil* and *Satan,* who *deceives* the whole world, was hurled to the earth, and his angels were hurled down with him.

¹⁰Then I heard a loud voice in heaven, saying: "Now has come the salvation, power, and kingdom of our God and the rule of His Christ, because he who *accused* our fellow Christians day and night before our God has been thrown out. ¹¹But they conquered him because of *the blood of the Lamb* and the truth they spoke and didn't love their life but were willing to die. ¹²For this *be glad, you heavens,* and you who live in them. Woe to the earth and the sea — the devil has come down to you and is very angry because he knows he has only a little time left."

The Devil and the Church

¹³When the dragon saw he had been hurled to the earth, he persecuted the woman who had given birth to the Boy. ¹⁴The woman was given two wings of the big eagle to fly to her place in the desert, away from the snake, where she is fed for *three and a half years.*·ᶜ ¹⁵Then the snake poured from his mouth a stream of water after the woman to sweep her away. ¹⁶But the earth helped the woman; it opened its mouth and swallowed the stream that the dragon poured from his mouth.

¹⁷The dragon was angry with the woman and went away to fight with her other children, those who were observing the commandments of God and holding on to the witness of Jesus. ¹⁸He stopped on the sandy shore of the sea.

13 Then I saw *a beast coming up out of the sea. He had ten horns* and seven heads, and on his horns were ten crowns, and on his heads were blasphemous names. ²The beast I saw was *like a leopard* and had feet *like a bear* and a mouth *like a lion.* The dragon gave him his power, his throne, and great authority. ³One of his heads seemed to have received a deadly wound, but his deadly wound had been healed.

The whole world was amazed as it followed the beast ⁴and worshiped the dragon because he had given power to the beast, and it worshiped the beast. "Is there anyone like the beast?" they asked. "And is there anyone who can fight with him?"

⁵He was allowed *to speak arrogant* and blasphemous *things* and was given authority to *act* for 42 months. ⁶He opened his mouth to slander God, His name, His home and those who live in heaven. ⁷He was allowed *to fight with the holy people and to conquer them* and was given authority over every *tribe, people, language,* and *nation.* ⁸Everyone who lives on earth will

8 Dan 2:35   9-10 Gen 3:1,13; Zech 3:1   11 Ex 12:5,7   12 Is 44:23; 49:13
14 Dan 7:25; 12:7   1 Dan 7:3,7,20,24   2 Dan 7:4-6 5-7 Dan 7:8,11,20,21; 11:36
7 Dan 3:4; 7:14

c - 14   Literally: "a time and times and half a time."

worship him — everyone whose name *isn't written in the book of life of* the *Lamb* Who was *slain* from the beginning of the world.

⁹You have ears; then listen. ¹⁰*If anyone is to be taken prisoner, he'll be taken prisoner.* If anyone kills with a sword, he must be killed by a sword. Here is where the holy people will need to endure and trust.

¹¹Then I saw another beast come up out of the ground, and he had two horns like a lamb but talked like a dragon. ¹²He is acting for the first beast with all his authority. He makes the earth and those living on it worship the first beast, whose deadly wound has been healed. ¹³He also does great miracles, even makes fire come down from the sky to the ground before people. ¹⁴He deceives those who live on the earth because of the wonders he is allowed to do for the beast, and he tells those who live on the earth to make a statue for the beast that was wounded by a sword and yet lived. ¹⁵He was allowed to put a spirit into the beast's statue so that the beast's statue could talk, and to have *all who would not worship the* beast's *statue* killed. ¹⁶He forces all, great and small, rich and poor, free and slave to be branded on their right hands or on their foreheads, ¹⁷and only he who has the brand — the beast's name or the number of its name — can buy or sell.

¹⁸Here we need to be wise. If you can understand, figure out the beast's number, because it is a man's number. His number is 666.

The New Song

14Then I saw the Lamb standing on Mount Zion and with Him 144,000 people who had His name and His Father's name *written on their foreheads.*

²And I heard *a sound* from heaven like *the noise of many waters* and of loud thunder. The sound I heard was also like the singing of musicians playing on their lyres. ³They were *singing a new song* before the throne, before the four living beings and the elders. And only the 144,000 who had been bought from the earth could learn the song.

⁴These are the men who have not soiled themselves with women; they are pure. They follow the Lamb wherever He goes. They were bought as the first ones among men to belong to God and the Lamb. ⁵*They've never been known to tell a lie.* They're without fault.

The Angel with the Good News

⁶I saw another angel flying high in midair with everlasting good news to tell those living on the earth, every *nation, tribe, language,* and *people.* ⁷"*Fear God* and give Him glory," he called out with a loud voice; "*the time has*

---

8 Ex 32:32-33; Ps 69:28; 139:16; Is 4:3; Mal 3:16; Dan 12:1; Ex 12:6,21; Lev 1:11; Is 53:7; Jer 11:19   10 Jer 15:2   15 Dan 3:5-6   1 Ezek 9:4,6
2 Ezek 1:24; 43:2   3 Ps 33:3; 40:3; 96:1; 98:1; 144:9; 149:1; Is 42:10
5 Ps 32:2; Is 53:9; Zeph 3:13   6 Dan 3:4; 7:14

come for Him to judge. And worship Him *Who made heaven, the earth, the sea,* and springs of water."

Babylon Has Fallen

[8]A second angel followed him. "*She has fallen!*" he said. "*The great Babylon has fallen* — she who made all *the nations drink of the wine of her immoral passion.*"

[9]A third angel followed them. "If *anyone worships the* beast and his *statue,*" he called out with a loud voice, "and is branded on his forehead or on his hand, [10]he must also *drink of the wine of God's anger,* poured out *unmixed into the cup* of *His punishment,* and must be tortured by *fire and sulfur* before the holy angels and before the Lamb. [11]*The smoke* of their torture *goes up forever.* There's no rest *day and night* for *those who worship the beast* and his *statue* and for anyone branded with his name."

[12]Here the holy people need to stand their ground as they keep on observing what God has commanded and trusting in Jesus.

[13]Then I heard someone say from heaven: "Write, blessed are the dead who die in the Lord!"

"Certainly," says the Spirit, "let them rest from their hard work; what they have done goes along with them."

Swing the Sickle

[14]Then I saw a white cloud, and *on the cloud sat One Who was like the Son of Man,* with a gold crown on His head and a sharp sickle in His hand. [15]And another angel came out of the temple, calling out loud to Him Who sat on the cloud: "*Swing Your sickle* and reap, because the *time has come to cut the grain. The crop* on the earth *is very ripe.*" [16]And the One Who sat on the cloud *swung His sickle* over the earth, and its grain was cut.

[17]Another angel came out of the temple in heaven, and he, too, had a sharp sickle. [18]And another angel came from the altar with power over fire. He called out with a loud voice to the one with the sharp sickle: "*Swing your* sharp *sickle* and gather the bunches of grapes from the vine of the earth, because the grapes on it are ripe."

[19]The angel *swung his sickle* on the earth and gathered the grapes from the vine of the earth and threw them into the great winepress of *God's anger.* [20]*The grapes were trodden in the winepress* outside the city, and the *blood* flowed from the winepress as high as the horses' bridles for about 200 miles.[d]

7 *Prov 3:7; Jer 51:6; Gen 14:19,22; Ex 20:11; Neh 9:6; Ps 146:6*
8 *Is 21:9; Jer 25:15; 50:2; 51:7-8; Dan 4:30*   **9** *Dan 3:5-6*
10 *Ps 75:8; Is 51:17; Jer 25:15*   **10-11** *Gen 19:24,28; Ezek 38:22; Is 34:10*
11 *Dan 3:5-6*   **14** *Dan 7:13*   **15** *Joel 3:13; Jer 51:33*   **16-19** *Joel 3:13*
19-20 *Is 63:2-3*

d - 20   Gk: 1600 Stadia

Seven Plagues

15 Then I saw in heaven another sign, great and wonderful: seven angels with *seven plagues*; the last plagues, since in them the anger of God was completed.

²And I saw what looked like a sea of glass mixed with fire, and standing on the glassy sea were those who had come away victorious from the beast, its statue, and the number of its name. They were holding God's lyres ³and singing *the song of Moses, God's servant*, and the song of the Lamb:

> Great and wonderful are Your works, Lord God Almighty.
> Righteous and true are Your ways, King of the ages.
> ⁴Is there anyone, Lord, who will not fear and glorify Your name?
> You alone are holy.
> All the nations will come and worship You,
> because they have seen Your righteous acts.

⁵After this I saw the temple of *the tabernacle containing God's Word* in heaven opened, ⁶and the seven angels with the *seven plagues* came out of the temple. They wore clean, shining linen and gold belts fastened around their chests. ⁷Then one of the four living beings gave to the seven angels seven gold bowls full of the anger of *God, Who lives forever.* ⁸*God's glory* and power *filled the temple with smoke*, and no one *could go into* the temple until the *seven plagues* of the seven angels were over.

16 Then I heard *someone from the temple* call out with a loud voice to the seven angels: "Go, *pour out* the seven bowls of *God's anger on the earth.*"

²The first went and poured out his bowl on the earth, and terrible and *painful sores came on the people* who had the brand of the beast and *worshiped its statue.*

³The second poured out his bowl into the sea, and *it turned to blood* like that of a dead man, and every living thing in the sea *died.*

⁴The third poured out his bowl into the *rivers* and the springs of water and *they turned to blood.*

⁵I heard the angel of the waters say: "*O holy One, You are* and You *were. You are just in judging* this way; ⁶*they have poured out the blood* of holy people and prophets, and You gave *them blood to drink* as they deserve."

---

1 Lev 26:21   3 Ex 15:1; Josh 14:7; Ex 34:10; Deut 32:4; Ps 111:3; 139:14; Ps 145:17
4 Jer 10:7; Mal 1:11; Ps 22:27; 86:9; Is 66:23; Jer 16:19
5 Ex 38:21; Num 1:50,53; 9:15; 10:11; 17:7,8; 18:2; II Chr 24:6
6 Lev 26:21   7 Dan 4:34; 6:26; 12:7
8 Ex 40:34-35; I Kings 8:10-11; Is 6:1,4; Ezek 44:4; Lev 26:21
16:1 Is 66:6; Ps 69:24; Jer 10:25; Zeph 3:8   16:2 Ex 9:10-11; Deut 28:35; Dan 3:5-6
16:3-4 Ex 7:17-21; Ps 78:44   16:5 Ex 3:14; Ps 19:9; 119:137; 145:17
16:6 Ps 79:3; Is 49:26

⁷I heard the altar answer: "Yes, *Lord God Almighty, Your judgments are true and just.*"

⁸The fourth poured out his bowl on the sun, and it was allowed to burn people. ⁹When they were badly burned, they blasphemed the name of God, Who controlled these plagues, and they did not repent to give Him glory.

¹⁰The fifth poured out his bowl on the throne of the beast; and its kingdom *turned dark*. People gnawed their tongues in anguish, ¹¹cursed *the God of heaven* for their pains and their sores but did not repent of what they had done.

¹²The sixth poured out his bowl on *the big Euphrates river*. Then *the water in it dried up*, to prepare the road for the kings *from the east.*

¹³Then I saw three unclean spirits, like frogs, come out of the mouths of the dragon, the beast, and the false prophet.ᵉ ¹⁴They were spirits of demons who were doing miracles. They went out to the kings of the whole world to gather them for war on the great day of the Almighty God.

¹⁵"See, I am coming like a thief. Blessed is he who stays awake and keeps his clothes, so he will not have to go naked and let others see his shameful parts."

¹⁶The spirits gathered the kings at the place the Jews call Armageddon.

¹⁷Then the seventh poured out his bowl over the air, and someone *called* out with a loud voice *from* the throne in *the temple*: "It is done!" ¹⁸*There were flashes of lightning, rumblings*, and peals of thunder, and a great earthquake. *There never was such* an earthquake *since there were* people *on earth.* ¹⁹The great city split into three parts, and the other cities of the nations fell. And God remembered to give *the great Babylon the cup of the wine of His* fierce *anger.* ²⁰Every island vanished, and the mountains couldn't be seen anymore. ²¹*Huge hailstones*, weighing about a hundred pounds each, *fell* from the sky *on people*, and they blasphemed God for the plague of hail, so *terrible* was that plague.

The Woman and the Beast

17 One of the seven angels who held the seven bowls came and told me: "Come, I will show you how the great prostitute who sits *on many waters* is judged. ²*The kings of the earth lived in sexual sin with her, and the people on earth got drunk on the wine of her* sexual vice.

³He took me in spirit to a desert. There I saw a woman sitting on a scarlet *beast* covered with blasphemous names, and it *had* seven heads and *ten horns.* ⁴The woman wore purple and scarlet and ornaments of gold, jew-

7 Ps 19:9; 119:137   *10 Ex 10:21-22*   *11 Dan 2:19*
12 Gen 15:18; Deut 1:7; 11:24; Josh 1:4; Is 44:27; Jer 50:38; Is 41:2,25
17 Is 66:6   *18 Ex 19:16,18; Dan 12:1*
19 Is 21:9; Jer 25:15; 50:2; 51:7-8; Dan 4:30; Ps 75:8; Is 51:17
21 Ex 9:24-25   *1 Jer 51:13*   *2 Is 23:17; Jer 51:7*   *3 Dan 7:7,20,24*

e - 13   The second beast, 13:11-18; 19:20; 20:10

els, and pearls. In her hand she held a *gold cup* full of the abominations and the unclean things of her sexual vice, ⁵and on her forehead was written a name with a hidden meaning: *THE GREAT BABYLON*, THE MOTHER OF PROSTITUTES AND OF THE ABOMINATIONS OF THE EARTH. ⁶I saw the woman was drunk with the blood of the holy people and the blood of the witnesses of Jesus. And I was very much surprised to see her.

⁷"Why are you surprised?" the angel asked me. "I'll tell you the hidden meaning of the woman and of the *beast* she rides *that has* the seven heads and the *ten horns.* ⁸*The beast* you saw once was but is no more, and it will *come up from* the bottomless pit and go to its destruction. And the people living on the earth whose names since the world was made have not been *written in the book of life* will be surprised to see the beast — it was and is no more and will come again.

⁹"Here is something for an intelligent person to think about. The seven heads are seven hills on which the woman is sitting. ¹⁰They are also seven kings: five have fallen, one is ruling now, the other hasn't come yet, and when he comes, he must stay a little while. ¹¹The beast that was and is no more is the eighth king; he comes from the seven and goes to his destruction.

¹²"*The ten horns* you saw *are ten kings* who have not yet started to rule but for an hour get authority as kings with the beast. ¹³They have one purpose and give their power and authority to the beast. ¹⁴They will go to war against the Lamb, but the Lamb, and the called, chosen, and faithful people with Him, will conquer them because He is *the Lord of lords and the King of kings.*

¹⁵"The waters you saw where the prostitute was sitting," he told me, "are *peoples*, crowds, *nations*, and *languages.* ¹⁶*The ten horns* you saw and the beast will hate the prostitute, lay her waste, strip her, devour her flesh, and burn her with fire. ¹⁷God has put it into their hearts to do what He has decided, to carry out one purpose, and to give their kingdom to the beast until what God has said is carried out. ¹⁸The woman you saw is the great city that rules over *the kings of the earth.*"

Babylon Has Fallen

18 After that I saw another angel come down from heaven. He had great power, and his glory lit up the earth. ²He called out with a loud voice: *"She has fallen, the great Babylon has fallen and has become a home for demons*, a dungeon for every unclean spirit and for every foul *bird* we loathe. ³All *the nations* fell by *the wine of her* immoral passion. *The kings of the earth have lived in sexual sin with her.* And the wealth of her luxury

---

4 *Jer 51:7*   5 *Dan 4:30*   7 *Dan 7:7,20,24*
8 *Dan 7:3; Ex 32:32-33; Ps 69:28; 139:16; Is 4:3; Mal 3:16; Dan 12:1*
12 *Dan 7:7,20,24*   14 *Deut 10:17; Dan 2:47*   15 *Dan 3:4; 7:14*
16 *Dan 7:7,20,24*   18 *Ps 2:2; 89:27*   2 *Is 21:9; Jer 50:2; 51:7-8; Dan 4:30; Is 13:20-21; 34:11,14*   3 *Is 21:9; Jer 25:15; 50:2; 51:7; Dan 4:30; Is 23:17*

has made the merchants of the earth rich."

> [4]Then I heard Someone else call from heaven:
>> *Come out of her, My people*,
>> so you will not share her sins
>> or suffer from any of her plagues.
> [5]Her sins *have reached up to heaven*.
>> And God has remembered her crimes.
> [6]*Pay her back, even as she has paid*,
>> and give her double *for what she has done*.
>> Mix a double drink for her in the cup she mixed for others.
> [7]Give her as much torture and misery
>> as she gave glory to herself and *lived in luxury*,
>> because *she thinks*, "I'm a queen on a throne,
>> *I'm no widow, and I'll never feel miserable.*"

[8]"For that reason her plagues — death and misery and hunger — *will come on one day*, and she will be *burned with fire*, because the *Lord* God, *Who has judge*d her, is *mighty*.

[9]"*The kings of the earth who lived in sexual vice* and luxury with her *will weep and mourn over her* when they see the smoke rise where she burns. [10]Frightened by her torture, they will stand far off and say: 'Woe, woe to the great city, *the mighty city of Babylon*! In one hour *judgment has come* on you.'

[11]"And the merchants of the earth *weep and mourn* over her because no one buys their loads of goods anymore, [12]their loads of gold, *silver*, jewels, pearls, fine linen, purple, silk, and scarlet cloth, all kinds of citrus wood, all kinds of ivory goods, and all kinds of articles made of very costly wood, of *copper, iron*, and marble; [13]and *cinnamon*, ointment, incense, perfume, frankincense, wine, olive oil, fine wheat flour, wheat, cattle, sheep, horses, wagons, *slaves — even human beings.* [14]The fruit you longed for is gone, all your fat and your splendor have perished, and no one will ever find them again. [15]The people who traded in those things and whom she has made rich, frightened by her torture, will stand far off, *weeping and mourning*. [16]They will say, 'Woe, woe to the great city that wore fine linen and purple and scarlet and ornaments of gold, jewels, and pearls. [17]In one hour all this wealth has been laid waste.'

"Every pilot and all who go anywhere in a ship, *sailors* and all others whose work is on the sea, *stood far off* [18]*and shouted* when they saw the smoke rise where she was burning. 'Was there ever a city as great as this?' they asked. [19]*They threw dust on their heads*, and *weeping and mourning*, they called:

---

4 Gen 19:14; Is 48:20; 52:11; Jer 50:8; 51:6,45   *5* Jer 51:9
6 Ps 137:8; Jer 50:29   *7-8* Is 47:8-9   *8* Jer 50:32,34   *9-10* Is 23:17; Ezek 26:17; Jer 51:6,8; Dan 4:30
11 Ezek 27:30-33   *12-13* Ezek 27:12-13,22   *15* Ezek 27:30-33
17-19 Ezek 27:29-33; Ezek 26:19

'Woe, woe to the great city,
whose treasures have made everyone *rich*
who had a ship on the sea.
In one hour *she's been laid waste.'*
[20]*"Be happy* over her, *heaven,*
holy *people,* apostles and prophets,
because God has punished her for you."

[21]Then a mighty angel lifted up *a stone* like a large millstone, *threw it into* the *sea,* and said: "With *such* violence *will Babylon, the great* city, *be hurled down* and *never be found again.* [22]Singing with lyres and the *playing of musical instruments,* of flutes and trumpets, *will never be heard in you again.* No skilled worker will ever be found in you again. The sound of a millstone will never be heard in you again. [23]*The light of a lamp* will never shine in you again. *The voices of a groom and a bride* will never be heard in you again. Your *merchants were the great men of the world,* but your witchcraft deceived all the nations, [24]and there was found in you the blood of prophets and holy ones, of *all who had been slaughtered on the earth."*

Praise the Lord!

19 After that I heard what sounded like a large crowd in heaven calling out: *"Praise the Lord*! Salvation, glory, and power belong to our God [2]because *His judgments are true and just* and He has sentenced the great prostitute who corrupted the world with her sexual vice and *has punished* her *for the blood of His servants.*

[3]Again they called: *"Praise the Lord! The smoke goes up from her forever."*

[4]And the 24 elders and the four living beings *bowed down and worshiped God, sitting on the throne.* They answered: *"So be it! Praise the Lord!"*

[5]Then a voice came from the throne and said: *"Praise* our God, *all His servants, you who fear Him, small and great."*

---

20 Deut 32:43; Is 44:23; 49:13; Jer 51:48
21-22 Jer 51:63-64; Dan 4:30; Is 24:8;Ezek 26:12-13,21
23 Jer 7:34; 16:9; 25:10; Is 23:8   24 Jer 51:49
1 Ps 104:35; 105:45; 106:1,48; 111:1; 112:1; 113:1; 115:18; 116:19; 117:1-2; 135:1,3,21; 146:1,10; 147:1,20; 148:1,7,14; 149:1; 150:1,6
2 Ps 19:9; 119:137; Deut 32:43; II Kings 9:7
3 Ps 104:35; 105:45; 106:1,48; 111:1; 112:1; 113:1; 115:18; 116:19; 117:1-2; 135:1,3,21; 146:1,10; 147:1,20; 148:1,7,14; 149:1; 150:1,6; Is 34:10
4 Ps 22:27; 86:9; Is 45:14; 49:23; 60:14; 66:23; Jer 16:19; I Kings 22:19; Ps 47:8; Is 6:1; II Chr 18:18; Ps 104:35; 105:45; 106:1,48; 111:1; 112:1; 113:1; 115:18; 116:19; 117:1-2; 135:1,3,21; 146:1,10; 147:1,20; 148:1,7,14; 149:1; 150:1,6
5 Ps 22:23; 115:13; 134:1; 135:1

The Lamb's Wedding

[6]Then I heard what sounded *like the voices of a* large *crowd* and *the noise of many waters* and loud peals of thunder, saying: "*Praise the Lord! The Lord our God, the Almighty, is King.* [7]*Let us rejoice and be delighted* and give Him glory because the marriage of the Lamb has come, and His bride has prepared herself. [8]She has been permitted to put on dazzling and pure linen. Her fine linen is the righteous living of the holy people."

[9]Then he said to me: "Write: Blessed are those who are invited to the Lamb's wedding dinner. These," he told me, "are God's true words."

[10]I *bowed down at his* feet *to worship him.* "Be careful! Don't do that!" he told me. "I'm a fellow servant of yours and of your fellow Christians who are speaking the truth told by Jesus. Worship God. The truth Jesus told is the Spirit's Word.

The King of Kings

[11]Then *I saw heaven opened*, and there was a white horse, and its Rider is called Faithful and True. *He is righteous when He judges* and goes to battle. [12]*His eyes are flames of fire*, and on His head are many crowns, and there's a name written on Him, but only He knows what it is. [13]He wears a *garment* dipped *in blood* and is called the Word of God. [14]Heaven's armies, dressed in pure, white linen, have been following Him on white horses. [15]A sharp sword comes *out of His mouth to strike down* the nations, and He *will rule them with an iron rod* and will *tread the winepress of* the fierce *anger of Almighty God.* [16]On His garment and on His thigh He has a name written:

KING OF KINGS AND LORD OF LORDS!

[17]Then I saw an angel standing in the sun, and he called out with a loud voice *to all the birds flying* in midair: "*Come together for* God's great banquet, [18]*to eat the bodies of* kings, generals, *warriors, of horses and their riders, of all people*, free and slave, small and great."

[19]Then I saw the beast and the *kings of the earth* with their armies *gathered* to fight against the Rider on the horse and His army. [20]And the beast was captured and with it the false prophet who had done miracles for the beast by which he deceived those who had received the beast's brand and *worshiped its statue*. Both were thrown into the fiery lake of *burning sulfur.* [21]And the sword that came out of the mouth of the Rider on the horse killed the rest, and *all the birds gorged themselves on* their *bodies.*

---

6 *Dan 10:5-6; Ezek 1:24; 43:2; Ps 93:4; 104:35; 105:45; 106:1,48; 111:1; 112:1; 113:1; 115:18; 116:19; 117:1-2; 135:1,3,21; 146:1,10; 147:1,20; 148:1,7,14; 149:1; 150:1,6; Ps 93:1; 96:10; 97:1; 99:1*

7 *Ps 118:24*   **10** *Ps 22:27; 86:9; Is 45:14; 49:23; 60:14; 66:23; Jer 16:19*

11 *Ezek 1:1; Ps 9:8; 96:13; 99:9; Is 11:4-5*   **12** *Dan 10:6*   **13** *Is 63:3*

15 *Is 11:4; Ps 2:8-9; Joel 3:13; Is 63:2-3; Lam 1:15*   **16** *Deut 10:17; Dan 2:47*

17-18 *Ezek 39:4,17-20*   **19** *Ps 2:2*   **20** *Dan 3:5-6; Is 30:33*

The Devil's Last Battle

20 Then I saw an angel coming down from heaven with the key to the bottomless pit in his hand, and a big chain. ²He took the dragon, the old *snake*, that is, the *devil* or *Satan*, bound him for a thousand years, ³threw him into the bottomless pit, and locked and sealed it over him to keep him from deceiving the nations any more until the thousand years are over. After that he must be set free for a little while.

⁴Then *I saw thrones*, and those who sat on them were *given authority to judge*. I also saw the souls of those who had been beheaded for speaking the truth told by Jesus and God's Word. They had not *worshiped the* beast and its *statue* and were not branded on their foreheads and hands. *They lived* and *ruled* with Christ a thousand years. ⁵The rest of the dead didn't live until the thousand years were over. This is the first resurrection.

⁶Blessed and holy are those who share in the first resurrection; the second death has no power over them, but they will be *priests of God* and of Christ and will rule with Him during the thousand years.

⁷When the thousand years are over, Satan will be freed from his prison ⁸and will come out to deceive the nations in all parts of the world — that is, *Gog and Magog* — to gather them for battle; they will be as many as the sand by the sea.

⁹So they came up, *spreading over the earth*, and surrounded the camp of the holy people and the city He loves. But *fire came down from heaven and consumed them.* ¹⁰And the devil who deceived them was thrown into the lake of *fire and sulfur*, where the beast and the false prophet are, and they will be tortured day and night forever.

The Judgment

¹¹Then *I saw a* great white *throne* and *Him sitting on it from Whom the* earth and the sky *fled* so far *they couldn't be found anywhere.* ¹²Then I saw the dead, great and small, standing before the throne, and *books were opened*. Another book also was opened — it was *the book of life*. And the dead were judged *according to what they had done* as it was written in the books. ¹³The sea gave up the dead that were in it, and death and the grave gave up the dead that were in them, and each one was judged *according to what he had done.*

¹⁴Then death and the grave were thrown into the fiery lake. The fiery lake is the second death. ¹⁵And if anyone wasn't found *written in the book of life*, he was thrown into the fiery lake.

21 Ezek 39:4, 17-20   2 Gen 3:1, 13; Zech 3:1   4 Dan 7:9,18,22,27; Dan 3:5-6
6 Is 61:6; Dan 7:18,22,27   8 Ezek 38:2
9 Hab 1:6; II Sam 22:9; II Kings 1:10,12; Is 26:11; Jer 5:14
10 Gen 19:24
11 I Kings 22:19; Ps 47:8; Is 6:1; Dan 7:9; II Chr 18:18; Ps 114:3,7; Dan 2:35
12 Dan 7:10; Ex 32:32-33; Ps 69:28; 139:16; Is 4:3; Mal 3:16; Dan 12:1
12-13 Ps 28:4; 62:12; Prov 24:12; Jer 17:10

The New Jerusalem

21 Then I saw *a new heaven and a new earth*, because the first heaven and the first earth had passed away. And there was no longer any sea. [2]And I saw *the holy city*, New *Jerusalem*, coming down from God in heaven, *dressed as a bride*, ready to meet her husband.

[3]And I heard a loud voice from the throne say: "Look! *God's home is among the people*, and He will live with them. *They will be His people*, and *God Himself will be with them.* [4]*He will wipe* every *tear from their eyes*. There will be *no* more *death*, and there will be *no more* grief or *crying* or pain, because the *first things* have passed away."

[5]"Look! *I am making* everything *new*," said *He Who sat on the throne*. And He added: "Write this because these words are true and you can trust them." [6]Then He said to me: "It is done! I am the Alpha and Omega [the A and Z], *the Beginning and the End. To anyone who is thirsty* I will give *water, without cost*, from the spring of the *water of life*. [7]Be victorious, and you will have these things, and *I will be your God, and you will be My son*.

[8]"But cowardly, unfaithful, and detestable people, and those who murder, sin sexually, practice witchcraft, and worship idols, and all liars will find themselves in the lake *burning with fire* and *sulfur*; this is the second death."

[9]Then came one of those seven angels with the seven bowls full of the *seven* last *plagues*. "Come," he said to me, "I will show you the bride, the Lamb's wife."

[10]He carried me in spirit *to a* large and *high mountain* and showed me *the holy city of Jerusalem* coming down from God in heaven. [11]*It had God's glory* and a brilliance like a very precious stone, like jasper that is clear as crystal. [12]It had a large, high wall with *twelve gates*, and at the gates twelve angels, and on the gates *were written the names of the twelve tribes of Israel.* [13]There were *three gates on the east side, three gates on the north, three gates on the south, and three gates on the west.* [14]And the wall of the city had twelve foundation stones, and on them were the twelve names of the twelve apostles of the Lamb.

[15]The angel who was talking to me had a gold *measuring rod* to measure the city, its gates, and its wall. [16]The city was *square* — it was as wide as it was long. He measured the city with the rod — it was 1500 miles.[f] Its length, breadth, and height were the same. [17]Then he measured its wall; it

15 Ex 32:32-33; Ps 69:28; 139:16; Is 4:3; Mal 3:16; Dan 12:1   *1 Is 65:17; 66:22*
2 Is 52:1; 61:10   *3 Gen 17:7-8; Ex 29:45-46; Deut 4:20; 26:18; 29:13; Is 7:14;*
8:8,10; Jer 7:23; 11:4; 24:7; 30:22; 31:1,33; 32:38; Ezek 11:20; 14:11; 34:24; 36:28;
37:23,27; Zech 2:10-11; 8:8; 13:9; Is 7:14; 8:8,10   *4 Is 25:8; 65:17,19*
5 Is 43:19; I Kings 22:19; Ps 47:8; Is 6:1; II Chr 18:18
6 Is 44:6; 48:12; Prov 10:11; 13:14; 14:27; 16:22; Is 55:1; Zech 14:8
7 Gen 17:7-8; Deut 4:20; 26:18; 29:13; II Sam 7:14; Jer 7:23; 11:4; 24:7; 30:22; 31:1;
32:38; Zech 8:8; 13:9   *8 Is 30:33*   *9 Lev 26:21*   *10 Is 52:1; Ezek 40:2*
11 Is 58:8; 60:1-2,19   *12-13 Ex 28:21; Ezek 48:31-34*

was 72 yards[g] according to human measurement, which the angel was using.

[18]Its wall was made of jasper, but the city was of gold as pure as clear glass. [19]*The foundations* of the city wall were made beautiful with all kinds of precious stones: the first foundation stone was jasper, the second *sapphire*, the third agate, the fourth emerald, [20]the fifth sardonyx, the sixth carnelian, the seventh chrysolite, the eighth beryl, the ninth topaz, the tenth chrysoprase, the eleventh jacinth, the twelfth amethyst. [21]The twelve gates were twelve pearls; each gate was made of one pearl. The street of the city was of gold as pure as clear glass.

[22]But I didn't see any temple in it, because the *Lord God, the Almighty,* and the Lamb are its temple. [23]And the city doesn't need *any sun or moon to give it light,* because God's *glory is* its *light,* and the Lamb is its lamp. [24]*The nations will walk by* its *light, and the kings* of the earth *will bring* their glory into it. [25]Its *gates will never be shut any day,* because *there will be no night* there. [26]People will bring the glory and *wealth of the nations* into it. [27]But *nothing unclean will ever come into it,* or anyone who does anything detestable or tells lies, only those who are *written in the Lamb's book of life.*

22

Then he showed me a river of the *water of life* bright as crystal, *flowing from* the throne of God and of the Lamb [2]and down the middle of the street of the city. *On each side of the river is a tree of life, producing* twelve kinds of *fruit, for each month its own fruit, and the leaves of the tree are to heal* the nations. [3]*There will no longer be anything that is cursed.*

The throne of God and of the Lamb will be in the city. His servants will worship Him [4]and *see Him,* and His name will be on their foreheads. [5]*There will be no more night,* and they will not need any light of a lamp or of *the sun,* because *the Lord God will shine* on them, and *they will be kings forever.*

I Am Coming Soon.

[6]"You can trust these words," he told me; "they are true. And the Lord, the God of the spirits of the prophets, has sent His angel to show His servants *what must happen* soon. [7]Remember, *I am coming* soon! Blessed is he who keeps what the prophecy of this book tells him."

[8]I, John, heard and saw these things, and when I had heard and seen them, I *bowed down to worship* at the feet of the angel who showed them to

---

15-16 *Ezek 40:3,5; Zech 2:1-2; Ezek 43:16*   **19** *Is 54:11*   **22** *Is 40:10; Mal 3:1*
23 *Is 60:1-2,19*   **24-26** *Ps 89:27; 138:4; Is 60:3,5,11; Zech 14:7*
27 *Is 52:1; Ex 32:32-33; Ps 69:28; 139:16; Is 4:3; Mal 3:16; Dan 12:1*
1 *Ezek 47:1,12; Joel 3:18; Zech 14:8* **2** *Gen 2:9; 3:22,24; Prov 3:18; 13:12; 15:4; Ezek 47:7,12*   **3** *Zech 14:11*   **4** *Ps 17:15; 42:2*   **5** *Zech 14:7; Is 60:19; Dan 7:18,22,27*
6 *Is 48:6; Dan 2:28-29,45*   **7** *Is 40:10*

---

f - 16   This seems to be the length of one side. Gk: 12,000 stadia g - 17   Gk: 144 cubits

me.

⁹"Be careful! Don't do that!" he told me. "I'm a fellow servant of yours and of the other Christians, the prophets, and those who keep what this book says. Worship God.

¹⁰"*Don't keep secret* what the prophecy of *this book* tells you," he said to me, "because the *time* is near when it will come true. ¹¹Let *the wrongdoer still do wrong*, the filthy one still be filthy, and let the righteous one still do right and the holy one still be holy."

¹²"Yes, *I am coming* soon and *will have My reward with Me* to *pay everyone according to what he has done.* ¹³I am the Alpha and the Omega [the A and the Z], *the First and the Last*, the Beginning and the End. ¹⁴Blessed are those who *wash their robes* so that they have the right to *the tree of life* and go through the gates into the city. ¹⁵Outside are the dogs and people who do witchcraft, sin sexually, murder, worship idols, and everyone who loves lies and tells them.

¹⁶"I, Jesus, have sent My angel to tell you these truths for the churches. I am *David's Descendant* and the bright Morning Star."

¹⁷"Come!" say the Spirit and the bride. "If you hear this, say, 'Come!' *If you are thirsty, come.* If you want it, take *the water of life as a free gift.*

¹⁸"I warn everyone who hears what the prophecy of this book tells him: If you *add anything to this*, God will *add to you* the plagues *written in this book.* ¹⁹And if you *take away* any words in this book of prophecy, *God will take away* your share in *the tree of life* and in the holy city that are described in this book."

²⁰He who spoke these truths says: "Yes, *I am coming* soon!" Amen! Come, Lord Jesus!

²¹The grace of the Lord Jesus be with all the holy people. Amen.

8 Ps 22:27; 86:9; Is 45:14; 49:23; 60:14; 66:23;   *10* Dan 8:26; 12:4-9
11 Dan 12:10   *12* Is 40:10; 62:11; Ps 28:4; 62:12; Prov 24:12; Jer 17:10
13 Is 44:2,6; 48:12   *14* Gen 49:11; Gen 2:9; 3:22,24; Prov 3:18; 13:12; 15:4
16 Is 11:1,10; Jer 23:5   *17* Is 55:1; Zech 14:8
18-19 Prov 30:6; Deut 4:2; 13:1; 29:19-20
19 Gen 2:9; 3:22,24; Prov 3:18; 13:12; 15:4   *20* Is 40:10

PSALMS
AND
PROVERBS

THE PSALMS

The Blessed Man

1 Blessed is the man
   who doesn't go with the wicked in their planning,
   stand in the ways of sinners,
   or sit in the company of mockers,
² but delights in what the LORD teaches
   and reads it thoughtfully day and night.

³ He's like a tree planted by streams of water:
   It produces its fruit in its season,
   and its leaves don't wither.
   He succeeds in everything he does.

⁴ The wicked are not like that
   but like chaff that the wind blows away.
⁵ And so when they're judged the wicked will not stand,
   nor will sinners in the congregation of the righteous.

⁶ You see, the LORD cares about what happens to the righteous,
   but the wicked go their way and perish.

God's Son

2 *Why are the nations getting together so noisily*
and the people plotting so uselessly?
² *The kings of the earth are taking their stand,*
and the rulers are planning together
*against the LORD and His Anointed,*ᵃ saying
³ "Let us tear their ropes in pieces and throw the cords away."
⁴ Sitting on His throne in heaven,
the Lord laughs and mocks at them.
⁵ Then He talks to them angrily
and by His fury terrifies them:
⁶ "I installed My King on Zion, My holy hill."

1-2 Acts 4:25-27; Rev 6:15; 11:15; 17:18; 19:19

---

a - 2   "Anointed" means "Christ," and this is the name the New Testament writers read
here in their Greek translation of the Old Testament.

(The Anointed:)

[7] I will tell about the decree of the LORD:
He said to Me,
"You are My Son, today I have begotten You.
[8] Ask Me and *I will give* You *the nations* as Your inheritance
and the most distant parts of the earth as Your possession.
[9] *You will break them in pieces with an iron rod*
and smash them like a potter's jar."

[10] Now then, you kings, be wise;
be warned, you rulers of the world.
[11] Serve the LORD with fear
and rejoice with trembling.
[12] Kiss the Son
or He'll get angry and you'll perish on your way;
because His anger can blaze quickly.
Blessed are all who find shelter in Him.

My Shield

David's psalm when he fled from his son Absalom.

3 O LORD, how my enemies have increased!
Many are attacking me;
[2] many are saying of me, "God will not save him." (Music)[b]

[3] But You, O LORD, are a Shield around me;
You give me glory and lift up my head.
[4] I call aloud to the LORD,
and He answers me from His holy hill. (Music)[b]

[5] I lie down and sleep and then wake up
because the LORD supports me.
[6] I'm not afraid of an army of tens of thousands,
that attacks me from all sides.

[7] Come, O LORD! Save me, my God!
Hit all my enemies in the face,
and smash the teeth of the wicked.
[8] Only You can save, O LORD;
so bless Your people. (Music)[b]

---

7 *Mt 3:17; 17:5; Mk 1:11; 9:7; Lk 3:22; 9:35; Acts 13:33; Heb 1:5; 5:5; 7:28; 2 Pet 1:17*
8-9 *Rev 2:26-27; 12:5; 19:15*

b - 2,4,8 The word "Selah [Music]" is conjectured by most to be a musical notation.

In the Evening

For the choir leader; with stringed instruments; a psalm by David.

4 When I call, answer me, O God, Who declares me righteous.
   I'm hard-pressed — set me free.
   Be kind to me and hear my prayer.
2 You mortals, how long are you going to turn My honor to shame?
   You love worthless things and seek falsehood. (Music)[b]
3 You should know that the LORD makes the one He loves
   someone special to Him.
   The LORD hears me when I call to Him.

4 *Tremble and don't sin.*
   Think about it on your beds and weep. (Music)[b]
5 Bring the proper sacrifices in the right spirit,
   and trust the LORD.

6 Many are saying, "If only someone could show us prosperity!"
   Let the light of Your face shine on us, O LORD.
7 You put more joy in my heart
   than a season with plenty of new grain and wine.
8 I can lie down and sleep in peace,
   because You alone, O LORD, enable me to live without fear.

In the Morning

For the choir leader; upon the flutes;[c] a psalm by David.

5 Listen to what I'm saying, O LORD: understand what I'm
   sighing about.
2 Listen to me when I call for help, my King and my God,
   because I'm pleading with You.
3 O LORD, in the morning listen to me;
   in the morning I lay my needs before You and look up.

4 You are not a God Who likes wickedness.
   Evil can't live with You.
5 Those who brag can't stand before Your eyes.
   You hate all who do wrong
6 and destroy those who tell lies.
   The LORD detests anyone who murders and cheats.

7 Your great kindness makes me come to Your house
   and worship in Your holy temple with a sense of awe for You.

---

4 Eph 4:26

b - 2,4   The word "Selah [Music]" is conjectured by most to be a musical notation.
c - 1   The meaning is uncertain.

⁸ O LORD, lead me in Your righteousness
     as I face those who hate me.
     Make Your way smooth before me.
⁹ There's no truth in what they say,
     but treachery is in their hearts.
     Their throat is an open grave.
     When they talk, they flatter.
¹⁰ O God, make them suffer for their sins
     and fall by their own plans.
     Throw them out because they did so much wrong
     and rebelled against You.
¹¹ Then all who find their shelter in You
     will be glad forever, shouting happily.
     You will shelter them.
     And those who love Your name will delight in You.
¹² O LORD, You bless the righteous man;
     You surround him with kindness as with a big shield.

Because You Love Me

For the choir leader; with stringed instruments, for bass
voices;^d a psalm by David.

6 O LORD, don't be angry and punish me,
     don't be furious and correct me.
² Be kind to me, O LORD, because I am miserable.
     Heal me, O LORD, because I'm shaken to my bones;
³ my *spirit is terribly upset.*
     O LORD, how long will you wait?
⁴ Come back, O LORD, rescue me;
     save me because of Your mercy.
⁵ Once a person is dead, he can't remember You.
     Can anyone in the grave praise You?
⁶ My groaning wears me out.
     Every night I make my bed swim and my couch flow with
       tears.

⁷ My eyes are hollow with grief
     and grow old because of all my enemies.
⁸ *Get away from me, all you who do wrong,*
     because the LORD has heard my crying,
⁹ the LORD has heard me ask for mercy,
     the LORD accepts my prayer.
¹⁰ All my enemies will be miserable and terrified and suddenly
     turn back in disgrace.

---

9 Rom 3:13   *3 Jn 12:27*   *8 Mt 7:23; Lk 13:27*

d - 1   The meaning is uncertain. Literally "on the eighth."

Trust in a Righteous God

A complaint David sang to the Lord about Cush, a descendant of Benjamin.

7 O LORD, my God, You are my Shelter.
   Save me from all who pursue me, and rescue me,
² or like a lion they will tear me to pieces,
   dragging me off with no one to save me.
³ O LORD my God, if I did this:
   if there's wrong in my hands,
⁴ if I paid back my friend with evil,
   or plundered anyone who opposed me without a reason,
⁵ then may an enemy chase me and catch me,
   trample my life into the ground,
   and lay my honor in the dust. (Music)ᵇ
⁶ Arise and be angry, O LORD;
   rise against the fury of my enemies;
   awake, my God, order a trial;
⁷ have an assembly of peoples gather around You
   and over them reign on high.
⁸ O LORD, judge the nations.
   Judge me, O LORD, according to my integrity;
      judge me according to my innocence, O Most High.
⁹ O may the wickedness of the wicked end,
   while You make the righteous secure —
   You are a righteous God who *examines minds and hearts.*
¹⁰ God Most High is my Shield.
   He saves those whose heart is right.
¹¹ God is a just Judge,
   a God Who is angry every day.
¹² If anyone will not repent, He sharpens His sword;
   He bends His bow and strings it;
¹³ He aims His arrows to kill him,
   making them blaze with fire.
¹⁴ Here's one who conceives evil,
   is pregnant with harm for others,
   and gives birth to a lie.
¹⁵ He digs a hole and keeps on digging
   until he falls into the hole he was making.
¹⁶ The harm he plans comes back on his own head.
   The crime he means to do comes down on his own skull.
¹⁷ I will thank the LORD — He is righteous.
   I will sing about the name of the LORD Most High.

9 Rev 2:23

Without God, Then Glory

For the choir leader; on a stringed instrument; a psalm by David.

8 O LORD, our Lord,
  how wonderful is Your name all over the earth!
  Your glory is sung over the heavens.
² *From the mouths of children and babies*
  You have established strength[e] despite Your foes,
  in order to silence the enemy and the avenger.

³ When I look at Your heavens that Your fingers made,
  the moon and the stars that You set up,
⁴   *what is man that You should think of him,*
  or the son of man that You should come and visit him?

⁵ *You make Him do without God for a little while;*
  then crown Him with glory and majesty
⁶ *and make Him ruler over what Your hands have made,*
  putting everything under His feet:
⁷ All the sheep and cattle, and the wild animals too,
⁸ birds in the air,
  and fish swimming in the paths of the seas.

⁹ O LORD, our Lord,
  how wonderful is Your name all over the earth!

The Judge Is My Refuge

For the choir leader; about the death of the oppressor;[f] a
  psalm by David.

9 I thank You, O LORD, with all my heart;
  I tell of all the wonderful things You did;
² I am happy and delighted in You
  and sing to praise Your name, O Most High.

³ My enemies turned back,
  stumbling and perishing before You.
⁴ You judged me and showed I am right.
  You sat on Your throne and judged fairly.
⁵ You denounced nations, destroyed the wicked,
  and wiped out their name forever.
⁶ The enemy is finished, destroyed forever.
  You uprooted their towns, and they are forgotten.

---

2 Mt 21:16   *4-6 Heb 2:6-9; I Cor 15:27,28; Eph 1:22*

e - 2   Or "praise"
f - 1   Conjectural; The Hebrew may be a musical notation

⁷ The LORD is sitting on His throne forever;
    He has set up His throne to judge.
⁸ *He judges the world with justice*
    and gives the people a fair trial.
⁹ The LORD is a Mountain Refuge for the oppressed,
    a Refuge in times of trouble.
¹⁰ Those who know You trust You
    because You don't forsake those who come to You for help.

¹¹ Sing to the LORD Who lives in Zion;
    tell among the people the great things He does.
¹² He cares for those who mourn, remembers them,
    and doesn't forget the cries of those who suffer.
¹³ O LORD, be kind to me;
    see how those who hate me make me suffer;
    pick me up from the gates of death
¹⁴ so I can proclaim Your praise.
    In the gates of Zion's people
    I will delight in Your salvation.

¹⁵ Nations are sunk in the pit they themselves made;
    their feet are caught in the very net they hid.
¹⁶ The LORD shows Who He is by His justice.
    The wicked were trapped by their own doings. (Solemn
      music)ᵍ
¹⁷ The wicked go back to the grave like all people who forget God.

¹⁸ The poor will not always be forgotten
    or those who suffer lose hope forever.
¹⁹ Rise, O LORD, to keep men from being triumphant.
    Nations will be judged before You.
²⁰ O LORD, frighten them —
    so nations will know they're only human.

Help the Oppressed

10 Why are You staying so far away, O LORD? Why do You
    hide whenever there's trouble?
² The wicked proudly hunt down the oppressed;
    may they be caught by their own schemes.
³ The wicked man boasts of his selfish lust.
    He is greedy for a blessing but scorns the LORD.
⁴ Because of his arrogance the wicked won't ask Him for help.
    God is left out of all his plans,
⁵ but he seems always to succeed.

---

8 *Acts 17:31; Rev 19:11*

g - 16   Selah Higgaion

Your judgments are too high for him to see.
He puffs at all his enemies.
⁶ He thinks, "Nothing can shake me.
I'll never have any trouble."

⁷ *His mouth is full of cursing,* deception, and oppression;
under his tongue lurk mischief and wrong doing.
⁸ He sits in ambush in the villages;
from his hiding places he kills the innocent;
his eyes are looking for victims.
⁹ He lies in his hiding place like a lion in his den,
waits there to catch the helpless,
and takes the poor away, dragging him in his net.
¹⁰ The victim is crushed and sinks down;
because of his power he falls helpless.
¹¹ But the wicked man says to himself, "God doesn't care.
He hides His face and will never see it."
¹² Come, O LORD God! Lift Your hand,
and don't forget the oppressed.
¹³ Why should the wicked despise God
and think that You won't punish?
¹⁴ See for Yourself the trouble and look at the grief,
so You can take it in hand.
The victim entrusts himself to You,
for You are the One who helps the orphan.
¹⁵ Break the arm of the wicked and evil man;
punish his wickedness until it is gone.

¹⁶ *The LORD is King forever.*
The heathen must perish from His land.
¹⁷ O LORD, You hear the desire of the oppressed.
Encourage them and listen to them.
¹⁸ Give the orphan and the oppressed fair treatment
so that no one on earth will terrify them again.

The Lord Loves Righteousness

For the choir leader; by David.

11 I take refuge in the LORD. How can you tell me:
"Flee like a bird to your hills"?
² Look at the wicked:
They bend their bow, and fix their arrows on the string,
to shoot in the dark at those who are honest.
³ When the foundations are torn down,
what does the Righteous One do about it?

7 *Rom 3:14*   16 *Rev 11:15*

⁴ The LORD is in His holy temple;
    the LORD's throne is in heaven —
    His eyes see, yes, His eyes examine mortal man.
⁵ The LORD tests the righteous.
    He hates anyone who is wicked and loves crime.
⁶ He has snares come down like rain on the wicked.
    Fire, sulfur, and a scorching wind will be the drink in
        their cup.
⁷ Yes, the LORD is just and loves righteousness.
    The righteous will see His face.

When People Lie

For the choir leader; for bass voices;[h] a psalm by David.

12 Help, O Lord, for there are no more godly people!
    The faithful have vanished from the world.
² Everyone tells lies.
    They talk with flattering lips and a double mind.
³ May the LORD cut off every lip that flatters and every
        tongue that talks big,
⁴ saying, "We'll show with our tongues how mighty we are.
    We say what we please. Who can be our master?"

⁵ "Because the poor are robbed and the needy groan,
    I will now rise," says the LORD.
    "I will provide safety to the one who longs for it."
⁶ The words of the LORD are pure,
    like silver refined in a furnace
    purified seven times.
⁷ O LORD, You watch over us,
    You keep us safe forever from this world,
⁸ where the wicked prowl around
    praising what is vile among people.

How Long?

For the choir leader; a psalm by David.

13 How long, O LORD? Will You forget me forever?
    How long will You hide Your face from me?
² How long should I be planning by myself,
    and my heart be grieving during the day?
    How long is my enemy going to triumph over me?

h - 1   Conjecture

³ Look and answer me, O LORD my God!
  Give light to my eyes,
  or I'll sleep the sleep of death,
⁴ and my enemy will say, "I overpowered him,"
  and my foes will be delighted because I've fallen.
⁵ But I trust Your kindness.
  I'll take delight in Your saving me.
⁶ I'll sing to the LORD,
  because He has done so much for me.

We Are Sinners

For the choir leader; by David.

14 A fool says in his heart, "There is no God."
  They do corrupt and detestable things.
  No one does anything good.
² The LORD looks at the world from heaven
  to see if *there is anyone wise, who comes to God for help.*
³ *They have all turned away together and become corrupt.*
  Not one does right, not a single one.
⁴ Don't all these who do wrong know,
  don't these who devour my people know
  that if anyone eats the bread the LORD gives
⁵ without calling on Him, panic will overtake them,
  because God is among righteous people?
⁶ You would make the poor man disappointed in his planning.
  But the LORD is his Refuge.
⁷ If only Someone would come from Zion to save Israel.
  When the LORD restores His people,
  Jacob will be delighted and Israel will be glad.

Close to God

A psalm by David.

15 (Congregation:)
O LORD, who may come to stay in Your tabernacle?
  Who may live on Your holy hill?

(Leader:)
² If you live perfectly, do what is right,
  and tell the truth from your heart.
³ If you don't use your tongue to do wrong to another
  or bring shame on your neighbor.

1-3 Rom 3:10-12

⁴ You despise one whom God rejects
    but honor those who fear the LORD.
    When you swear, you don't change it even if it hurts you.
⁵ You don't take interest on money you loan
    or take a bribe against an innocent person.
    If you do these things, you will never fail.

Victory over Death

    An inscription by David.

16 Keep me safe, O God — You are my shelter.
² I told the LORD, "You are my Lord.
    My well-being is only in You."
³ But as for those on earth who are holy, they are noble
    ones in whom is my total delight.
⁴ Those who buy another god quickly multiply their sorrows.
    I will not pour out drink offerings of blood for them
    or take their names on my lips.

⁵ The LORD is my measured portion and my cup;
    You firmly hold my destiny.
⁶ The land allotted to me is in pleasant places;
    yes, my inheritance is something beautiful.
⁷ I praise the LORD Who gives me counsel;
    also, at night my deepest feelings show me what is right.
⁸ *I always keep the LORD before Me.*
    With Him at My right hand, I can't fail.
⁹ *That is why My heart is glad, and My soul is delighted.*
    Also My body will rest securely
¹⁰ *because You will not leave Me in the grave*
    nor let Your Holy One experience decay.
¹¹ *You show Me the path of life —*
    plenty of joy in Your presence,
    delightful things at Your right hand forever.

In the Shadow of Your Wings

    A prayer by David.

17 O LORD, listen to a just case.
    Hear my cry, listen to my prayer,
    for there's no dishonesty on my lips.

8-11 Acts 2:25-28,31; 13:35

² Let me get justice from You;
    Your eyes see what is right.
³ Test my heart, examine me at night, test me in fire;
    You will find no evil intentions in me;
    nor do they cross my lips.
⁴ As for what others do —
    by Your word of warning I've kept myself from violent ways.
⁵ My steps have not strayed from Your paths;
    my feet have not slipped.

⁶ I call You, O God, because You answer me.
    Turn Your ear to me; listen to what I say.
⁷ Do Your wonderfully kind acts.
    With Your right hand save from their enemies
    those who trust in You.
⁸ Keep me like the pupil of Your eye.
    Hide me in the shadow of Your wings
⁹ from the wicked who violently mistreat me,
    from my mortal enemies who surround me.
¹⁰ They are given over to arrogance,
    their mouths talk proudly.
¹¹ They track me down and then gather around me
    looking determined to throw me to the ground.
¹² Each is like a lion longing for prey,
    like a young lion lying in his hiding place.
¹³ Rise, O LORD, oppose him to his face,
    put him down on his knees,
    with Your sword save me from the wicked,
¹⁴ with Your hand from men, O LORD,
    from men whose fulfillments are only in this life.
    As for those You treasure — fill their stomachs;
    may their sons be satisfied
    and leave what they have left to their infants.

¹⁵ With righteousness I will see *Your face*,
and be satisfied, when I awake, by seeing You.

David's Victory

    For the choir leader. By David the LORD's servant, who
    spoke this song to the LORD when the LORD
    rescued him from Saul and all his enemies. He said:

18 I love You, O LORD, my Strength.

---

15 *Rev 22:4*   2 *Heb 2:13; Lk 1:69*

i - 2   Or "my King"

² The LORD is my Rock, my Fortress, my Rescuer,
     my God, my Rock *where I find shelter*,
     my Shield,ⁱ *my Horn of salvation*, my Mountain Refuge.

³ I called on the LORD Who deserves praise
     and was saved from my enemies.
⁴Death surrounded me with its snares;
     torrents of destruction overwhelmed me;
⁵ the grave was all around me to catch me;
     death came toward me to trap me.

⁶ In my trouble I called the LORD; I cried to my God for help.
     In His temple He heard me call,
     and my *cry* for help *came to His ears*.
⁷ Then the earth swayed and quaked;
     the foundations of the mountains shook
     and rocked because He was angry.
⁸ Smoke went up from His nostrils,
     and *from His mouth came a devouring fire*
     that made coals glow.
⁹ He spread apart the heavens and came down
     with a dark cloud under His feet.
¹⁰ He rode on a cherubʲ and flew,
     darting along on wings of the wind.
¹¹ He made the darkness hide Him;
     dark water and thick clouds became His shelter.
¹² Light shone ahead of Him as dark clouds passed by,
     with hail and glowing coals.
¹³ The LORD thundered from heaven;
     the Most High spoke out; there was hail and glowing
       coals.
¹⁴ He shot His arrows and scattered them;
     He shot His lightning flashes and threw them into a
       panic.
¹⁵ Then the floor of the sea could be seen;
     the foundations of the earth were laid bare
     at Your rebuke, O LORD,
     at the blast of the breath of Your nostrils.

¹⁶ He reached down from above and took hold of me;
     He pulled me out of many waters
¹⁷ and rescued me from my strong enemies,
     from those who hated me,

---

6 *James 5:4*   **8** *Rev 11:5*

j - 10   An angelic being, usually symbolized in animal form.

because they were too strong for me.
[18] They came against me on the day I faced disaster,
    but the LORD helped me
[19] and brought me out to a place where I was free.

So He rescued me because He took delight in me.

[20] The LORD rewarded me according to my righteousness.
    He gave me what my clean hands deserve,
[21] because I've kept the LORD's ways
    and haven't wickedly turned away from my God.
[22] His laws are all before me;
    I don't lay aside His rules.
[23] I am blameless before Him;
    I have kept myself from doing wrong,
[24] so the LORD will reward me according to my righteousness,
    because He sees my hands are clean.
[25] You are *kind to him who is kind,*
    sincere with him who is sincere,
[26] pure with him who is pure,
    but shrewd with a crooked person.

[27] Yes, You save a suffering people,
    but You humble those who look proud.
[28] You light my lamp, O LORD;
    my God lights up my darkness.
[29] With You I can run into a troop;
    with My God I can jump over a wall.
[30] God's way is perfect;
    the LORD's promise has been tested by fire.
    He's a Shield to all who go to Him for shelter.

[31] Is there any God beside the LORD?
    Is there any Rock beside our God?
[32] This God arms me with strength
    and makes my way perfect.
[33] He makes my feet like those of deer
    and gives me a sure footing on the heights.
[34] He trains my hands to fight
    so that my arms can bend a bronze bow.
[35] You gave me Your shield to save me;
    Your right hand supports me;
    Your coming down to help me is what makes me great.
[36] You make a wide path for me to walk on;

and my ankles don't waver.
[37] I chase my enemies and catch up with them
and don't go back until they're completely defeated.
[38] I smash them so they can't get up
but fall under my feet.
[39] You arm me with strength to fight
and make those who attack me bow at my feet.
[40] You enable me to put my feet on the back of my enemies,
so I wipe out those who hate me.
[41] They cry for help, but there's no one to save them;
they cried to the LORD, but He doesn't answer them.
[42] I beat them fine like dust flying in the air;
like mud on the streets I clear them away.

[43] You free me from the quarreling of the people,
and make me a leader of nations.
[44] People I don't know serve me
and obey me as soon as they hear of me.
Foreigners cringe before me.
[45] Foreigners wilt like leaves
and come trembling out of their fortifications.

[46] The LORD lives!
Praise be to my Rock! Let high honor come
to God Who saves me,
[47] the God Who takes vengeance for me
and subdues people under me.
[48] He rescues me from my enemies;
You lift me above those who attack me;
You rescue me from the men of violence.
[49] *For that I will thank You*, O LORD,
among the nations, and sing to praise Your name.
[50] He gives His king great victories;
He loves His anointed, David and his descendants, forever.

God's Wonders

For the choir leader; a psalm by David.

19 The heavens are telling how wonderful God is,
and the sky announces what His hands have made.
[2] One day tells the next a lively story,
and one night informs the next
[3] without talking, without words,
without a voice that can be heard.

---

49 Rom 15:9

⁴ Yet *their sound goes out all over the earth,*
        and what they say to the most distant parts of the world.
    He has set up a tent in the heavens for the sun,
⁵ and it comes like a bridegroom out of his chamber.
    Like a strong man it delights to run along its path,
⁶ starting from one end of the sky
        and moving around to the other.
    Nothing can hide from its glowing heat.

⁷ The LORD's word is perfect and gives new life.
        The LORD's truth can be trusted to make simple people wise.
⁸ The LORD's instructions are right, delighting the mind.
        The LORD's commandment is pure, a light for the eyes.
⁹ The LORD's command to fear Him is clean and forever the same.
        The LORD's decisions are true and altogether *right.*
¹⁰ We want them more than gold, more than plenty of fine gold.
        They're sweeter than honey, even when it flows from the
            honeycomb.
¹¹ Your servant gets light from them.
        If we keep them, we get a great reward.

¹² Who can know his unintentional errors?
        Cleanse me from hidden faults.
¹³ Above all keep Your servant from proud sins;
        don't let them get control over me.
    Then I'll be blameless and innocent of any great wrong.
¹⁴ May what I say please You and what I think be what You like,
        O LORD, my Rock and my Redeemer.

Before Battle

For the choir leader; a psalm by David.

20 (Chorus:)
    May the LORD answer you when you're in trouble!
        May the name of Jacob's God lift you up on a safe height.
² May He send you help from His holy place
        and support you from Zion.
³ May He remember all your gifts
        and accept your burnt offerings. (Music)ᵇ
⁴ May He give you your heart's desire
        and carry out all your plans.
⁵ Then we'll shout joyfully over the victory given you
        and in our God's name wave our banners.

---

4 Rom 10:18   *9 Rev 16:5,7; 19:2*

May the LORD give you everything you ask for.
(Solo:)
6 Now I'm sure the LORD will give His anointed a victory
    as He answers him from His holy heaven
    with mighty deeds by His right hand.
7 For some it's chariots; for others, horses;
    but we will boast in the name of the LORD our God.
8 They will totter to their knees and fall,
    but we will rise and stand up.
(People:)
9 O LORD, save!

May the King answer us when we call.

After Battle

For the choir leader; a psalm by David.

(Chorus:)
21 O LORD, in Your power the king rejoices;
    in Your victory how very delighted he is!
2 You've given him what his heart desired
    and didn't keep from him what he asked for. (Music)[b]
3 You come to him blessing him with good things
    and put on his head a crown of fine gold.
4 He asked You for life — You gave it to him,
    long life, forever and ever.
5 His glory is great because of the victory You gave him,
    You have laid honor and majesty on him.
6 You have given him blessings that last forever.
    You have made him glad as he joyfully looks at You.

(Solo:)
7 Yes, the king is trusting the LORD,
    and the kindness of God above doesn't let him fail.
8 Your hand finds out all your enemies,
    your right hand all who hate you.
9 O LORD, when You appear,
    You will burn them as in a blazing furnace.
    In His anger the LORD will devour them,
    like a *fire consuming* them.
10 By destroying their children you will rid the earth of them,
    and the world of their descendants.
11 When they plan evil against you, scheming and plotting,
    they can't succeed.

9 James 5:3

¹² You make them turn their backs
    by shooting your arrows at their faces.

(People:)
¹³ O LORD, rise in Your might!
    Then we'll sing songs and praise Your power.

The Suffering Savior

    For the choir leader, on the Doe of Dawn, a psalm by David.

22 *My God, My God, why did You forsake Me?*
    Far away from Him Who can save Me,
    I cry out.

² My God, I call by day, but You don't answer,
    at night, and I get no rest.
³ But You are holy, on Your throne;
    You are praised by Israel.
⁴ Our fathers trusted You;
    they trusted You, and You rescued them.
⁵ They cried to You and were saved;
    they *trusted* You and were *not disappointed.*

⁶ But I am a worm and no man,
    scorned by men and despised by people.
⁷ All who see Me *mock* Me;
    with mouths wide open they are *wagging their heads* (saying):
⁸ *"Put Your trouble on the Lord. —*
    Let Him rescue Him and save Him, seeing He delights in Him!"

⁹ You drew Me out of My mother's womb
    and made Me feel safe on My mother's breasts.
¹⁰ I was cast on You from before I was born;
    from My mother's womb You have been My God.

¹¹ Don't go far away from Me—
    trouble is near and there's no one to help Me.
¹² Many bulls gather around Me;
    strong bulls from Bashan surround Me.
¹³ They come for Me with mouths opened wide —
    lions tearing and roaring.
¹⁴ I am poured out like water, and all My limbs are torn apart.
    My heart is like wax, melted within Me.

---

1 Mt 27:46; Mk 15:34   5 Rom 5:5
6-8 Mt 27:39,43-44; Mk 15:29,31-32; Lk 22:63,65; 23:35

¹⁵ My strength is dried up like a piece of broken pottery;
    My tongue sticks to My jaws.
    You are placing Me down in the dust of death.
¹⁶ Dogs gather around Me;
    a gang of villains surrounds Me.
    They have dug holes in My hands and feet.
¹⁷ I can count all My bones.
    They watch; they gloat over Me.
¹⁸ *They divide My clothes among themselves*
    and throw dice for My garment.

¹⁹ But You, O LORD, don't go far away;
    O My Strength, hurry to help Me.
²⁰ Save My life from the sword,
    My one life from the clutches of a dog.
²¹ *Save Me from the lion's mouth,*
    and from the horns of the wild bull.
    You answered me!

²² *I will spread Your fame among My brothers;*
    I will praise You in the congregation:
²³ "You *who fear* the LORD, *praise Him!*
    All you descendants of Jacob, glorify Him!
    Fear Him, all you descendants of Israel!
²⁴ For He did not despise or abhor the Sufferer's suffering,
    nor hide His face from Him.
    But when He called to Him for help,
    He listened to Him."
²⁵ For You I give thanks in the great congregation;
    I do what I vowed before those who fear Him.
²⁶ Let the humble eat and be satisfied,
    and those who go to the LORD for help praise Him —
    may you live forever!

²⁷ In all parts of the world people will remember
    and come back to the LORD;
    all the families of *the nations will worship You*
²⁸ because *the LORD is King and rules* the nations.
²⁹ All the rich people in the world will eat and worship,
    and all who go down to the dust, who can't live,
    will bow before Him.
³⁰ There will be descendants that serve Him

---

16 Rev 1:7   *18 Mt 27:35; Mk 15:24; Lk 23:34; Jn 19:24*
21 II Tim 4:17   *22 Heb 2:11-12,17; Jn 17:6*   *23 Rev 19:5*
27 Rev 3:9; 4:10; 5:14; 11:16; 15:4; 19:4,10; 22:8   *28 Rev 11:15*

when those of a coming age are told about the Lord.
[31] They will come and tell a people still to be born
about His righteousness—He *has done* it!

My Shepherd

A psalm by David.

23 The LORD is my Shepherd —
I have everything I need.
[2] He makes me lie down in fresh green pastures
and *leads* me *to water* where I can rest.
[3] He restores my life.
He leads me on paths of righteousness
for His name's sake.
[4] Even though I walk in a very dark valley,
I fear no harm because You are with me;
Your rod and Your staff give me comfort.
[5] You set a table before me
right in front of my enemies.
You have anointed my head with oil;
my cup is running over.

[6] Surely goodness and mercy will follow me all my life,
and I will live in the LORD's house forever.

Welcome the King of Glory!

A psalm by David.

(Congregation in procession:)
24 *The earth is the LORD's and everything in it,*
the world and those who live in it.
[2] He laid its foundation over the seas
and set it firmly above the rivers.

(Voice:)
[3] Who can go up on the LORD's hill?
Who can stand in His holy place?
(Leader:)
[4] The person whose hands are clean,
whose *mind* is *pure,*
who doesn't set his heart on worthless idols,
or lie when under oath.
[5] Such a person will get a blessing from the LORD

and righteousness from God Who saves him.
⁶ Such are the people who are searching for Him
    and coming to You for help, God of Jacob. (Music)ᵇ

(Congregation entering:)
⁷ O gates, rise O doors of the everlasting One,
    that the King of glory may come in!
(Voice:)
⁸ Who is the King of glory? (Leader:)
    The LORD, strong and mighty!
    The LORD, a hero in battle!
(Congregation:)
⁹' O gates, rise O doors of the everlasting One,
    that the King of glory may come in!
(Voice:)
¹⁰ Who is the King of glory?
(Congregation:)
The LORD of armies, He is the King of glory. (Music)ᵇ

Forgive and Help, Lord

By David.

25 I long for You, O LORD. ²I trust You, O my God;
    don't let me down; don't let my enemies triumph over me.
³ *No one who looks* to You *for help will be disappointed,*
    but those who for no reason are unfaithful
        will be disappointed.
⁴ O LORD, help me know Your ways
    and teach me Your paths.
⁵ Lead me in Your truth and teach me,
    because You are the God who saves me.
    I am always looking to You for help.
⁶ Remember, O LORD, how merciful
    and kind You've always been.
⁷ Don't remember how I sinned and did wrong when I was young.
    You are so kind — remember me
    and show how good You are, O LORD.
⁸ Because the LORD is good and righteous;
    He shows sinners how to live.
⁹ He enables the humble to live right,
    teaching them His way.
¹⁰ The LORD is kind and true in everything He does
    for those who keep His covenant and His truth.

---

3 Rom 5:5

¹¹ Glorify Your name, O LORD,
        and forgive My sin—it is great.
¹² If you are one who fears the LORD,
        He will teach you the way you should choose.
¹³ You will enjoy good things in your life,
        and your children will inherit the land.
¹⁴ The secret of the LORD is known to those who fear Him;
        He will show them what His covenant means.

¹⁵ I'm always looking to the LORD
        because He can get my feet out of the trap.
¹⁶ Turn to me and be kind to me —
        I am lonely and miserable.
¹⁷ The troubles of my heart have become great.
        Take me out of my distress.
¹⁸ See how poor and miserable I am,
        and take away all my sins.
¹⁹ See how many enemies I have
        and how violently they hate me.
²⁰ Protect and rescue me.
        Don't let me *be disappointed* —
        because I've come to You for shelter.
²¹ May innocence and honesty protect me
        because I look to You for help.
²² O God, free Israel from all their troubles!

Help Me—I'm Innocent

        By David.

26 Give me justice, O LORD — I've lived innocently
        and trusted the LORD without wavering.
² Examine me, O LORD, and test me,
        probe my heart and my mind.
³ I see how kind You are;
        I live in Your truth.
⁴ I don't sit with men who lie;
        I don't keep company with hypocrites.
⁵ I hate every assembly of those who do wrong
        and will not sit with the wicked.

⁶ I wash my hands in innocence
        and march around Your altar, O LORD,
⁷ to praise You with a loud voice
        and tell all the wonderful things You've done.

---

20 Rom 5:5   *2 Rev 2:23*

⁸ O LORD, I love the house You've made Your home,
    the place where Your glory dwells.
⁹ Don't take away my life with sinners and murderers,
¹⁰ whose hands are busy with vice
    and whose right hands are full of bribes.
¹¹ I am living innocently—
    free me and be kind to me.
¹² My foot stands on even ground.
    In the congregations I will praise the LORD.

Nothing to Fear

By David.

27 The LORD gives me light and saves me—
    of whom should I be afraid?
    The LORD is a fortress where my life is safe —
    whom should I fear?
² When wicked men attack me to tear me in pieces,
    my enemies and foes will stumble and fall.
³ Though an army besieges me,
    I'm not afraid.
  Even if a battle is waged against me,
    I'll still be confident.

⁴ I ask the LORD for one thing —
    this is what I want:
    to stay in the LORD's house as long as I live,
    and see how delightful the LORD is,
    and to meditate in His temple.
⁵ He hides me in His shelter when there's trouble,
    keeps me hidden in His tent,
    and sets me high up on His rock.
⁶ Then my head is raised over my enemies around me.
    I want to bring sacrifices into His tabernacle
    with happy shouting;
    I want to sing and play music for the LORD.

⁷ O LORD, hear me as I call out;
    be kind to me and answer me.
⁸ My heart says for You, "Come to Me for help."
    I am coming to You, O LORD.
⁹ Don't hide Your face from me;
    in anger don't turn away Your servant,
    but help me.
  Don't leave me or forsake me, O God, my Savior!
¹⁰ If my father and my mother forsake me,

the LORD will take care of me.
[11] O LORD, teach me Your way,
and lead me on an even path
as I face those who hate me.
[12] Don't give me up to the will of my enemies,
because they appear against me as false witnesses,
breathing out accusations of crime.
[13] I'm sure I will see the goodness of the LORD
in the land of the living.
[14] Wait for the LORD to help you.
Be strong and full of courage.
Yes, wait for the LORD.

Prayer and Thanks

By David.

28 I'm calling You, O LORD,
O my Rock, don't turn silently away from me.
If You are silent,
I will be like those who go down to the grave.
[2] Listen to me plead as I call to You for help,
as I raise my hands toward Your most holy place.
[3] Don't drag me away with the wicked,
with those who do wrong,
who talk of peace with their neighbors
but have evil in mind.
[4] Pay them back *according to what they have done,*
according to their wicked deeds.
Pay them back according to what their hands have done,
and give them what they deserve.
[5] Because they don't consider what the LORD has done
or what His hands have made,
He will tear them down
and never build them up again.

[6] Praise the LORD —
He has heard my call for mercy.
[7] The LORD is my Strength and my Shield.
My heart trusts Him and so I'm helped;
I'm delighted and praise Him in my song.
[8] The LORD is our Strength and a fortress for His anointed one.
[9] Save Your people and bless Your inheritance!
Be their Shepherd and carry them forever!

---

14 I Cor 16:13   *4 Rev 20:12-13; 22:12*

Everything Says, "Glory!"

A psalm by David.

29 Give to the LORD, O sons of God,
    give to the LORD glory and power;
² give to the LORD the glory due His name.
    Worship the LORD in holy splendor.
³ The LORD's voice is over the waters;
    the God of glory is thundering;
    the LORD is over many waters.
⁴ The LORD's voice is powerful;
    the LORD's voice is majestic.
⁵ The LORD's voice shatters the cedars;
    the LORD smashes the cedars of Lebanon.
⁶ He makes Lebanon jump like a calf,
    and Mount Hermon like a young wild bull.
⁷ The LORD's voice cuts down with flames of fire.
⁸ The LORD's voice shakes the wilderness;
    the LORD shakes the wilderness of Kadesh.
⁹ The LORD's voice makes the deer give birth
    and strips the forests bare.
    In His temple everything is saying, "Glory!"

¹⁰ The LORD sits enthroned over the flood;
    the LORD is a king on His throne forever.
¹¹ The LORD gives His people power;
    the LORD blesses His people with peace.

Thank You for Saving My Life

A psalm sung at the dedication of the Temple. By David.

30 I praise You, O LORD, for pulling me out
    and not letting my enemies rejoice over me.
² O LORD my God, I called to You for help,
    and You made me well.
³ O LORD, You lifted me up from the grave
    and saved me from going down to the pit.
⁴ Sing to the LORD, you people that He loves,
    and praise Him as you remember how holy He is.
⁵ His anger lasts for only a moment,
    but His favor lasts for a lifetime.
Weeping may last for a night,
    but there's happy shouting in the morning.

---

3 Acts 7:2

⁶ When all was well with me, I thought, "I'll never fail."
⁷ O LORD, by Your kindness
    You made me like a mighty mountain.
    But when You hid Your face,
    I was terrified.
⁸ I called to You, O LORD;
    I pleaded with my Lord:
⁹ "What's the good of my being killed and going down to the grave?
    Can the dust praise You or tell how faithful You are?
¹⁰ Listen, O LORD, and be merciful to me!
    O LORD, help me!
¹¹ You have changed my weeping to dancing;
    You have taken off my sackcloth and fastened joy like a
    robe around me.
¹² Now my heart can sing to You and not weep.
    O LORD my God, I will praise You forever."

When Friends Run Away

    For the choir leader; a psalm by David.

31 I've taken refuge in You, O LORD;
    don't let me be disappointed.
Because of Your righteousness rescue me.
² Listen to me — hurry to save me.
    Be my Rock of Refuge, a strong fortress to save me.
³ You are my Rock and my Fortress;
    for the honor of Your name lead me and guide me.
⁴ Pull me out of the trap secretly laid for me,
    because You are my Refuge.
⁵ *Into Your hands I entrust my spirit —*
    You have redeemed me, O LORD, my faithful God.
⁶ I hate those who worship worthless idols,
    but I trust the LORD.
⁷ I rejoice and take delight in Your kindness —
    You see my misery and care about me in my troubles.
⁸ You haven't surrendered me to the enemy,
    but You have set my feet in a place where I can move freely.
⁹ O LORD, be kind and help me—I'm in trouble.
    My eyes, my throat, and my belly waste away with grief.
¹⁰ My life is consumed with sorrow, and my years with groaning.
    My grief breaks down my strength and wastes away my limbs.
¹¹ I'm scorned by all my enemies;
    I'm a curse to my neighbors, and I frighten my friends —
they look at me on the street and run away from me.

5 *Lk 23:46*

¹² I'm forgotten like one who is dead.ᵏ I'm like a broken dish.

¹³ I hear many slander, frightening me from all sides.
    Scheming together against me, they plot to take my life.

¹⁴ But I trust You, O LORD. I say, "You are my God."

¹⁵ What happens to me is in Your hands —
    rescue me from my enemies who pursue me.

¹⁶ Let Your face shine on Your servant,
    and save me by Your kindness.

¹⁷ I have called to You, O LORD;
    don't let me be disappointed,
    but let the wicked end in shame and be thrown into a grave.

¹⁸ May their lying lips be muzzled when in proud scorn
    they dare to talk against the righteous.

¹⁹ What great kindness
    You secretly reserve for those who fear You,
    and do for those who trust in You, for all the world to see.

²⁰ You hide them in the shelter of Your presence,
    from the schemes of men;
    You keep them safe in a shelter from quarrelsome tongues.

²¹ The LORD be praised
    for being wonderfully kind to me in a besieged city.

²² I said when panic-stricken,
    "I'm cut off so that You can't see me,"
    but You heard me plead and call to You for help.

²³ Love the LORD, all you whom He loves.
    The LORD preserves the faithful
    but pays back in full those who act proudly.

²⁴ *Be strong and full of courage,*
    all you who look hopefully to the LORD.

Your Sins Are Forgiven

A psalm by David, to be played skillfully.ˡ

32 *How blessed you are if your wrongs are forgiven*
    and your sins are covered.

² *How blessed you are if the LORD doesn't count sins against you,*
    and if *there is no deception in your* spirit.

³ When I kept silent,ᵐ
    I wore out my limbs, groaning all day long.

⁴ Day and night Your hand was heavy on me;
    my vitality was drained by the summer heat. (Music)ᵇ

---

24 *I Cor 16:13*   **1-2** *Rom 4:7-8*   **2** *I Pet 2:22; Rev 14:5*

k - 12   Or "shriveled like corpse"

l - 1   Conjecture. Perhaps "A Wisdom Song"

m - 3   Or "devised mischief"

⁵ I told You my sin and didn't cover my wrong.
  I said, "I will confess, O Most High;
      I will confess my wrongs, O LORD."
      And You took away my sin and guilt. (Music)ᵇ

⁶ That is why all Your devoted ones pray to You.
  When distress comes, or a flood of raging waters,
      it will not reach them.
⁷ You are my Hiding Place;
      You protect me against trouble.
  You surround me with people who are rescued,
      and shouting happily about it. (Music)ᵇ
  (The LORD:)
⁸ I will instruct you
      and teach you the way you should go.
  I'll advise you, keeping My eye on you.
⁹ Don't be like a horse or a mule without sense;
      with a bit and bridle their rebellion must be restrained
      so you can come near them.

¹⁰ The wicked suffer much!
      But if you trust the LORD,
      He will surround you with mercy.
¹¹ Delight in the Lord and be glad, you who are righteous,
      and sing happily, all you whose hearts are honest.

A Happy People

      Shout happily in the LORD, O righteous people!

33 You devout people, it is beautiful to praise.
² Praise the LORD with a lyre;
      praise Him with a ten-stringed lute.
³ *Sing* to Him *a new song*;
      play well on the instruments with happy shouting.
⁴ The LORD's Word is right, and all His works are faithful.
⁵ He loves what is right and just.
      The earth is full of the LORD's goodness.

⁶ The LORD made the heavens by His Word,
      and all the stars by the Breath of His mouth.
⁷ He gathers the water of the sea in a jar
      and puts the deep waters in storage.
⁸ The whole earth should fear the LORD,

---

3 Rev 5:9; 14:3

and all who live in the world be in awe of Him.
⁹ He spoke and it was,
    He ordered and it came into being.

¹⁰ *The LORD makes the plans of the nations fail;*
    He hinders them in what they propose to do.
¹¹ But what the LORD plans stands firm forever;
    what He proposes is for all generations.
¹² Blessed is the nation whose God is the LORD,
    the people He chose to be His own.
¹³ The LORD looks down from heaven and sees all humanity.
¹⁴ From the place where He sits enthroned
    He looks down on all who live on earth.
¹⁵ He Who forms the hearts of all of them,
    also is well aware of everything they do.
¹⁶ A king can't win victory just with a large army,
    or a hero save himself just by his great strength.
¹⁷ It isn't true that a horse brings victory;
    despite its great strength it can't help you escape.

¹⁸ Remember the LORD's eye is on those who fear Him,
    who look hopefully to His mercy,
¹⁹ to save them from death and keep them alive when starving.
²⁰ We long for the LORD, Who helps us and shields us.
²¹ Yes, our hearts delight in Him, and we trust His holy name.
²² May Your mercy be on us, O LORD,
    as we look hopefully to You.

God Rescues Us

    By David when he changed his behavior before Abimelech,
    causing Abimelech to drive him away.

34 I will always bless the LORD;
    my mouth will continually praise Him.
² My soul will glory in the LORD;
    humble people will be glad to hear it.
³ Honor the LORD with me,
    and let us lift up His name together.

⁴ I went to the LORD for help, and He answered me
    and rescued me from everything I dreaded.
⁵ Look to Him and be radiant;
    don't let your[n] face be downcast.

---

10 I Cor 1:19   *8 I Pet 2:3*

n - 5   Versions; Heb; "their face"

⁶ This poor man called, and the LORD heard him
    and rescued him from all his troubles.
⁷ The Angel of the LORD camps around those who fear Him
    and rescues them.

⁸ *Taste* and see *how good the LORD is*;
    happy is the man who takes refuge in Him.
⁹ Fear the LORD, you who are His holy ones;
    fear Him, and you will lack nothing.
¹⁰ Young lions may be in need and go hungry,
    but those who go to the LORD for help have every good thing.
¹¹ Come, sons and daughters, listen to me,
    and I will teach you how to fear the LORD.
¹² Do *you love life*?
    Do you desire to live long, and enjoy good things?
¹³ Then *stop talking evil and saying deceitful things*;
¹⁴ *turn away from wrong and do good;*
    be eager for peace and pursue it!
¹⁵ *The LORD's eyes are on the righteous;*
    His ears hear their cry for help.
¹⁶ *But the LORD's face is against those who do wrong,*
    and He will wipe out all memory of them from the earth.

¹⁷ When the righteous cry, the LORD hears
    and rescues them from all their troubles.
¹⁸ The LORD is near you when you're brokenhearted
    and saves you when you're crushed in spirit.
¹⁹ If you're righteous, you have many griefs,
    but the LORD rescues you from all of them,
²⁰ and protects every *bone* in you
    so that *not one* of them *is broken.*
²¹ Evil kills the wicked,
    and those who hate the righteous will be punished.
²² But the LORD ransoms the life of His servants,
    and all who take refuge in Him will not be punished.

When You Feel Hunted

    By David.

35 O LORD, oppose those who are opposing me;
    fight those who are fighting me;
² grab small and large shields and come to help me;
³ draw a spear and a battle axe to meet those who pursue me.

12-16 I Pet 3:10-12; Heb 12:14   **20** *Jn 19:36*

Give me assurance that You will save me.
4 May those who are trying to kill me be humiliated
and disgraced;
may those who plan disaster for me
be turned back with shame;
5 may they be like chaff blown by the wind —
the Angel of the LORD throwing them down;
6 may their path be dark and slippery —
the Angel of the LORD chasing them.
7 Without a reason they secretly lay their net over a pit for me,
digging it for me without a reason.
8 May they be destroyed suddenly when they least expect it;
may the net they hid catch them;
may they fall into it and be destroyed.

9 I delight in the LORD; I am glad He saves me.
10 My whole being says, "Who is like You, O LORD?
You rescue a poor man from one who is stronger,
a poor and needy person from one who robs him."

11 Men get up and accuse me of crime;
they ask me questions I can't answer.
12 They pay me back evil for good,
making me feel as if I had lost my children.
13 When they were sick, I wore sackcloth
and denied myself by fasting.
(May my prayer come back to my bosom.)
14 I walked around as if it were my friend or my brother;
as if it were for my mother, I bowed down in mourning.
15 But when I stumble they gather with glee;
they band together against me,
striking me when I least expect it.
They tear me apart and never stop.
16 With ungodly mocking while they're eating,
they grind their teeth at me.

17 My Lord, how long will You look on?
Rescue me from their destruction,
my precious life from the lions.
18 I will thank You in the great congregation
and praise You in a large gathering of people.
19 Don't let those who are my enemies without a reason gloat
over me, nor let those who *hate me without a reason*
give me an evil look.

---

19 Jn 15:25

20 They don't talk of peace
    but plot to betray people living quietly in the land.
21 They open their mouths wide at me, saying, "Aha! Aha!
    We saw it ourselves."
22 O LORD, You have seen it — don't be silent.
    O Lord, don't be far away from me.
23 Rouse Yourself and give me justice;
    O my God and Lord, awake and defend my cause.
24 O LORD, since You are righteous, give me justice;
    O my God, keep them from gloating over me.
25 Don't let them think, "Aha! That's what we want," or say,
    "We have ruined him!"
26 May those who gloat over my trouble
    be altogether ashamed and disgraced;
    may those who boast against me
    be covered with shame and disgrace.
27 But those who are pleased when I receive justice
    should shout and be glad and keep on saying,
    "Great is the LORD, Who delights to see His servant happy."
28 Then my tongue will tell how righteous
    You are and praise You all day long.

The Spring of Life

For the choir leader; by David, the LORD's servant.

36 The wicked man has rebellion in his heart.
    God doesn't terrify him.
2 He flatters himself in his own eyes,
    and is not aware of his sin to hate it.
3 He talks only of doing wrong and deceiving,
    and has stopped doing what is wise and good.
4 Lying on his bed, he plans to do wrong
    and sets himself on a course that's no good.
    He doesn't reject evil.

5 O LORD, Your mercy is high as the heavens,
    Your faithfulness reaches to the clouds.
6 Your righteousness is like God's mountains;
    Your justice like the deep ocean.
    You save men and animals, O LORD.
7 How precious is Your kindness, O God.
    People come for shelter under the shadow of Your wings;
8 they are satisfied with rich foods at Your house,
    and You let them drink from Your river of delights.

1 Rom 3:18

⁹ With You is the spring of life,
>> and in Your light° we shall see light.
¹⁰ Keep on being kind to those who know You
>> and show yourself righteous to those whose heart is right.

¹¹ Don't let the feet of proud men step on me
>> or the hand of the wicked throw me down.
¹² Then those who do wrong will fall,
>> pushed down never to get up.

Don't Envy the Wicked

By David.

37 Don't get upset about evil people
>> or jealous of those who do wrong.
² Like grass they soon wither
>> and fade away like a green plant.
³ Trust the LORD and do good;
>> live in the land, practice being faithful.
⁴ Delight in the LORD,
>> and He will give you your heart's desire.
⁵ Commit your ways to the LORD, trust Him,
>> and He will act (for you).
⁶ He will make your righteousness shine like a light
>> and your just cause like sunshine at noon.
⁷ Stand still and look to the LORD for help.
>> Don't get upset when somebody is successful
>> and accomplishes the evil he plans.
⁸ Stop being angry, quit raging;
>> don't be upset, it only leads to doing wrong.
⁹ The wicked will be destroyed,
>> but those who look to the LORD for help,
>> will take possession of the land.

¹⁰ In a little while the wicked will be gone;
>> then look carefully where he was — he won't be there!
¹¹ *The humble will possess the land*
>> and enjoy great well-being.
¹² The wicked man plots against the righteous,
>> grinding his teeth at him.
¹³ The Lord laughs at him
>> because He sees his day coming.
¹⁴ Wicked men draw their swords

11 Mt 5:5

o - 9   Or "land"

and bend their bows to strike down the poor and needy
and slaughter those who live right.
¹⁵ Their swords will pierce their own hearts,
and their bows will be smashed.
¹⁶ Better is a little that the righteous man has
than the wealth of many wicked people.
¹⁷ The arms of the wicked will be broken,
but the LORD helps the righteous.
¹⁸ The LORD takes care of the innocent day by day,
and their inheritance will last forever.
¹⁹ They will not be miserable in bad times
and in days of famine they will eat all they want.
²⁰ But the wicked will perish;
the LORD's enemies will vanish like the glory of the meadows;
they will vanish in smoke.
²¹ A wicked man borrows and doesn't pay back,
but a righteous man is kind and gives.
²² If the LORD blesses you, you will own the land,
but if He curses you, you will be cut down.

²³ The LORD makes a man walk firmly
and He is pleased with his way.
²⁴ He may fall but will not be thrown down
because the LORD's hand holds him.
²⁵ I was young and now I'm old,
but never have I seen the righteous forsaken
or his children begging for bread.
²⁶ He is always generous and lends money,
and his children will be blessed.
²⁷ Shun evil and do good
and live in the land forever.
²⁸ The LORD loves what is right
and will not desert those devoted to Him.
They will be preserved forever,
but the descendants of the wicked will be cut down.
²⁹ The righteous will own the land and live there forever.
³⁰ The mouth of the righteous man talks wisdom;
his tongue says what is right.
³¹ The teaching of his God is in his mind
and his steps do not falter.
³² A wicked man spies on the righteous
and tries to kill him.
³³ But the LORD will not leave him in his power
or condemn him when he is tried.
³⁴ Look to the LORD for help and live in His way,
and He will lift you up to own the land,

and you will see the wicked cut down.

³⁵ I have seen the wicked as a tyrant,
    spreading out^p like a native tree full of leaves.
³⁶ But he passed away, and now he's gone.
    I looked for him but couldn't find him.
³⁷ Keep an eye on the blameless man,
    and watch the honest man; that man will finally have peace.
³⁸ The wicked will be completely destroyed
    and their future cut off.
³⁹ But the LORD saves the righteous
    and keeps them safe when trouble comes.
⁴⁰ The LORD helps them and rescues them;
    He rescues them from the wicked and saves them
    because they came to Him for shelter.

My Sin and Suffering

A psalm by David. For praying.^q

38 Lord, don't correct me in Your anger
    and punish me in Your fury.
² Your arrows have gone deep into me,
    and Your hand presses down on me.
³ Because You're angry, there's not a healthy spot in my body;
    because I've sinned, there's nothing sound in my limbs.
⁴ My sins overwhelm me,
    like a heavy load they burden me down.
⁵ Because I was foolish,
    my wounds stink and fester.
⁶ I'm twisted and very bowed down.
    All day I go about mourning.
⁷ My loins are all inflamed,
    and there's nothing healthy in my body.
⁸ I am numb and badly crushed.
    I groan because my heart is moaning.
⁹ O Lord, You know all my longing,
    and my sighing isn't hidden from You.
¹⁰ My heart is throbbing — I've lost my strength;
    even the light of my eyes is gone.

¹¹ Those who love me, my *friends*,
    stand back at the sight of my disease,
    and my relatives *stand at a distance*.

---

11 Lk 23:49; Mt 27:55; Mk 15:40

p - 35   meaning uncertain
q - 1   meaning uncertain

¹² Those who try to kill me lay snares for me;
   out to harm me, they talk of my ruin;
   all day long they think of ways to deceive.
¹³ I am like a deaf man, who cannot hear,
   and like a mute, who cannot speak.
¹⁴ I have become like a man who doesn't hear anything
   and has no arguments to offer.
¹⁵ But I look to You, O LORD, for help.
   O Lord, my God, You will answer.
¹⁶ For I have already said, "Don't let them gloat over me.
   When my foot slips, don't let them ridicule me."
¹⁷ I'm about to break down — I'm always in pain.
¹⁸ I'm going to tell about my wrong — I'm worried about my sin.
¹⁹ The enemies of my life are strong,
   and there are many who hate me deceitfully.
²⁰ They pay me back evil for good
   and bitterly accuse me for trying to do good.
²¹ Don't desert me, O LORD;
   O my God, don't be far away from me.
²² Come quickly to help me;
   O Lord, hasten to save me.

Life Is a Vapor

For the choir leader. For Jeduthun. A psalm by David.

39 I said: I will watch my ways and not sin with my tongue;
   I will keep a muzzle on my mouth while I face the wicked man.
² I kept completely silent and said nothing;
   then my grief was stirred up,
³and my heart burned in me. As I meditated it blazed.
   Then I spoke with my tongue:
⁴ "O LORD, tell me about my end, how many days I have left,
   so that I know how fleeting my life is.
⁵ You made my days a few inches,
   and my whole life is nothing to You.
⁶ Every man stands there as just a vapor; (Music)^b
   each one walks around in the dark;
   he makes a lot of fuss about nothing;
   he heaps up things without knowing who will get them."

⁷ And so, what is there for me to look forward to, Lord?
   You are my hope!
⁸ Save me from all the wrong I've done,
   and don't make me the scorn of fools.
⁹ I am silent and don't open my mouth —
   if You would only act!

¹⁰ Take away from me the suffering You inflicted;
     because You have struck me with Your hand, I am finished.
¹¹ When You punish men by correcting their sin,
     You make what is precious to them crumble
     as if eaten by a moth.
     Surely every man is just a vapor. (Music)ᵇ
¹² Listen to my prayer, O LORD, and hear my cry for help.
     Don't be deaf to my tears.
     I'm a *stranger* staying with You,
     a *guest* like all my ancestors.
¹³ Spare me and I'll be happy
     before I pass away and am gone.

Help Me

          For the choir leader; a psalm by David.

40 I waited patiently for the LORD,
          and He turned and listened to my cry for help.
² He pulled me out of the pit that would destroy me,
     out of the mire and clay,
     and set my feet on a rock, helping me walk firmly.
³ He put a *new song* in my mouth, a praise to our God.
     Many shall see it and fear, and trust in the LORD.
⁴ Blessed is the man who puts his trust in the LORD,
     and doesn't turn to those who are arrogant
     and are entangled in lies.
⁵ You have done many wonderful things for us,
     O LORD my God. You have made many wonderful plans;
     no one can be compared with You.
     I want to announce them and tell about them,
     but they are more than I can tell.
⁶ *You were not pleased with sacrifice and offering —*
     You have opened my ears;
     You didn't want burnt offerings and sacrifices for sin;
⁷ *then I said, "I have come!*
     (The writing in the scroll of the book tells about Me).
⁸ I delight *to do what You want*, O My God.
     Your law is in My heart."

⁹ I tell the news of righteousness in the great congregation,
     and I don't shut my mouth —
     O LORD, You know it.
¹⁰ I don't keep Your righteousness a secret in my heart;
     I tell how faithful You are and how You save.

---

12 I Pet 2:11   *3 Rev 5:9; 14:3*   *6-8 Heb 10:5-10; Eph 5:2*

I have not hid from the great congregation how kind
and true You are.

[11] You, O LORD, don't hold back Your kindness from me.
May Your kindness and Your truth always protect me;
[12] for evils surround me until they can't be counted. My sins
have caught up with me until I can't see;
they are more than the hairs on my head.
I have lost my courage.
[13] Hurry, O LORD, to rescue me!
O LORD, come quickly to help me!
[14] May those who are trying to destroy me,
all be disappointed and ashamed,
and those who delight in harming me
turn back in disgrace.
[15] May those who say to me, "Aha! Aha!"
be appalled by their own shame.
[16] But may all who look to You for help find joy
and delight in You.
May those who love You for saving them always say,
"The LORD is great!"
[17] I am poor and needy; but my LORD plans for me.[r]
You are my Helper and Deliverer. O my God, don't delay!

Gossip and a Bad Friend

For the choir leader; a psalm by David.

41 Blessed is he who treats the poor with understanding.
When trouble comes, may the LORD rescue him.
[2] May the LORD protect him and keep him alive.
May he enjoy happiness in the land,
and not be surrendered to the greed of his enemies.
[3] May the LORD strengthen him on his sickbed —
sustain him on his bed and overthrow his sickness!

[4] I say, "O LORD, be kind to me.
Heal me — I have sinned against you."
[5] My enemies talk evil of me:
"When will he die and his name disappear?"
[6] When one of them comes to see me, he tells lies.
He keeps all the gossip in mind,
and then goes outside and tells others.
[7] All who hate me whisper together about me.

---

r - 17   Or with Psalms 70:5 "O Lord, come to me quickly."

They mean to harm me, saying:

8 "May a deadly disease be poured out on him;
    may he lie there and never get up again!"
9 Even My friend whom I trusted,
    who ate My food, gives Me a hard kick.

10 But You, O LORD, be kind to me;
    help me get up and I will pay them back.
11 Then I will know You are pleased with me,
    if my enemy doesn't triumph over me.
12 As for me, You have taken hold of me in my innocence
    and have set me before You forever.
13 *Praise be to the LORD, the God of Israel*
    from everlasting to everlasting! So be it, yes, so be it!

Longing for God

For the choir leader; by Korah's descendants;
to be played skillfully.[s]

42 As a deer pants for streams of water,
    so my soul pants for You, O God.
2 I thirst for God, the living God:
    O when will I come and *appear* before *God?*
3 My tears have been my food day and night
    because I'm asked all day long, "Where is your God?"
4 As I pour out my soul before Him,
    I recall how I used to go in the crowd
    and lead them to God's house,
    with happy shouting and praise
    as the crowd celebrated a festival.
5 Why am *I so discouraged,*
    and why am I in such turmoil?
    I must look to God for help,
    and praise Him Who is my Saviour and 6my God.
    When *I'm so discouraged* I will remember
    You from the land of Jordan,
    the peaks of Hermon, and at the hill Mizar,
7 where the floods resound and the waterfalls roar,
    where all Your billows and waves passed over me.
8 During the day the LORD sent His kindness;
    and at night His song was with me;
    my prayer was to the God of my life.

---

9 Mk 14:18; Jn 13:18   *13 Lk 1:68*   *2 Rev 22:4*
5-6,11 Mt 26:38; Mk 14:34

s - 1   "skillfully" is conjectural

⁹ I will ask God, "My Rock, why did You forget me?
    Why must I go mourning while the enemy oppresses me?"
¹⁰ My enemies insult me — it's a crushing of my bones —
    by asking me all day long, "Where is your God?"

¹¹ Why am *I so discouraged*,
    and why am I in such turmoil?
    I must look to God for help,
    and praise Him as my Savior and my God.

Send Your Light

43 Defend me, O God, and plead my case.
    From an unkind nation,
    from deceitful and evil people rescue me.
² You are my Mountain Refuge, O God! Why do You reject me?
    Why must I go mourning while the enemy oppresses me?
³ Send Your light and Your truth to guide me
    and take me to Your holy hill, the place where You live.
⁴ Then I will go to the altar of God, to God, the Joy of my life;
    and I will praise You on the lyre, O God, my God.

⁵ Why am *I so discouraged*
    and why am I in such turmoil?
    I must look to God for help,
    and praise Him as my Savior and my God.

Why Do You Hide Your Face?

For the choir leader; by Korah's descendants;
to be played skillfully.

44 O God, we heard it ourselves;
    our fathers told us what Your hand accomplished
    in their days, the days of long ago.
² You drove out peoples and planted our fathers there;
    You shattered nations and let our fathers spread out.
³ Not by their sword did they take the land,
    nor did their arms win the victory.
    No, Your right hand, Your arm,
    and the light of Your face did it,
    because You were kind to them.
⁴ It was You, my King, my God, Who ordered victories for
Jacob.
⁵ With You we pushed down our enemies;

---

5 Mt 26:38; Mk 14:34

in Your name we trampled on those who attacked us.

6 I don't trust my bow, and my sword can't save me.

7 No, You saved us from our enemies
and put to shame those who hated us.

8 We have always boasted in our God
and will praise Your name forever. (Music)ᵇ

9 But now You have rejected us and brought disgrace on us;
You don't go out with our armies.

10 You make us turn back from the enemy,
and those who hate us plunder us as they please.

11 You surrender us like sheep to be slaughtered, and scatter us
among the nations.

12 You sell Your people cheap,
and don't make much by the price You get.

13 You make our neighbors scorn us,
and those around us to mock and make fun of us.

14 You make us an object of ridicule among the nations so that
people shake their heads at us.

15 All day long I see my disgrace,
and my face is covered with shame,

16 because of the voice of those who insult and revile us, because
of the enemy and the avenger.

17 While all this happened to us, we didn't forget You, nor were
we untrue to Your covenant.

18 Our hearts didn't turn away,
and our feet didn't leave Your way,

19 though You crushed us in a place for jackals and covered us
with deep gloom.

20 If we had forgotten the name of our God
and stretched out our hands to a foreign god,

21 wouldn't God find it out,
since He knows the secrets of the heart?

22 No, *because of You we are killed all day long and considered
sheep to be butchered.*

23 Wake up! Why are You sleeping, O Lord?
Awake! Don't reject us forever.

24 Why do You hide Your face
and forget how we suffer and are oppressed?

25 Our necks are bowed down in the dust, and our bellies cling
to the ground.

26 Rise and help us!
Save us because You are kind to us!

---

22 Rom 8:36

The King and His Bride

For the choir leader, according to "Lilies,"
by Korah's descendants; to be played skillfully.
A love song.

45 A fine theme stirs in my heart.
I will recite what I'm writing about the King.
My tongue is the pen of a skillful writer.

² You are the most beautiful of men;
Your lips pour out grace;
so God has blessed You forever.
³ Strap Your sword on Your thigh, O mighty One;
march on in Your splendor;
⁴ with Your majesty drive to victory. Ride in the cause of truth,
and be concerned with justice.
And may Your right hand teach awesome things.
⁵ May people fall beneath You,
with Your sharp arrows in the hearts of the King's enemies.

⁶ *Your throne, O God, is forever and ever;*
You rule as a King with a righteous scepter.
⁷ *You love righteousness and hate wickedness;*
that is why God, Your God, has anointed You
with the oil of joy above Your companions.
⁸ All Your garments are fragrant with myrrh,
scented wood, and cassia.
From ivory palaces the music of stringed instruments
delights You.
⁹ Among Your noble women are kings' daughters;
The queen in gold from Ophir
will take her place at Your right hand.
¹⁰ Listen, daughter, look, and turn your ear to me:
Forget your people and your father's home.
¹¹ The King longs for your beauty —
He's your Lord — bow down to Him.

¹² The people of Tyre, the richest of the people,
want to win your favor with a gift.
¹³ In her rooms the King's daughter is altogether wonderful;
her dress is interwoven with gold.
¹⁴ In her many-colored robes she is led to the King;
the virgins, her friends, following her, are brought to You.
¹⁵ With joy and delight they are brought in

6-7 Heb 1:8-9

and come into the King's palace.

16 Your sons will take the place Your ancestors had,
and You will make them rulers all over the earth.
17 I will cause Your name to be remembered
by all the people of the coming ages;
and that is why the nations will praise You forever and ever.

God Is Our Refuge

For the choir leader; a song by Korah's descendants;
for soprano voices. A song.

46 God is our Refuge and Strength,
our very great Help in time of trouble.
2 We're not afraid
even when the earth quakes,
the mountains topple into the sea;
3 even when its waters roar and foam,
and the mountains shake in the middle of it. (Music)[b]

4 There is a river whose streams delight God's city,
the holy place where the most high God lives.
5 God is in the city — she can't fall.
God will help her when the morning dawns.
6 Nations are in confusion and kingdoms totter —
when God utters His voice, the earth trembles.

7 The LORD of armies is with us;
the God of Jacob is our Refuge. (Music)[b]
8 Come, see the works of the LORD,
what terrible things He does in the world!
9 He stops wars all over the earth,
smashing bows, cutting off spears, and burning chariots.
10 "Stop and realize that I am God!
I am high over the nations, exalted over the world!"

11 The LORD of armies is with us;
the God of Jacob is our Refuge. (Music)[b]

The King of the World

For the choir leader; a psalm by Korah's descendants.

47 All you people, clap your hands;
shout to God with loud rejoicing.
2 The LORD, the Most High, is awesome;

He is the great King over all the earth.
[3] He made people bow down to us and put nations under our feet.
[4] He chose our land for us,
the pride of Jacob whom He loved. (Music)[b]

[5] God has gone up with a shout of joy,
the LORD with the sound of the trumpet.
[6] Sing to God, praise Him! Sing to our King, praise Him!
[7] God is King of the whole world — sing with skillful music.
[8] God is King of the nations;
God is sitting on His holy *throne.*
[9] May the princes among the nations gather together
as a people for Abraham's God.
The shield-bearers of the earth belong to God;
He is highly exalted.

God's City

A song, a psalm by Korah's descendants.

48 The LORD is great and worthy of much praise.
In the city of our God is His holy hill,
[2] rising beautifully, the joy of all the world.
Mount Zion is on the northern ridge;
it is *the city of the great King.*
[3] God is in her fortified palaces;
He has shown Himself to be a mountain ridge.

[4] Indeed, the kings have gathered!
They advanced together;
[5] then they looked and were amazed,
and in a panic ran away.
[6] Panic seized them there;
they were in anguish like a woman having a child,
[7] as when an east wind wrecks the ocean going ships of Tarshish.
[8] What we had heard of,
we saw in the city of the LORD of armies,
the city of our God.
God makes it stand firm forever. (Music)[b]

[9] We think of Your kindness, O God,
while we're in Your temple.
[10] Like Your name, O God,
Your praise goes to the ends of the earth.
Your right hand is full of justice.

---

8 Rev 4:2,9,10; 5:1,7,13; 6:16; 7:10,15; 19:4; 20:11; 21:5   *2 Mt 5:35*

¹¹ May Mount Zion be happy and Judah's towns be glad,
>   as they see Your just actions.
¹² Walk around Zion, go around her;
>   count her towers, ¹³examine her ramparts;
>   walk through her fortified palaces,
>   so you can tell your descendants in the future:
¹⁴ God is here, our eternal and everlasting God.
>   He will lead us forever.

You Can't Take It with You

For the choir leader; a psalm by Korah's descendants.

49 Hear this, all you people;
>   listen, all you who live in the world,
² human beings, high and low, rich and poor.
³ My mouth will speak wisely
>   and my mind think with understanding.
⁴ I will turn my ear to a wise saying,
>   and with a lyre clarify my puzzling thoughts.
⁵ Why should I be afraid in times of trouble,
>   or of the evil of the treacherous enemies who surround me,
⁶ who trust their wealth and brag about how very rich they are?
⁷ No one can buy anyone's freedom
>   or pay God a ransom for him.
⁸ The price to be paid for their soul is too costly,
⁹ for a man to live forever and avoid the grave.
¹⁰ No, God looks at wise men and they die.
>   He gazes on fools and brutish men and they perish,
>   leaving their wealth to others.
¹¹ Their graves become their long-term homes,
>   their dwellings for all the generations.
>   They call their lands by their names.
¹² But man with his precious things can't go on living;
>   he's like the animals that perish.
¹³ This is the fate of confident fools
>   and those coming after them who like what they said.
¹⁴ Like sheep they have to lie down in the grave
>   with death as their shepherd;
>   and honest people will tramp on them in the morning.
>   Their limbs will be consumed in the grave,
>   away from their princely homes.
¹⁵ But God will ransom me from the power of the grave
>   because He will receive me. (Music)^b

¹⁶ Don't be afraid when a man gets rich
>   and his household becomes more and more wealthy.

¹⁷ When he dies, he can't take anything with him;
  his wealth can't follow him down there.
¹⁸ While he's living, he may think he's happy
  and be praised for doing well for himself;
¹⁹ but he will join his fathers who lived before him,
  never to see the light.
²⁰ A man with precious things but no understanding
  is like the animals that perish.

God Comes to Judge

   A psalm by Asaph.

50 The mighty God, the LORD speaks, and He calls the earth,
  from where the sun rises to where it sets.
² God is shining from Zion, the perfection of beauty.
³ Our God comes and isn't silent;
  in front of Him a fire is devouring,
  and around Him a storm is raging.
⁴ He summons the heavens above
  and the earth to His people's trial:
⁵ "Gather around Me My holy ones,
  who made a pledge with Me by sacrifice."
⁶ The heavens tell about His righteousness,
  for God Himself is doing the judging. (Music)ᵇ

⁷ "Listen, My people, and I will speak;
  listen, Israel, and I will testify against you:
  I am God, your God!
⁸ I do not criticize you for your sacrifices,
  for regularly bringing Me your burnt offerings.
⁹ But I need not take a bull from your homes
  or a male goat from your folds,
¹⁰ since all the animals in the forest are Mine
  and the cattle on the hills by the thousand.
¹¹ I care for every bird in the hills,
  and everything stirring in the field is present before Me.
¹² If I were hungry, I need not tell you
  because the world is Mine and everything in it.
¹³ Do I eat the meat of bulls or drink the blood of goats?
¹⁴ *Bring God your thanks as a sacrifice,*
  and do for the most high God what you vowed.
¹⁵ *Call Me in time of trouble!*
  When *I rescue you,* you should honor Me."

14 Heb 13:15; Mt 5:33 15 Mt 21:22

¹⁶ But God tells the wicked:
  "What business is it of yours to recite My laws
  and talk about My covenant?
¹⁷ You hate to be corrected,
  and toss My words behind you.
¹⁸ When you see a thief, you want to be with him
  and share the life of adulterers.
¹⁹ You let your mouth talk evil, and your tongue plans deceit.
²⁰ You sit and talk against your brother,
  slandering your own mother's son.
²¹ You do this, and should I say nothing?
  You plan to destroy; should I be like you?
  I will correct you and lay it before your eyes.
²² Consider this, you who forget God,
  or I'll tear you in pieces and no one will rescue you.
²³ If you *bring* your *thanks as a sacrifice*, you can honor Me.
  If you set your life in order,
  I will have you drink your fill of God's salvation."

Wash Me Clean

For the choir leader; David's psalm when the prophet
Nathan had come to him after he had sexual relations
with Bathsheba.

51 O God, You are so kind — be merciful to me,
  Your grace is so great — wipe out my wrong;
² wash me thoroughly from my guilt,
  and cleanse me from my sin.
³ I realize the wrong I've done,
  and my sin is always before me.
⁴ I sinned against You, against You only,
  and did what is wrong in Your sight;
  *so that You are just when You speak
  and* pure *when You judge.*
⁵ Yes, I was born guilty,
  and when my mother conceived me I was in sin.
⁶ You desire truth in my heart;
  You want to teach me to be wise in my inner being.
⁷ Cleanse me from sin with hyssop and I'll be clean;
  wash me and I'll be whiter than snow.
⁸ Make me to hear joy and gladness;
  then the limbs You crushed will be glad again.
⁹ Hide Your face from my sins, and wipe out all my wrongs.

23 Heb 13:15   4 Rom 3:4

¹⁰ Create a *clean heart* for me, O God,
      and give me a steady new spirit.
¹¹ Don't banish me from Your presence
      or take Your Holy Spirit from me.
¹² Give me again the joy of Your salvation
      and a willing spirit to strengthen me.

¹³ Then I will teach the rebellious Your ways,
      and sinners will come back to You.
¹⁴ O God, rescue me from bloody wrong,
      O God Who saves me, and my tongue will sing aloud
      about Your righteousness!
¹⁵ O Lord, open my lips, and my mouth will praise You.
¹⁶ If You wanted sacrifice I would give it,
      but a mere burnt offering doesn't please You.
¹⁷ The sacrifice which God wants is a broken spirit.
      A broken and crushed heart, O God, You won't despise.
¹⁸ By Your kindness be good to Zion,
      and build the walls of Jerusalem.
¹⁹ Then You will delight in the right kind of sacrifices,
      burnt offerings and whole offerings.
      Then young bulls will be sacrificed on Your altar.

My Enemy Is in God's Hands

For the choir leader; to be played skillfully; David's psalm
when Doeg, a descendant of Esau, went and told Saul,
"David has come to Ahimelech's home."

52 You tyrant, why do you brag about behaving wickedly?
      God's love is forever!
² Your tongue is like a sharp razor,
      scheming to destroy and doing deceitful things.
³ You love evil instead of good,
      lying instead of saying what is right. (Music)^b
⁴ You love every kind of destructive speech,
      you deceitful tongue!
⁵ God, too, will destroy you forever,
      knock you down and snatch you out of your tent,
and pluck you by the roots out of the land of the living. (Music)^b

⁶ The righteous will look at him in awe,
but they will laugh at him:
⁷ "Look at the man who wouldn't make God his fortress

10 Mt 5:8

but trusted his great wealth
and got strong by destroying others."

⁸ But I am like a flourishing olive tree in God's house,
    trusting God's mercy forever.
⁹ I thank You forever for what You did
    and announce to Your holy ones how good Your name is.

We Are Sinners

For the choir leader; for sickness;
to be played skillfully; by David.

53 A fool says in his heart, "There is no God."
    They do corrupt and detestable things.
    No one does anything good.
² God looks at the world from heaven
    to see if *there is anyone wise, who comes to God for help.*
³ *They have all turned away together and become corrupt.*
Not one does right, not a single one.
⁴ Don't these who do wrong know,
    don't these who devour my people know
    that if anyone eats the bread God gives
⁵without calling on Him, panic will overtake them?
    Certainly there will be panic
    when God scatters the bones of those who besiege you.
They will be put to shame because God will reject them.

⁶ If only Someone would come from Zion to save Israel!
When God restores His people,
    Jacob will be delighted and Israel will be glad.

Help!

For the choir leader; to be played skillfully on stringed
instruments; by David when the people of Ziph went and
told Saul, "Isn't David hiding among us?"

54 O God, save me by Your name,
    and by Your power get me justice.
² Listen to my prayer, O God, and hear what I say.
³ Strangers attack me, and tyrants try to kill me —
    they don't keep God before them. (Music)ᵇ

⁴ But look, God is my Help! The Lord supports me.
⁵ May He pay back evil to my enemies.

1-3 Rom 3:10-12

> With Your truth destroy them!
> [6] Then I will gladly sacrifice to You
> > and praise Your name, O LORD, because it is good;
> [7] for You have rescued me from every trouble,
> > and my eye can gaze now at my enemies.

When a Friend Turns Against You

> For the choir leader; to be played skillfully on stringed instruments; by David.

55 Listen to my prayer, O God;
> > don't hide from me when I plead.
> [2] Turn to me and answer me.
> > I am restless and troubled,
> [3] and confused by the shouting of the enemy
> > and the oppression of the wicked.
> For they bring me misery and angrily pursue me.
> [4] My mind is in anguish
> > as the terrors of death fall on me;
> [5] I fear and tremble and shudder all over.
> [6] I say if I only had wings like a dove,
> > I would fly away and rest.
> [7] Yes, I would run far away and stay in the desert. (Music)[b]
> [8] I would hurry to my shelter
> > from the raging wind and storm.

> [9] Destroy them, O Lord! Confound their tongues,
> > because I see violence and conflict in the city.
> [10] Day and night they go around on its walls;
> > trouble and misery are in the city,
> [11] and destruction is also there;
> > oppression and cheating remain in its streets.

> [12] If it were the enemy who insulted me —
> > that I could bear;
> > if it were one that hated me who attacked me —
> > I could hide from him.
> [13] But it's you, a man who is my equal;
> > my friend and one I knew so well!
> [14] We talked in sweet fellowship
> > and walked with a crowd into God's house.

> [15] May death take them suddenly;
> > may they go down alive to the grave
> > because wickedness is in their hearts.
> [16] I will call on God, and the LORD will save me.

¹⁷ In the evening, in the morning,
  and at noon I will complain and groan,
  and He will hear me.

¹⁸ He will ransom me by His peace,
  from the war waged against me,
  for my adversaries are beside me.
¹⁹ May God who sits on His ancient throne hear
  and put them down (Music)^b
  because they never change and don't fear God.
²⁰ Each lays hands on his friends and violates his pledge.
²¹ His talk is smoother than butter,
  but he means to fight;
  his words are softer than oil,
  but they are like drawn swords.
²² *Throw your burden on the LORD,*
  and He will support you.
  He will never let the righteous fail.
²³ But You, O God, will throw the others down into a deep grave.
  Men who murder and deceive will not live out half their days.
  But I'm trusting You.

In God I Trust

  For the choir leader; according to "The Dove of Distant
  Oaks;" David's inscription when the Philistines arrested
  him in Gath.

56 Be kind and help me, O God, men trample on me.
  They fight all day long and they oppress me;
   ² all day long my enemies hound me,
  as many fight against me.
  O Most High, ³when I'm afraid, I put my trust in You.

⁴ In God — I praise His Word —
  In God I trust — I'm not afraid;
  what can flesh do to me?

⁵ All day long they cause me grief,
  thinking only to harm me.
⁶ They start a fight and then hide.
  They watch where I go
  because they're eager to kill me.
⁷ With the wrong they do, can they escape?
  In Your anger, O God, put down the peoples.

---

22 I Pet 5:7 *4,11 Heb 13:6*

8 Write down how I have to flee;
   put my tears in Your water-skin —
   aren't they in Your scroll?
9 Then my enemies will have to turn back on the day I call;
   for this I know: God is with me.

10 In God — I praise His Word —
   In the LORD — I praise His Word —
11 *In God I trust* — I'm not afraid;
   what can man do to me?
12 I'm under vows to You, O God;
   I will carry them out by praising You.
13 You have rescued me from death,
   and kept my foot from stumbling,
   that I might walk before God in the light of the living.

In the Shadow of Your Wings

For the choir leader; "Don't Destroy;" David's inscription
when he fled from Saul into the cave.

57 Be merciful to me, O God, be merciful to me
   because in You my life finds protection.
   I take cover in the shadow of Your wings
   until the threat of destruction passes by.
2 I call to God, the Most High, Who does things for me.
3 He sends help from heaven and saves me
   from the slander of him who hounds me. (Music)[b]
   God sends His mercy and His faithfulness.
4 But I myself must lie down among lions —
   men who devour. Their teeth are spears and arrows,
   and their tongues are sharp swords.

5 You are high above the heavens, O God,
   and Your glory is over all the earth.

6 They prepared a net for my feet; my soul is bowed down.
   They dug a pit in front of me; then they fell into it. (Music)[b]
7 I am confident, O God, I am confident.
   I will sing and play music.
8 Wake up, my glorious soul! Wake up, O lute and lyre! I will
   wake up the dawn!
9 I will thank You among the nations, O Lord,
   and play music to praise You among the people,
10 because Your kindness is as great as the heavens,
   and Your faithfulness reaches the clouds.
11 You are high above the heavens, O God,

and Your glory is over all the earth.

God Will Judge

For the choir leader; "Don't Destroy;" an inscription by David.

58 Will you, O judges, really say what is right?
Will you judge the people fairly?
2 No, you act with perverse minds,
and your hands commit violence in the land.
3 The wicked are wrong from the womb;
from their birth they go astray and tell lies.
4 Their poison is just like the venom of a snake.
They are like a deaf cobra shutting its ears,
5 unable to hear the sound of the charmers,
or anyone trained to cast spells.

6 O God, break the teeth in their mouths!
Knock out the lions' fangs, O LORD!
7 May they disappear like water flowing away,
and shoot their arrows as if they were blunted.
8 May they pass on like a snail that leaves a slimy track,
or a stillborn child that didn't see the sun.
9 Before your pots feel the burning thorns,
whether still green or burning,
may God sweep them away.[t]

10 The righteous will be glad when he sees vengeance
and washes his feet in the blood of the wicked.
11 Then people will say, "The righteous are still rewarded,
and there still is a God who judges the earth."

Rescue Me

For the choir leader; "Don't Destroy;" David's inscription
when Saul sent men to watch his home and kill him.

59 Rescue me from my enemies, O my God!
Provide for me a high refuge from those who attack me.
2 Rescue me from those who do wrong,
and save me from murderers.
3 There they lie in ambush for me,
fierce men attacking me for no wrong or sin of mine, O LORD.
4 I've done no wrong, but they run and get ready for me.
Be aware of my encounter and see.
5 You, O LORD God of armies, God of Israel,

---

t - 9   Following some Greek versions. The translation verse 9 is tentative.

awake to punish all the nations;
show no mercy to any treacherous wrongdoer. (Music)[b]
[6] When evening comes they return,
howling like dogs and prowling around in the city.
[7] See what belches from their mouths —
swords from their lips.
They think, "Can anyone hear it?"
[8] But You, O LORD, will laugh at them
and mock at all the nations.
[9] O my Strength, I am watching for You.
because God is my Mountain Refuge.
[10] God, Who loves me, comes to me;
God lets me gloat over my enemies.
[11] Do not kill them, or my people may forget.
By Your power make them stagger;
then throw them down, O LORD, our Shield.
[12] For the sin of their mouths and the words of their lips —
let them be caught in their arrogance.
For the curses and lies they tell;
[13] in anger destroy them, destroy them until they're gone.
Then they'll know God rules over Jacob
and to the most distant parts of the world. (Music)[b]
[14] When evening comes they return,
howling like dogs and prowling around the city.
[15] They wander around to devour,
and if they don't get all they want, they go on all night.
[16] But I will sing about Your power
and in the morning shout loudly about Your kindness.
You are my Mountain Refuge
where I can flee when I'm in trouble.

[17] O My Strength, I am watching for You
because God is my Mountain Refuge.

After a Defeat

For the choir leader; according to "Lilies"; a word of truth
to be taught; David's inscription when he fought the
Arameans of Mesopotamia and the Arameans of Zobah,
and Joab came back and struck down 12,000 Edomites
in the Valley of Salt.

60 O God, You have rejected us and broken us;
You have been angry — restore us.
[2] You have made the land quake and split open —
heal its fractures because it is tottering.
[3] You have made Your people suffer cruel things

and given us wine to drink that makes us stagger.

4 Give those who fear You a banner
    to display because of the truth. (Music)[b]
5 Save us by Your right hand
    and answer us in order to free Your dear people.
6 God spoke from His sanctuary:
    "I will be exultant and divide up Shechem,
    and measure off the valley of Succoth.
7 Gilead is Mine, and Manasseh is Mine;

    Ephraim is a helmet on My head; Judah is My scepter;
8 Moab is the basin I wash in; I will plant My sandal on Edom
    — I have shouted in triumph against Philistia."

9 Who, then, will bring me into the fortified city?
    Who will lead me to Edom?
10 Didn't You reject us, O God?
    Didn't You, O God, refuse to go out with our armies?
11 Give us help against the enemy,
    for human deliverance is useless!
12 With God we'll do great things.
    He will trample down our enemies.

Far from Home

For the choir leader; on stringed instruments; by David.

61 Listen to my cry, O God: hear my prayer!
2 From a distant spot on earth I'm calling You,
    because I feel faint.
Lead me to a rock that towers above me.
3 Yes, be my Shelter, a strong tower
    to protect me against the enemy.
4 I want to live in Your tabernacle forever
    and take refuge under the Shelter of Your wings. (Music)[b]
5 O that You, God, would hear my vows
    and give me the inheritance of those who fear Your name.
6 Add days to the king's life;
    may his years go on and on,
7 and may he sit enthroned before God forever.
May kindness, and truth be appointed to keep him safe.
8 Then I will sing of Your name forever
    as I daily fulfill my vows.

Look to God

> For the choir leader; according to Jeduthun;
> a psalm by David.

62 Surely my heart is calm before God,
　　　for He saves me.
² Surely He is my Rock and my Savior,
　　　my Mountain Refuge where I'll not be severely shaken.

³ How long will you assail a man;
　　　how long will you be intent on murder?
　You are all like a leaning wall,
　　　a sagging fence.
⁴ Yes, they plan to hurl him from his high position,
　　　delighting in lies.
　They bless with their mouths
　　　but curse in their hearts. (Music)ᵇ

⁵ Surely my heart is calm before God, for He gives me hope.
⁶ He alone is my Rock and my Savior,
　　　my Mountain Refuge where I'll not be shaken.

⁷ The Most High God is my Salvation and Glory;
　　　God is my strong Rock and my Shelter.
⁸ Trust Him always, you people!
　Pour out your hearts before Him.
　God is our Shelter. (Music)ᵇ
⁹ Mortal men are only a breath,
　　　even important men a delusion.
　When they are weighed the scales rise;
　　　they are altogether less than a vapor.
¹⁰ Don't trust to get anything by extortion or scheme
　　　to get anything by robbery.
　When you get rich, don't rely on it.
¹¹ God said it once, twice I heard it:
　　　"Power belongs to God."
¹² And to You, O Lord, belongs kindness,
　　　for You *pay a man according to what he does.*

Your Love Is Better than Life

> David's psalm when he was in the wilderness of Judah.

63 O God, You are my God;
　　　I'm eagerly looking for You, I'm thirsting for You.

---

12 Mt 16:27; Rom 2:6; II Tim 4:14; Rev 2:23; 20:12-13; 22:12

My body faints with longing for You,
>in a dry and parched land where there is no water.
² So I look for You in the sanctuary to see Your power and glory.

³ Because Your kindness is better than life,
>my lips praise You.
⁴ I will bless You as long as I live,
>raising my hands in Your name.
⁵ You satisfy my hunger as with rich food;
>I praise You with jubilant lips.
⁶ When I remember You on my bed
>and think of You during the night —
⁷ how You are my Help,
>how in the shadow of Your wings I shout happily,
⁸ then my heart clings to You
>and Your right hand holds me up.
⁹ But as for those who try to destroy my life,
>may they go into the depths of the earth.
¹⁰ May they be thrust through by the sword,
>and left as food for the jackals.

¹¹ But the king will delight in God.
Everyone who swears by Him will be happy,
>but the mouths of those who tell lies will be shut.

Men's Arrows and God's

>For the choir leader; a psalm by David.

64 Hear my voice, O God, when I complain.
Protect my life against an enemy who frightens me.
² Hide me from men secretly talking about doing evil,
>from the mob of wicked men.
³ They sharpen their tongues like swords,
>and aim their bitter words like arrows
⁴ to shoot at the innocent from their hiding places.
They shoot suddenly, without fear.
⁵ They encourage one another in some evil plan
>to lay snares secretly.
They think: Who will see us?
⁶ They search for wicked crimes:
>we have devised a well-laid plan!
What is inside a man, in his mind, is deep.

⁷ God will shoot them with an arrow,

striking them down suddenly.
[8] Their own tongues ruin them.
All who see them shake their heads.
[9] Everybody will be afraid and declare,
"God did that," and will learn a lesson from what He did.
[10] The righteous are delighted in the LORD
and find shelter in Him,
and all whose heart is right will feel happy.

Thank You, God

For the choir leader; a psalm by David; a song.

65 It is fitting to praise You, O God, in Zion.
One should do for You what he vowed.
[2] You are the One Who hears prayer,
and everyone should come to You.
[3] Our sins overwhelm us,
but You forgive our wrongs.

[4] Blessed is anyone You choose,
everyone You bring to live in Your courts.
We are satisfied with the blessings of Your house,
and the holiness of Your temple.
[5] O God, our Savior, in Your righteousness
and with Your awesome deeds cause us to triumph!
On You depend all the distant parts of the earth
and the faraway places in the sea.
[6] You are girded with strength;
You set up the mountains by Your power.
[7] You quiet *the raging seas,* their *roaring waves,*
and the noisy tumult of the nations.
[8] People who live far away stand in awe of Your wonders.
All the way from the rising of the sun to its setting
there is a happy shout.
[9] You visit the earth and water it,
making it fruitful with showers.
You fill God's rivers with water, and grow grain for them.
For that You prepare the ground,
[10] water its furrows, soften its clods,
dissolve it with showers,
and bless what grows on it.
[11] You crown the year with Your bounty.
From Your tracks the abundance drips,
[12] dripping on the meadows in the desert;

---

7 *Lk 8:24; 21:25*

the hills are wreathed with joy,
13 pastures are clothed with flocks
     and valleys wrapped in grain.
They shout to one another — yes, they sing.

Thank God for a Wonderful Rescue

For the choir leader; a song; a psalm.

66 Shout with joy to God, everyone on earth.
2 Sing about the glory of His name;
     glorify Him with praise.
3 Tell God, "How awesome are the things You do!
     Your power is so great Your enemies cringe before You.
4 The whole world should bow to You,
     sing to You, and praise Your name." (Music)[b]

5 Come and see what God has done.
     What He does for people is awesome:
     6He changed the sea to dry land,
     and they went through the river on foot.
     So let us delight in Him.
7 By His power the everlasting One rules;
     His eyes watching the nations
     to keep rebels from rising against Him. (Music)[b]
8 Bless our God, O you nations!
     Let all hear how you praise Him;
     9 for He kept us alive and didn't let our feet slip.

10 But, O God, You have tested us;
     You have purified us like silver.
11 You caught us in a net,
     and put misery on our bodies.
12 You let men drive over our heads;
     we went through fire and water;
     but then You brought us out to have plenty.
13 I will enter Your temple with burnt offerings
     and do for You what I vowed,
14 what my lips said and my mouth promised
     when I was in trouble.
15 I will sacrifice to You fattened livestock as burnt offerings
     with the fragrant smoke of sacrificed rams.
     I will offer cattle and goats. (Music)[b]

16 Come, listen, all you who fear God,
     and I'll tell you what God did for me.
17 When I called to Him with my mouth,

high praise was on my tongue.
[18] If I had meant to do wrong,
  the Lord would not have listened to me.
[19] But God did listen to me and heard me pray.
[20] Praise God for not rejecting my prayer
  or withdrawing His kindness from me.

God Bless Us!

For the choir leader; on stringed instruments; a psalm; a song.
May God be merciful to us and bless us!

67 May His face shine on us, (Music)[b]
[2] that the world might know Your way
  and the *nations know how You save.*
[3] May the people praise You, O God;
  may all the people praise You.
[4] Then the nations will be glad and shout happily
  because You judge the people with justice
  and guide the nations in the world. (Music)[b]
[5] The people should thank You, O God;
  all the people should thank You —
[6] the land has produced its crop,
  and God, our God, has blessed us.
[7] May God go on blessing us
  and all the most distant parts of the world worship Him.

God's Victory

For the choir leader; a psalm by David; a song.

68 God arises — His enemies scatter,
  and those who hate Him run away from Him.
[2] Like smoke that is blown, You blow them away.
Like wax melted by a fire, the wicked perish before God.
[3] But the righteous are glad,
  rejoicing before God and overflowing with joy.

[4] Sing to God, sing to praise His name!
Make a highway for Him to drive through the deserts!
His name is the LORD.
Be very happy before Him.
[5] In His holy dwelling God is the Father of the fatherless
  and the Defender of widows.
[6] God gives the lonely a home to live in;
He releases prisoners, making them happy.

---

2 Acts 28:28

But the rebellious must live in a parched land.

⁷ O God, when You went out in front of Your people
and marched through the desert, (Music)ᵇ
⁸the earth quaked and the sky poured down rain,
before God, the One of Sinai,
before God, the God of Israel.
⁹ You poured out plenty of rain, O God;
and when Your land was exhausted,
You refreshed it.

¹⁰ Your living family settled there;
being kind, God, You provided for the poor.

¹¹ The Lord uttered the word;
a big crowd of women told the good news.
¹² The kings and their armies fled; they fled
and the woman staying home got her share of the spoil.
¹³ Even if you lie down among the sheepfolds,
you are like the wings of a dove covered with silver,
its feathers with yellow gold.
¹⁴ Meanwhile the Almighty was still scattering kings there,
like snow falling on Mount Zalmon.

¹⁵ Bashan's mountain is God's mountain;
Bashan's mountain has peaks.
¹⁶ Mountains and peaks, why do you look with envy
at the mountain where God likes to live?
Yes, the LORD will live there forever.
¹⁷ God's chariots are twice ten thousand,
thousands upon thousands.
The Lord is among them, as at Sinai, in His holy place.
¹⁸ *You went up on high, You took prisoners captive.*
You received *gifts from men*,
even from the rebellious
so that the LORD God will live there.

¹⁹ Praise the Lord!
Day by day He carries our load for us.
This is the God Who saves us. (Music)ᵇ
²⁰ Our God is the God Who saves us;
the Lord God is our escape from death.
²¹ Yes, God crushes the heads of His enemies,
the hairy scalps of those who go on in their guilt.

---

18 Eph 4:8-10

u - 22   Or, "from the Serpent"

²² The Lord says, "I will bring them back from Bashan;ᵘ
  I will bring them back even from the depths of the sea
²³ so that you can bathe your feet in blood
      and your dogs' tongues can get a share of the enemy."

²⁴ One can see Your festive procession, O God,
      the procession for my God, my King, into the holy place.
²⁵ First come singers, then those who play instruments,
      surrounded by girls beating tambourines:
²⁶ "In the meetings of the congregation,
      bless God, the Lord, you who are born of Israel."
²⁷ Look, Benjamin, the youngest, is leading them!
  Judah's leaders with their shouting crowd,
      Zebulun's leaders, Naphtali's leaders.
²⁸ Summon Your power, O God!
  Exert Your strength, O God, in what You do for us,
²⁹ from Your temple over Jerusalem!
  Kings will bring You presents.
³⁰ Rebuke that beast among the reeds,
      and his herd of bulls with its calves.
  He trampled on the nations in his lust for silver;
      He scattered the people who delight in war.
³¹ Princes will come from Egypt;
      Ethiopia quickly will stretch out her hands to God.
³² O kingdoms of the world, sing to God,
      sing to praise the Lord, (Music)ᵇ
³³ Who drives through the highest heavens,
      the ancient heavens.

  Listen, His voice thunders mightily —
³⁴ acknowledge the power of God;
      His majesty is over Israel,
      and His power is in the skies.
³⁵ O God, *You are awesome*
      when You come from Your holy place.
  But the God of Israel is the One
      Who gives His people strength and power.
  Praise God!

God's Servant Suffers

For the choir leader; according to "Lilies," by David.

---

35 II Thess 1:10

69 Save Me, O God, the waters come up to My neck.
² I'm sunk in deep mud where there's nothing to stand on.
I have come into deep water where streams sweep Me away.
³ I'm tired of calling, My throat is hoarse.
My eyes are bleary looking for My God.

⁴ Those who *hate Me without a reason*
     are more than the hairs on My head.
Those who are out to destroy Me are mighty.
They have no real reason to be My enemies.
 I have to pay back what I didn't rob.

⁵ O God, You know My foolishness;
My guilt isn't hidden from You.
⁶ Don't let those who look to You for help be disgraced
     because of Me, O Lord, the LORD of armies.
Don't let those who eagerly come to You
     be put to shame for My sake. O God of Israel.
⁷ Yes, for You I took insults and blushed with shame;
⁸I've become a stranger to My brothers
     and a foreigner to My mother's sons.
⁹ *The zeal for Your house consumed Me,*
     and the insults of those who insult You fell on Me.
¹⁰ I wept and ate nothing and was insulted for it.
¹¹ I made sackcloth My garment
     and became the butt of their jokes.

¹² Those who sit at the gate gossip about Me,
     and drunkards make up songs about Me.
¹³ As for Me, My prayer is to You,
     if now You'll accept it, O LORD.
You're so great in kindness,
     answer Me, O God. By Your faithful help,
¹⁴ pull Me out of the mud—I don't want to sink into it.
I want to be rescued from those who hate Me
     and from the deep water.
¹⁵ Don't let the flood sweep Me away,
     or the deep water swallow Me,
     or the pit shut its mouth over Me.

¹⁶ Answer Me, O LORD, Because Your kindness is precious.
     Your mercy is so great, turn to Me.
¹⁷ Don't hide Your face from Your servant;

4 Jn 15:25   9 Jn 2:17; Rom 15:3; Heb 11:26

because I'm in trouble — answer Me quickly.
¹⁸ Come near Me and redeem Me;
     because of My enemies, set Me free.
¹⁹ You know how I'm insulted, put to shame, and disgraced —
     My enemies are all before You.
²⁰ Insults have broken My heart and I am sick.
   I'm looking for sympathy and there's none,
     and for comforters and can't find any.
²¹ And they put gall in My food
     and *for My thirst give Me vinegar to drink.*
²² May *their table, spread before them, become a snare,*
     and a trap when they feel all is well.
²³ *May their eyes turn dark so they can't see*
     and their loins *continually* shake.
²⁴ *Pour Your anger on* them;
     may Your blazing fury catch them.
²⁵ *May their camp turn to ruins;*
     and no one live in their tents,
²⁶because they pursue Him whom You struck
     and talk about the pains of those You wounded.
²⁷ Charge them with one sin after another.
   Exclude them from Your righteousness.
²⁸ May they *be blotted out of the book of life*
     and *not be listed* with the righteous.

²⁹ But I am suffering and in pain.
   By Your saving power lift Me to a safe height, O God.
³⁰Then I will praise God's name in a song
     and with thanks tell how great He is.
³¹ The LORD will like that better
     than a young bull with horns and hoofs.
³² Look, you who are oppressed and rejoice;
     you who go to God for help, may your spirits be refreshed.
³³ For the LORD listens to the needy
     and doesn't despise His own when they are in prison.

³⁴ Heaven and earth praise Him, the seas
     and everything moving in them,
³⁵ because God saves Zion and builds Judah's towns
     so that people can settle there and own them.
³⁶ His servants' descendants will inherit the land,
     and those who love His name will live there.

---

21 *Mt 27:34,48; Mk 15:36; Lk 23:36; Jn 19:28-29*   **22-23** *Rom 11:9-10*
24 *Rev 16:1*   **25** *Acts 1:20*   **28** *Phil 4:3; Rev 3:5; 13:8; 17:8; 20:12,15; 21:27*

Help Me

For the choir leader; by David, as a prayer.

70 Come quickly, O God, to rescue me,
O LORD, to help me.
² May those who are trying to destroy me
be disappointed and ashamed,
and those who delight in harming me
turn back in disgrace.
³ May those who say, "Aha! Aha!"
be appalled by their own shame.
⁴ But may all who look to You for help
find joy and delight in You.
May those who love You for saving them
always say, "God is great!"
⁵ I am poor and needy, O God, come to me quickly.
You are my Helper and my Deliverer;
O LORD, don't delay!

When I'm Old

71 O LORD, in You I take shelter;
don't ever let me be disgraced.
² By Your righteousness rescue me and help me escape.
Listen to me and save me.
³ Be my Mountain Refuge where I can always go.
You gave the order to save me
because You are my Rock and my Fortress.
⁴ My God, rescue me from the hands of the wicked,
from the hands of those who are unjust and cruel.

⁵ You are my Hope, O Lord GOD,
You have been my Confidence from my youth.
⁶ I have depended on You from birth;
You took me from my mother's body.
I praise You continually.
⁷ To many I am a wonder,
but You are my strong Shelter.
⁸ My mouth is full of praise of You
and of Your glory all day long.
⁹ Don't discard me when I'm old
or leave me when I lose my strength,
¹⁰because my enemies talk about me,
and those who watch to take my life plan together.

¹¹ They say, "God has abandoned him.
  Pursue and grab him — there's no one to rescue him."
¹² O God, don't be far away from me;
  O my God, come quickly to help me.
¹³ May those who accuse me come to a shameful end,
    and those who are out to harm me
    be covered with disgrace and humiliation.
¹⁴ But I will always have hope
    and praise You more and more.
¹⁵ I will tell how righteous You are,
    about Your saving deeds every day,
    although they're more than I can number.

¹⁶ I will enter Your house, O Lord GOD,
    and recite the triumphs You alone perform.
¹⁷ O God, You taught me from my youth;
    I still talk about the wonderful things You have done.
¹⁸ Even when I get old and gray, don't forsake me, O God,
    until I tell this age what Your arm has done;
    and tell all who come about Your mighty action
¹⁹ that Your righteousness reaches to heaven, O God.
  You have done great things, O God. Who is like You?
²⁰ Though You made me endure many troubles and miseries,
    You will restore me to life again,
    and lift me up from the depths of the earth again.

²¹ You make me very great
    and come to comfort me.
²² Then I will praise You with a lute
    for being faithful, my God.
  I will play on a lyre to praise You,
    O Holy One of Israel.
²³ My lips will shout happily as I praise You,
    my very being that You have freed.
²⁴ All day long my tongue will loudly tell how righteous You are,
    and those who are out to harm me
    will then be ashamed and disgraced.

The Coming King

By Solomon.

72 O God, give the King Your justice
    and the King's Son Your righteousness,
  ² that He may judge Your people with righteousness
    and Your poor with justice.

³ May mountains bring well-being to the people
   and the hills righteousness.
⁴ Then He will give justice to those who suffer,
   save the children of the poor, and crush the oppressor.
⁵ They will fear You^v as long as there's a sun
   and a shining moon, throughout the generations.
⁶ He will come down like rain on mown grass,
   like showers that water the earth.
⁷ In His days the righteous man will flourish,
   and peace will abound until the moon is no more.
⁸ He will rule from sea to sea
   and from the Euphrates to the ends of the world.
⁹ The desert people will *bow to Him*,
   and His enemies will lick the dust.
¹⁰The kings of Tarshish and the islands will *pay tribute*;
   the kings of Sheba and Seba will *bring gifts*.
¹¹ All the kings will *worship Him*,
   and all the nations serve Him;
¹² because He will rescue the needy who call for help
   and the oppressed who have no one to help them.
¹³ He will pity the weak and the poor
   and save the lives of the needy.
¹⁴ He will free them from oppression and violence;
   their blood will be precious in His sight.
¹⁵ May He live long and may the *gold* of Sheba be *given to Him*.
   Let prayer be made for Him continually,
   and may they praise Him all day long.
¹⁶ May there be plenty of grain in the country;
   may it grow even on top of mountains,
   its fruit blossom like Lebanon,
   and the people from the city will flourish like grass
   on the ground.
¹⁷ May His name endure forever,
   and His name increase as long as the sun shines.
   May *all nations be blessed in Him* and call Him blessed.
¹⁸ *Blessed be the LORD God, the God of Israel*;
   Who alone does wonderful things.

¹⁹ May His glorious name be blessed forever,
   and His glory will fill the whole world.
   Let it be so! Let it be so!
²⁰ The prayers of David, Jesse's son, end here.

9-11 *Mt 2:11*   **15** *Mt 2:11*   **17** *Acts 3:25*   **18** *Lk 1:68*

v - 5   Or with Greek: "He will endure. . ."

Does It Pay to Be Good?

A psalm by Asaph.

73 Surely God is good to Israel,
to *those whose hearts are pure.*
2 But my feet almost slipped,
and I almost lost my footing
3 because I was jealous of those who are proud
and saw how the wicked prosper.
4 They suffer no pains.
Their bodies are healthy.
5 They have no drudgery like ordinary people
and aren't plagued like others.
6 Therefore, pride is their necklace
and crime the garment that covers them.
7 Their eyes stand out in their fat faces.
Their imagination goes too far.
8 They mock and speak wickedly,
talking about oppression with arrogance.
9 They set up their mouths against the heavens
and their tongues wag against the earth.
10 So His people turn to them,
swallow their words[w]
11 and ask, "How can God know
and the Most High understand?"

12 Look! They are wicked,
and with never a worry they've piled up wealth.
13 Yes, it was for nothing I kept my heart pure
and washed my hands in innocence.
14 I am plagued all day long
and take my beating every morning.
15 If I had decided to talk like that,
I would have betrayed Your people.
16 So I thought this over to understand it —
it looked too difficult to me,
17 until I came into God's holy place
and saw the end in store for them.
18 Surely You will set them in slippery places
and make them fall into ruin.
19 How quickly they will be destroyed,
completely wiped out in terrifying ways!
20 Like a dream when one wakes up,

1 Mt 5:8

w - 10   or "plenty of water"

so You, Lord, will awake
and despise the very thought of them.

21 When my heart is filled with bitterness
and stirred up inside,
22 I'm stupid and don't understand,
like an animal in Your presence.

23 But I'm always with You —
You hold my right hand.
24 You will guide me with Your advice
and finally take me to glory.
25 Who is mine in heaven?
Having You, I don't want anything else on earth.
26 My flesh and my heart waste away,
but God is the Rock my mind rests on
and my inheritance forever.

27 Those who wander far from You are lost;
You destroy all who go lusting away from You.
28 So it is best for me to come close to God.
I've made You, O Lord GOD, my Shelter;
so I can talk of everything You've done.

Think of Your Defeated People

By Asaph; to be played skillfully.

74 O God, why do You reject us forever;
why does Your anger blaze against *the sheep* of Your pasture?
2 Remember Your *congregation that You bought,*
the tribe You redeemed long ago to be your own people,
Mount Zion which You made Your home.

3 Direct your steps toward these permanent ruins —
the enemy has wrecked everything in the sanctuary.
4 Your foes have roared in the place where the assembly met
and set up their own emblems as banners.
5 From the entrance on
they hacked like a woodsman in a forest;
6   they smashed all its carved work with axes and crowbars.
7 They set Your holy place on fire,
polluted and tore down the sanctuary bearing Your name.
8 They thought, "We will crush them altogether,"
and they burned every place in the land

1-2 Acts 20:28

where God met with us.
⁹ We no longer see signs,
    and there are no prophets anymore,
    or anyone who knows how long this will last.

¹⁰ How long, O God, will the enemy insult us?
    Will the enemy scorn Your name forever?
¹¹ Why do You withdraw Your hand
    and keep Your right hand in Your bosom?

¹² Yet from long ago God has been my King,
    performing victories throughout the country.
¹³ By Your power You stir up the sea
    and crush the heads of sea monsters in the water.
¹⁴ You smash the heads of Leviathan
    and give them as food to the sharks in the sea.
¹⁵ You cut openings for springs and brooks
    and dry up rivers that always flowed.
¹⁶ The day is Yours, and the night is Yours —
    You set up the moon and the sun.
¹⁷ You set all the boundaries of the earth.
    You make summer and winter.

¹⁸ Remember how the enemy has defied You,
    O LORD, how a foolish people have scorned Your name.
¹⁹ Don't let wild beasts take the life of Your dove,
    or forever forget the lives of Your suffering servants.
²⁰ Have regard for Your covenant,
    because darkness and dens of violence have filled the land.
²¹ Don't let the down-trodden return in disgrace;
    let the poor and needy praise Your name.
²² Rise, O God, fight for Your cause.
    Remember how a fool defies You all day long.
²³ Don't forget the shouting of Your enemies,
    the continuous noise of those attacking You.

God Will Judge

For the choir leader; "Don't Destroy!" A psalm by Asaph;
a song.

75 We thank You, O God;
    we praise Your name, O One Who is near;
    we tell of the wonderful things You have done.
    (The Lord:)

² "I will seize the appointed time,
  and judge men fairly.
³ When the earth totters with all who live on it,
  I will make its pillars stand firm. (Music)ᵇ
⁴ Tell those who brag, 'Don't brag,'
  and the wicked, 'Don't raise your horns,
⁵ don't raise your horns so high
  or speak so proudly against the Creator.'
⁶ No one from the east or the west
  or from the desert will help us rise."
⁷ Yes, God is the Judge;
  He puts one down and raises the other.
⁸ In the Lord's hand there's a *cup* of foaming *wine*
  thoroughly *mixed with spices,*
  and He will pour from it —
  surely all the wicked on earth
  will drink it down to the very last drop.
⁹ I will glorify the Eternal One, and sing to praise Jacob's God.
¹⁰ I will cut off all the horns of the wicked,
  but the horns of the righteous will be raised high.

The Lord Triumphs

For the choir leader; on stringed instruments; a psalm by
Asaph; a song.

76 God has shown Himself in Judah; His name is great in Israel.
² His tent is in Salem; His home is in Zion.
³ There He broke the flaming arrows,
  the shield, the sword, and war itself. (Music)ᵇ
⁴ You are shining with might more splendidly
  than the mountains of prey.ˣ
⁵ Valiant men were plundered and went to the sleep of death
  — not a fighting man could lift a hand.
⁶ At Your rebuke, O God of Jacob, chariots
  and horses were paralyzed.
⁷ As for You, You terrify —
  who can stand before You
  when once You are angry?
⁸ From heaven You announce a verdict,
  the earth hushed in fear.
⁹ When You rise to judge, O God,
  to save all who suffer on earth, (Music)ᵇ

---

8 Rev 14:10; 16:19

---

b - 3,3,9 Selah
x - 4   Or "the eternal mountains."

> You will wrap the remaining anger around You.
> [11] Make vows to the LORD your God and keep them.
>   Let all around Him bring gifts
> to the One Who is to be feared.
> [12] He cuts off the lives of rulers
> and terrifies the kings of the world.

I Will Remember

> For the choir leader; according to Jeduthun; a psalm by Asaph.

77 With my voice I call to God —
        to God, with my voice; and He hears me.
[2] When I'm in trouble, I go to my Lord for help.
        At night I stretch out my hands without getting tired;
            I refuse to calm down.

[3] I remember God, and I sigh.
        I think of Him, and my spirit faints. (Music)[b]
[4] You keep my eyelids open; I'm so troubled I can't talk.
[5] I think of the early days, the years of long ago.
[6] At night I remember my song,
        my mind thinking and my spirit searching:
[7] Is my Lord rejecting me forever
        and not going to be kind again?
[8] Has His kindness stopped forever,
        and His promise been forever canceled?
[9] Has God forgotten to be merciful,
        or in anger locked up His mercy? (Music)[b]
[10] Then I said, "It makes me weak,
        that the right hand of the Most High might change.
[11] I recall the LORD's accomplishments;
        I remember the wonders You did long ago,
[12] and meditate on all Your work;
        I think of what You have done.
[13] O God, Your way is holy.
    Is any god as great as our God?
[14] You are the God Who does wonders,
        You have shown Your power among the nations.
[15] By Your arm You freed Your people,
        both Jacob's and Joseph's descendants. (Music)[b]
[16] The waters saw You, O God,
        the waters saw You and shook;
yes, they were stirred to the depths.
[17] The clouds poured down water;

---

b - 3,9   Selah

the skies thundered and Your arrows darted.
  [18] Your thunder rumbled in the sky;
       lightning flashes lit up the world;
       the earth trembled and shook.
  [19] You tread through the sea;
       Your path went through great waters;
       yet no one could tell where You walked.
  [20] You led Your people like a flock
       by the hands of Moses and Aaron.

The Lord's Wonderful Way with His People

By Asaph, to be played skillfully.

78 My people, listen to my instruction;
       pay attention to what I say.
  [2] *I will open my mouth with a parable*
      and speak of the ancient mysteries
        [3]that we have heard and known and our fathers told us;
  [4] we'll not hide them from their children
      but will tell the next generation
      about the LORD's wonderful deeds,
      His power and the marvelous things He did:
  [5] how He established the truth in Jacob
      and set up the law in Israel,
      how He ordered our fathers to teach their children,
        [6] so a coming generation would know it;
      and children yet to be born
      might grow up and tell their children
        [7] to trust in God
      and not forget the things God did,
      but do what He ordered.
        [8] They should not be stubborn and rebellious like their fathers,
      whose hearts didn't stand firm,
      whose spirits were unfaithful to God.
  [9] Ephraim's men, armed with bows,
      turned back on the day of battle.
  [10] They hadn't kept God's covenant
      and refused to live as He ordered.
  [11] They forgot what He did and His wonders that He showed them.

  [12] In the presence of their fathers He did wonders in Egypt,
      in the land of Zoan.
  [13] He divided the sea and led them through,
      making the water stand up like a wall.

---

2 Mt 13:35

¹⁴ During the day He led them by a cloud
   and all night by the light of a fire.
¹⁵ He split rocks in the wilderness,
   and let them drink as from deep water,
¹⁶ making streams come out of a rock
   and water flow like rivers.

¹⁷ But they kept on sinning against Him,
   rebelling against the Most High in the desert.
¹⁸ In their hearts they tested God
   by demanding the food they craved.
¹⁹ They talked against God, asking,
   "Can God set a table in the desert?
²⁰ He struck a rock, water gushed out, and streams flowed down
   — but can He also give bread or provide meat for His people?"
²¹ So, when the LORD heard it, He became angry;
   His fire burned against Jacob and His anger blazed at Israel,
      ²² because they did not trust God or believe He could save them.
²³ Yet He commanded the clouds above,
   and opened the doors of heaven.
²⁴ He rained on them *manna to eat,*
   and *gave them the bread of heaven.*
²⁵ So man ate the bread of angels,
   and He sent them plenty of food.
²⁶ He let loose the east wind from the heavens
   and drove the south wind by His power.
²⁷ He rained meat on them like dust
   and winged birds like sand by the sea.
²⁸ He let them fall in the middle of their camp,
   all around their tents.
²⁹ So they ate and were filled;
   He brought them what they craved,
      ³⁰ but they didn't get over their craving.
   Their food was still in their mouths
      ³¹ when God became angry with them
   and killed some of their husky men
   and struck down Israel's young men.
³² In spite of all this they kept on sinning
   and didn't believe His wonders.
³³ So He made their days vanish like a vapor,
   and their years came to an end in terror.

³⁴ When He struck them down, they searched for Him,
   turned back, and eagerly looked for God.
³⁵ They remembered God was their Rock,

24 Jn 6:31; Rev 2:17

and the Most High their Redeemer.
³⁶ But with their mouths they flattered Him
and with their tongues they lied to Him.
³⁷ In their *hearts* they *didn't stand true* to Him
but were unfaithful to His covenant.

³⁸ Yet being merciful, He forgave their sin
and didn't destroy them.
Many times He restrained His anger
and didn't stir up all His fury.
³⁹ He remembered they were only flesh,
a breeze that blows and doesn't come back.
⁴⁰ How often they rebelled against Him in the wilderness
and grieved Him in the desert!
⁴¹ Over and over they tempted God
and grieved Israel's Holy One.
⁴² They didn't remember what His hand did
when He freed them from those who oppressed them,
⁴³by doing His signs in Egypt
and His wonders in the land of Zoan.
⁴⁴ He *turned their rivers into blood*
so they couldn't drink from their streams.
⁴⁵ He sent among them swarms of flies that devoured them
and frogs that destroyed them.
⁴⁶ He gave their crops to grasshoppers
and what they worked for to locusts.
⁴⁷ He killed their vines with hail
and their figs with frost.
⁴⁸ He let the hail strike their cattle
and bolts of lightning strike their flocks.
⁴⁹ He sent them His blazing anger, wrath, fury, and trouble —
an escort of messengers of woe.
⁵⁰ He cleared a path for His anger
and didn't spare them from death.
He let the plague take their lives.
⁵¹ He struck down every firstborn in Egypt,
the very first son of their vigor in the tents of Ham.

⁵² But His own people He led out like sheep
and guided them like a flock through the desert.
⁵³ He led them safely, without fear,
while the sea covered their enemies.
⁵⁴ He brought them into His holy land,
to these hills His right hand had won.
⁵⁵ He drove out the nations before them,

37 Acts 8:21   *44 Rev 16:4*

and gave them their land as an inheritance.
He settled Israel's tribes in their tents.

[56] Still they tempted God and rebelled against the Most High
and didn't live by His truth.
[57] They left Him and became traitors like their fathers,
turning like a bow you can't trust.
[58] They made Him angry by worshiping on their high places,
and made Him jealous with their idols.

[59] God heard them and became furious.
He vehemently rejected Israel
[60] and abandoned His home in Shiloh,
the tabernacle where He lived among people.
[61] He let His strength[y] be captured
and His glory go into the enemies' hands.
[62] He let the sword kill His people
and was furious with His own.
[63] Fire consumed their young men,
and no wedding song praised their girls.
[64] The sword struck down their priests,
and their widows couldn't even weep.
[65] Then the Lord awoke like one who had been sleeping,
like a strong man shouting from wine.
[66] He beat His enemies back and disgraced them forever.
[67] He rejected Joseph's tents, and didn't choose the tribe of Ephraim.
[68] He chose rather the tribe of Judah
and Mount Zion that He loved.
[69] He built His sanctuary like the high heavens
and founded it forever like the earth.

[70] He chose His servant David
and took him from the sheepfolds.
[71] From tending the sheep nursing their young,
He brought him to be the shepherd of Jacob, His people,
and Israel, His possession.
[72] So he shepherds them with a pure heart
and leads them with skillful hands.

Jerusalem Is in Ruins — Help!

A psalm by Asaph.

79 O God, the heathen have invaded Your inheritance,
and defiled Your holy temple,

    and laid Jerusalem in ruins.
2 They have given the dead bodies of Your servants
    as food to the birds of the sky,
    and the flesh of Your loved ones to the beasts of the earth.
3 They have *shed* their *blood* like water around Jerusalem,
    and nobody buried them.
4 Our neighbors insult us;
    those around us mock and scoff at us.
5 *How long, LORD?* Will You be angry forever?
    Will Your zeal go on burning like fire?

6 Pour out Your fury on *the nations who don't know You*
    and on the kingdoms that haven't called on Your name.
7 They have devoured Jacob and made his home a deserted ruin.
8 Don't hold our fathers' sins against us.
    Hurry to come to us with Your mercy — we are helpless.
9 O God, our Savior, help us;
    because of Your glorious name rescue us;
    yes, forgive our sins for Your name's sake.

10 Why should the nations ask,
    "Where is their God?"
    May Your vengeance for the shed blood of Your servants
    become known among the nations while we watch.
11 May the groaning of the prisoners come before You;
    with Your strong arm keep alive those doomed to die.
12 Pay back our neighbors seven times
    for the insults with which they defied You, Lord.
13 Then we, Your people, the sheep that You shepherd,
    will thank You forever and tell from age to age
    the wonderful things You have done.

Save Your Vine, Lord!

    For the choir leader; according to "Lilies;"
    Asaph's testimony; a psalm.

80 O Shepherd of Israel, listen.
    You who led Joseph like a flock,
    O One enthroned between the cherubim, shine!
2 As You lead Ephraim, Benjamin, and Manasseh,
    stir up Your power and come to save us.
3 O God, restore us and let Your face shine to save us.

4 O LORD God of armies, how long will You be angry

---

3 Rev 16:6   *5 Rev 6:10*   *6 I Thess 4:5; II Thess 1:8*

with the prayer of Your people?
5 You have fed them on the bread of tears,
    and have given them plenty of tears to drink.
6 You make us something for our neighbors to quarrel about,
    and our enemies mock us.
7 O God of armies, restore us and let Your face shine to save us.

8 You plucked up a vine from Egypt,
    drove out nations, and planted it.
9 You cleared the ground before it
    so that it struck roots and filled the country.
10 Its shade covered mountains;
    its branches covered the mighty cedars.

11 It sent out its branches to the sea and its shoots to the river.
12 Why did You break down its stone fences?
    All who pass by are picking its fruit;
13the boar from the woods devours it;
    the animals of the field feed on it.
14 God of armies, come back;
    look from heaven and see.
  Come to help this vine.
15 Take care of what Your right hand planted,
    the son You strengthened for Yourself.
16 May those who burned it with fire and cut it off
    perish before Your angry face.

17 May Your hand be on the man at Your right hand,
    the son of man You strengthened for Yourself.
18 Then we will not leave You.
    Give us life, and we'll call on Your name.
19 LORD God of armies, restore us and let Your face shine to
    save us.

If You Will Only Listen

For the choir leader; on the gittith; z by Asaph.

81 Sing joyfully to God,
    our Strength; shout in triumph to Jacob's God.
2 Sing a psalm and beat the tambourine;
    play the lyre with its pleasant music and the lute.
3 Blow the trumpet on the first of the month,
    at the full moon, on the day of our festival.

---

z - 1   according to the tune used when trampling grapes

⁴ This is a law for Israel,
    an ordinance from Jacob's God.
⁵ This is the testimony God gave in behalf of Joseph
    when He went to war against Egypt:
  "When I heard a language I didn't understand,
⁶ I took the burden off his shoulder,
    and his hands were freed from the basket.
    ⁷When you called in distress, I rescued you;
    hidden in thunder, I answered you.
  I tested your loyalty at the Water of Meribah. (Music)ᵇ

⁸ Listen, My people, and I will warn you.
  O Israel, if you will only listen to Me!
⁹ Don't ever have a strange god among you;
    don't ever worship a foreign god.
¹⁰ I am the LORD your God, Who took you out of Egypt.

  Open your mouth wide and I will fill it.
¹¹ But My people didn't listen to Me;
  Israel didn't want to follow Me.
¹² So I let them go their stubborn way
    and follow their own plans.
¹³ If only My people would listen to Me
    and Israel would live in My ways,
¹⁴how quickly I would make their enemies surrender
    as I turn My hand against their foes.
¹⁵ May those who hate the LORD cringe before Him,
    may they have everlasting trouble.
¹⁶ But I would feed Israel with the finest wheat
    and satisfy him with honey from a rock."

God Judges the Judges

A psalm by Asaph.

82God takes His place in His own congregation
    and does the judging among the "gods":
² "How long are you going to judge unjustly
    and favor the wicked?" (Music)ᵇ
³ "Give justice to the weak and fatherless
    and those who suffer and are poor.
⁴ Rescue the weak and the needy;
    save them from the hands of the wicked."
⁵ They don't know or understand anything
    as they walk around in the dark,

and all the foundations of the world are shaken.
⁶ It was I Who said, *"You are gods*;
    all of you are sons of the Most High;
⁷ but as human beings you die
    and fall like any of the princes."
⁸ Come, O God, judge the world
    because all the nations belong to You.

Like a Forest Fire

A song, a psalm by Asaph.

83 O God, don't keep silent;
    don't be quiet, O God, and fail to act.
² Your enemies are raging,
    and those who hate You hold their heads high.
³ They discuss shrewd plots against Your people
    and plan against those You treasure.
⁴ They say, "Come, let us wipe them out as a nation,
    so no one will remember Israel's name any longer."

⁵ All of them agree on their plan
    and make an alliance against You:
    ⁶ Edom's tents and Ishmael's descendants,
      Moab and Hagar's descendants,
    ⁷ Gebal, Ammon, and Amalek,
      Philistia and those who live at Tyre;
    ⁸ Assyria also has joined them,
      becoming an arm of Lot's descendants. (Music)ᵇ

⁹ Do to them what You did to Midian,
    to Sisera and Jabin at the brook Kishon,
    ¹⁰who were destroyed at Endor
    and became fertilizer for the ground.
¹¹ Make their noblemen like Oreb and Zeeb,
    all their leaders like Zebah and Zalmunnah.
¹² They said, "We'll take God's pastures for ourselves."
¹³ O my God, make them like tumbleweed,
    like chaff the wind blows away.
¹⁴ As a fire burns a forest, as flames set ablaze the hills,
    ¹⁵so hunt them down with Your storm
    and terrify them with Your tornado.
¹⁶ Let their faces blush with shame
    when they seek Your name, O LORD.
¹⁷ May they be ashamed and terrified forever

6 Jn 10:34

and perish in disgrace.

[18] Then they will know that You Whose name is the LORD —
that You alone are high over all the earth.

I Long to Be in God's House

For the choir leader; on the gittith; a psalm by
Korah's descendants.

84 How lovely is the place where You live,
O LORD of armies!
[2] I yearn, yes, I'm wearing out with longing
for the courts of the LORD.
My heart and my body shout happily to the living God.
[3] Even a bird finds a home and a swallow a nest for herself,
where she can hatch her young at Your altars,
O Lord of armies, my King and my God.

[4] Happy are those who live at Your house,
always praising You. (Music)[b]
[5] Blessed are those whose refuge is in You:
their minds are on the pilgrim roads.
[6] As they pass through the valley of weeping
they make it a place of springs.
The early rains also cover it with blessings.
[7] They get stronger and stronger
until each appears before God in Zion.

[8] O LORD God of armies, hear me pray;
listen, O God of Jacob. (Music)[b]
[9] O God, our Shield, look
and see the face of Your anointed one.
[10] A day in Your courts is better than a thousand elsewhere.
I would rather stand at the threshold of the house of my God
than live in the tents of wickedness.

[11] The LORD is a sun and a shield;
God bestows grace and honor.
The LORD doesn't keep back anything good
from those who live innocently.

[12] O LORD of armies, blessed is the person who trusts in You.

You Have Forgiven, Now Make Us Happy

For the choir leader; a psalm by Korah's descendants.

85 You have been gracious to Your country, O LORD;

You have brought back Jacob from captivity.
² You have taken away Your people's wrongs
    and covered all their sins. (Music)ᵇ
³ You have withdrawn all Your fury,
    You don't let it blaze anymore.

⁴ O God, our Saviour, restore us,
    and don't be provoked with us again.
⁵ Will You be angry with us forever,
    and pour out Your anger throughout the generations?
⁶ Will You not restore our lives again
    so Your people can delight in You?
⁷ O LORD, show us your kindness and give us Your saving help.
⁸ I want to listen to what God the LORD says,
    because He promised His people and His godly ones
    that they will be happy.
    But they mustn't go back to foolishness.
⁹ Surely He is near those who fear Him to save them,
    that His glory may rest on our country.
¹⁰ Kindness and truth have met,
    righteousness and peace have kissed.
¹¹ Truth sprouts from the ground,
    and righteousness looks down from heaven.
¹² The LORD will also give us what is good,
    and our land will produce its crop.
¹³ Righteousness will go ahead of Him
    and make His footsteps a way to walk in.

Help Me — You Alone Are God

A prayer by David.

86 Listen, O LORD, and answer me,
    for I am miserable and poor.
² Protect me for I am one You love.
My God, save Your servant who is trusting You.
³ Have mercy on me, O Lord, because I call You all day long.
⁴ Give Your servant joy, because I lift up my heart to You;
⁵ You, O Lord, are kind and forgiving,
    full of mercy for all who call to You.
⁶ O LORD, listen to my prayer and hear my plea for mercy.
⁷ When I'm in trouble, I call You because You answer me.

⁸ There's no god like You, O Lord,
    and no accomplishment like Yours.

9 Rev 3:9, 4:10; 5:14; 11:16; 15:4; 19:4,10; 22:8

⁹ *All the nations*, whom You made,
  will come and worship You, O Lord, and honor Your name.
¹⁰ Indeed, You are great and do wonders;
  You alone are God.
¹¹ Teach me Your way, O LORD; I want to live in Your truth;
  make me respect Your name with all my heart.

¹² I thank You, O Lord my God, with all my heart
  and honor Your name forever,
¹³ because Your loving kindness toward me is great,
  and You have saved me from the deepest grave.
¹⁴ O God, proud men attack me,
  and a cruel mob wants to kill me.
  They don't have any respect for You.
¹⁵ But You, O Lord, are *a merciful and kind God*,
  slow to get angry and full of kindness and truth.
¹⁶ Turn to me and have mercy on me.
  Give Your servant Your strength,
  and save Your maiden's son.
¹⁷ To prove to me it is well, show a sign,
  that those who hate me may see it and feel ashamed,
  because You, O LORD, are my Help and my Comfort.

Born in Zion

A psalm by Korah's descendants; a song.

87 His foundation is on holy mountains.
² The LORD loves Zion's gates more than all of Jacob's dwellings.
³ Wonderful things are told about you, O city of God! (Music)ᵇ

⁴ "I will count Egypt and Babylon among those who acknowledge Me.
  There is Philistia, Tyre, and Ethiopia —
  each one claims that he was born there."
⁵ But it will be said of Zion, "Every nation is born in her,
  and the Most High Himself will make her secure."
⁶ The LORD will write down in His record of the nations:
  "This one was born there." (Music)ᵇ
⁷ There will be singing and dancing,
  for all will find their home in you.ᵃ

Why Do You Reject Me, Lord?

A song; a psalm by Korah's descendants; by Heman the
native-born; for the choir leader; to be sung about afflic-

---

15 James 5:11

a - 7   Gk; Heb: "all my springs are in you"

tion and played skillfully.

88 O LORD God, You can save me.
During the day I call, and at night I'm before you.
2 May my prayer come into Your presence;
listen to my cry.
3 I've had enough troubles;
my life has come close to the grave.
4 I'm counted with those who go down to the pit
and am like a man without strength.
5 Like those that are slain,
I join the dead who lie in the grave.
You don't remember them anymore,
cut off as they are from Your helping hand.
6 You put me in a deep pit, in dark and deep places.

7 Your anger lies heavily on me;
with all Your waves You overwhelm me. (Music)[b]
8 You have taken my *friends far away* from me a
and made them loathe me.
I am shut in and can't get out.
9 My eyes get weak with grief.
Every day I call You, O LORD,
and spread out my hands to You.
10 Do You do wonderful things for the dead?
Do their spirits get up and praise You? (Music)[b]

11 Does anyone in the grave tell about Your kindness;
do they talk about Your faithfulness in that place of decay?
12 Does anyone in that dark place know Your wonders
or anyone in the land of forgetfulness know
Your righteousness?
13 But I call to You for help, O LORD;
in the morning my prayer comes to You.
14 Why do You reject me, O LORD, and hide Your face from me?
15 I've been suffering and close to death from my youth.
I have endured Your terrors — I'm bewildered.
16 Your blazing anger swept over me;
Your terrors have destroyed me.
17 All day long they surrounded me like a flood
and attacked me from all sides.
18 You have removed from me anyone who might love me
or be a friend.
The friend I know is — darkness!

---

8 *Lk 23:49; Mt 27:55*

Are You Breaking Your Promise to David, Lord?

By Ethan, the native-born; to be played skillfully.

89 O LORD, I will sing of Your kindness forever,
I will make known to all the coming generations
how faithful You are.
[2] I will tell how Your grace is forever built in the heavens;
how You firmly set up Your faithfulness there.
[3] "I made a covenant with the man I chose;
I *swore to* My servant *David*:
[4] I will have *your line*[b] continue forever
and build *your throne* for all the generations." (Music)[b]
[5] The heavens praise Your wonders, O LORD,
and Your faithfulness in the congregation of the holy ones.

[6] Who in the sky can be compared to the LORD?
Who among God's sons is like the LORD?
[7] God, terrifying *in the* council of *holy beings*,
is great and more awesome than any around Him.
[8] O LORD God of armies, who is like You?
Your strength and faithfulness surround You.
[9] You rule the raging sea;
when its waves rise, You quiet them.
[10] You crushed Rahab[c] like a carcass;
with Your strong *arm* You *scattered* Your enemies.
[11] Heaven is Yours and the earth is Yours,
the world and everything in it — You made them.
[12] The north and the south—You created them;
Tabor and Hermon sing Your name joyfully.
[13] Your arm is mighty, Your hand is strong,
Your right hand is lifted high.

[14] Your throne is built on righteousness and justice.
Mercy and truth come to serve You.
[15] Blessed are the people who know that shout of joy,
O LORD, as they walk in the light of Your face.
[16] They delight in Your name all day long,
and Your righteousness lifts them up.
[17] You are their Glory and their Strength,
and by Your favor we raise our horns high,
[18] because the LORD is our Shield
and Israel's holy One our King.

3-4 Acts 2:30   *7 II Thess 1:10*   *10 Lk 1:51*

---

b - 4   Or: "Descendant"; cf Is 9:7; Luke 1:30
c - 10   A reference to Egypt

¹⁹ Once in a vision You said to Your faithful ones:
"I set a boy above a warrior
and promoted one chosen from the people.
²⁰ *I found* My servant *David*
and anointed him with My holy oil.
²¹ With a firm hand I will help him
and strengthen him with My arm.
²² No enemy will attack him by surprise
and no wicked person mistreat him.
²³ I will crush his enemies before him
and strike down those who hate him.
²⁴ But I will be faithful to him and love him;
My name will raise his horn high.
²⁵ I will put the sea under his power
and the rivers under his right hand.
²⁶ He *will call to* Me, 'You are my *Father*,
my God and my Rock, Who saves me,'
²⁷ Yes, I will make him *the first-born*,
the *highest of the kings of the earth.*
²⁸ I will always be merciful to him,
and be faithful in My covenant with him.
²⁹ I will have his *Descendant go on forever*
and His throne like the days of heaven.

³⁰ If his sons forsake My law and don't live by My rules,
³¹ if they violate My laws and don't do what I order,
³² I will punish their wrongs with a rod
and their sins with blows.
³³ But I will not stop loving him or prove Myself unfaithful.
³⁴ I will not violate My covenant or break My promise.
³⁵ One thing I swore by My holiness — I will not lie to David:
³⁶ His *Descendant will go on forever,*
and His throne will be like the sun before Me;
³⁷like the moon it will stand forever,
and *faithful* is the *One Who tells the truth* in heaven."ᵈ (Music)ᵇ

³⁸ But You put away, rejected,
and became angry with the one You anointed.
³⁹ You have given up the covenant with Your servant
and made his crown unholy in the dust.
⁴⁰ You tore down all his walls

---

20 *Acts 13:22*   **26** *I Pet 1:17*   **27** *Rev 1:5; 17:18; 21:24*   **29** *Jn 12:34*
36 *Jn 12:34*   **37** *Rev 1:5; 3:14*

---

d - 37   Or "His throne will be more reliable than the heavens."

and laid his fortified cities in ruins.
⁴¹ All who went along the road plundered him,
and his neighbors insulted him.
⁴² You held high the right hand of his enemies
and made all his foes happy.
⁴³ Yes, You turned back his sharp sword
and didn't support him in battle.
⁴⁴ You put an end to his splendor
and hurled his throne to the ground.
⁴⁵ You cut short the days of his youth
and covered him with disgrace. (Music)ᵇ

⁴⁶ How long, O LORD? Will You hide forever?
How long will Your anger burn like fire?
⁴⁷ Remember O Lord, how short my life is.
Why have You made all human beings for vanity?
⁴⁸ Does any man live without experiencing death;
can any rescue his life from the grave? (Music)ᵇ
⁴⁹ Where is the kindness You showed at first, O Lord,
and faithfully promised David with an oath?
⁵⁰ Remember, O Lord, how *Your servants* are *scorned.*
I carry in my heart all those nations
⁵¹ whom Your enemies have scorned, O LORD,
who also *scorn* every step of *the one You anointed.*
⁵² *Blessed be the LORD* forever. So be it! So be it!

Our Everlasting God

A prayer by Moses, the man of God.

90 O Lord, You are our home through all the ages.
² Before the mountains were born
or You gave birth to the earth and the world —
O God, You exist from everlasting to everlasting.
³ You turn man back to dust,
saying, "Return, children of men."
⁴ *A thousand years* pass in Your sight
like yesterday,
like a watch in the night.
⁵ As by a flood You sweep them away—they are sleeping.
In the morning they grow up new like grass.
⁶ In the morning they blossom and are fresh;
in the evening they will wither and dry up.
⁷ Yes, Your anger consumes us; Your fury terrifies us.

⁸ You have set our sins before You,
　　our hidden sins before the light of Your face.
⁹ When You pour out Your anger, all our days vanish;
　　we finish our years like a sigh.
¹⁰ We live as long as 70 years,
　　and if we're strong enough get to be 80.
Yet what we are proud of[e] is but toil and trouble;
　　it's gone so quickly and we fly away.
¹¹ Who knows how fierce Your anger is?
　　Your fury is as great as the fear due You.
¹² Teach us to count our days that we learn to be wise.

¹³ How long until You return, O LORD?
　　Have pity on Your servants.
¹⁴ In the morning satisfy us with Your mercy;
　　then we'll shout happily and be glad as long as we live.
¹⁵ Make us glad as many days as You made us suffer,
　　as many years as we've seen misery.
¹⁶ May Your servants see what You can do,
　　and may Your glory be on our children.
¹⁷ May the kindness of the Lord our God be upon us;
　　give us success in what we're doing;
　　yes, give us success in what we're doing.

Under the Wings of the Almighty

91 Let him who lives in the shelter of the Most High
　　and stays in the shadow of the Almighty,
² say to the LORD, "My Refuge and my Fortress,
　　my God Whom I trust!"
³ He is the One Who will rescue you from the snare
　　and from the deadly plague.
⁴ He will *cover you with His feathers,*
　　and under His wings you will find refuge.
　　His truth is a shield and an armor.
⁵ You need not be afraid of anything dreadful at night,
　　an arrow flying during the day,
⁶ the pestilence moving in the dark,
　　or the plague ravaging at noon.
⁷ A thousand may fall at your side
　　and ten thousand at your right,
　　but it will not come near you.
⁸ You will only watch it with your eyes
　　and see how the wicked are paid back.

---

4 II Pet 3:8

e - 10　　Or "their arrogance brings. . ."

⁹ If you have made the LORD, who is my Refuge,
    the Most High, your Home,
¹⁰He will not let any harm come to you
    or disaster come near your home,
¹¹ because *He orders His angels to be with you*
    and protect you everywhere you go.
¹² *They will carry you in their hands*
    and not let you stub your foot against a stone.
¹³ You *will step on* a lion or *a cobra*
    and trample on a young lion or a serpent.

(The Lord:)
¹⁴ "Because he clings to Me in love, I will rescue him
    and put him in a safe high place,
    because he knows My name.
¹⁵ When he calls Me, I will answer him,
    be with him in trouble, rescue him, and honor him.
¹⁶ With a long life I will satisfy him
    and have him drink his fill of My salvation."

Like Flowers

A psalm to be sung on the Sabbath day.

92 It is good to thank the LORD
    and sing about Your name, O Most High,
²and talk in the morning about Your kindness
    and at night about Your faithfulness
³ with a ten-stringed instrument, a lute, and music on a lyre.

⁴ You made me glad, O LORD, by what You did;
    I will shout about what Your hands accomplished.
⁵ How great are Your works, O LORD,
    and very deep Your thoughts!
⁶ A dull person can't understand it,
    and a fool can't grasp it.
⁷ The wicked come up like grass,
    and all who do wrong blossom like flowers
    only to be killed off forever.
⁸ But You, O LORD, are most high forever.
⁹ Look at Your enemies, O LORD; see how Your enemies perish,
    and all who do wrong are scattered.

¹⁰ But You have given me strength like that of a wild bull,
    and fresh oil is poured on me.

11-12 Mt 4:6; Lk 4:10-11 13 Lk 10:19

¹¹ My eyes see those who watch for me;
    my ears hear the evildoers attacking me.
¹² The righteous flourish like palm trees
    and grow tall like cedars in Lebanon.
¹³ They are planted in the LORD's house;
    they blossom like flowers in the courts of our God.
¹⁴ Even when they're old, they still bear fruit,
    being green and full of sap,
¹⁵ to show that the LORD is righteous.
    He's my Rock, and there's no iniquity in Him!

Our Everlasting King

93 *The LORD is King! He* is clothed with majesty.
    The Lord dresses in power, fastening His belt.
    The world also was made to stand firm
        and can't be moved.
² Long ago Your throne was made to stand firm —
    You are from everlasting.
³ O LORD, the rivers make a noise;
    the rivers make their roaring noise;
    the rivers make a crashing noise—
⁴ but more than *the noise of vast waters*
    and mightier than the waves of the sea
    is the might of the LORD above!

⁵ The truths You wrote are absolutely trustworthy.
    In Your temple, O LORD, holiness is beautiful forever.

A Just God Helps

94 God of vengeance; O LORD,
    God of vengeance, shine!
² Rise, Judge of the world, give the proud what they deserve.
³ How long, O LORD, how long will the wicked rejoice?
⁴ Gushing and talking boldly,
    all who do wrong brag about themselves.
⁵ They trample on Your people, O LORD,
    and make Your own suffer.
⁶ They kill the widow and the stranger and murder orphans,
      ⁷saying, "The LORD doesn't see it;
    Jacob's God doesn't even notice it."
⁸ You mindless ones among the people, understand;
    you fools, when will you get wise?
⁹ He planted the ear — can't He hear?

93:1,4 Rev 19:6   94:1 I Thess 4:6

He formed the eye — can't He see?
[10] He disciplines nations — can't He correct?
He teaches people — doesn't He know?
[11] *The LORD knows that what man thinks is nothing.*

[12] Blessed is the man whom You, O LORD,
correct and teach from Your Word,
[13] to give him rest after a time of trouble,
while a pit is dug for the wicked.
[14] *The LORD doesn't reject His people* or forsake His own.
[15] The decisions of judges will again become just,
and all whose heart is right will pursue justice.
[16] Will anyone rise against the wicked in my behalf?
Will anyone stand by me against those who do wrong?

[17] If the LORD hadn't helped me,
I soon would have gone down to silence.
[18] When I think my foot is slipping,
Your mercy, O LORD, holds me up.
[19] When there's much troubling me inwardly,
Your comforts delight me.

[20] Can anyone on a throne of wickedness be Your partner,
when he uses laws to do mischief?
[21] They band together to attack the life of the righteous
and condemn innocent people to death.

[22] But the LORD has been my Mountain Refuge,
and my God is the Rock Who shelters me.
[23] He made their wickedness lash back on them,
and for their evil He will wipe them out —
Yes, the LORD our God will wipe them out.

Our King and Shepherd

95 Come, let us sing joyfully to the LORD;
let us shout happily to the Rock Who saves us.
[2] Let us come before Him with praise
and shout happily to Him with psalms.

[3] The LORD is a great God,
the great King above all gods.
[4] In His hand are the deep places of the earth;
the mountain peaks are His;
[5] the sea is His — He made it,

---

11 *I Cor 3:20*   14 *Rom 11:1-2*

and His hands formed the dry land.

⁶ Come, let us worship and bow down
and kneel before the LORD Who made us.
⁷ He is our God;
we're the people of His pasture, the flock of His hand.
Today, hear if you will, His voice:
⁸ *"Don't get stubborn as at Meribah,*
as on that day at Massah in the wilderness, ⁹where your fathers
tested Me and tried Me out, although they had seen what I could do.
¹⁰ *For 40 years I was disgusted with those people;*
I said, *'They're a people* whose *hearts are going astray; they*
haven't learned My ways.'
¹¹ *So in My anger I took* a solemn oath:
'They will never come to My place of rest!'"

Worship the Lord!

96 *Sing* to the LORD a *new song!*
   Sing to the LORD, all the world!
² Sing to the Lord! Bless His name!
   From day to day tell the news of how He saves.
³ Among the nations tell about His glory,
   about the wonderful things He does among all the people.
⁴ The LORD is great and should be praised very highly,
   and should be held in awe above all gods.
⁵ All the other gods of the nations are worthless idols,
   but the LORD made the heavens.
⁶ Splendor and majesty are before Him;
   power and beauty are in His holy place.

⁷ Give the LORD, O families of the nations,
   give the LORD glory and power;
   ⁸give the LORD the glory due His name.
   Bring an offering and come to His courts;
   ⁹worship the LORD in holy garments.
   Tremble before Him, all the world!
¹⁰ Tell among the nations: *"The LORD is King!"*
   He made the earth stand firm so that it can't be moved.
   He will judge the peoples fairly.
¹¹ Let the heavens rejoice and the earth be glad;
   let the sea roar like thunder and everything in it,
   ¹²the fields be delighted and everything in them.

7-11 Heb 3:7-11,13,15-18; 4:3,5-7,10-11   *1* Rev 5:9; 14:3   *10* Rev 19:6

> Then all the trees in the forest will sing joyfully
> [13] before the LORD because He is coming.
>> When He comes to judge the earth,
>> *He'll judge the world fairly* and the people faithfully.

We're Happy in Our King

97 *The LORD is King.* Let the earth rejoice,
>> and the many islands be glad.
> [2] Clouds and darkness are around Him.
>> His throne is built on righteousness and justice.
> [3] Fire goes ahead of Him, burning up His enemies all around.
> [4] His lightnings light up the world —
>> seeing it, the earth trembles.
> [5] The mountains melt like wax as they face the LORD,
>> the Master of the whole earth.
> [6] The heavens tell about His righteousness,
>> and all the people of the world see His glory.
> [7] All who worship images, and brag about vain idols,
>> will come to a shameful end.
>> All the gods *bow down to Him.*
> [8] Zion is happy to hear it;
>> Judah's towns are delighted with Your judgments, O LORD.
> [9] You, O LORD, are high above the earth,
>> very high above all gods.
> [10] If you love the LORD, hate evil.
>> He who preserves the lives of His devoted ones
>> will rescue them from the hands of the wicked.
> [11] Light dawns for the righteous,
>> and joy for those whose hearts are right.
> [12] Be happy in the LORD, you righteous,
>> and praise Him as you remember how holy He is.

Sing to Our Victorious King!

A psalm.

98 *Sing to the LORD a new song —*
>> He has done wonderful things;
>> His right hand and His holy arm have won Him victory.
> [2] The LORD has shown how He saves
>> and revealed His righteousness for the nations to see.
> [3] He *has remembered His kindness* to Israel
>> and His faithfulness to them.

---

13 Acts 17:31; Rev 19:11 **1** Rev 19:6   **7** Heb 1:6
1 Rev 5:9; 14:3   **3** Lk 1:54; Acts 28:28

All the distant parts of the world have seen
 how our God *can save.*
⁴ Shout to the LORD, all the world;
 break into happy shouting, and sing to praise Him.
⁵ Make music to the LORD with a lyre,
 with a lyre and the sound of music,
  ⁶with trumpets and the blowing of a horn.
Shout before the King, the LORD.

⁷ May the sea roar like thunder and everything in it,
 the world and those who live in it.
⁸ May the streams clap their hands,
 and the hills shout happily together
  ⁹before the LORD, because He will come to judge the world;
He will judge the world fairly and the people with justice.

He Is Holy

99 *The LORD is King — the people tremble;*
 He's on a throne among the angels — the earth shakes.
² Great is the LORD in Zion
 and high above all the peoples.
³ They should praise Your great and awesome name;
 it is holy.

⁴ O Mighty King, You love justice and establish fairness!
 You do what is just and right in Jacob.
⁵ Honor highly the LORD our God and worship at *His footstool* —
 He is holy.

⁶ Moses and Aaron were among His priests,
 and Samuel was among those who called on His name.
They called the LORD, and He answered them,
 ⁷and talked to them from a pillar of cloud.

They kept the truth He wrote and the law He gave them.
⁸ O LORD, our God, You answered them.
 You were their God Who forgave them
 but punished their wrongs.
⁹ Honor highly the LORD our God and worship at His holy hill
 because the LORD our God is holy.

---

9 *Acts 17:31; Rev 19:11* **1** *Rev 11:17-18; 19:6* **5** *Mt 5:35*

Thank God

A psalm to give thanks.

100 Shout to the LORD, all the world;
² serve the LORD with joy;
come before Him shouting happily.
³ Know that the LORD is God:
He made us, and not we ourselves.
We are His people and the flock of His pastures.
⁴ Come into His gates to give thanks,
into His courts to praise.
Thank Him, bless His name
⁵ because the LORD is good and merciful forever
and is faithful through all the generations.

The King Hates Wrong

A psalm by David.

101 I will sing of kindness and justice
and make music to You, O LORD.
² I want to understand the perfect way.
O when will You come to me?
I will live with a pure heart in my own home.
³ I will not put anything wicked before my eyes.
I hate what the unfaithful do;
I want no part of it.
⁴ I will stay away from crooked thoughts.
I will not be friendly with evil.
⁵ I'll silence anyone who secretly slanders his neighbor;
I won't put up with anyone who looks proud and is conceited.
⁶ I look for the faithful people in the land,
so they may live with me.
When anyone lives a pure life,
he may serve me;
⁷ but no one who does deceitful things shall live in my home;
no one who tells lies can stay with me.
⁸ Every morning I'll destroy all the wicked in the land,
to purge the LORD's city of all who do wrong.

Help Me-I'm Suffering

A prayer by one who is suffering when he is faint and
pours out his troubles before the LORD.

102 O LORD, listen to my prayer,

and let my cry for help come before You.
² Don't hide Your face from me when I'm in trouble;
   turn Your ear to me; when I call, answer me quickly.
³ My days vanish like smoke,
   and my limbs burn as on a hearth.
⁴ My heart is parched and withered like grass —
   I forget to eat my food.
⁵ As I groan my bones cling to my flesh.

⁶ I have become like an owl in the desert,
   like a night-owl among ruins;
⁷ I'm always awake, like a bird alone on a roof.
⁸ All day long my enemies insult me;
   raging at me, they bind themselves with an oath against me.
⁹ Yes, I eat ashes like bread and mix my drink with tears.

¹⁰ You were so angry and furious
   You picked me up and threw me down.
¹¹ My days are like a shadow getting longer,
   and I wither away like grass.
¹² But You, O LORD, are on Your throne forever;
   You are remembered through all the ages.
¹³ You will rise and be merciful to Zion —
   it's time to be kind to her,
   the time that was set has come.
¹⁴ Your servants delight even in Zion's stones
   and pity even her dust.

¹⁵ The nations will fear the LORD's name,
   and all the kings of the world His glory.
¹⁶ When the LORD builds Zion,
   He will be seen there in His glory.
¹⁷ He will listen to the prayer of those stripped of everything;
   He doesn't despise their prayer.

¹⁸ This will be written down for a future generation,
   so a people still to be created can praise the LORD.
¹⁹ The LORD looked down from His high and holy place;
   He looked from heaven at the earth,
²⁰ to hear the prisoner groan and to free those doomed to die,
²¹ to hear those in Zion tell about the LORD's name,
   and His praise in Jerusalem,
²² when the people and kingdoms are gathered to serve the LORD.
²³ When on the way, He weakened my strength
   and shortened my life;
²⁴ so I said, "My God, don't take me away in the middle of my life.

Your years last forever.
²⁵ *Long ago You laid the earth's foundation,*
   and Your hands made the heavens.
²⁶ *They perish, but You go on;*
   they will all wear out like a garment;
   You will change them like clothes, and they will pass away,
      ²⁷ *but You are the same and Your years never end.*
²⁸ Your servants' children will live undisturbed,
   and their descendants will stand firm before You."

Like a Father

By David.

103 My soul, praise the LORD,
   and everything in me, praise His holy name.
² My soul, praise the LORD,
   and don't forget all the good He does:
   ³He forgives all my wrongs, heals all my sicknesses,
   ⁴saves my life from being destroyed,
   crowns me with kindness and mercy,
   ⁵and satisfies me with good things as long as I live
   so that like an eagle my youth is renewed.
⁶ The LORD does what is right
   and just for all who are oppressed.

⁷ He let Moses know His ways
   and Israel the great things He did.
⁸ *The LORD is merciful and kind,*
   slow to get angry, and rich in kindness.
⁹ He will not always accuse us of wrong
   or be angry forever.
¹⁰ He hasn't dealt with us as we deserve for our sins
   or paid us back for our wrongs.
¹¹ No, as high as heaven is above the earth,
   that's how great His *kindness is to those who fear Him.*
¹² As far as the rising of the sun is from its setting,
   so far has He put our sins away from us.
¹³ As a father has compassion for His children,
   so the LORD has compassion for those who fear Him.

¹⁴ He knows how we are made and remembers we are dust.
¹⁵ A man's days are like grass;
   he blossoms like a flower in the field;
      ¹⁶the wind blows over him, and he is gone;

25-27 Heb 1:10-12   8 James 5:11   11 Lk 1:50

and his home doesn't know him anymore.
¹⁷ But from everlasting to everlasting
the LORD has mercy on those who fear Him
and gives His righteousness to children's children,
¹⁸ to those who keep His covenant
and remember to do what He orders.

¹⁹ The LORD set up His throne in heaven
and as King rules everything.
²⁰ Praise the LORD, you angels of His,
mighty beings that listen when He speaks
and do what He says.
²¹ Praise the LORD, all His armies,
His servants that do what He wants.
²² Praise the LORD, all His creatures
in all places of His kingdom.
My soul, praise the LORD!

Give Thanks

104 My soul, bless the LORD!
O LORD my God, You are very great.
You dress in majesty and splendor,
²wrap Yourself in light as a garment,
stretch out the heavens like tent curtains,
³lay the beams of Your home in water,
make the clouds Your chariot,
and move on the wings of the wind.
⁴ *You make Your angels winds*
and Your servants flames of fire.
⁵ You set the earth on its foundations
never to be shaken.
⁶ You covered it with deep water as a garment,
the waters standing over the mountains.
⁷ When You threatened the waters, they fled,
when You thundered at them, they ran away —
⁸ the mountains rising and the valleys sinking down
to the place You appointed for them.
⁹ They can't cross the boundary You set
or come back to cover the earth.
¹⁰ You make water gush from springs into the ravines
and flow between the hills
¹¹ to let every animal in the field drink,
so the wild donkeys can quench their thirst.

---

17 Lk 1:50   *4 Heb 1:7*

¹² Beside the water *nest the birds of the air,*
    singing among the leaves.
¹³ From Your home above You water the hill-country,
    and satisfy the world by what You do,
¹⁴ making grass grow for the cattle
    and plants for man to cultivate
    to get food from the ground:
    ¹⁵wine to cheer up a man,
    olive oil to make his face shine,
    and bread to strengthen him.
¹⁶ The LORD's trees, the cedars of Lebanon that He planted,
    drink their fill.
¹⁷ Birds make their nests in them,
    the stork having his home in the fir trees.
¹⁸ The high mountains are for the wild goats;
    the rocks are a shelter for badgers.
¹⁹ You made the moon to mark the seasons,
    the sun that knows when to go down.
²⁰ When You make it dark, it is night;
    then all the animals in the woods move around;
²¹ the young lions roar for their prey,
    seeking their food from God.
²² When the sun rises, they slink away
    and lie down in their dens.
²³ Then man goes out to work and to toil until the sun goes down.
²⁴ O LORD, how many are the things You made;
    You made them all by wisdom.
  The earth is full of Your creatures,
²⁵ living things large and small.
    There is the sea, great and wide,
    with countless things moving in it.
²⁶ There go the ships, and Leviathan You formed to play in it.
²⁷ All of them are looking to You
    to give them their food at the right time.
²⁸ You give it to them — they pick it up;
    You open Your hand —
    they are satisfied with good things.
²⁹ You hide Your face — they are terrified;
    You take away their breath —
    they die and turn again to dust.
³⁰ You send out Your Breath — they are created;
    You make new the surface of the ground.

³¹ May the LORD's glory go on forever,

---

12 Mt 13:32; Mk 4:32; Lk 13:19

and the Lord be delighted with what He made.
[32] He looks at the earth and it trembles;
  He touches the mountains and they smoke.
[33] I will sing to the LORD as long as I live
  and make music to my God as long as I exist.
[34] May my meditation please Him —
  I will delight in the LORD.
[35] May sinners vanish from the world and the wicked be no more!
  My soul, bless the LORD!
  Praise the LORD!

God's People, from Abraham to the Taking of Canaan

105 Thank the LORD, call out His name,
  tell among the nations what He has done.
[2] Sing to Him and play instruments before Him;
  meditate on all the wonderful things He has done.
[3] Glory in His holy name.
  You who look for the LORD, be glad at heart.
[4] Search for the LORD and His strength;
  look for Him continually.
[5] Remember the marvelous works He did,
  His wonders and the judgments He pronounced.
[6] O descendants of Abraham, His servant!
  O descendants of Jacob, whom He chose!
[7] He is the LORD our God Who judges the whole world.
[8] *He always remembers His covenant*
  that He ordered for a thousand generations,
[9] the oath He made *with Abraham, and swore* to Isaac.
[10] He confirmed it as a law for Jacob
  as an everlasting covenant for Israel.
[11] "I give you the land of Canaan," He said,
  "as your property measured out to you."
[12] They were then only a few, a little group,
  and strangers in the country.
[13] They wandered from nation to nation,
  from one kingdom to another.
[14] He let no one oppress them
  and for their sake warned kings.
[15] He said, "Don't touch My anointed ones
  or harm My prophets."

---

35 Rev 19:1,3,4,68-9 Lk 1:72-73

¹⁶ He called for a famine on the land
    and broke every staff of bread.ᶠ
¹⁷ He sent one ahead of them: Joseph,
    who was sold as a slave.
¹⁸ They hurt his feet with chains,
    and iron cut into his neck,

¹⁹ until the time when what he said came true,
    and the LORD's Word proved he was right.
²⁰ The king sent someone to release him;
    the ruler of the nation sent and gave him liberty.
²¹ *He made him the master of his palace*
    and the ruler of everything he had,
²²to train the king's officers the way he wanted,
    and teach his elders wisdom.

²³ Then Israel came to Egypt,
    and Jacob lived as a stranger in Ham's country.
²⁴ He made His people grow rapidly in number
    and stronger than their enemies.
²⁵ They changed their minds so that they hated His people
    and dealt treacherously with His servants.
²⁶ He sent His servant Moses,
    and Aaron whom He had chosen.
²⁷ They did His signs among them
    and wonders in Ham's country:
²⁸ He sent darkness, and it got dark —
    they did not rebel against His word.
²⁹ He turned their waters to blood and so killed their fish.
³⁰ Their country swarmed with frogs,
    even getting into their kings' bedrooms.
³¹ He spoke, and swarms of flies came
    and gnats all over their country.
³² He gave them hail instead of rain
    with fire flashing through their country.
³³ He struck their vines and fig trees
    and smashed the trees in their country.
³⁴ He spoke, and grasshoppers came,
    wingless ones that couldn't be counted.
³⁵ They devoured all the plants in their country,
    everything that grew on their ground.
³⁶ He struck down every firstborn in their country,
    the first ones born of all their manly strength.

---

21 Acts 7:10

· **f** - 16   Loaves were hung on a staff to keep them from mice, etc.

³⁷ He brought Israel out with silver and gold,
    and among His tribes no one stumbled.
³⁸ The Egyptians were glad they were leaving
    because they were afraid of them.
³⁹ He spread out a cloud to protect them
    and a fire to light up the night.
⁴⁰ They asked, and He brought quail
    and satisfied them with bread from heaven.
⁴¹ He opened a rock, and water gushed out
    and flowed in a stream through the dry places.
⁴² Yes, He remembered His holy promise
    and His servant Abraham.
⁴³ He led out His people with joy,
    His chosen ones shouting happily.
⁴⁴ He gave them the lands of other nations,
    and they took what others had worked for —
    ⁴⁵ so that they might do what He ordered and keep His laws.
Praise the LORD!

God's People Rebelled

106 *Praise the LORD!*
    Thank the LORD because
    He is good and merciful forever.
² Who can say what mighty things the LORD has done
    and tell about everything we should praise Him for?
³ Blessed are those who practice justice
    and always do what is right.

⁴ Remember me, O LORD, when You are kind to Your people;
    come and help me when You save them,
    ⁵ so I may see the prosperity of Your chosen ones,
    enjoy the happiness of Your people,
    and boast with those who are Your own.

⁶ We have sinned like our fathers,
    doing wrong and wicked things.
⁷ Our fathers in Egypt didn't understand Your wonders
    or remember how merciful You were;
    so they rebelled beside the sea, the Red Sea.
⁸ Yet He saved them to honor His name,
    to let them know His power.
⁹ He rebuked the Red Sea, and it dried up;
    He led them through the floods as through a desert.

---

45 Rev 19:1,3,4,6   *1 Rev 19:1,3,4,6*

[10] So He *saved* them *from the power of those who hated* them,
and freed them *from the enemy.*
[11] Water covered their enemies,
and not one of them was left.
[12] Then they believed what He said and sang His praise.
[13] But they soon forgot what He did
· and didn't wait for His advice.
[14] So they lusted in the wilderness
and tested God in the desert.
[15] He gave them what they demanded
but also sent a disease that made them waste away.
[16] They were jealous of Moses in the camp
and of Aaron, the LORD's holy one.
[17] The ground opened and swallowed Dathan
and buried Abiram's group.
[18] Fire consumed their group;
flames burned up the wicked.
[19] At Horeb they made a calf
and worshiped an image of poured metal.
[20] *So they traded their glorious God*
for a statue of a bull that eats grass.
[21] They forgot God Who saved them,
Who did great things in Egypt,
[22]wonders in Ham's country,
and terrible things at the Red Sea.
[23] He said He would destroy them —
if Moses, whom He chose, hadn't stood in His way
to turn back His fury and keep Him from destroying them.
[24] They scorned the delightful country,
didn't believe what He said,
[25]grumbled in their tents,
and didn't obey the LORD.
[26] Raising His hand, He swore to them
to strike them down in the wilderness,
[27] disperse their descendants among the nations,
and scatter them in the various countries.
[28] But they went to serve Baal at Peor
and ate what was sacrificed to dead idols.
[29] So they made Him angry by what they did,
and sudden death broke out among them.
[30] Then Phinehas stood up between God and the people,
and the plague was stopped;
[31] and it was credited to him as righteousness
through all the generation forever.

---

10 Lk 1:71   *20 Rom 1:23*

³² They made Him angry by the water of Meribah
        and got Moses into trouble,
    ³³making him feel bitter and talk rashly.
³⁴ They didn't destroy the people as the LORD told them,
    ³⁵but mingled with the nations.
    They learned to do what they did,
        ³⁶ and worshiped their idols,
        which were a trap for them.
³⁷ They *sacrificed* their sons and daughters to *demons,*
    ³⁸poured out innocent blood,
    the blood of their own sons and daughters
    whom they sacrificed to the idols of Canaan.
    The land was polluted by bloodshed.
³⁹ They defiled themselves by what they did;
        they behaved like prostitutes.
⁴⁰ Then the LORD became angry at His people
        and was disgusted with His own.
⁴¹ He put them into the hands of other nations,
        and those who hated them ruled over them.
⁴² Their enemies oppressed them,
        and they became subject to their power.
⁴³ Many times He rescued them,
        but they planned rebellion and sank lower in their sin.
⁴⁴ He saw they were in trouble
        when He heard them crying.
⁴⁵ *He remembered His covenant* with them
        and relented according to His great mercy.
⁴⁶ He made all their captors pity them.

⁴⁷ Save us, O LORD our God,
        and gather us from the nations
        to give thanks to Your holy name
        and to glory in praising You.

⁴⁸ *Praise the LORD, the God of Israel,*
        from everlasting to everlasting.
    And let all the people say *Amen. Praise the LORD!*

Back from Exile

107 "Thank the LORD because He is good
        and merciful forever!"

---

37 I Cor 10:20   45 Lk 1:72   48 Lk 1:68; Rev 19:1,3,4,6

² That's what those should say
    whom the LORD rescued from the enemy
    ³and gathered from other countries,
    from the east and from the west,
    from the north and from the south.
⁴ Men wandered around on a desert road in the wilderness
    without finding a town to live in.
⁵ Hungry and thirsty, they were desperate.
⁶ Then they cried to the LORD in their trouble,
    and He rescued them from their distress.
⁷ He led them in the right way to go to a town to live in.
⁸ Let them thank the LORD for His goodness,
    for doing wonderful things for men.
⁹ When they were thirsty, He gave them plenty to drink;
    when they were hungry, He filled them with good things.

¹⁰ *Men sat in darkness and gloom,*
    as prisoners in misery and iron chains
¹¹ because they rebelled against the words of God,
    and scorned what the Most High had planned.
¹² So He made them weary with work to humble them,
    and when they fell there was no one to help them.
¹³ Then they cried to the LORD in their trouble,
    and He saved them from their distress.
¹⁴ He took them out of the darkness and gloom
    and tore off the ropes that bound them.
¹⁵ Let them thank the LORD for His goodness,
    for doing wonderful things for men,
    ¹⁶for smashing the gates of bronze
    and cutting the iron bars in pieces.

¹⁷ Fools suffer for their wicked ways
    and the wrongs they do.
¹⁸ They detest every kind of food,
    and come near the gates of death.
¹⁹ Then they cried to the LORD in their trouble,
    and He saved them from their distress.
²⁰ *He sent* His *Word* and made them well
    and rescued them from the grave.
²¹ Let them thank the LORD for His goodness,
    for doing wonderful things for men.
²² Let them bring sacrifices to thank Him,
    shouting happily as they tell what He did.

---

9 Lk 1:53   *10 Lk 1:79*   *20 Acts 10:36; 13:26*

²³ Those who go down to sail the sea in ships,
 who do their business on the high seas,
²⁴ saw what the LORD can do
 and His wonders in the deep waters.
²⁵ He spoke and raised a storm
 and made its waves dash high.

²⁶ Men went up to the *heights* and down to the *depths;*
 the disaster melted their courage;
²⁷ reeling and staggering like drunkards,
 all their skills became useless.
²⁸ Then they cried to the LORD in their trouble,
 and He brought them out of their distress.
²⁹ He made the storm calm down,
 and the waves around them were still.
³⁰ They were glad it was quiet.
 So He brought them to the haven they longed for.
³¹ Let them thank the LORD for His goodness,
 for doing wonderful things for men.
³² Let them glorify Him in the congregation of the people,
 and praise Him where elders sit.

³³ He changes rivers into a desert,
 springs of water into thirsty ground,
³⁴ and fertile ground into a salt flat
 because the people living there are wicked.
³⁵ He changes the desert into pools of water
 and dry ground into springs of water.
³⁶ There He settles those who are hungry
 and they build towns to live in.
³⁷ Then they sow fields and plant vineyards
 that produce a crop.
³⁸ He blesses them; they get to be very many,
 and He doesn't let them lose any cattle.
³⁹ Their numbers had become few and they sank down
 under oppression, disaster, and grief.
⁴⁰ He had poured contempt on their noblemen
 and had made them wander in a pathless wilderness.
⁴¹ But now He lifts the poor from misery
 and makes their families like a flock.
⁴² The righteous are glad to see it,
 and all wickedness shuts its mouth.
⁴³ Are you wise? Then watch for these things
 and see for yourself the goodness of the LORD.

26 Rom 10:6-7

Give Us Victory

A song, a psalm by David.

108 I am confident, O God.
I want to sing and make music even with my soul.
² Wake up, lute and lyre,
that I might wake up the dawn.
³ I will thank You among the nations, O LORD,
and play music to praise You among the people,
⁴ because Your kindness is greater than the heavens,
and Your faithfulness reaches the skies.
⁵ O God, be high over the heavens,
and let Your glory be over all the earth.
⁶ Save us by Your right hand
and answer us so Your dear people may be free.
⁷ God promised from His holy place:
"I will triumph, divide Shechem,
and measure off the valley of Succoth.
⁸ Gilead is Mine, and Manasseh is Mine;
Ephraim is a helmet on My head;
Judah is My scepter,
⁹ Moab is the basin I wash in;
I will toss My shoe to Edom;
I will shout in triumph over Philistia."

¹⁰ Who can bring me into the fortified city?
Who can lead me to Edom?
¹¹ O God, haven't You rejected us,

O God, haven't You refused to go out with our armies?
¹² Help us against the enemy — man's help is worthless!
¹³ But with God we'll fight valiantly;
He will trample down our enemies.

A Curse on the Evil Man

For the choir leader, a psalm by David.

109 O God, Whom I praise, don't be silent.
² Wicked and deceitful men have opened their mouths against me,
spoken to me with lying tongues,
³ surrounded me with hateful talk,
and fought against me without a reason.
⁴ In return for my love they accuse me,
but I pray for them.ᵍ

---

g - 4   "for them" with Syriac; Heb omits

⁵They give me evil for good and hate for my love.
⁶ Appoint a wicked man over him;
    let one stand at his right to accuse him.
⁷ When he's tried, may he come away guilty;
    let his prayer become a sin.
⁸ May his days be few,
    and *another take over his office!*
⁹ May his children be orphans and his wife a widow!
¹⁰ May his children wander around and beg
    and look for help far from their ruined homes!
¹¹ May a creditor grab everything he has
    and strangers plunder what he produced by his work!
¹² May no one be kind to him anymore
    or pity his fatherless children!
¹³ May his descendants be cut off
    and their name be wiped out in the next generation!
¹⁴ May the LORD remember the guilt of his fathers
    and not wipe out his mother's sin;
      ¹⁵may they always be before the LORD!
May He cut off the memory of them from the earth!
¹⁶ For he didn't remember to be kind
    but hunted down the poor,
    needy and brokenhearted to kill them.
¹⁷ He loved to curse — let a curse come on him!
    He didn't like to bless — may a blessing be far from him.
¹⁸ He wore cursing like his clothes —
    may it enter into his body like water
    and into his bones like oil.
¹⁹ May it be wrapped around him like a garment,
    like a belt he always wears!
²⁰ That is what the LORD should pay back
    to those who accuse me and talk evil against me.

²¹ But You, O Lord GOD,
    deal with me according to Your reputation;
    Your kindness is so good, rescue me.
²² I am poor and needy,
    and my heart is troubled within me.
²³ Like a shadow getting longer, I am gone;
    I'm shaken off like a grasshopper.
²⁴ My knees give way because of fasting,
    and my body is lean, without any fat.
²⁵ I'm a victim of their insults;
    they look at me and *shake their heads.*

---

8 Acts 1:20   *25 Mt 27:39; Mk 15:29*

²⁶ Help me, O LORD my God!
>   You are so kind; save me!
²⁷ Then they will know this is Your hand,
>   that You, O LORD, have done it.
²⁸ They may curse, but You bless.
>   May those who attack me come to a shameful end,
>   but may Your servant be glad.
²⁹ May those who accuse me put on disgrace as a garment
>   and be wrapped in their shame as in a robe.
³⁰ I will thank the LORD very much
>   and praise Him among many people,
³¹ for He stands at the right side of the needy man
>   to save him from those who condemn him to die.

Our King, Priest, and Judge

A psalm by David.

110 *The LORD says to my Lord, "Sit at My right*
>   *until I make Your enemies Your footstool."*
² From Zion the LORD will send out the scepter of Your power:
>   "Rule in the middle of Your enemies."
³ Your people willingly offer themselves
>   when You call up Your army.
>   From the womb of the dawn like dew,
>   Your youth will come to You in beautiful, holy garments.
⁴ *The LORD has sworn and will not change His mind:*
>   *"You are a Priest forever like Melchizedek."*

⁵ At your right the Lord will smash kings when He's angry.
⁶ He will pass judgment on the nations
>   and fill valleys with dead bodies;
>   He will smash the rulers over the wide earth.
⁷ Along the way, He will drink from a brook;
>   therefore He will hold His head high.

The LORD Is Kind and Faithful

111 *Praise the LORD!*
>   I will thank the LORD with all my heart
>   in the fellowship of the righteous and in the congregation.
² The LORD has done great things,

---

1 Mt 22:44; 26:64; Mk 12:36; 14:62; 16:19; Lk 20:42-43; 22:69; Acts 2:34-35; I Cor 15:25: Eph 1:20,22; Col 3:1; Heb 1:3,13; 8:1; 10:12-13; 12:2;I Pet 3:22
110:4 Heb 5:6,10; 6:20; 7:3,11,15,17,21,24,28   111:1 Rev 19:1,3,4,6

things studied by all who delight in them.
3 *His work is glorious* and majestic,
and He will be righteous forever.
4 He made His wonders something to be remembered.
The LORD is kind and merciful:
5 He gives food to those who fear Him;
He will always remember His covenant.
6 He showed His people His power by His works,
by giving them the land of the nations.

7 Faithful and just are the works of His hands;
all His guiding principles are reliable.
8 They are unshakably firm forever;
they are faithfully and correctly put into action.
9 *He sent liberty to His people*
and ordered His covenant to be forever.
His name is holy and awesome.

10 To be wise, first fear the LORD;
it is good sense for all to do that.
He will be praised forever.

Give to the Poor

112 *Praise the LORD!*
How blessed is the man who fears the LORD,
who takes great delight in His commandments!
2 His descendants will grow strong in the world
and be blessed as an honest generation.
3 There will be wealth and riches in his home.
His righteousness goes on forever.

4 The Light will dawn in the darkness for the righteous;
that is the *Kind, Merciful,* and Righteous *One.*
5 It is good for a man to be generous and ready to lend
and fair in doing his business.
6 Such a man will never fail.
A righteous man will always be remembered.
7 He will not have to fear bad news.
As he trusts the LORD, his courage doesn't waver.
8 His heart is steady, and he's not afraid.
Finally he will look in triumph on his enemies.

---

3 Rev 15:3 *4 James 5:11* ***9** Lk 1:49,68*
***112:1** Rev 19:1,3,4,6* ***3** II Cor 9:9* ***4** James 5:11*

9 *He gives freely to the poor.*
   His righteousness goes on forever.
   His head will be raised in honor.
10 The wicked will see it and not like it;
   he will grind his teeth and vanish.
   The wicked will never get what he wants.

The LORD Helps the Poor

113 *Praise the LORD!*
   Praise Him, O servants of the LORD;
      praise the LORD's name!
2 Bless the LORD's name from now on and forever!
3 From the rising of the sun to its going down,
      praise the LORD's name!
4 The LORD is high above all nations
   and His glory above the skies.

5 Who is like the LORD our God,
      seated on His high throne?
6 He bends to look down on heaven and earth.
7 He raises the poor from the dust,
      and lifts up the needy from the manure pile.
8 He enables him to sit with noblemen,
      the noblemen of his people.
9 He makes the childless woman live in her own home,
      as the happy mother of children.
   Praise the LORD!

A Song of the Exodus

114 When Israel came out of Egypt
      and Jacob's family left a people who talk a strange language,
2 Judah became His holy place and Israel His kingdom.
3 The sea saw it and *fled;*
      the Jordan turned back.
4 The mountains danced like rams; the hills like lambs.
5 Why have you fled, O sea?
      And Jordan, what made you turn back?

6 O mountains, what made you dance like rams,
      O hills, like lambs?
7 O *earth,* tremble *before the Lord,* before Jacob's God —

9 *II Cor 9:9*   **113:1** *Rev 19:1,3,4,6*   **9** *Rev 19:1,3,4,6*
114:3 *Rev 20:11*   **7** *Rev 20:11*

⁸He changed the rock into a pool of water
and the flint into springs of water.

God Blesses Us

115 Not to us, O LORD, not to us
but to Your name give glory,
because of Your mercy and faithfulness.
² Why should other nations say, "Where is their God?"
³ Our God is in heaven
and does anything He wants to do.
⁴ Their idols are *silver and gold made by human hands.*
⁵ They have a mouth but can't talk,
eyes but *can't see,*
⁶ears but *can't hear,*
a nose but can't smell,
⁷hands but can't feel,
feet but *can't walk.*
They can't make a sound with their throats.
⁸ Those who make them are like them,
and so are all who trust them.

⁹ (Leader:)
Israel, trust the LORD.
(Choir:)
He helps and shields them.
¹⁰ (Leader:)
Aaron's family, trust the LORD.
(Choir:)
He helps and shields them.
¹¹ (Leader:)
You who fear the LORD, trust the LORD.
(Choir:)
He helps and shields them.
¹² (Leader:)
The LORD has been thinking of us and He will bless us.
(Choir:)
He will bless Israel's family;
He will bless Aaron's family;
¹³ He will bless *those who fear* the LORD, *small and great.*
¹⁴ The LORD will cause you and your children to increase.
¹⁵ You will be blessed by the LORD Who made heaven and earth.
¹⁶ The highest heaven belongs to the LORD,
but the earth He gave to men.

4-7 Rev 9:20   *13 Rev 11:18; 19:5*   *18 Rev 19:1,3,4,6*

¹⁷ The dead can't praise the LORD
　　or any who go down to silence.
¹⁸ But we will bless the LORD from now on and forever.
　　Praise the LORD!

How Can I Thank the LORD?

116 I love the LORD because
　　He hears me call and plead.
² Because He turns His ear to me,
　　I will call on Him as long as I live.
³ The snares of death came around me;
　　the distress of the grave took hold of me;
　　I experienced anguish and grief.
⁴ So I prayed in the LORD's name: "Please, O LORD, rescue me!"

⁵ The LORD is kind and righteous; our God is merciful.
⁶ The LORD protects the helpless;
　　He saved me when I was weak.
⁷ O my soul, go back to your rest,
　　the LORD has been kind to you.
⁸ You saved my life from death,
　　my eyes from tears and my feet from stumbling,
　　⁹so I might walk before the LORD in the land of the living.
¹⁰ (*I believed* even when I had *to speak* of my suffering so much.
¹¹ I had said in my panic, "*Everyone is lying.*")
¹² How can I pay back the LORD
　　for all the good He has done for me?
¹³ I will raise the cup of salvation
　　and pray in the LORD's name.
¹⁴ I will fulfill my vows to the LORD before all His people.
¹⁵ Precious to the LORD is the death of His holy ones.
¹⁶ O LORD, I am Your servant;
　　I am Your servant, the son of Your maid-servant.
　　You freed me from the ropes that bound me.
¹⁷ With a sacrifice I will thank You
　　and pray in Your name, O LORD.
¹⁸ I will fulfill my vows to the LORD before all His people,
　　¹⁹in the courts of the LORD's temple, in Your midst,
　　O Jerusalem.
　　Praise the LORD!

---

18 Rev 19:1,3,4,6　　*10 II Cor 4:13*　　*11 Rom 3:4*　　*19 Rev 19:1,3,4,6*

Praise the LORD!

117 *Praise the LORD,* all you nations!
Praise Him, all you people!
[2]His mercy toward us is great,
and the LORD is faithful forever.
Praise the LORD!

Procession to the Temple

118 (On the way:)
Thank the LORD because
He is good and merciful forever.
[2] Israel should say, "He is merciful forever."
[3] Aaron's family should say, "He is merciful forever."
[4] Those who fear the LORD should say,
"He is merciful forever."

[5] In my trouble I called on the LORD.
The LORD answered me and set me free.
[6] *The LORD is for me, I'm not afraid.*
What can man do to me?
[7] *The LORD* is for me; He *helps me.*
I will gloat over those who hate me.
[8] It is better to take refuge in the LORD
than to trust men.
[9] It is better to take refuge in the LORD
than to trust the best of men.

[10] All the nations surrounded me—
in the LORD's name I have defeated them;
[11] they surrounded me, yes, surrounded me —
in the LORD's name I have defeated them;
[12] they surrounded me like bees;
but like burning thorns they were extinguished;
in the LORD's name I have defeated them.

[13] You pushed hard to make me fall,
but the LORD helped me.
[14] The LORD is my strength and song;
He has saved me.
[15] Listen to the happy shouting of victory
in the tents of the righteous!
The LORD's right hand is working mightily;
[16]the LORD holds high His right hand;

117:1-2 *Rom 15:11; Rev 19:1,3,4,6*   **6-7** *Heb 13:6*   **17-18** *II Cor 6:9*

the LORD's right hand is working mightily.
¹⁷ I will *not die but live* and tell what the LORD has done.
¹⁸ The LORD sharply *corrected* me *but didn't let* me *die.*
¹⁹ (Entering:)

Open the gates of righteousness for me;
    I will go into them and thank the LORD.
²⁰ This is the LORD's gate —
    the righteous go into it.
²¹ (Inside:)
I thank You, for You have answered me
    and have become my Deliverer.
²² *The Stone the builders rejected*
    has become the Cornerstone.
²³ *The LORD has done this, and we think it is wonderful.*
²⁴ The LORD made this day;
    let us rejoice and be glad in Him.
²⁵ O LORD, *please save. Lord,*
    please give us success.
²⁶ *Blessed is He Who comes in the LORD's name.*
    We bless You in the LORD's temple.

²⁷ The LORD is God, and He gives us light.
    March in festive procession with branches
    up to the horns of the altar.
²⁸ You are my God, and I thank You;
    My God, I honor You highly.
²⁹ Thank the LORD because He is good and merciful forever!

God's Word

119 Happy are those whose lives are innocent,
    who live by what the LORD teaches.
² Happy are those who keep the truths He wrote,
    searching for Him with all their hearts;
    ³who do no wrong but walk in His ways.
⁴ You ordered us to give diligent attention to Your directions.
⁵ O how I want my life to conform to Your laws!
⁶ I will never be ashamed
    when I study all Your commandments.
⁷ I will praise You sincerely as I learn Your righteous decrees.
⁸ I will keep Your laws—don't utterly forsake me.
⁹ How can a young man keep his life pure?

22-23 *Mt 21:42; Mk 12:10-11; Lk 20:17; Acts 4:11; I Pet 2:7*   **24** *Rev 19:7*
25-26 *Mt 21:9,15; 23:39; Mk 11:9; Lk 13:35; 19:38; Jn 12:13; Rev 1:4,8; 4:8*

By living as You tell him to.
10 With all my heart I search for You.
   Don't let me stray from Your commandments.
11 I treasure in my heart what You say,
   so I won't sin against You.
12 Blessed are You, O LORD — teach me Your laws.
13 With my lips I tell of every decree that comes from Your mouth.
14 I delight in the way of Your written instructions
   as much as in all kinds of riches.
15 I think about how You want me to live and watch Your ways.
16 I delight in Your laws and will not forget what You say.

17 Kindly help Your servant,
   that I may live and do what You say.
18 Open my eyes,
   and I will see wonderful things in what You teach.
19 I'm a stranger on earth —
   don't hide Your commandments from me.
20 At all times my soul craves
   and longs for Your regulations.
21 You rebuke the proud who are cursed,
   for going astray from Your commandments.
22 Remove insults and contempt away from me
   because I keep the truths You wrote.
23 Even while princes sit and plot against me,
   Your servant thinks about Your laws.
24 Yes, I delight in the truths You wrote —
   they are my advisers.

25 My spirit clings to the dust —
   give me a new life as You promised.
26 When I tell You about my life, answer me;
   teach me Your laws.
27 Help me understand how You want me to live,
   and I will think of the wonderful things You do.
28 My misery deprives me of sleep —
   strengthen me as You promised.
29 Turn me away from falsehood,
   and kindly give me Your instructions.
30 I have chosen the way of faithfulness
   and set Your decrees before me.
31 I cling to the truths You wrote —
   O LORD, don't let me come to shame.
32 I will run the way of Your commandments
   because You give me a *broader understanding*.

32 II Cor 6:11

³³ O LORD, teach me the way You prescribe,
    and I will keep it to the end.
³⁴ Give me understanding, and I will keep what You teach
    and do it with all my heart.
³⁵Lead me in the path of Your commandments —
    I am delighted with it.
³⁶ Make me interested in the truths You wrote
    and not in greedy profit.
³⁷ Turn my eyes away from watching worthless things.
    Give me a new life in Your way.
³⁸ Do what You promised Your servant,
    that I may respect You.
³⁹ Take away the scorn I dread,
    because Your decrees are good.
⁴⁰ I long for Your guiding principles;
    by Your righteousness give me life.

⁴¹ O LORD, may Your mercy come to me;
    save me as You promised.
⁴² Then I'll have an answer for him who insults me,
    for I trust Your promise.
⁴³ Never take any of the word of truth from my mouth
    because I put my hope in Your regulations.
⁴⁴ Then I will continually and forever
    be careful to do what You teach.
⁴⁵ I will walk in freedom
    because I have studied how You want me to live.
⁴⁶ I will speak of Your written truths before kings
    and not feel ashamed.
⁴⁷ I delight in Your commandments, which I love;
⁴⁸ I stretch out my hands for Your commandments,
    which I love, and meditate on Your laws.

⁴⁹ Remember Your promise to Your servant
    for by it You have given me hope.
⁵⁰ This is my comfort in my misery:
    that Your word gives me life.
⁵¹ Proud men bitterly scorn me,
    but I don't turn away from Your teaching.
⁵² O LORD, I remember Your righteous acts of long ago
    and am comforted.
⁵³ The wicked, who forsake Your teaching,
    make me hot with anger.
⁵⁴ Your laws have been my songs here where I'm a stranger.
⁵⁵ At night I think of Your name, O LORD,
    and I carefully do what You teach.

⁵⁶ It is good for me to follow the way You want me to live.

⁵⁷ O LORD, You are my portion;
    I promise to do what You say.
⁵⁸ With all my heart I want You to be friendly to me;
    be kind to me as You promised.
⁵⁹ I have thought about my life,
    and so I have come back to the truths You wrote.
⁶⁰ I hurry without a delay to do what You ordered.
⁶¹ The wicked put the ropes of their traps around me,
    but I don't forget Your teaching.
⁶² I get up at midnight to thank You for judging what is right.
⁶³ I'm a friend to all who fear You
    and follow the way You want them to live.
⁶⁴ The earth is full of Your kindness, O LORD.
    Teach me Your laws.

⁶⁵ O LORD, You have treated Your servant well,
    as You promised.
⁶⁶ Teach me good judgment and knowledge
    because I trust Your commandments.
⁶⁷ Before I suffered, I was going wrong,
    but now I do what You say.
⁶⁸ You are good, and You do good — teach me Your laws.
⁶⁹ Proud men have smeared me with lies,
    but with all my heart I follow the way You want me to live.
⁷⁰ Their heart is like fat without feeling,
    but I delight in Your teaching.
⁷¹ It is good for me to have suffered in order to learn Your laws.
⁷² Your teaching is worth more to me
    than thousands in gold and silver.

⁷³ Your hands made me and formed me—help me understand,
    and I will learn Your commandments.
⁷⁴ Those who fear You will see me and be glad
    because I trust Your promise.
⁷⁵ O LORD, I know Your judgments are just,
    and You were faithful when You made me suffer.
⁷⁶ May Your kindness comfort me
    as You promised Your servant,
⁷⁷ and Your mercies come to me
    so that I may live because I delight in Your teaching.
⁷⁸ May proud men come to shame
    because they wronged me with lies,
    but I'll think of how You want me to live.
⁷⁹ Those who fear You should turn to me

and learn the truths You wrote.
80 May my heart be blameless in Your laws
    that I might not come to shame.

81 I am worn out as I long for You to save me —
    I trust Your promise.
82 My eyes have become strained as I look for Your promise
    and ask, "When will You comfort me?"
83 Although I've become like a wineskin in smoke,
    I haven't forgotten Your laws.
84 What is left of Your servant's life?
    When will You punish those who pursue me?
85 Proud men have dug pits for me —
    not according to Your instructions.
86 All Your commandments are true,
    but those men persecute me with lies — help me!
87 They almost wiped me off the earth,
    but I didn't forsake the way You want me to live.
88 According to Your love give me a new life,
    and I will keep the truths You spoke.

89 O LORD, Your word stands forever firm in heaven.
90 You are faithful through all the ages.
    You formed the earth, and it continues to stand.
91 By Your decrees they stand firm today
    because all things serve You.
92 If I hadn't been delighted in Your teaching,
    I would have perished in my misery.
93 I will never forget Your directions —
    by them You gave me a new life.
94 I am Yours — save me,
    because I've studied how You want me to live.
95 The wicked have waited for me, to destroy me,
    but I want to understand the truths You wrote.
96 I have seen how everything perfect comes to an end,
    but Your commandment extends very far.

97 How I love Your teaching—I think about it all day long.
98 Because I always have Your commandments,
    I'm wiser than my enemies.
99 I have a better insight than all my teachers
    because I think of the truths You wrote.
100 I understand better than the old men
    because I follow the way You want me to live.
101 I keep my foot from walking on any evil path —
    I want to do what You say.

¹⁰² I haven't turned away from Your regulations
     because You have taught me.
¹⁰³ How pleasant Your words taste,
     better than honey in my mouth.
¹⁰⁴ I get understanding from Your decrees;
     that is why I hate all deception.

¹⁰⁵ Your Word is a lamp for my feet and a light on my path.
¹⁰⁶ I made a promise with an oath and will keep it,
     an oath to carry out Your righteous decisions.
¹⁰⁷ I am suffering so very much, O LORD,
     give me the new life You promised.
¹⁰⁸ Please accept, O LORD, the praise I gladly give,
     and teach me Your regulations.
¹⁰⁹ I always hold my life in my hand,
     but I never forget Your teaching.
¹¹⁰ The wicked set a trap for me,
     but I have never wandered
from the way You want me to live.

¹¹¹ The truths You wrote are mine forever
     because they are my heart's delight.
¹¹² I'm always, and to the very end,
     interested in doing what Your laws say.

¹¹³ I hate two-faced people,
     but I love Your teaching.
¹¹⁴ You are my Hiding Place and my Shield —
     I wait for Your promise.
¹¹⁵ Go away from me, wicked men —
     I want to do what my God orders.
¹¹⁶ Help me as You promised so that I may live,
     and don't let me be disappointed in my hope.
¹¹⁷ Strengthen me so I may be saved,
     and I will always respect Your laws.
¹¹⁸ You reject all who leave Your laws to go wrong—
     with a lie they deceive themselves.
¹¹⁹ You get rid of all the wicked on earth like dross,
     but I love the truths You wrote.
¹²⁰ My flesh shudders in fear of You;
     I stand in awe of Your judgments.

¹²¹ I have done what is just and right;
     don't leave me to those who oppress me.
¹²² Guarantee Your servant's welfare—
     don't let proud people oppress me.

¹²³ My eyes are strained as I look for You to save me
    and for the righteousness You promised.
¹²⁴ Deal with Your servant according to Your kindness,
    and teach me Your laws.
¹²⁵ I am Your servant —
    help me understand and know the truths You wrote.
¹²⁶ O LORD, it is time to act —
    they have violated Your teaching.
¹²⁷ But I love Your commandments more than gold or even fine gold.
¹²⁸ I agree with all Your regulations, and hate all deception.

¹²⁹ The truths You wrote are wonderful;
    that's why I keep them.
¹³⁰ Your word is a door that lets in light
    and helps the simple person understand.
¹³¹ I open my mouth wide and pant
    as I long for Your commandments.
¹³² Turn to me and be merciful to me
    as is right for those who love Your name.
¹³³ Make my steps firm by Your word,
    and don't let wrong have control over me.

¹³⁴ Free me from the oppression of men,
    and I will follow the way You want me to live.
¹³⁵ Let Your face shine on Your servant,
    and teach me Your laws.
¹³⁶ Tears stream down from my eyes
    because others don't follow Your teaching.

¹³⁷ *You are righteous,* O LORD, and *right when You judge.*
¹³⁸ When You gave Your truth,
    it was fair and completely dependable.
¹³⁹ My zeal consumes me
    because my enemies forget Your word.
¹⁴⁰ Your word is very pure, and Your servant loves it.
¹⁴¹ I am unimportant and despised,
    but I don't forget how You want me to live.
¹⁴² Your righteousness is everlasting,
    and Your word is the truth.
¹⁴³ I have suffered trouble and anguish,
    but I delight in Your commandments.
¹⁴⁴ The truths You wrote are always right;
    make me understand them that I might live.

137 Rev 16:5,7; 19:2

[145] I call with all my heart — answer me, O LORD;
  I will keep Your laws.
[146] As I call You, save me;
  then I will follow the truths You wrote.
[147] I was up before dawn calling for help—
  I wait for You to keep Your promise.
[148] I'm wide awake throughout the night watches
  to study Your word.
[149] Since You love me, listen to me calling;
  according to Your justice, O LORD, give me a new life.
[150] Those who pursue vice have come near;
  they are far from Your teaching.
[151] You are near, O LORD,
  and all Your commandments are true.
[152] Long ago I learned from the truths You wrote
  that You established them forever.

[153] See what I suffer, and rescue me
  for I never forget Your teaching.
[154] Take my side in this conflict and free me;
  give me a new life as You promised.
[155] The wicked are far from being saved
  because they don't study Your laws.

[156] Your mercies are great, O LORD;
  according to Your justice give me a new life.
[157] Many pursue me and oppress me,
  but I don't turn away from the truths You wrote.
[158] I'm disgusted to see those who are unfaithful,
  because they haven't followed Your word.
[159] See how I love Your guiding principles.
  In Your kindness, O LORD, give me a new life.
[160] Your whole word is true,
  and all Your righteous decrees are everlasting.

[161] Princes pursue me without a reason;
  before Your word I stand in awe.
[162] I am delighted with Your word
  like one finding much spoil.
[163] I hate lying and am disgusted with it,
  but I love Your teaching.
[164] Seven times a day I praise You
  for Your righteous decrees.
[165] Those who love Your teaching are very happy,
  and nothing can make them fall.

¹⁶⁶ I wait for You to save me, O LORD,
    and I do what You order.
¹⁶⁷ I keep the truths You wrote and love them very much.
¹⁶⁸ I keep Your regulations and the truths You wrote
    because all my ways are before You.

¹⁶⁹ Let my loud cry come before You, O LORD;
    give me understanding as You promised.
¹⁷⁰ Let my plea come before You;
    rescue me as You promised.
¹⁷¹ My lips will pour out praise
    because You teach me Your laws.
¹⁷² My tongue will sing about Your word
    because all Your commandments are righteous.
¹⁷³ May Your hand be ready to help me
    because I have chosen the way You want me to live.
¹⁷⁴ I long for You to save me, O LORD,
    and delight in Your teaching.
¹⁷⁵ Give me a new life, and I'll praise You,
    and help me by Your righteous action.
¹⁷⁶ If I wander away like a lost sheep,
    search for Your servant
    because I never forget Your commandments.

Rescue Me

A song for going up to worship.

120 In my trouble I call on the LORD and He answers me.
² O LORD, save me from lips that lie
    and from tongues that deceive.
³ What will He give you, O deceiving tongue;
    what more will He do to you?
⁴ A warrior's sharpened arrows
    and glowing coals of the broom shrub.

⁵ Woe to me — I live as a stranger in Meshech
    and dwell near Kedar's tents.
⁶ I have lived too long with those who hate peace.
⁷ I talk of peace but they talk only of war.

Our Guardian Doesn't Sleep

A song for going up to worship.

121 I look up to the hills — where can I get help?
² I get help from the LORD who made heaven and earth.
³ Does He let your foot slip?

Does He Who guards you slumber?
[4]No, He Who guards Israel doesn't slumber or sleep.
[5] The LORD is your Guardian;
the LORD is your Shade at your right hand.
[6] *The sun will not strike* you *during the day*
or the moon at night.
[7] The LORD protects you against every harm;
He protects your life.
[8] The LORD protects you as you come and go, now and forever.

May It Be Well with Jerusalem

David's song for going up to worship.

122 I was glad they said to me,
"Let us go to the LORD's house."
[2] Our feet are standing inside your gates, Jerusalem.
[3] Jerusalem is a well-built city,
[4]where the tribes, the LORD's tribes, go up.
It is a law in Israel to praise the LORD's name.
[5] There stand the seats for judges to try cases,
seats for the men of David's family.

[6] Pray for the peace of Jerusalem:
"May it be well with those who love you!
[7]Peace be inside your walls
and undisturbed happiness in your palaces!"
[8] Thinking of my relatives and friends I say,
"Peace be with you!"
[9] Thinking of the house of the LORD our God,
I will look for your welfare.

I Look Up to You

A song for going up to worship.

123 I look up to You on Your throne in heaven.
[2] Yes, like servants looking to their masters' hand,
like a maid looking to her mistress' hand,
so we look to the LORD our God until He has mercy on us.
[3] Have mercy on us, O LORD, have mercy on us
because we've had more than enough contempt.
[4] We've had our fill of being mocked by those who are at ease,
our fill of being despised by the proud.

If We Didn't Have the LORD

David's song for going up to worship.

124 "If we didn't have the LORD," Israel should say,
2 "If we didn't have the LORD
when men attacked us,
3 then they would have swallowed us alive
when their anger blazed against us;
4 then the water would have swept us away,
a torrent going over us;
5 then the proudly raging waters would have gone over us."
6 Praise the LORD who didn't give us up
as a prey to their teeth.
7 We escaped like a bird from the hunters' trap —
the trap is broken and we got away.
8 Our help is in the name of the LORD
Who made heaven and earth.

The Mountains Around Us

A song for going up to worship.

125 Those who trust the LORD are like Mount Zion,
never shaken but standing forever.
2 Like the mountains around Jerusalem
the LORD is around His people now and forever.
3 The scepter of the wicked will not rest
on the land allotted to the righteous,
and the righteous will not need to stretch out their hands
to do wrong.
4 Do good, O LORD, to those who are good,
whose hearts are right.
5 But when people turn to crooked ways,
the LORD will take them away with the criminals.
Peace be on Israel!

Glad to Be Home

A song for going up to worship.

126 When the LORD restored the captives of Zion,

we were like those who dream.
2 Then our mouths were filled with laughter,
and our tongues were shouting happily.

5 Gal 6:16

Then it was said among the nations,
    "The LORD did great things for them."
³ The LORD has done great things for us — we are glad!
⁴ O LORD, make us prosperous again
    as the streams return in the South.
⁵ Though you may sow with tears,
    you will reap with shouts of joy.
⁶ Though you may go out weeping, carrying your seed bag,
    you will surely come home singing, carrying your sheaves.

If the Lord Is with Us

Solomon's song for going up to worship.

127 If the LORD doesn't build a house,
    it's no use working so hard building it.
If the LORD doesn't protect a city,
    it's no use to guard and protect it.
² It's no use for you to get up early and go to bed late,
    O you who eat the bread of strenuous labor,
    for surely He gives to those He loves while they sleep.

³ Behold, children are an inheritance from the LORD;
    His reward is a fruitful womb.
⁴ Like arrows in a warrior's hand
    are a man's children who are born when he's young.
⁵ Happy is the man who has filled his quiver with them:
    He will not come to shame
    when he speaks with his enemies at the city gate.

A Happy Family

A song for going up to worship.

128 Blessed is everyone who fears the LORD
    and lives in His ways.
² You will eat what your hands have worked for.
    Blessings to you!
May all go well with you!
³ Your wife will be like a fruitful vine inside your home;
    your children will be like olive plants around your table.
⁴ So you can see how a man is blessed if he fears the LORD.
⁵ May the LORD bless you from Zion —
    may you see prosperity in Jerusalem as long as you live!
⁶ May you see your children's children!
Peace be on Israel!

6 Gal 6:16

The Lord Defeats Our Enemies

A song for going up to worship.

129 Let Israel say, "Men have often attacked me
from the time I was young.
² They have often attacked me from the time I was young
but have never overpowered me.
³ They have plowed my back and made their furrows long.
⁴ But the LORD, Who is righteous,
has cut me loose from the ropes of the wicked."
⁵ May all who hate Zion be turned back in disgrace.
⁶ May they be like herbs growing on the housetops
that wither before being plucked,
⁷so no reaper can take a handful of it,
no gatherer can take it to his bosom,
⁸and no one who passes by can say,
"The LORD bless you!
We bless you in the LORD's name!"

You Forgive

A song for going up to worship.

130 Out of the depths I call to You, O LORD.
² O LORD, listen to me calling;
let Your ears be alert to hear my plea.
³ If You remembered sins, O LORD,
who could survive?
⁴But You forgive us to have us fear You.
⁵ I wait for the LORD;
I wait and look for Him to do what He said.
⁶ I turn to the LORD more than those who watch for the morning,
yes, more than those who watch for the morning.
⁷ Israel, put your hope in the LORD;
the LORD is gracious
and there is unlimited forgiveness with Him.
⁸*He will rescue* Israel *from all* their *sins.*

A Quiet Trust

David's song for going up to worship.

131 O LORD, I don't feel proud or look haughty
or meddle in things too great and wonderful for me.
² No, I've calmed down and silenced my ambitions

---

8 Titus 2:14; Rev 1:5

like a weaned child rests in its mother's arms;
my spirit in me rests like a weaned child.
³ Israel, put your hope in the LORD, now and forever!

Zion, the Lord's Home

A song for going up to worship.

132 O Lord, remember for good all of David's troubles,
²how he swore to the LORD,
and vowed to the Mighty One of Jacob:
³ "I will certainly not go home,
or go to lie on the bed made for me,
⁴or let my eyes sleep or slumber,
⁵ until I *find* a place for the LORD,
a home for the Mighty *One of Jacob.*"

⁶ We heard about the sacred ark in Ephrathah;
we found it in the woods.
⁷ Let us go to His dwelling and worship at His footstool.
⁸ Come, O LORD, to Your resting place,
You and Your mighty ark.
⁹ Your priests dress in righteousness, and Your devoted ones
shout happily.
¹⁰ For Your servant David's sake
don't turn away from Your anointed.
¹¹ *With an oath the LORD promised David —*
He certainly will not fail to keep it:
"*I will put your own offspring on your throne.*
¹² If your sons keep My covenant
and My written truths that I teach them,
their descendants also will sit on your throne forever."

¹³ The LORD chose Zion, wanting it for His home:
¹⁴ "Here is where I will stay forever.
Here I will be on My throne because that is what I want.
¹⁵ I will certainly bless her food
and satisfy her poor with bread.
¹⁶ I will dress her priests in salvation,
and her people, whom I love, will shout happily.

¹⁷ Then I will *make a Horn sprout up for David*
and will prepare a Lamp for My anointed.
¹⁸ I will cover His enemies with shame as with a garment,
but on Him His crown will sparkle."

5 Acts 7:46   *11 Acts 2:30*   *17 Lk 1:69*

Living in Harmony

David's song for going up to worship.

133 See how good and pleasant it is for brothers to live in unity!
² It is like the fine oil on the head,
   flowing down on the beard, Aaron's beard, flowing down
   over the collar of his garment,
      ³like the dew of Hermon coming down on Zion's mountains.
There, the LORD promised His blessing of life forever.

The Lord's Servants

A song for going up to worship.

134 Now bless the *LORD, all you servants of the LORD,*
   who stand in the LORD's temple through the night;
² raise your hands toward the holy place and bless the LORD.
³ The LORD Who made heaven and earth bless you from Zion!

Israel's God

135 *Praise the LORD! Praise* the LORD's name!
   Praise Him, *you servants of the LORD,*
      ²who stand in the LORD's temple,
   in the courts of the temple of our God!
³ *Praise the LORD* — the LORD is good.
   Sing to His name—it is delightful.
⁴ The LORD chose Jacob to be His own
   and Israel to be His treasure.

⁵ I know the LORD is great
   and our Lord is above all gods.
⁶ The LORD does anything He wants to do
   in heaven, on earth, in the seas
   and all the depths of the ocean.
⁷ He has fog come up from the distant parts of the earth;
   He makes lightning flashes for the rain
   and brings wind out of His storerooms.
⁸ He struck down the firstborn of men and animals in Egypt.
⁹ He sent signs and wonders into the middle of Egypt
   against Pharaoh and all his men.
¹⁰ He struck down many nations and killed mighty kings:
      ¹¹Sihon king of the Amorites, Og, king of Bashan,
   and all the kingdoms of Canaan.

134:1 Rev 19:5   135:1 Rev 19:1,3,4,5,6   3 Rev 19:1,3,4,6

¹² He gave their land as a possession
    to His people Israel.
¹³ O LORD, Your name is forever.
  O LORD, You will be remembered through all the ages.
¹⁴ *The Lord provides justice for His people,*
    and has compassion on His servants.

¹⁵ *The idols* of the nations *are silver and gold made by human hands.*
¹⁶ They have a mouth but can't talk,
    eyes but *can't see,*
      ¹⁷ears but *can't hear,*
    and there is no breath in their mouths.
¹⁸ Those who make them are like them,
    and so are all who trust them.

¹⁹ O Israel's family, bless the LORD!
  O Aaron's family, bless the LORD!
²⁰ O Levi's family, bless the LORD!
  You who fear the LORD, bless the LORD!
²¹ Blessed be the Lord in Zion!
  Blessed be He Who lives in Jerusalem!
  Praise the LORD!

136 Thank the LORD for He is good —
    His mercy endures forever!
² Thank the God of gods —
    His mercy endures forever!
³ Thank the Lord of lords —
    His mercy endures forever!

⁴ He alone does great wonders —
    His mercy endures forever!
⁵ He made the heavens with understanding —
    His mercy endures forever!
⁶ He made the earth stand above the waters —
    His mercy endures forever!
⁷ He made great lights —
    His mercy endures forever!
    ⁸the sun to rule the day —
    His mercy endures forever!
    ⁹the moon and the stars to rule the night —
    His mercy endures forever!

¹⁰ He struck down the firstborn of the Egyptians —

---

14 Heb 10:30   *15-17 Rev 9:20*   *21 Rev 19:1,3,4,6*

His mercy endures forever!
¹¹and took Israel out from among them —
His mercy endures forever!
¹²with a strong hand and an outstretched arm —
His mercy endures forever!
¹³ He divided the Red Sea — His mercy endures forever!
¹⁴and had Israel go through the middle of it —
His mercy endures forever!
and shook Pharaoh and his army
¹⁵into the Red Sea —
His mercy endures forever!

¹⁶ He led His people through the wilderness —
His mercy endures forever!
¹⁷ He struck down great kings —
His mercy endures forever!
¹⁸and killed mighty kings —
His mercy endures forever!
¹⁹Sihon, king of the Amorites —
His mercy endures forever!
²⁰Og, king of Bashan —
His mercy endures forever!
²¹and gave their land as a possession —
His mercy endures forever!
²²as a possession of His servant Israel —
His mercy endures forever!
²³ When we were humbled, He thought of us —
His mercy endures forever!
²⁴ and snatched us from our enemies —
His mercy endures forever!

²⁵ He gives food to all living beings —
His mercy endures forever!
²⁶ Thank the God of heaven —
His mercy endures forever!

In Exile

137 By the rivers of Babylon,
there we sat down and wept as we thought of Zion.
² There we hung our lyres on the poplars.
³ Those who hold us captive there asked us for a song,
and those who mocked us wanted us to be cheerful —
"Sing us a song of Zion!"
⁴ How could we sing the LORD's song in a foreign land?

⁵ If I forget you, Jerusalem,
　　may my right hand wither
⁶and my tongue stick to the roof of my mouth,
　　if I don't remember you,
　　if I don't put Jerusalem above my highest joy!

⁷ LORD, keep in mind what the people of Edom did
　　on the day Jerusalem fell.
　They said, "Down with it, down with it,
　　to its very foundation!"
⁸ O people of Babylon who destroy,
　　happy is he who *pays you back*
　　with the same treatment you gave us!
⁹ Happy is he who grabs *your* little *children*
　　and *dashes them* against a rock!

Your Great Promise

By David.

138 I thank You with all my heart.
　　Before the false gods I sing to praise You
²and bow toward Your holy temple.
　　I thank Your name because You are kind and faithful,
　　and have made Your name
　　and Your promise greater than everything.
³ When I called, You answered me
　　and made me bold and strong.
⁴ *All the kings on earth* will thank You, O LORD,
　　when they hear the words of Your mouth.
⁵ They will sing of the LORD's ways,
　　that the LORD's glory is great.
⁶ The LORD is high above but He regards the lowly
　　and knows a proud man from a distance.
⁷ Even though I live in the middle of trouble,
　　You keep me alive.
　You stretch out Your hand against my angry enemies,
　　and Your right hand saves me.
⁸ The LORD accomplishes His purpose for me.
　O LORD, You are merciful forever —
　　don't drop the work You started.

You Know Me

For the choir leader; a psalm by David.

---

8 Rev 18:6　　　*9 Lk 19:44*　　　*4 Rev 21:24*

139 O LORD, You have searched me and You know me:
>   [2]You know when I sit down and when I get up;
>   You understand from far away what I think.
[3] You watch me when I travel and when I lie down
>   and know intimately all my ways.
[4] Before there's a word on my tongue,
>   O LORD, You know all about it.
[5] You besiege me from behind
>   and in front and lay Your hand on me.
[6] Your knowledge is too wonderful for me,
>   too high for me to reach.

[7] Where can I go from Your Spirit?
>   Where can I flee from Your face?
[8] If I go up to heaven, You are there,
>   or make the grave my bed,
>   You are there.
[9] If I take the wings of the dawn
>   and stay at the most distant part of the sea,
>   [10]even there Your hand would lead me,
>   and Your right hand would hold on to me.
[11] If I say, "Surely, darkness overwhelms me
>   and the light that was around me is now night,"
[12] even the dark isn't too dark for You,
>   but the night shines like the day,
>   and darkness is like light.

[13] You created my inner being
>   and wove me together in my mother's womb.
[14] I thank You for how marvelously and wonderfully I am made.
>   *What You do is wonderful,* and I am fully aware of it.
[15] My limbs weren't hidden from You when I was made in secret
>   and skillfully woven as in an underground workshop.
[16] Your eyes saw me before I was formed;
>   before a single one of my days took shape,
>   they were all prepared and *written in Your scroll.*
[17] How precious to me are Your thoughts, O God!
>   How very many they are!
[18] If I count them—they are more than the sand.
>   When I wake up, I am still with You.
[19] O God, if You would only kill the wicked —
>   you murderous men, get away from me.
[20] They speak blasphemy against You,
>   and, as Your enemies, insult You.

---

14 Rev 15:3   *16 Rev 13:8; 17:8; 20:12,15; 21:27*

²¹ O LORD, shouldn't I hate those who hate You
    and be disgusted with those who attack You?
²² I hate them with a perfect hatred;
    they have become my enemies.
²³ Search me, O God, and know my mind.
    Test me, and know my thoughts,
        ²⁴and see if there's anything in me that leads to pain,
    and lead me on the everlasting way.

Rescue Me from My Enemies

For the choir leader; a psalm by David.

140 Rescue me, O LORD, from wicked men;
    protect me from criminals,
        ²who in their hearts plan evil and always stir up fighting.
³ They make their tongues sharp like a snake's,
    their lips hide a viper's poison. (Music)ᵇ
⁴ Keep me, O LORD, from the hands of the wicked;
    protect me from criminals who plan to trip me.
⁵ Arrogant men have hidden a snare for me,
    and spread a net with ropes,
    and set traps for me along the path. (Music)ᵇ
⁶ I say to the LORD, "You are my God;
    O LORD, hear me pleading for mercy."
⁷ O Lord GOD, the mighty One Who saves me,
    cover my head in battle.
⁸ O LORD, don't let the wicked have what they want
    or succeed with their plans. (Music)ᵇ

⁹ Those who surround me raise their heads —
    may the mischief they talk about overwhelm them.
¹⁰ May burning coals be thrown on them;
     may they be thrown into watery pits, never to rise again.
¹¹ May the slanderer not stand in the land,
     and disaster pursue the criminal, blow after blow.

¹² I know the LORD will uphold the case of the poor
     and the rights of those who suffer.
¹³ Yes, the righteous will praise Your name,
     and those who are honest will live before You.

Keep Me from Sinning with Others

A psalm by David.

3 Rom 3:13

141 I call You, O LORD; hurry to help me.
    Listen to me when I call You.
2 May my *prayer* be set *as incense* before You,
    and the raising of my hands as an evening sacrifice.
3 O LORD, set a guard on my mouth,
    guard the door of my lips.
4 Don't let my mind be inclined to talk of evil
    or to become involved with wickedness
    with people who are evildoers;
    don't let me eat their delicacies.
5 When a righteous person strikes me —
    it's a kindness; when he corrects me —
    it is oil for the head.
    Let not my head refuse it.
    But I will keep on praying against their evil deeds.
6 When their judges are thrown down from the sides of a cliff,
    then they will listen to what I say —
    it will sound pleasant.
7 Their bones will lie scattered at the opening of the grave,
    like something broken and shattered on the ground.

8 But I look to You, Lord GOD;
    I go to You for shelter, O God; protect my life.
9 Keep me from the trap they set for me
    and the snares of those who do wrong.
10 May the wicked fall into their own nets while I escape.

Rescue Me

    David's prayer when he was in the cave;
    to be played skillfully.

142 I call out to the LORD and plead with the LORD for mercy;
2 I pour out my complaint before Him
    and tell Him my trouble.
3 When I am weak enough to give up,
    You know my way.
    On the path where I have to go
    they have hidden a snare for me.
4 Look to the right and see — no one's concerned about me.
    My escape is cut off — no one cares about me.
5 I call You, O LORD, and say, "You are my Refuge,
    my own Portion in the land of the living!"
6 Listen to me calling loud — I am very low.

2 Rev 5:8; 8:3-4

Rescue me from those who pursue me —
    they are too strong for me.
⁷ Get me out of prison so that I can praise Your name.
    The righteous will crowd around me
    when You do good to me.

Like a Thirsty Ground

A psalm by David.

143 O LORD, listen to my prayer, hear my plea;
    You are faithful and righteous — answer me!
² Don't bring Your servant into court
    because *no one living is righteous before You.*

³ The enemy has pursued me, stamped my life to the ground,
    and made me live in dark places like those long dead.
⁴ I am weak enough to give up and am numb inside.
⁵ I remember the days of long ago, think of all You have done,
    and meditate on what Your hands have made.
⁶ I spread out my hands to You,
    longing for You like thirsty ground. (Music)ᵇ
⁷ Answer me quickly, O LORD —
    my spirit wears out with longing.
Don't hide Your face from me,
    or I'll be like those who went down to the grave.

⁸ In the morning let me hear about Your kindness,
    because I trust You.
Teach me the way I should go,
    because I long for You.
⁹ Rescue me from my enemies, O LORD —
    I hide in You.
¹⁰ Teach me to do what You want —
    You are my God.

May Your good Spirit lead me on even ground.
¹¹ For Your name's sake, O LORD, give me a new life.
    You are righteous — get me out of trouble.

¹² You are kind — silence my enemies,
    and destroy all who trouble me,
    because I am Your servant.

---

2 Rom 3:20; Gal 2:16

For Victory and Every Blessing

By David.

144 Blessed be the LORD, my Rock,
Who trained my hands to fight and my fingers to do battle.
² He is my merciful One, my Fortress, my Refuge
and my Rescuer, my Shield in Whom I trust.
He makes my people obey me.
³ O LORD, what is man that You should care about him,
the son of man that You should think about him?
⁴ Man is like a vapor, his life like a shadow passing away.

⁵ O LORD, bend Your heaven low, and come down;
touch the mountains so they'll smoke,
⁶ hurl lightning and scatter them,
shoot Your arrows and confuse them,
⁷ stretch out Your hands from above,
snatch me and rescue me from a great flood,
from a foreign people.
⁸ They tell lies and with their right hands they pledge to lies.

⁹ O God, I will *sing* You *a new song*
and play music to You on a lute with ten strings.
¹⁰ You give victory to kings
and rescue Your servant David from a murderous sword.
¹¹ You snatch me and rescue me from a foreign people.
They tell lies and with their right hands they pledge to lies.

¹² May our sons be like plants nurtured from their youth.
May our daughters be like corner pillars,
carved in a shape to fit a palace.
¹³ Our full granaries provide us
with one good thing after another.
Our sheep are producing thousands
and tens of thousands in our fields.
¹⁴ Our oxen are loaded down.
No one is breaking into our cities
or going out to war or crying loud in our streets.
¹⁵ Blessed are the people with whom this is so;
happy are the people whose God is the LORD!

---

9 Rev 5:9; 14:3

Great in Power and Love

A song of praise by David.

145 I will praise You highly, my God and King,
and bless Your name forever.
² I will bless You every day and praise Your name forever.
³ The Lord is great; He deserves high praise.
His greatness is unsearchable.
⁴ Those of one generation will praise to the next what You have done
and tell about Your mighty acts.
⁵ I will think of the splendid glory of Your majesty
and the wonderful things You have done.
⁶ People will speak about the power of Your awesome deeds,
and I will tell about Your greatness.
⁷ They will tell what they remember of Your great goodness
and shout out loud about Your righteousness.
⁸ *The LORD is gracious and merciful,*
slow to get angry and great in kindness.
⁹ The LORD is good to everyone
and shows compassion on everything He made.
¹⁰ Everything You made praises You, O LORD,
and Your devoted ones bless You.
¹¹ They talk of the glory of Your kingdom
and tell of Your power.
¹² They teach the world His mighty acts
and the wonderful glory of His kingdom.
¹³ Your kingdom is an everlasting kingdom;
You rule through all the generations.ʰ
¹⁴ The LORD holds up all who are falling
and raises all who are bowed down.

¹⁵ The eyes of all look to You,
and You give them their food at the right time;
¹⁶ You open Your hand to satisfy every living thing with what it wants.
¹⁷ The LORD *is just in* all *His ways*
and kind in everything He does.
¹⁸ The LORD is near all who call Him,
all who call Him sincerely.

¹⁹ He does what those who fear Him want;
He hears their call for help and saves them.
²⁰ The LORD protects all who love Him

---

8 James 5:11   17 Rev 15:3; 16:5

h - 13   One Hebrew manusript and the Greek, Latin, and Syriac add "The LORD is faithful in everything He says and kind in everything He does."

but destroys all the wicked.
[21] My mouth will praise the LORD,
    and all people will praise His holy name
    forever and ever.

Trust the Lord!

146 *Praise the LORD!*
    O my soul, *praise the LORD!*
[2] I will praise the LORD as long as I live
    and sing to my God as long as I exist.

[3] Don't put your trust in the best of men,
    or in human beings who can't save.
[4] When a man stops breathing, he goes back to the ground,
    and that day his plans perish.

[5] Blessed are you if your help is Jacob's God,
    and your hope is the LORD your God,
    [6]Who made heaven and earth,
    the sea and everything in them.
    He will always be faithful,
    [7]provide justice for the oppressed,
    and give the hungry food.
    The LORD sets prisoners free;
[8] the LORD gives sight to the blind;
    the LORD raises those who are bowed down;
    the LORD loves the righteous;
[9] the LORD protects strangers;
    He makes orphans and widows happy again,
    but ruins the way of the wicked.
[10]The LORD will rule forever;
    your God, O Zion, will rule through all the ages.
    Praise the LORD!

Praise Our God!

147 *Praise the LORD!*
    It is good to sing hymns to our God
    because He is delightful, and praise is beautiful.
[2] The LORD is rebuilding Jerusalem
    and gathering those of Israel who were driven away.
[3] He heals the brokenhearted and bandages their wounds.

---

1 Rev 19:1,3,4,6   *6 Acts 4:24; 14:15; Rev 10:6; 14:7*   *10 Rev 19:1,3,4,6*
          1 Rev 19:1,3,4,6

⁴ He decides how many stars there should be
  and gives all of them names.
⁵ Our Lord is great and very strong,
  and there's no limit to what He knows.
⁶ The LORD makes those who suffer happy again
  but throws the wicked down on the ground.
⁷ Sing a hymn of thanks to the LORD;
  play on the lyre to our God.
⁸ He covers the sky with clouds, prepares rain for the ground,
  and makes grass grow on the hills.
⁹ He gives food to the animals
  and to the young crows that call.
¹⁰ He doesn't delight in a horse's strength
  or take pleasure in a man's legs.
¹¹ The LORD takes pleasure in those who fear Him,
  who look for His mercy.
¹² Jerusalem, praise the LORD! Praise your God, Zion!
¹³ He made the bars of your gates strong
  and blessed your children within you.
¹⁴ He brings peace to your border
  and gives you plenty of the finest wheat.

¹⁵ *He sends His order* throughout the earth;
  His word runs very fast.
¹⁶ He gives snow like wool
  and scatters hoarfrost like ashes.
¹⁷ He throws down His hailstones like bread crumbs —
  who can stand before His icy blast?
¹⁸ *He sends His word* and melts the ice,
  makes the wind blow and the waters flow.
¹⁹ He speaks His word to Jacob, His laws and decrees to Israel.
²⁰ He hasn't done this for any other nation;
  they do not know His decrees.
  Praise the LORD!

All Should Praise Him

148 *Praise the LORD!*
  Praise the LORD from the heavens;
  praise Him from the heights!
² Praise Him, all you His angels;
  praise Him all His heavenly army!

---

15 *Acts 10:36; 13:26*   18 *Acts 10:36; 13:26*
20 *Rev 19:1,3,4,6*   1 *Rev 19:1,3,4,6*

³ Praise Him, sun and moon;
  praise Him, all you shining stars!
⁴ Praise Him, you highest heavens,
  and waters above the sky!
⁵ They should all praise the LORD's name —
  He ordered and they were created;
⁶ He put them in their places forever,
  and gave a law that none can break.

⁷ *Praise the LORD* from the earth,
  you sea monsters and all ocean depths,
  ⁸fire and hail, snow and fog,
  stormy wind doing what He tells you,
  ⁹mountains and all hills, fruit trees and all cedars,
  ¹⁰wild animals and all that are tame, crawling things
  and winged birds,
  ¹¹kings of the world and all peoples,
  officials and all judges in the world,
  ¹²young men and also girls, old men and boys.
¹³ They should all praise the LORD's name
  because it alone is exalted.
  His glory is above the earth and heaven,
  ¹⁴and He has raised a horn for His people,
  something praise-worthy for those devoted to Him,
  for the sons of Israel, the people who are close to Him.
  Praise the LORD!

Praise — and Punish

149 *Praise the LORD!*
  Sing to the LORD *a new song,*
  praising Him in the congregation of His devoted ones.
² Israel should be happy in Him Who made them,
  and the people of Zion delight in their King.
³ They should praise His name with dancing
  and play on the tambourine and lyre to Him.
⁴ The LORD delights in His people;
  He glorifies the humble with victory.
⁵ His devoted ones should rejoice in this honor
  and shout happily on their beds.
⁶ High praise to God should be in their throats—
  and two-edged swords in their hands
  ⁷to take vengeance on the nations and correct the peoples,
  ⁸to bind their kings with chains

---

7 *Rev 19:1,3,4,6*   14 *Rev 19:1,3,4,6*   1 *Rev 19:1,3,4,6; 5:9; 14:3*

and their leaders with iron fetters,
⁹to punish them as it is written.
This is an honor which belongs to all His devoted ones.
Praise the LORD!

With Musical Instruments

150 *Praise the LORD!*
Praise God in His holy place!
Praise Him for the sky spread out by His power,
² praise Him for His mighty acts,
praise Him according to His great majesty!
³ Praise Him with a blast of a ram's horn,
praise Him with lutes and lyres,
⁴ praise Him with tambourines and dancing,
praise Him with stringed instruments and flutes,
⁵ praise Him with loud cymbals,
praise Him with crashing cymbals!
⁶ Everything that breathes should *praise the LORD!*
Praise the LORD!

---

9 Rev 19:1,3,4,6   *1 Rev 19:1,3,4,6*   *6 Rev 19:1,3,4,6*

THE PROVERBS

1 The Proverbs of Solomon, David's son, king of Israel:

2   to give people wisdom and discipline
    to understand intelligent speech
3   and to learn the discipline of understanding,
    to be righteous, just and fair.
4   They should make the simple shrewd
    and give young people knowledge and skill.
5   A wise person will listen and add to his learning;
    an intelligent person will learn how to lead
6   and help others understand proverbs and puzzling statements,
    the teachings of wise men and difficult sayings.
7   Fearing the LORD is the best way to know anything,
    but fools despise wisdom and training.

8   My son, listen to your father's criticism,
    and don't neglect your mother's teaching
9   because they are a beautiful garland on your head
    and an ornament around your neck.

Don't Be Enticed

10   My son, if sinners tempt you, don't be willing to sin;
11   if they say, "Come with us, we'll set an ambush to kill;
     we'll hide to get the innocent just for fun.
12   Like the grave, we'll swallow them alive,
     like those who go down to the pit in good health.
13   We'll get all kinds of valuable possessions
     and fill our houses with robbed goods.
14   Throw in your lot with us.
     We'll all have just one purse."
15   My son, don't go with them.
     Keep your foot away from their path
16   because their *feet* are *running* to do evil,
     and they *hurry to shed blood*.
17   If the birds see it spread,
     the net is spread in vain.
18   These men set an ambush for their own bloody execution;

they go into hiding only to lose their own lives.
19 This is what happens to all who get goods by robbing;
those who have such goods lose their lives.

Wisdom Speaks

20 Wisdom shouts in the streets.
She is calling in the market places;
21 she calls at the corners of noisy streets,
and speaks at the entrances of city gates:
22 "How long, you thoughtless people,
will you love to be thoughtless,
and you mockers delight in your mocking,
and fools go on hating knowledge?
23 Turn to me as I correct you,
and I'll pour out my mind for you
and make known to you what I have to say.
24 Since I called and you refused to listen,
since *I stretched out my hands* to you
and no one paid attention,
25 and you *ignored all my advice*
and didn't want me to correct you,
26 I, too, will laugh at your calamity;
I'll mock when you're struck with panic,
27 when panic comes on you like a thunderstorm
and disaster like a whirlwind,
when trouble and anguish come on you.
28 Then they will call me, but I won't answer.
They'll look for me but not find me
29 because they hate knowledge
and would rather not fear the LORD.
30 They don't want my advice and despise all my correction.
31 They must eat the fruit of their ways
and be fed with their own schemes.
32 By turning away, thoughtless men kill themselves,
and by overconfidence, fools destroy themselves.
33 But listen to me and you'll live securely;
you'll have peace of mind and not fear disaster."

Listen to Wisdom

2 My son, if you accept what I say
and keep my instructions close to you
2 and listen to wisdom
and in your mind reach for understanding;

---

24 Rom 10:21   25 Lk 7:30   28 Jn 7:34

3   yes, if you will ask for insight and call for *understanding*,

4   if you will look for it as if it were money
      and dig for it like *hidden treasure*,

5   then you will know how to fear the LORD
      and will get to know God,

6   because *the LORD gives wisdom*
      and from His mouth comes knowledge and understanding.

7   He has reserved sound wisdom for honest people
      and protection for those who live innocently,

8   to guard those on the right paths
      and watch over the ways of His saints.

9   Then you will understand what is right and just,
      what is fair and leads to a prosperous life.

10   Wisdom will come into your heart,
      and it will be your pleasure to know things.

11   Intelligence will watch over you,
      and insight will guard you,

12   in order to save you from any evil way,
      from anyone saying deceitful things.

13   Such people leave the right paths
      and walk along dark roads.

14   They are glad to do wrong
      and delight in being evil and perverse.

15   Their paths are crooked,
      and their ways are twisted.

16   Wisdom will also save you from the immoral woman,
      from the loose woman with her smooth talk,

17   who leaves the man she married when she was young
      and forgets the covenant with her God.

18   Her house sinks down to death,
      and her ways lead you to the shades of death.

19   None who have sexual intercourse with her come back
      or ever reach the paths of life.

20   I want you to walk on the way of good men
      and keep on the paths of righteous men,

21   because *the righteous will live in the land*
      and the innocent will stay there.

22   But the wicked will be killed off in the land,
      and those who are disloyal will be driven out of it.

The Way to Wisdom

3 My son, don't forget what I teach you,
      and keep my instructions in mind,

2   because they will give you a long,

---

good life and you will be happy.

3   May kindness and truth never leave you.
     Fasten them around your neck.
     Write them on the tablet of your heart.
4   Then you will see how *kind* and sympathetic
     God and people will be to you.
5   Trust the LORD with all your heart,
     and don't depend on your own understanding.
6   Acknowledge Him in everything you do,
     and He will make your paths smooth.
7   *Don't think you are wise.*
     Fear the LORD and turn away from evil.
8   Then your body will be healthy,
     and your bones will be refreshed.

9   Honor the LORD with your wealth
     and with the best of all your produce.
10   Then your barns will be filled with plenty,
     and your vats will overflow with the juice of grapes.

11   *My son, don't reject the LORD's training*
     or get disgusted with His correction,
12   *because the LORD corrects the one He loves,*
     like a father corrects *a son he delights in.*

Wisdom Is the Best

13   Happy is a man who finds wisdom,
     a man who gets understanding;
14   you get a higher gain with wisdom than with money;
     it's more profitable than fine gold.
15   It is more precious than jewels,
     and nothing you desire can equal it.
16   In her right hand she offers a long life
     and in her left riches and honor.
17   Her ways are pleasant,
     and all her paths lead to happiness.
18   She is *a tree of life* for those who hold her,
     and she *makes happy those who cling* to her.

19   By wisdom the LORD laid the foundation of the earth,
     and by understanding He set up the sky.
20   By His knowledge the deep waters broke out

---

3 *II Cor 3:3*   4 *Lk 2:52; Rom 12:17; II Cor 8:21*
7 *Rom 12:16; Mt 10:28; Lk 12:5; Acts 10:2,22,35; 13:16,26; I Pet 2:17; Rev 14:7*
11-12 *Eph 6:4; Heb 12:5-8; Rev 3:19*   18 *Rev 1:3; 2:7; 22:2,14,19*

and the clouds dropped dew.

21 My son, don't lose sight of these things;
   use common sense, and plan carefully.
22 They will mean life for you
   and be an ornament on your neck.
23 Then you will go safely on your way, and you won't stub your foot.
24 When you lie down, you won't be afraid,
   and lying there, your sleep will be sweet.
25 Don't be afraid *of anything that could* suddenly *terrify you*
   or of the destruction of the wicked when it comes,
26 because you trust the LORD
   and He will keep your foot from getting caught.

Be Fair

27 Don't keep back anything good from those who have a right to it
   when you're able to do it.
28 When you have it with you, don't tell your neighbor,
   "Go, and come back; tomorrow I'll give it to you."
29 Don't plan to do wrong to your neighbor
   while he's sitting there with you, suspecting nothing.
30 Don't quarrel with a man without a reason,
   when he's done you no harm.
31 Don't envy a criminal
   or wish you had any of his ways,
32 because the LORD is disgusted with anyone doing wrong
   but is close to those who are righteous.
33 The LORD's curse is on a wicked person's house,
   but He blesses the home of the righteous.
34 *He mocks those who mock but is gracious to the humble.*
35 Wise people will be honored, but fools will bear disgrace.

Get Wisdom

4 Listen, my sons, to a father's instruction;
   pay attention to get understanding.
2 The learning I give you is good,
   so don't give up anything I teach you.
3 Once I was a boy with my father,
   a tender and only child around my mother.
4 He used to teach me by telling me:
   "With your heart cling to what I say.
   Keep my instructions and you will live.
5 Get wisdom, get understanding.
   Don't forget what I tell you or turn away from it.
6 Don't leave wisdom, and she'll watch over you.

---

25 *I Pet 3:6*   **34** *James 4:6; I Pet 5:5*

Love her, and she'll protect you.

7 The most important thing to get is wisdom.
Purchase understanding with all you have.

8 Cherish her and she'll raise you up.
Hug her and she'll honor you,

9 give you a lovely wreath for your head,
and hand you a beautiful crown."

10 Listen, my son, accept what I say,
and you'll live many years.

11 I have taught you wisdom's way
and led you in the right paths.

12 When you walk, your steps will not be hindered;
even if you run, you won't fall.

13 Cling to discipline and don't let it go;
keep it because it means your life.

14 Don't go in the way of the wicked
or walk in the path of evil people.

15 Keep away from it, don't walk on it,
turn away from it, and pass on.

16 For they can't sleep unless they do wrong;
they're robbed of their sleep unless they bring people down.

17 They eat food gotten by doing wrong
and drink wine taken by violence.

18 But the path of the righteous is like the morning light
that gets brighter until it has reached the brightest of the day.

19 *The way of the wicked is completely dark,*
so they don't know what they stumble over.

20 My son, pay attention to what I tell you,
and listen to what I say.

21 Don't let these things get out of your sight,
but keep them in the center of your heart,

22 because they are life to those who find them a
nd health to their whole bodies.

23 More than anything else watch your heart,
because from it flows your life.

24 Put away from you a mouth that says crooked things;
put far away from you lips that deceive.

25 Let your eyes look forward,
your gaze be straight ahead.

26 Walk a *straight path,*
and all your ways will be sure.

27 Don't turn to the right or to the left,
and walk away from evil.

---

19 John 12:35   *26* Heb 12:13

Love, Impure and Pure

5 My son, pay attention to my wisdom;
    listen to the understanding I give you,

2   that you may conduct yourself wisely and talk intelligently.

3   The lips of an adulteress woman drip with honey
    and her mouth is smoother than oil,

4   but in the end she's bitter as a poisonous plant
    and sharp as a double-edged sword.

5   Her feet go down to death;
    her steps go straight to hell.

6   She doesn't take into account the path of life;
    she doesn't know where her paths wander.

7   Now, my sons, listen to me;
    don't turn away from what I tell you.

8   Keep far away from her,
    and don't go near the door of her house,

9   or you will give your honor to others
    and your years to some cruel person.

10 Strangers will benefit from your strength,
    and your labors will enrich a stranger's home.

11 Then you will moan when your end comes,
    when your body and flesh are consumed,

12 and you say, "How I hated discipline
    and in my heart scorned correction.

13 I didn't listen to what my teachers taught me
    or hear what my instructors said.

14 I had almost reached total ruin
    in the assembly and the congregation."

15 Drink water from your own cistern,
    water flowing from your own well.

16 Why should the water from your spring flow outside,
    like streams of water out on the streets?

17 Keep them for yourself alone,
    and don't share them with strangers.

18 Let your own fountain be blessed;
    have pleasure with the wife you married when you were young —

19 a deer to be loved and a graceful wild goat.
    Always let her breasts satisfy you;
    always be intoxicated with her love.

20 Why should you, my son, fall for an adulterous woman
    and hug a stranger's bosom?

21 *The LORD's eyes see the road every person takes;*
    He observes all his paths.

---

21 Heb 4:13

22 A wicked person is trapped by his wrongs
and caught in the ropes of his sin.
23 He dies because he had no discipline
and by all his foolish lust he's lost.

The Rash Pledge

6 My son, if you guarantee a loan for a neighbor
or pledge yourself by a handshake with a stranger,
2   you are trapped by what you say,
caught by your promise.
3   Now do this, my son, and free yourself
because you have put yourself into your neighbor's hands.
Go, humble yourself; pester your neighbor.
4   Don't give your eyes any sleep or your eyelids any slumber.
5   Free yourself like a gazelle from what holds you
and like a bird from the bird-catcher.

Sloth

6   Go to the ant, you lazy one!
Watch her ways and get wise.
7   She had no judge, overseer, or governor.
8   In summer she prepares her nourishment;
in the harvest she gathers her food.
9   How long are you going to lie there, you lazy one?
When are you going to get up from your sleep?
10   "Just a little sleep, a little more slumber,
a little more folding the hands to rest" —
11   So your poverty will come like a drifter
and your need like a bandit.

The Villain

12   A worthless person and a villain is a man who is dishonest in speech.
13   He winks his eyes, shuffles his feet, points his fingers.
14   With a devious mind he is always scheming and spreading discord.
15   That is why disaster will come on him suddenly;
in a moment he will be crushed beyond recovery.

Seven Vices

16   Six things the LORD hates, even seven He detests:
17   Proud-looking eyes, a lying tongue,
hands that kill innocent people,
18   a mind making wicked plans, feet that are quick to do wrong,

17 Mt 23:35; James 5:6

19   a dishonest witness telling lies,
and the man who stirs up quarrels between brothers.

Adultery Leads to Trouble

20   My son, do what your father orders,
and don't reject your mother's teaching.
21   Fasten them forever on your heart;
tie them around your neck.
22   When you walk around, they'll lead you;
when you lie down, they'll watch over you,
and when you wake up, they'll talk to you
23   because a commandment is a lamp and a teaching is a light,
and the rules of discipline are the path of life,
24   keeping you from a bad woman
and from the smooth tongue of a loose woman.
25   *Don't use your mind to lust for her beauty,*
and don't let her catch you with her eyes.
26   A prostitute's price is a loaf of bread,
but a married woman hunts a man's very life.[a]
27   Can a man take fire into his lap without getting his clothes burned?
28   Or can anyone walk on red-hot coals
without getting his feet scorched?
29   So it is with the man who has sexual relations with his neighbor's wife;
anyone who touches her will not escape punishment.
30   People don't despise a thief if he steals to satisfy his appetite
when he's hungry.
31   But when he's caught, he has to pay back seven times
and give up all the goods in his house.
32   Anyone who commits adultery with a woman doesn't have any sense.
When he violates her he destroys himself.
33   He will get wounds and dishonor,
and his disgrace will not be blotted out
34   because jealousy makes a husband furious.
He will have no mercy when he takes revenge.
35   No money you pay him will move him,
and the biggest bribe will not satisfy him.

The Prostitute

7 My son, keep my word,
and treasure my instruction.
2   Do as I order you and live;
guard my teachings like the pupil of your eye.
3   Tie them on your fingers,

---

25 Mt 5:28

a - 26   A married woman committing adultery with a man brought on him the death
penalty (Lev 20:10; Deut 22:22).

write them on the tablet of your heart.

4 Tell wisdom, "You are my sister,"
and call understanding your relative —

5 so they will keep you from the adulterous woman,
from the loose female with her smooth talk.

6 At a window of my house I looked through my lattice.

7 Looking at the silly fellows,
I saw among them a lad without much sense.

8 He was walking along a street near her corner
and approaching her house.

9 In the twilight, in the evening of the day,
in the dark hours of the night —

10 a woman came to meet him, dressed as a prostitute,
with secret plans in mind,

11 lusty and rebellious — her feet won't stay home;

12 one moment she's on the street and the next she's in the square,
waiting at every corner to catch someone.

13 She grabs him and kisses him,
puts on a bold face, and tells him,

14 "I have some sacrificial meat; today I paid my vows.

15 That's why I came out to meet you,
to look for you until I found you.

16 I have spread blankets on my bed,
covers of colored yarn from Egypt.

17 I have sprinkled my bed with myrrh, aloes, and cinnamon.

18 Come, let us have our fill of love until morning;
let's enjoy making love.

19 My husband isn't home; he's gone on a trip far away.

20 He took a bag of money with him.
He won't come home until the full moon."

21 With all her seductive charms she persuades him;
with her smooth lips she misleads him.

22 Immediately he's following her —
like an ox going to be butchered,
like a ram hobbling into captivity —[b]

23 until an arrow pierces him; like a bird rushing into a snare,
he doesn't know it will cost him his life.

24 Now, my son, listen to me,
and pay attention to what I say.

25 Don't let your heart turn to her ways,
don't wander off on her paths;

26 many are those she throws down dead,
and those she has killed are numerous.

---

3 *II Cor 3:3*

b - 22   The Heb is obscure

27 Her house is the way to hell,
which goes down to the inner chambers of death.

Wisdom's Call

8 Isn't wisdom calling
and understanding raising her voice?
2 She's standing on top of the high place
at a place where paths meet.
3 Beside the gates to the city, where people enter the doors,
she's calling loud:
4 I'm calling you, O men,
and talking to you, O people.
5 You silly people, learn how to be shrewd;
you fools, become intelligent.
6 Listen because I tell you important things;
my lips say what is right.
7 My mouth expresses the truth,
and my lips detest evil.
8 Everything I say is right,
and there's nothing twisted or crooked in it.
9 All of it is correct to an intelligent person
and right for one who's getting knowledge.
10 Take my instruction, not silver,
and my knowledge rather than the best gold,
11 because wisdom is better than jewels,
and nothing else you desire can equal it.

12 I, wisdom, have lived with shrewdness
and have discovered knowledge and skill.
13 Fear the LORD and you'll hate evil. I hate conceit and pride,
wicked behavior and perverse speech.
14 I plan wisely.
I am intelligent and I have strength.
15 By me kings have dominion,
and rulers decide what is right.
16 By me princes and leaders rule —
all who govern the earth.
17 I love those who love me;
look for me eagerly and you'll find me.
18 I have riches and honor,
enduring goods with righteousness.
19 What I produce is better than gold, fine gold;
my product is better than the best silver.
20 I walk in the way of righteousness and in the paths of justice,
21 giving wealth to those who love me,
and filling their storerooms.

God's Son

22 *The LORD became My Father at the beginning of His way,*
long ago before any of His works.
23 *I was set up from everlasting,*
from the first, before the earth was.
24 Before there was any ocean, I was born,
before there were springs, or sources of water.
25 Before the mountains were settled in their places
and before the hills — I was born.
26 When He hadn't yet made the earth or its fields
or the first dust of the world,
27 when He set up the heavens, I was there.
When He marked the horizon on the surface of the ocean,
28 when He made firm the skies above,
when He made the mighty fountains of the ocean,
29 when He set limits for the sea
and wouldn't let the water flow farther than He ordered,
when He set up the foundations of the earth —
30 then *I was beside Him* as the Master Workman.
From day to day I was delighted,
always happy before Him,
31 rejoicing in His inhabited world,
and delighted with people.

32 And now, My son, listen to Me!
Blessed are those who keep My ways.
33 Listen to instruction and don't reject wisdom.
34 Happy is anyone who listens to Me,
watching daily at My gates, waiting by My doorposts.
35 The person who finds Me finds life,
and the LORD will be delighted with him.
36 But anyone who sins against Me hurts himself.
All who hate Me love death.

Wise or Foolish?

9 Wisdom has built her house.
She has carved out her seven pillars.
2 She has butchered her meat, mixed her wine,
and spread her table.
3 She has sent away her maids
and calls from the highest spots in the city:
4 "If you're untaught, turn in here."
If you don't have understanding, she tells you,

22-23 Jn 1:1-2; Col 1:15,17; Rev 3:14   30 Jn 1:1-2   32 Lk 11:28

5   "Come, eat my bread,
     and drink the wine I mix.
6   Leave ignorant people and begin to live;
     walk the road that leads to understanding."

7   *If you correct a scoffer, you get insulted.*
     If you criticize a wicked person, you get hurt.
8   Don't correct a scoffer or he will hate you;
     correct a wise person and he will love you.
9   Give advice to a wise person and he'll be wiser still.
     Teach a righteous man and he will learn more.

10   The fear of the LORD is the beginning of wisdom;
     knowledge of the Holy One is understanding.

11   By me you live longer
     and add years to your life.
12   If you're wise, your wisdom will help you.
     If you scoff, you hurt only yourself.

13   A foolish woman is loud.
     Being simple, she doesn't know anything.
14   She sits at the door of her house,
     on a seat at the high places in the city,
15   calling to those who pass by,
     who are minding their own business:
16   "If you're untaught, turn in here."
     To those who don't have understanding, she says:
17   "Stolen waters are sweet,
     and food eaten in secret is pleasant."
18   He doesn't know the dead are there,
     and that her guests are in the depths of hell.

The Proverbs of Solomon:

10 A wise son makes his father happy,
     but a foolish son makes his mother sad.
2   Treasures gotten dishonestly don't help anyone,
     but righteousness saves a person from death.
3   The LORD doesn't let a righteous person starve;
     He pushes aside the desire of the wicked.
4   If you do things carelessly, you'll be poor,
     but the hands of busy people make them rich.
5   You're a wise son if you gather in summer,
but you're a disgrace if you sleep at harvest time.

7 Mt 7:6

⁶ Blessings are on a righteous person's head,
but the mouth of the wicked hides[c] violence.
⁷ The memory of the righteous is blessed,
but the name of the wicked will rot away.

⁸ If you're wise, you take orders;
but if you talk without thinking, you fall down headlong.
⁹ Live innocently, and you'll live securely;
but if you're dishonest you'll be found out.
¹⁰ He who winks with his eyes causes heartache,
and if you talk without thinking you fall down headlong.
¹¹ The mouth of *the righteous is a fountain of life,*
but the mouth of the wicked hides violence.
¹² Hate stirs up quarrels,
but *love covers* every *wrong.*
¹³ You will find wisdom on the lips of an intelligent person,
but a rod is for the back of one who lacks understanding.
¹⁴ Wise men store up knowledge,
but a fool's mouth threatens ruin.
¹⁵ A rich man's wealth is his strong city,
but it is poverty that ruins the poor.
¹⁶ The reward of a righteous man is life;
but the harvest of a wicked man is sin.
¹⁷ If you practice discipline you're on the way to life,
and if you ignore criticism you'll go wrong.
¹⁸ Anyone who conceals hatred has lying lips,
and whoever spreads slander is a fool.
¹⁹ If you talk a lot, you're bound to make an error,
but if you hold your tongue, you're wise.
²⁰ What a righteous person says is pure silver,
but what the wicked thinks is worthless.
²¹ What a righteous person says feeds many,
but fools die for lack of sense.
²² It is the LORD's blessing that makes a man rich,
and hard work can't add anything to it.
²³ Doing something immoral is fun for a fool,
but wisdom is the intelligent person's fun.

²⁴ What a wicked person dreads happens to him,
and what righteous persons want is given to them.
²⁵ *When the storm has passed the wicked man vanishes,*
but a righteous person has an everlasting foundation.
²⁶ Like vinegar to the teeth and smoke in the eyes
is a lazy person to him who sends him.

---

11 Jn 4:14; Rev 7:17; 21:6   12 James 5:20; I Pet 4:8   25 Mt 7:25,27

c - 6   or "covers"

27 Fear the Lord and you will add to your life,
   but the years of the wicked are shortened.
28 The hope of the righteous is a happy thing,
   but the eager waiting of the wicked comes to nothing.
29 The LORD's way is a fortress for the innocent,
   but ruin to those who do wrong.
30 A righteous person will never be shaken,
   but the wicked will not continue to live in the land.
31 The mouth of a righteous one flows with wisdom,
   but the perverse tongue will be cut off.
32 The lips of the righteous pour out good will,
   but the mouth of the wicked is perverse.

11 The LORD hates dishonest scales,
   but accurate weights please Him.
2 Pride comes and then comes shame,
   but wisdom is with the humble.
3 Honest people are guided by their innocence,
   but the hypocrisy of unfaithful people leads them to ruin.
4 Riches will not help anyone on the day of God's fury,
   but righteousness will save a person from death.
5 The righteousness of the innocent makes their road smooth,
   but the wicked fall by their wickedness.
6 Righteous people are rescued by their righteousness,
   but the unfaithful are trapped by their greed.
7 When a wicked person dies his hope comes to nothing,
   and his confidence in strength comes to nothing.
8 When a righteous person is rescued from trouble,
   the wicked man succeeds him in it.
9 With his talk a godless person tries to ruin his neighbor,
   but by knowledge the righteous are rescued.
10 When the righteous prosper a city is glad;
   when wicked people perish there's happy shouting.
11 With the blessing of honest people a town prospers,
   but the talk of the wicked tears it down.
12 It is senseless to despise your neighbor,
   but it is intelligent to keep silent.
13 A person who gossips gives away secrets,
   but a trustworthy mind can keep a secret.
14 Where there's no one to lead them,
   an army will fall, but many advisers can save it.
15 A man who guarantees a stranger's loan will get into trouble,
   but if you avoid making rash bargains you're safe.
16 A gracious woman wins respect, but ruthless men grasp riches.
17 *A kind man does himself a favor,*

---

17 Mt 5:7

but a trouble maker hurts himself.

18 A wicked person earns counterfeit wages,
but if you sow righteousness your pay is genuine.

19 The one who upholds righteousness will live,
but anyone who pursues evil will die.

20 The LORD detests those who are crooked at heart,
but He is delighted with those whose ways are innocent.

21 It is certain, an evil person will not go unpunished,
but the family of the righteous will escape.

22 A beautiful woman who lacks taste
is like a golden ring in a pig's snout.

23 The desire of the righteous brings about good,
but the hope of the wicked brings about fury.

24 *One man gives freely only to get richer;*
another holds back what he should spend only to be in need.

25 Be generous to others and you'll grow prosperous;
refresh others and you'll be refreshed.

26 Hold back grain and people will curse you;
sell it and a blessing will be on your head.

27 If you're eager to do good, you'll win good will;
if you look for trouble, you'll get it.

28 If you trust your riches, you'll wither,
but the righteous will flourish like green leaves.

29 If you neglect your family, you'll inherit the wind;
being a fool you will be a slave of the wise.

30 Righteous behavior is a tree of life.
If you take others into your care, you're wise.

31 If a *righteous* person is paid back on earth,
how much more a *wicked and sinful person!*

12 If you delight in discipline, you'll love to learn;
but whoever hates correction is like a dumb animal.

2 The LORD delights in a good man
but condemns a malicious schemer.

3 A man can't stand firm on a wicked basis,
but the root of the righteous cannot be shaken.

4 A good wife is her husband's crown,
but one who brings disgrace is like rot in his bones.

5 The thoughts of the righteous are honest,
but the thoughts of the wicked are treacherous.

6 What the wicked say brings about bloodshed,
but what the honest say saves people.

7 When the wicked are overthrown and gone,
the house of the righteous will stand.

8 A man is praised according to his intelligence,

_____

24 II Cor 9:6   31 I Pet 4:18

but if his mind is twisted, he will be despised.

9   It is better to be thought unimportant and have a slave
    than to act important and have nothing to eat.

10 A righteous person is concerned about the life of his animals,
    but the compassion of the wicked is cruel.

11 If you work your ground, you'll have plenty to eat,
    but the stupid chase after fantasies.

12 A wicked person desires the plunder of evil men,
    but the root of the righteous produces for others.

13 A bad man is trapped by the wrong things he says,
    but a righteous person finds his way out of trouble.

14 A man can enjoy good things as a result of his speaking ability,
    and he will be paid according to what his hands have accomplished.

15 A fool considers his own way right,
    but a wise man listens to advice.

16 When a fool is irritated, he shows it immediately,
    but a shrewd man hides the offense.

17 A true witness speaks honestly,
    but a lying witness utters deceit.

18 A man's careless talk stabs like a sword,
    but what a wise man says heals.

19 Truthful lips endure forever,
    but a lying tongue lasts for only a moment.

20 Deceit is in the heart of those who plan evil,
    but those who plan for people's welfare are happy.

21 No harm can come to the righteous,
    but the lives of the wicked are filled with trouble.

22 The LORD detests lips that lie,
    but He is delighted with those that are honest.

23 A sensible man doesn't display what he knows,
    but the foolish mind proclaims its foolishness.

24 Diligent hands will gain control,
    but a lazy person will be doing slave work.

25 Anxiety in a person's mind will weigh him down,
    but an encouraging word makes him glad.

26 A righteous person spies out what will harm him,
    but the path of the wicked leads them astray.

27 A lazy hunter does not catch his prey,
    but a diligent man becomes wealthy.

28 On the road of righteousness there is life;
    it is the path that leads to immortality.

13   A wise son is corrected by his father,
    but a scoffer doesn't listen to criticism.

2   A man can eat well as a result of his speaking ability,
    but the appetite of the faithless feeds on violence.

3   Watch your mouth and you'll protect your life,

but talk a lot and you'll invite ruin.

4   A lazy man craves food and gets none,
     but busy people are well fed.

5   A righteous person hates lying,
     but a wicked person behaves shamefully and disgracefully.

6   Righteousness protects the innocent,
     but it is wickedness that overthrows a sinner.

7   One person pretends to be rich and has nothing;
     another pretends to be poor and is very rich.

8   A man with riches may need them to ransom his life,
     but a poor man doesn't listen to threats.

9   The light of the righteous shines brightly,
     but *the lamp of the wicked goes out.*

10   Pride produces only quarreling;
     but those who take advice are wise.

11   Get wealth by injustice and it will dwindle away,
     but gather it little by little and you'll have plenty.

12   An expectation that drags on and on makes you sick at heart,
     but a hope that comes true is *a tree of life.*

13   If you despise the Word, you'll pay the penalty for it;
     respect the commandment and you'll be rewarded.

14   The teaching of a wise person is *a fountain of life;*
     it turns away the snares of death.

15   A fine understanding brings favor,
     but the way of the treacherous is rough.

16   Any sensible man will act intelligently,
     but a fool displays his folly.

17   A bad messenger makes trouble,
     but a dependable one heals trouble.

18   To refuse correction brings poverty and shame;
     if you pay attention to criticism, you will be honored.

19   A desire realized is a pleasant experience,
     but fools hate to turn from evil.

20   Walk with wise men and you'll be wise,
     but keep company with fools and you'll suffer for it.

21   Disaster hunts down sinners,
     but the righteous are rewarded with good.

22   A good man leaves property to his grandchildren,
     but a sinner's wealth is stored away for the righteous.

23   When people are able to plow, there is much food,
     and a person is swept away where there's no justice.

24   If you fail to use your stick, you hate your son.
     But if you love him, you will diligently discipline him.

25   A righteous person eats to satisfy his appetite,
     but the belly of the wicked is never filled.

---

9 Mt 25:8   12 Rev 2:7; 22:2,14,19   14 Jn 4:14; Rev 7:17; 21:6

14 Every wise woman builds her home,
but a foolish one tears it down with her own hands.

2 The man who lives right fears the LORD,
but if you live wrong you'll despise Him.

3 Because of a fool's words, a whip is lifted against him,
but the lips of the wise men protect them.

4 Where there are no cattle, the manger is empty,
but an ox's strength produces a large crop.

5 *A witness you can trust* doesn't lie,
but *a dishonest witness* breathes lies.

6 A scoffer searches for wisdom without finding it,
but for an intelligent person knowledge comes easily.

7 Stay away from a fool;
you won't learn anything from his lips.

8 The wisdom of a shrewd person causes him to behave intelligently,
but the stupidity of fools misleads them.

9 Fools make fun of guilt, but the house of [d] the honest is blessed.

10 The heart knows its own bitterness,
and no one else can share its joy.

11 The house of the wicked will be destroyed,
but the tent of the honest people will prosper.

12 There is a way a man thinks is right,
but it finally becomes the way of death.

13 Even while laughing a heart may be aching,
and joy can end in grief.

14 A heart that has left the LORD may be satisfied without His ways,
but only with Him does anyone find what is good.

15 A simpleton believes everything,
but a shrewd person watches where he's going.

16 A wise person is cautious and turns away from evil,
but a fool is careless and overconfident.

17 Lose your temper and you act foolishly,
and a man plotting evil is hated.

18 Simpletons are gifted with foolishness,
but the shrewd wear knowledge as a crown.

19 Evil people will bow before the good,
and the wicked at the gates of the righteous.

20 Even his neighbor dislikes a poor man,
but many love a rich man.

21 If you despise your neighbor, you sin,
but *if you're kind to him, you'll be blessed.*

22 Don't those who plan evil go astray?
But those who plan good are kind and true.

---

5 *Acts 6:13; Rev 1:5; 3:14*   **21** *Mt 5:7*

d - 9   Gk; Heb "among the. . ."

23 In all hard work there's something gained,
but just talking causes poverty.

24 The crown wise people wear is their wealth,
but the foolishness of fools is just that—foolishness!

25 An honest witness saves lives,
but one who tells lies is a betrayer.

26 In fearing the LORD you can have confidence and strength,
and your children will have security.

27 The fear of the LORD is *a fountain of life*
to help us avoid the snares of death.

28 In a large population a king has honor,
but without people a ruler is ruined.

29 If you have great understanding, you'll be *slow to get angry,*
but a hot temper is the height of foolishness.

30 A calm mind makes a healthy body,
but jealousy means a rotting of the bones.

31 If you oppress the poor, you insult his Maker,
but if you're kind to the poor, you honor Him.

32 By his wrongdoing a wicked person is thrust down,
but a righteous person has a refuge even when he's dying.

33 Wisdom finds rest in the heart of an intelligent person,
and even among fools it is revealed.[e]

34 Righteousness lifts up a nation, but sin is the disgrace of people.

35 A king is delighted with *a servant who acts intelligently,*
but he's angry with one who acts shamefully.

15 A kind answer turns away anger, but harsh words stir it up.

2 The tongue of the wise drips with knowledge,
but the mouth of fools pours out nonsense.

3 *The LORD's eyes are everywhere,*
watching the wicked and the good.

4 A soothing tongue is *a tree of life,*
but a deceitful tongue breaks the spirit.

5 A fool scorns his father's correction,
but if you accept criticism you show good sense.

6 In the righteous man's house is great treasure,
but trouble comes along with the income of the wicked.

7 The lips of the righteous spread knowledge,
but the mind of fools does not.

8 The LORD detests any sacrifice brought by the wicked,
but delights in the prayer of the righteous.

9 The LORD detests the behavior of the wicked,
but loves anyone who pursues righteousness.

---

27 *Jn 4:14; Rev 7:17; 21:6*   **29** *James 1:19*   **35** *Mt 24:45-46; Lk 12:42*
3 *Heb 4:13*   **4** *Rev 2:7; 22:2,14,19*

---

e - 33   Gk and other versions; Heb: "it becomes unknown"

10 Anyone who leaves the right path will be severely punished;
   anyone who hates criticism will die.

11 The grave and destruction lie open before the LORD:
   how much more the hearts of people!

12 A scorner doesn't like to be corrected;
   he stays away from the wise.

13 A happy mind makes a bright face,
   but a sad heart breaks the spirit.

14 The mind of an intelligent person searches for knowledge,
   but fools feed on nonsense.

15 Those who suffer are always miserable,
   but a cheerful mind is always feasting.

16 It is better to possess little with the fear of the LORD
   than to have riches with turmoil.

17 A dish of vegetables where there's love is better
   than fattened beef with hate.

18 A hot-head stirs up quarrels,
   but one who is slow to get angry stops them.

19 A lazy man's path is overgrown with thorns,
   but the road of honest people is a highway.

20 A wise son makes his father happy,
   but a fool despises his mother.

21 Foolishness is fun to a stupid person,
   but an intelligent person forges straight ahead.

22 Plans go wrong without advice,
   but with many advisers they succeed.

23 A man is delighted to hear an answer from his own mouth;
   how fine is something said at the right time.

24 The path of life leads upward for the wise,
   to turn him from the grave below.

25 The LORD tears down the house of the proud
   but firmly fixes the boundary of the widow.

26 The LORD detests the thoughts of an evil man,
   but friendly words are pure.

27 The greedy man brings trouble to his home,
   but if you refuse bribes you will live.

28 A righteous person tries to think of an answer,
   but the mouth of the wicked pours out malice.

29 The LORD is far from the wicked,
   but He hears the prayer of the righteous.

30 Shining eyes delight the heart;
   good news refreshes the body.

31 If you listen to criticism,
   you'll live and be at home among the wise.

32 If you fail to take criticism, you despise yourself;
   but if you listen to correction, you gain understanding.

³³ When you fear the LORD, you are trained in wisdom;
humility comes before honor.

16 A man may plan what he's going to say,
but the answer on the tongue comes from the LORD.

² A man may think all his ways are pure,
but the LORD weighs the heart.

³ Entrust your work to the LORD,
and your plans will be fulfilled.

⁴ The LORD has made everything for its own purpose,
and also the wicked for the day of trouble.

⁵ The LORD detests everyone who is proud;
let me assure you he will not escape punishment.

⁶ In kindness and faithfulness sin is forgiven,
and in fearing the LORD we turn away from evil.

⁷ When the LORD is pleased with anyone's ways,
He makes even his enemies become his friends.

⁸ A few possessions gained honestly
are better than many gotten by injustice.

⁹ A man's mind may plan his journey,
but the LORD directs his steps.

¹⁰ When a divine revelation is on a king's lips,
he cannot speak wrong in a legal decision.

¹¹ The LORD has an honest balance and scale;
all the weights in the bag are of His making.

¹² Kings hate wrongdoing,
because doing right makes a throne stand secure.

¹³ Kings delight in honest words; anyone telling the truth is loved.

¹⁴ A king's anger comes as a messenger of death,
but a wise man can pacify it.

¹⁵ A king's shining face means life,
and his favor is like a spring cloud bringing rain.

¹⁶ How much better it is to get wisdom than gold,
and to gain understanding rather than silver.

¹⁷ The highway of honest people turns away from evil;
if you watch your step, you can preserve your life.

¹⁸ Pride leads to disaster,
and a proud spirit leads to a fall.

¹⁹ Better to be humble with the lowly
than to share plunder with the proud.

²⁰ Whoever gives attention to the LORD's Word prospers,
and happy is the man who trusts in the LORD.

²¹ A wise man is considered intelligent,
but it is charming speech that helps others learn.

22 To those who possess understanding, it is *a fountain of life*,
   but fools punish themselves with their foolishness.
23 A person with a wise mind talks intelligently,
   and what he says helps others learn.
24 Pleasant words are a honeycomb,
   sweet to the spirit and healthy for the body.
25 There's a way that a man thinks is right,
   but it ends up as the way to death.
26 A laborer's appetite works for him
   because his hunger drives him on.
27 A worthless person plots trouble,
   and on his lips is a *searing flame.*
28 A malicious man starts quarrels,
   and a slanderer can break up a friendship.
29 A criminal deceives his neighbor
   and leads him on a way that isn't good.
30 One who winks his eyes is plotting something crooked;
   one who bites his lips has finished his evil work.
31 Silver hair is a beautiful crown
   when found on a person who has lived a righteous life.
32 Being slow to get angry is better than being a fighter,
   and controlling your spirit is better than capturing a city.
33 A lot is cast into a lap,
   but how it will come out is decided by the LORD.

17 A bite of dry bread in peace
   is better than a house filled with feasting and quarreling.
2 An intelligent slave will rule over a shameless son;
   he'll have a share of the property as one of the brothers.
3 The crucible is for refining silver and the smelter for gold,
   but the One Who purifies hearts by fire is the LORD.
4 A wrongdoer is interested in wicked words;
   a liar pays attention to a slanderous tongue.
5 If you mock a poor man, you insult your Maker;
   if you're happy to see someone in distress,
   you will not escape punishment.
6 Grandchildren are the crown of the elderly,
   and parents are the glory of their children.
7 Fine talk doesn't fit a fool;
   how much less does lying fit a noble person?
8 A bribe looks like a jewel to one who gives it;
   wherever he turns he prospers.
9 If you cover a friend's wrong, you seek his goodwill,
   but if you repeat the thing, you will break up the friendship.
10 Criticism to an intelligent person

has more effect than a hundred lashes on a fool.

11 A wicked man is looking for nothing but trouble;
so a cruel messenger will be sent against him.

12 Better to meet a bear robbed of her young
than a fool involved with his nonsense.

13 The person who pays back evil for good
will always have trouble at home.

14 Starting a quarrel is like opening a flood gate;
so quit before the quarrel starts.

15 One judges the bad to be good, another the good to be bad —
the LORD detests both of them.

16 Why should a fool have money in his hand to buy wisdom
when he doesn't have a mind to grasp it?

17 A friend will always love you,
and a brother is born to share trouble.

18 A man without good sense will make a bargain with a handshake,
and guarantee a debt in the presence of his neighbor.

19 Anyone who loves wrong loves a quarrel,
anyone who builds a high gate invites a crash.

20 A twisted mind will not find happiness,
and one with a malicious tongue will get into trouble.

21 If you are the parent of a fool,
you'll have grief; the father of a fool has no joy.

22 A happy mind is good medicine,
but a broken spirit saps one's strength.

23 When a wicked person secretly accepts a bribe,
he perverts the ways of justice.

24 An intelligent person finds wisdom in front of his face,
but a fool's eyes are looking for it all over the earth.

25 A foolish son irritates his father
and is a bitter grief to his mother.

26 To punish the innocent is not good,
nor is it right to strike noble people.

27 If you control your tongue, you're really wise;
if you're even-tempered, you have good sense.

28 Even a fool is thought wise if he remains silent,
and considered intelligent if he keeps his lips closed.

18 The unsociable man is out to get what he wants for himself;
he opposes every wise undertaking.

2 A fool doesn't delight in understanding,
but only in expressing what he thinks.

3 When a wicked person appears, he brings shame,
and with contempt there's insult.

4 The words that come from the mouth are like deep water;
the fountain of wisdom is a gushing stream.

⁵ It isn't right to favor the guilty
   or to deprive the innocent of justice.
⁶ By talking, a fool gets into a quarrel,
   and his mouth calls out for a beating.
⁷ A fool's mouth ruins him,
   and his lips trap him.
⁸ The words of a gossip are swallowed greedily
   and they go down deeply into a person's being.
⁹ If you're lazy in your work,
   you're a brother to him who loves to destroy.
¹⁰ The LORD's name is a strong tower;
   a righteous person runs into it and is safe.
¹¹ A rich man's wealth is his strong city;
   in his imagination it is like a high tower.
¹² Before he's destroyed a man is proud;
   humility comes before honor.
¹³ If you answer before you listen,
   you are foolish and shameful.
¹⁴ A man's spirit can sustain him in sickness,
   but who can bear a broken spirit?
¹⁵ The mind of an intelligent person acquires knowledge,
   and if you're wise, your ears keep listening for knowledge.
¹⁶ Giving a gift provides access for a person
   and brings him before great men.
¹⁷ The first to state his case seems right,
   until another comes and examines him.
¹⁸ Casting lots settles a quarrel
   and keeps strong opponents apart.
¹⁹ It is harder to win a wronged brother than to take a strong city,
   and such quarrels are like the locked gate of a castle.
²⁰ What a man says can provide food to fill his belly;
   the fruit of his lips can provide him a living.
²¹ The tongue has power over death and life,
   and those who love to talk will have to eat what they say.
²² If you have found a wife, you've found something good,
   and the LORD will be pleased with you.
²³ A poor person must beg,
   but a rich man gives harsh answers.
²⁴ A man and his friends can destroy one another,
   but there is a friend who sticks closer than a brother.

19 Better to be poor and live innocently
   than to be one who talks dishonestly and is a fool.
² Enthusiasm without knowledge isn't good;
   a man in a hurry makes mistakes.
³ When a man by his own foolishness is a failure,

his heart rages against the LORD.

4 Wealth brings many friends,
but a poor person may be separated from his only friend.

5 A lying witness will be punished,
and one who utters lies will not escape.

6 Many try to win the kindness of a generous person,
and everyone is a friend to one who gives gifts.

7 All of a poor man's brothers shun him;
even more do his friends keep their distance from him;
when he goes after them and calls to them, they are gone.

8 A person who gains wisdom loves himself;
one who fosters understanding finds what is best.

9 A lying witness will be punished,
and one who utters lies will perish.

10 It isn't fitting that a fool should have luxury;
how much less that a slave should rule over princes.

11 It is intelligent to control your anger
and beautiful to forgive a wrong.

12 A king's anger is like a lion's roar,
but his being pleased is like dew on the grass.

13 A foolish son ruins his father,
and a nagging wife is like water dripping continually.

14 A home and wealth are inherited from our fathers,
but a sensible wife comes from the LORD.

15 Laziness puts you into a deep sleep,
and an idle person will go hungry.

16 He who keeps the commandment preserves his life,
but he who despises the LORD's authority will die.

17 *When you're kind to the poor, you lend to the LORD,*
and He'll pay you back for what you do.

18 Discipline your son while there's hope;
do not be the one responsible for his death.

19 A person who becomes really angry will pay a price for it;
if you rescue him you will have to do it again.

20 Listen to advice and take criticism
if you want to be wise the rest of your life.

21 A man has many plans in his mind,
but the LORD's plan will stand firm.

22 It is attractive to be kind;
and better to be poor than a liar.

23 Fearing the LORD leads to life;
such a person will rest satisfied without suffering harm.

24 A lazy person buries his hand in a dish
and won't even bring it back to his mouth.

17 Mt 25:40

²⁵ Strike a scorner and the simple person may learn a lesson;
     correct an intelligent person and he will become more intelligent.
²⁶ A son who brings insult and shame
     assaults his father and drives away his mother.
²⁷ Stop, my son, and listen to criticism,
     before you turn your back on words of knowledge.
²⁸ A worthless witness mocks at justice,
     and the mouth of the wicked gulps down wrong.
²⁹ Punishments are ready for scorners,
     and blows for the backs of fools.

20 Wine makes people scoff, and liquor makes them noisy;
     anyone under its influence isn't wise.
²   A king's terror is like the roar of a lion;
     anyone who makes him angry puts his life in danger.
³   A man is honorable when he stays away from a quarrel;
     any fool can start a fight.
⁴   A lazy person will not plow in the fall;
     he will look for something in the harvest and find nothing.
⁵   The motive in a man's mind is like deep water,
     but an understanding person will draw it out.
⁶   Many a man will profess to be kind,
     but where can you find someone you can trust?
⁷   If you live right and you're honest,
     your children after you will be blessed.
⁸   When a king sits on his throne to judge
     he sifts out every evil with his eyes.
⁹   Who can say, "I have made my heart pure;
     I am cleansed from my sin"?
¹⁰ A double standard of weights and measures —
     the LORD detests them both.
¹¹ Even a child shows what he is by what he does,
     whether his work is pure and right.
¹² A hearing ear and a seeing eye —
     the LORD made both of them.
¹³ Don't love sleep or you'll be poor;
     keep your eyes open and you'll have plenty to eat.
¹⁴ "Bad! Bad!" says the buyer;
     then as he goes away, he brags about his purchase.
¹⁵ There is gold and plenty of jewels,
     but what a precious thing the lips of the wise are!
¹⁶ Take the garment of one who guarantees a stranger's debt,
     and hold the man responsible
     who makes a pledge in behalf of a foreigner.
¹⁷ Food gotten dishonestly tastes good,
     but afterwards your mouth will be filled with gravel.

¹⁸ Advice brings plans to realization;
with shrewd guidance one carries on a war.

¹⁹ A gossip goes around and tells secrets;
don't have anything to do with a person whose mouth is always open.

²⁰ *If anyone curses his father and his mother,*
his light will go out in total darkness.

²¹ An inheritance quickly obtained in the beginning,
will not be blessed in the end.

²² *Don't think you can pay back evil for evil;*
trust the LORD and He will save you.

²³ The LORD detests unequal weights,
and a dishonest scale is wicked.

²⁴ The LORD is the One Who directs a man's steps;
how else can a man understand which way to go?

²⁵ It is dangerous to say, "This is a holy gift"
and then to have second thoughts after vows have been made.

²⁶ A wise king scatters the wicked
and drives the wheel over them.

²⁷ A man's spirit is the LORD's lamp
searching his whole inner being.

²⁸ Mercy and truth protect a king,
and by kindness he strengthens his throne.

²⁹ Young men feel proud of their strength,
but silver hair is the beauty of the elderly.

³⁰ Blows and wounds cleanse away wickedness,
and a beating reaches the soul.

21 The LORD holds in His hands the king's mind;
like canals of water, He diverts it any way He wants.

² *A man thinks all his ways are right,*
but the LORD weighs hearts.

³ Doing what is right and fair
is more pleasing to the LORD than sacrifice.

⁴ A conceited look, a proud mind —
the hallmark of the wicked is sin.

⁵ The planning of an industrious man surely leads to plenty,
but if you try to get it quick, you only get poor.

⁶ Getting riches by lying is a fleeting vapor;
such people are looking for death.

⁷ The plundering done by the wicked will sweep them away
because they refuse to do what is right.

⁸ The way of a guilty man is crooked,
but a pure man does what is right.

⁹ Better to live on the corner of a roof

---

20 *Mt 15:4; Mk 7:10*   **22** *Rom 12:17,19; I Thess 5:15; I Pet 3:9*   **2** *Lk 16:15*

than to share a home with a quarreling woman.

10 The mind of a wicked person wants to do wrong
and has no compassion on his fellow man.

11 When a scoffer is punished, a simple person gets wiser,
and when a wise person is instructed, he gains knowledge.

12 The Righteous One considers the thoughts of the wicked;
He overthrows the wicked and ruins them.

13 If you shut your ears to the crying of the poor,
you too will call and get no answer.

14 A secret gift calms anger,
and a present slipped in the bosom calms great fury.

15 The practice of justice delights the innocent
but terrifies those who do wrong.

16 Anyone who wanders off from the way of understanding
will arrive at the assembly of the dead.

17 If you love pleasure, you will be poor;
if you love wine and oil, you will not get rich.

18 The wicked will be made a ransom instead of the righteous,
and the treacherous man will take the place of the honest man.

19 Better to live in a desert
than with a quarreling and nagging woman.

20 There's costly treasure and oil in the home of the wise;
but a foolish man devours it.

21 If you eagerly seek to be righteous and kind,
you will find life, righteousness, and honor.

22 A wise man can attack a city of warriors
and push down the strong defenses they trust in.

23 Guard your mouth and your tongue,
and you'll keep out of trouble.

24 A proud and conceited person is called a scoffer;
there is arrogance and conceit in what he does.

25 The wants of a lazy person kill him
because his hands refuse to work.

26 He is always feeling greedy;
but a righteous person gives and doesn't hold back.

27 The sacrifice of the wicked is an abomination,
especially if they bring it with some evil intent.

28 A lying witness will perish,
but a man who listens to advice will continue to speak.

29 A wicked person puts on a bold face,
but an honest person is sure of his way.

30 No wisdom, no intelligence,
and no planning can stand up against the LORD.

31 Horses may be made ready for the day of battle,
but the victory belongs to the LORD.

22 A good name is more desirable than great wealth;
to be gracious is better than silver or gold.

2 A rich man and poor man meet —
the LORD made them both.

3 A shrewd person foresees trouble and avoids it,
but thoughtless people go ahead and suffer for it.

4 Humility and fearing the LORD
are rewarded with riches, honor, and life.

5 A crooked person has thorns and snares ahead of him;
to protect yourself, keep far away from them.

6 Train a child in the way he should go,
and even when he's old he will not leave it.

7 A rich person rules over poor people,
and if you borrow you're a slave of him who lends.

8 *If you sow* injustice, *you reap* disaster,
and this weapon of your own anger will be destroyed.

9 If you have a kindly eye, you'll be blessed
because you share your food with the poor.

10 Drive out a scorner, and quarreling will leave;
disputing and abusing each other will cease.

11 If you love a pure heart and speak with charm,
you'll have a king as your friend.

12 The LORD's[f] eyes are watching over knowledge,
but He overturns those who talk disloyally.

13 A lazy person says, "There's a lion outside.
I'll be killed on the streets."

14 The mouth of an adulterous women is a deep pit;
anyone with whom the LORD is angry will fall into it.

15 Foolishness is deeply ingrained in a boy's mind;
a rod to chastise him will rid him of it.

16 One man oppresses the poor and makes himself rich;
another gives to the rich and makes himself poor.

Sayings of the Wise Men

17 Listen and hear what wise men say;
set your mind on the knowledge I give you.

18 It's pleasant if you keep it within you
and have it firmly settled on your lips.

19 I'm telling you this today, yes you,
so that you will trust the LORD.

20 Didn't I write you important advice and knowledge,

21 to teach you the very words of truth,
so you can give a true report to him who sent you?

---

8 *II Cor 9:6-7*

---

f - 12   With Gk; Heb omits "The LORD"

22 Don't rob the weak because he's helpless
or trample on the rights of the needy at the gate,

23 because the LORD will defend them
and will take the lives of those who rob them.

24 Don't be a friend of one who has a temper,
and don't accompany a hot-head,

25 or you will learn his ways and get yourself into a trap.

26 Don't be among those who make pledges for others,
among those who guarantee other people's debts.

27 If you haven't got anything to pay it with,
why should your bed be taken from under you.

28 Don't push back the ancient boundary line your ancestors set up.

29 You see a man who is efficient in his work;
he will serve kings;
he will not serve unknown people.

23 When you sit and eat with a ruler,
pay close attention to what is set before you.

2 If you're a big eater, put a knife at your throat.

3 Don't crave his delicacies.
This is a food that deceives you.

4 Don't wear yourself out to get rich.
Be smart enough to stop.

5 Won't you only catch a glimpse of it before it is gone?
Wealth makes wings for itself, like an eagle flying away into the sky.

6 Don't eat the food of anyone who is stingy
or crave his delicacies,

7 because he is like one who makes provision for his own appetite.
"Eat and drink," he tells you,
but his heart isn't with you.

8 You will vomit up the morsel you've eaten
and spoil your pleasant talk.

9 Don't talk to a fool
because he will despise the wise things you say.

10 Don't move back an ancient boundary line,
or trespass into the fields of orphans,

11 because their Redeemer is strong;
He will take up their cause against you.

12 Put your heart into your training,
and listen to intelligent words.

13 Don't withhold discipline from a boy.
If you punish him with a stick he won't die.

14 Take a stick to him yourself
and save him from the grave.

15 My son, if you have a wise mind,
I will be glad.

16 My heart will be delighted when you say what is right.
17 Don't let your mind envy sinners,
      but always fear the LORD.
18 Surely there's a future,
      and your hope will not be disappointed.
19 Listen, my son, and be wise,
      and keep your mind going in the right direction.
20 Don't keep company with those who drink too much wine
      or eat too much meat for pleasure,
21 because a drunkard and a glutton will get poor,
      and drowsiness will dress a person in rags.
22 Listen to your father — you are his son,
      and don't despise your mother when she's old.
23 Buy truth and don't sell it;
      acquire wisdom, training, and understanding.
24 A righteous man's father can surely rejoice;
      one who has a wise son will take delight in him.
25 May your father and your mother be happy,
      and may she who gave birth to you rejoice.
26 My son, give me your heart;
      may your eyes take delight in my ways.
27 A prostitute is a deep ditch,
      and an immoral woman a narrow well.
28 She's like a robber, lying in ambush;
      she makes more and more men unfaithful.

29 Who has woe? Who has misery?
      Who has quarrels and who is groaning?
      Who gets wounded without a reason?
      Whose eyesight is blurred?
30 Those who linger over their wine;
      those who keep coming to taste mixed wine.
31 *Don't look at wine when it is red,*
      when it sparkles in the cup and goes down smoothly.
32 Finally it bites like a snake and stings like an adder.
33 Your eyes will see strange sights,
      and your mind will say confused things.
34 You will be like one lying down in the middle of the sea
      or lying down on top of a mast:
35 "They strike me, but I don't feel any pain.
      They beat me, and I don't know it.
      As soon as I wake up
      I'm going to look for another drink."

---

31 Eph 5:18

24 Don't envy evil men or wish you were with them,
2   because they're busy planning crime,
      and what they say brings misery to others.
3   Wisdom builds a house, and understanding establishes it;
4   knowledge fills the rooms with everything precious and pleasant.
5   A wise man is strong,
      and an intelligent man builds up strength.
6   With the right strategy you can fight a war,
      and plenty of advisers mean victory.
7   Wisdom is beyond a fool;
      he can't open his mouth at the gate.
8   Anyone who plans to do wrong becomes known as a schemer.
9   The purpose of a fool is sin.
      A scoffer gets hated by everyone.
10 If you faint when trouble comes,
      you have too little strength.
11 Rescue the captives from death,
      and spare those staggering toward their slaughter.
12 If you say, "Look, we didn't know this,"
      won't He who weighs hearts consider it?
      And He who guards your life—won't He know it,
      and *won't He pay back everyone according to what he does?*
13 Eat honey, my son, because it is good;
      honey that flows from the comb tastes sweet.
14 And realize that is what wisdom is to your soul.
      If you have found it, you have a future,
      and your hope will not be disappointed.
15 O wicked man, don't lie in ambush at the home of the righteous;
      don't rob his resting place.
16 A righteous person may fall seven times and get up again;
      but when wicked people fall, it is disaster.
17 Don't be happy when your enemies fall,
      and don't feel glad when they go down.
18 Or the LORD may see you and not like it,
      and turn His anger away from the wicked.
19 Don't fret over evildoers or envy wicked people,
20 because an evil man has no future,
      and *the lamp of the wicked will go out.*
21 *Fear the LORD, my son, and the king;*
      don't mix with those who insist on change,
22 because disaster will come on them suddenly,
      and who knows what misery both may bring on them?

---

12 Mt 16:27; Rom 2:6; II Tim 4:14; Rev 2:23; 20:12-13; 22:12   *20 Mt 25:8*
21 I Pet 2:17

23 These are also the sayings of the wise men:
It isn't good to show partiality in court.

24 If anyone says to the guilty, "You are innocent,"
people will curse him and nations will detest him.

25 Things will go well for those who convict the guilty,
and they will have prosperity.

26 Giving the right answer is like a kiss on the lips.

27 Give attention to your work outside
and make provision for yourself in the field
and after that build your house.

28 Don't testify against your neighbor without a reason,
nor deceive anyone with your lips.

29 *Don't say, "I'll do to him as he did to me;
I'll pay back a man according to what he did to me."*

30 I passed by the field of a lazy man
and the vineyard of a man without sense.

31 It was all overgrown with thorns,
and the ground was covered with weeds,
and its stone wall was torn down.

32 When I saw this, I considered it well;
I saw it and learned my lesson.

33 "A little more sleep, a little more slumber,
a little folding of the hands to rest" —

34 then your poverty will come like a drifter,
and your need like that of a bandit.

25 These also are Solomon's proverbs which were copied
by the men of Hezekiah, king of Judah:

2 It is God's glory to hide a thing,
but the glory of kings to search it out.

3 Like the high heaven and the deep earth,
the mind of kings can't be searched.

4 Take impurities away from the silver
and the vessel will shine for the silversmith.

5 Take away a wicked man from serving a king,
and his throne will be made secure by justice.

6 Don't glorify yourself before a king
or stand in the place that belongs to the nobles.

7 It is better to *be told, "Come up here,"*
than to be put down in front of a prince whom your eyes have seen.

8 Don't be in a hurry to go to court,
for what will you do in the end if your neighbor disgraces you?

9 Present your argument to your neighbor,
but do not reveal another person's secret;

---

29 Rom 12:17; I Thess 5:15; I Pet 3:9   7 Lk 14:10

10   otherwise, when he hears about it, he will denounce you,
    and his evil report about you will never disappear.

11   A word spoken at the right time
    is like golden apples in a silver background.

12   Like a gold ring and a necklace of fine gold
    is a wise criticism to the ear of one who listens.

13   Like the coolness of snow on a harvest day
    is a trustworthy messenger to those who send him;
    he refreshes his master.

14   Like misty clouds and a wind without rain
    is a man who brags about a gift he doesn't give.

15   With patience you can persuade a judge,
    and kind words can break bones.

16   When you find honey, eat only as much as you need;
    if you get too much you may vomit it.

17   Step infrequently into your neighbor's house,
    or he'll see too much of you and hate you.

18   A man who lies in testifying against his neighbor
    is like a club, a sword, and a sharp arrow.

19   Trusting a treacherous person when you're in trouble
    is like having a crumbling tooth and a lame foot.

20   Like taking off a coat in cold weather and like vinegar on soda
    is the singing of songs to one in a bad mood.

21   *If your enemy is hungry, give him something to eat.*
    If he's thirsty, give him a drink,

22   *because you will put fiery coals on his head,*
    and the LORD will reward you.

23   As the north wind produces rain,
    a whispering tongue brings angry looks.

24   Better to live on a corner of the roof
    than to share a home with a quarreling woman.

25   Like cold water to one famishing from thirst
    is good news from far away.

26   Like a spring trampled by animals and a polluted well
    is a righteous person who yields to the wicked.

27   Eating too much honey isn't good,
    and searching for honor is not honorable.

28   Like a city broken into, like a city without a wall
    is a man without self-control.

26 Like snow in summer and rain in the harvest,
    so honor doesn't fit a fool.

2   Like a flitting sparrow and a darting swallow,
    so a curse without a reason doesn't come true.

3   A whip for a horse, a bridle for a donkey,

21-22 Rom 12:20

and a rod for the back of fools.

⁴ Don't answer a fool according to his foolishness,
or you too will be like him.

⁵ Answer a fool according to his foolishness,
or he will think he's wise.

⁶ To send a message by a fool
is to cut off one's own feet and get abused.

⁷ Like a lame man's legs, hanging useless,
so is a proverb in the mouth of fools.

⁸ Like tying a stone in a sling,
so is one who gives honor to a fool.

⁹ Like a thorn going into a drunkard's hand,
so is a proverb in the mouth of fools.

¹⁰ Many are the wounds of all who pass by
when one hires a fool or a drunkard.

¹¹ Like *a dog going back to his vomit,*
so is a fool repeating his foolishness.

¹² Do you see a man who is wise in his own eyes?
There's more hope for a fool than for him.

¹³ A lazy person says, "There's a lion on the road;
there's a lion loose in the streets."

¹⁴ As a door turns on its hinges,
so a lazy man turns on his bed.

¹⁵ A lazy person buries his hand in the dish,
but it wears him out to bring it back to his mouth.

¹⁶ A lazy person is wiser in his own eyes
than seven who answer intelligently.

¹⁷ You may as well pull a dog's ears
as to mix in a quarrel that isn't yours.

¹⁸ Like a crazy person who shoots flaming arrows, arrows and death,

¹⁹ is a man who cheats his neighbor and says, "I was only joking!"

²⁰ Without wood a fire goes out,
and without slandering a quarrel dies down.

²¹ Like fuel for hot coals and wood for a fire,
a quarrelsome man rekindles a dispute.

²² The words of a gossip are greedily swallowed
and they go down deeply into a person's being.

²³ Fervent lips with a wicked heart
are like pottery covered with impure silver.

²⁴ One filled with hate disguises it with his lips,
but inside he harbors deceit.

²⁵ When he talks charmingly, don't trust him,
because he has seven abominations in his mind.

²⁶ His hatred is deceitfully hidden,
but his wickedness will show up in the community.

11 II Pet 2:22

²⁷ If you dig a pit, you may fall into it;
   if you roll a stone, it may come back on you.
²⁸ A lying tongue hates its victims,
   and a flattering mouth causes ruin.

27 Don't brag about tomorrow
because you don't know what a day may bring.
² Another person should praise you
   and not your own mouth; a stranger, and not your own lips.
³ A stone is heavy and sand weighs much,
   but a fool's annoyance is heavier than both.
⁴ Anger is cruel and fury a torrent,
   but who can stand before jealousy?
⁵ Open criticism is better than hidden love.
⁶ Well meant are the wounds made by a friend,
   but an enemy's kisses are too much to bear.
⁷ When you've had plenty to eat, you despise honey,
   but when you're hungry even what is bitter tastes sweet.
⁸ Like a bird wandering from her nest,
   so is a man wandering from his home.
⁹ Perfume and incense delight the heart,
   but pleasant is a friend giving helpful suggestions from his heart.
¹⁰ Don't forsake your friend or your father's friend.
   Don't go to your brother's home only when you're in trouble.
   A neighbor living nearby
   is better than a brother far away.
¹¹ Be wise, my son, and make me glad,
   so I can answer anyone who insults me.
¹² A shrewd person foresees trouble and avoids it,
   but thoughtless people go ahead and suffer for it.
¹³ Take the garment of one who guarantees a foreigner's debt,
   and hold the man responsible
   who makes a pledge in behalf of a stranger.
¹⁴ When anyone gets up early in the morning
   and blesses his friend in a loud voice,
   the friend may consider it a curse.
¹⁵ A constant dripping on a rainy day and a nagging wife are alike.
¹⁶ The one who can control her can control the wind
   and pick up olive oil with his right hand.
¹⁷ As iron sharpens iron,
   so one man sharpens the wits of another.
¹⁸ Anyone who takes care of a figtree can eat its fruit,
   so anyone who protects his master is honored.
¹⁹ As you can see your face reflected in water,
   so you can see yourself reflected in the heart of another man.

1 James 4:13-16

20 The grave and destruction are never satisfied,
   and a man's eyes are never satisfied.
21 Silver is refined in a melting-pot and gold in a furnace,
   but a man is tested by the praise he receives.
22 Crush a fool in a mortar, into pieces with a pestle,
   and even then his nonsense won't leave him.
23 Know how your flock is,
   and pay good attention to your herds,
24 for possessions aren't forever,
   and a crown certainly isn't for all generations.
25 When hay is stored away, tender grass can be seen,
   and vegetables are gathered from the hills.
26 Lambs will provide you with clothes,
   and the money you get for male goats will buy a field.
27 There will be enough goats' milk to feed you
   and your family and it will keep your maids alive.

28 The wicked flee when no one chases them,
   but the righteous feel safe as a young lion.
2 When a country is in revolt, it has many rulers,
   but only with a man of intelligence and knowledge will it last long.
3 A poor man who oppresses the poor
   is like a sweeping rain that leaves no food.
4 Those who forsake the law praise the wicked,
   but those who keep the law oppose them.
5 Wicked men don't know right from wrong,
   but those who seek the LORD's help have discretion.
6 Better to be poor and innocent than rich and dishonest.
7 An intelligent son does as he is instructed,
   but a friend of gluttons disgraces his father.
8 One who gets wealthy by taking interest and making loans
   will gather it only to benefit him who is kind to the poor.
9 If anyone refuses to listen to divine instruction,
   even his prayer is an abomination.
10 If anyone leads honest people astray he will fall into his own pit,
   but the innocent will inherit prosperity.
11 A rich man may think he is wise,
   but a poor man with understanding can see through him.
12 When the righteous triumph, everything is fine,
   but when the wicked rise, people hide.
13 If you cover your wrong, you will not succeed,
   but if you confess it and forsake it, you will be treated mercifully.
14 You will be blessed if you always stand in awe,
   but if you get stubborn, you will get into trouble.

---

14 Rom 2:5

15 A wicked man ruling over poor people
is like a roaring lion and a prowling bear.

16 A ruler without understanding is a great oppressor,
but those who hate unjust gain will live longer.

17 A man guilty of murder will take refuge in a pit,
but no one should help him.

18 If you live honestly, you will be safe,
but if you're dishonest, you will fall into a pit.[g]

19 If you work your ground, you'll have plenty to eat,
but if you chase after fantasies, you'll get plenty of nothing.

20 A trustworthy man has many blessings,
but one who is in a hurry to get rich will not stay innocent.

21 It is not good to show special favors to anyone;
a man will do wrong even for a bite of food.

22 A greedy person is in a hurry to get rich,
not realizing that want is about to overtake him.

23 Criticize a man, and afterwards he'll be kindlier
than if you had flattered him.

24 Anyone who robs his father and his mother and says, "It isn't wrong,"
might as well be a destroyer.

25 A greedy person stirs up trouble,
but one who trusts the LORD will prosper.

26 If you trust your own mind, you're a fool,
but if you live wisely, you will survive.

27 If you give to the poor, you lack nothing,
but if you shut your eyes (to their need),
you will get many a curse.

28 When the wicked rise, men hide,
but when they perish, the righteous flourish.

29

One who is often corrected and gets stubborn,
will be ruined suddenly and there will be no cure.

2 When there are many righteous, people are happy,
but when a wicked person rules, people groan.

3 If you love wisdom, you make your father happy,
but one who keeps company with prostitutes wastes his wealth.

4 By justice a king strengthens a country,
but one who takes gifts tears it down.

5 A man who flatters his neighbor
spreads a net for his feet.

6 To an evil man sin is a snare,
but a righteous person sings and is glad.

7 A righteous person knows the just cause of the poor;
a wicked person has no understanding of this.

---

g - 18   Or, "fall suddenly"; Heb "in one"

8   Scoffers put a city in an uproar,
    but wise men turn away anger.

9   When a wise person argues with a fool,
    the fool may rage or laugh, but there is no peace.

10 Bloodthirsty men hate an innocent person,
    but just people are concerned for his life.[h]

11 A fool expresses all his spirit,
    but a wise person holds it back.

12 If a ruler listens to lies,
    all his servants will be wicked.

13 A poor man and an oppressor have this in common —
    the LORD gives light to the eyes of both.

14 When a king honestly provides justice for the poor,
    his throne will be secure forever.

15 Disciplining a boy with a stick produces wisdom,
    but when he has his own way, he brings disgrace on his mother.

16 Where there are many wicked, crime increases,
    but the righteous will see their downfall.

17 Correct your son, and he will give you peace of mind
    and delight your soul.

18 Where there is no divine revelation, the people run wild,
    but anyone who keeps the law is happy.

19 You can't correct a slave with words;
    though he may understand, he won't respond.

20 Do you see someone who is quick to talk?
    There is more hope for a fool than for him.

21 If you pamper your slave from the time he's a child,
    he will end up a spoiled son.

22 An angry person starts a fight,
    and a hot-head does a lot of wrong.

23 *A man's pride will bring him low,*
    but a man with a lowly spirit will get honor.

24 Anyone who is partner with a thief hates himself;
    he will not testify under oath.

25 A man's fear lays a trap for him,
    but one who trusts the LORD is protected.

26 Many want a ruler to be kind to them,
    but justice comes from the LORD.

27 The righteous detest the unjust,
    and the wicked detest the honest.

30 This revelation was spoken by Agur, Jakeh's son.
The man said: I'm tired out, O God; I'm tired out and exhausted, O God.

2   I'm only an animal and don't have any human intelligence.

---

23 *Mt 23:12; Lk 18:14*

h - 10   Heb "seek his life"

³ I haven't learned wisdom
  and I don't know the Holy One!
⁴ *Who has gone up to heaven and come down?*
  Who has grabbed the wind in His hand?
  Who has wrapped up water in a garment?
  Who has set up the boundaries of the earth?
  What is His name, or His Son's name, since you must know?

⁵ Everything God said has proven to be true.
  He's a Shield to those who come to Him for protection.
⁶ *Don't add anything to what He says*
  or He will correct you,
  and you will be found a liar.

⁷ I have asked you for two things.
  Don't keep them from me before I die.
⁸ Keep nonsense and lies far away from me.
  Don't give me poverty or riches.
  Feed me with the food I need.
⁹ Or I may feel satisfied and deny You,
  saying, "Who is the LORD?"
  Or I may get poor and steal,
  and profane the name of my God.

¹⁰ Don't slander a slave to his master,
   or he will curse you, and you will have to pay for it.
¹¹ There are those who curse their fathers
   and don't bless their mothers.
¹² There are those who think they are pure
   but aren't washed from their filth.
¹³ There are those who have proud looks
   and a haughty appearance.
¹⁴ There are those whose teeth are like swords
   and whose jaws are like knives
   to devour the poor from the earth
   and the needy from the land.

¹⁵ The blood-sucker has two daughters — Give and Give.
   There are three things that are never satisfied,
   yes, four that never say, "Enough":
¹⁶ the grave, a barren womb,
   a land in need of water,
   and a fire that doesn't say, "Enough."

¹⁷ An eye that mocks a father and scorns a mother

---

4 Jn 3:13; Rom 10:6   6 Rev 22:18   8 Mt 6:11

will be picked out by crows in the valley
and eaten by vultures.

¹⁸ Three things are too wonderful for me,
and four things I can't understand:

¹⁹ How an eagle makes his way through the sky,
how a snake makes his way on a rock,
how a ship makes its way in the middle of the sea,
and how a man makes his way with a virgin.

²⁰ This is the way of an adulterous woman:
She eats, wipes her mouth,
and says, "I've done nothing wrong."

²¹ The earth trembles under three things
and can't bear up under four:

²² A slave getting to be king, a fool being filled with food,

²³ a shunned woman getting married,
and a maid taking the place of her mistress.

²⁴ There are four things on earth that are small,
but they are very wise:

²⁵ The ants are a species that isn't strong,
but they prepare their food in summer.

²⁶ Rock badgers aren't a mighty species,
but they make their home on a cliff.

²⁷ The locusts have no king,
but all of them march in ranks.

²⁸ You can take a lizard in your hands,
and yet he's found in royal palaces.

²⁹ There are three things that move with stately steps,
yes, four that stride with dignity:

³⁰ A lion, the mightiest among animals, turning back from no one;

³¹ a war horse[i] or a male goat,
and a king at the head of his army.[j]

³² If you are so foolish as to honor yourself,
or if you scheme evil, you had better put your hand on your mouth;

³³ for just as churning milk produces curds,
and squeezing a nose produces blood,
so stirring up anger produces a fight.

31 The sayings of King Lemuel, a revelation which his mother taught him:

² What, O my son? What, O son of my womb?

---

i - 31   Meaning obscure. Some read "greyhound," others "a strutting cock".

j - 31   Meaning also obscure

What (should I say), son of my vows?
3   Don't give your strength to women
     or your power to those who ruin kings.
4   It is not for kings, O Lemuel,
     not for kings to drink wine,
     nor for rulers to love liquor.
5   By drinking, they may forget what is right
     and deny justice to all the poor.
6   Give liquor to those who are perishing
     and wine to those who feel bitter.
7   When such a person drinks, he forgets his poverty
     and doesn't think of his misery anymore.
8   Speak out for those who can't speak,
     for the rights of those who are doomed.
9   Speak out, render fair decisions,
     and defend the rights of poor and needy people.

The Ideal Wife — An Alphabetic Poem

Aleph
10   Who can find a good wife?
     She is far more precious than jewels.

Beth
11   Her husband trusts her,
     and he doesn't lack anything of value.

Gimel
12   She helps him and doesn't harm him
     as long as she lives.

Daleth
13   She plans to get wool and flax
     and works with willing hands.

He
14   She is like a merchant ship,
     bringing food from far away.

Waw
15   She gets up when it is still dark
     and gives food to her family
     and assigns jobs to her maids.

Zain
16   She considers a field and buys it;
     with what her hands have produced she plants a vineyard.

Heth
17   She puts on strength like a garment
     and goes to work with energy.

Teth
18   She sees she's making a fine profit;
     so her lamp never goes out at night.

Yod
19   She puts her hands on the distaff [k]
     and with them holds a spindle.

Kaph
20   She opens her hands to the poor
     and stretches them out to the needy.

Lamed
21   She doesn't fear for her family when it snows
     because her whole family is dressed in scarlet.

Mem
22   She makes coverings for herself;
     her clothes are linen and purple.

Nun
23   Her husband is known at the gates
     when he sits with the elders of the country.

Samek
24   She makes linen garments and sells them;
     she delivers sashes to the merchant.

Ain
25   She dresses in strength and nobility;
     and she smiles at the future.

Pe
26   She speaks with wisdom,
     and on her tongue there is kindly instruction.

Sade
27   She watches well the conduct of her family
     and she doesn't eat the food of idleness.

---

k - 19   "Distaff" means a staff for holding the yarn or wool in spinning.

Qoph

²⁸ Her children stand up and call her blessed;
   her husband too, sings her praises:

Resh

²⁹ "Many women have done fine work,
   but you have done better than all of them."

Shin

³⁰ Charm deceives, and beauty vanishes,
   but a woman who fears the LORD, she is to be praised.

Tau

³¹ Give her credit for what she has done,
   and let her deeds praise her at the gates.

THE LAND OF JESUS' MINSTRY

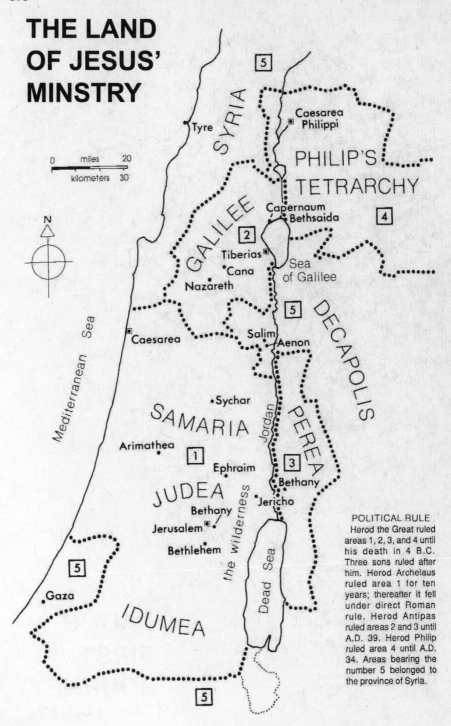

0 miles 20

kilometers 30

N

Mediterranean Sea

SYRIA

Tyre

Caesarea Philippi

PHILIP'S TETRARCHY

5

4

GALILEE

Capernaum
Bethsaida

Tiberias
2
Cana
Nazareth

Sea of Galilee

DECAPOLIS

Caesarea

Salim
Aenon
5

Sychar

SAMARIA

Jordan

PEREA

Arimathea

1
Ephraim

3
Bethany

JUDEA

Jericho

Bethany
Jerusalem
Bethlehem

the wilderness

Dead Sea

5
Gaza

IDUMEA

5

POLITICAL RULE
Herod the Great ruled areas 1, 2, 3, and 4 until his death in 4 B.C. Three sons ruled after him. Herod Archelaus ruled area 1 for ten years; thereafter it fell under direct Roman rule. Herod Antipas ruled areas 2 and 3 until A.D. 39. Herod Philip ruled area 4 until A.D. 34. Areas bearing the number 5 belonged to the province of Syria.

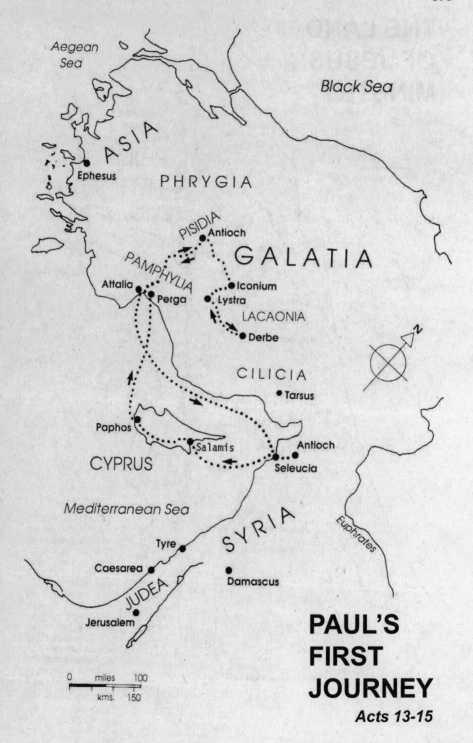

**PAUL'S
FIRST
JOURNEY**

Acts 13-15

MACEDONIA

Thessalonica
Apollonia
Berea
Amphipolis
Philippi
GREECE
Neapolis

Samo-
thrace
THRACE

Corinth
Cenchrae
Athens
Troas
Black Sea

MYSIA
BITHYNIA

Ephesus
ASIA
PONTUS

CRETE
PHRYGIA
GALATIA

Antioch

Mediterranean Sea
Lystra
Iconium

Derbe

CILICIA

CYPRUS
Antioch

Alexandria
Euphrates

SYRIA

Caesarea

EGYPT
Jerusalem

Nile

0   miles   150

kms.   200

**PAUL'S
SECOND
JOURNEY**

Acts 16-18

MACEDONIA

Danube

Berea
Thessalonica
Philippi

Black Sea

Corinth

Troas
Assos
Mitylene

GREECE

Chios

ASIA

Samos

Ephesus

CRETE

Cos
Miletus

PHRYGIA

Rhodes

Antioch

GALATIA

Mediterranean Sea

Patara

Iconium
Lystra

Derbe

CILICIA

CYPRUS

Antioch

Alexandria

SYRIA

Ptolemais
Caesarea

Tyre

EGYPT

Jerusalem

Nile

0   miles   150

kms.   200

**PAUL'S
THIRD
JOURNEY**
Acts 19-23

PAUL'S FOURTH JOURNEY

Acts 24-28

SPAIN

GAUL

Corsica

Sardinia

DALMATIA

AFRICA

Rome

Three Taverns

Puteoli

Forum of Appius

ITALY

ILLYRICUM

Danube

Sicily

Malta

Rhegium

Syracuse

MACE-
DONIA

Nicopolis

Thessalonica

Black Sea

GREECE

Phoenix

Crete

Lasea

Ephesus

Cyrene

Fair
Havens

Cnidus

ASIA

LIBYA

Mediterranean

Myra

GALATIA

Sea

Cyprus

Antioch

Alexandria

SYRIA

Sidon

EGYPT

Caesarea

Nile

Jerusalem

Euphrates

0   miles   300

kilometers   400

ARABIA

WHY THE LUTHERAN TRANSLATION OF THE BIBLE ON THE 500TH ANNIVERSARY OF THE REFORMATION

On October 31, 1517, Martin Luther nailed his 95 theses to the door of the Castle Church in Wittenberg, Germany. This event marked the beginning of the Reformation. Now, some 500 years later, Christendom is in far greater need of another Reformation. In 1517 the Catholic Church was denying justification by faith alone. However, few within the church of that day would have denied the Genesis account of creation, the virgin birth, the deity and resurrection of Jesus Christ, the Trinity and the absolute certainty of the Bible. Today theologians within almost all the major denominations deny basic doctrines of the Christian faith, promote evolution and universalism, and reject what the Bible says about abortion, homosexuality, same sex marriage and procreation.

Martin Luther responded to the theological ignorance and confusion of his day by translating the Bible into the language of the people.

This translation, more than any other modern English translation, is the work of many dedicated confessional Lutheran theologians who have helped revise and polish Dr. William Beck's original translation of more than 40 years ago. The Lutheran theologians and scholars, who confess historic Christian doctrine, such as inerrancy, the Trinity, the virgin birth, the two natures of Christ, and His vicarious satisfaction for the sins of the world, intend, as did Luther, to clearly communicate God's Word to every reader.

This translation is intended for all who want a translation of the Bible which is absolutely faithful to the Hebrew and Greek text. It is for all who appreciate true Biblical textual scholarship and a Bible in the language of today.

It is for Roman Catholics, Orthodoxy, Lutherans, Baptists, Methodists, Episcopalians, Assemblies of God, Seventh Day Adventists, Mormons, Jehovah's Witnesses, Muslims, Jews, etc. This translation may be called "the Ecumenical Bible."

Martin Luther was the master Bible translator. Those who follow his principles of translation are the master translators of today.

In the April, 1948, Professor John T. Mueller, of Concordia Seminary, St. Louis, wrote an article titled "Can We Trust Modern Versions?" in the "Concordia Theological Monthly," where he stated:

"The objection that we Lutherans should not use a Bible translation different from others no longer holds, since the various churches are divided on the use of various translations. Would, it then, not make for unity, rather than disunity to have a reliable Lutheran translation?"

Since 1948 many more new translations of both the New Testament and the Bible have been published.

In 1963 Concordia Publishing House (CPH) published William Beck's "An American Translation of the Bible" (AAT) and said it would publish Beck's entire translation. It was directed to do so by a convention of the Lutheran Church-Missouri Synod (LCMS). Beck's translation was hailed as the most accurate and reliable modern translation of the Bible in the language of today. Beck noted that his translation was closer to Luther's than any other not because he followed Luther, but because both he and Luther followed the original Hebrew and Greek text. Both Luther and Beck were particularly careful in their translation of key messianic prophecies that show Jesus Christ is at the heart and center of both the Old and New Testament. Note the statement by Beck on the back of this translation of the New Testament, Psalms and Proverbs and the explanation by Beck (p. i) of the symbol on the cover.

Beck wrote in the preface of the AAT New Testament published by CPH:

"God wants to use our language to talk to the world-before the end! He means to reach every man, woman, and child everywhere. We hold in our hands the doorknob to millions of hearts...

"In His Word the Spirit of the living God is talking to us, and His book is the book of life. His vital touch is on every word. And when we let God speak the living language of today, a reader can instantly get into the spirit of the words to the point where the printed book seems to vanish, and he hears the truth fresh from the lips of his God. He reads on and on, delighted with the meaning that shines to light up his way.

"When we personally ground everything we believe in His Word, we have God so near; we will not go wrong. We will sharply distinguish what God says from what men say and we will know what is true and false, what is right and wrong.

"We need a spiritual missile. This is it – the sword of the Word in its unveiled power. As we find in the atom a kind of pure power of God, so we get in His unencumbered

Word a pure power that cleanses and creates life.

"Let His full power work on you and grip you, and you will feel secure, ready to stand your ground alone, like Jesus answering every challenge with the invincible 'It is written.'

"And so you get the kind of faith with which you can stand strong and free, ready to face anything, a faith that makes you want to tell everybody about it, a certainty that will enable you to say 'yes' even when all the world says 'no'."

Holman Bible Publishers, the oldest publishers of Bibles in America, published Dr. Beck's entire AAT. The preface read:

"Dr. Beck, well trained in both Hebrew and Greek, spent the major portion of his professional life translating the Bible, meticulously working through ancient manuscripts and newly discovered papyri to get the exact meaning from the original texts. The results of his labors are immediately apparent in this translation into simple, precise English.

"William F. Arndt, noted New Testament scholar and co-translator of A Greek-English Lexicon of the New Testament, calls Dr. Beck's translation a grand piece of work. Other scholars have echoed this commendation.

"Dr. Beck was not content to confine his translation to the textus receptus of the beloved King James Version. Rather, he diligently compared many of the 5,000 manuscripts of the New Testament, including recent discoveries which have illuminated the meaning of the sacred text. He examined every scrap of lexicographical, grammatical, and archaeological evidence."

"The publisher takes great pride in presenting this excellent translation to the Christian world."

The text of the entire AAT published in 1976 is the text approved by CPH editors Erich Allwardt, Rudolf Norden, Elmer Foelber and Reinhold Stallmann who worked hundreds of hours at CPH on the translation. Improvements suggested by such scholars as Erich Kiehl, Elmer Smick and members of the Bible version committee of the LCMS's Commission on Theology and Church Relations were incorporated in the first printing of the AAT. A copy of the AAT was sent to all 6,000 congregations of The Lutheran Church-Missouri Synod. At that time all pastors of the LCMS were still expected to have some knowledge of Greek and Hebrew. The preface concluded: "No translation is perfect. Suggestions for any future printing will be gratefully accepted and considered."

A revision committee of leading confessional Lutheran theologians and laymen then evaluated the many suggestions for improvements. A good number of improvements were made. Confessional Lutheran scholars involved in revisions of the AAT included Martin Scharlemann, Siegbert Becker, Rudolf Honsey, Phillip Giessler, Horace Hummel, Robert Hoerber, Peter Prange, Robert Preus, Larry Marquardt, Reu Beck, Oswald Skov, Harold Buls, James Voelz, G. Waldemar Degner, Walter Maier Jr. and Raymond Surburg.

In preparation for the Fourth Edition, John Drickamer, a qualified Hebrew and Greek translator, an expert in the English language, spent the better part of a year refining some of the English. He also incorporated any valid changes made in the "New Testament – God's Word to the Nations" edited by Phil Giessler and other confessional Lutherans, including David Kuske and Jack Cascione.

John Drickamer

Dr. Drickamer wrote in 1999 in an article titled: "What Do You Want in a Bible?": "The beauty of the AAT is its simplicity. No other modern Bible translation can compare to it for combining clarity and accuracy. Some are fairly clear but not very accurate. Some are fairly accurate but not very clear. Among modern translations only AAT is very clear and very accurate."

Louis Brighton of the LCMS

Few knew William Beck better than Louis Brighton, now a retired professor at Concordia Seminary, St. Louis. He is the author of CPH's scholarly commentary on Revelation. When Beck died in 1966 Brighton wrote:

"Of all the learned essays and pronouncements and the thousands of words in print from the official offices and theological professional gatherings so little of it means anything at all or has any significant influence in the life of the Church. But the work and words and spirit of this man, William F. Beck, will long speak to the heart and needs of people."

Henry Koch of the WELS

Henry Koch of the Wisconsin Evangelical Lutheran Synod, who taught for some years at the LCMS's Concordia College, Bronxville, New York, earned his Ph.D. at the University of Leipzig in 1919. When the entire AAT was published, Koch wrote: "Dr. Beck was a Christian scholar and I cherish his translation much more than any other, because he is at the same time a truly Lutheran and Christian scholar. For many others scientific renown means more than anything else. I want scholarly and truly Christian fidelity to the text. Dr. Beck serves this cause in every respect."

Dr. Koch wrote,

"I heartily endorse the truly Lutheran translation of Dr. Beck together with the added improvements mentioned above, but I cannot endorse the NIV for reasons of conscience bound by Scriptures and mentioned in my evaluation. Here we have a chance of obtaining a Lutheran translation of our own minting. I hope that we can work together for an even better translation and edition whenever necessary. To me it seems as though our dear Lord of the Church is showing us a way of reaching the noble goal of a truly Lutheran translation of the Bible in these later days."

Rudolph Honsey of the ELS

Rudolph Honsey is a retired professor of the Evangelical Lutheran Synod's Bethany College. He was a member of the AAT revision committee and the author of the WELS's Northwestern Publishing House's "The People's Bible Commentary on Job". Honsey wrote about Job Chapter 19:

"The NIV, in which the text for this book is given, translates the verb in the first line of verse 26 'has been destroyed.' Most English versions translate it similarly. The King James Version adds the word 'worms': 'Worms destroy this body.' As the italics in the KJV indicate, that word is not in the Hebrew text. The translation 'has been destroyed,' as in the NIV, is surely a possible translation.

"Although most versions translate the verb with the meaning of 'destroy,' it can be translated differently. In his German Bible, Martin Luther translates that word with the German expression 'umgeben werden,' which means 'be surrounded.' William F. Beck also translates it in that manner in his American Translation. That translation has support from two early translations of the Old Testament: the Greek translation known as the Septuagint, a few centuries before Christ, and the Latin translation known as the Vulgate, about A.D. 400" (132-133).

"The author of this volume of The People's Bible also prefers the translation 'surround.' While it is certainly true that our bodies will decay and our skin will be destroyed in death, it is equally true that each of us will be raised up with the same body and one's own skin, but in a glorified condition. It appears to this writer that the entire verse (26) speaks of the resurrection" (133).

Jack Cascione

Jack Cascione, who worked on revision of the AAT by God's Word to the Nations Bible Society, wrote in "Unique Features of Beck's Old Testament" (*Christian News*, August 22, 2011):

"First and foremost Dr. William Beck was an Old Testament scholar. His goal was to have readers gain a deeper understanding of the Biblical text in his "An American Translation." Beck's translation of Micah 1:8-16 is an example of his attempt to translate the meaning of a text rather than present a strictly literal translation. One of the arts of translation is to decide when God is intending a literal meaning versus a figurative or metaphoric meaning."

"Beck is clearly an innovator. His insights into the Old Testament have no equal in 20th Century English translations, which is why the NIV and others have borrowed his innovations and incorporated them into their own translations. His daring translation is partly due to the fact that he is more certain of his theology than other translators. We have yet to find a translator who captures the rhythm of the text and intended meaning of the Minor Prophets more than Beck."

Diatheke

Matthew 26:28, Mark 14:24, Luke 22:20 1 Corinthians 11:25
AAT, Fourth Edition, KJV: "This is My blood of the New Testament"
ESV, NIV, NASB, NKJV: "This is my blood of the covenant."

Baptists, Pentecostals, and nearly all Reformed denominations say the word should be "covenant" instead of "testament." One new translation of the Bible after another show the legalistic, law-loving, I-gave-my-life-to-Jesus Baptist/Reformed bias, by using the word "covenant." "Is it 'New Testament' or 'New Covenant': What does Luther Say" by Jack Cascione, Luther Today – What Would He Do or Say, pp. 92, 97. "We have to ask why Concordia Publishing House doesn't publish a Bible that agrees with Luther on the Lord's Supper? (Why Does CPH now promote the ESV rather than the AAT?)," Jack Cascione. Note what the "New Testament – God's Word to the Nations" (GWN) says about Diatheke, pp. 531-540.

"Following Jerome and Luther, the King James (KJV) or Authorized Version (A.V.) translated diatheke with 'covenant' and 'testament' according to the basic guidelines laid down by Luther" (p. 534). "Luther, who translated the Bible into very down-to-earth German, often decided to avoid the simpler **Bund** in favor of the more complex **Testaments** in the New Testament portion of his translation.

"This would indicate that the 'testament' approach, followed for over 1,400 years in the history of the New Testament translation, had been used after much thought had been given to it. The occurrence of 'covenant' in one passage and 'testament' in another was not arbitrary" (536-537).

Scott Meyer

Scott Meyer, Retired Attorney and President of the Concordia Historical Institute wrote

"• As a confessional and orthodox Lutheran layman, I confess the authority, inerrancy, efficacy, and sufficiency of the Bible, and that Scripture interprets Scripture. Hebrews 2:9 clearly teaches that the preceding verses 6-8 which it cited from Psalm 8:4-6, refer to Jesus. Therefore, the confessional and orthodox Lutheran interpretation of Psalm 8, as in Luther and AAT, must be that it teaches of Christ the "son of man," rather than "man."

"• The foregoing interpretation of Psalm 8 is consistent with the Confessions of the Lutheran Church, as seen from the Formula of Concord, Solid Declaration, Article VIII, 'Person of Christ,' The Book of Concord, Kolb/ Wengert, p. 621. It is also consistent with the Missouri Synod's leading dogmatician, F. Pieper, Christian Dogmatics, Vol. 11, The Doctrine of Christ," at pp. 158-159, "Communicated Omnipotence" and p. 329, "Christ's Session at God's Right Hand." According to David P. Scaer, Christology, pp.105-106, in *Confessional Lutheran Dogmatics*, Vol. VI, Pieper is in agreement with what the 'older Lutheran teachers-Martin Chemnitz, John Gerhard, John Quenstadt, David Hollaz' -- have written on this issue. In summary, *Christian News* has it right."

The LCMS's CTCR and the ESV promoted through CPH in most LCMS churches disagree with Luther and say Psalm 8 does not refer to Jesus Christ.

A Comparison of Some Bible Translations

Genesis 4:1

AAT: "She said, 'I have gotten a man, the Lord'."

ESV (English Standard Version), RSV (Revised Standard Version), NASB (New American Standard Bible), NIV (New International Version), KJV (King James Version) "I have gotten a man with the help of the Lord."

(Luther: Ich habe den Mann, den Herrn.)"

Eve was mistaken that she was to be the mother of the Messiah but she correctly understood that Genesis 3:15 referred to Jesus, the coming Messiah.

Genesis 49:10

AAT: "The scepter will not pass away from Judah or a ruler between his feet Till SHILOH (Man of Rest) comes whom the nations will obey."

ESV, RSV, NIV: "The scepter shall not depart from Judah nor the ruler's staff from between his feet, until tribute comes to him and to him shall be the obedience of the people."

Psalm 8:5

AAT: "You make Him do without God for a little while: then crown Him with glory and honor."

ESV, RSV, NASB, NIV: "Yet you have made him a little lower than the heavenly beings and crowned him with glory and honor."

Luther insisted that Psalm 8:5 referred to Jesus Christ. The LCMS's CTCR in it's The Creator's Tapestry, supports the ESV and disagrees with Luther and says it refers to a human and not Jesus Christ, (*Christian News*, April 26, 2010).

Proverbs 8:22
AAT: "The LORD became My Father at the beginning of His way. . ."
This Lutheran translation makes it clear that here God's Son, who is eternal, is mentioned.
ESV, RSV, NIV, NASB: "The Lord possessed me at the beginning of his work. . ."

Jeremiah 23:6
AAT: "This is the name that He will be called: The Lord-Our-Righteousness."
ESV, RSV: "And this is the name by which he will be called: The LORD is our righteousness."
By adding "is" the RSV and ESV take the name "Lord" from Messiah.

Micah 5:2
AAT: "From you (Bethlehem) there will come out for Me, One who is to rule Israel Who comes from eternity."
ESV, RSV, NIV: "From you (Bethlehem) there comes out for Me, One who is to be ruler of Israel, whose origin is of old, from ancient days."
(We speak of the "ancient Egyptians" but they are not from eternity)

Hebrews 5:8
AAT: "Although Jesus is the Son, He learned from what He suffered what it means to obey."
ESV, RSV, NIV, NASB: "Although he was a son, he learned obedience through what he suffered."

Philippians 2:5,6
AAT: "Think just as Christ Jesus thought: Although He was God: He did not consider His being equal with God as a prize to be displayed. . ."
ESV, RSV, NIV, NASB: "Have this mind among yourselves, which is yours in Christ Jesus, who, though he was in the form of God, did not count equality with God a thing to be grasped."

These translations make "equality with God" something that Jesus did not have; it is "a thing to be grasped" in the future. There is no future in the text, which clearly states that Jesus is equal with God without reaching for such equality.

C. T. Craig, one the RSV translators, reports that all nine translators of the New Testament agreed on this rendering without a discussion, and he comments on this passage, " 'Jesus is Lord' – not God." William Beck, We Need A Good Bible, *Christian News*, December 1, 1975.

John 1:3
AAT, KJV: "Everything was made by Him."
ESV, RSV, NIV, NKJV (New King James Version) "All things were made through Him."

"By" or "through" (Greek: dia) – While the Bible sometimes speaks of Jesus as the agent "through" whom the Father acts, it also presents Jesus as an independent Creator, Redeemer, and Judge. But in all the statements where Jesus is the Creator (John 1:3, 10; 1 Cor.8:6; Col. 1:16) the RSV-ESV has changed "by" as it is in the KJV to "through." "Through" is incorrect as well as awkward language. "By" is correct and idiomatic. Other passages in which Jesus is the original cause but which the RSV-ESV translates with "through" are: Rom. 1:5; 5:17, 21; 8:37; 2 Cor. 1:20; Gal. 1:1.

The RSV translates this preposition when it is used with "prophet" and with "Jesus" as follows:

	"by"	"through"
Prophet	21	1
Jesus	8	46

Here the RSV clearly shows its bias. It uses "by" with "prophet" in all cases except one in order to make the prophets independent, uninspired writers, as far as that can be done by a preposition. It uses "by" with Jesus only eight times and "through" forty-six times: This presents Jesus as far as possible as a dependent agent of God. (The RSV always uses "by" with angels.)

The ESV follows the RSV and similarly translates dia with "through" in John 1:3, John 1, 10; 1 Cor. 8:6; Col. 1,16.

ESV also translates dia with "through" in Romans 1,5; Romans 5,17; Romans 5,21; Romans 8:37; 2 Cor. 1,20; Gal. 1:1.

The NIV translates dia with "through" in John 1:3; John 1:10; 1 Cor. 8:6; Romans 1:5; Romans 5:17; Romans 5:21; Romans 8:37; 2 Cor. 1:20.

The New King James Version translates dia with "through" in John 1:3; John 1:10; 1 Cor. 8:6; and Col. 1:16.

King James Version translates **dia** with "by" in John 1:3; John 1:10; 1 Corinthians 8:6; and Col. 1:16.

Direct – Rectilinear
Messianic Prophecy

Matthew 2:15
"I called My Son from Egypt."

The AAT and NKJV mention that this passage refers to Numbers 24:8 and Hosea 11:1. The NIV, ESV, NASB only list Hosea 11:1. This passage is often cited by those who ridicule defenders of direct messianic prophecy and observe that the context in Hosea 11 indicates that Hosea 11:1 refers to the nation Israel. However, as such ancient church fathers as Eusebius and Cyprian noted, the passage refers to Numbers 24:8. The fourth edition of the AAT at Numbers 24:8 cites Matthew 2:15. See "A Solution to a "Problem Prophecy" An Examination of Matthew 2:15" *Christian News*, March 23, 1992, *Christian News Encyclopedia*, p. 3321.

The Language of Today

The preface to the Revised Standard Version of the National Council of Churches says that "The Revised Standard Version is not a new translation in the language of today" (p. ix). A review of the ESV in the April 2005 *Concordia Journal* of Concordia Seminary, St. Louis, said that the "archaic English" of the ESV is not helpful and that "the AAT provides a more readable and understandable translation." The Fall 2006 *Wisconsin Lutheran Quarterly* said that the language of the ESV is "very archaic and hard to understand like the King James" and "in many places sounds quite stilted." Mark L. Strauss of Bethel Seminary, San Diego, who has been a consultant for several Bible translations, says that the ESV "is not suitable as a standard Bible for the church. This is because the ESV too often fails the test of 'standard English'." A survey (*Christian News*, August 24, 2009, pp. 16, 17) comparing the AAT and ESV showed that some 90% who responded preferred the language and doctrinal accuracy of the AAT over the ESV.

Distribution of the New Testament, Psalms & Proverbs, the most accurate translation in the language of today, is a noble mission project. Studies have shown that people everywhere do not believe in the One True God, the Holy Trinity, Father, Son and Holy Ghost, as the one and only way to heaven. The Lord asks us to help spread His Word. He says: "Therefore, wherever you go, disciple all nations, baptizing them in the name of the Father, and the Son, and of the Holy Spirit, teaching them to observe everything as I have commanded you; and remember, I am with you always until the end of the age." (Matthew 28: 19-20).

No translation is perfect. Suggestions for any future printing will be gratefully accepted and considered by the publisher.